Atlas of Rome

The City of Rome

Atlas of Rome

The Form of the City on a 1:1000 Scale Photomap and Line Map

Aerofoto Consult / Automap
Compagnia Generale Ripreseaeree
Marsilio

Editor
Italo Novelli

Translated from the Italian by
Chris Heffer and David Kerr

© 1991 Marsilio Editori, Venice, Italy
English Language Edition © 1992 Marsilio Publishers
853 Broadway, New York, N. Y. 10003

Distributed in the U.S.A. by Rizzoli International
300 Park Avenue South, New York, N. Y. 10010

ISBN 0-941419-70-3

All rights reserved
Printed in Italy

Contents

Paolo Marconi
11 A new tool for an improved city

Eugenio Baldari   Bruno Cussino   Luigi Prestinenza Puglisi
35 Objectives and contents of the new cartographic system for Rome

    35 Preface
    35 A paradoxical image
    36 The cartography of the centre of Rome: a simple conceptual model
    38 Techniques, materials and problems
    38 Archives and processing
    39 System architecture

Gabriella Maltese   Daniele Tinacci
43 Mapping technology

    43 General features: databanks and local-area databanks
    46 The Rome City Council local-area databank
    46 Hardware
    46 Software

Licinio Ferretti
49 A photomap in the making

53 ATLAS OF ROME

609 日本語編

St Peter's Basilica and square

Paolo Marconi
A new tool for an improved city

The development of Rome, which more than any other city, and especially from the Augustan age on, has universally been considered the heart of the western world, has been accompanied by a wealth of cartographic material unrivalled both in quality and quantity. The best source for such material is a monumental work by Amato Pietro Frutaz. After a lifetime dedicated to topography and cartography, in 1962 Frutaz published three weighty volumes entitled *Le Piante di Roma* (Plans of Rome). From the days of Septimius Severus to the most recent postwar period, hundreds of plans (vertical projections from above), but also hundreds of "bird's-eye views", have described the Tiber as it meanders round the Campus Martius, the distinctively fish-shaped Isola Tiberina, the Colosseum with the nearby Roman Forum, and even the tiniest dwellings in Trastevere.

Christendom's Mecca, as the incorrigible Voltaire described it, Rome inevitably invited an enormous cartographic output. The fact it harboured such great architectural treasures and was the destination of so many pilgrimages (not only religious ones, but also the secular and cultural pilgrimages of the Grand Tour) meant that the maps of the city were permanently being updated according to new developments and the needs of the great variety of people who used them. Almost all of the numerous cartographic techniques have been applied to the city of Rome: late-ancient "narrative" rolls, thirteenth-century symbolic representations (Rome *a modo de lione*), *ichnographic* plans projected from above, *plastigraphic* bird's-eye views from the sixteenth to eighteenth centuries, and twentieth-century aerial photography. In the last three techniques, the position of the cardinal points inevitably required some care, given that they were inscribed in a square or rectangular background. The orientation thus becomes interesting and often expresses powerful cosmographic philosophies. Among these we see that the position of North, shown by a prominent North Pole at the top of the plan, only occurs in more recent versions. Yet it is commonly believed that this orientation is as old as the world itself.

Ichnographic plans are particularly well suited for cadastres: the streets, churches and houses are represented in their "real" full-blown development (except for their reduction to the metric scale), and appear as if drawn at ground level at the time of their foundation. They are stripped of any information about vertical architectural features and the altimetric growth of the city. These kinds of plans are built with rudimentary but nonetheless accurate tools. They are useful for gathering horizontal distances between points on buildings and on the ground. This information is then transferred to a drawing. They do not require controlling from above, though every now and then controls may be useful to avoid accumulated errors and consequent graphical inaccuracies.

Septimius Severus' plan of Rome, better known as *Forma Urbis Romae* (AD 203-211, format approx. 13 x 18.10 metres), is a colossal marble mosaic representing Rome ichnographically. It is not only a guide, but an itinerary and, above all, a cadastre; fashioned by the authorities, it was a public document that could be referred to by all citizens. Leonardo Bufalini's 1551 woodcut, showing Rome within its walls as well as some of the immediate surrounding area, is also ichnographic. G.B. Nolli's eighteenth-century plan is along similar ichnographic lines. Apart from differences in accuracy and aims (the latter two are not primarily meant for cadastral purposes), these ichnographic plans

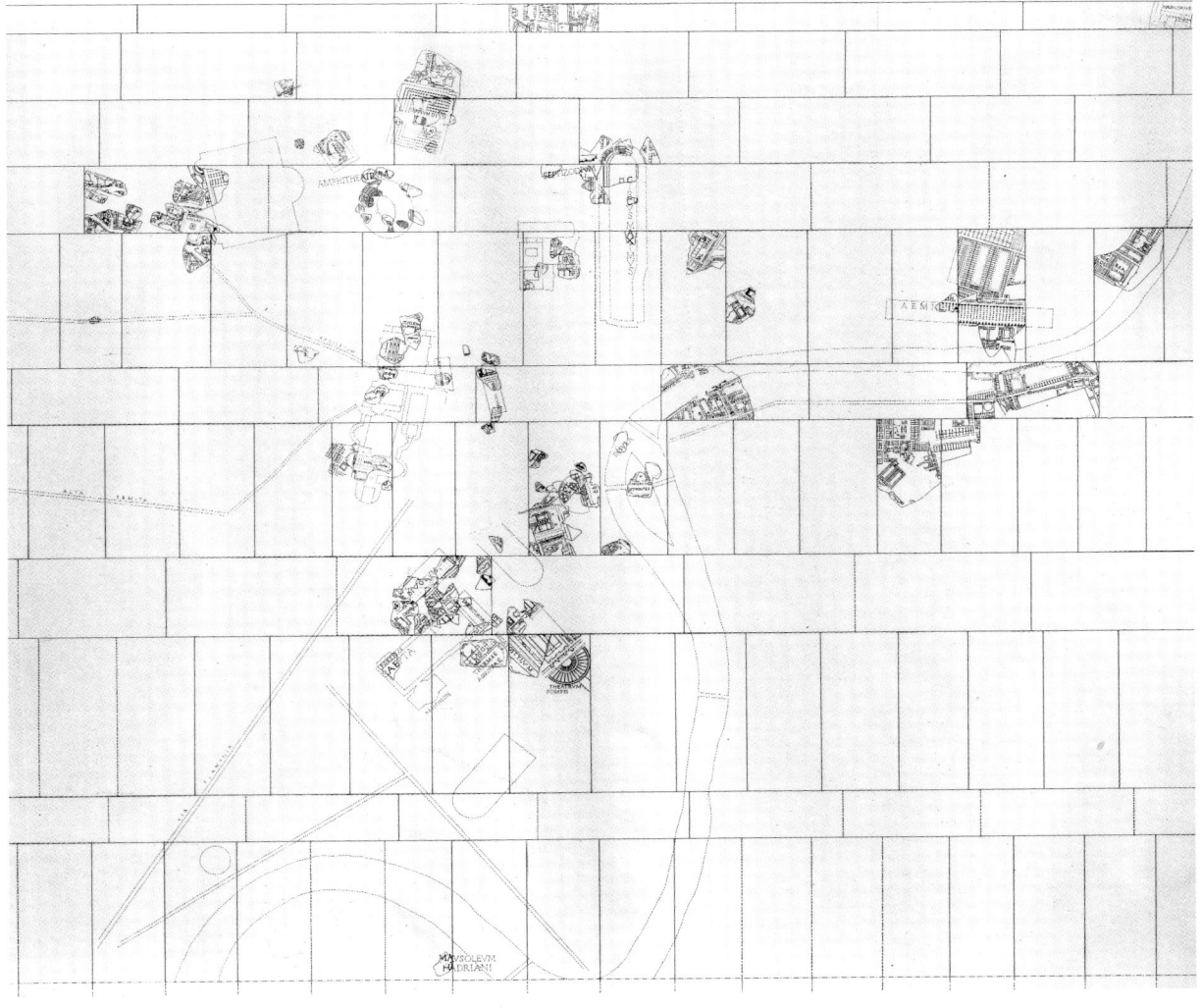

1. *Plan of Rome at the time of Septimius Severus* (AD 203-11). *This plan was engraved on marble and fixed on a wall in a huge hall adjacent to the Temple of Peace. The hall dates from Vespasian times but was restored during Severus' reign. The large marble wall, which once rested on a base covered in coloured marble slabs, is now an external wall of the monastery adjoining the Basilica of Santi Cosma and Damiano. The scale of the engraving is approximately 1:240. Now in 993 pieces, the size of the original was 13 x 18.10 m. Orientation: approximately Southeast at the top. This plate is a reproduction of the more complete edition of the plan edited by G. Carettoni, A.M. Colini, L. Cozza and G. Gatti,* La Pianta marmorea di Roma antica etc., *Rome 1960 (from A.P. Frutaz,* Le Piante di Roma, *Rome 1962)*

2. Fragment from the plan of Rome at the time of Septimius Severus (cf. ill. 1) with the Porticus Liviae and the Theatrum Traiani (from A.P. Frutaz)

3. Plan of Rome in 1551 by Leonardo Bufalini. A 1560 reprint of the original wood-engraving, now lost, by A. Trevigi da Lecce. Orientation: Northeast at the top. This first ichnographic plan of Rome since the Severian engraving was the outcome of field surveys by Leonardo Bufalini from Udine. Extraordinarily precise for its time, the work was probably checked from above from the Loggia of Villa Lante on the Janiculan hill, a position which allowed Bufalini and his many emulators to observe the bend in the Tiber from at least 1521 (from A.P. Frutaz)

differ from plastigraphic representations because of their greater planimetric precision. They do not give information about the elevation of the represented objects, but make up for this shortcoming by their wealth of precise documentary material.

Although arising from a pre-logical instinct to produce a synoptic three-dimensional representation of objects, *plastigraphic* plans may be considered an improvement in information about cities, supplying details that could not be possible in ichnographic plans. In addition to providing information about the communications networks and the plan of the cities and buildings, they also give altimetric details about the city: its streets, houses and chimneys, roofs, trees, etc. This synoptic information thus provides much deeper knowledge but is also more difficult for the cartographer to manipulate. While being a much more instinctive form of knowledge, or even animal-like as the analogy with the "bird's-eye" view suggests, plas-

tigraphic plans are much nearer to the modern systems of spatial representation known as axonometric projections, where drawings can reproduce the three dimensions of an object even from a single observation point. Cartographers must, therefore, not only survey the city and houses but also the elevations, roofs, and spot heights where the terrain varies. And their task does not stop here, for they are involved in complex gradual work, taking care not to conceal background elevations with those in the foreground and so on. Moreover, in order not to lose sight of the overall view and avoid having to carry out detailed surveys of all the elevations that "look towards" the observer, it is a considerable advantage to have a hill or bell-tower as an observatory to check the features of what is to be represented.

We see, in fact, that the providential presence of a hill overlooking and parallel to the growth of the city was crucial for the development of plans of

Rome. It even conditioned the choice of orientation, especially in the centuries after the invention and spread of the telescope. In other words, the convenience of having a hill, or an open lodge on a hill, was so important that it even conditioned conventional cartographic choices of orientation for geographic and plastigraphic maps. This phenomenon, confirmed by sixteenth- and seventeenth-century maps, is worth going into in more detail.

But what do we mean by "conventional cartographic choices of orientation"? The aforementioned *Forma Urbis Romae* by Severus is a clear example. Here the city is presented with South at the top, North at the bottom, East to the left and West to the right. This more or less corresponds to the view from Monte Mario, but is conducted with the precision of an ichnographic representation. The photographic map presented here, eighteen centuries later, has North at the top, South at the bottom, East to the right and West to the left. This corresponds to a view from a raised point, which might coincide with the view from the Aventine, in the southern sector of the city. The latter is thus a complete reversal of older conventional cartography. But when did such a reversal begin and why have North and South switched places in recent centuries?

The reversal was not gradual but sudden and goes back to the Age of the Enlightenment. The first ichnographic map of Rome with North at the top was G.B. Nolli's plan carried out at his own expense between 1736 and 1748. Before this plan, the cartographic tradition was never truly consistent but the vast majority of maps were oriented with East at the top. There are also ichnographic or plastigraphic plans with South at the top, as at the time of Septimius Severus, but they only appear in the fifteenth and sixteenth centuries and were obviously influenced by the discovery and publication of Vitruvius' treatise on architecture, dating back to the Augustan age. The Roman architect's influence was so strong that a whole spate of Renaissance plans placed South at the top: Taddeo di Bartolo (1414); an early fifteenth-century anonymous engraver; Masolino da Panicale (1453); an anonymous engraver of 1447; G. da Besozzo (early sixteenth century); and Pietro del Massaio (1469, 1471 and late-sixteenth century). But the most significant admirer of Vitruvius was Leon Battista Alberti. In his *Descriptio Urbis Romae* (1423-34) he places South at the top in Roman style, showing that he had fully understood the passage from Vitruvius (I,6) where a description is given of how to establish

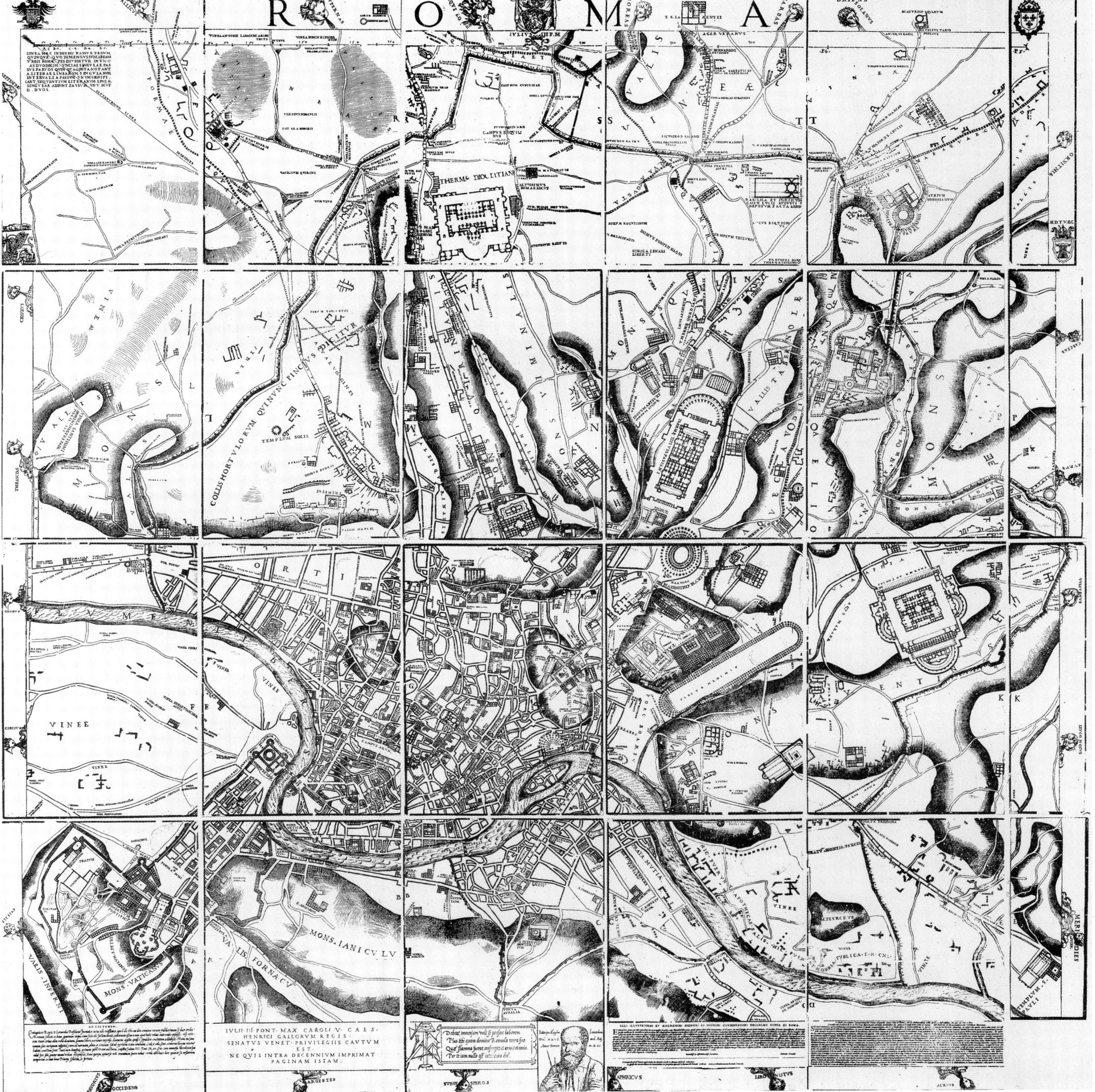

4. *Plan of Rome by Giovanni Battista Nolli (small), 1748. The engraving for the second ichnographic plan of Rome after Bufalini's was made by G.B. Piranesi and C. Nolli to accompany the large Plan (see ills. 20, 21, 22).*
Orientation: magnetic North at the top, as can be deduced from the windrose inset in the Porta Portese area. Nolli's plan certainly owes a good deal to Bufalini's, which Nolli partly reprinted. It was executed with equally elementary optical operations involving a back-sight without a telescope and a small table on a tripod, shown in a detail of the large Plan (cf. ill. 21) (from A.P. Frutaz)

the orientation. This system was to last until the compass was invented. The last to place South at the top was Dosio, an antiquarian and humanist from Raphael's circle, who could not resist making an erudite reference to his ancient forefathers as late as 1561-2, well into the Modern age.

But what was Vitruvius' technique for establishing the cardinal points, and why did South have a privileged position at the top of the map? Vitruvius, in reality, was not alone in using such a method. It had been practised for who knows how many centuries earlier and was the basis of not only the Greek and Roman ways of organizing their cities and dividing property, but also the famous method used by the land surveyors who accompanied the Roman legions to divide up conquered territories in lots of a hundred. Practised in the two hours before and after noon, the method involved sticking a gnomon (originally a long brass pin, but now the arm of a sundial) vertically in the ground. At around an hour before midday, the tip of the shadow cast by the pin was marked off. A pair of compasses was then opened from the centre of the pin to the tip of the shadow and a circumference traced out on the ground. In the afternoon, the shadow of the gnomon gradually moved away until it touched the circumference traced earlier, and the intersection point was marked. Placing the pair of compasses on these two points, an "X" was traced. A line was marked from here to the centre and this line gave the North-South direction, while the line joining the two shadows gave the East-West direction. Naturally the heart of the operation was the sun, as the two points marked off literally defined the course of the sun from dawn to sunset. As the whole operation took place facing the sun it was only natural to place South in the top position if the results were drawn on a wall or a sheet of paper. North, on the other hand, took on a negative role, as it was the point on the horizon where there was no light, and thus the opposite of South. This, of course, also depended on the fact that writing ran from top to bottom and from left to right. It would be a completely different story if we looked at the context of the "other" way of writing, including the Islamic world, but to do so would sidetrack us in a long and unnecessary way.

The cartographic convention of placing South at

5. *Fifteenth-century plan of Rome by Taddeo di Bartolo, painted in the vestibule of the internal chapel in the Palazzo Comunale, Siena. Orientation: South at the top (from A.P. Frutaz)*

6. *Early fifteenth-century plan of Rome. A miniature in the codex containing the works of Sallust. Orientation: South at the top (from A.P. Frutaz)*

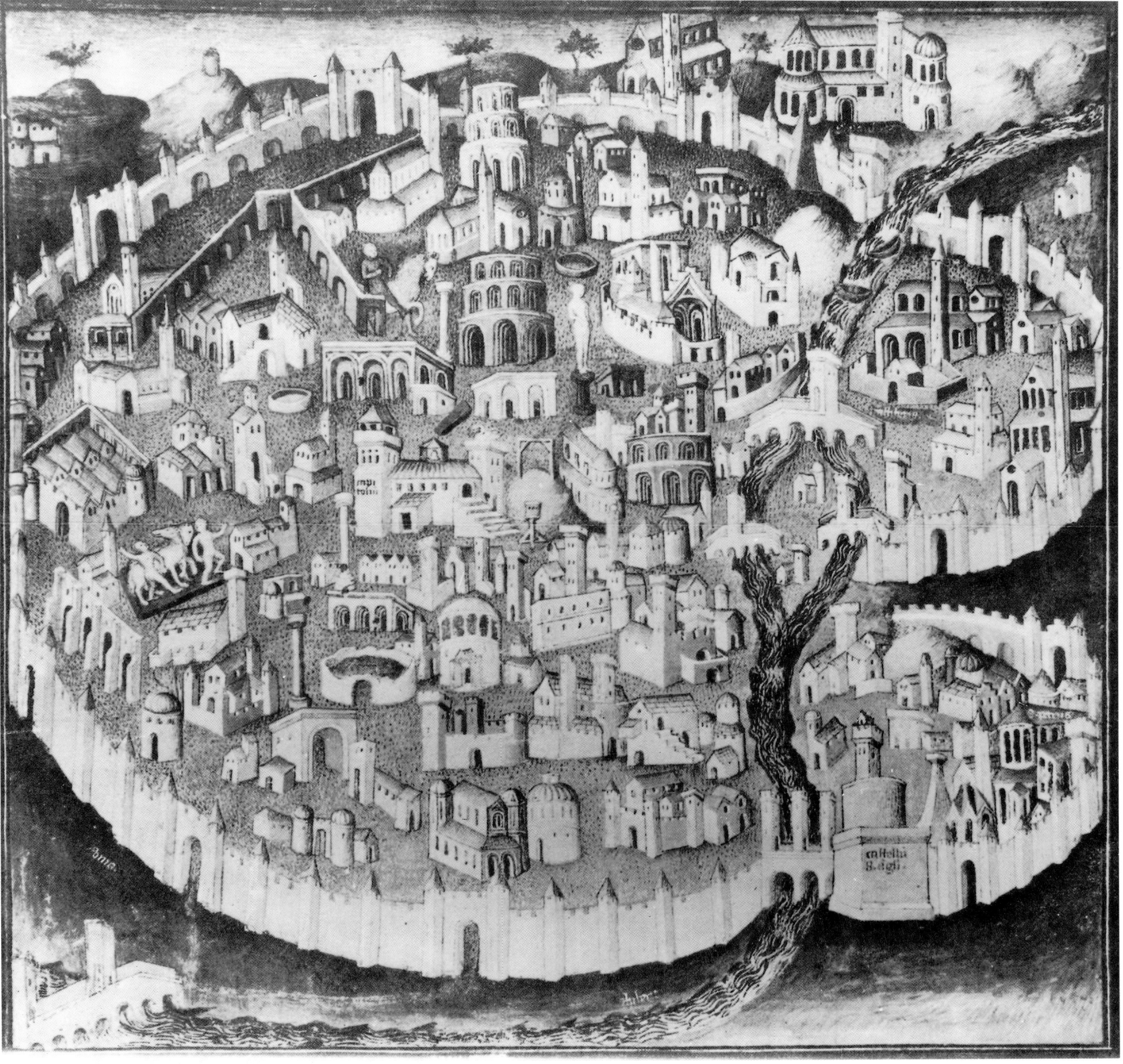

7. *Plan of medieval Rome: miniature executed in 1447 to illustrate the* Dittamondo *by Fazio degli Uberti. Orientation: South at the top (from A.P. Frutaz)*

the top lasted until the late Middle Ages, but there was an important alternative from the eleventh to the fourteenth century, when world maps and plastigraphic and ichnographic plans (including those of Rome) placed East at the top. During the Crusades, maps not only had East at the top but at times identified the East with Christ's face, often depicted in a special inset. To the left and right (North and South) Christ's crucified hands were depicted, while his feet were to the bottom (West). Similarly, the "navel" of the world was made to coincide with Jerusalem. There were even mapmakers like Opicinus de Canistris at the Court of Avignon who took personification to extreme lengths, producing "moralized" geographical maps of Europe and Asia Minor. One such effort by this monk, who has even been described as "schizoid", shows a crowned knight with the "boot of Italy" as the leg of Christ, Spain as his head and Yugoslavia as the other leg, engaged in a struggle with an Islam-like monster situated in the Middle East. This delirious imagery from a vision which sees God incarnate as Man is born out of a world identified with its creator; thus, the head of the world inevitably assumes the position of the head of Man.

From Opicinus' Vatican manuscripts to late medieval world maps – an anonymous twelfth-century map in which the earth is represented as a circle with Jerusalem at the centre and the Orient at the top; the Ebdorf world map from around 1255, again with Jerusalem at the centre and Christ's head at the top; the late fifteenth-century Borgia world map, which is more "secular", but still strictly oriented with East at the top, etc. – the *orientation* of maps reflects the etymology of the word (the *Orient* is the most important cardinal point). It was only with the discovery of America and the commercial spread of the compass that North was to reacquire the importance given it by the Arabs and was once more returned to prominence at the top of maps.

Although this widespread change affected most regional or world scale maps, it was not so common in town and city plans, which became highly popular with the invention of printing in Europe from the mid-sixteenth century. One only needs to glance at the rich collections of ichnographic and plastigraphic plans of Italian and other European cities, published by Pierre Mortier or Braun & Hogenberg and their successors, to realize that these prints, usually collected by publishers on local markets and thus heavily indebted to more or less deeply-rooted cartographic traditions, are not

*8. Fifteenth-century plan of Rome illuminated by Pietro del Massaio in 1469.
Orientation: South at the top (from A.P. Frutaz)*

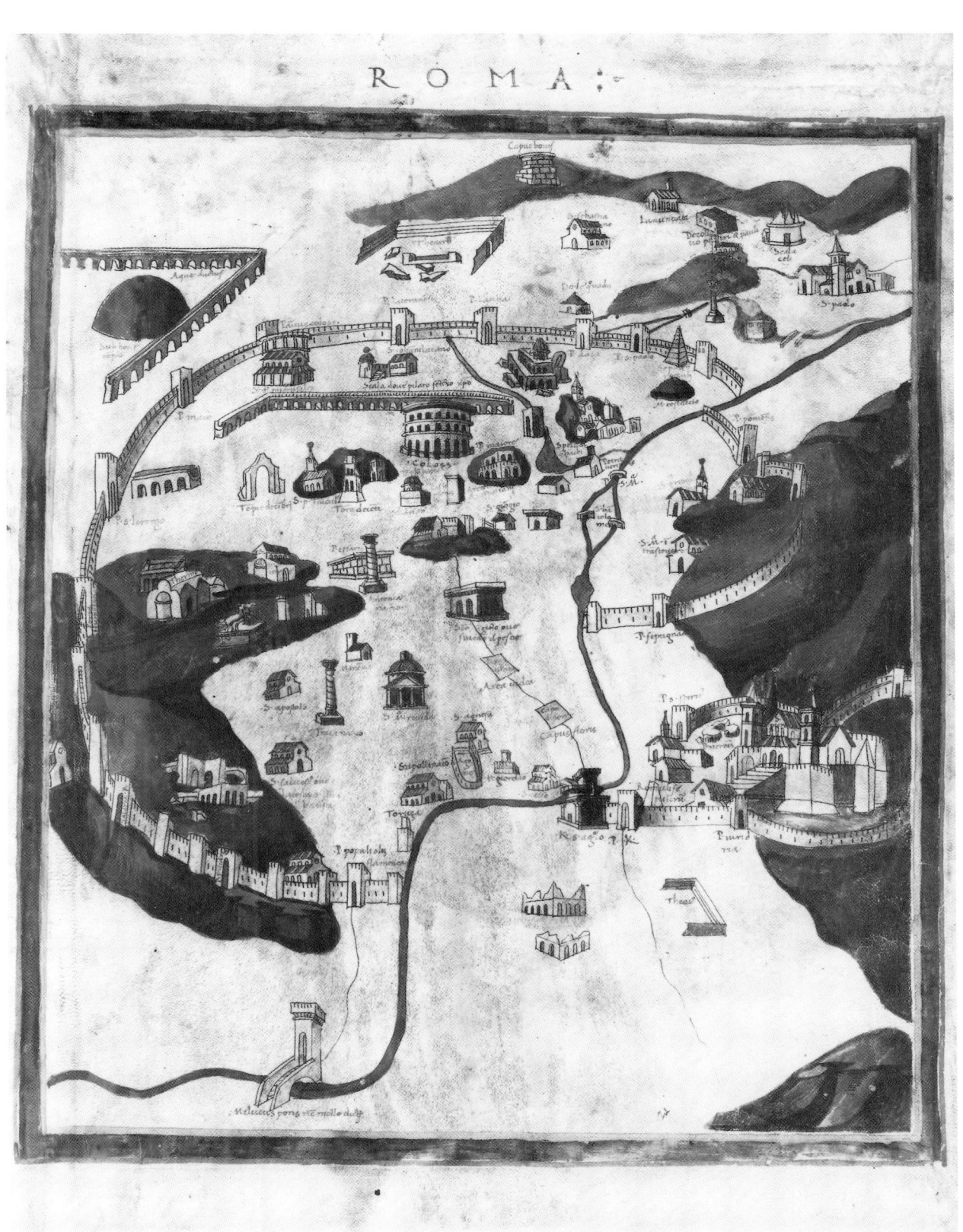

always oriented to North, and often prefer East. In the Mortier collection, to take an example at random, Cherasco, L'Aquila and La Valletta (Malta) are drawn with the Orient at the top. This collection is clearly the outcome of buying previously-engraved bronze plates. The original author's name is then omitted or the publisher writes his own name over that of the original author. In the same collection, for some mysterious reason, Ascoli Piceno is represented with South at the top, while Gubbio has North at the top. The latter orientation can be explained by the fact that Gubbio can only be seen clearly from the South, as it backs on to a hill to the north of the town. The same can be said of L'Aquila, but not of La Valletta or Cherasco. In the case of La Valletta, it may well be that the engraver chose a view to fit in with the rectangular format of the sheet, and the longest side is North-South. On examining these plans we gradually begin to realize that the orientation in the sixteenth century was increasingly influenced by "secular" and utilitarian considerations, such as the best view available or the shape of the sheet. Is it possible that plans of Rome also had a similar utilitarian background?

An answer is provided by a brief examination of the plans in Frutaz's volumes. From the fundamental 1551 ichnographic woodcut by Leonardo Bufalini, based on Eufrosino della Volpaia's slightly earlier regional map (1547), right up to the aforementioned "enlightened" ichnographic plan by G.B. Nolli, published in 1748, all the plans of post-Renaissance Rome are oriented with East at the top, except for the plan by Dosio (South at the top in Roman style) and those by Beatrizet (1557), Bertelli-Ballino (1567), Du Pérac-Lafrery (1557) and S. del Re (1557), which are oriented with West at the top.

The plans with East at the top include the famous works by Pirro Ligorio (1552), U. Pinard (1555), F. Licinio (1557), F. Paciotto (1557), S. Peruzzi (1564-5), G.F. Camocio (1569), G. Braun, S. Novellanus and F. Hogenberg (1575), M. Cartaro (small, 1575 and large, 1576), A. Brambilla (1590), A. Tempesta (1597), T. De Bry (1597), P. Bertelli (1599), M. Florimi (late-sixteenth century), G. Maggi (1600), A. Giovagnoli (1616), M. Greuter (1618), F. Paoli (1623), G. Maggi (1625), G. Van Schayck (1630), G. De Rossi (1637), A. Tempesta (reprint, 1661-62), G. Blaeu (1663), V. Van Cruyl (1665), F. Agnelli (1666), G.B. Falda (small, 1667 and large, 1676), A. Tempesta (1693), G. De la Feuille (1691-1700), A. Barbey (1697), N. De Fer (1700), F. Nodot (1706), Anonymous (1727), and

9. *Plan of Rome according to measurements by L.B. Alberti. The plan was conceived by D. Gnoli using the pamphlet* Descriptio Urbis Romae *written in Rome by L.B. Alberti between 1432 and 1434 and published by G.B. De Rossi in 1879. Drawing by A. Capannari in 1884. Orientation: South at the top (from A.P. Frutaz)*

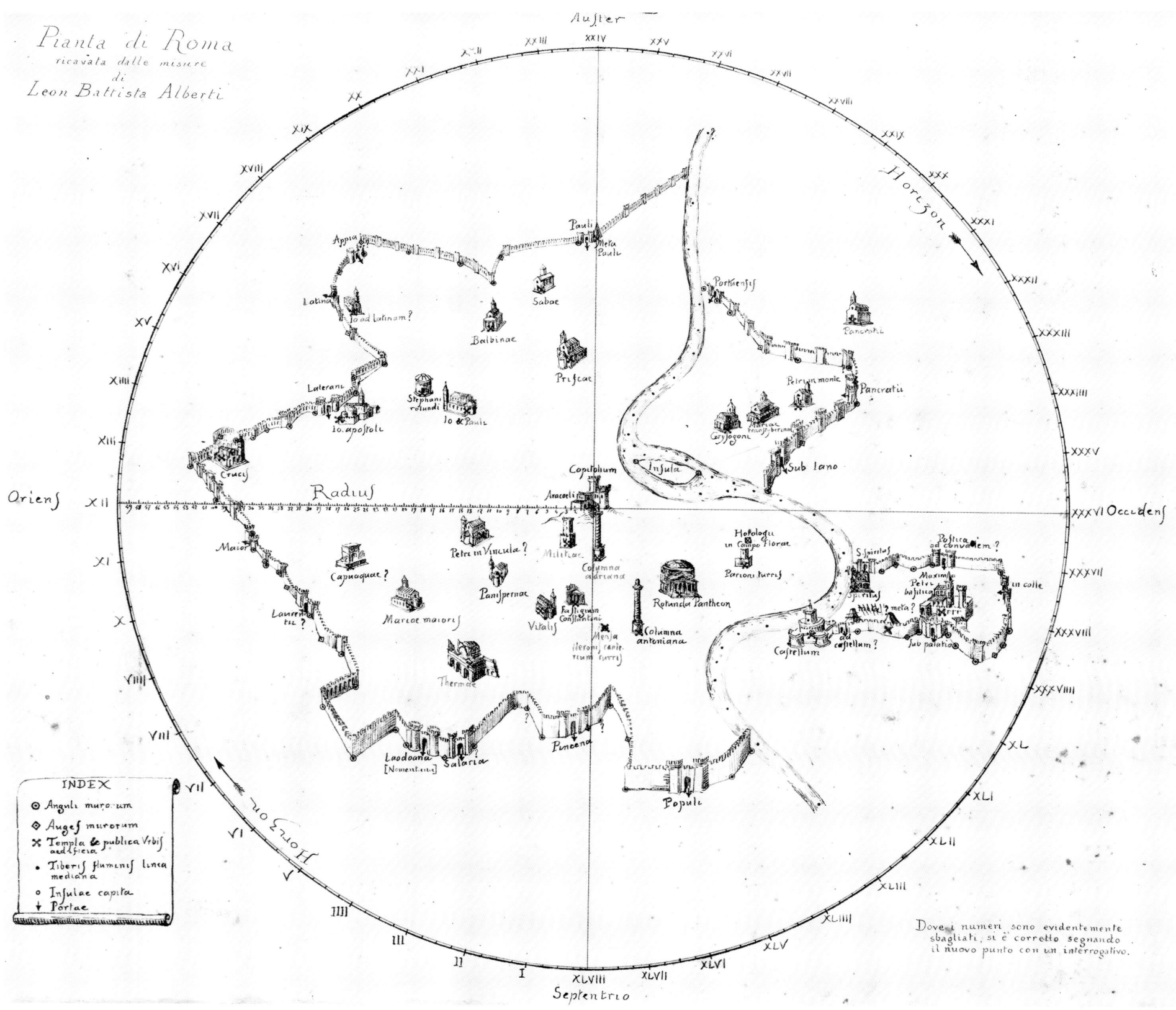

10. Twelfth-century anonymous world map, with Jerusalem at the centre and the Orient at the top (from L. Bagrow, History of Cartography, *London 1964)*

11. The Ebdorf world map from around 1255. At the centre is Jerusalem with a Macrocosm and Christ's head at the top, towards the Orient, while his hands and feet stretch towards the other cardinal points. Orientation: East at the top (from L. Bagrow)

Strindbeck-Bodenehe (circa 1730).

The reason why all these cartographers placed East at the top can be explained by a closer examination of Bufalini's 1551 map. He possessed a compass and used it well, but had no "ideological" preferences for any particular cardinal points. In fact he made good use of the convenient vantage-point of the Janiculan hill, which he certainly did not wish to relinquish for the sake of any cosmographic prejudices. Bufalini, then, took the Janiculum as his observation point, which was two compass points to the west of the centre of Rome. The vertical direction of the sheet is thus North-east/Southwest, as is perfectly demonstrated by the North-East line that he traces on the sheet itself, using a magnetic compass. In Bufalini's ichnographic plan, this detail is obvious, though the same cannot be said of the plastigraphic plans, which usually have a summary indication of East at the top.

But where exactly on the Janiculum did the cartographers work from? The most convenient and suitable point is undoubtedly the Loggia of the Villa Lante, high up on the crag which still dominates the Villa Farnesina. The terrace of the church of San Pietro in Montorio, or its bell-tower, are also fine observation points, but the Loggia must have been more attractive. Built for himself and his friends by the refined humanist and *bon viveur* Cardinal Turini da Pescia, who was a datary to Pope Leo X, the villa was designed by Giulio Romano and had stuccoes by Giovanni da Udine. From as early as 1521 the villa must have been a luxurious observatory from which to survey and control the building of the *Urbe*.

HINC TOTAL LICET AESTIMARE ROMAM
1531

This inscription can still be seen on the plaque on the central door of the Loggia, along with images of the deeds of Pope Leo X and Pope Clement VII, Cardinal Turini's protectors, and the stories of Aeneas and Numa Pompilius. The magnificent villa was built before 1531, which was probably the date of restoration work required after the Sack of Rome in 1527. The villa was the first to fall, as visitors are reminded by elegant graffiti engraved over the frescoes in the main salon:

a di 6 de magio 1527
fo la presa de Roma
(On 6 May 1527 Rome was taken)

The villa was certainly completed by 1521, at

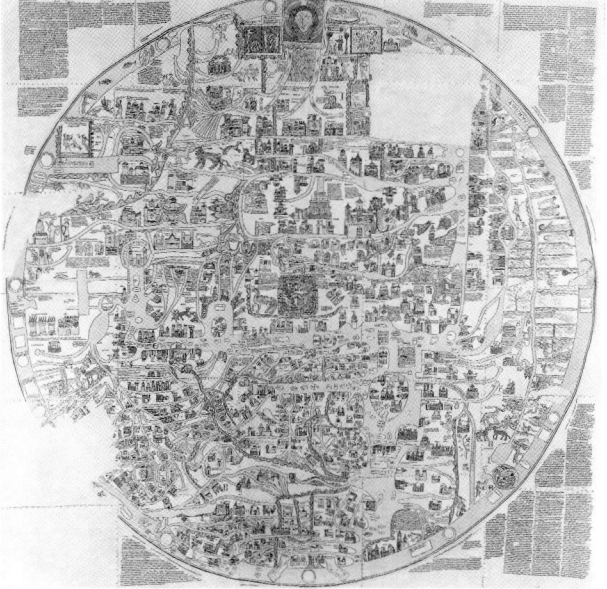

least as regards the rustication, and with the exception of some external stucco decorations. The Latin phrase scrawled by the graffiti writer is a paraphrase from Martial

UNDE TOTAM LICET AESTIMARE ROMAM
ET LONGAM VALLEM NEBULAS TEGENTES

and it was almost certainly an erudite comment made by some of the Cardinal's guests, who climbed up to the villa to enjoy the banquets in the attractive surroundings of Giulio Romano's licentious frescoes, now no longer to be seen.

Since Cardinal Turini's time the Loggia has been known as the observatory of Rome, protecting cartographers from the rain, if not from the north wind. Along with San Pietro in Montorio, it is included in the early plans of Renaissance Rome, beginning with Bufalini's highly accurate version and followed by a series of variations which, if nothing else, leave a record of building developments. From the Janiculan hill there is a view of sunrise. A view with East to the top thus becomes imperative, although it does require a slight twisting of the compass, since in reality – as the conscientious Bufalini points out – to be truly accurate Northeast would be at the top. But why take such great pains over accuracy if, by cheating slightly, a reference point could be had from which to make plans with means that may well have been obsolete but nonetheless, once exercised, had considerable charm? The symbolist cosmographic tradition using the figure of Christ was thus complied with, but the more pressing demands of some Sancho Panza accompanying the map-maker on a mule up the slopes of the Janiculan hill must also have been met. This assistant probably not only had the Praetorian Tables in hand, with which to look for the observations already made by a simple optical back-sight, but he was also equipped – from the late-sixteenth century on – with a heavy crystal and brass telescope which, unlike its inventor, Galileo, had never really been excommunicated.

With Bufalini's plan as a very fine precedent, from the mid-sixteenth to the mid-eighteenth century maps of Rome abounded. After the enormous labours of the poor carpenter, engraver, surveyor, military architect, and even entrepreneur (in the building of the Borgo Walls), undertaken with the typical industriousness of a native of Udine, for two whole centuries map-makers had a ready reference – and many still marvel at its accuracy given the means available. They used Bufalini's plan as the basis for their bird's-eye views or other ich-

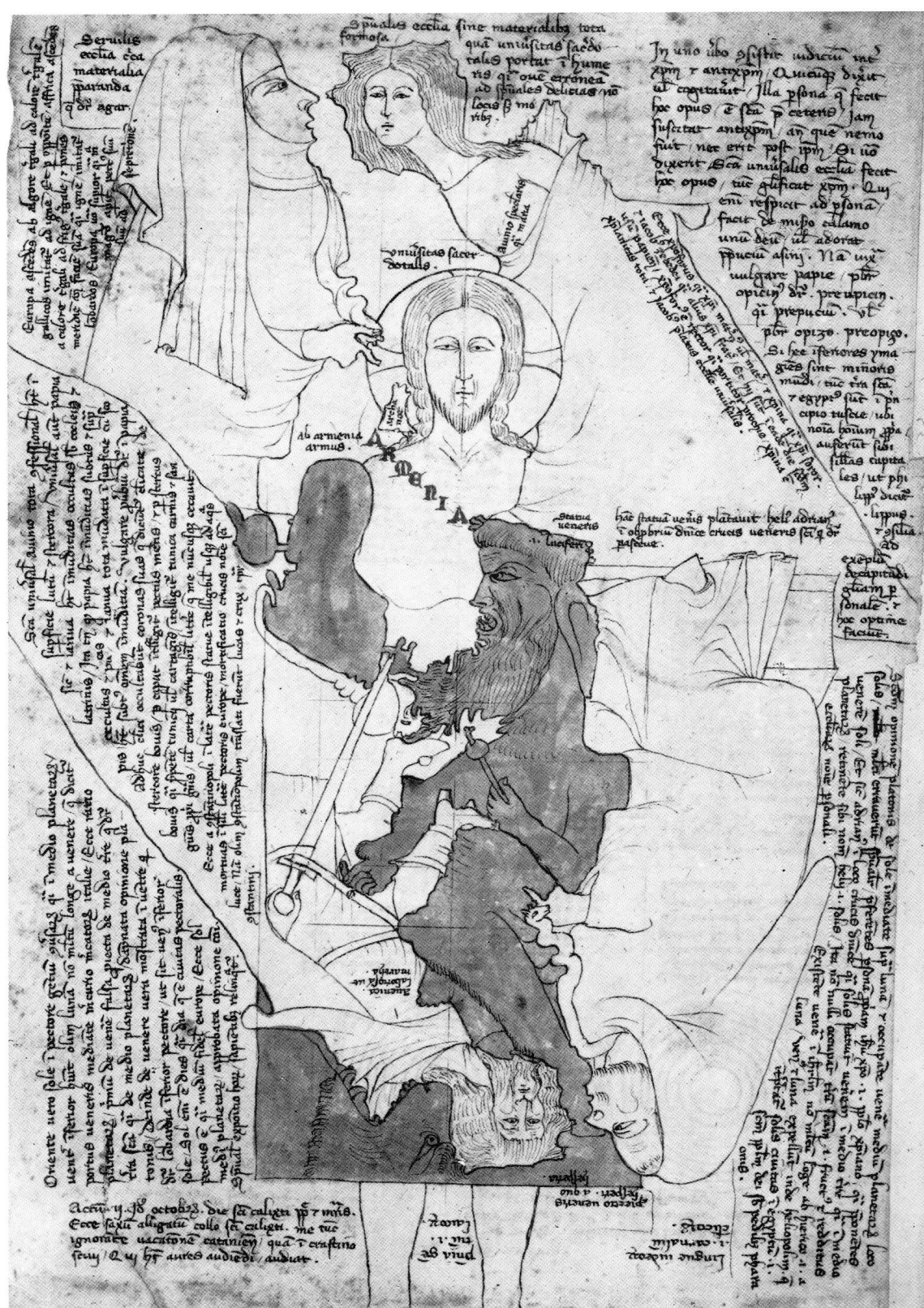

12. *Opicinus de Canistris*, a monk from Pavia at the court of Avignon in the fourteenth century. This "moralized" chart of the Mediterranean and Europe comments on contemporary history. The orientation is given by Christ's head, which gives form to the chart (ms. Palatino Latino no. 6435, fol. 69v, Biblioteca Apostolica Vaticana)

nographic plans with different details. All had East at the top, apart from the rare exceptions already mentioned.

Two centuries later, another industrious northerner appeared on the scene: Giovan Battista Nolli from Como. After twelve years of indefatigable field-work at his own expense, Nolli produced a second splendidly drawn and engraved ichnographic plan of the city of Rome. This was the first ever plan to be made with North at the top and it even has a magnificent rose of winds with not only the astronomic, but also the magnetic, orientation. From Nolli on, the numerous descriptive and cadastral ichnographic plans of Rome are all oriented with North at the top. And, in fact, it was from the mid-eighteenth century that the custom of making the North Pole the protagonist of our world maps prevailed.

From the eighteenth century to the early twentieth century, cartographic techniques made no great advances, and improvements were limited to perfecting optical and typographic instruments. For example, the sophisticated and accurate geographical and topographical charts made by the Istituto Geografico Militare in Florence after the unification of Italy were still the result of field surveys. They were, however, part of a geodetic network for the whole country that ensured adjacent sheets were collimated.

At this point it is evident that the invention and spread of technical means such as the aeroplane and photography paved the way to a considerable qualitative step forward. This would finally free cities and regions from the same old observation and control points and permit complete zenithal accuracy in maps. Once again Rome was in the vanguard, as it was one of the first cities to be photographed from above for topographic purposes. The result was the 1900 topographic map made by the Photographic Section of the Third Regiment of Italian Army Engineers on a 1:10,000 scale. The city was most likely photographed from an aerostatic balloon, for a photographic survey from an aeroplane was not made until after World War I. An unknown twenty-four-year-old lieutenant, Umberto Nistri, made the negatives that were used to produce the first aerial photograph of the city in an approximate scale of 1:10,000. The Italian Air Force chivalrously dedicated the result to Rodolfo Lanciani, a famous topographer of Ancient

13. Opicinus de Canistris: the Mediterranean takes on an explicitly diabolical form, while it changes the sex of Europe and the Maghreb (ibid., fol. 84r)

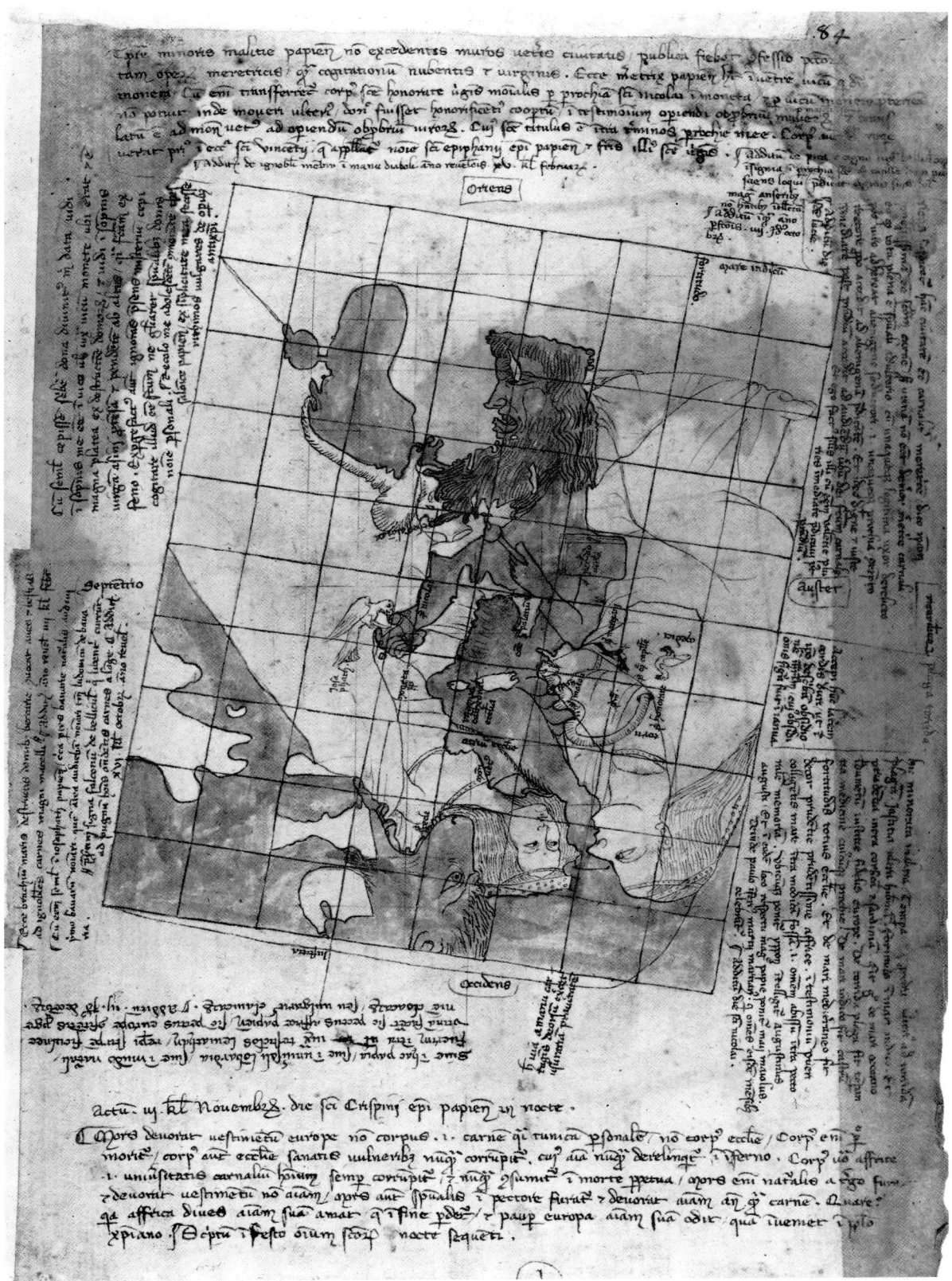

Rome who was still alive at the time (1919). Umberto Nistri, who was the inventor and shrewd custodian of the aerophotogrammetric survey, took another aerial photograph from an altitude of 3000 metres in 1934. The result was to form the basis of the aerophotogrammetric survey carried out with the "Nistri" system by ETA to produce a 1:5000 scale as an aid in the 1962 town-planning scheme for Rome. This latter survey was based on a mosaic of photos taken between December 1959 and February 1960 (around the time of the Winter solstice). Nistri's first photographs were also taken at this time of year, in February 1919.

How can this choice of timing be explained? Good black-and-white aerial photography should be carried out with optimal ground visibility, namely with a clear sky (best when there is a north wind) and with vegetation as bare as possible. Another condition, which obviously contrasts with the preceding, is that of having the slightest shadow possible cast from roofs onto the ground. But this condition can only be found at the Summer solstice, when there is little chance of a north wind, and trees, bushes and grass are at their lushest.

In general, then, the best conditions for a good aerophotogrammetric survey are to be had in winter, when there is a minimum of vegetation. Why, in that case, was the survey for this book carried out around the Summer solstice rather than the Winter solstice? There is an easy answer. Black-and-white photography obviously does not render colour differences in the objects reproduced. In a black-and-white photo nearly all tree foliage looks the same – cluster-pines resemble oaks – and all bricks and tiles have a similar greyish hue. Only a very fine resolution would be able to produce a palette that varied for every object. And even then there would still be a large degree of uncertainty. In Rome a yellowish roof means that the tiles have come from the Valle delle Fornace, near the Vatican. From the fifteenth century to the early 1950s these quarries supplied clays that, when fired, gave tiles and bricks a characteristic golden colour. A reddish roof reveals that the tiles come from quarries in the Tiber Valley, which have supplied bricks and tiles since the more convenient Vatican quarries were closed under the pressure of the building boom and property speculation that reduced them to a pathetic ruin of industrial archaeology. Nowadays a completely yellowish roof is something of a rarity. Not only because roofs are covered in dust, but like all tiled roofs in the world they are also subject to regular maintenance involving replace-

14. *Plan of Rome in 1557, associated with the War of Naples, drawn and engraved by Niccolò Beatrizet and published by A. Lafrery in 1557. Temporary fortifications are much in evidence. The observatory used to check the map may have been on the Trinità de' Monti (the Pincio). Orientation: West at the top (from A.P. Frutaz)*

15. *Plan of Rome in 1561, drawn by G.A. Dosio, engraved by S. Del Re and published by F. Faleti. The antiquarian interests of the artist explain the emphasis on ancient monuments and the choice of orientation. Orientation: South at the top (from A.P. Frutaz)*

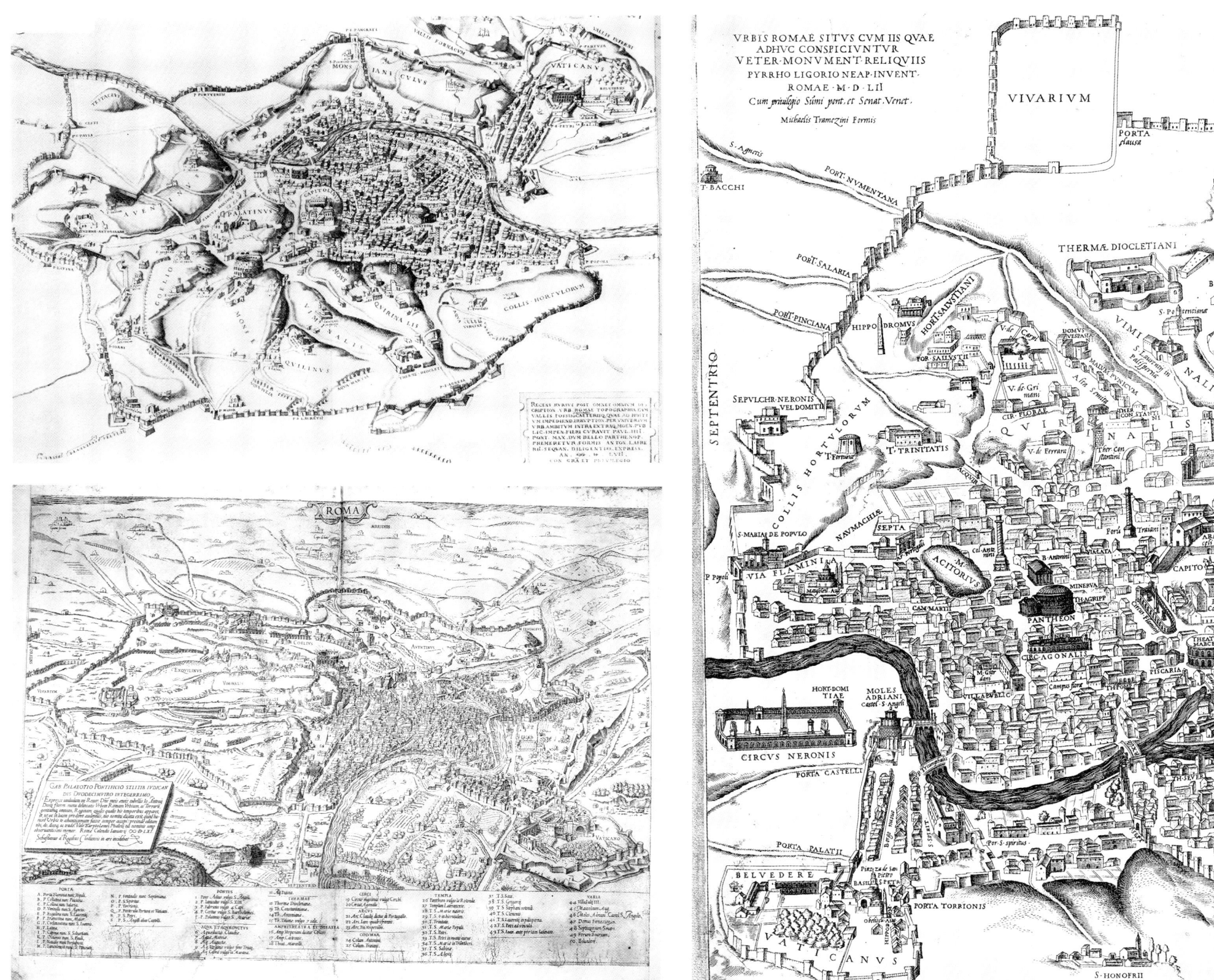

16. *Plan of Rome in 1552, drawn by Pirro Ligorio, engraved by an anonymous artist with initials G.L.A. and published by M. Tramezino. Note the fairly detailed representation of the Villa Lante, then owned by Cardinal Baldassarre Turini da Pescia, indicated by Ligorio with the inscription "Villa B. de Pescie". The villa is shown with a saddle roof and a small shed in the garden to the south of the main building. This covering must have been provisional since the final roofing was a hip roof. It may well be that the drawing was made during a phase of building and we know that the villa was not even completely finished by 1531. The importance attached to the villa in this context would appear to be further proof that its Loggia afforded the best panoramic view of Rome. Orientation: East at the top (from A.P. Frutaz)*

ments. A well-trained eye, however, can make out yellow "patches" from red "patches" and date them. Such dating can often speak more clearly than archive documents which, understandably in a city under great property pressure, often involve giving the benefit of the doubt.

Continuing on the subject of roof coverings, another example of detail that would elude black-and-white photography is the differences in testudo roofing over the twin churches in Piazza del Popolo and the Pantheon. All that would show up would be a difference in pattern and not in materials. In fact the roofs in Piazza del Popolo are made of slate, through the stubbornness of a Ligurian cardinal, and the slight difference in colour is enough to distinguish them from the lead sheets over the Pantheon, which were a lavish gift of Pope Nicholas I to the pagan temple that was redeemed and included in the circuit of the Universal Jubilee in 1450.

As regards pavings, we see that an iron grey gives way to a reddish colour where recent consumerism has preferred Alpine porphyry to the beautiful Latian volcanic flint. The latter is less amenable to mass production because it is found in layers spread across the region in lava-streams. The quarries are therefore subject to boundary disputes, plundering from authorized and unauthorized builders, and depletion because of the serpentine nature of the lava-streams. The fan-like arrangement of the porphyry cubes is morphologically akin to the Roman flints, although the more malleable porphyry produces more uniform paving, which thus provides a clue to its nature. Their reddish colour makes them immediately identifiable, however, and this could be used in any rightful battle the City Council might wish to wage for a return, or at least improvements, to the uneconomical flint paving. But why should improvements only be made in favour of competitive products? Any such schemes should help products to become competitive once more, or at least to be able to survive with dignity in a climate in which decisions are also based on critical taste and not simply on economic expedient. This is an area in which the concept of "assisted industries" is no affront to common sense; there is, above all, a need to help small or medium-sized businesses concerned with conserving and upgrading the architectural heritage, help them to keep alive materials and crafts that the brutal logic of the market would simply sweep away to the detriment of living standards in the historic centres, which are strictly linked to their aesthetic quality.

In conclusion, then, colour aerial photography

17. *Plan of Rome in 1557*, drawn by F. Paciotti (Paciotto), engraved by N. Beatrizet and published in Rome by A. Lafrery in 1557. Although plastigraphic, the plan was based on Bufalini's work. Here, too, Villa Lante is in evidence, indicated by the inscription "Villa bald. de pescie". This time the roof is drawn in hip form, almost as if further work had been carried out since Ligorio's drawing, which was probably the case. Orientation: East at the top (from A.P. Frutaz)

18. *Plan of Rome in 1575*, drawn and engraved by M. Cartaro in 1575 (small). Here Villa Lante appears without a caption but with the same kind of roof as described by Paciotto – a hip roof with two characteristic pillars framing the facade in a marked way. Two arched arbours framing the perspective of the entrance are also represented. Orientation: East at the top
(from A.P. Frutaz)

must be carried out between June and August to obtain all the information possible about the vegetation and permit a thorough survey of trees and bushes as well as the other surveys mentioned above. And it must be carried out in these months even if tree foliage at this time of year sometimes covers underlying objects. The obvious advantages of colour photography also include being able to discern the colour of river water. Note, for example, the green stretches in the Tiber between Ponte Sisto and Ponte Sant'Angelo. If the river were healthy, the algae on the bed would not show up so strongly. Incidentally, the ancient popular name of *biondo* ("fair one") was coined to describe the excellent condition of the river and not the dried-up state that in recent years droughts have extended right up to its source in Tuscany.

The timing of colour photography obviously also has its own influences. It is not only best to photograph around the Summer solstice when shadows are at their shortest, the time must also be as near as possible to solar noon so that the sun is at its zenith and shadows are at an absolute minimum. As in Vitruvius' time, then, the recording must take place within an hour either way of midday. The photomap published here enables us to make a fairly accurate guess at the time when at least one of the photographs – that of the Janiculan hill – was taken, and therefore the approximate time when the whole photomap was recorded. Below the square on the Janiculan hill with its monument to Garibaldi, a transparent patch of mist floats near the retaining wall the tourists are looking over. This is actually the autograph of the midday cannon shot. At this time the city traffic is reduced to a minimum because the people of Rome have all arrived at their offices, or are buying or selling in shops. Their cars are parked in single or double file along the pavements and the already scorching sun is left to heat the tarmac and the motionless metal bodies.

We must now turn to the almost immobile city, before the rush of homeward-bound traffic. What we notice most clearly about the urban fabric is the

19. *Plan of Rome in 1551, designed and engraved by A. Bufalini (cf. ill. 3). The woodcut form emphasizes the North-South line, overlaid on the ichnographic representation of the Via Salaria area. The chosen orientation clearly demonstrates how Bufalini preferred the convenience of the Loggia in the Villa Lante on the Janiculum, which he used to control the field measurements, to any cartographic criteria, and he was undoubtedly helped in this choice by the fact he could rely on the compass. Many cartographers were to use Bufalini's plan as a prototype, but, especially in plastigraphic plans, East was set at the top. Orientation: Northeast (from A.P. Frutaz)*

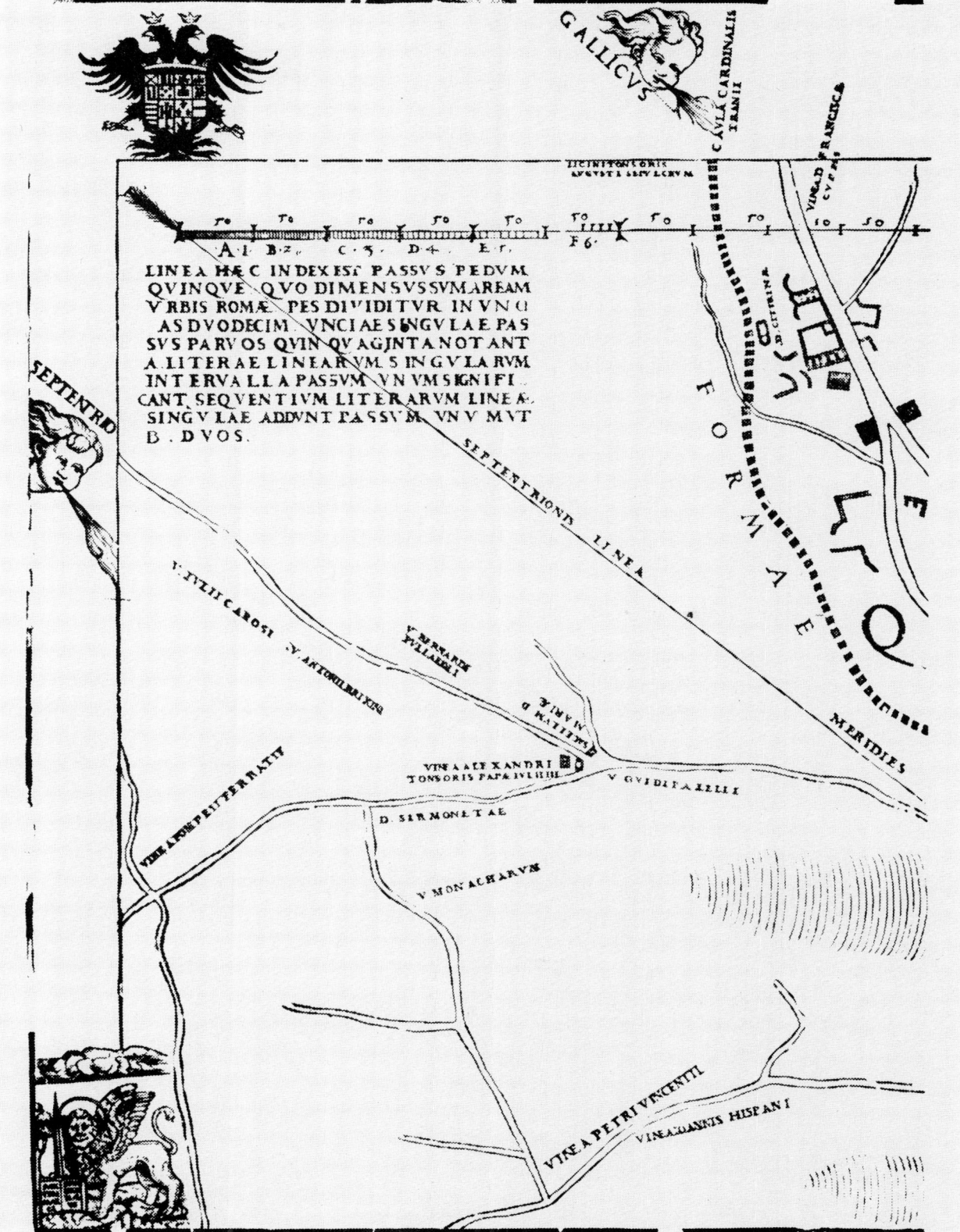

condition of the roofs and terraces. The photomap gives extremely precise information about them, including their altimetric heights, and the subject deserves to be dealt with in greater depth than a series of disconnected comments could provide. A study of the roofs of Rome with the help of the photomap could be an incentive for the local authorities to wage a battle that is not only abstractly worthwhile but highly feasible and with good prospects of victory: the battle against the unauthorized raising of buildings, the most obvious sign of architectural corruption in the city, especially when seen from above, as in the photomap.

Dormer window garrets, sunlights cut into roofs, solariums, and even small swimming pools, clutter up the roofs. But the most common form of unauthorized building are the "penthouses" built on top of blocks in the historic centre during a wave of unauthorized building in the 1960s which transformed so-called "technical volumes" into greatly sought-after dwellings. In the urban development plan these homes were concealed as washing or clothes-drying areas. It was as if washing machines had not yet come onto the market and "washing areas" were places where housewives still met each week, on appointed days arranged by porters straight out of neo-realistic films, to hang their double sheets in the sun, like mainsails or nightshirts resembling Penelope's peplos.

After cluttering up the hills of Parioli with thousands of blocks bristling with deluxe finished "technical volumes", the building culture of the penthouse spread to the historic centre, exporting its capacity for finding loopholes and camouflaging the new with the old on a holiday weekend, or even overnight. Since the times of Pinelli, immortalized by the poet Belli, the old centre had been inhabited by a destitute urban class that managed to survive thanks to welfare in the form of frozen rents. Moreover, the centre inevitably attracted a flow of well-off people due to the induced economy associated with the seats of economic and political power: Parliament, Senate, the Prime Minister's and President's official residences, banks, offices of Roman and non-Roman newspapers. The people linked to these seats of power, for various and increasingly pressing reasons, sought above all to occupy the ground-floor shops and upgrade them along with all the available housing. As the traditional floors for housing – the *piano nobile*, and other floors built above them in various stages between the eighteenth and nineteenth centuries – were occupied by tenants with frozen rents, the only possible

20. *Plan of Rome by G.B. Nolli (large), 1748. Frontispiece (from A.P. Frutaz)*

21. *Plan of Rome by G.B. Nolli (large), 1748. Sheet showing the area of San Giovanni in Laterano and Santa Croce in Gerusalemme. The windrose reveals that Nolli orients the plan to magnetic North. He was the first to do so in the history of Roman cartography (from A.P. Frutaz)*

22. *Plan of Rome by G.B. Nolli (large), 1748. Sheet depicting an architectural background with the Piazza del Campidoglio, the dome of St Peter's and the Porta Latina area. There is also a putto playing with a "praetorian table" on a tripod with a simple back-sight, the instrument used by the Como cartographer to make his excellent survey. Nolli owes a lot to Bufalini's work and acknowledges the "prototype" by reproducing it along with his engravings of a large and a small plan (from A.P. Frutaz)*

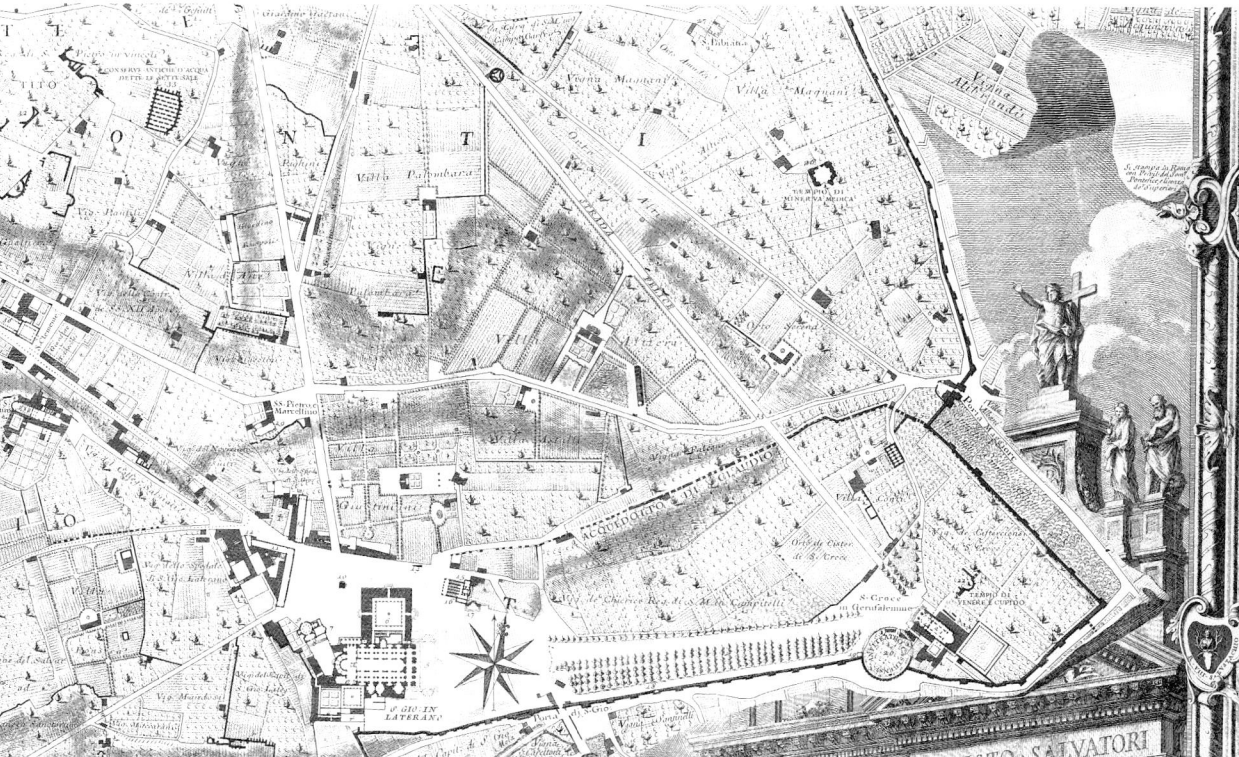

solution was to move the rich dwellings under and on top of the roofs. These new penthouses were in no way governed by the sort of legislative tradition existing in France, and, totally unlike the Parisian equivalents, were not destined for use by *bonnes* or penniless artists, but by a new ruling class.

The penthouses, furthermore, were built on top of a series of "natural" heights which were already at the physiological limit of the maximum height for masonry buildings. From the mid-eighteenth to the end of the nineteenth century, an average of two storeys were added to houses in the Renaissance area (the densest area of precious historic buildings), and similar additions were made to buildings throughout the entire city within the Aurelian Walls. Previously the average height of these houses had been three storeys, with many exceptions of two storeys. The first derogations on height regulations were granted to Renaissance princes for palaces used for ambassadorial or reception purposes. In the eighteenth century, rented houses as high as five storeys appeared on the edge of piazzas that would tolerate them. An example is to be found in Piazza Capranica, where one such building was the outcome of a property transaction

23. *Plan of Rome in 1900, drawn by the Third Regiment of Army Engineers in 1900. Scaccia Scarafoni and Frutaz are of the opinion that the plan was drawn with the "help of surveys made from an aerostatic balloon", as the comparison with the aerial view in ill. 24 would seem to confirm. Orientation: magnetic North at the top (from A.P. Frutaz)*

by a religious community which built for profit and extended the initial building to a whole block. Although significant from the point of view of experimentation and type, these were isolated phenomena. The most interesting building operations were those carried out around 1870 which led to whole streets extending upwards; Via del Corso, Via del Babuino and Via Giulia are just three examples. The ruling élite of the new unified Italy had already cast eyes on these streets as the city was undergoing complex and, on the whole, harmonious urban transformations, such as those in Corso Vittorio, the Prati quarter and the Esquilino area. The average height was limited to six storeys – as high as the building techniques of the time would permit – and new roads were built in suitable proportions.

At this time, buildings were raised with "natural" techniques and methods. Typological changes were made to the plan, starting with the arrangement of the entrance, the hall and stairway, which were all designed in accordance with the number of floors to be built (a practice described in the guidelines laid down by Gianfranco Caniggia's typological science, which is available to town-planning historians). But the penthouses, which were the outcome of property speculation in the 1960s, have nothing natural or physiological about them. They mushroomed on top of austere buildings like some infesting weed, debilitating and impoverishing in exactly the same way as fungi wear away old walls. Lifts were jammed into the already cluttered hallways. Excess weight pressed down on already weak upper floors and walls, which until around the 1950s had usually been built with a low quality mixture of tufa and bricks. New passages were even hammered open in the narrow walls for the sprouting service canalizations intended to rid the *nouveau riche* of their rubbish and provide them with refrigerated water or air, without ever worrying about possible damage or loss to the poor materials of the older part of the buildings – materials such as the wood of floors and beams, plaster, mortar and brittle tufa. This silent, furtive climbing upwards ended up making the lower floors uninhabitable. And it was here that the snake bit its own tail: the more lower storeys became uninhabitable, the more residential life had to move upwards, raising building heights in the absence of any mandatory regulations or, as was more often the case, the will to respect them where they did exist.

The loss of sunlight in historic centre buildings is also highlighted by the photomap, which, as we

24. *View of Rome in 1919, taken from the aeroplane of Lieutenant Umberto Nistri on 11 February 1919. Approximate scale of the original 1:10,000. Orientation: magnetic North at the top (from A.P. Frutaz)*

25. *Aerial view of Rome in 1934, taken by Umberto Nistri from an altitude of 3000 metres during the International Air Show and Conference on Aerophotogrammetry held in Paris in 1934. This detail shows the areas of Prati, Flaminio, the Pincio and Parioli. Orientation: magnetic North at the top (from A.P. Frutaz)*

26. *Aerophotogrammetric plan of Rome in 1961, photographed and printed in Rome by the Ente Topografico Aerofotogrammetrico (ETA) for the new Rome urban development scheme. Central area in a 1:5000 scale, reproduced in an approximate scale of 1:10,000. Orientation: magnetic North at the top (from A.P. Frutaz)*

explained, was the result of photography taken at the time of day and year when there was least shade and therefore the greatest amount of sunlight. At this point we should take a close look at an area of the historic centre with a great concentration of buildings of historic and economic interest. Via Condotti begins at Piazza di Spagna and runs straight down towards Tor di Nona, crossing Corso Umberto at right angles. As a good Roman *cardo*, Corso Umberto is oriented North-South (or, rather, inclined by a compass point to West), as prescribed by Vitruvius and the ancient Roman land surveyors, to avoid harmful and bothersome winds. Like its many parallels (and the whole area is almost a grid of right-angled streets, so we are talking about half of the total number), Via Condotti at midday is a deep furrow of shade, and only towards late afternoon, just before sunset, does it receive a little sunlight. The Corso and its parallels, on the other hand, receive a good deal of light at midday, but it is short-lived. By four in the afternoon the sun "sets" for good behind the roofs of the buildings facing east, and the Corso becomes just as dark as the streets perpendicular to it.

To sum up, then, frozen rents pushed the "new rich" in the 1960s to live over the heads of the "old poor" in the historic centre, thus raising houses to intolerable heights as far as statics and living conditions are concerned. There can be no doubt that staying within the limits set by nineteenth-century developments would be the optimum solution in a city not subject to demographic pressure. Of course this would have to be based on a healthy economic policy of restoring and improving buildings rather than worsening their condition, which is the case today due to the artificial nature of the property market.

Would this necessarily imply putting an end to the city's future as a services sector? But when has Rome, or at least the historic centre, ever had any other activity? Rome has been the archetypal service city for at least two thousand years. Its inhabitants have always worked in the service sector: innkeepers, hotel owners, bank clerks, craftsmen and even professionals involved in organizing services. And nowadays there are all kinds of professionals at all levels: the managers of all the offices of political, economic, bureaucratic and administrative power at a national, regional and local level.

We have listed the negative effects of the assault on the historic centre by service sector professionals, but we have also said that they had to move in very turbid conditions. Some sections of the

population still had the right to live in historic palaces of Renaissance princes or eighteenth-century cardinals at the same or even lower rents than those for low-cost popular housing built this century. Moreover, the proletarianization of the historic centre, only begun in Napoleonic times, had completely degraded an area which until the end of the seventeenth century had been the domain of bankers and courtiers – not to mention courtesans – who lived in more regal style than the greatest and most patronly Popes the city had ever seen. From the sixteenth-century Medici princes to Popes Urban VIII, Innocent X and Alexander VII, Via Giulia, Via dei Banchi Nuovi and Via del Corso were splendid and harmonious streets, but already much higher than the Renaissance golden mean that required height and width to be in a one to one ratio. The Villa Farnesina, Palazzo Spada, Palazzo Massimo and Palazzo Riario (later to become the Palazzo della Cancelleria) were among the most exclusive and representative dwellings in the world, and life proceeded in them according to ceremonial rites much more akin to religious services than bourgeois privacy.

Nowadays the palatial residences are moving to the suburbs, towards the green Roman countryside. Thanks to new means of transport and computer communications, they leave the few remaining residences to be swallowed up by service professionals – who finally have inherited the grounds and gardens of villas once owned by cardinals and princes – and to the services themselves, as is happening in almost all modern metropolises.

Given this situation, an increasingly less utopian vision emerges: the "thinning out" of the Renaissance centre of the city – the city of the political and administrative *Palazzi* – not in breadth but in height. There was, in fact, a too radical thinning out in breadth in the 1930s. But now the idea is to return the city's buildings to the form they had at the time of the creation of the Kingdom of Italy. This would be done in accordance with what we have already described as the physiological and natural height of buildings. Equally physiological and natural methods would be used, consisting in a return to the original typological and structural features of the buildings.

But have too many amnesties made the building situation solidify in an irremediably perverse structure? We believe the only way out from the harmful policy of amnesties, and the asphyxiating logic of fragmented public-owned property, is through the market. Naturally, the market can only take over once prices have been regulated. But this is the direction to be taken to avoid adopting a holier-than-though attitude and supplying the public with legislative tools that are no longer appropriate at a time of rapid and sweeping economic change.

With suitable historical and material research, it is now possible to reconstruct optimal street profiles that take into account the organic growth of the original buildings. Consequently we can reconstruct building typologies "stripped" of the contaminations created by the shortsighted boom in penthouses, and thus restore the buildings to the kind of dignity they had in the nineteenth century – if not earlier.

There is now an increasingly widespread and acknowledged tendency on the property market for owners to buy entire blocks or palaces, which are thus free of hindrances and the need to share with minor owners. The parties concerned can manage their capital, finally recognized as such, and their primary interest is to restore the building as an organic unit, rather than contributing to letting the asset they have just acquired at such a high price fall into ruin. These new owners are willing to relinquish ridiculous and harmful additions for the sake of the overall good of the whole building. Such moves could be encouraged in town-planning policies by offering tax benefits to the owners.

But perhaps all this is being a little over-ambitious in *Italietta*: the petty Italy of building amnesties and property transactions effected on long-weekend holidays. We should like to believe that it is feasible, however, especially bearing in mind that Italy is a country that will soon have to meet European standards. The great value of this photomap is that it will be the primary source of information for future restoration schemes and attempts to eliminate excess elevations from the city of Rome. Far from simply being a photographic souvenir of a beautiful but corrupt city at noon on a summer's day, the photomap is the fundamental working tool to be used in building a better city.

Eugenio Baldari   Bruno Cussino   Luigi Prestinenza Puglisi
Objectives and contents of the new cartographic system for Rome

Preface

According to Lao-Tze, "a house belongs to those who look at it and not those who live in it". We could equally apply this maxim to the whole built-up area of a city. Naturally we are not talking about property ownership, but the cultural and aesthetic aspects of the figurative nature of a city, which are of considerable importance in terms of enjoyable and intense spiritual experiences. Moreover, this will only be true insofar as we are able to grasp the "raison d'être des choses", to use Le Corbusier's phrase, or the innermost "meaning" that gives structure and life to built environments. As Goethe perceptively pointed out, "we cannot possess that which we do not understand". Accordingly, things will remain alien to us as long as we fail to understand them.

Over and above the functions described below, we should like this *Atlas of Rome*, with its photo-map and line map, to be used to make our city less alien, to help us better understand its structure revealed from an unusual angle. This publication should also prove useful for "specialists" trying to focus on the general problem of Rome's historical identity, which is connected to various specific problems concerning its "architectonic fabric", "urban morphology" and "architectural language" – problems that remain unsolved no matter how much they are debated.

On this subject, it is worth quoting art historian G.C. Argan on his experience as Mayor: "Rome is a unique city... it was never designed according to the calculations of economists or sociologists but has always been imagined... After 1870, Rome was no longer imagined. There was a desire to plan it. Unfortunately, the authorities who planned its development were all for property speculation and the city did not grow harmoniously, but its development was strictly linked to its exploitation... Rome has lost its historical identity."

A paradoxical image

In one of his works, Borges recounts how a group of cartographers, blinded by the myth of exact correspondences between an object and its representation, created such a perfect map on a life-size scale that it was no different from reality. The result was an enormous map that served no practical purpose and was as useless as it was true to life. Leaving aside the paradox, we see that Borges focuses on the interminable question of the relation between words and things, and leads us to surmise that if science progresses, it is thanks partly to the disingenuous efforts of those wishing to make models so close to the original that they are exact copies.

The efforts involved in producing this publication could be seen in the light of Borges' paradoxical tale. There is the same chimerical attempt to achieve an exact correspondence between reality and its images no matter what form they take – in this case by integrating a conventional plan with aerial photography.

Over and above the poetic image, it must be said that, for at least twenty years now, after a concern with purely economic analysis or attempts at classification according to function and techniques of urban zoning, there has been a greater emphasis on supplying images of cities simply as physical objects, the main purpose being to provide concrete information about their unique nature.

In line with now well-established works like Aldo Rossi's *L'architettura della città*, Giuseppe Samonà's *L'urbanistica e l'avvenire della città*, and Gianfranco Caniggia's *Le strutture dello spazio antropico*, other efforts in this direction include more recent analytic urban studies such as Bernardo Secchi's investigations, right up to "third generation plans". Along with these, we should also mention the countless studies on individual Italian towns produced by various publishers (the eighth volume of the *Storia dell'arte italiana* by Einaudi, the Laterza monographs and specialized reviews), as well as the city atlases with photogrammetric surveys (Marsilio), research into building techniques and modes, begun by Battisti and relaunched through publication (Edilstampa), and lastly, the *Manuali del recupero*, edited by the Rome City Council's Special Office for the Historic Centre.

The *Atlas of Rome* comes into the category of those projects seeking to establish models that represent cities in their concrete and unique nature. There can be no doubt that such projects have only been made possible thanks to computer science. The map published here is a fundamental part of a numeric system of cartography (processed and managed by computers) which associates alphanumeric information (information entries) with individual building units. Moreover, the system is able to generate particularly effective three-dimensional views and models.

This subject will be dealt with in greater depth below, but in the meantime I would like to return to Borges. In a work entitled *Words and Things*, he mentions a certain *Chinese Encyclopedia* in which animals are divided as follows: *a)* belonging to the Emperor; *b)* stuffed; *c)* tame; *d)* piglets; *e)* mermaids; *f)* fabulous; *g)* wild dogs; *h)* included in the present classification; *i)* frenetic; *j)* countless; *k)* drawn with a very fine camel-hair brush; *l)* et cetera; *m)* that make love; *n)* that look like flies from afar.

Like the paradox of the cartographers, this absurd and ironic taxonomy contains a hidden literary truth, as well as several scientific and philosophical notions. Indeed, Foucault was to base his attempt to found an archaeology of the human sciences on this text. The absurd nature of the classification contains a specific lesson for we computer people: although it is possible to create an almost infinite number of taxonomic series, not all of them have useful/practical truths. Many may even turn out to be less subtly absurd (and not at all ironical) than those in Borges' unlikely *Chinese Encyclopedia*. As McLaughlin has commented, it is senseless to gather an infinite multitude of "data". They will probably be too many and definitely unusable in constructing a model that, as far as possible, should be simple, well-oriented and made up of a controllable number of variables.

In the case of the historic centre of Rome, after many attempts at achieving a satisfactory approximation of the real, attempts are now being made to find models which, although partial, are able to meet the needs of different forms of knowledge. Among these are thematic maps and three-dimensional models. If we were to put ourselves in the place of Borges' absolutely accurate cartographers, we should have to raise a number of doubts. Thematic maps supply useful information, but they are impersonal and deliberately partial. Three-dimensional models, on the other hand, fail to capture the concrete reality of a building, its grain and material.

Personally, I have always found Nolli's plan quite extraordinary. In this seventeenth-century work, the external urban spaces and the plans of churches, seen as covered piazzas, appear side by side. Similar plans were also made of other cities, including Venice. Although partial, such plans provide a tool for understanding a single public space, for at that time churches were just as much public places and spaces as outside areas. Evidence of this even comes from the memoirs of some libertines, or, going even further back in time, from the Church's recommendations intended to eliminate

27. *Piazza della Madonna de' Monti; Fontana di Giacomo della Porta.* Three-dimensional computer image (project by F. Pecoraro, F. Berti and M. Panunti)

the excess number of naves and chapels that lent themselves to furtive encounters and immoral practices in the penumbra.

Equally remarkable are a number of three-dimensional views, such as the bird's-eye views, which, although far from accurate, do give a physical sense of the city, its colours and unique features.

Although it still has a number of shortcomings compared to the more intuitive productions of the cartographers and engravers mentioned here, computerized cartography has the advantage and potential of being a tool able to develop and grow in time, continually reorganizing its classifications and information.

The cartography of the centre of Rome: a simple conceptual model

When initiates to the world of computer science begin to see just how much information can be managed, processed and synthesized, they are often tempted to believe that highly complex and articulated realities can be controlled very easily. There then begins a kind of hunt for "data", seen as unitary, absolute and totally objective elements. But the realization soon dawns on them that these elements are far from unitary or objective, having been gathered either for definite purposes, which immediately annuls their objectivity, or according to approximate criteria, which set limits to their reliability.

A further misunderstanding, arising from the considerable power of both the hardware and software of computer systems, is that it is easy to manage huge quantities of data for different uses. Consequently there is a temptation to construct complex archives able to respond to thousands of potential user needs. The outcome may be compared to the sense of bewilderment felt in the dusty corridors of enormous traditional state archives. We know they are full of incredibly rich and interesting material, but it is necessarily classified in such a monotonous way that it is very difficult to identify and get at the elements we require.

Our case, however, is much simpler, or rather, the things of interest to us are few and well-defined. It is like going into a big department store which has thousands of articles on display but you only want a few at a time. If you do not come with a precise shopping list you are liable to end up with a bag full of unwanted items.

This *Atlas* is based on a few easily identified and commonly used elements. And the same can be said of the underlying information system. Even a base map, however, struggles to keep up with developments in the enormous area under the jurisdiction of the City of Rome (150,736 hectares), an area in continual evolution due to the growth of new zones and construction of new buildings. The same difficulty is encountered by the administrators, technicians and experts who have trouble in describing the situation that they are supposed to be working with every day. The ancient city is the largest historic centre in the world (almost 1500 hectares) and has a very dense urban fabric. Some of its buildings have existed for centuries, others for two millennia, but even they are continually being modified as they undergo both authorized and unauthorized elevations or demolitions, changes to street furniture, pavements, pedestrian precincts, and green areas in the form of parks and gardens.

Aerial photography now goes back some seventy years. But manual plotting times of good aerial photography are too slow for a metropolitan area, while automatic processing systems are fairly economic for public authorities and only require few specialized human resources to manage them.

Therefore, a flight plan and photographic survey provide an easy and rapid tool for updating and rectifying on the computer.

The principles underlying the approach adopted for the line map and photomap of the historic centre of Rome are relatively straightforward: an initial, accurate, traditional, plotted plan is transferred into numeric form and updated by successive flights; the stages are divided into suitable time gaps with immediate updating automatically managed by computer processing.

The plan opposite the photomap is not overloaded with information which would be of no interest to most users. It simply shows the internal and external shapes of buildings (external outline, courtyards – aerial photos are not always easy to read), street names, spot heights (there are many hills, rises, steps, etc.), and information about public property.

The result is a tool which can certainly be more easily read than necessarily more fragmentary traditional maps. The scale is small enough for an accurate overall view (each sheet covers over six hectares, 62,500 square metres) but large enough to make out even the tiniest houses, cars and trees.

28. *Piazza della Madonna de' Monti; Fontana di Giacomo della Porta. Detail of the new layout and street furniture scheme (F. Pecoraro, F. Berti and M. Panunti)*

29. *Piazza della Madonna de' Monti; Fontana di Giacomo della Porta. New layout (F. Pecoraro, F. Berti and M. Panunti)*

The cartographic system for the historic centre of Rome is based on the simplicity of the fundamental elements to be represented. The logical base is the urban block (a housing block or building identifiable as a unit delimited by streets, squares, etc.). This basic unit can be further divided into sub-units (courtyards, cloisters, internal areas, roofing elements, etc.). The base unit is associated with place names, though more directly with the abstract but commonly used administrative area, such as the *rione* (quarter) and census section. This makes it possible to build up complex data archives from a few elements.

Thanks to data processing, building surfaces and volumes and other classified features, population statistics, and ownership data can be directly derived or easily linked up, cross-checked and verified. More indirectly, through simple logical operational steps it is possible to build up complex archives starting from straightforward identification elements. Thus, what we have are not a few complex models but many modules which are individually or globally accessible and which can be mutually integrated with a common topographic matrix. This also makes it possible to construct typologies and models according to the various individual user needs, be they study, designing or public works.

Historical and traditional maps are certainly less impersonal and, in a rigorous representation, can provide rich pictorial imagery, which reflects not only the nature of the place but the way it is described, the "manner" of seeing it. Such maps often seem a personal narrative written by pen and embellished by drawings or small watercolours, and they are consequently study and research tools of matchless charm. Modern map-making cannot offer this kind of charm. But the photographic images (combined with automatic drawing) can provide a much more unusual idea of the city. For although the images are near enough to make out things and people, they have been taken from a privileged and unorthodox view point.

Images and pictorial views, palaces and places – the images from traditional views are almost in a different world from computer-generated images. But it would be an oversimplification merely to write off the latter as being impersonal. Each element represented has been carefully constructed in the mind before being transposed with a "pen" (though here the pen is actually an optomagnetic pointer in a computer programme). In a few hours, or even minutes, depending on its speed and

30. *Piazza Manfredo Fanti. Three-dimensional computer image of part of the new layout and street furniture scheme for the area in front of the Acquario Romano (F. Pecoraro, F. Berti and M. Panunti)*

power, a computer builds dozens of elevations with different light and shading. In this case the computer is used for planning. It helps us, but also others, understand the impact of an architectural design, of changes to a square, street or area. In the past, elevations were a means of visual representation and communication, often very striking, but just as often an end in themselves. Now they are part of a rapid technique for visualizing, understanding and communicating.

Rome is a very complex city to represent and, like many others, it is constantly evolving. By using the now well-established art of photography and the new tool of data processing, the whole local area can be represented, and without falling prey to the illusion of total objectivity. The resulting image may be conventionally structured, but if the larger scale of a public space, square or short itinerary is used, it can also arouse curiosity and excite the public imagination.

Techniques, materials and problems

Following the evolution of specific application programmes and developments in hardware, a specialized market has sprung up. User interfaces have been improved and both hardware and software can be accessed and used more easily. There has been a drastic fall in processing costs and a downward spread in technology and management systems, which until a few years ago were only possible on very expensive hardware in highly specialized computer centres.

Now it is possible, with a few restrictions of speed and screen quality, to manage fairly large cartographic archives on low-cost computers that can be utilized by non-specialist individual users. The results of processing can then be transferred onto paper or a photographic support by means and techniques which, though too expensive for individual users, can be produced economically enough in specialized service centres.

All this is possible because the cartographic system developed for the historic centre of Rome was designed from the outset with these factors in mind, at a time when the market still did not offer low-cost hardware for users like university students or researchers. Thus, one of the priorities to be developed is to supply data and archives in formats that can be easily and rapidly transferred into any other environment.

Here we come to what may be the most important feature of the system. Setting aside the initial quality of the archives, made with modest economic resources and therefore containing many initial defects (since corrected), the most important factor is the great ease with which this product can be corrected and updated, often as a result of direct inexpensive surveys effected by the parties concerned.

The three-dimensional models require more specific training. One of the main aims of the models is to act as a backup and checkpoint for working designs, often on an urban scale. Although necessarily schematic for organizational purposes, these models require a capacity for overall vision which normally can only really be acquired by those who have worked for long periods of time with analogous traditional techniques. But then again, even those operators with little experience of drawing and plotting can obtain fairly valid results.

Archives and processing

In addition to literary paradoxes, town-planners and administrators must come to terms with limited funds, restrictive laws, and established juridical practices that for centuries have governed the knowledge, use, management and control of a city's buildings. Codified in the statutes of the medieval city, and even represented schematically in some (mainly descriptive) cadastres as early as the fifteenth century, the customs and obligations connected with the construction and control of a city's buildings have always been a primary element in the

31. Piazza Manfredo Fanti. Three-dimensional computer image of part of the new layout and street furniture scheme for the area in front of the Acquario Romano (F. Pecoraro, F. Berti and M. Panunti)

growth of urban communities. There is a temptation, then, to include in plans and maps schematic information about the geometry of buildings and details of both public and private ownership. In the case of the historic centre of Rome, priority was accorded to quantitative information on buildings (surfaces, volumes and topographic location). Such information was derived from the aerophotogrammetric map and accompanied by information on ownership from the cadastral map, which was overlaid when necessary. Further study of this information led to a new thematic map (a map of publicly-owned properties in the historic centre of Rome).

More recently, as a direct consequence of the information system described above, it has been possible to gain access to, and cross-reference, information from other archives, such as public service company archives (SIP, ENEL and ITALGAS). These archives can provide complex functional pictures of daily public life in the city, and form the basis of attempts to improve spaces, routes and services.

The map based on aerophotogrammetry goes back to 1980, but was corrected and updated by a special survey flight in May 1990. The scales are 1:1000 for an area of around 1500 hectares and 1:500 for around 530 hectares. To this base, 1400 place names were added.

The cadastral map is derived from originals made available by the Ministry of Finance (Direzione generale del catasto e dei servizi tecnici erariali). Thematic information on property not directly derivable from cadastral sources is then added. This information is still being processed. An official trial run is planned by the appropriate cadastral offices.

With the aim of managing the architectural and monumental heritage more efficiently, a number of programmatic and operational agreements have been reached with research institutions (the CNR and the Commissione per la valutazione del rischio ambientale), the Heritage Superintendencies, university faculties (Dipartimento di storia e analisi della città), and planning organizations. The latter organizations, specially appointed to study and control the city's buildings, receive a great deal of help from the calculation system for three-dimensional representations, which can provide spatial and land models even over wide areas.

The future of part of our knowledge of the form and structures of the city will undoubtedly be linked to the evolution and spread of similar systems of archiving and management, now possible with even modest resources. The resultant functional and representational models will have their own autonomy as a dynamic cognitive aid. They do not, or cannot, claim to be alternatives to planning, but thanks to their intrinsic capacity for rapid processing of increasingly large information flows, they can generate qualitatively limited but quantitatively useful and effective planning information.

System architecture

The fundamental problem in the approach to a similar project is the study and development of a system architecture that allows for integration with existing or future models and systems.

Given the extremely fast-evolving nature of hardware and software, it is impossible to design a system architecture that is easily exportable and adaptable. Nonetheless, it is possible, as we have attempted to show, to structure archives, procedures and models with flexibility in mind. Both the cartographic and alphanumeric archives can be exported in a number of standard forms (ASCII, DXF and IGES). The procedures were written in both C and Fortran 77, following as closely as possible the most widespread specifications and standardized dialects, and gradually eliminating internal macroinstructions in non-standard languages, or, worse, calls to system – access to particular areas of hardware memory – that optimize the resources of a programme but bind its use to one particular piece of hardware.

Already widely acquired by the system, these features may be considered as the final stage and ideal state of a product whose use is already far-reaching, especially given the sweeping computerization process of information in public administration, research institutions, design and planning companies and even in the small- and medium-sized architectural and engineering studios.

The advantages to be had from producing protocols for the spread of data to be processed or reprocessed are beneficial to all. This was obvious when we considered the different categories of end users, but until recently it was less obvious to the

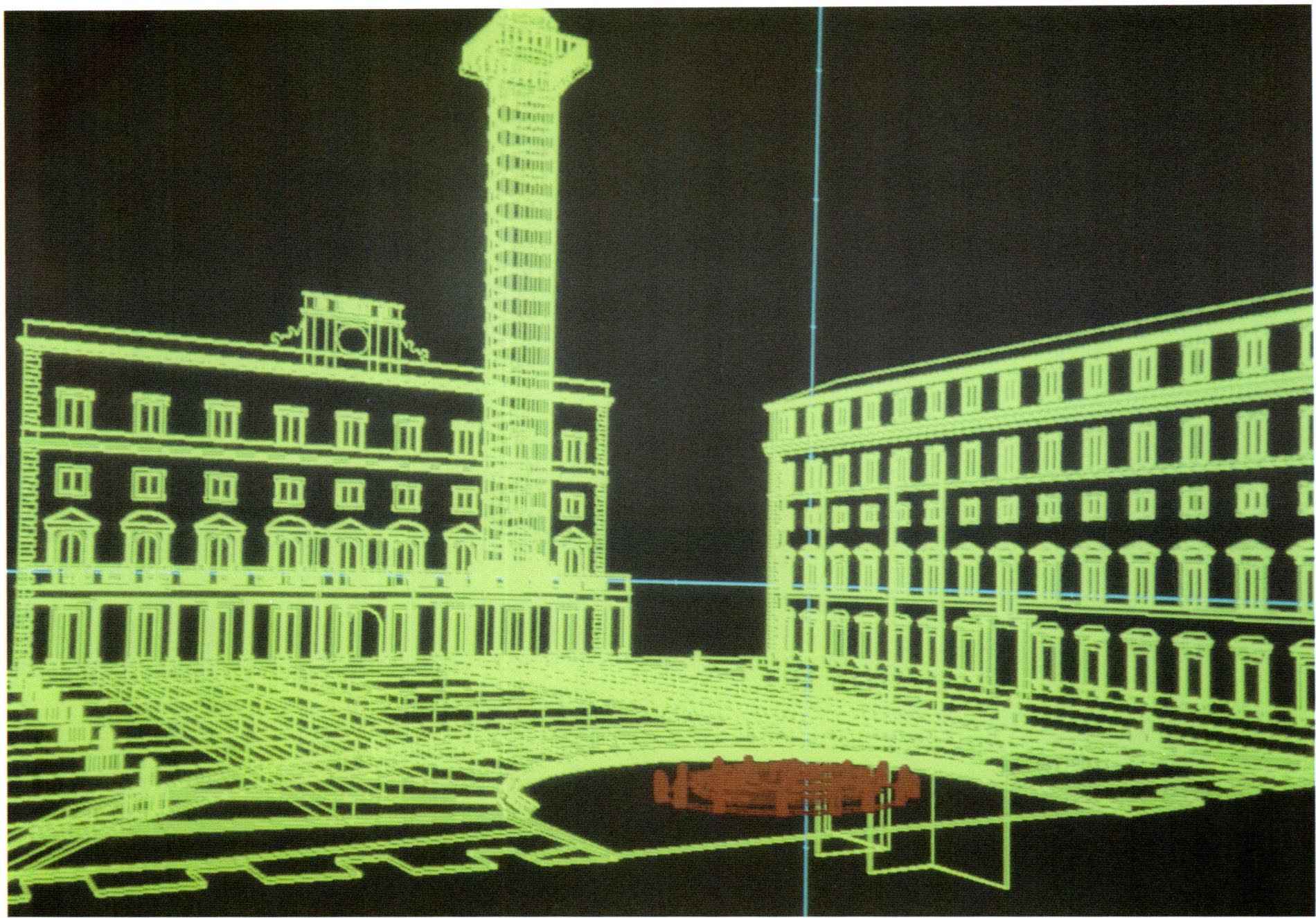

32. *Piazza Colonna. Wire-frame perspective view. Computer image for the new layout and street furniture scheme (A. Simbolotti and M. Martini; computer processing by F. Bramerini)*

firms distributing and/or producing applications programmes for cartography, town-planning and designing. In fact there was a tacit established practice of binding the programmes to limited homogeneous families of hardware. If in the past this could be justified by the need to make the most of high-performance hardware, the advent of new, incredibly high-performance systems and the collapse in market standards, along with the de facto imposition of standard operating systems and languages (UNIX System V, DOS, Windows, XWindows, C and Fortran), has led those who insisted on trying to impose one single direction into untenable positions.

Given the basic similarities in performance and prices, it is no longer economically viable or important to insist on one particular hardware system, and it is a big mistake to try and force customers to depend on long-term service contracts. This presupposes an elasticity in structure that the vast majority of software houses do not have. Moreover, it would mean they would have to dedicate their human resources to a permanent hunt to vary features in their systems as rapidly as possible. Even

33. *Piazza Colonna. Wire-frame perspective view. Computerized image of a new layout and street furniture scheme (A. Simbolotti and M. Martini; computer processing by F. Bramerini)*

34. *Piazza Colonna. Computerized wire-frame isometric view of a detail of the facade of the Palazzo Wedekind (computer processing by F. Bramerini)*

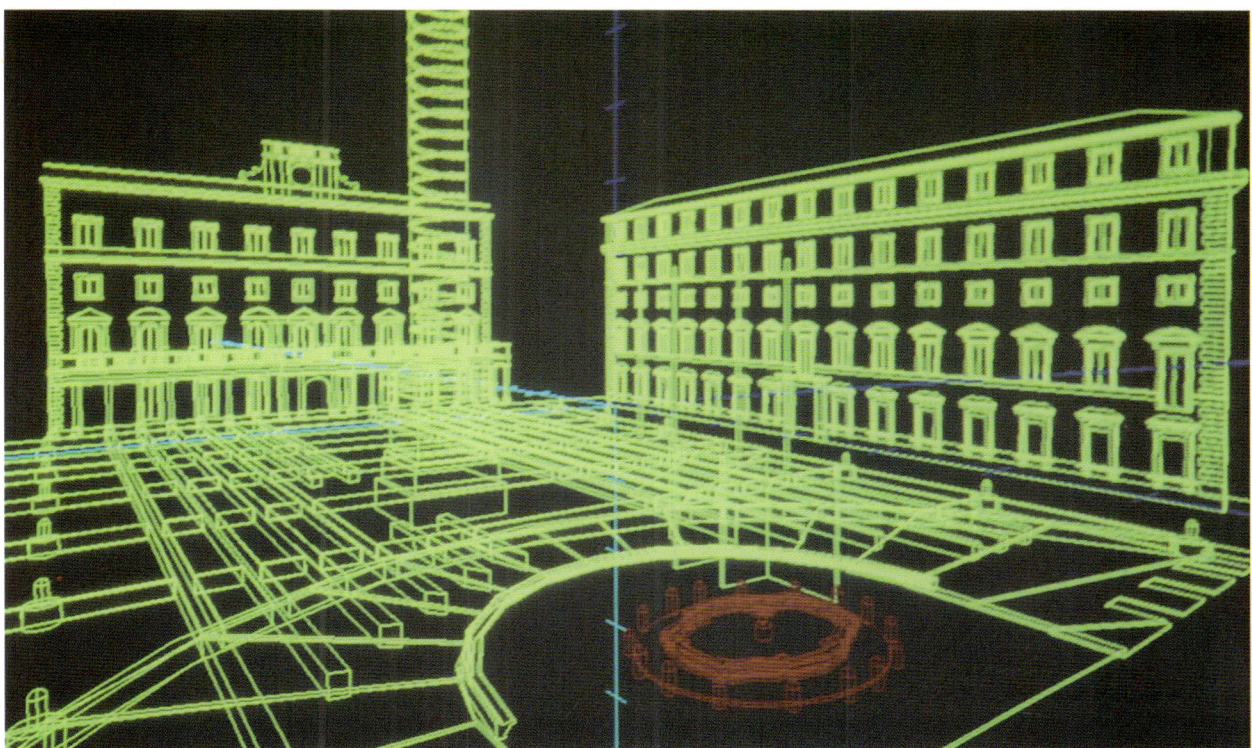

the parent companies producing both hardware and software now increasingly tend to quickly absorb software products that have already been successful on the market, as well as particularly successful malleable hardware parts (special graphics adapters, specially developed graphics microprocessors) produced by groups that cannot go beyond a certain production threshold, never mind marketing threshold.

In this brief overview of the systems environment, we must further note the fading of distinctions between families of computers in terms of some of their performances and features. There was (and still is) a distinction between personal computers (PCs), microcomputers, minicomputers, and the mainframe computer, often in terms of the processing speed of given procedures and in the capacity both to manage various jobs at the same time (multitasking) and provide this possibility for several users (multi-user mode). This articulated complex of possibilities defined the borderlines between families of computers and their respective operating systems. Today these classifying parameters are gradually disappearing, since multitasking is now possible on a good personal computer, and multi-user mode is available by using UNIX on low-cost hardware. This means that local networks (LAN), or even remote networks, have a de facto multi-user mode (still with a few limitations) for PCs, as they link up with each other and link up the user with more powerful processing units. There are now – and they are an aggressive presence on the market – "small", low-cost, extremely fast computers whose features can be compared to nominally superior categories of hardware.

Not without a certain difficulty, efforts are being made in the automatization project of urban-scale cartography, as well as of town planning and architectural schemes for the historic centre of Rome, to come to terms with current market conditions, since this project must address members of the public and specialized users with very different systems. While the public administration shows a growing demand for structured numeric information, planners, researchers and students expect archives to be able to adapt to the limits of their own resources and need access to data and procedures not only in paper form but also in numeric form.

Consequently the architecture of the cartographic and planning system of the Office for the Historic Centre is structured so that it is possible to work in the local network LAN, using either of the two most common operating systems (DOS or UN-

35. Piazza Colonna. Shaded perspective view (processing by F. Bramerini)

36. Piazza Colonna. Detail of the facade of the Palazzo Chigi. Shaded wire-frame computer image (processing by F. Bramerini)

ix), and in uniform environments (XWindows and Windows), with personal computers linked up to peripherals such as graphics printers, plotters and digitizers (for the acquisition and correction of data) and having programmes able to combine graphic data and alphanumeric archives. There will also be the possibility in the near future of long-distance links with archives and systems in other parts of the local administration (Rome City Council) or with the State (Superintendent for Historic Monuments).

The public administration's efforts to adapt presuppose elasticity on the part of the administrative structures and motivated technicians who are morally gratified but also often weighed down by everyday red tape problems that contrast with the dynamic nature of the problems they have to tackle.

The cartographic product only apparently has limits: a compromise was struck so as to show the possibilities for updating and correction, while the archive chosen (the publicly-owned property archive), produced in time for the Office for the Historic Centre, is soon to be radically updated and integrated.

As is generally the case in complex operations, there may be mistakes and omissions. Some very specialized users may feel the need for more technical and more detailed plans. Such plans are available, but how many "readers" would be interested, or able, to read them?

Having opted to present the great mass of information in another more specialized place, here we have simply provided an absolutely new and precious tool comprehensible to all. Although the final result may not have some of the pictorial beauty of the old drawings, from the unusual view point of the aerial photography it allows an effective comparison between an objective vision of reality and its practical conventional representation. Finally, this tool is all the more useful in that it is part of a dynamically updated system of production, and – despite the undeniably complex nature of the underlying technique – can easily be consulted and propagated.

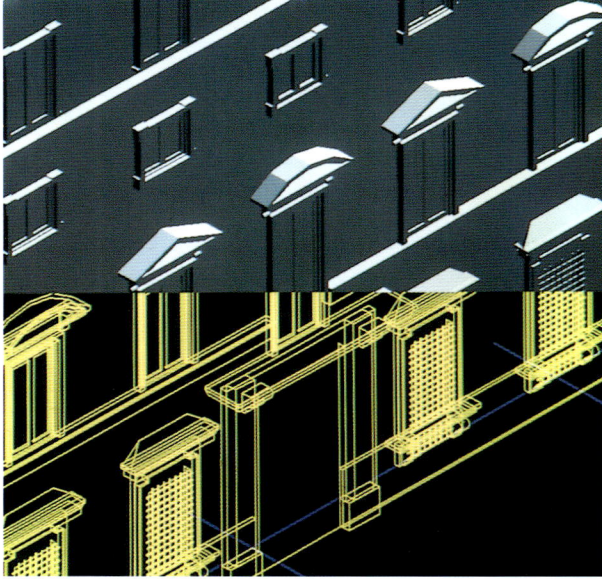

Gabriella Maltese   Daniele Tinacci
Mapping technology

Unlike the earlier work on Venice (Marsilio 1989), in *An Atlas of Rome* the aerial photographs are accompanied by a map that not only represents the topographical aspects of the area but also a number of unusual thematic features derived from non-cartographic sources: the "use" of buildings and spaces by a particular category of users, in this case public bodies.

This thematic content represents just one of many analyses of the area carried out by the Special Office for Works in the Historic Centre. The purpose of such analyses is to improve our knowledge of, and thus govern better, the dynamics of transformation in the complex urban system of the present-day historic centre of Rome.

The tool used for these analyses, for planning and monitoring, is the Sistema Informativo Territoriale (SIT). Created by AUTOMAP of Rome and AEROFOTO CONSULT with the aim of developing a databank, this computerized system uses multimedia techniques to integrate and manage complex detailed archives of cartographic, architectural, judicial, socioeconomic and administrative information.

The "heart" of the system is GEODIS (Geographic Distributed Information System), entirely developed by AUTOMAP, which moves and links up two "brains" – IBM computer systems with RISC technology – to graphic and alphanumeric peripherals for the input or output of data. Thanks to these instruments, for a number of years now a rationalization and interlinking process of data has been underway. The data in question had been gathered by the City Council offices over the years, but was only available in a variety of disaggregate forms, which could only be correlated by means of painstaking interpretations.

Bearing in mind these working conditions, we wish to illustrate the three main components of SIT – the databanks, software and hardware. But we should like to begin by making some general comments on the overall approach adopted.

General features: databanks and local-area databanks

A "databank" is generally considered to be a set of data on a specific theme organized in a structure designed so that the data may be used both individually or in an aggregate fashion.

A more or less complex structure is indispensable not only so that research methods are not restricted to scrolling through the entire collection, but also because it is often the "natural container" of further information determined by the interrelations intrinsic to a specific item of information. It would only be slight exaggeration to say that the structure is the container for "meta-information" that is often more important than the actual base information. The design of the data structure is strictly correlated to the *specific* aims of the databank itself.

In paper databanks, the structure is necessarily *rigid*. This means that a more or less radical change in purpose involves large-scale restructuring problems for the archives. In the case of large quantities of data, such operations are almost always so long and troublesome that they are a waste of time. This also applies to electronic archives. But it is much easier to create or maintain dense complex structures in electronic archives than in paper ones. Moreover, in recent times considerable efforts have been made to ensure that structures are more flexible or to create structures that are less dependent on the specific aims of cataloging.

Initially, software for managing database structures (DBMS – Data Base Management Systems) followed criteria meant to make the internal structures visible, forcing the user to maintain them manually. This was the case with hierarchy or network DBMS, which also suffered from a kind of rigidity. Consequently, the application of research criteria not contemplated in the design stage always turned out to be troublesome.

Currently, the best results are obtained from the so-called "relational" concept, whereby structures can be created dynamically from raw data, provided, of course, they are based on information

37. Rome. Historic Centre. Map of the Census sections and street blocks; overprint of the information sheet for a section (1981 ISTAT Census data)

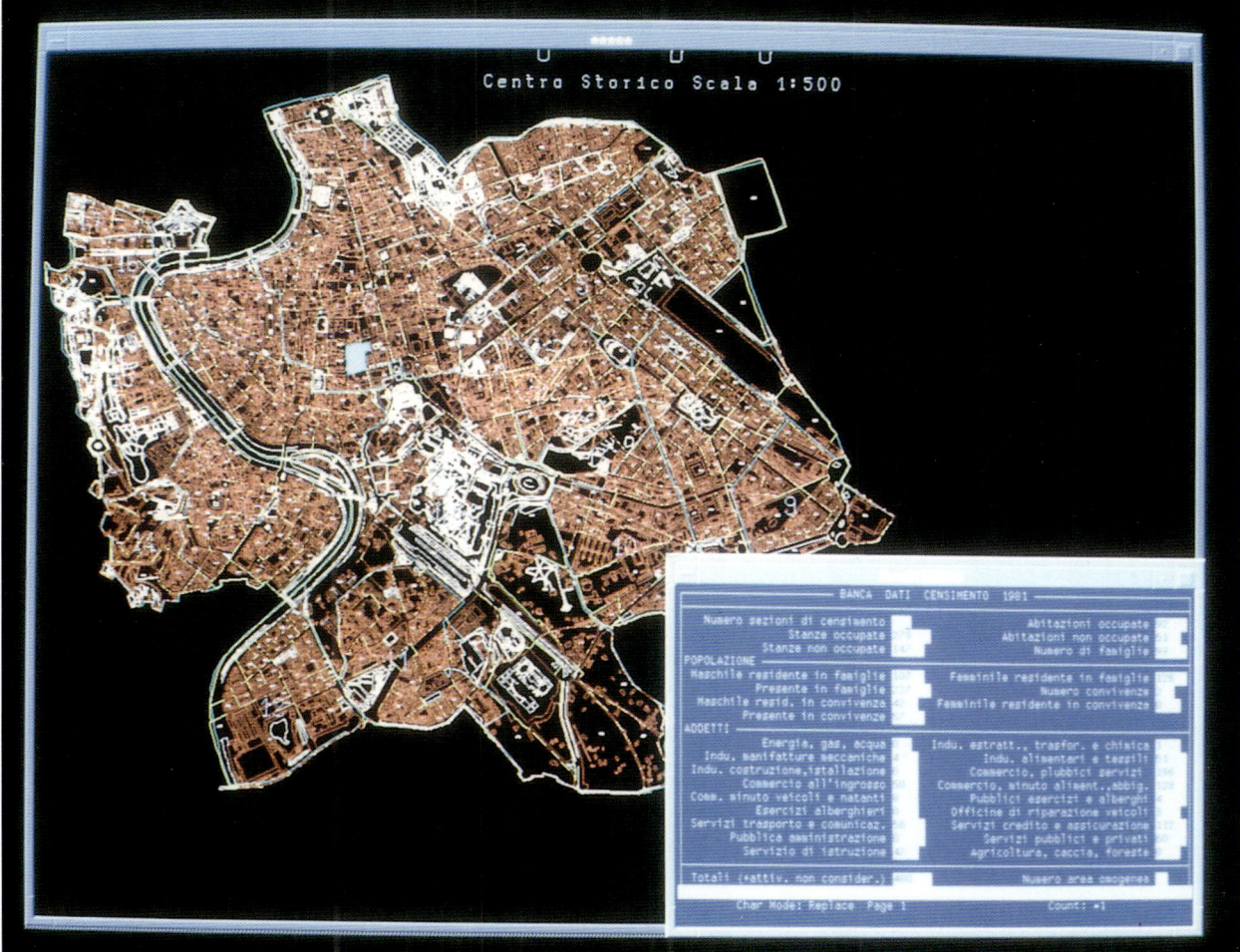

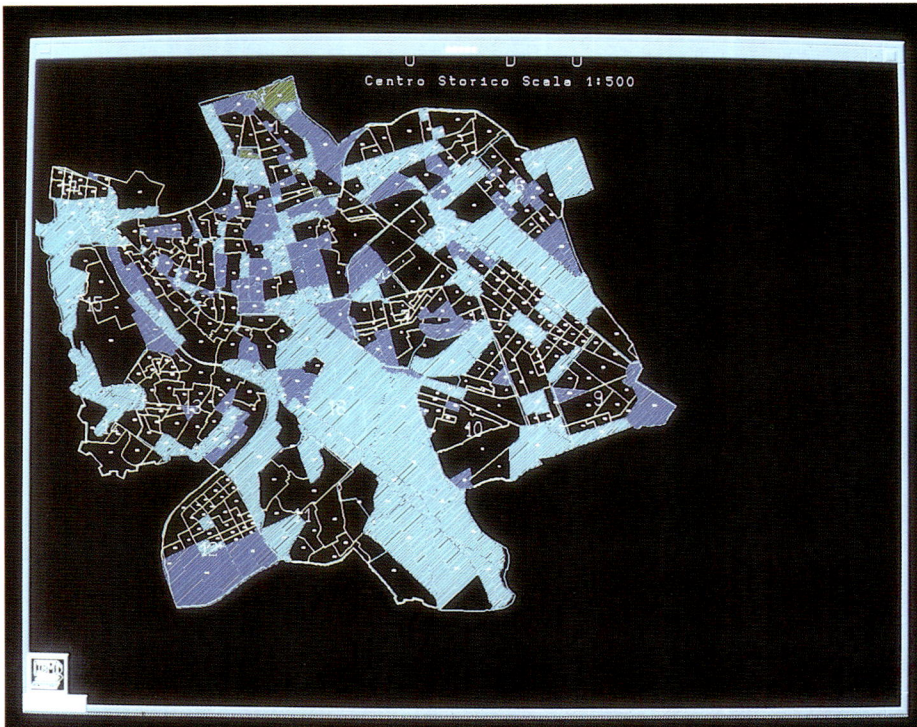
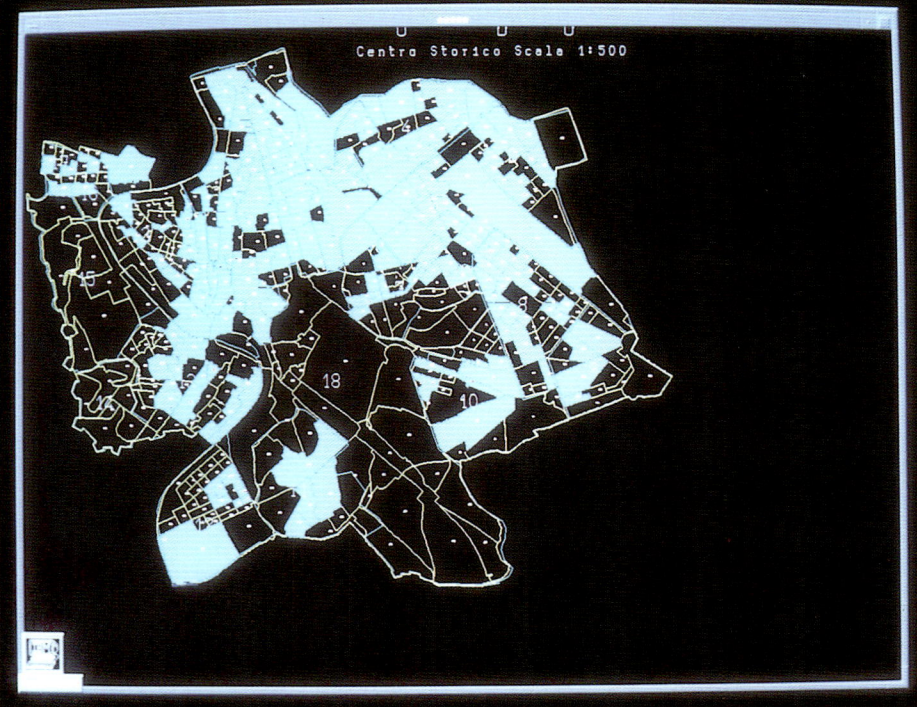

38. Rome. Historic Centre. Map of the Census sections and street blocks; sections with under 100 residents are indicated in light blue and those with under 200 residents in purple (1981 ISTAT Census data)

39. Highlighting of sections with more than 100 traders (from the databank for retail and wholesale traders; 1981 ISTAT Census data)

already contained in some form in the existing data. This was the solution adopted for the Rome City Council area.

In a relational DBMS, the fundamental concept is that of a table: a very simple column and row structure in which each row represents an item of information and each column a descriptive field. A relational DBMS enables the discovery of relations between data (implicit structures in the data itself, but which have not been precoded as such) through a definition of field "views" – selection criteria based on logical equations and various kinds of functions (mathematical, string, etc.). Views are not predetermined when designing databases and can be defined, and thus applied to the data, according to particular needs. Whenever a particular "view" is applied to the data, the DBMS produces the list required. Having been generated dynamically (i.e. at the time of application and not at the time of the definition of the view itself) this list takes into account all the modifications (cancellations, corrections, insertions) that have occurred right up to an instant earlier.

As long as access to computerized databases was rigid, their applications were necessarily limited to areas densely populated by data, but conceptually very simple, predictable and with standard accesses. Consequently, they only had a routine use. A typical example is provided by the City Council registry office. It has a densely populated universe of basic data (all the data for each individual citizen), but generally requires standard and temporally stable procedures.

The great flexibility of relational systems allows very ambitious objectives to be achieved. This has directly affected the aim of our project, since the value of a database attempting to describe phenomena in a given region – attempts, that is, to use structures containing localized relations – would be highly questionable if it did not entail great flexibility and dynamic access.

The phenomena covered by the administrative and geographical term "local" are so varied, fluid and changeable that a rigid design of a routine enquiry would be utterly vain. The will or, to be more precise, the need to think in terms of a varied typology of data in their natural location in the area in question implies the need to use software able to dominate the extremely dynamic phenomena concerned. Here the idea is to build a kind of container model in which each datum not only has a position but, above all, is managed and integrated through structures which, by means of extreme syntheses, make it possible to verify and discover transverse phenomena that only come together and are seen in the field.

We deliberately introduced the concepts of relational software systems to place them in strict correspondence with the needs just described. But from the point of view of computerized usage, although indispensable, a relational data management system is not enough for our purposes. Given that the data are in tables, the relational DBMS has difficulty in manipulating strictly local-area (geographical and geometrical) information which requires a kind of user interface that is as natural as a table is for other kinds of information. What is required is a graphic, or rather, cartographic interface. Just as relational system tables resemble tables in paper catalogues, a system which claims to represent a local area must also do so in cartographic form. This is not so much because we are accustomed to using maps, but, on the contrary, because cartography is the way of representing areas that man has worked out and perfected for thousands of years to meet his needs (thus it is cartography which is "accustomed" to man and not vice versa).

A local-area DBMS cannot fail to take into account the need to represent the area in all its relational spaces and must present them to the outside world (the user interface) in a cartographic form, just as a relational system presents its own data in a (natural) table form. The system must also manage more "conventional" information in table form and must

40. *Extract from the public property plan*

maintain references to items in both directions: i.e in the tables and on the maps whose reference points are correlated to table items thanks to "local-area" (i.e. spatial) relations. The system must easily create "views" of data using mixed criteria, both table and local-area (spatial), with output of the views in both table and cartographic form.

Once the database of all the information levels required has been loaded, this kind of system easily accommodates verification enquiries into the state of various phenomena in the area. If also based on a relational DBMS for maintaining table data, it is likewise easy to add supplementary additional elements from other information levels, as well as the gradual building up of databases according to the real needs that have emerged.

The Rome City Council local-area databank

This, then, was the underlying logic behind the building up of databanks for the historic centre of Rome. These databanks consist of cartographic, graphic and alphanumeric archives, all geo-referenced so that the information system covers the whole local area and can be completely integrated.

In building up the databanks the following cartographic sources were used:
– the 1980 aerophotogrammetric survey, partly on a 1:500 scale and partly 1:1000, included in the national geodetic system and thus using Gauss-Boaga coordinates;
– 1:1000 cadastral maps based on the Cassini-Soldner plane coordinates, cut differently from the base map and not divided irregularly in full sheets, but in closed parcels;
– the 1:2000 city toponymic plan, with no geographical background, containing the complete street plan, the perimeters and official numbering of the census sections and street blocks.

Overall, the archive consisted of just under 200 sheet maps, which were digitalized by AEROFOTO CONSULT using high-precision digitizers and by coding data in uniform information sets (buildings, blocks, cadastral parcels, census sections, etc.). For cross-reference purposes, all the cartographic data was managed in an integrated form using the most accurate map – the aerophotogrammetric map – as a reference. Around forty characteristic points, such as the edges of buildings, bridges or monuments, were identified on each sheet, and their Gauss-Boaga coordinates read directly from the database. These values were then overlaid on the corresponding points on the other maps so as to transfer them all into a single coordinate system, using the rotation-translation procedures in the AUTOMAP software, which was used in all phases to build the database.

The database consists of sets of data grouped together in uniform categories distinguished by codes assigned during digitalization. Individual, concrete or abstract "objects" are catalogued in these categories. By concrete we mean all objects that directly refer to natural or man-made features which can be seen and surveyed in the field, and thus also on the photomap. Abstract objects, on the other hand, are those items invented by man, such as administrative boundaries, that cannot be seen in the field and can only be surveyed from primary paper sources containing the product of human decision-making or calculated processes.

In addition to the cartographic level of information just described, there is also an alphanumeric information level – or table level – containing data associated with, or capable of being associated with, field objects. This alphanumeric information, however, is not directly represented in the field, but often describes fundamental phenomena for the identification of on-going emergent processes.

Following the logic described in the previous paragraph, the organization of digital cartography in a cartographic database has led to the distribution throughout the local area of a whole series of existing or surveyed data, which have also been organized in a relational database. The data already existing or specially surveyed by Rome City Council includes:
– cadastral data on ownership;
– data on public and publicly-controlled structures situated in the historic centre;
– ISTAT data from censuses;
– data on mobility, subdivided into means of transport and time zones;
– and various other kinds of information referred to characteristic uniform areas.

Hardware

The system's hardware is based on two IBM systems with RISC technology – a recent constructional approach that uses a limited number of basic instructions to increase considerably the performance of the computers. The two systems – a 6150 and a RISC 6000, equipped with large-format colour

41. Rome. Historic Centre. 1:1000 Roof-level map

graphics screens – are linked up so that there is common management both of the mass storage (620 MB) and the peripherals, comprising two PS/2 terminals, an alphanumeric terminal, a plotter and a Calcomp digitizer – both large format.

Software

The RISC IBM operational system is AIX, the IBM

abstract) objects in the field, and the set of relations between alphanumeric data and maps. Moreover, consistency between the geographic database and the alphanumeric database can be guaranteed by suitable updating.

Using GEODIS it is possible to situate and visualize on the map (and therefore in the field) any piece of information that is important for the local area. Conversely, geometric relations can be transferred to the alphanumeric database in the form of coded information. A typical example is the transferring of zoning codes in building unit records, obtained by comparing their inclusion in a graphically defined zone. Moreover, the results of alphanumeric database enquiries can be visualized on the cartographic support, thus creating a system whereby local area data may be "read".

One or more tables or views can be associated with each class of objects through a univocal code associating objects in the columns and rows in the tables.

GEODIS also supplies an interactive graphics environment equipped with a user-friendly simple-menu system, a powerful macro-language with structured flow control, and advanced "primitives". These primitives use artificial intelligence techniques to run complex operations concerning cartographic objects (calculations of area, volumes, global geometric and topological operations and transformations) as well as managing a library of external programmes and integration with the alphanumeric database.

The user can utilize the environment in various ways according to the circumstances. He can make macro-commands directly from the keyboard, use the standard menu system or customize it to speed up repetitive operations. The user can also construct complex procedures using the macro-language and external utilities, which effectively become further instructions or complex primitives.

Given their managerial agility and operational immediacy, and because of the consequent spread of the same technologies to offices in the Rome City Council, Province of Rome and the Region of Latium, these capabilities have been producing an equal number of complex information system nuclei, consistently built "by" and "between" different local government bodies. Although such offices may have different tasks, they all work on the same common heritage, following the same logic of protecting its image.

version of standard UNIX. GEODIS software, entirely developed by AUTOMAP, uses this system for the management of the local area.

GEODIS is a package of programmes for the automatic management of cartographically-based local-area databanks (i.e. not only alphanumeric data). With this package it is possible to manage the numeric cartography, an associated database – whatever its complexity, architecture and structure – of alphanumeric data concerning (real or

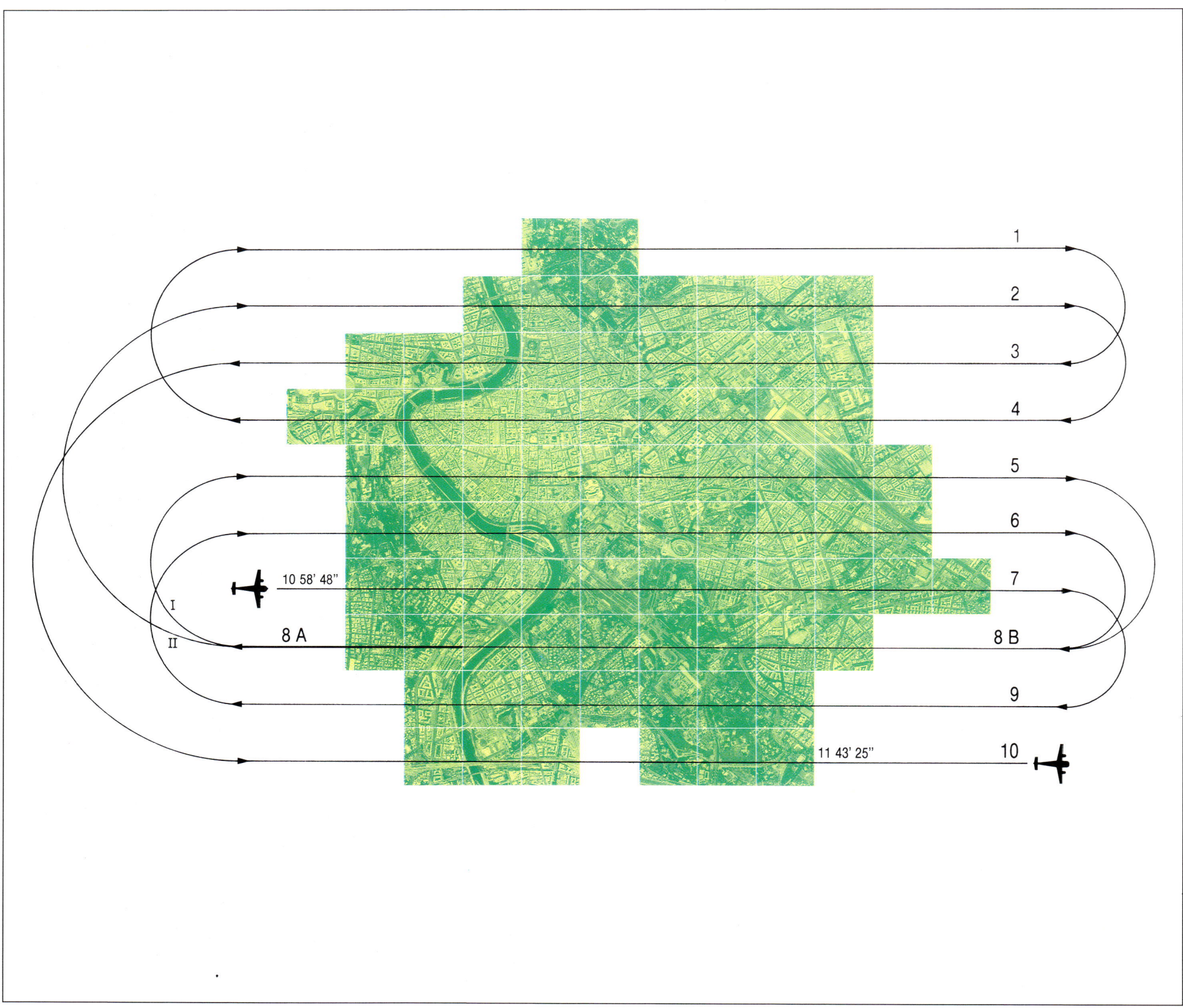

42. Diagram of the ten strips of film photographed from 10.58am to 11.43am on 11 June 1990 and used to produce the 81 plates of the photomap of the historic centre of Rome

Licinio Ferretti
A photomap in the making

The 1:1000 colour photomap of Rome covers the area circumscribed by the Aurelian Walls. A total of 81 plates in a 50 x 50 cm format make up a Cartesian orthogonal grid in accordance with the Gauss-Boaga coordinates. The choice of format, already used for *Venezia forma urbis*, was made after taking into consideration a number of factors. The main concern was to use a similar format to the original photogram. Given the need for exact alignment reflecting the precise moment when the photographs were taken, the square format was chosen to ensure a uniform perspective and resolution for each individual plate. Only the central area of each photo is used so that the perspective effects are minimal and resolution optimal.

The photographing and developing of the photomap were planned down to the slightest detail and effected by the Compagnia Generale Ripreseaeree, Parma, which was responsible for all the aerophotogrammetric operations and all the subsequent processing.

The survey was made on 11 June 1990 from a twin-engined Partenavia P68 I-ANCP equipped with a ZEISS RMK.A 30/23 whose focal length was 305.38 mm and format 23 x 23 cm. The photographs were taken at a relative height of about 1800 metres, with an average longitudinal overlap of 80%, using sensitive KODAK AEROCOLOR NEGATIVE FILM 2445 (Estar Base), which was then treated with Aeroneg continuous automatic developer. The aerophotogrammetric coverage of the historic centre of Rome required ten sorties oriented East-West, producing a total of 308 photograms on an average 1:5700 scale.

The photographic survey was effected in a very limited time span, from 10.58 am to 11.43 am (summer-time). The light conditions and position of the sun were ideal to ensure the best colour results with minimal shade, and to avoid the reflection of solar rays in the camera viewpoint (the so-called hot spot). As the graph of the flight plan shows, the eighth strip was taken in two stages: air traffic over Rome is very intense and authorization was not given to complete the run. The missing part was taken around 10 minutes later.

To obtain an absolute orientation for enlargement and rectifying purposes on a 1:1000 scale, suitable framing was carried out using aerial triangulation with a special photo at a higher altitude included in the IGMI national network and with points connected to the latter determined by direct measurement.

Made at 3000 metres of absolute altitude with a ZEISS RMK.A 30/23, focal length 305.38 mm and KODAK DOUBLE-X Aerographic Panchromatic film 2405, this survey produced 5 strips and 132 photograms, providing 8 control points for every rectification. The enlargement and rectification operations were carried out on ZEISS SEG VI instruments, fitted with colour heads and projection control units as well as a high resolution power lens finely adjusted for colour fidelity. The treatment of the sensitive material required particular care to ensure the greatest uniformity possible and the right definition.

Each section of the photomap was checked through a minimum of six known ground-level points until the residual deviations were under ± 0.4 graphic millimetres in the flat areas and just over that in the hilly areas typical of the morphology of the city of Rome. Each section was also checked for colour uniformity and the rendering of detail. Those residual deviations above the

Strip of film	Time
1	11 34' 40" - 11 34' 45"
2	11 26' 26" - 11 27' 10"
3	11 37' 24" - 11 38' 10"
4	11 29' 46" - 11 31' 47"
5	11 17' 33" - 11 18' 38"
6	11 06' 41" - 11 07' 45"
7	**10 58' 48"** - 10 59' 59"
8A	11 22' 29" - 11 22' 34"
8B	11 13' 44" - 11 14' 28"
9	11 02' 56" - 11 03' 38"
10	11 42' 18" - **11 43' 25"**

43. Table of the times required for each strip of film. The eighth sequence had to be shot in two stages

44. Diagram of the area covered by the 18 photograms in three strips. The dark grey bands indicate lateral overlaying

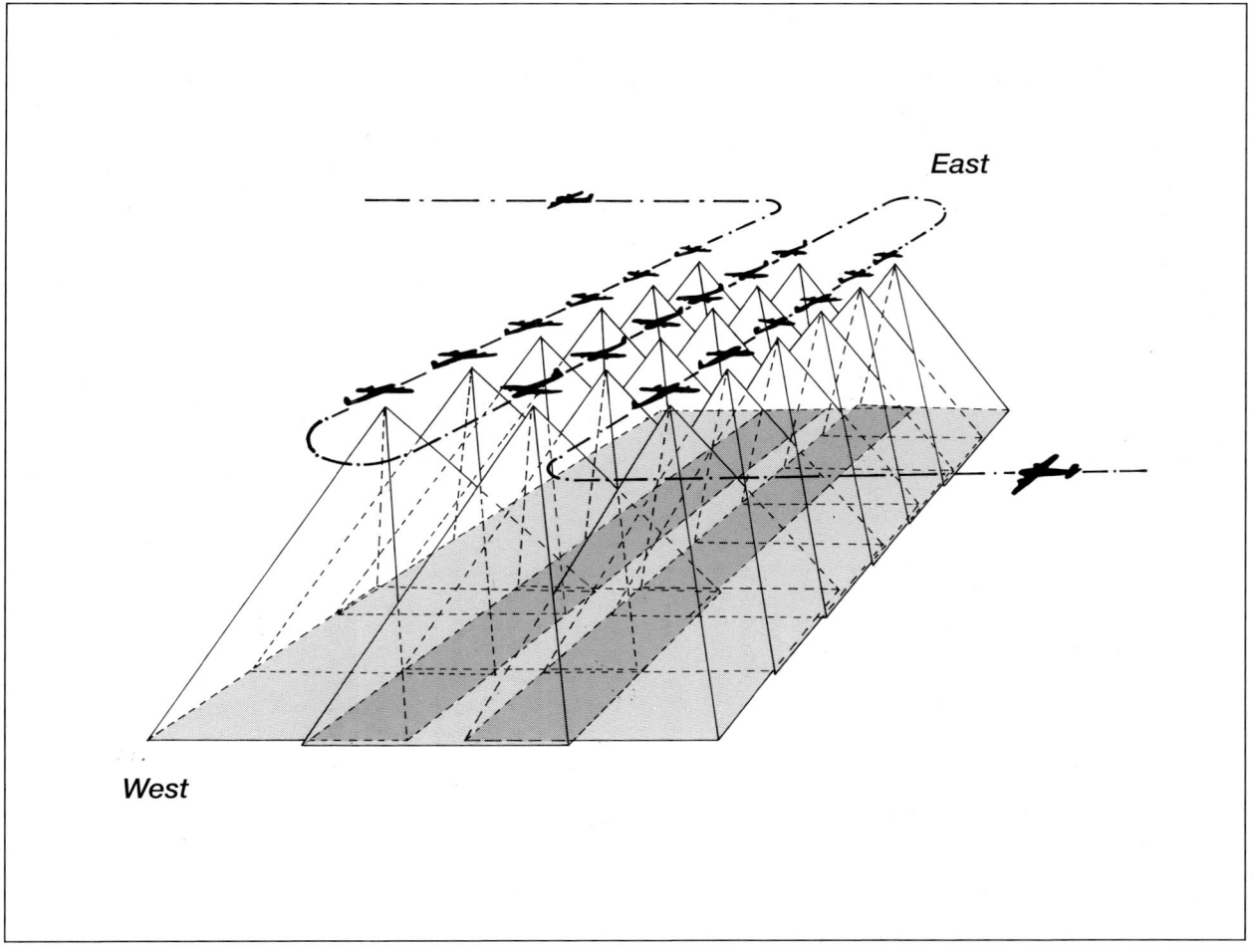

45. Diagram of a segment of Strip 3, made up of three photograms. Photograms 285 and 287 are presented in schematic form, while Photogram 286 is reproduced to its real size. Only the central portion of Photogram 286 was used in the final printing of the photomap (Plates 63, 64, 81 and 82). There is obviously a very wide overlap (80 per cent) to obtain as much material as possible. The picture actually used in the photomap comes from the central portion of each photogram to reduce to a minimum perspective effects and obtain the best resolution

tolerance threshold were still low enough for the purposes of providing excellent material for the creation of this *Atlas*. KODAK EKTACOLOR paper was used for printing on paper in a 50 x 50 cm format.

Four 25 x 25 cm plates were obtained from each colour photomap and, along with the corresponding line map on the same scale, form the substance of this publication.

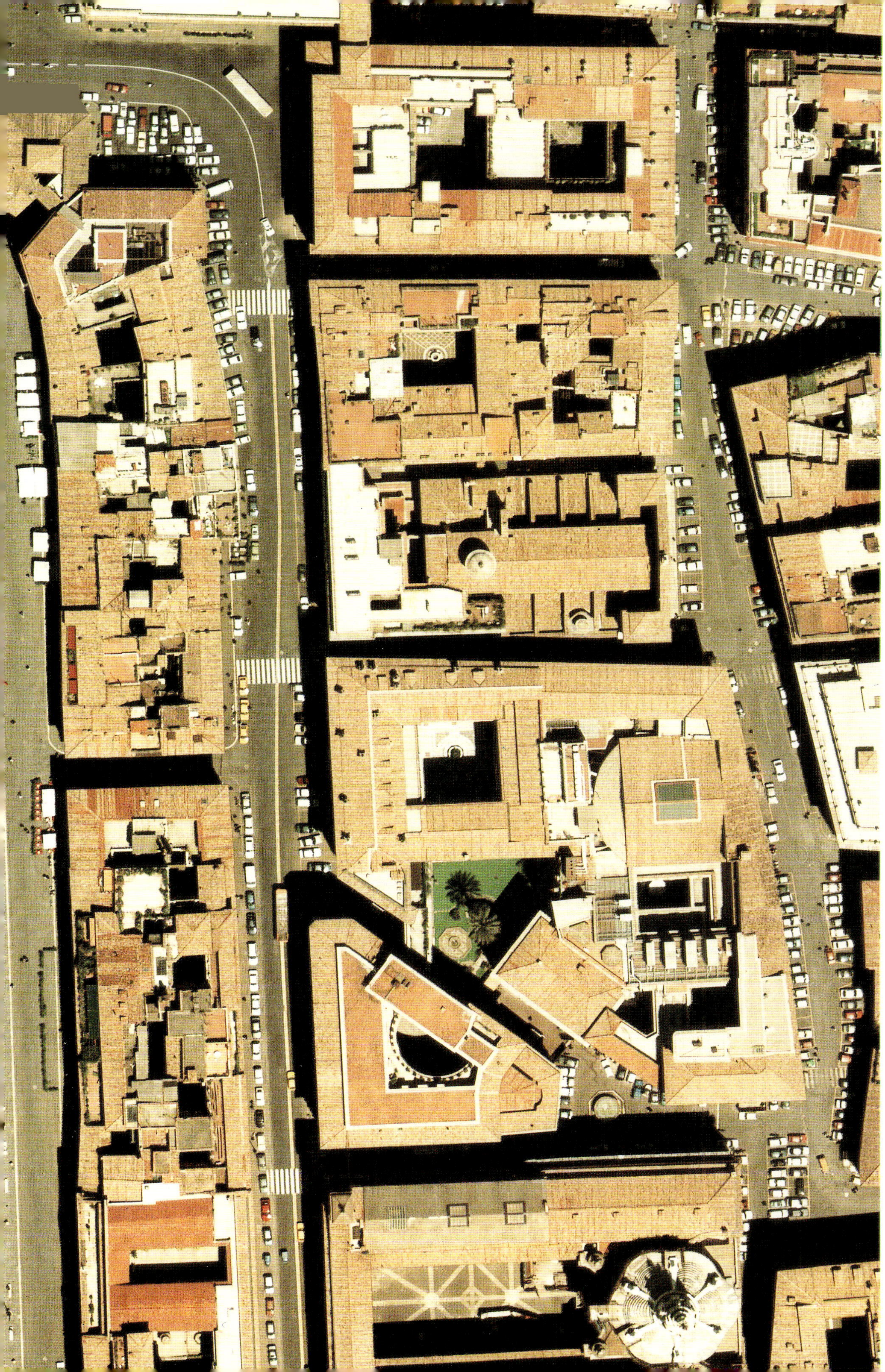

Atlas of Rome

LEGEND OF THE LINE MAP SHEETS

Symbol	Description
	Private property
	Public property
	Parliamentary and Presidential property
	State property, superintendencies, universities and the Bank of Italy
	City of Rome, Provincial and Regional property
	Property of the Church and related institutions
	Property belonging to more than one body
	Walls, reinforcing walls, architectural elements (fountains, stairs and ramps)
	Lawns, pavements, and paths
15.60	Spot heights

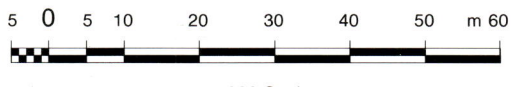

1:1000 Scale

THE BASE MAP WAS PRODUCED FROM AERIAL PHOTOGRAPHY AND SUBSEQUENT PLOTTING BY S.A.R.A. NISTRI IN 1978.

THE PHOTOMAP IS SUBJECT TO LAW NO. 68 (2.2.1960). IGMI AUTHORIZATION NO. 49 (25.2.1991).

x = 2311346   y = 4643296

The top right vertex of plate 3
has the Gauss-Boaga coordinates
x = 2311346
y = 4643296

Overall composite grid of sheets
in the line map

Overall composite grid of plates for the photomap

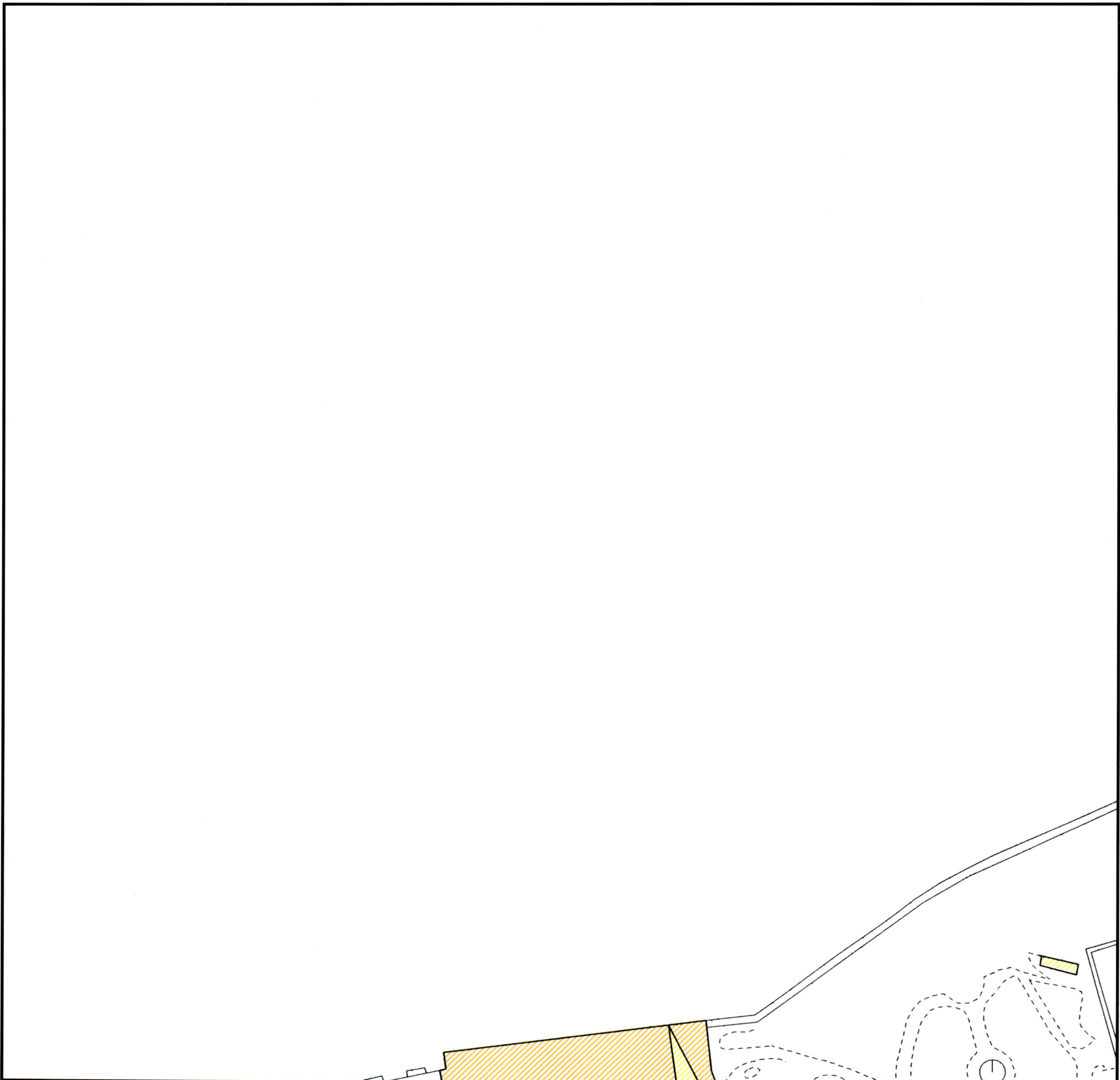

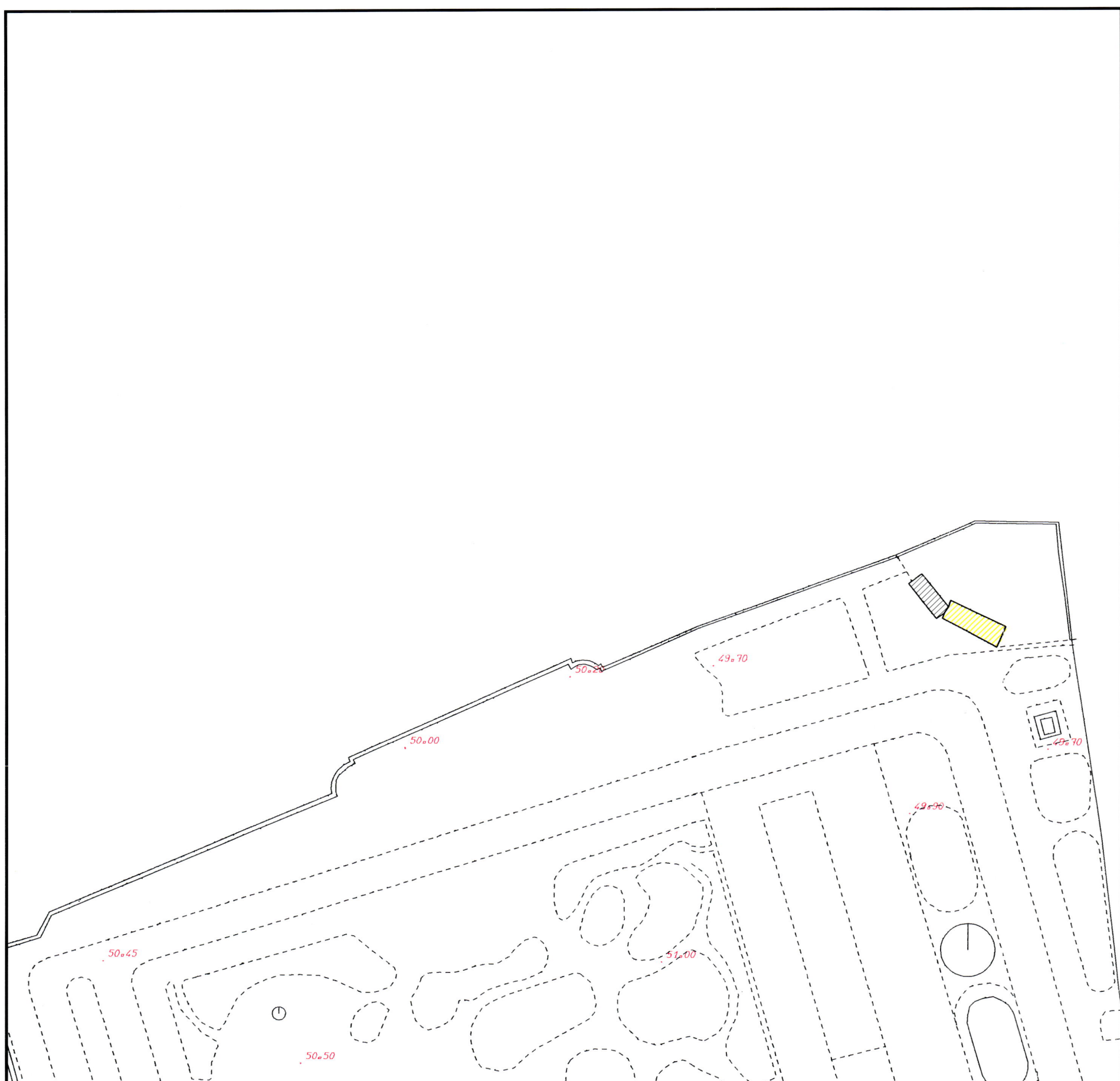

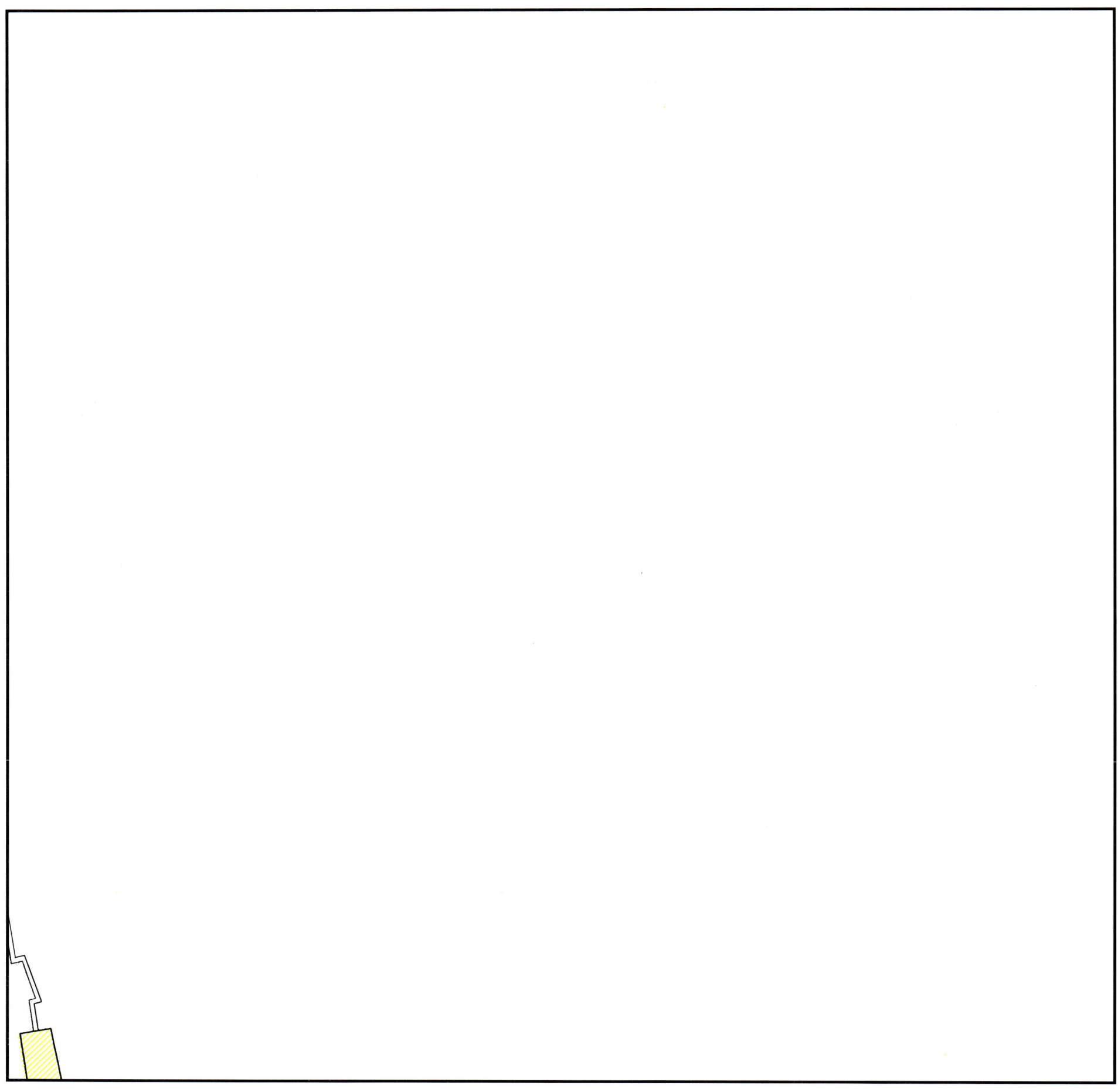

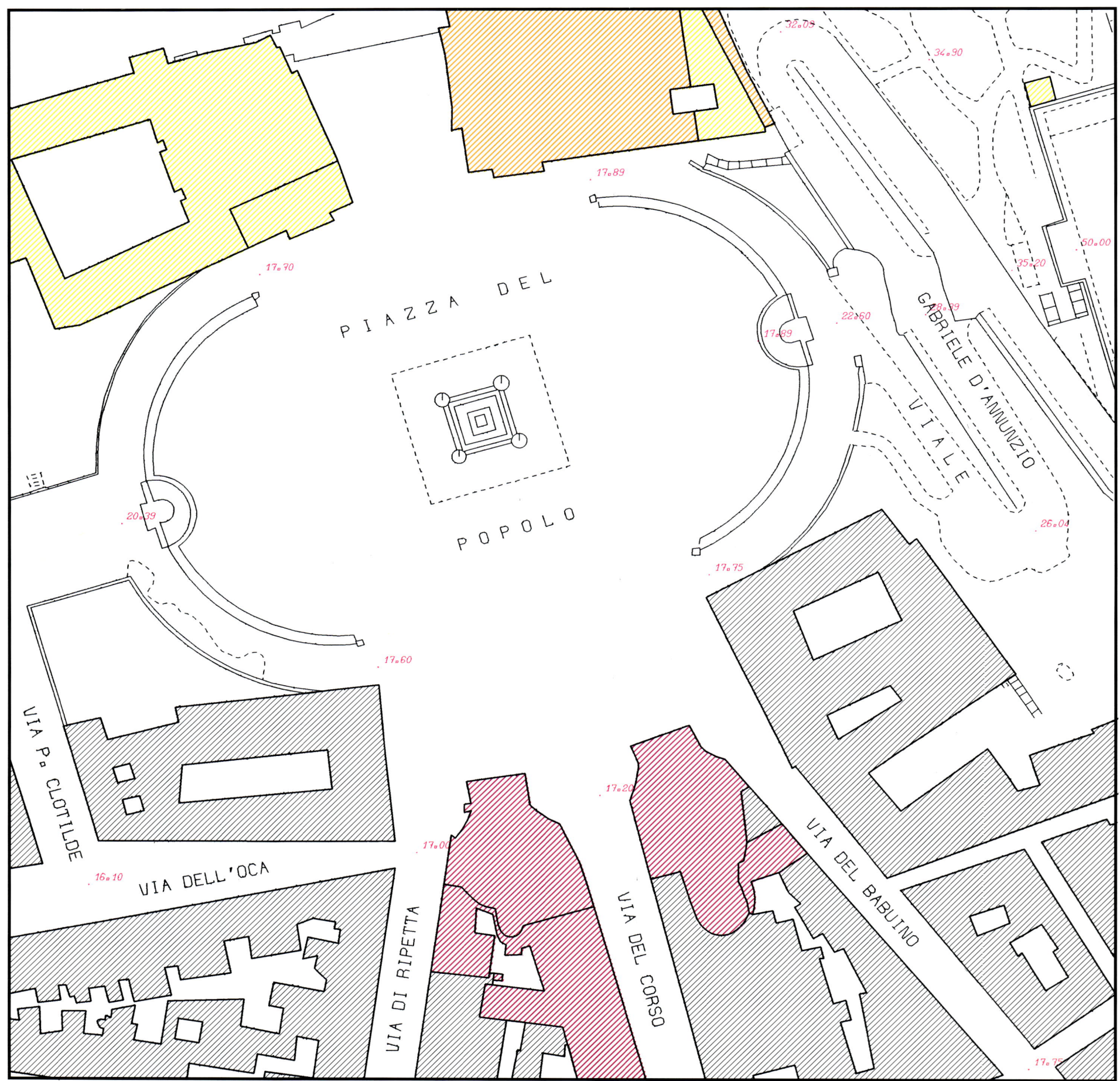

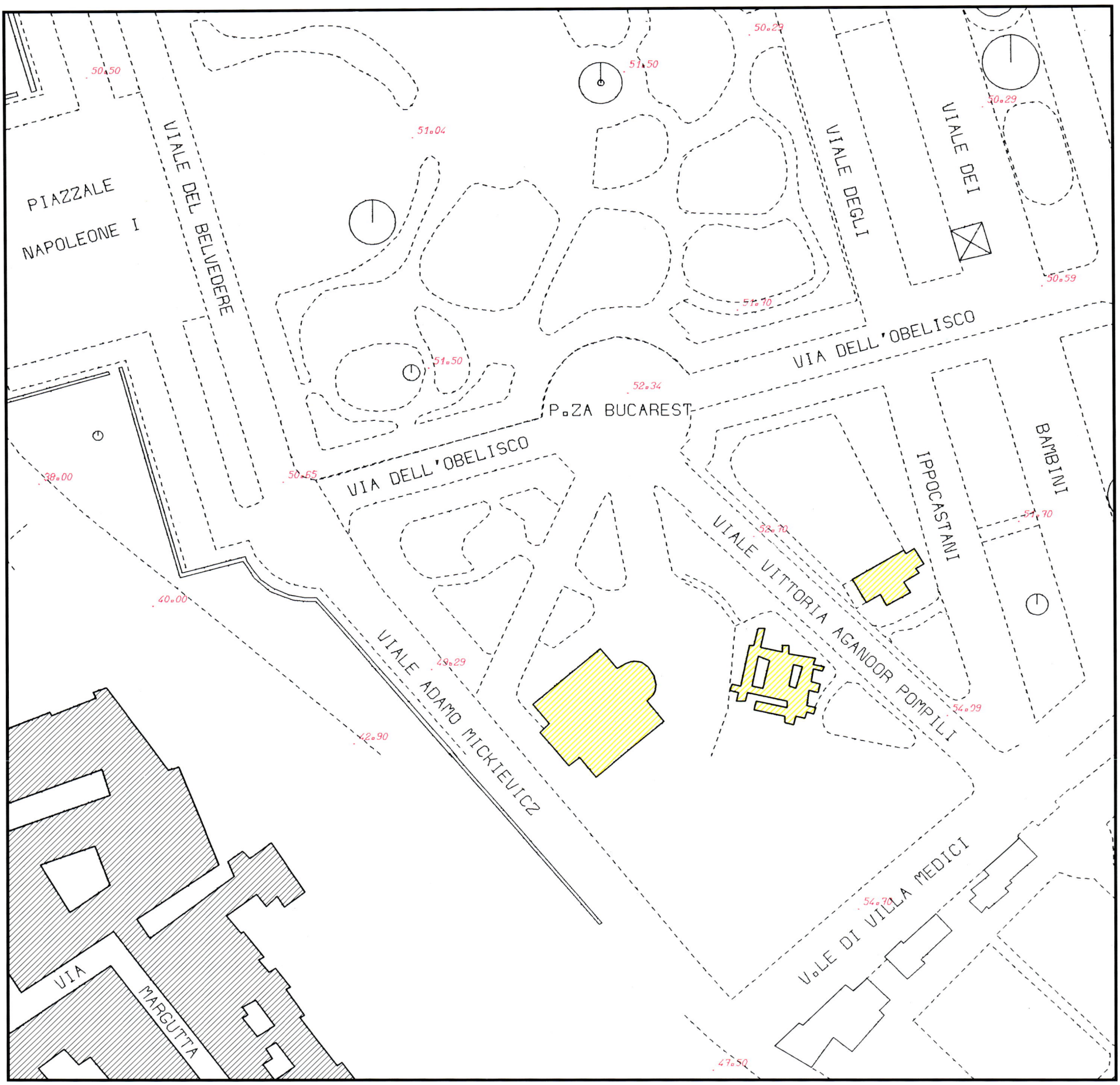

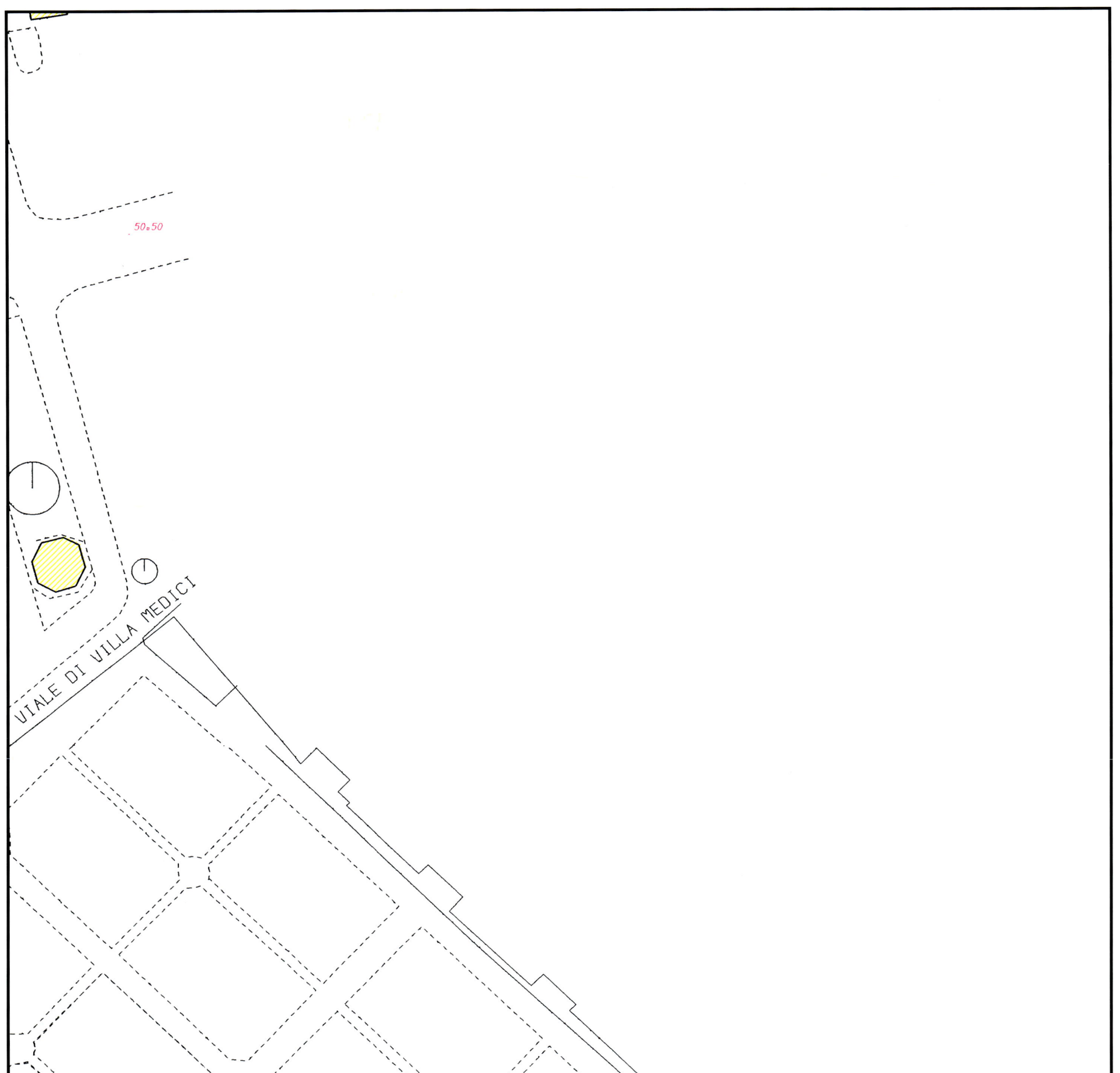

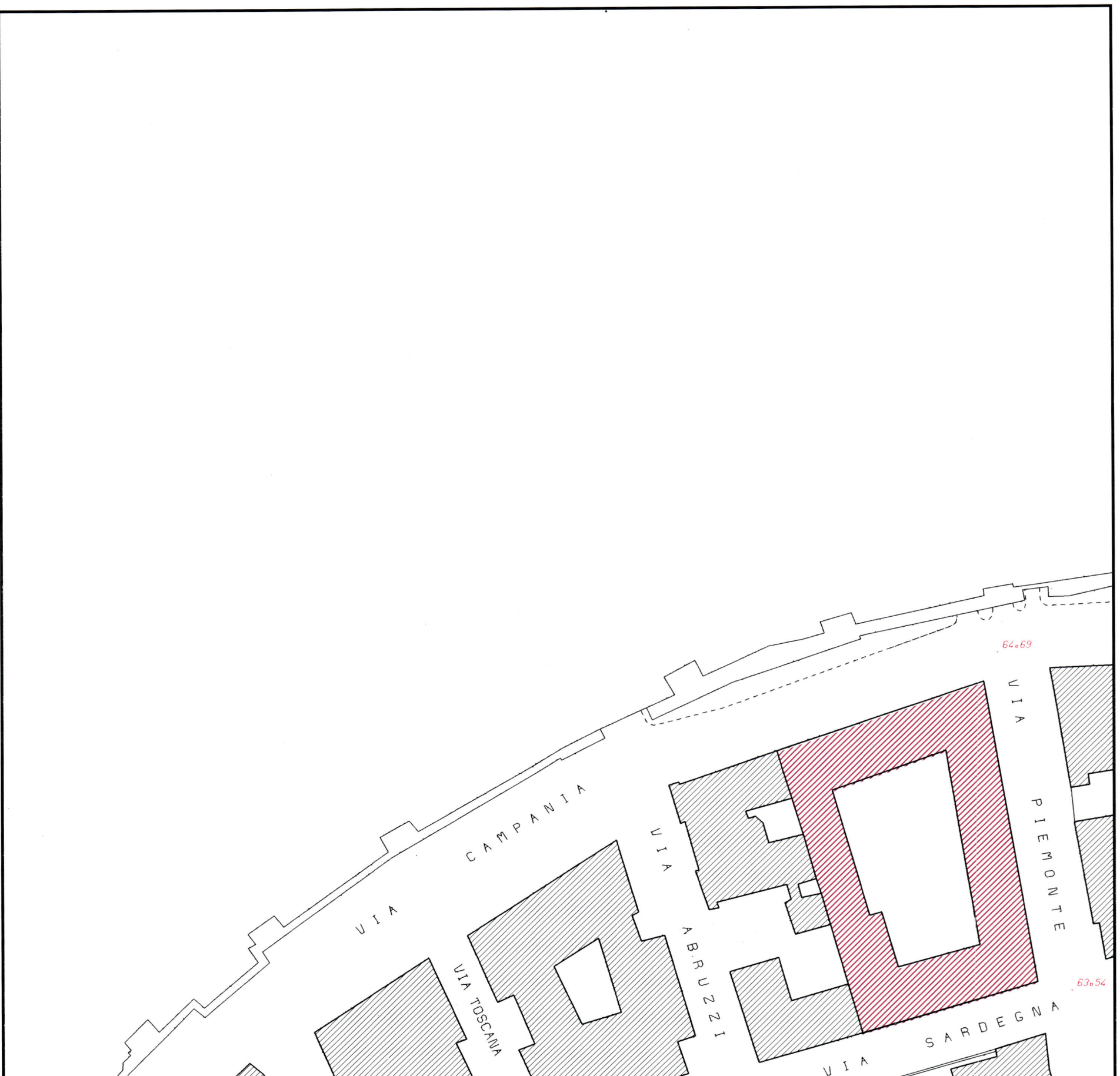

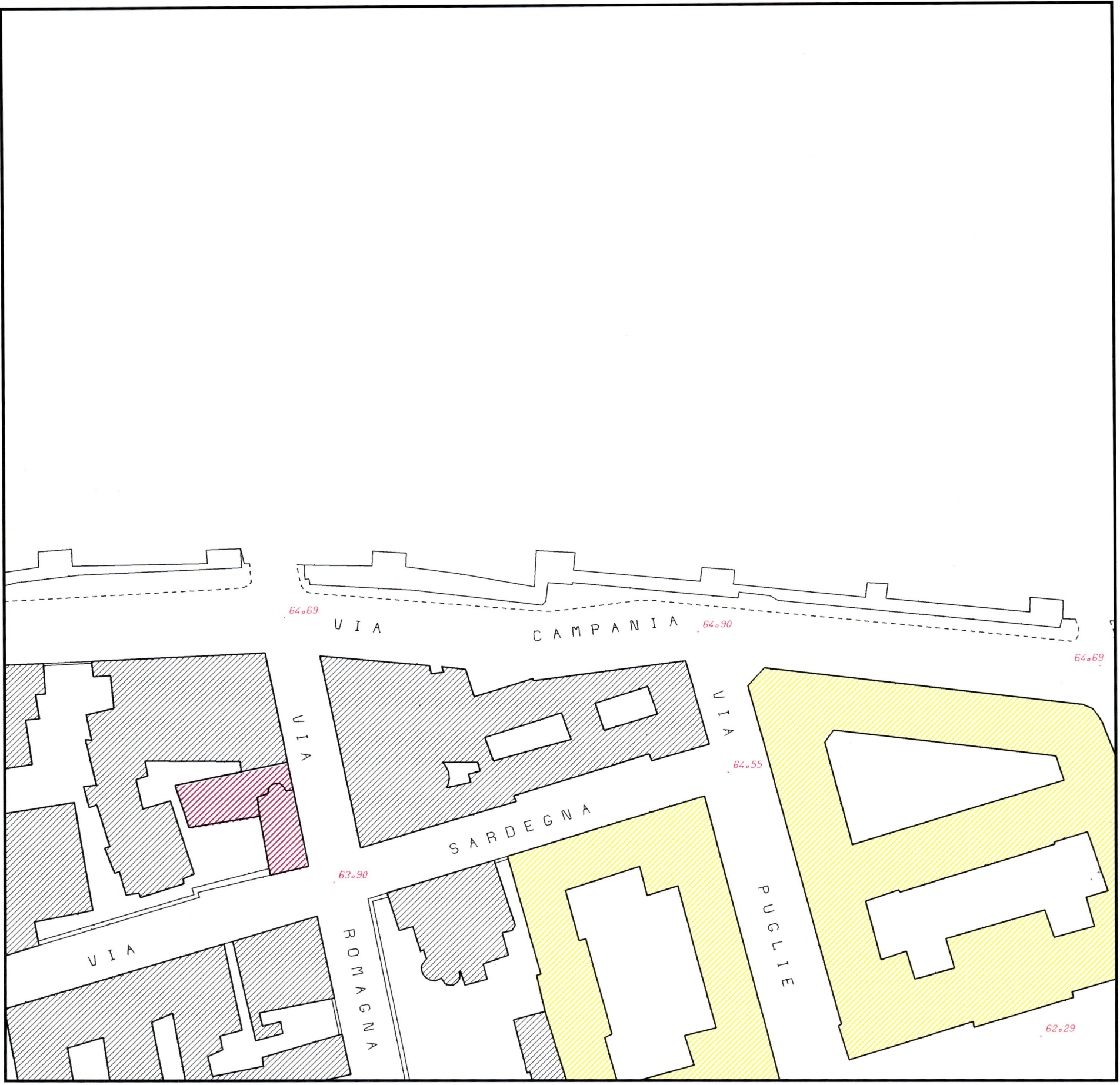

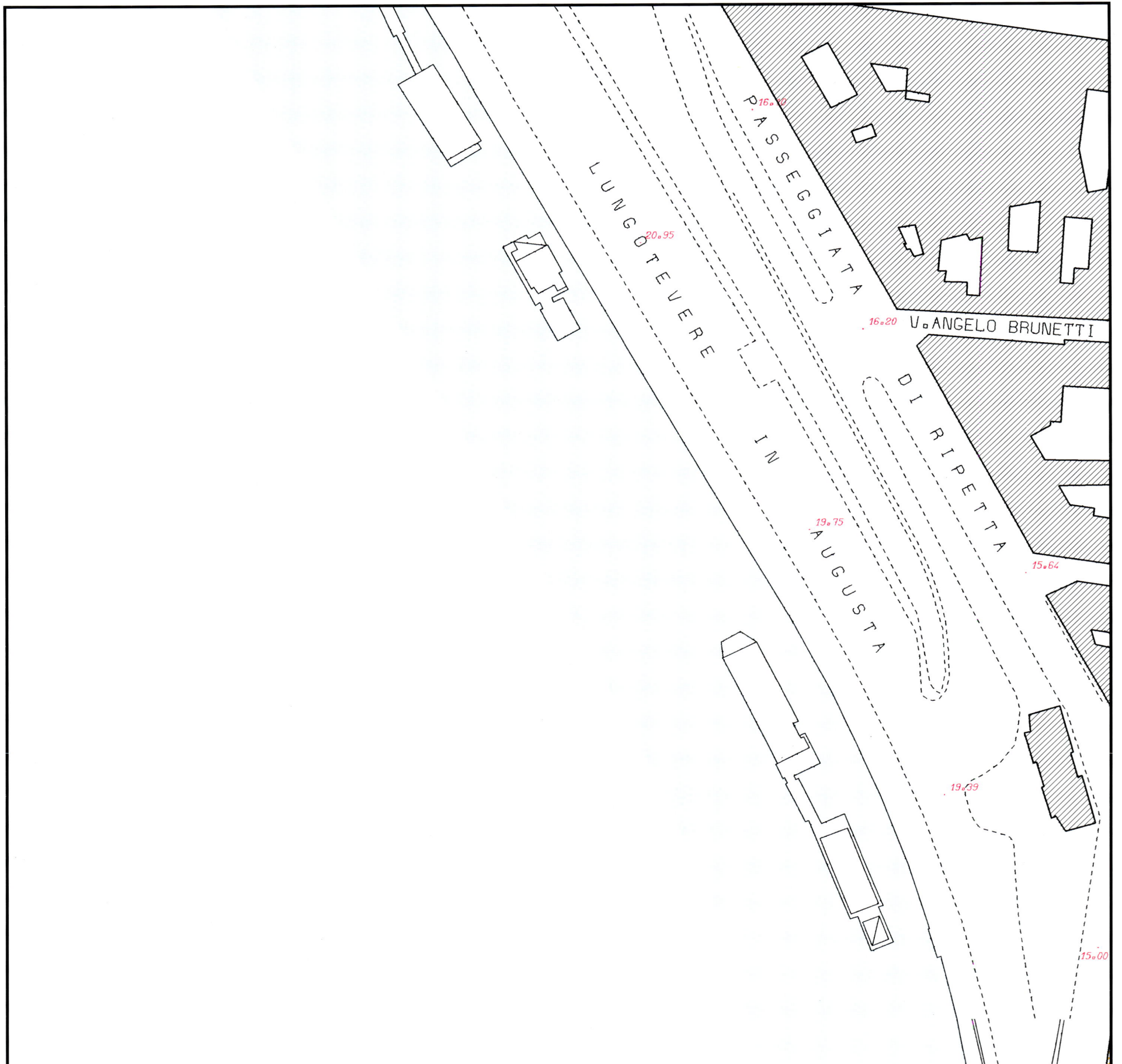

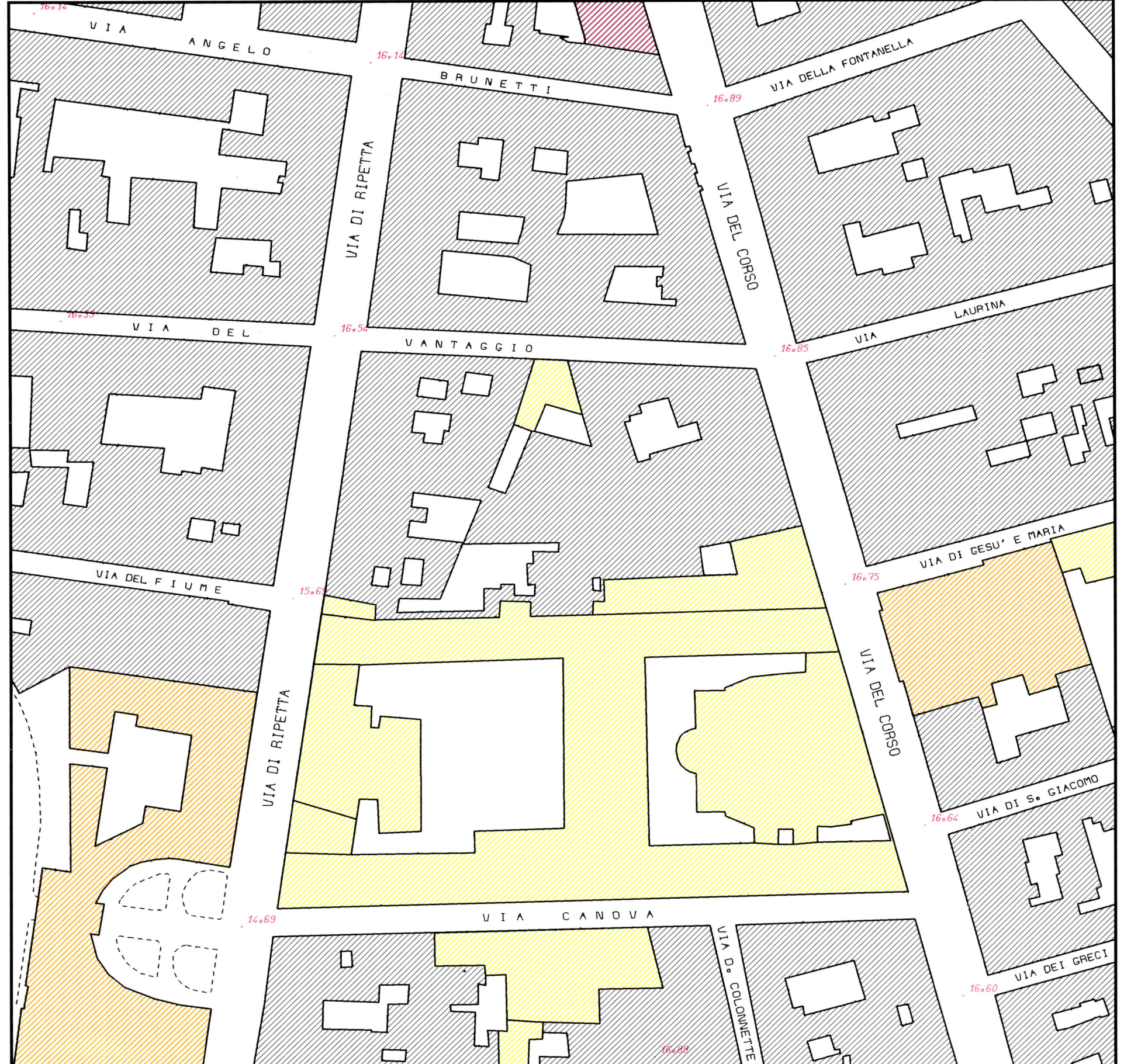

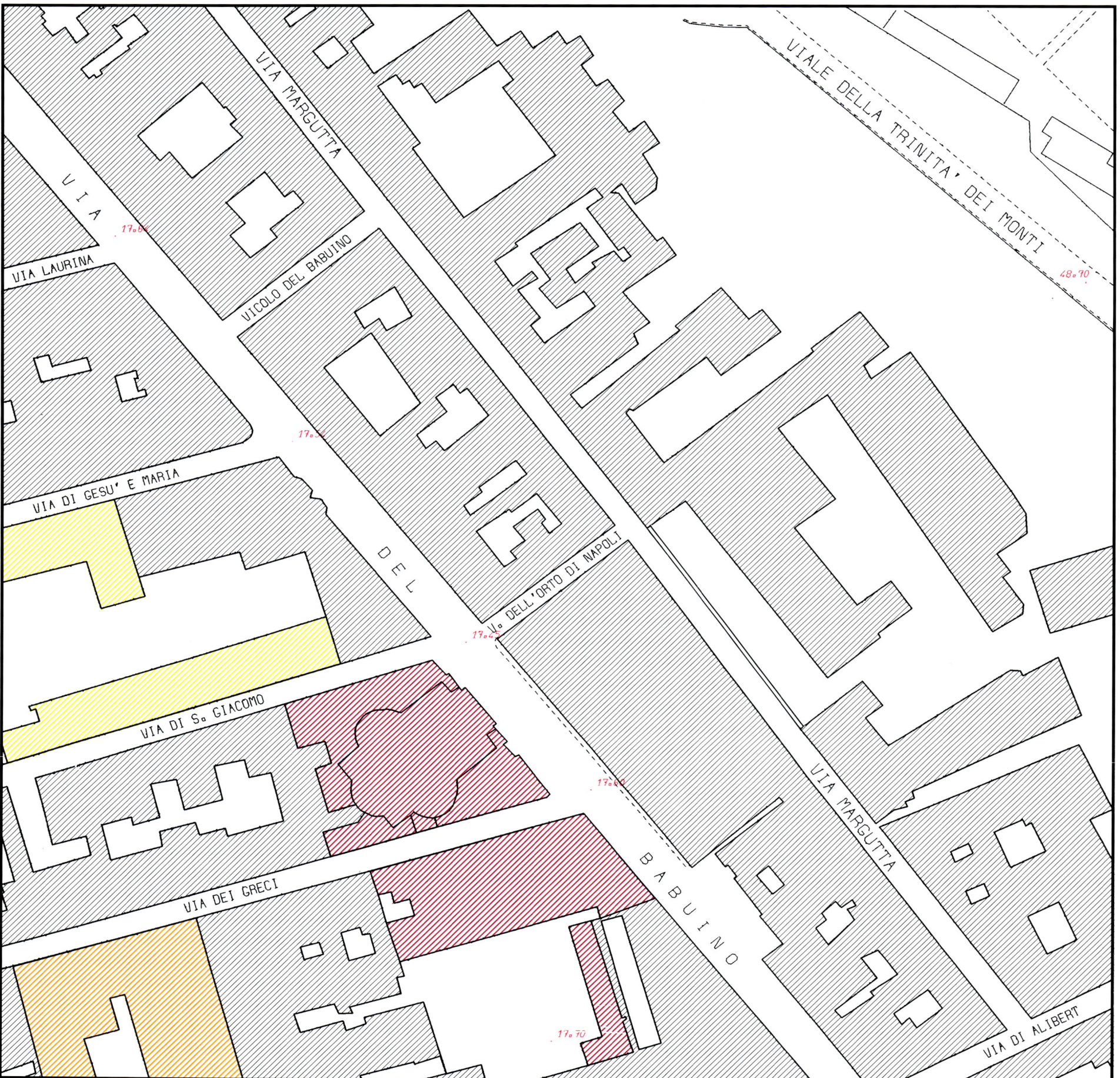

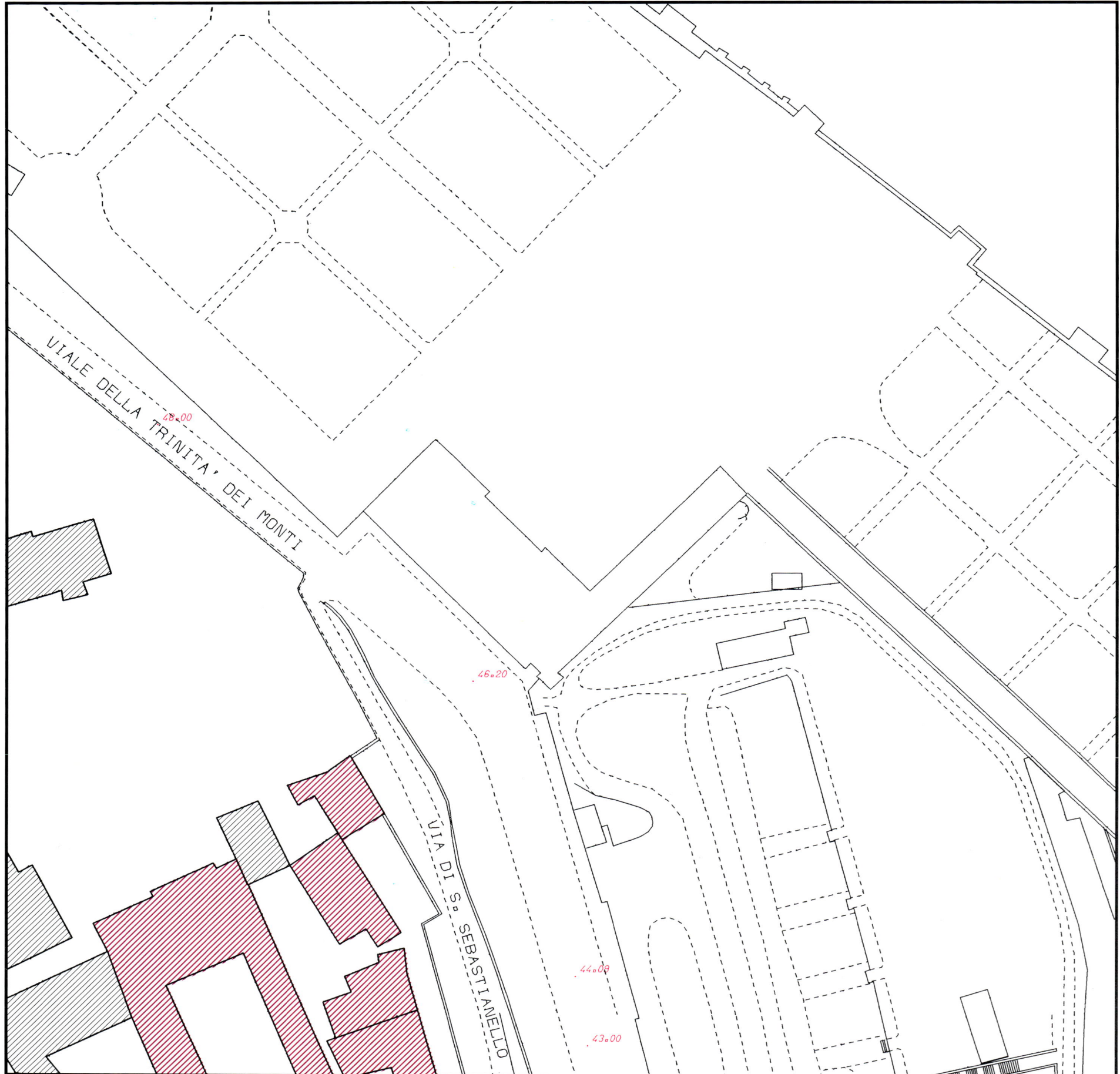

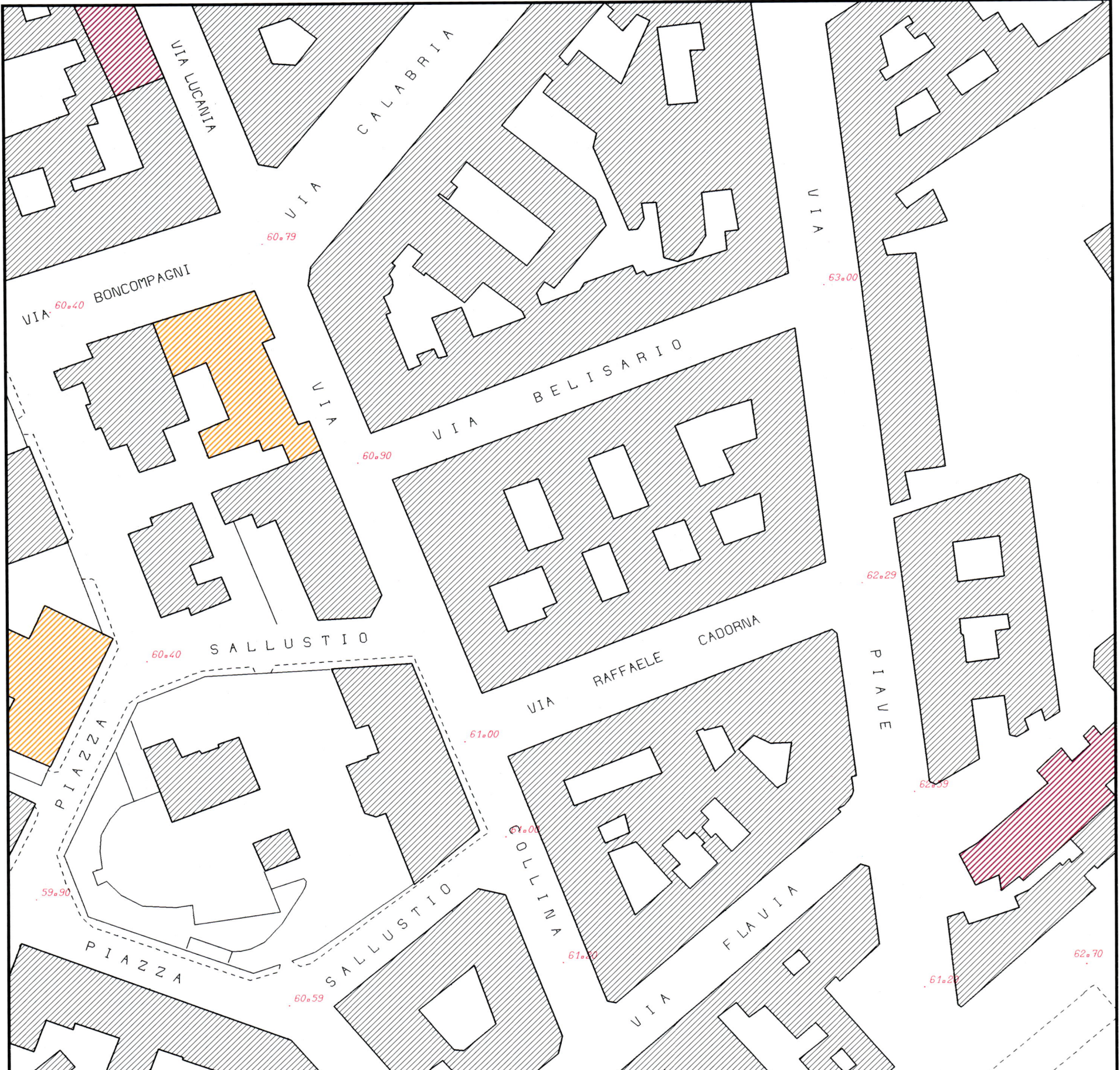

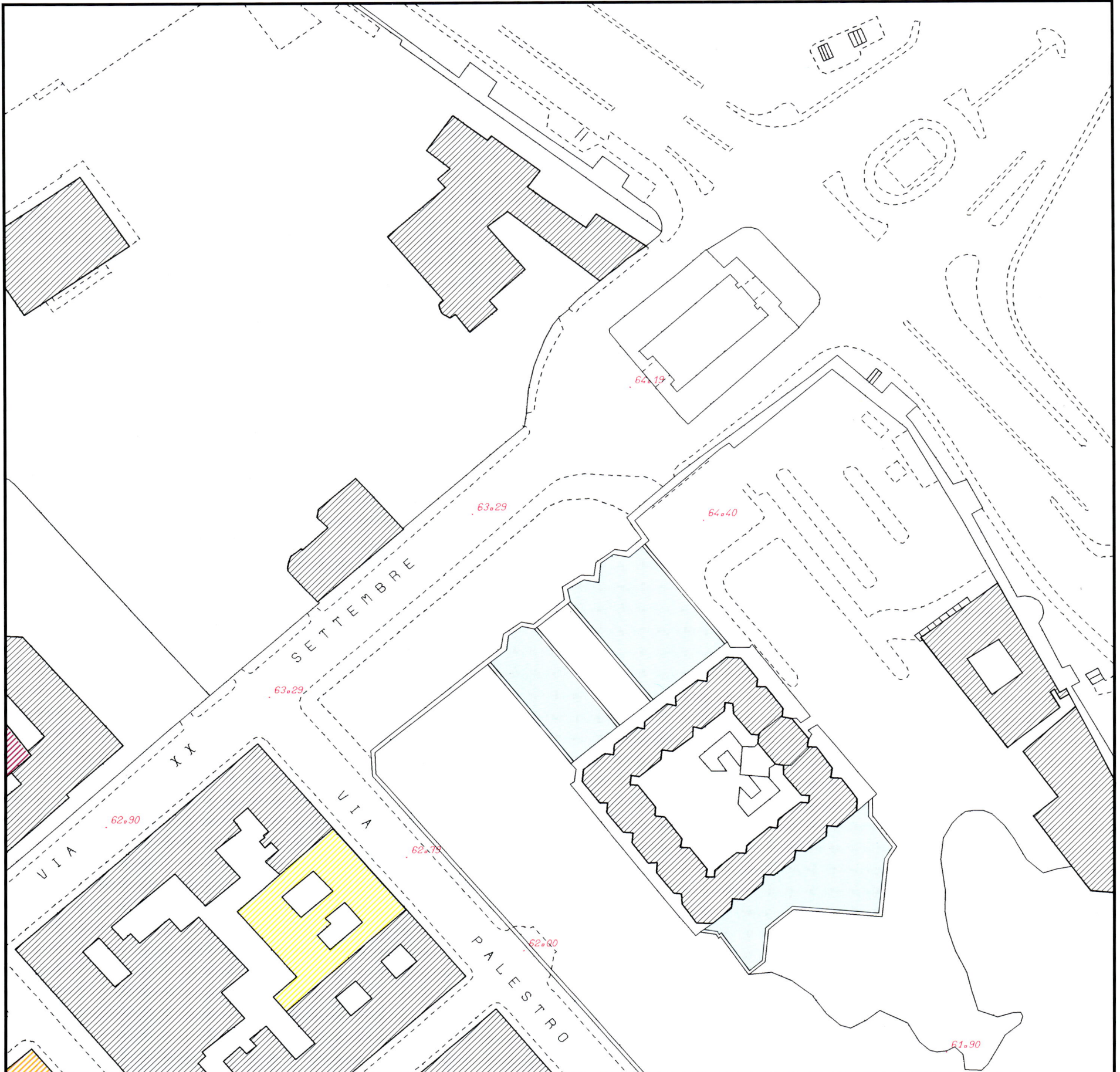

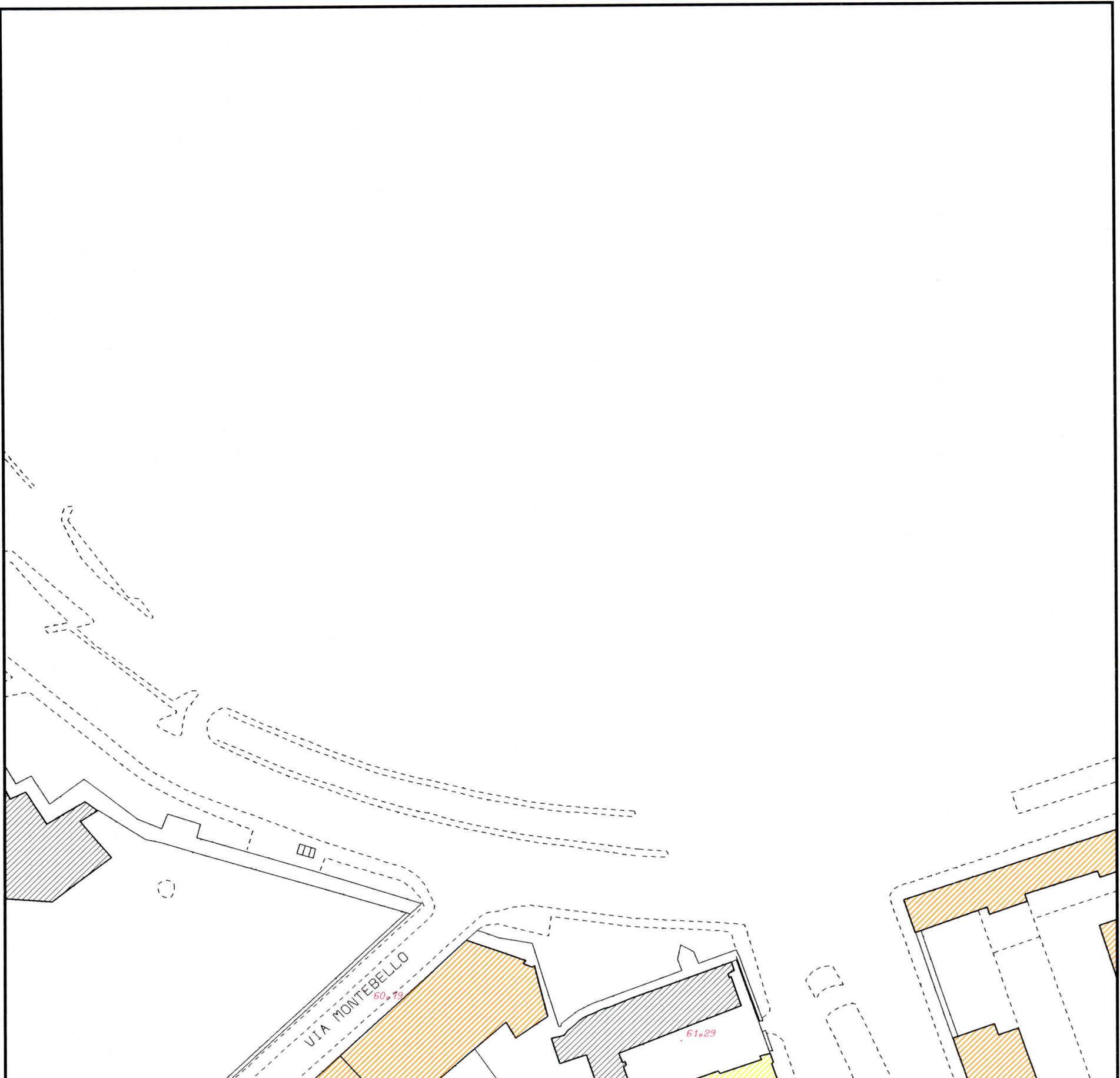

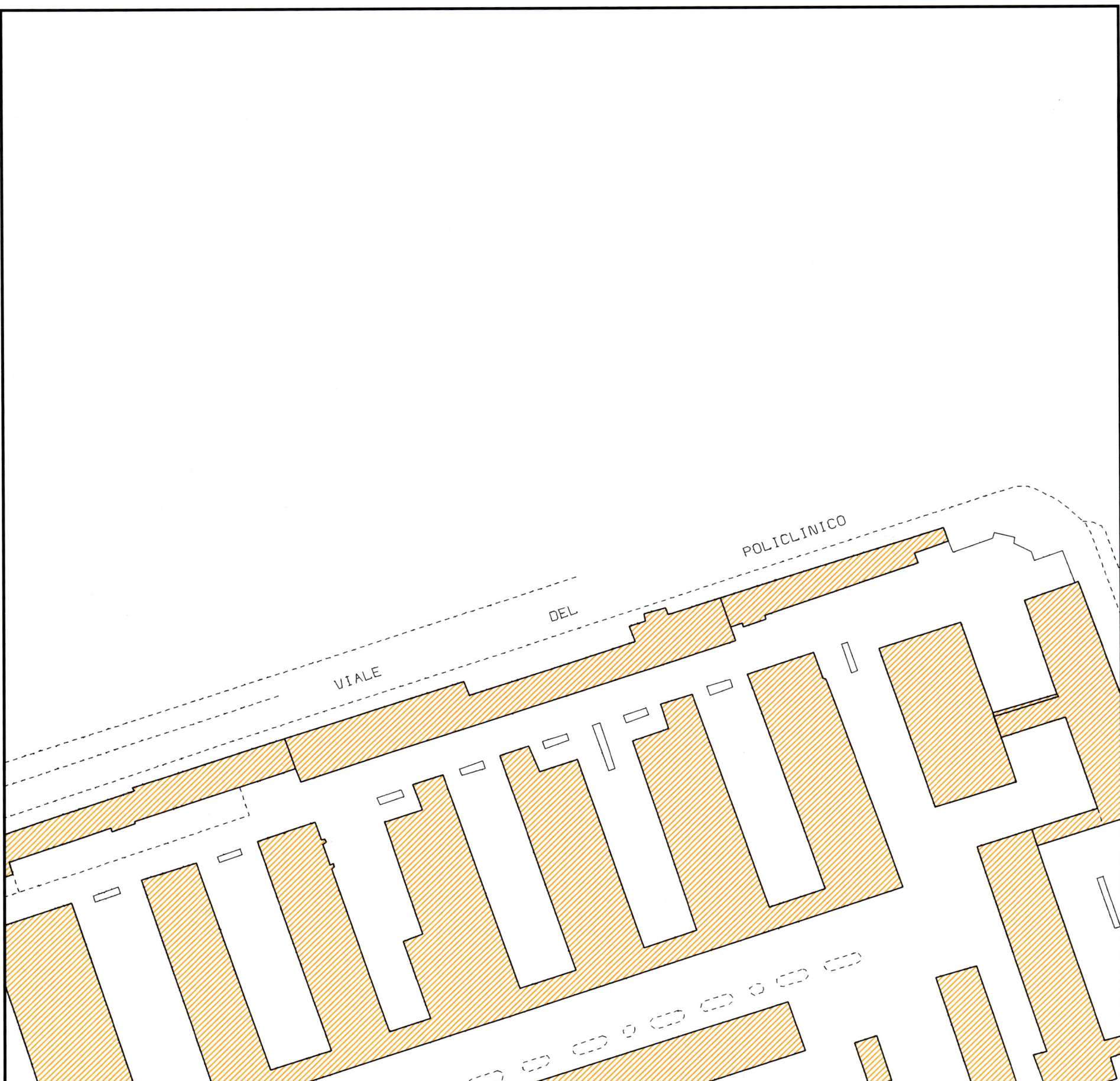

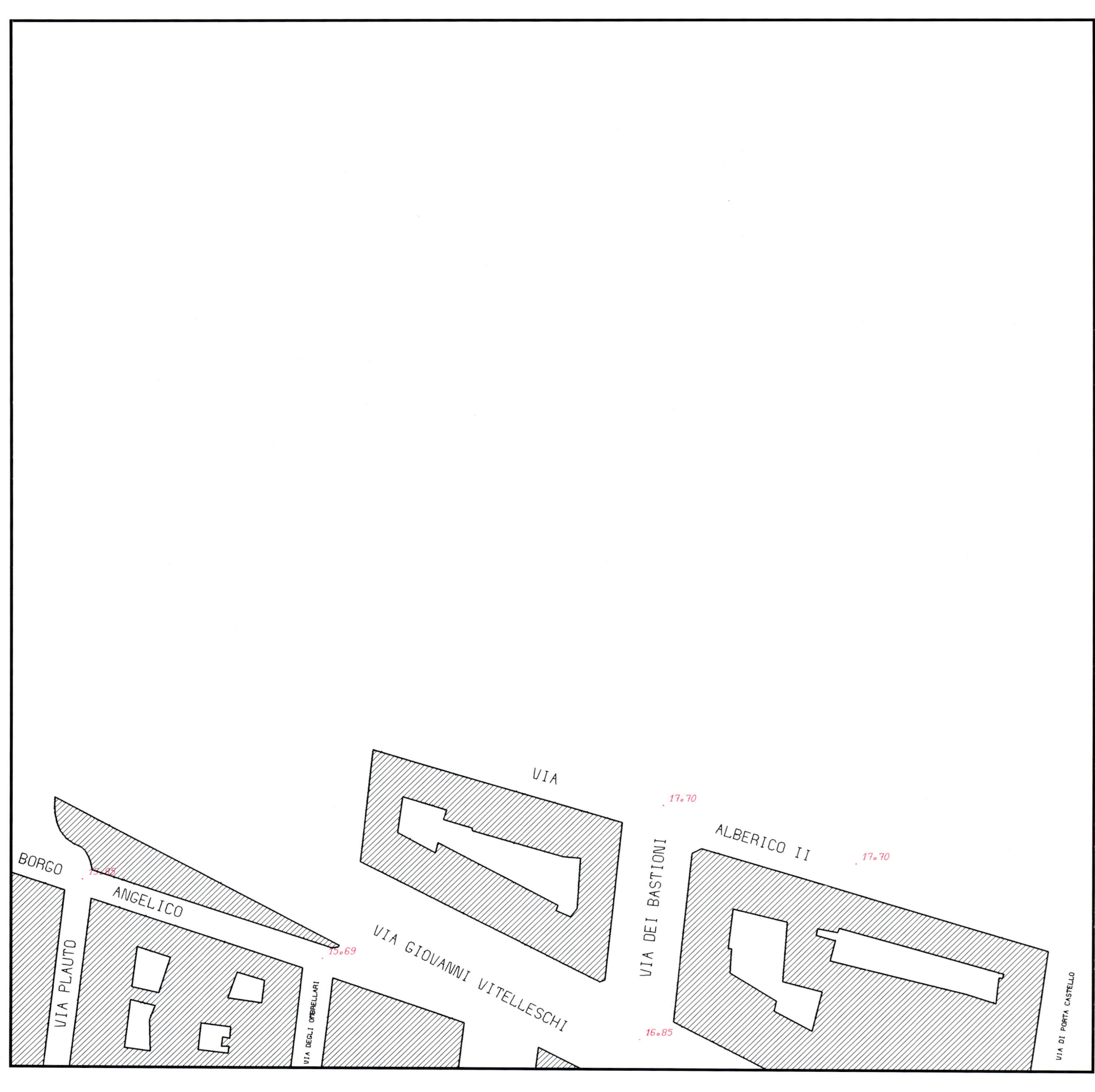

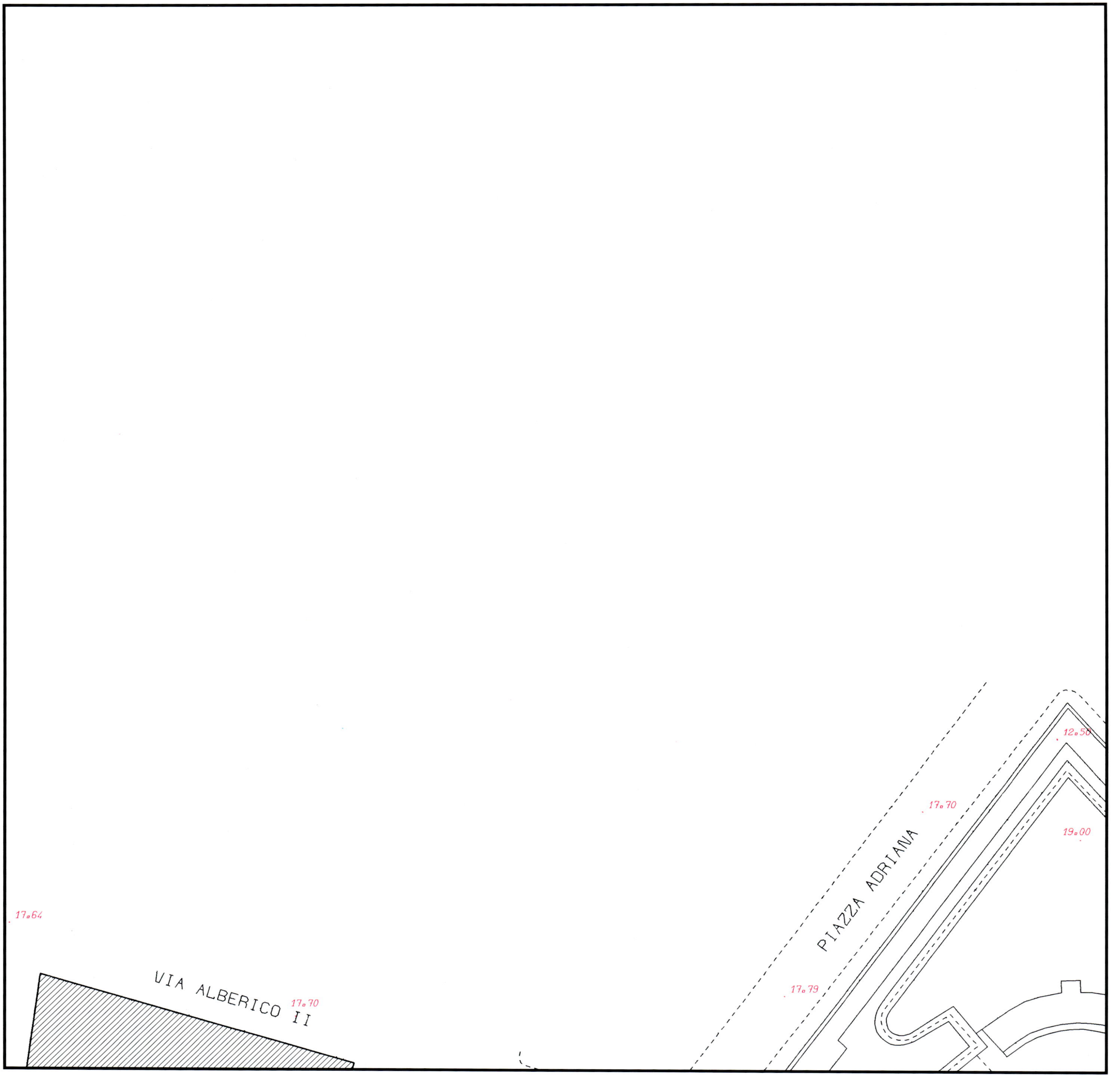

17.64

PIAZZA ADRIANA

12.50
17.70
19.00
17.79

VIA ALBERICO II 17.70

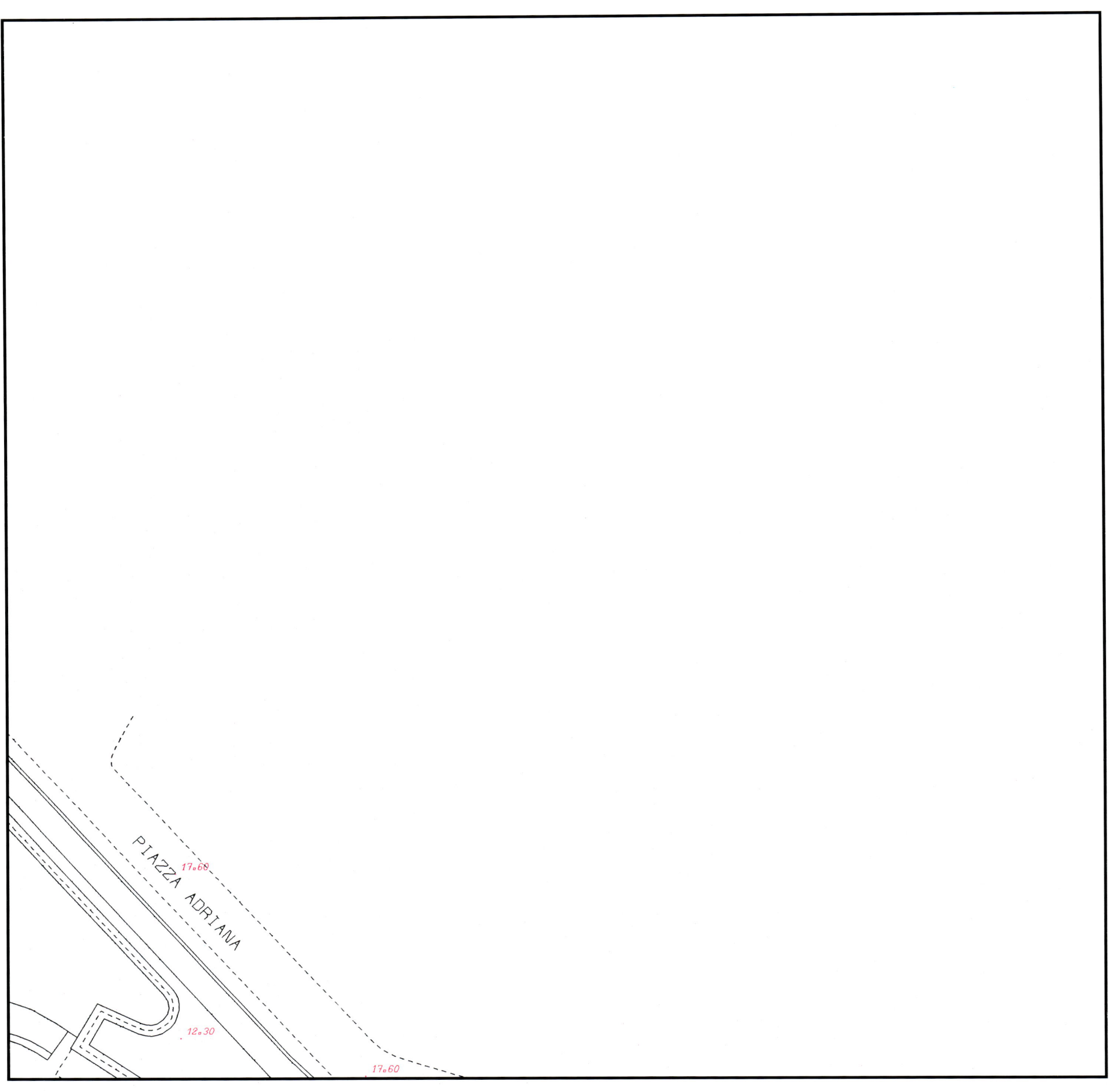

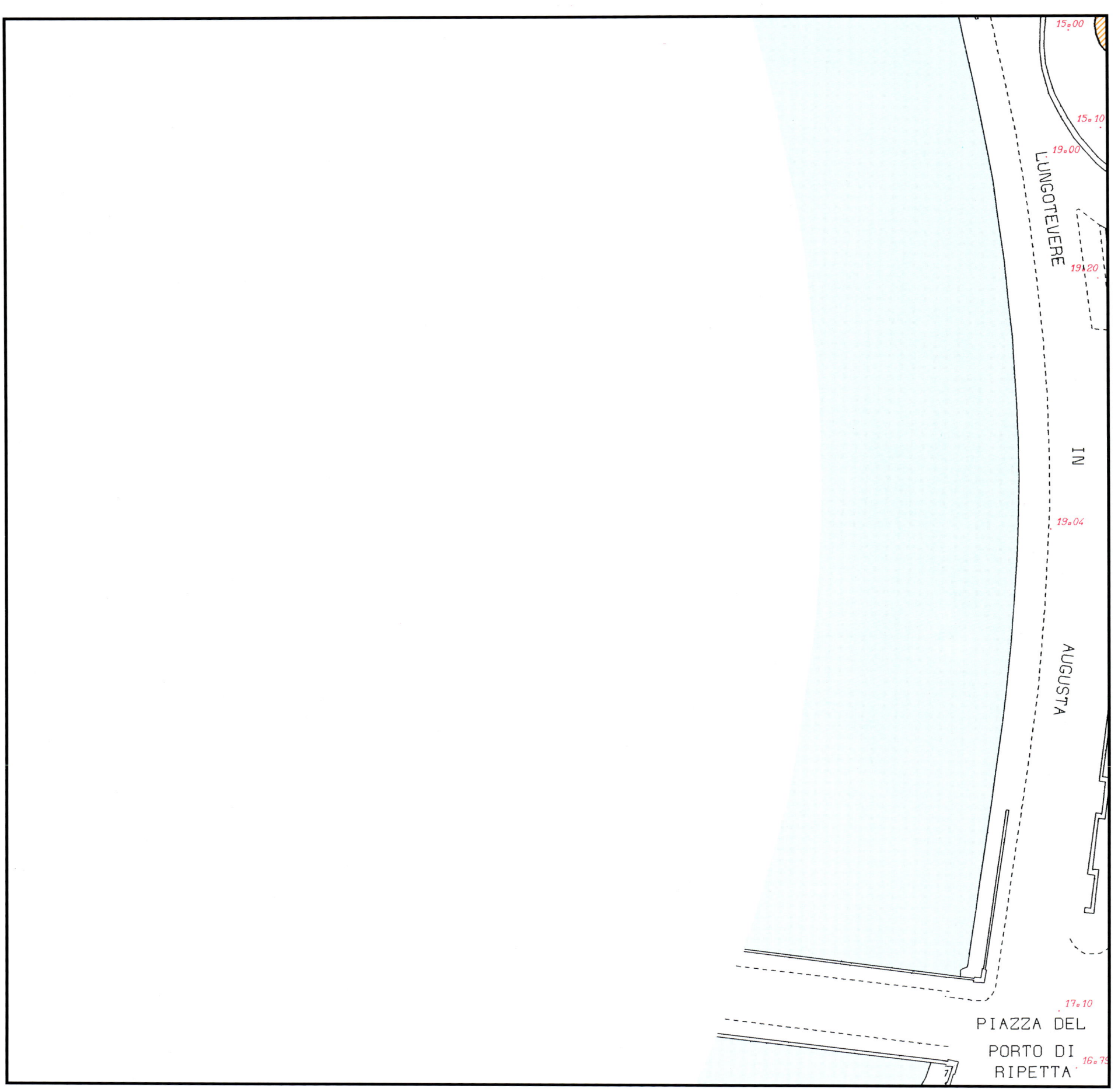

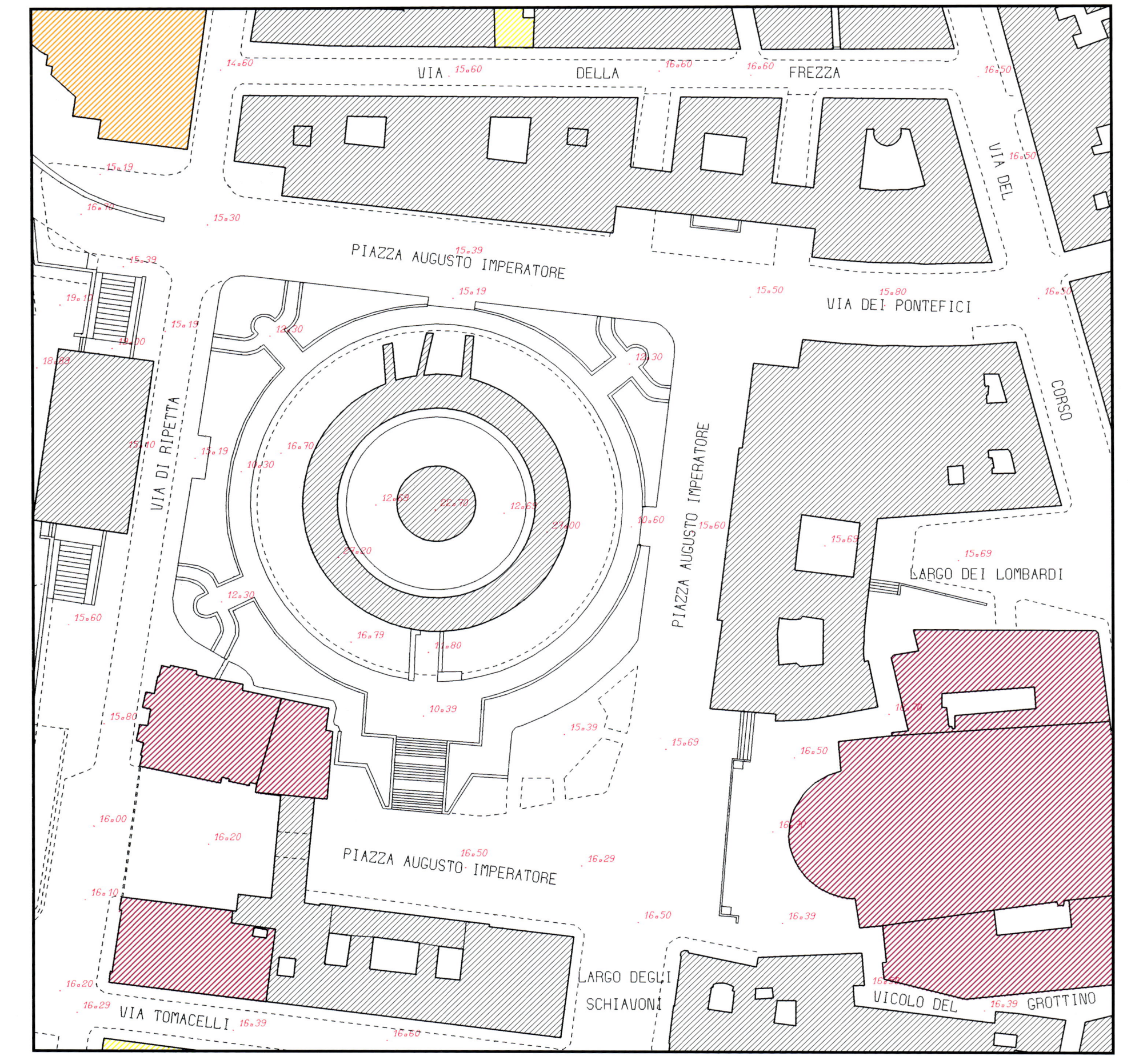

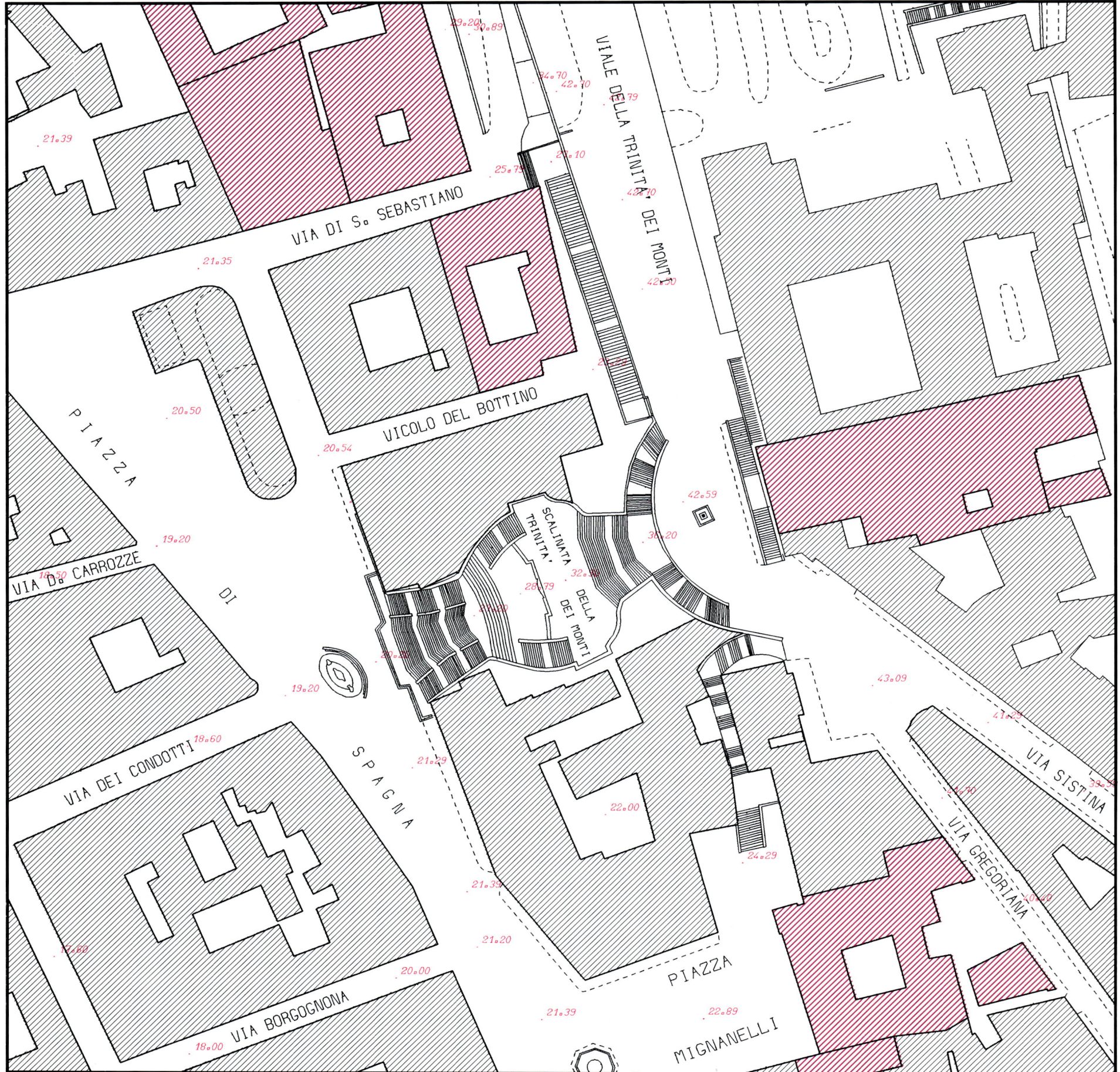

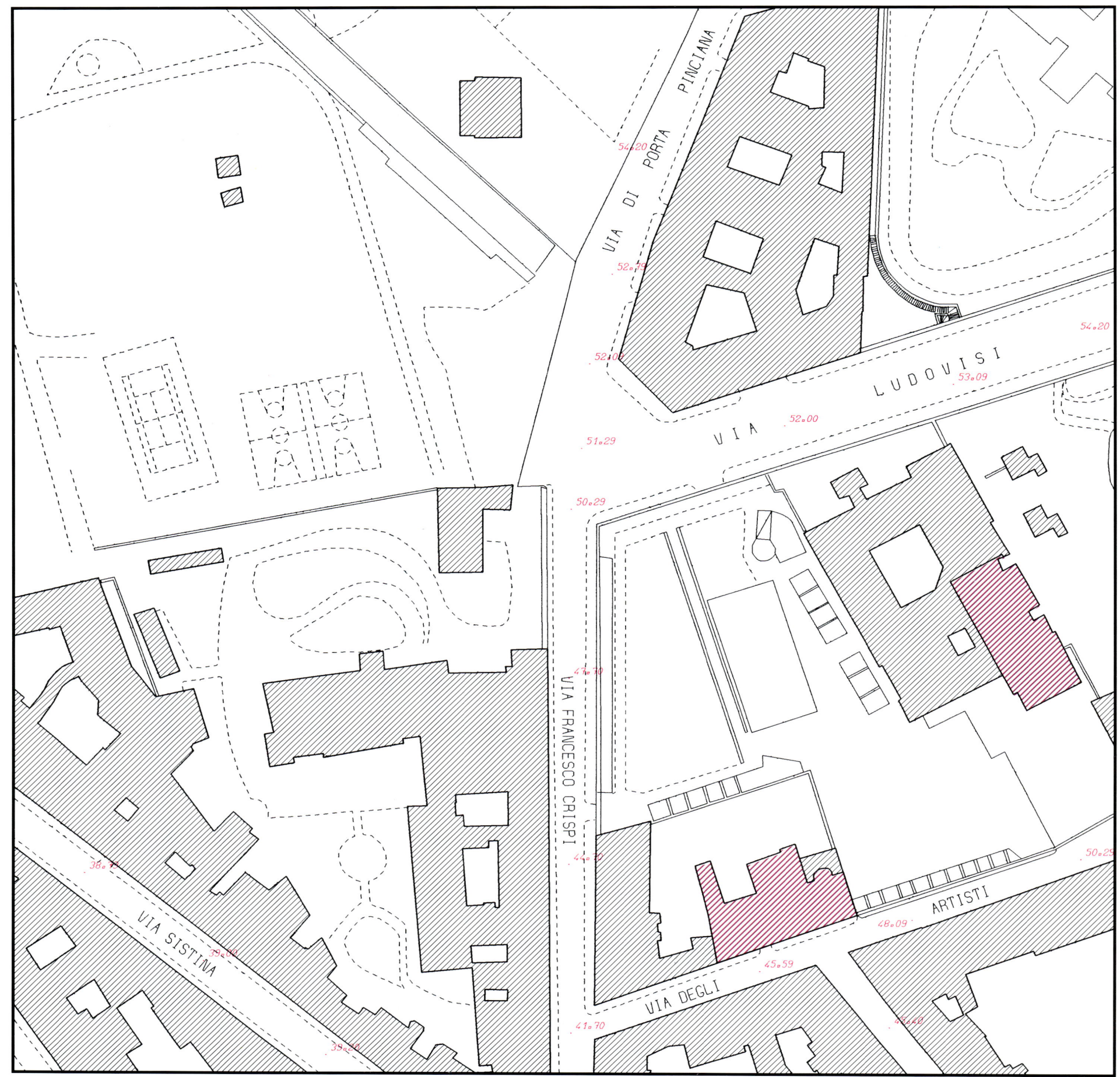

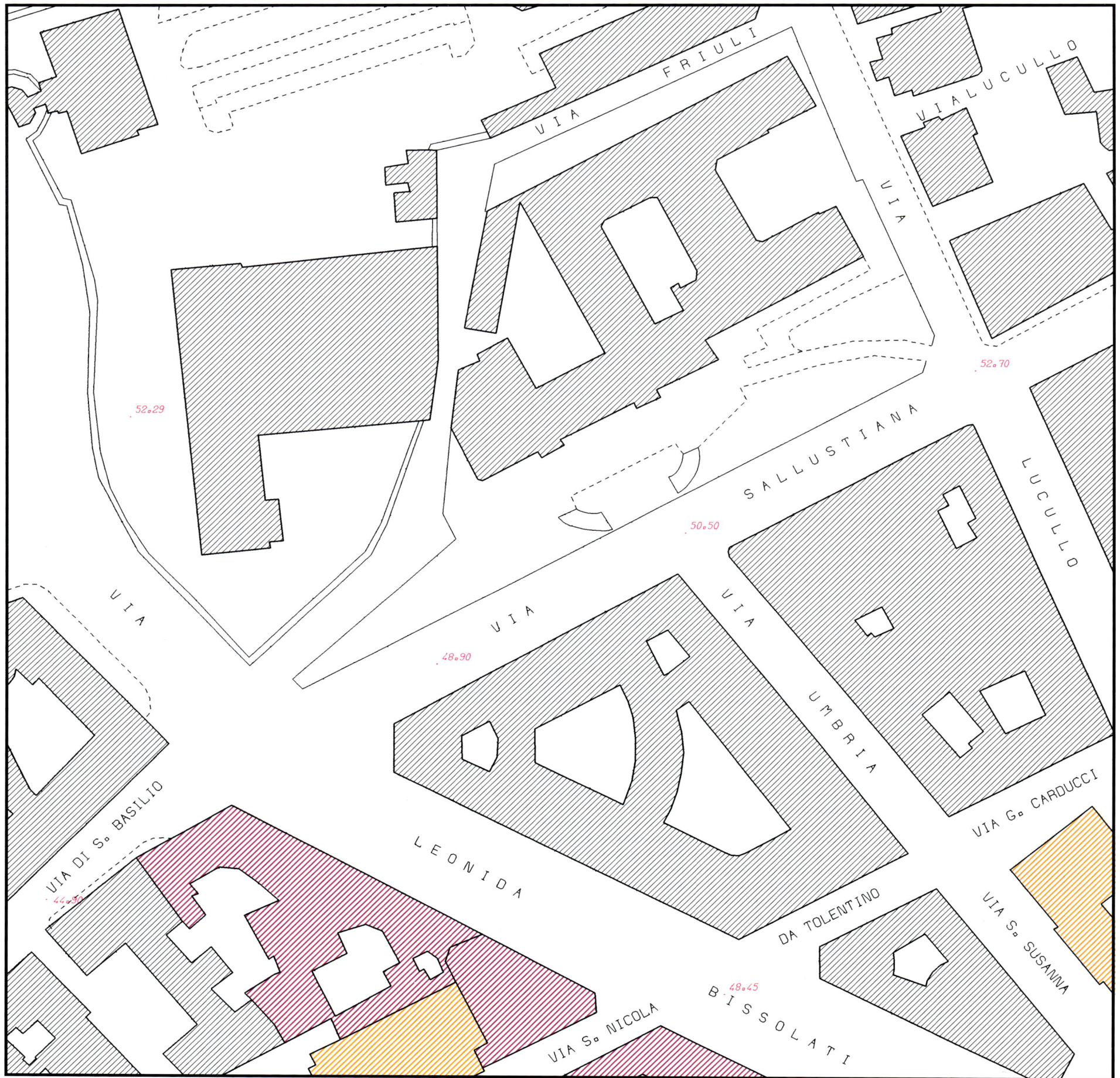

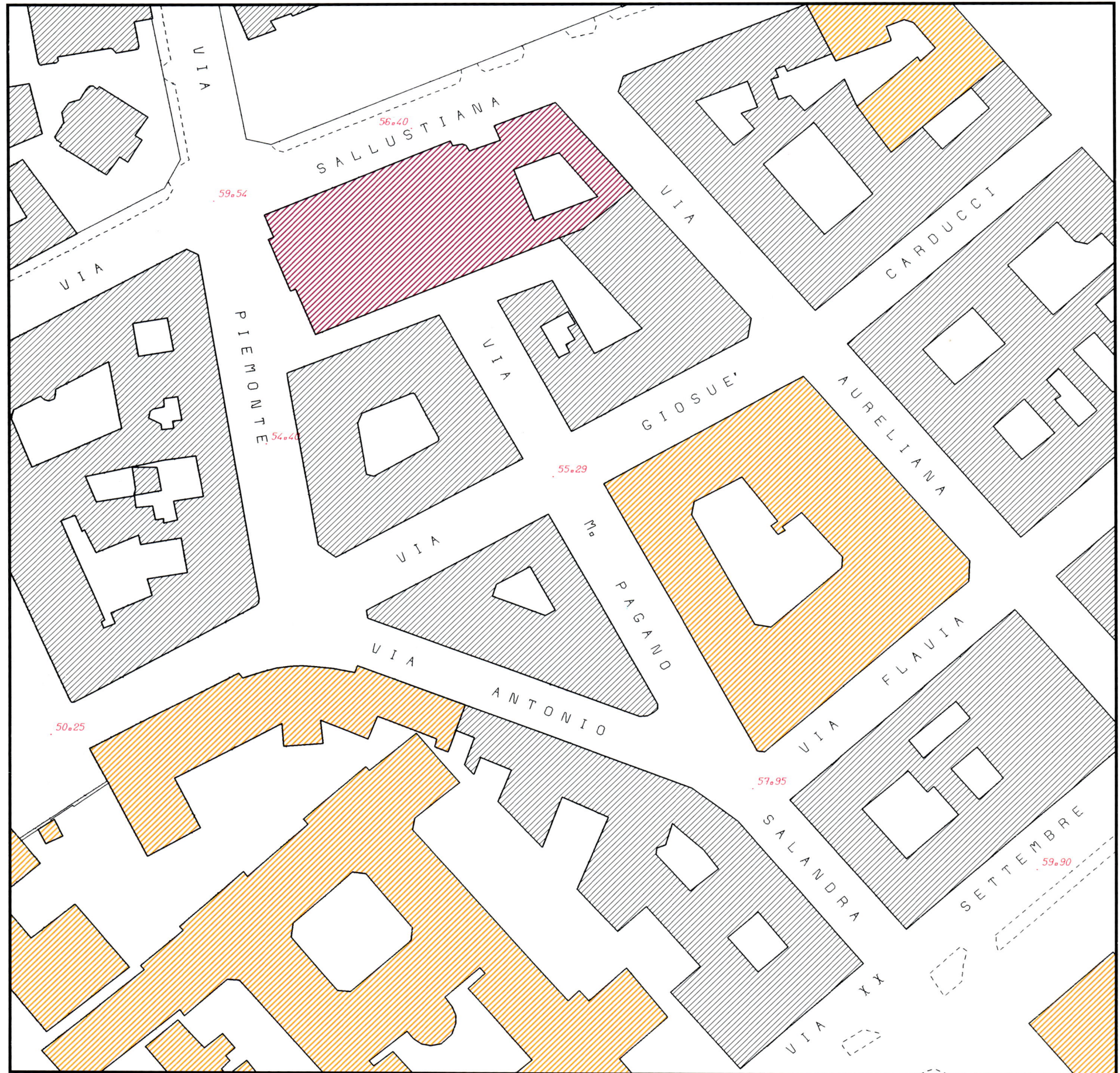

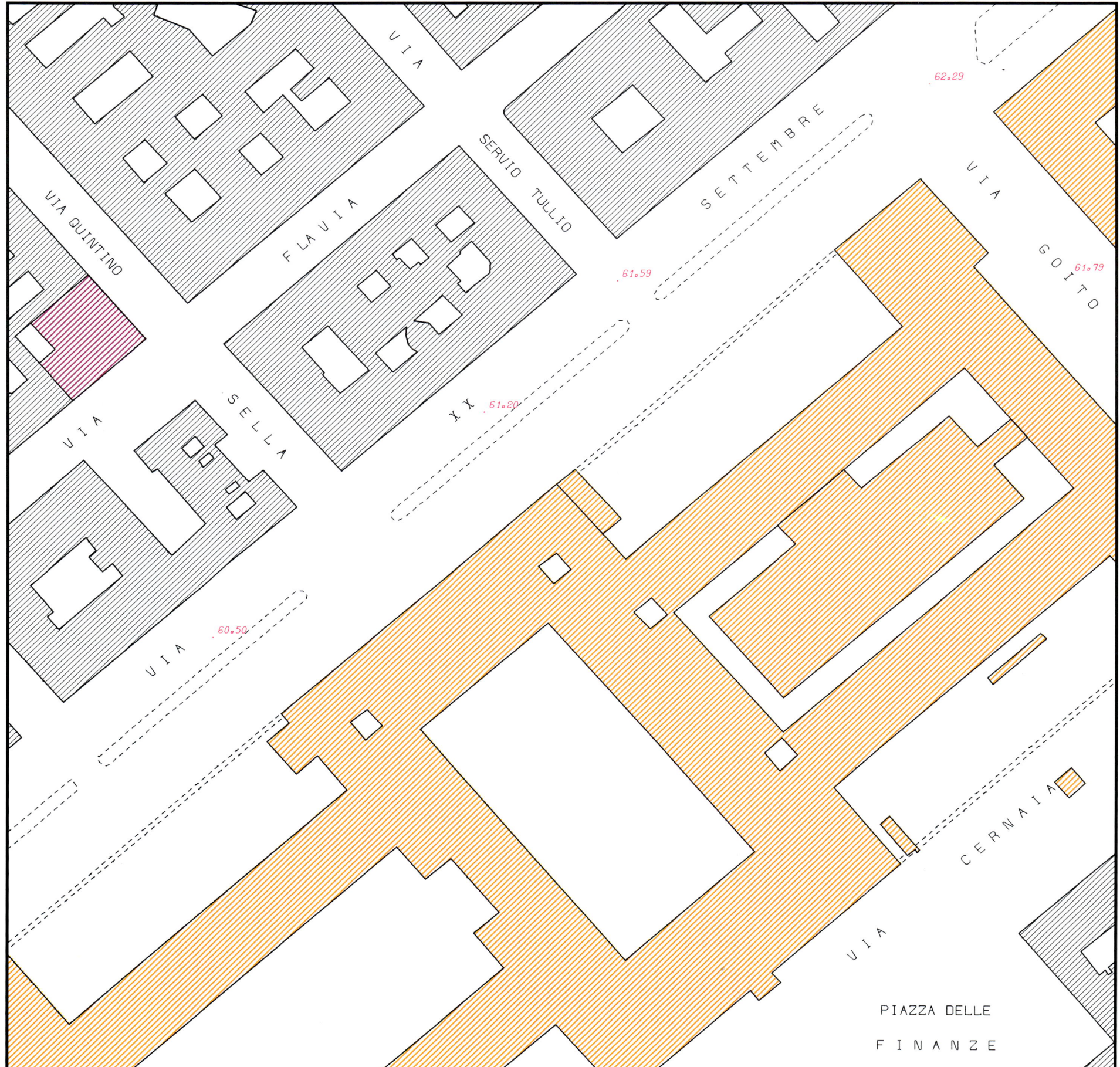

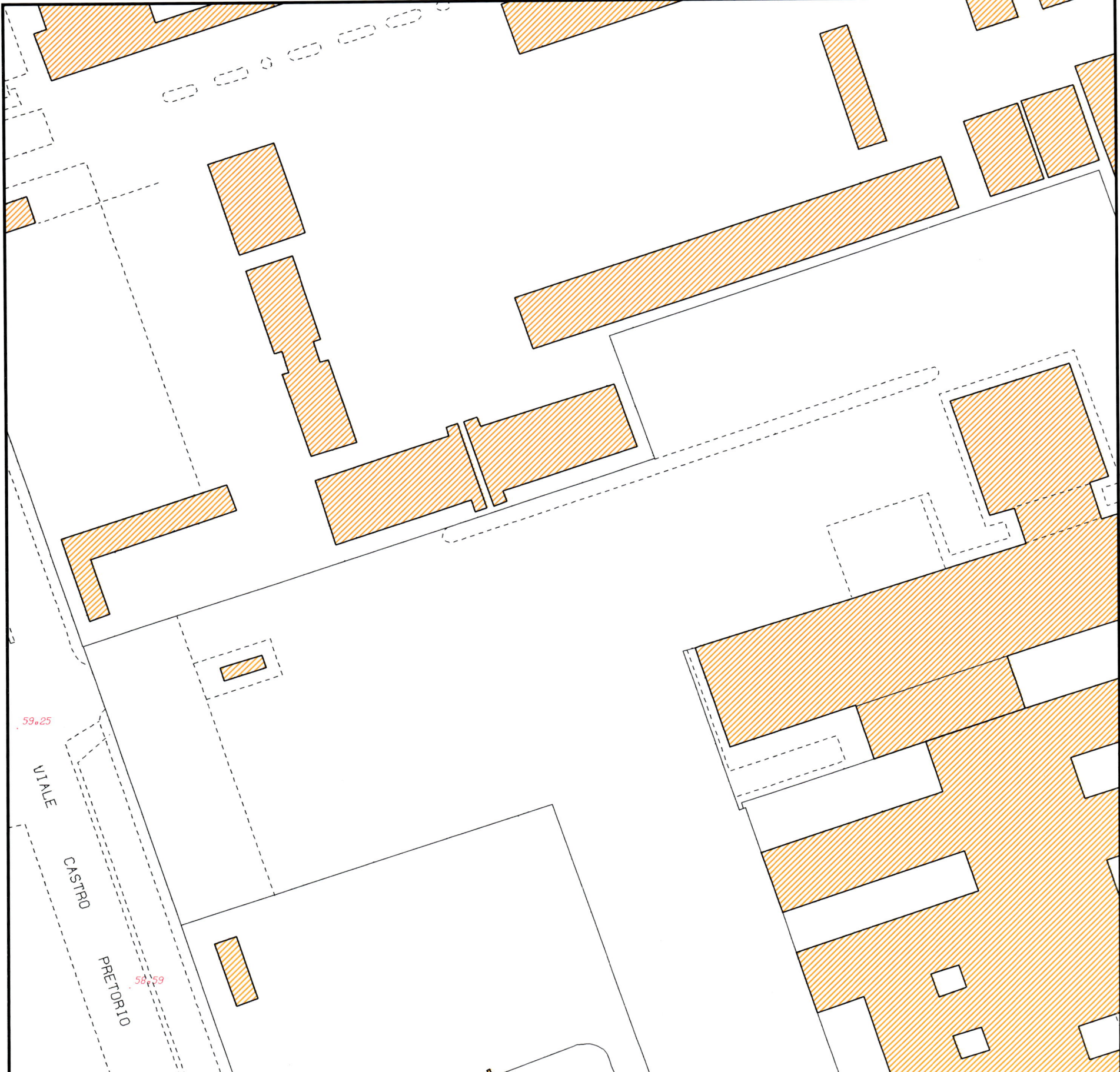

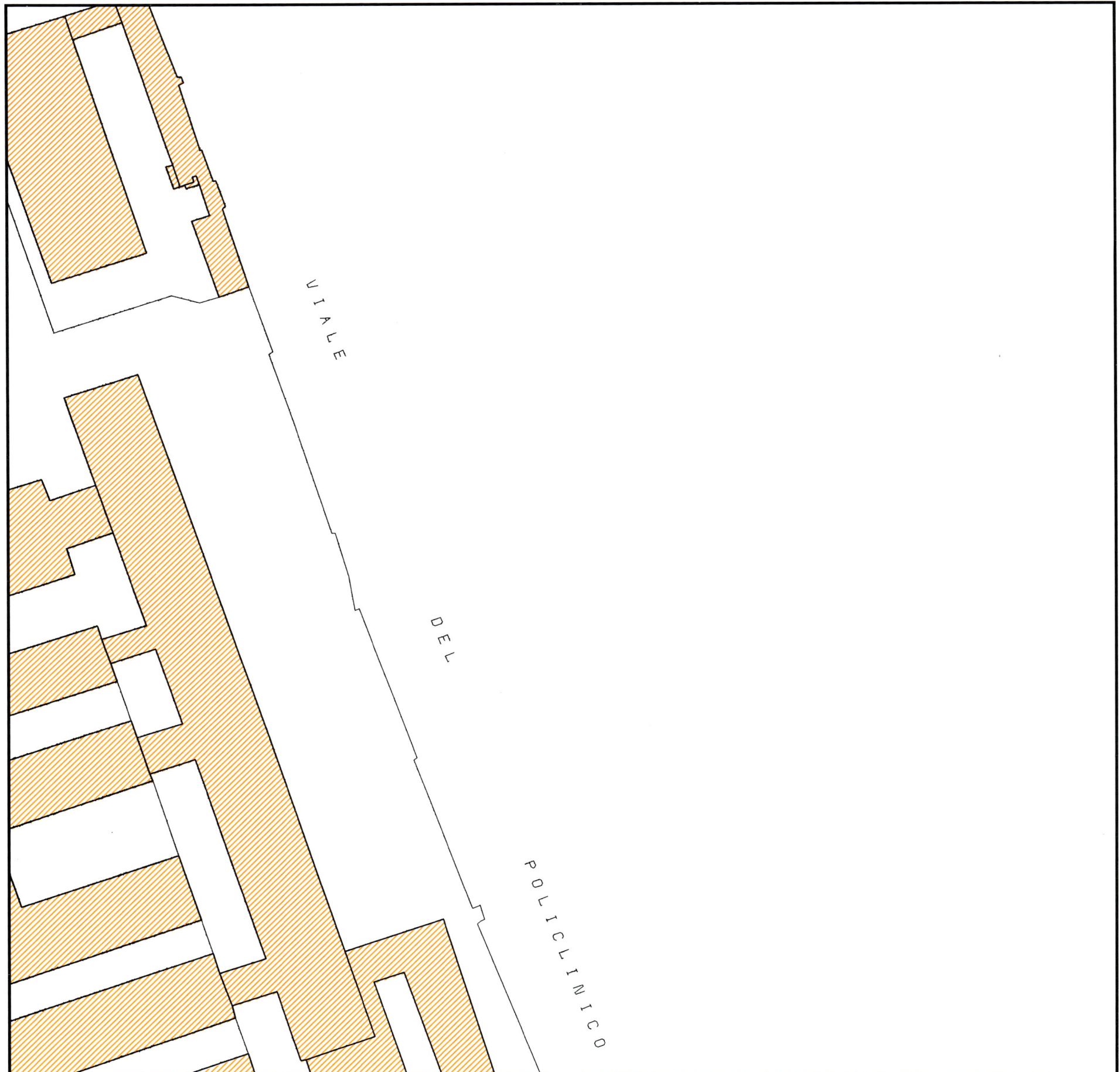

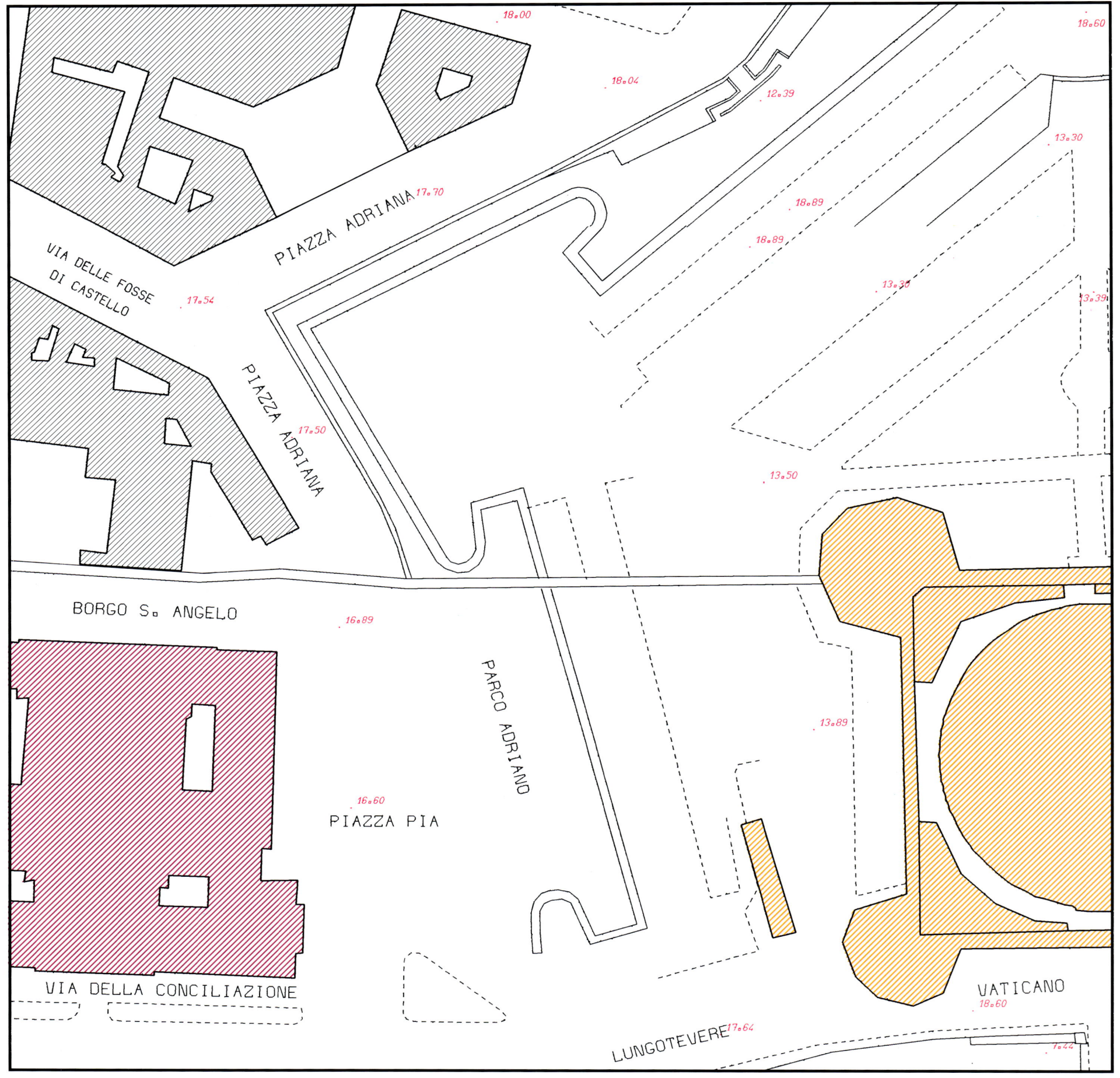

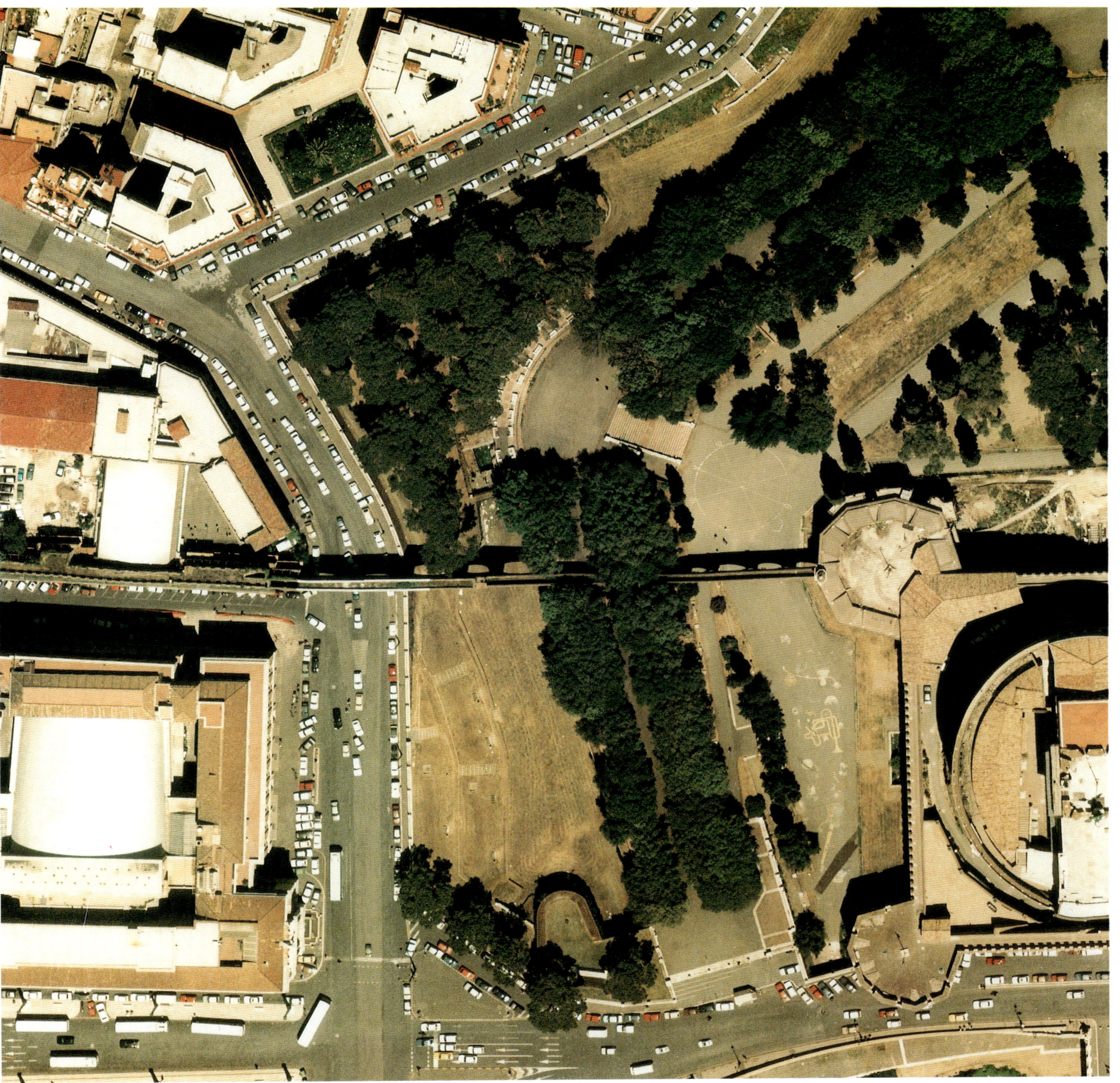

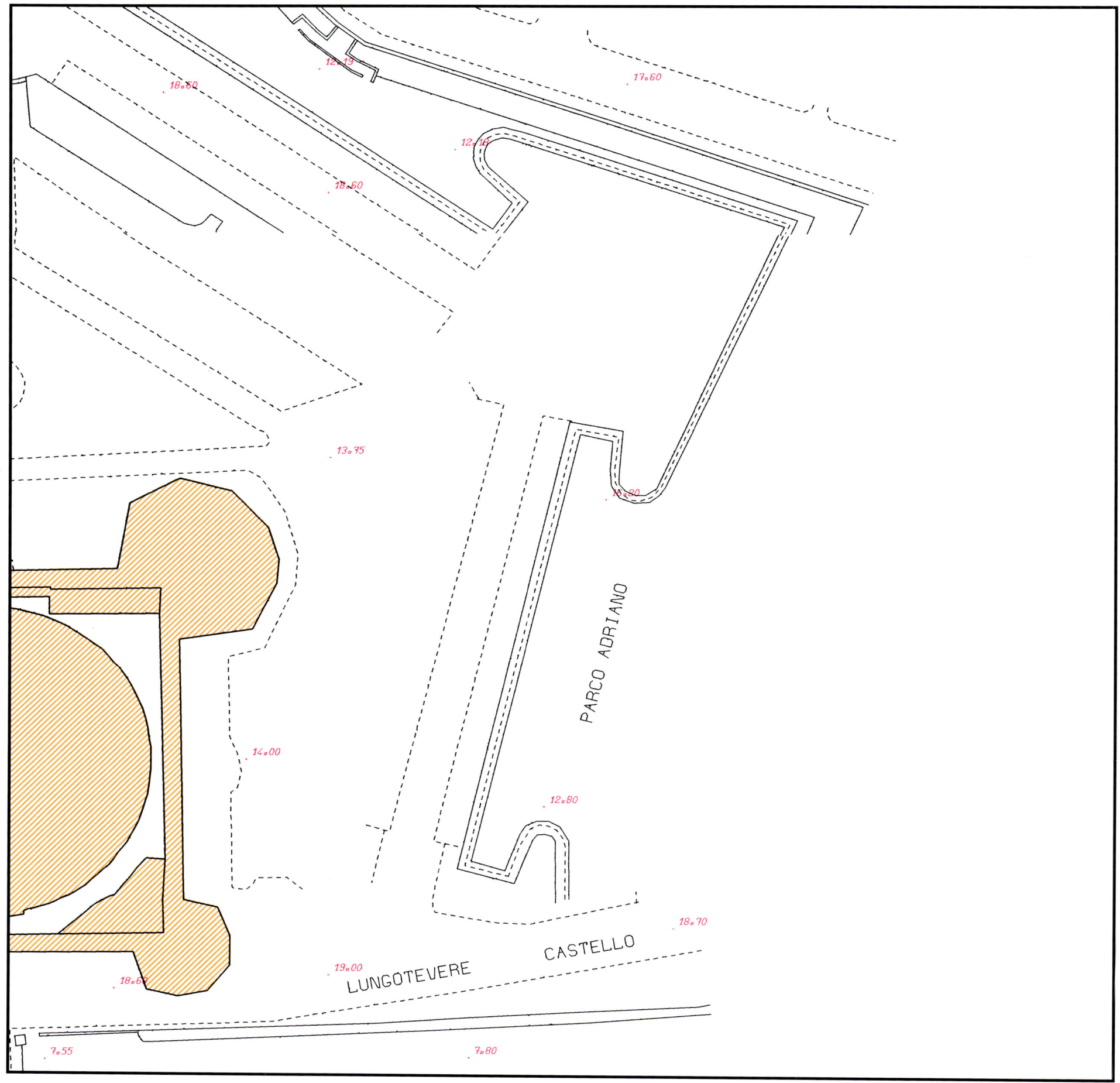

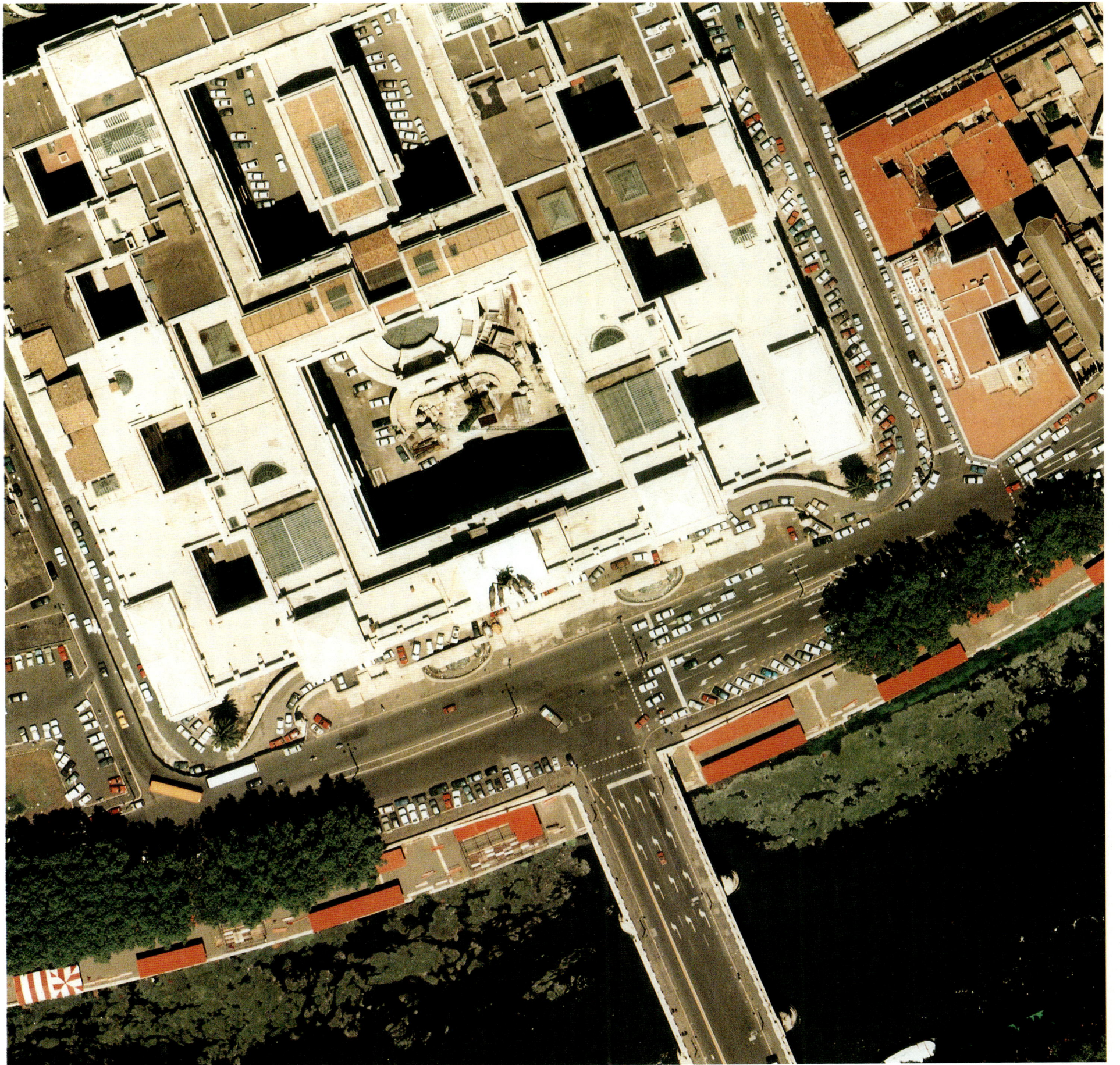

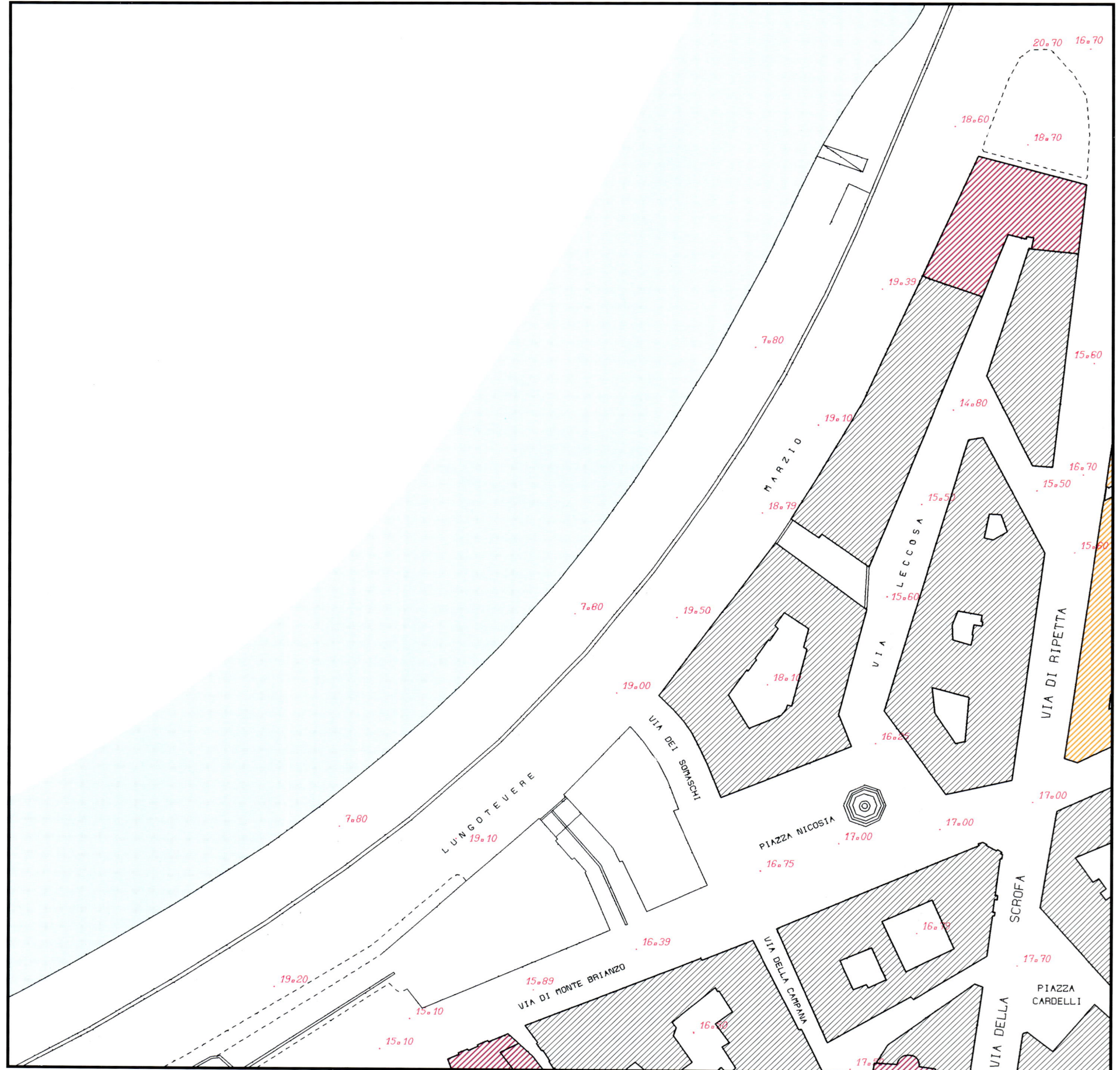

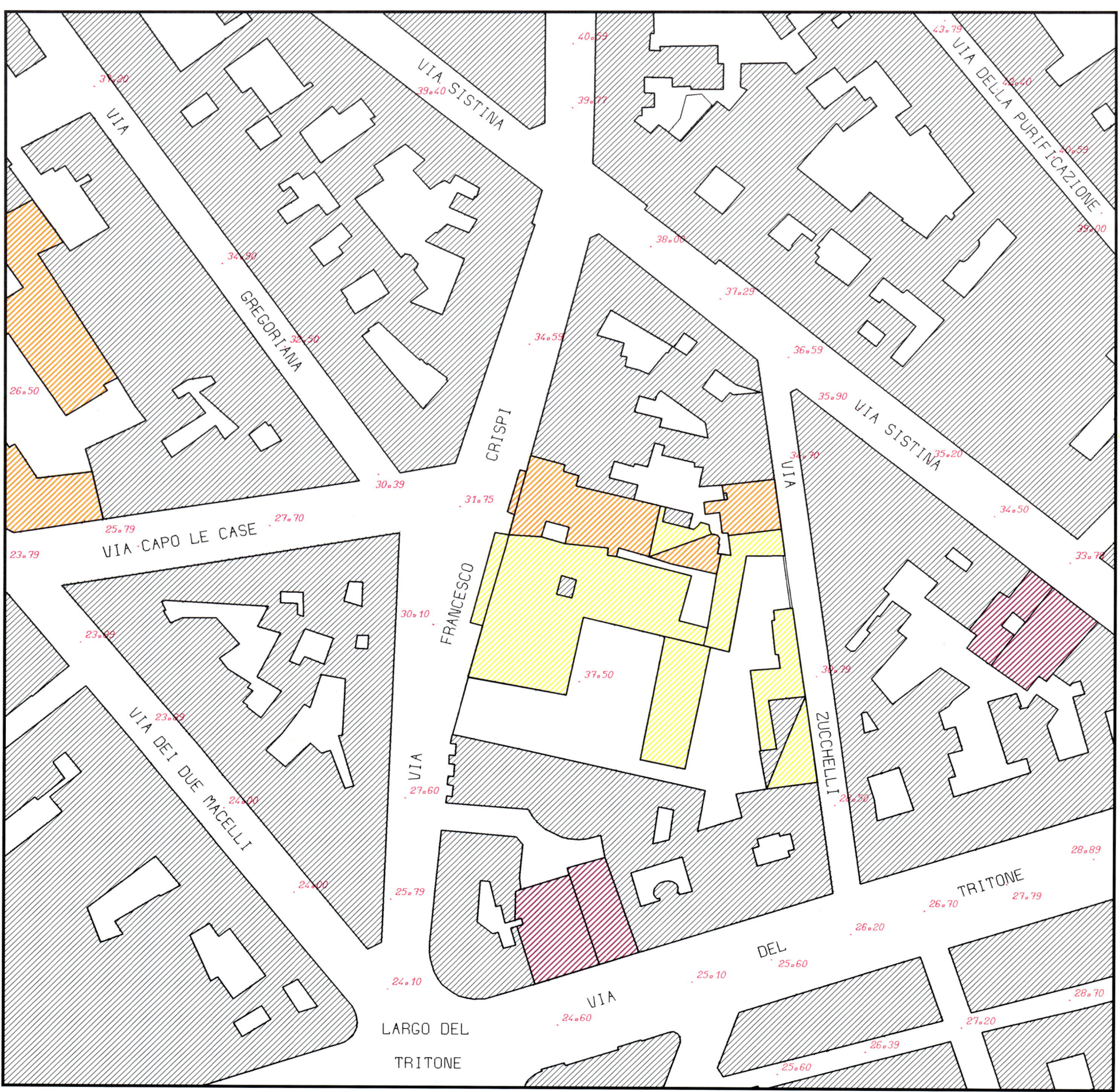

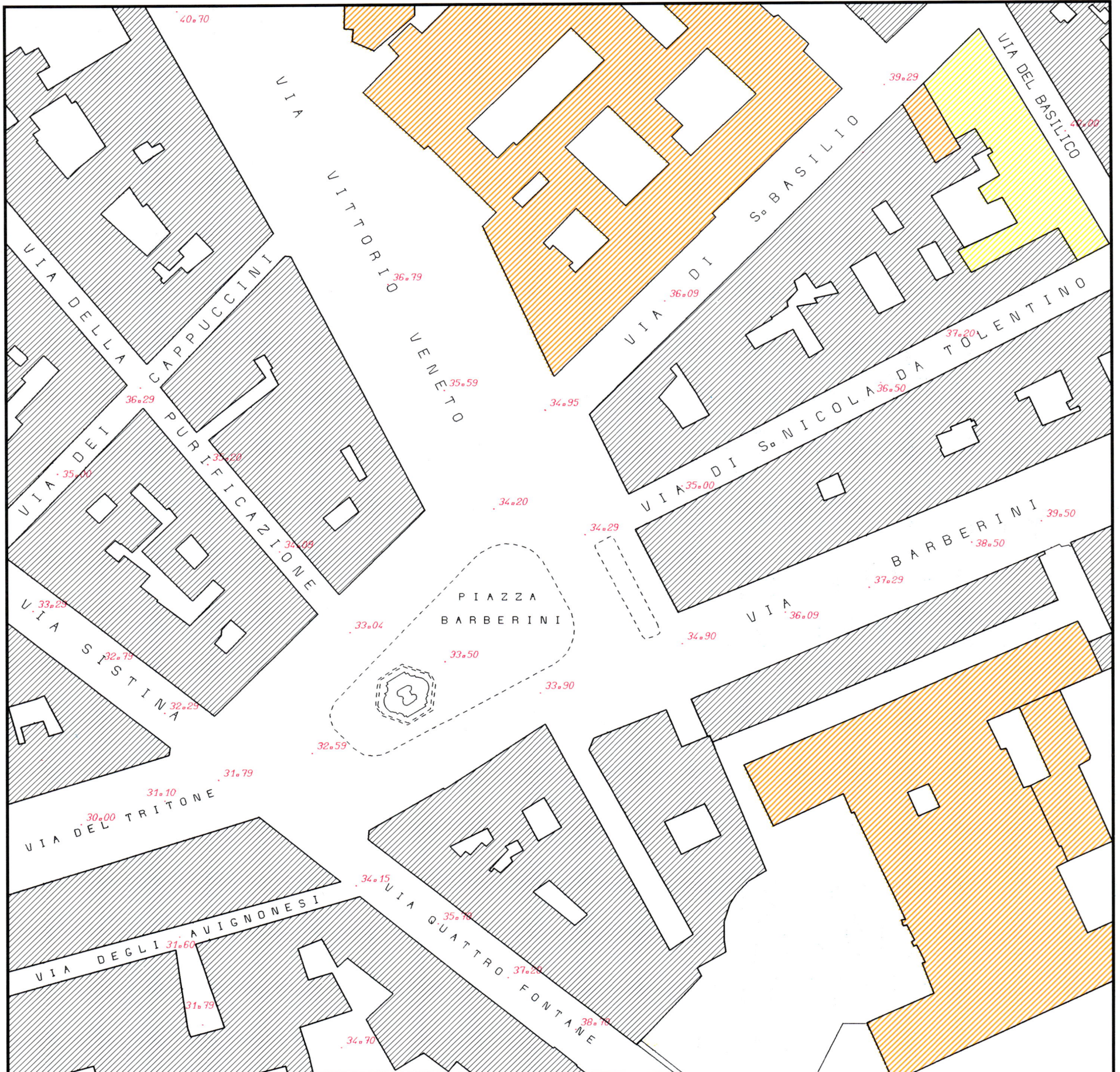

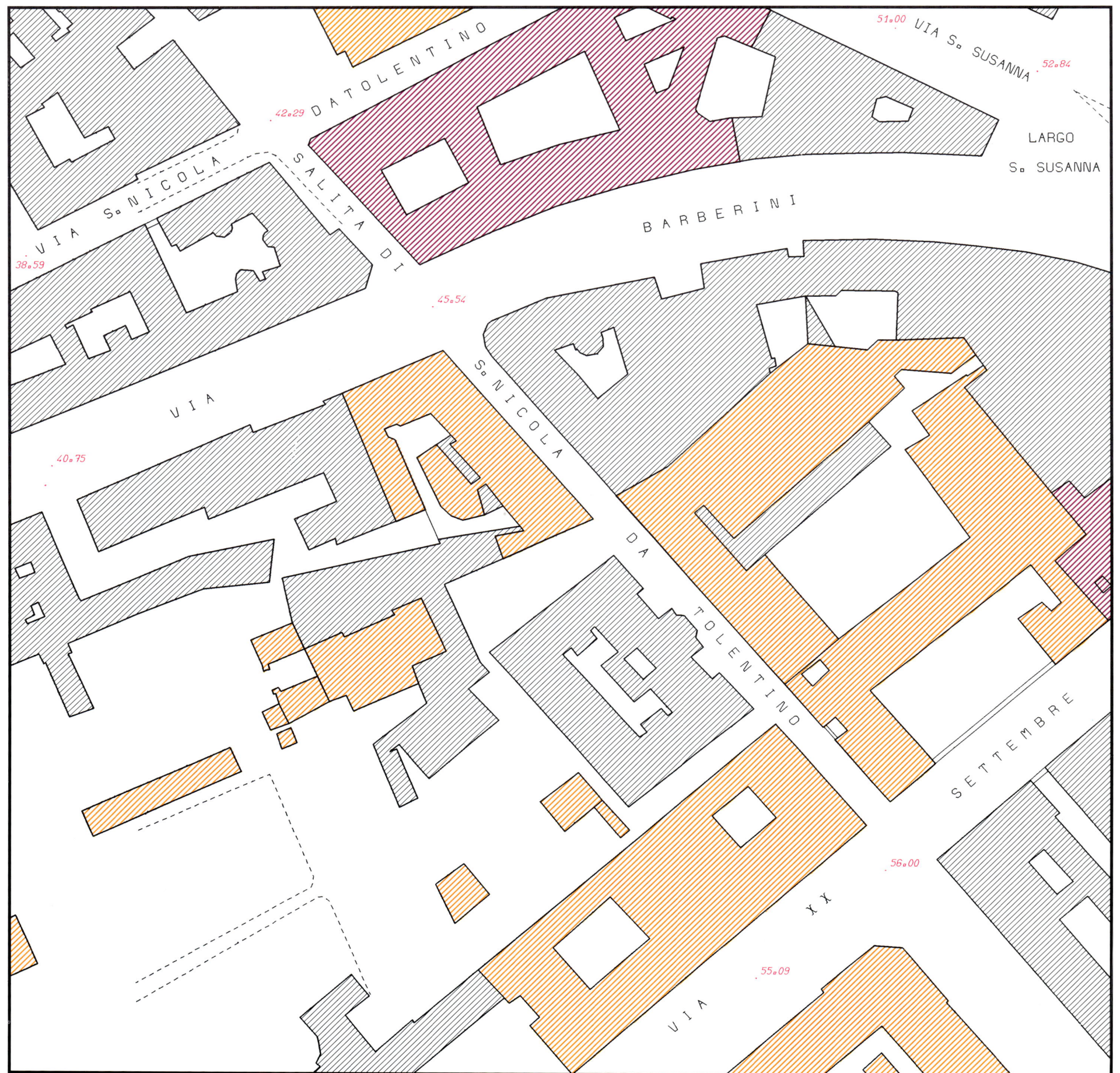

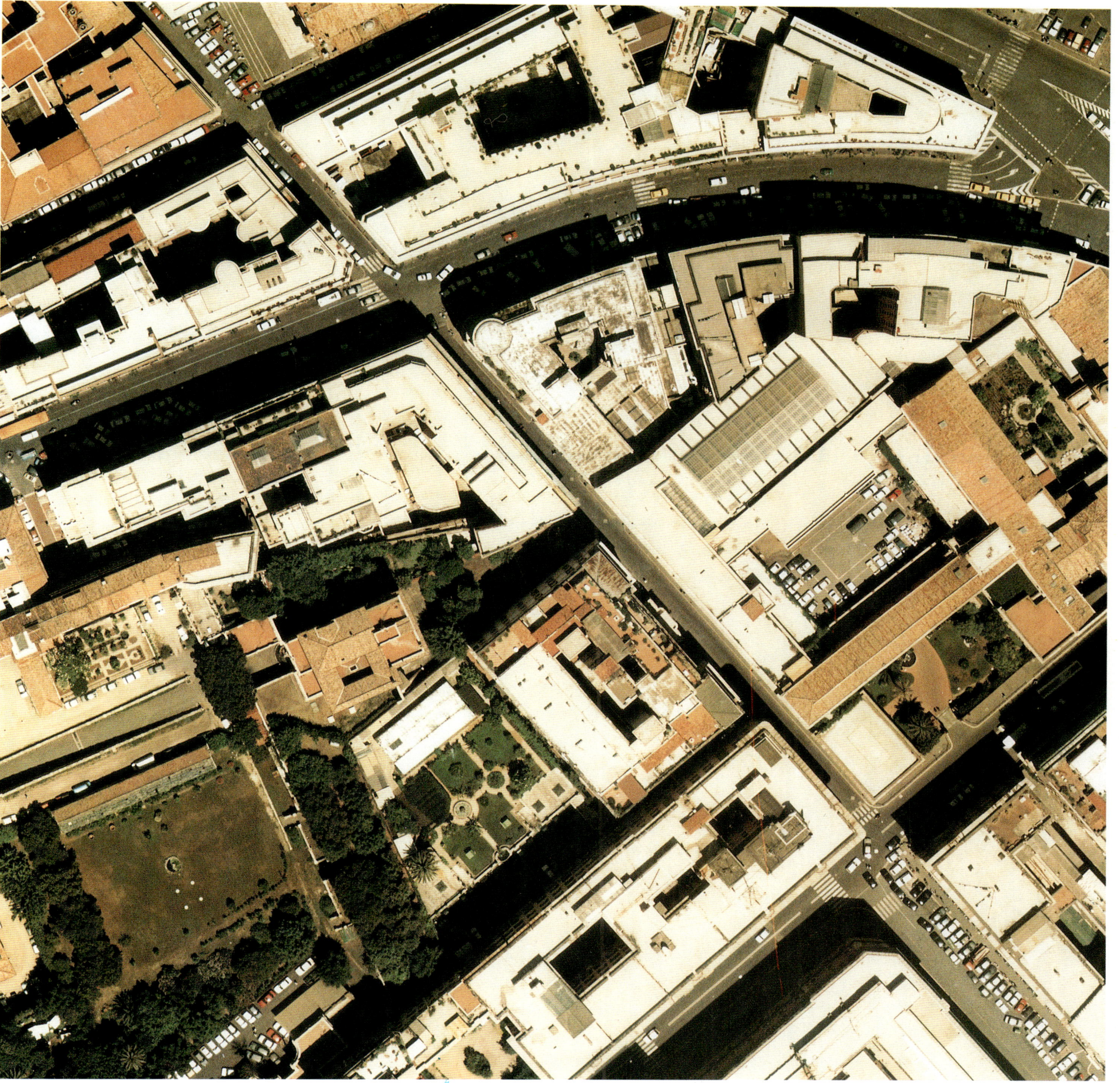

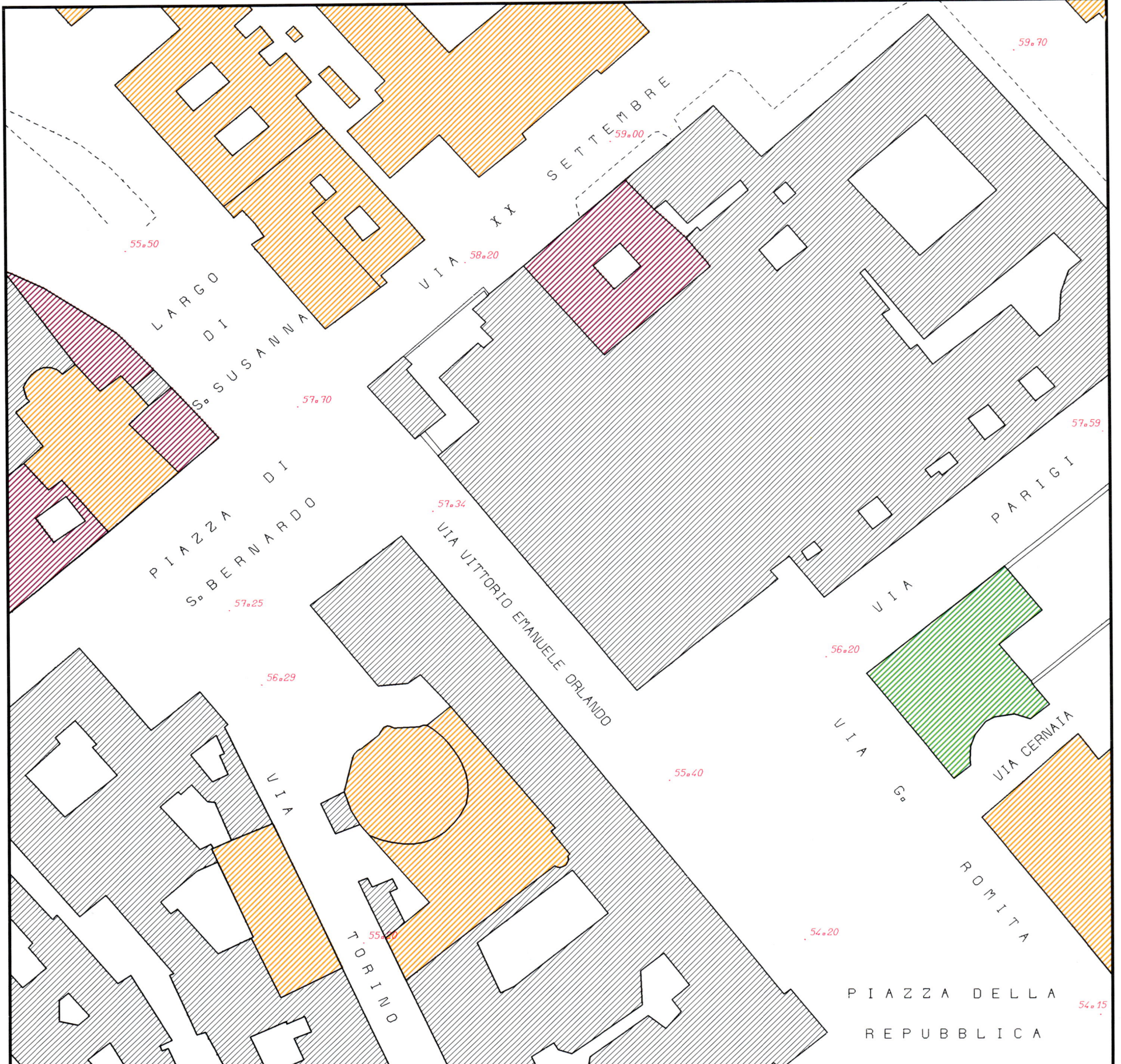

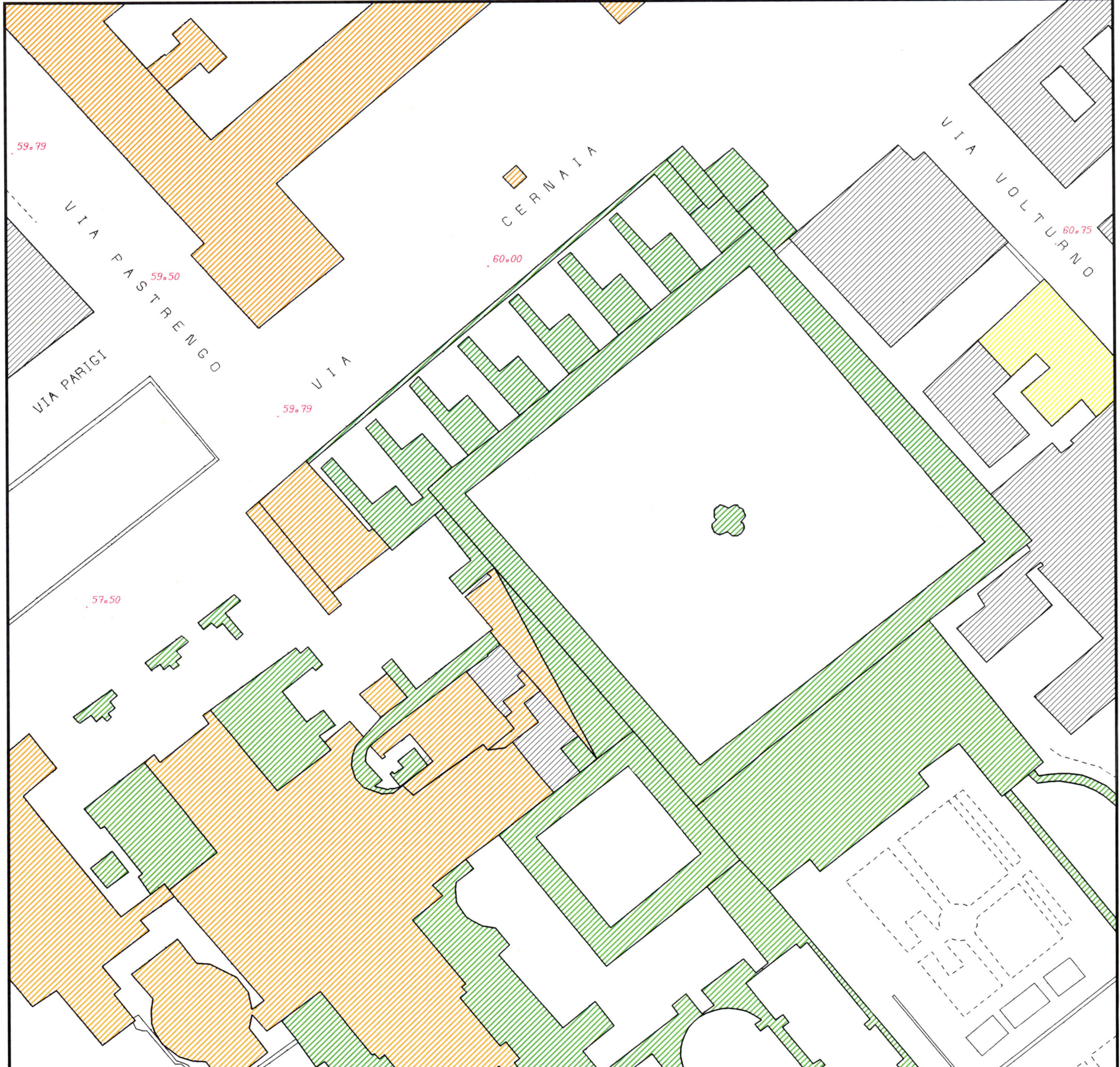

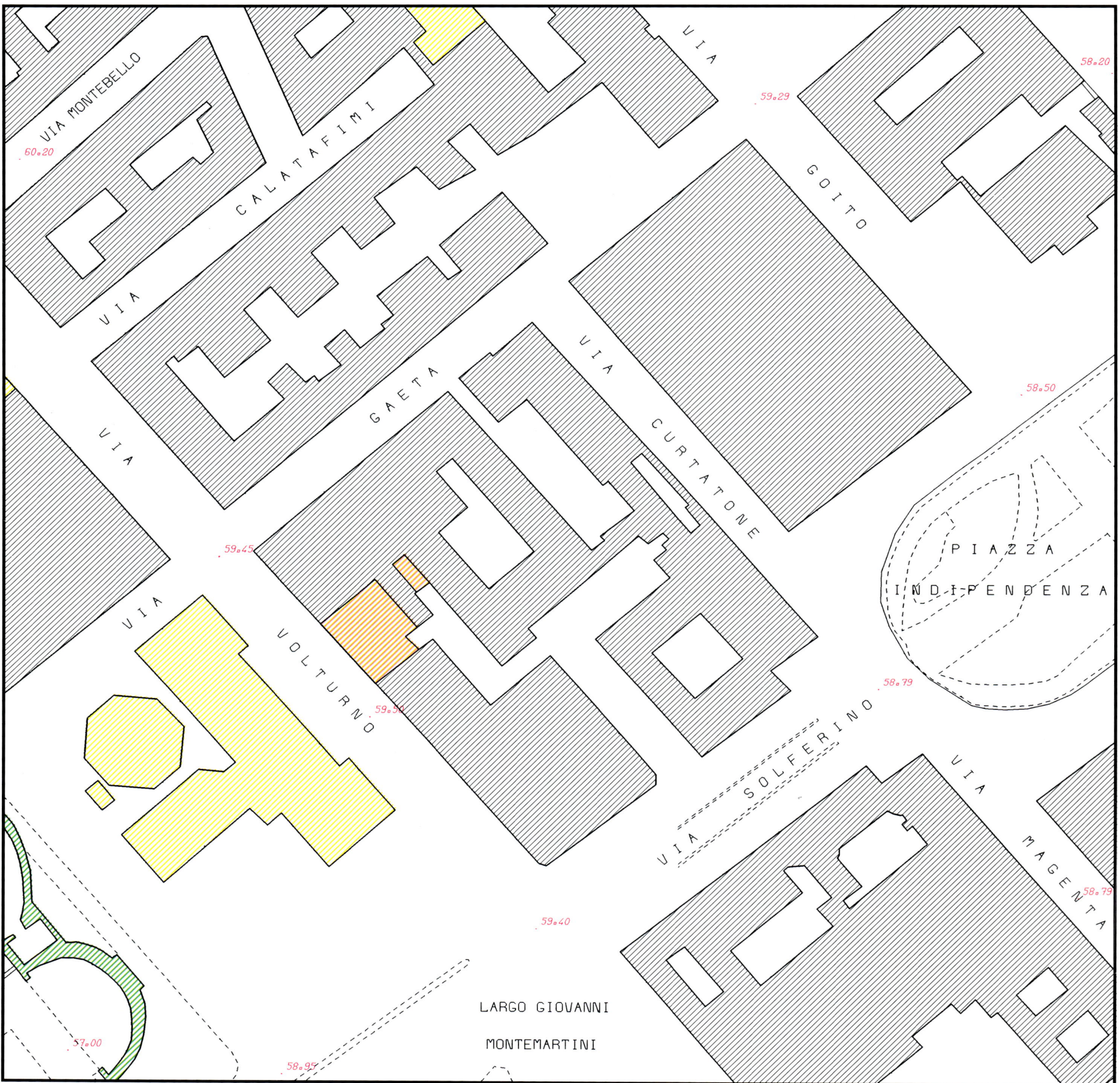

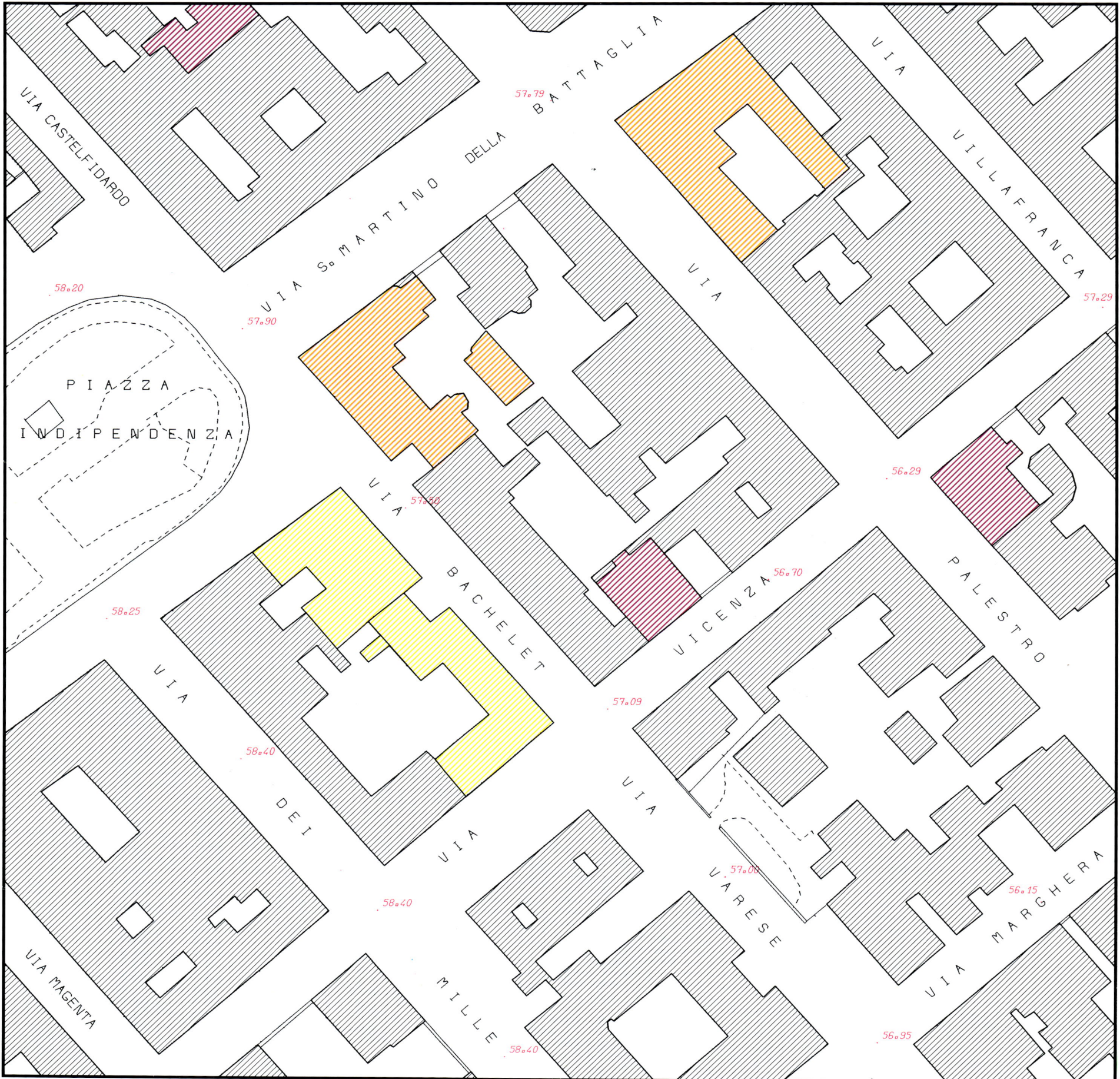

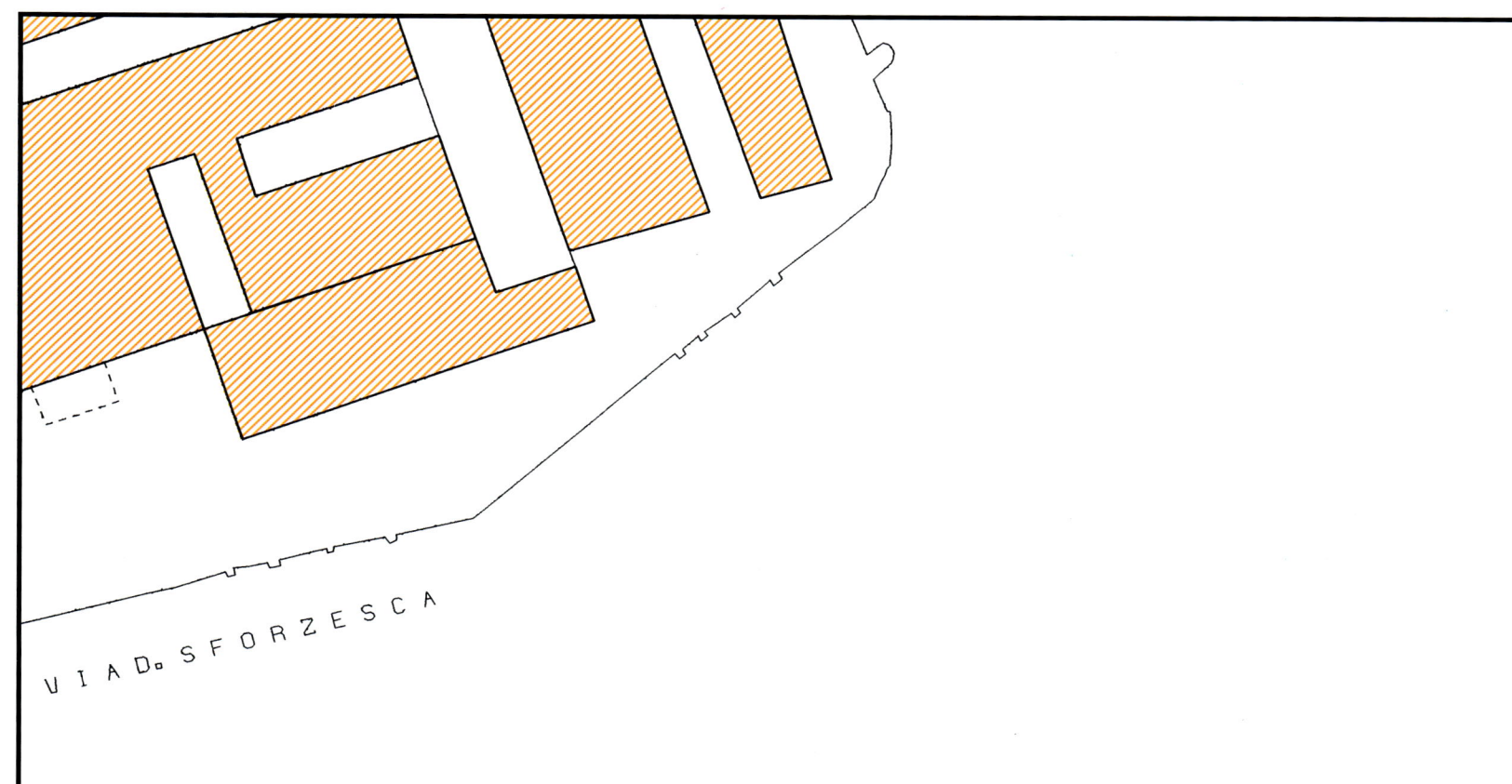

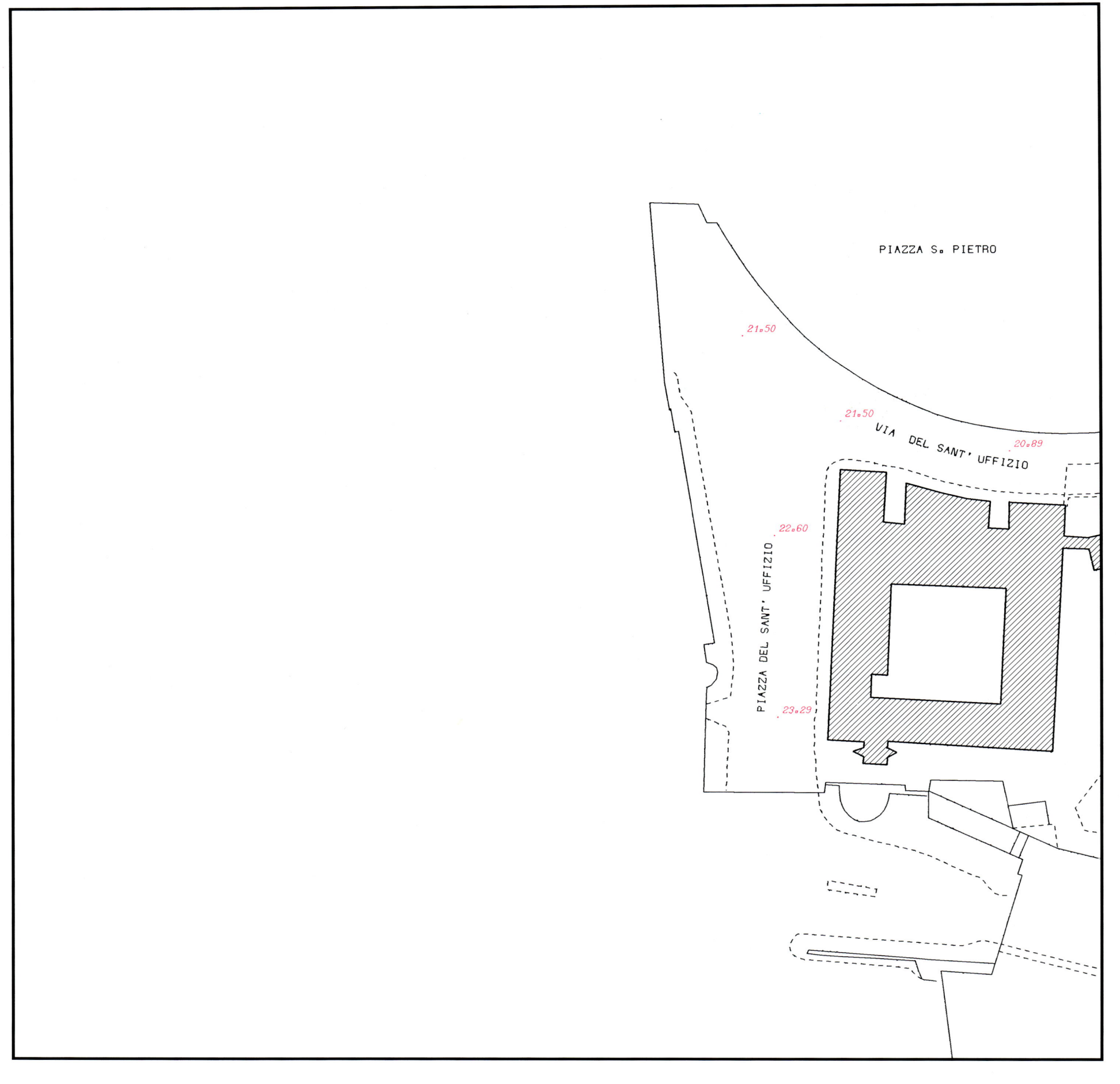

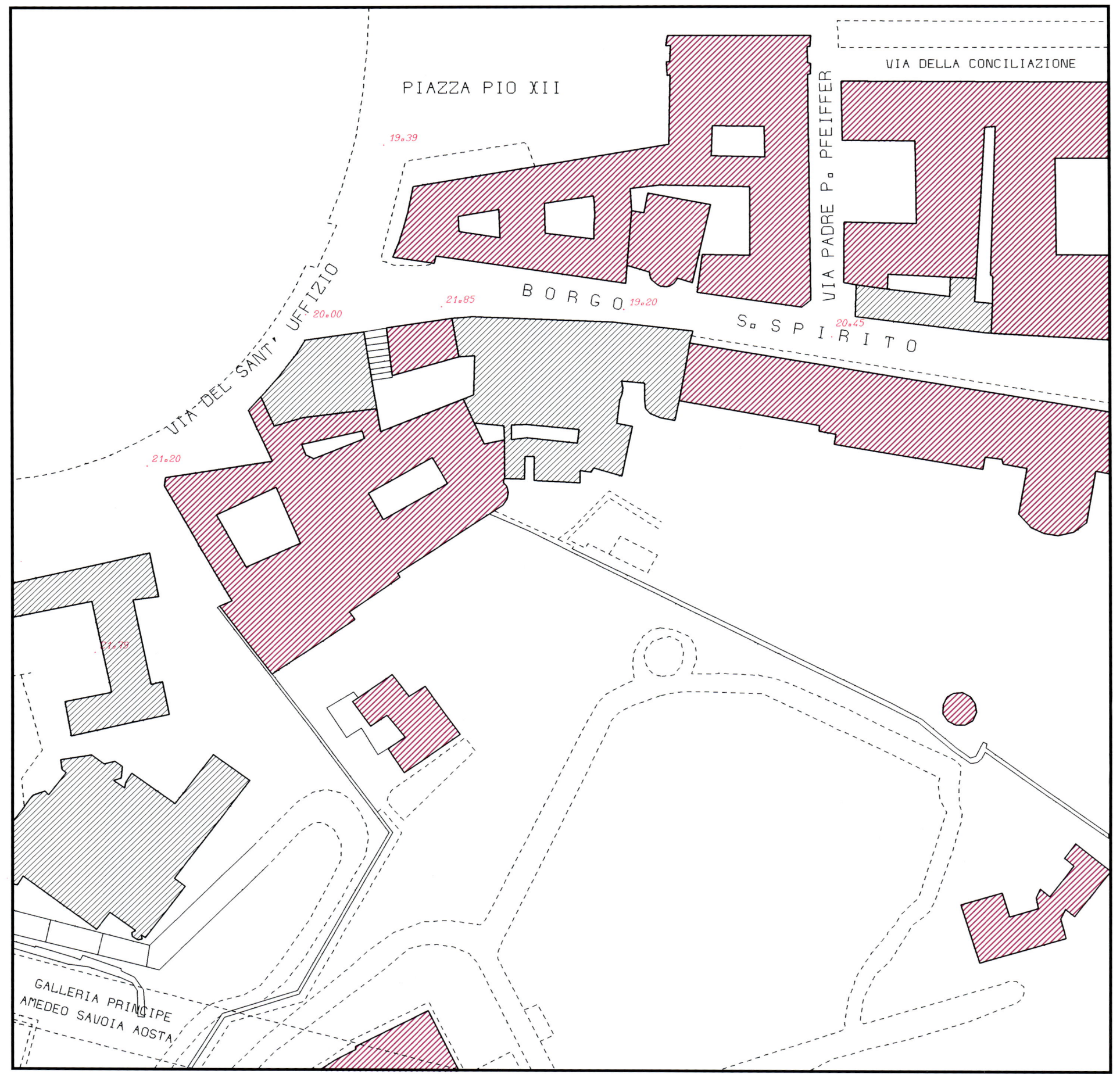

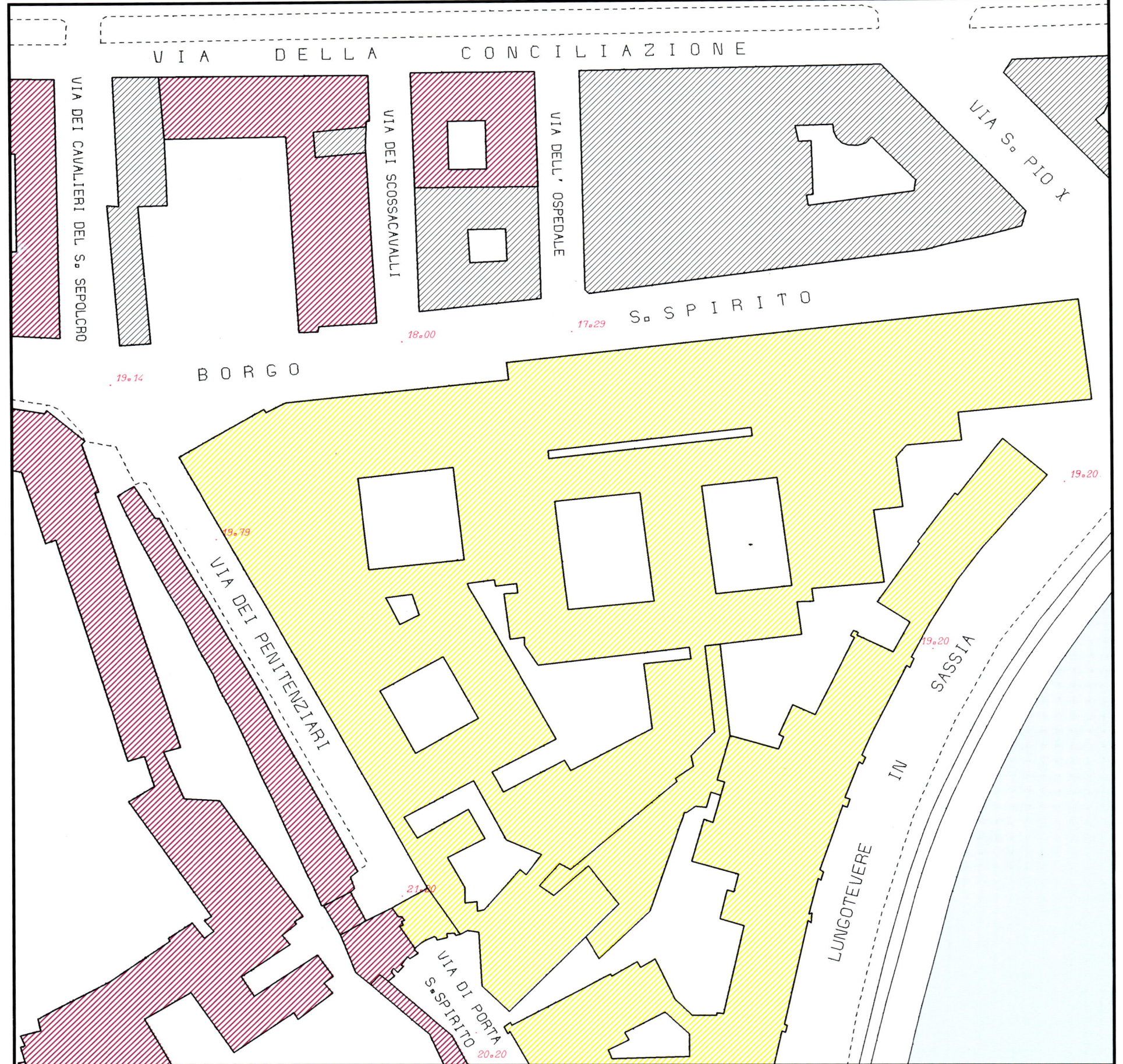

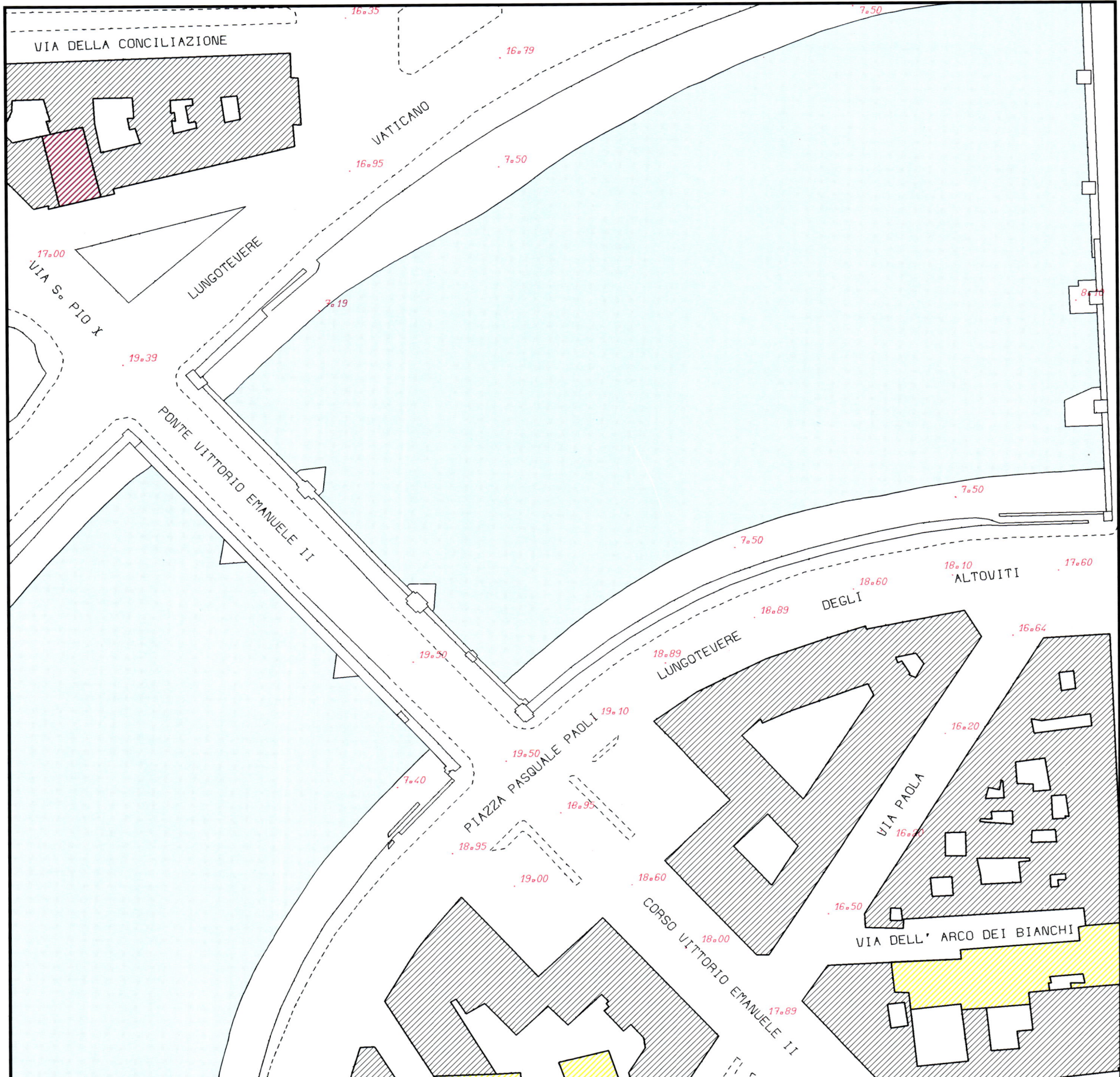

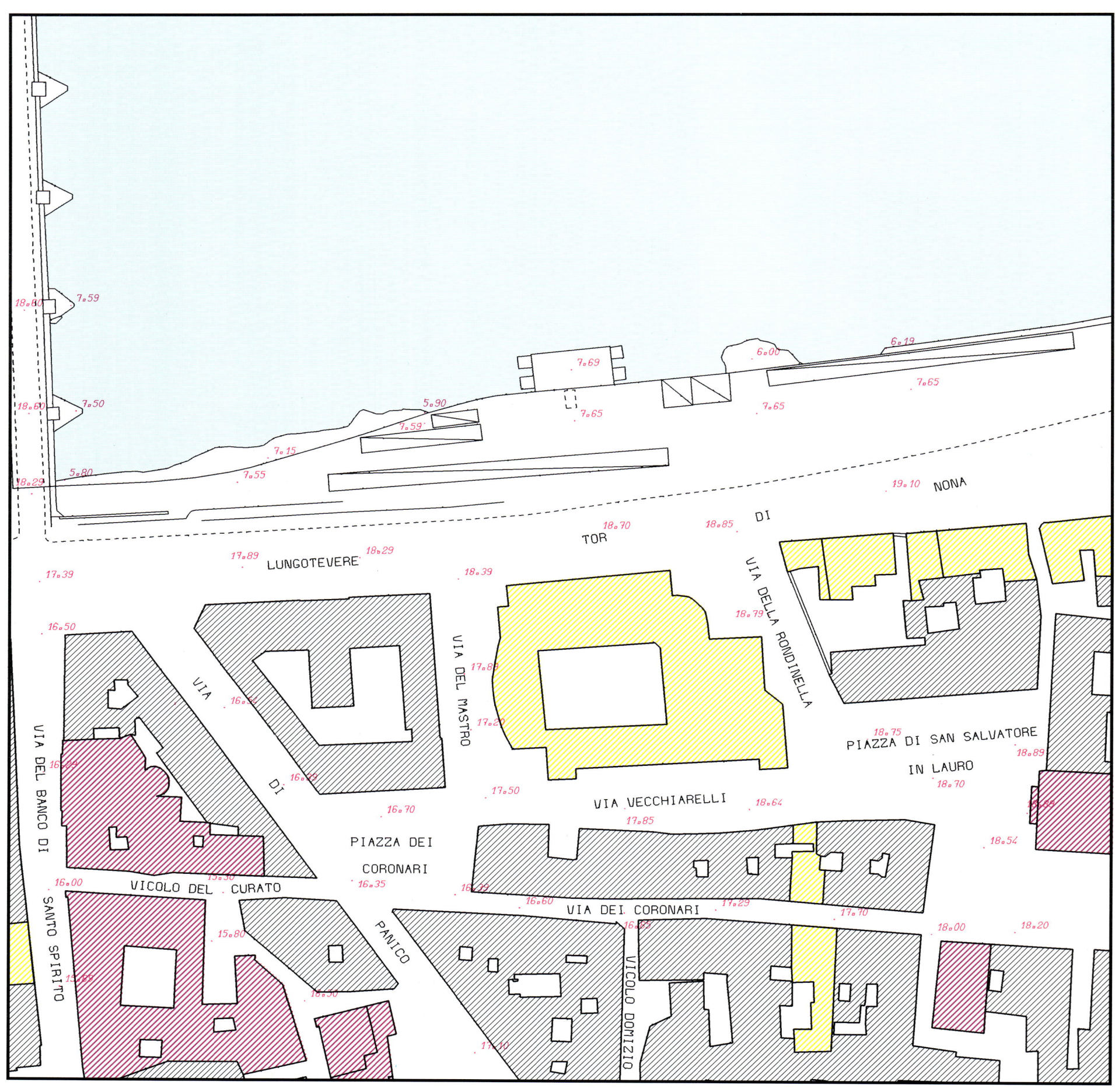

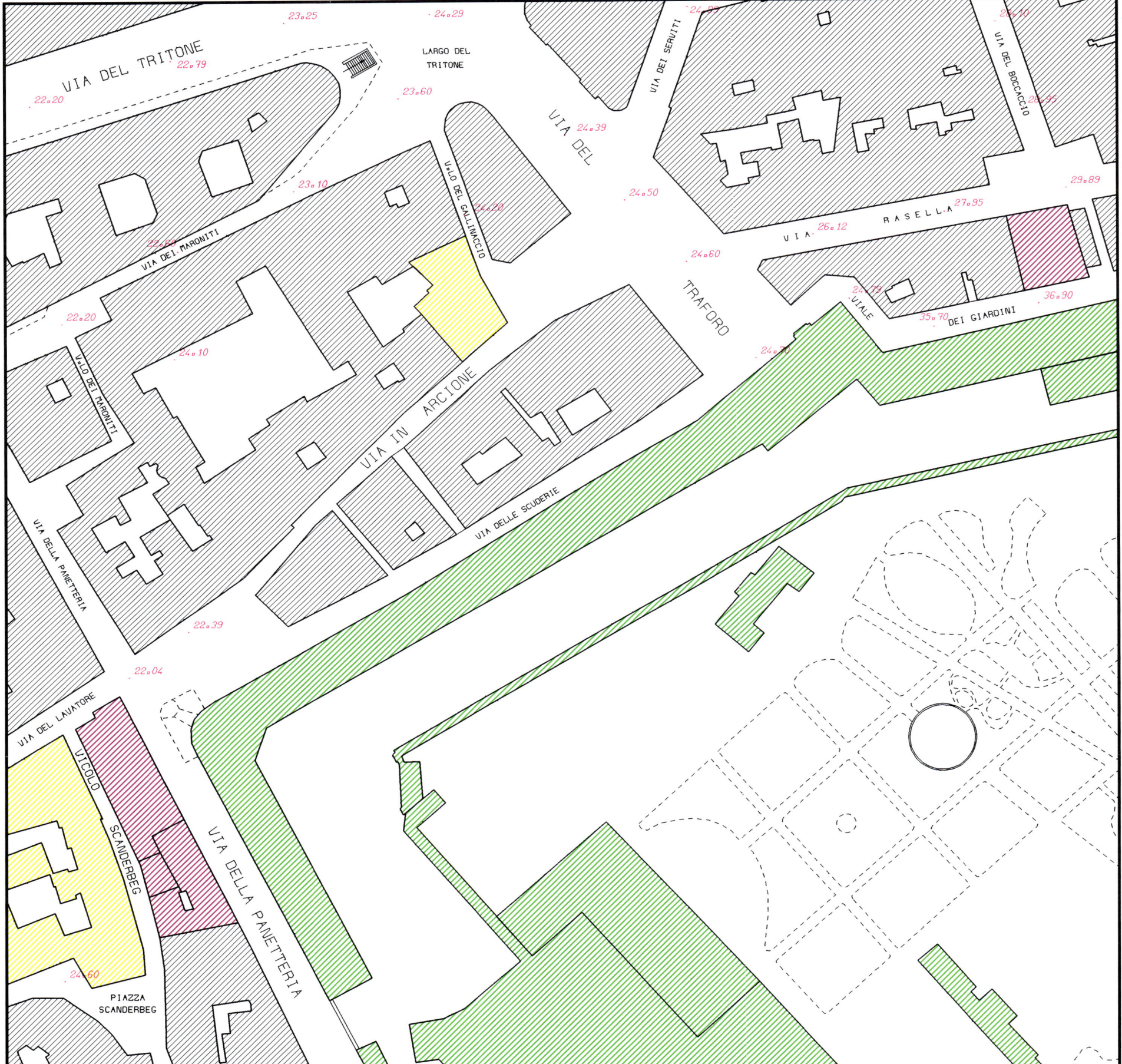

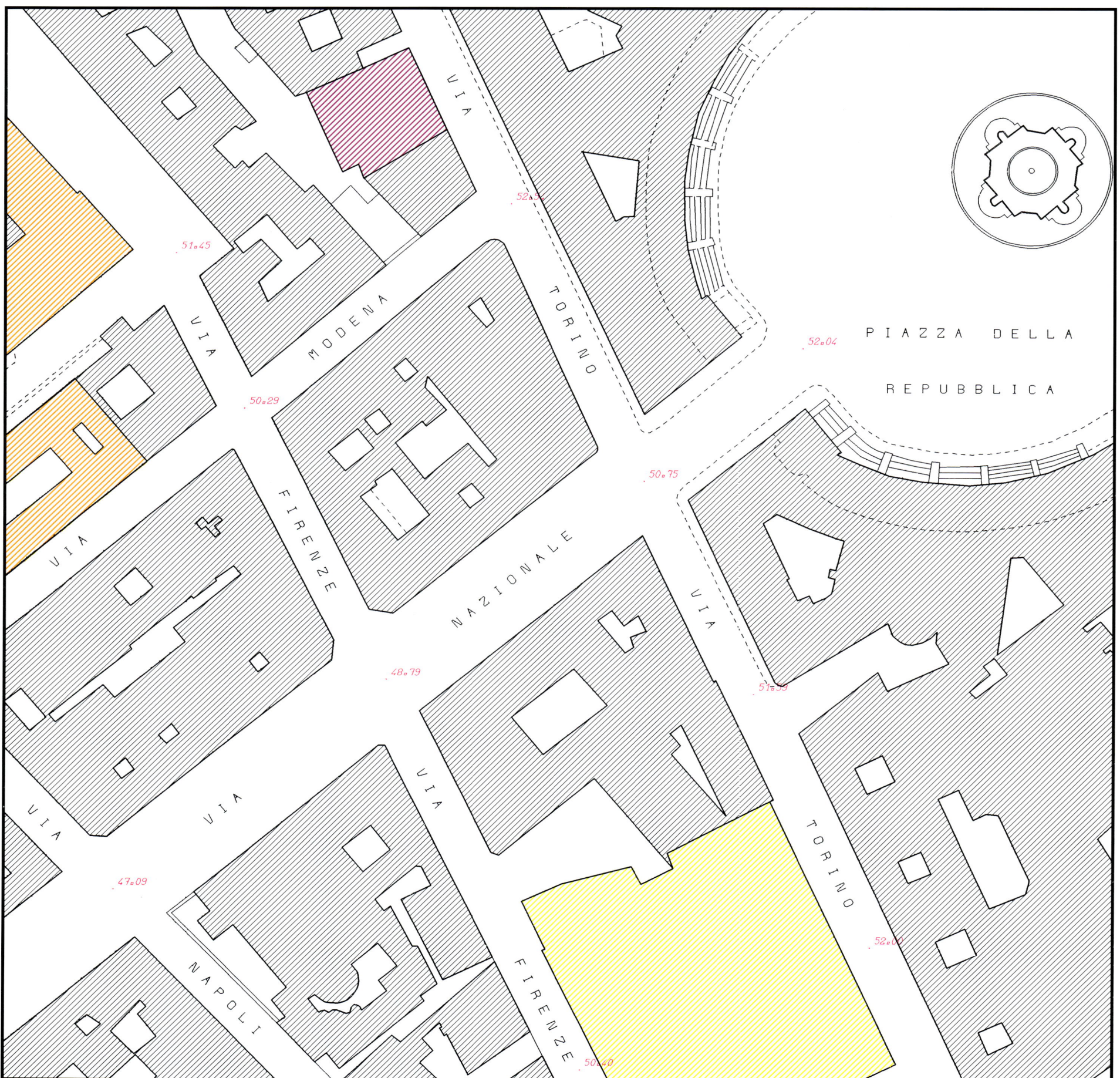

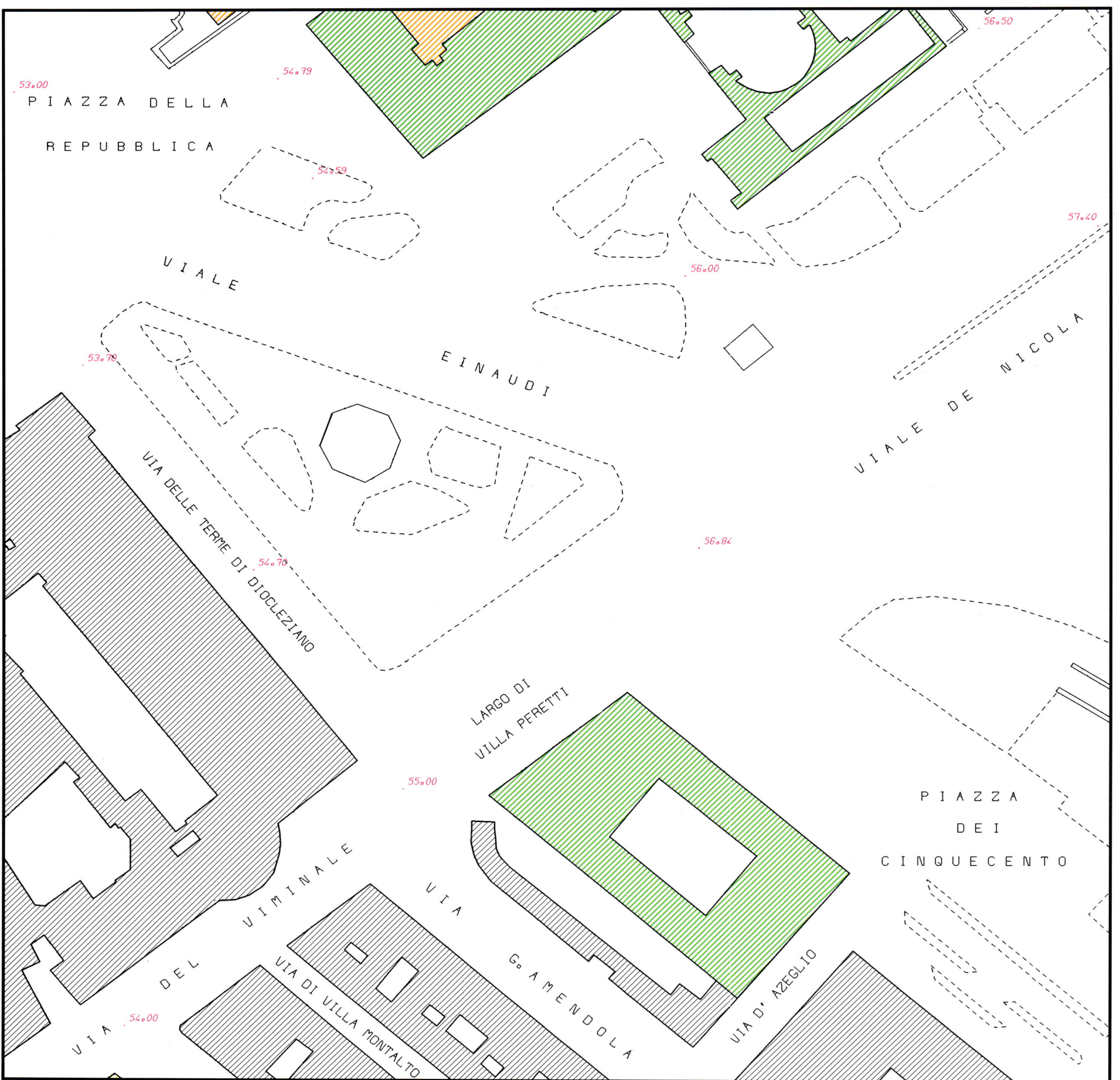

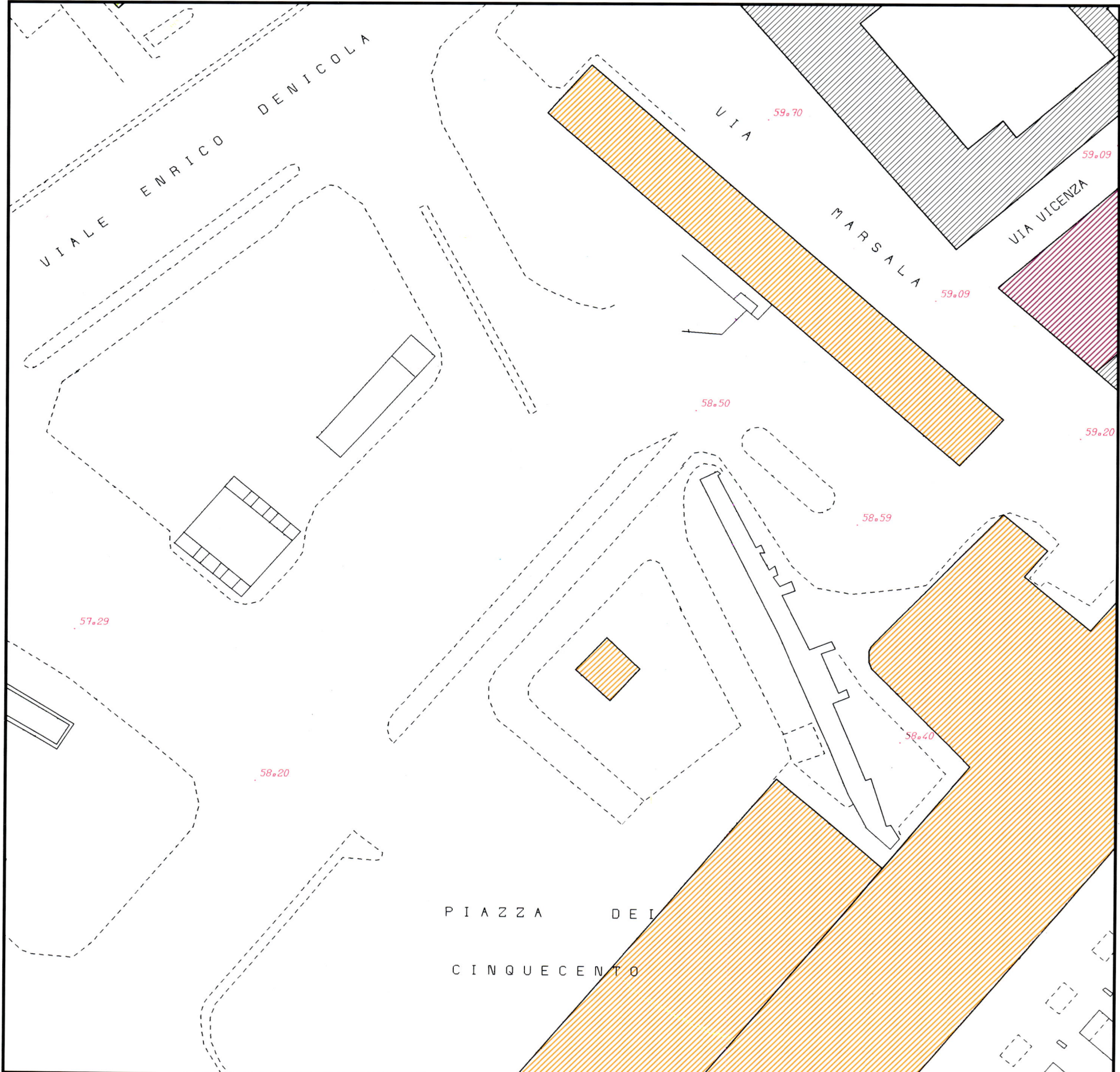

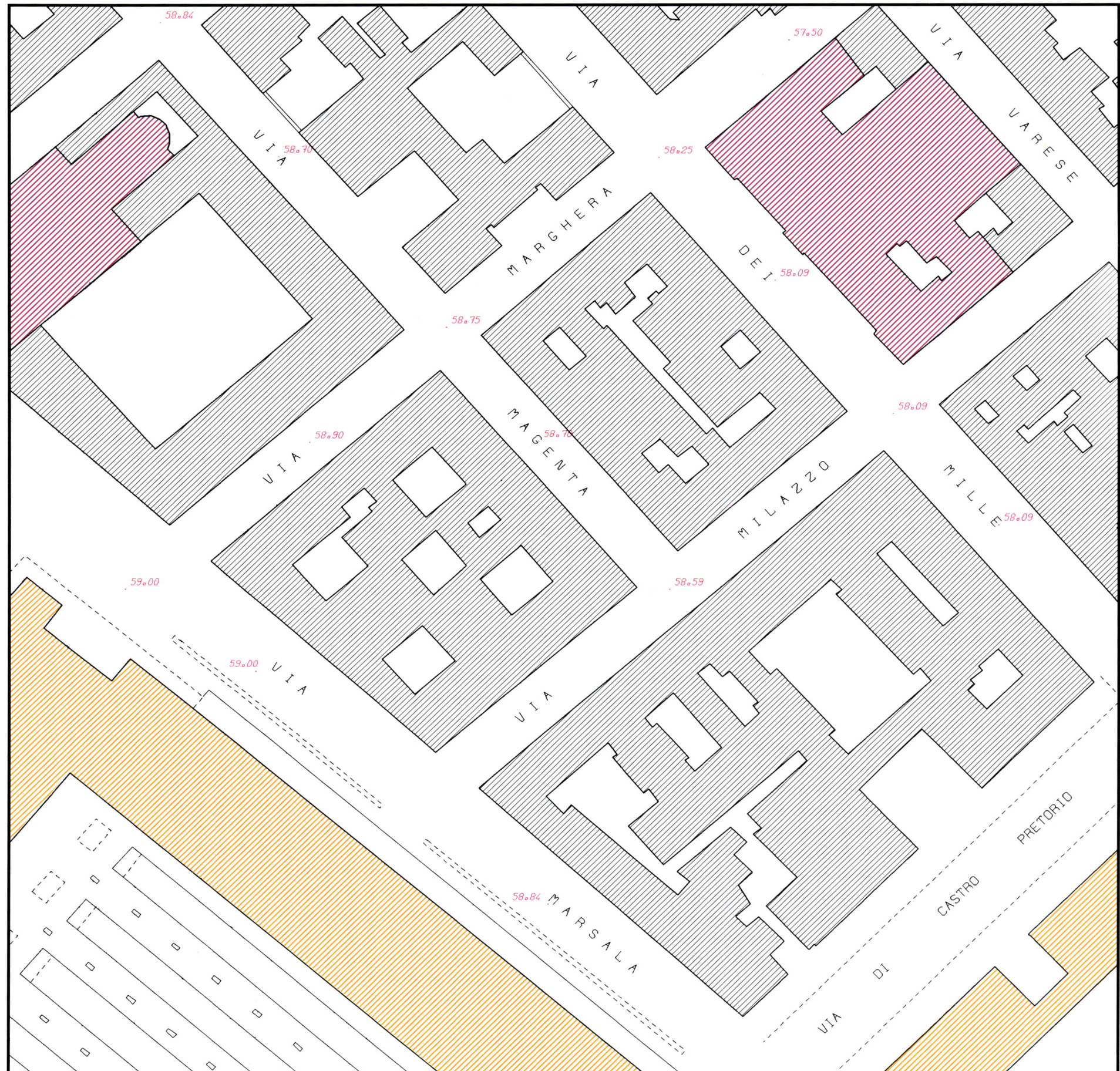

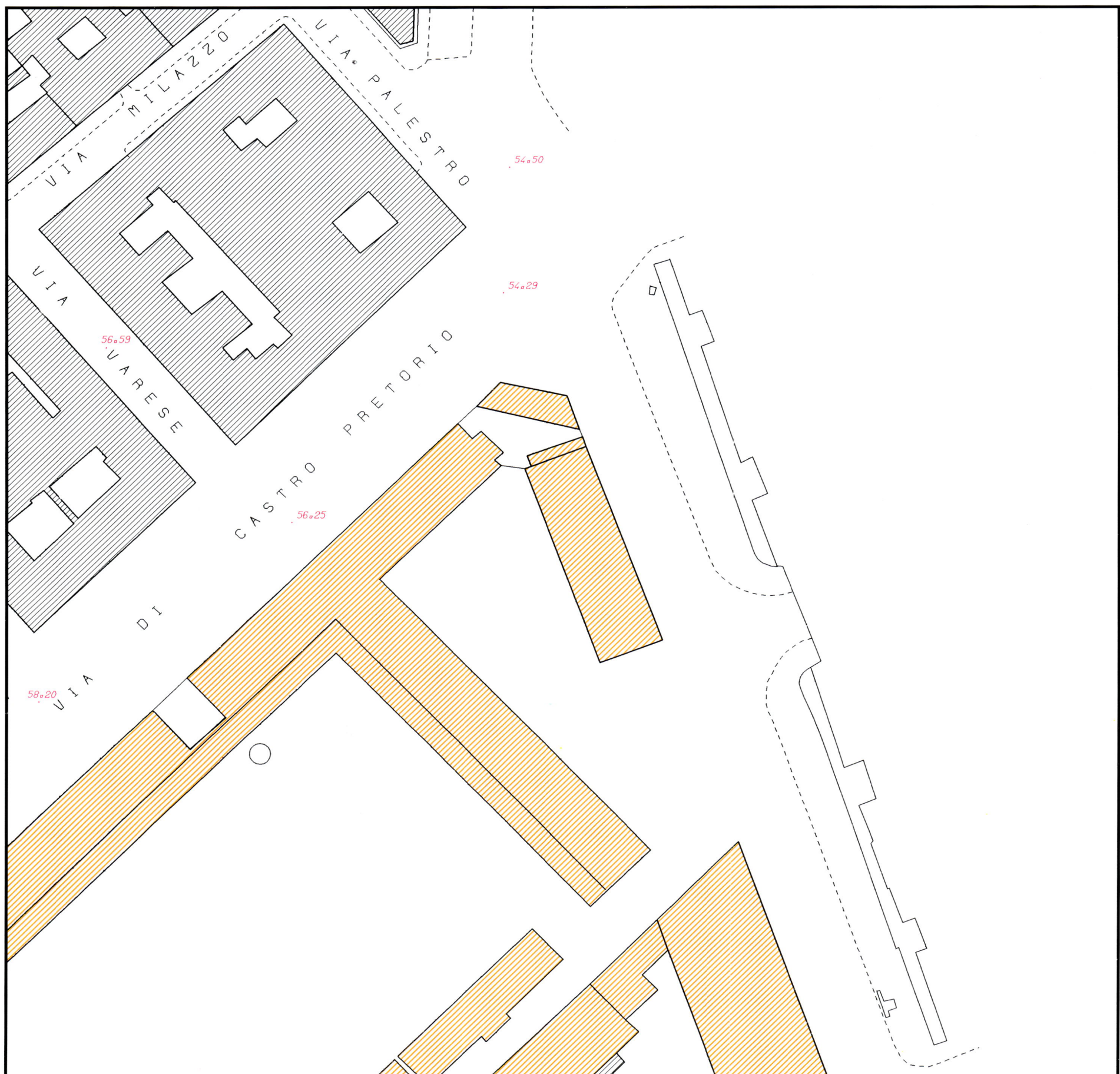

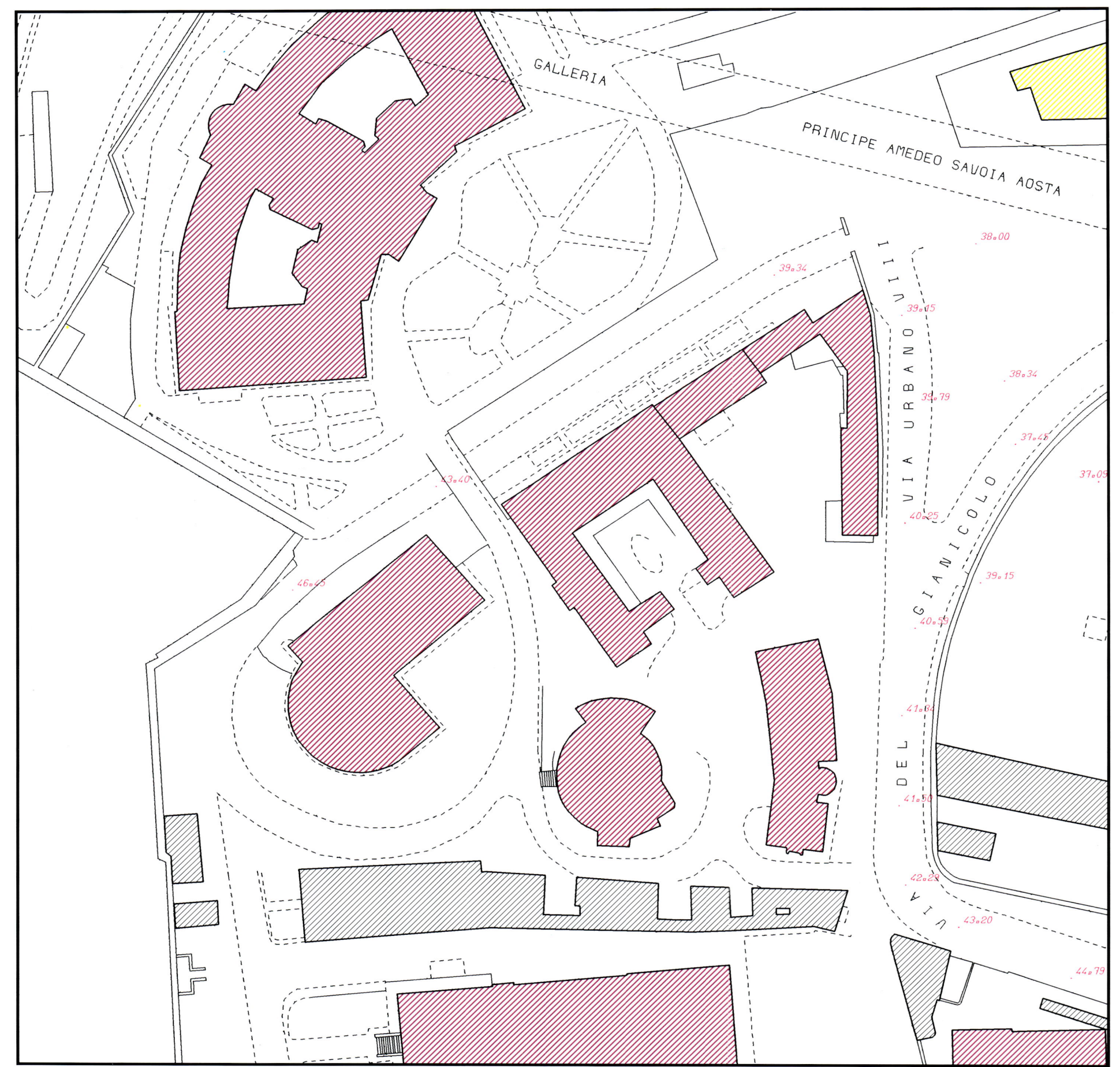

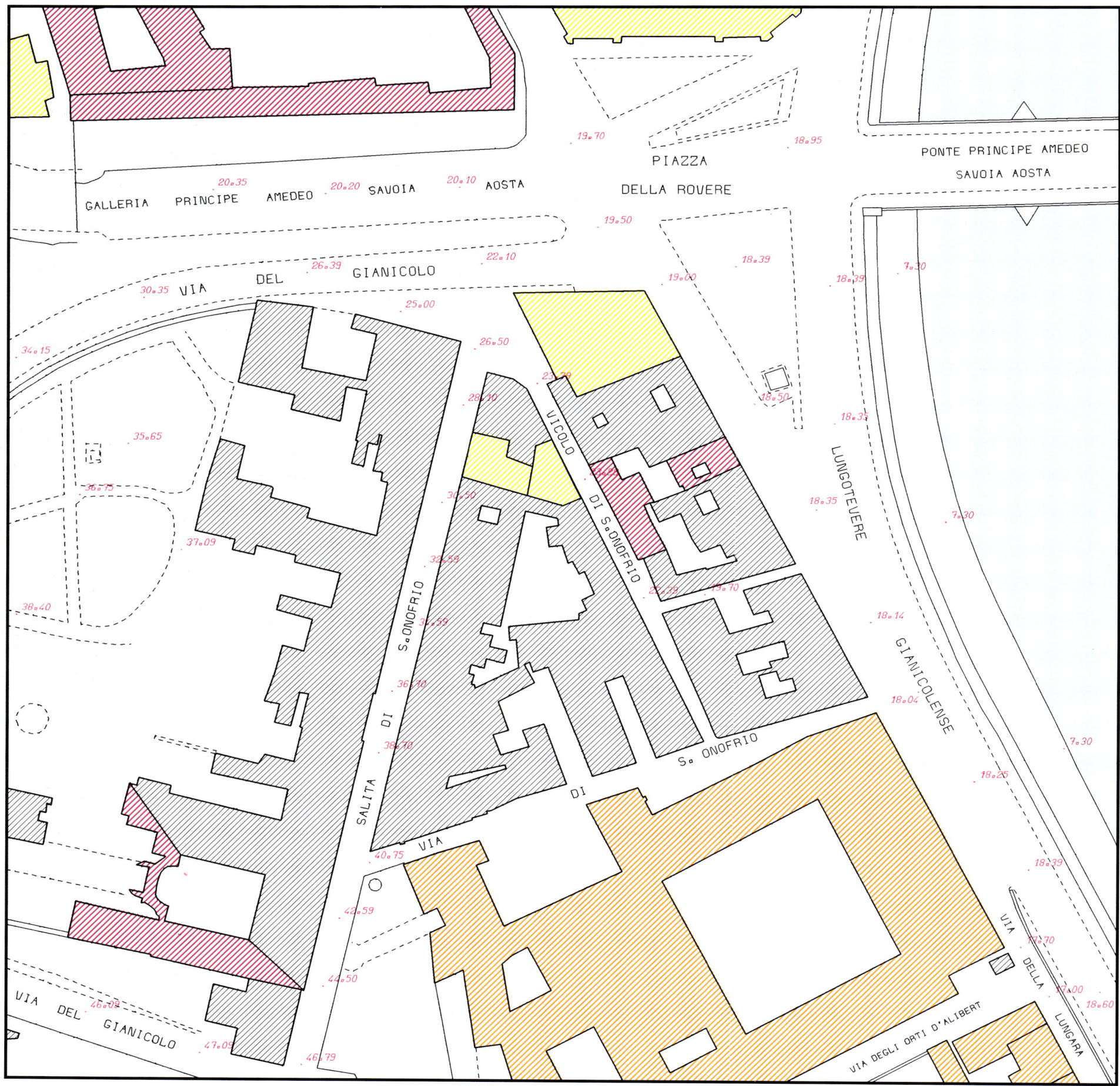

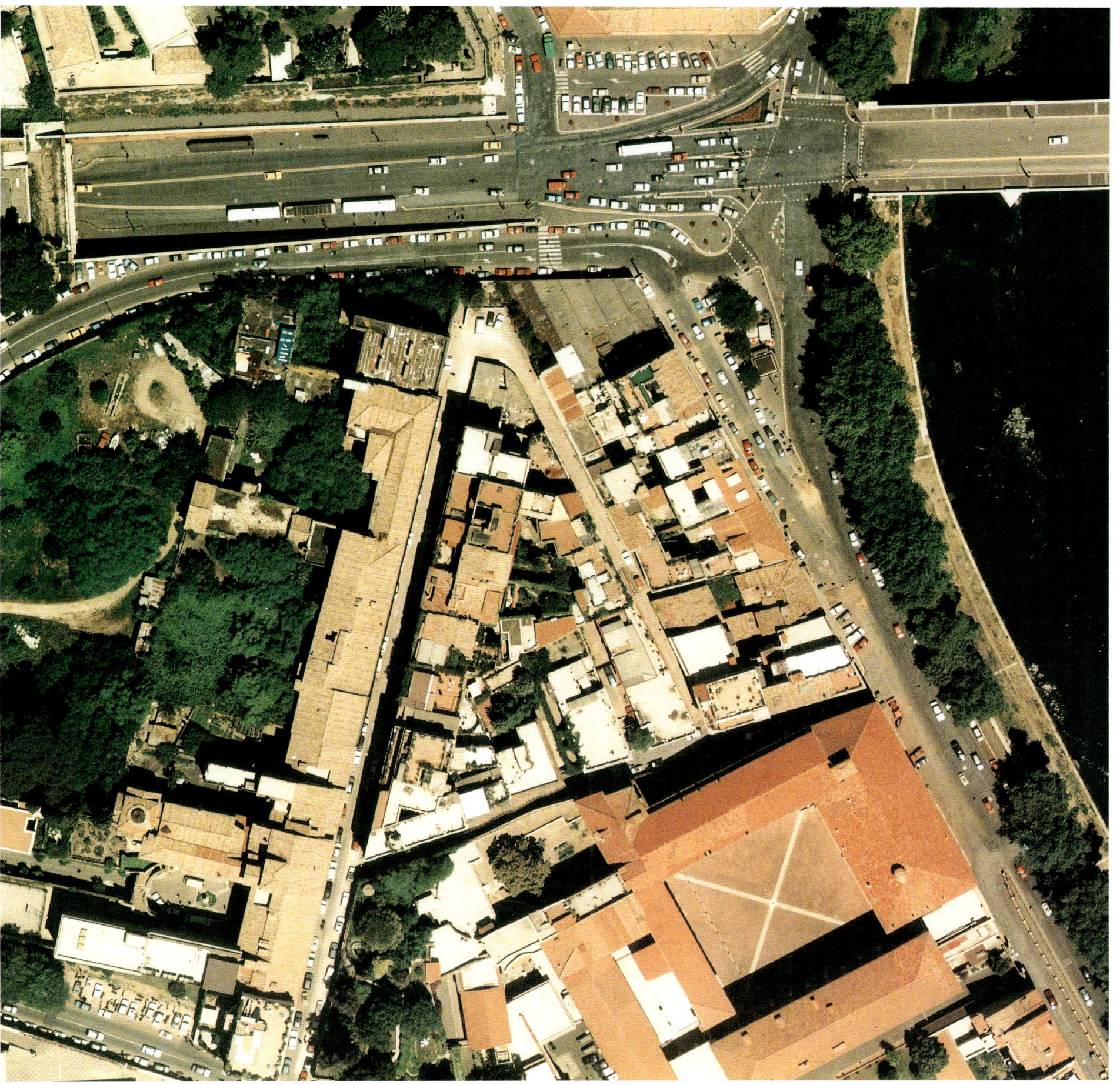

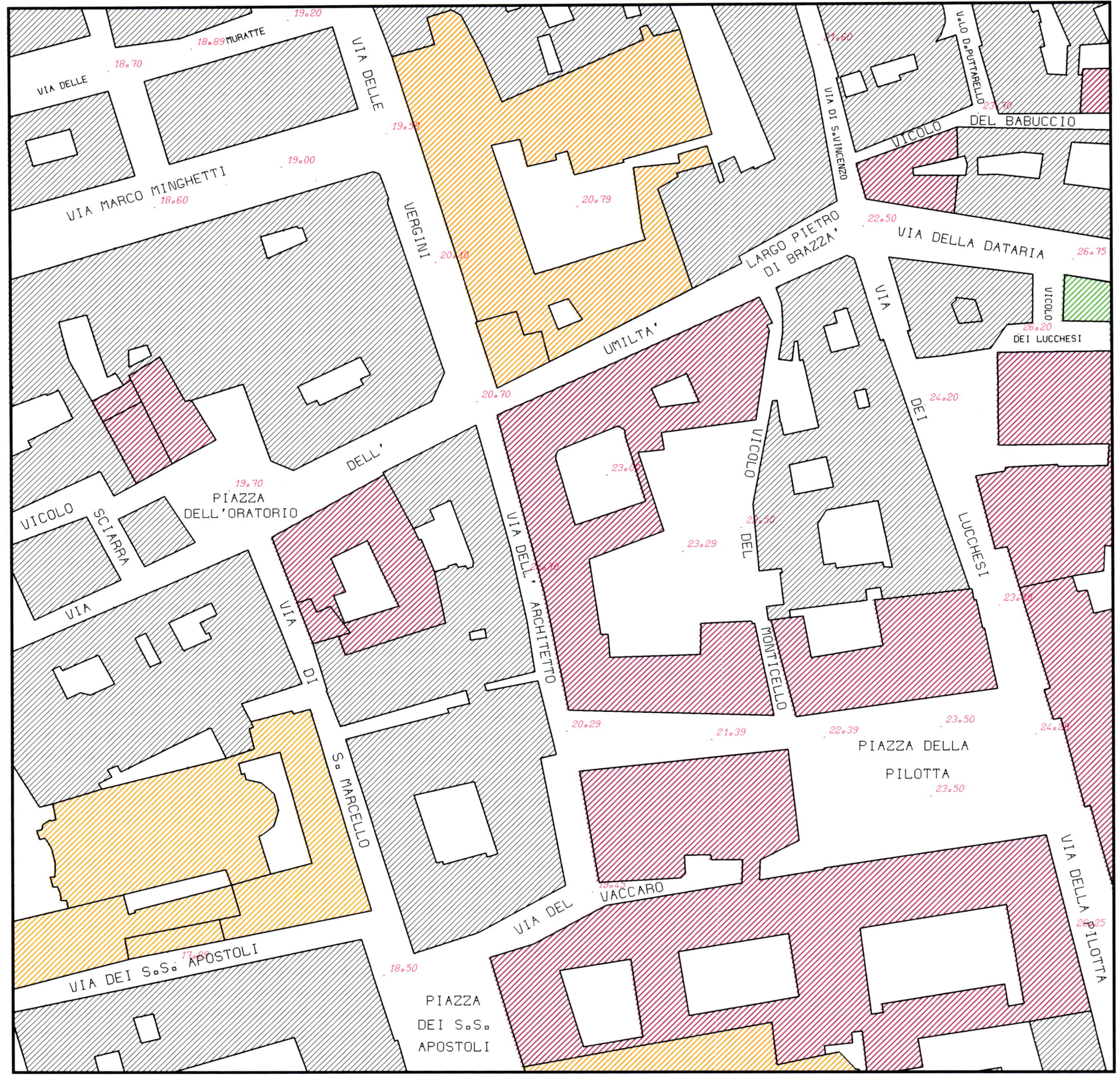

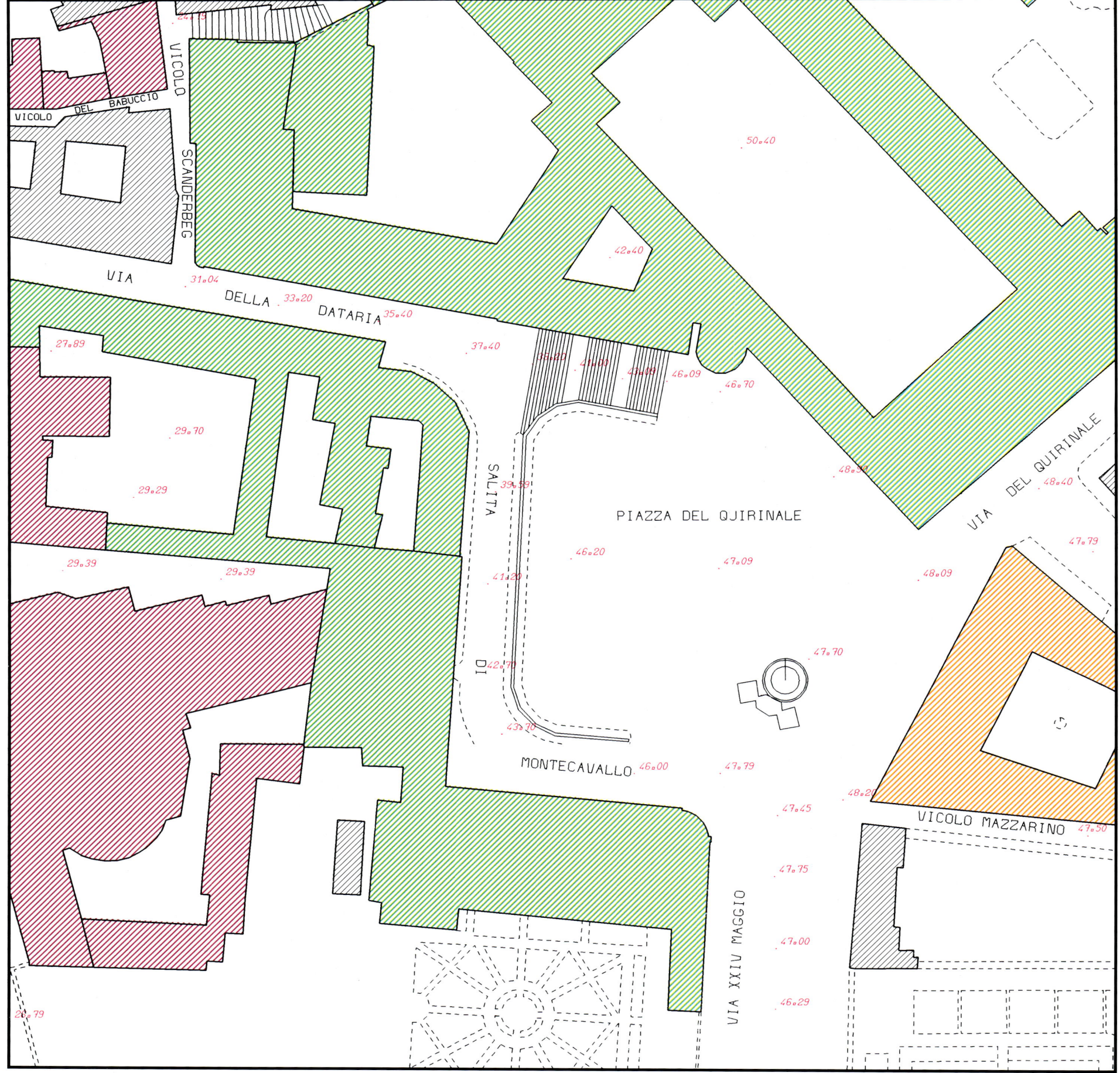

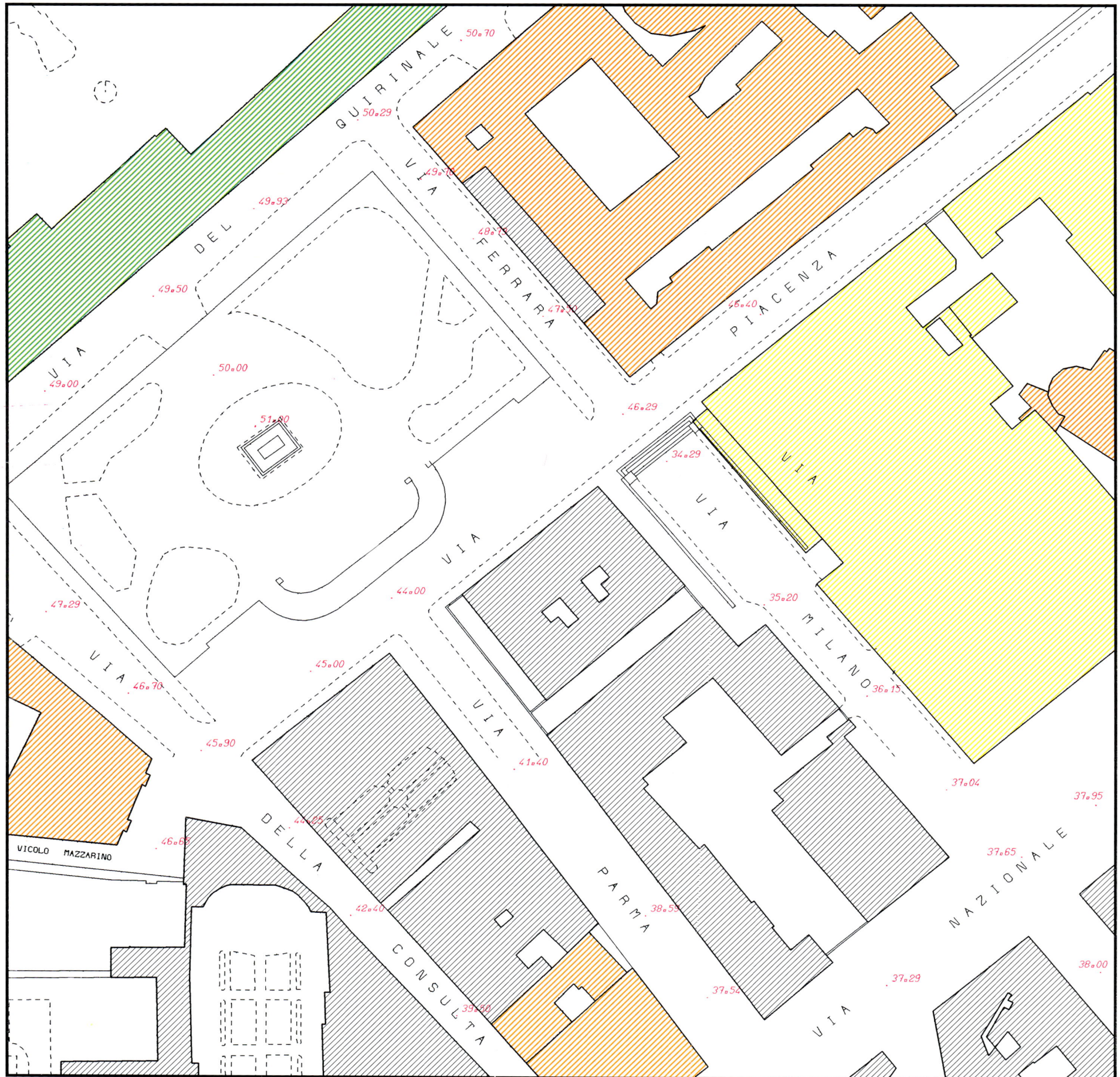

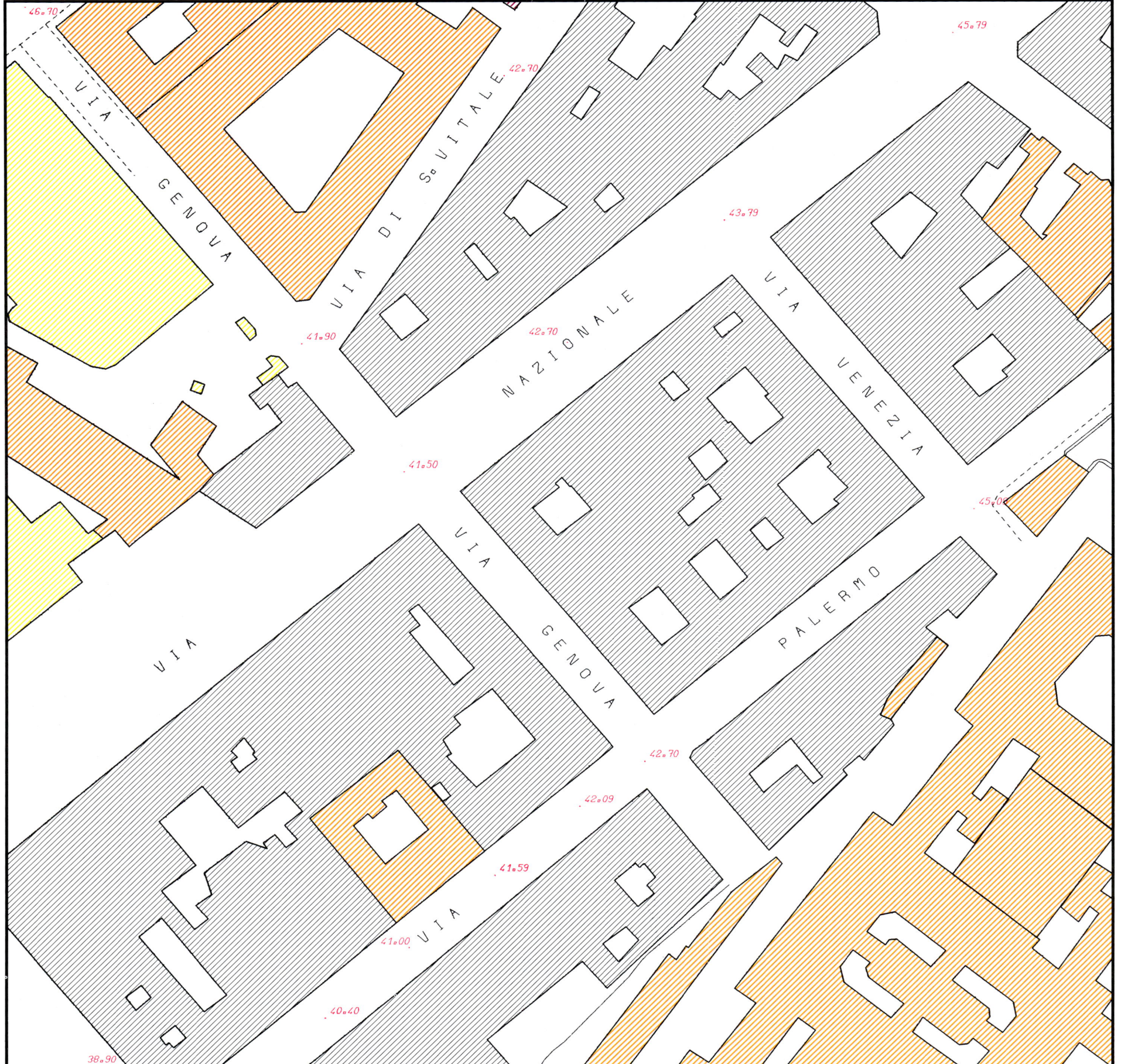

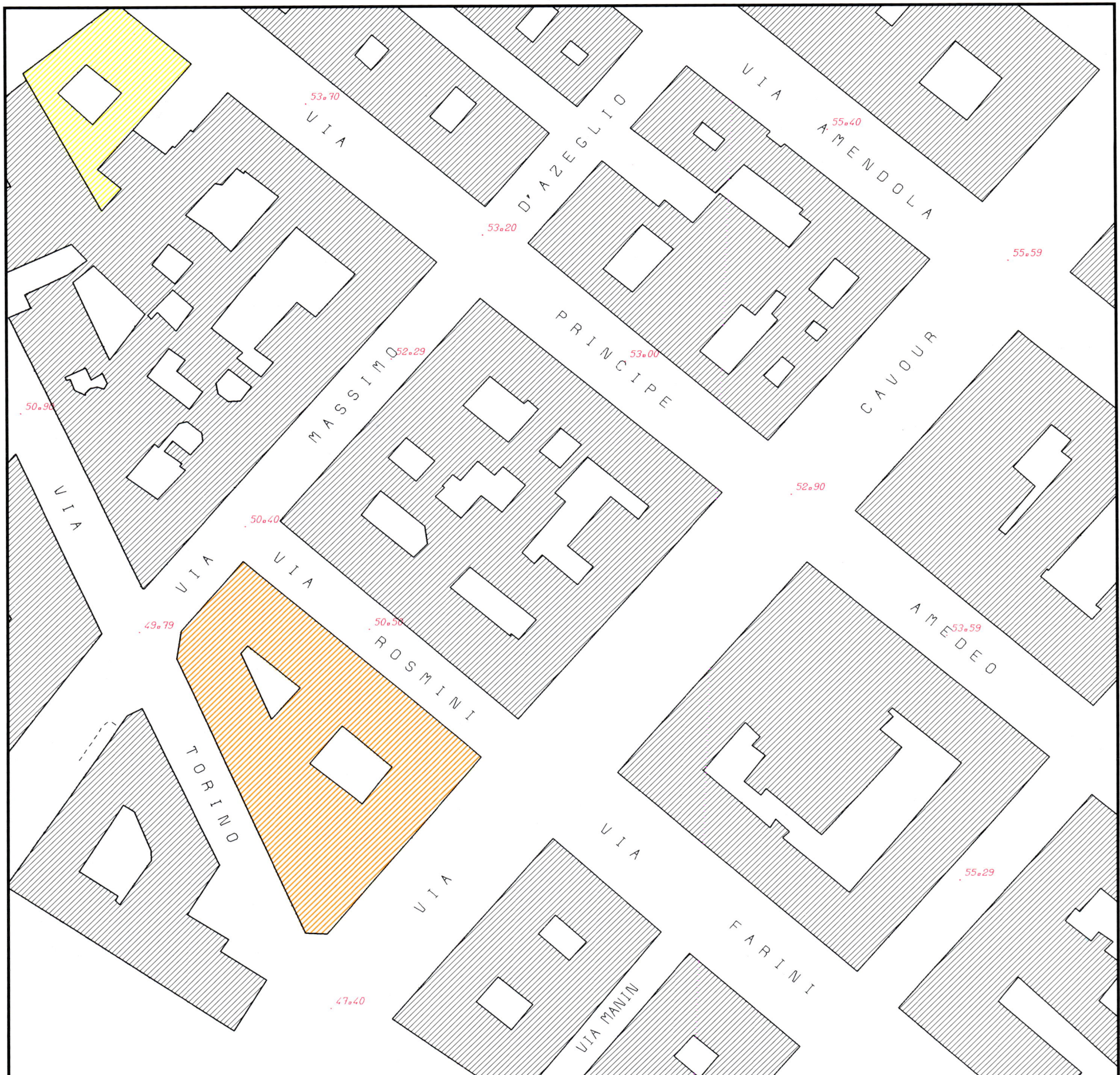

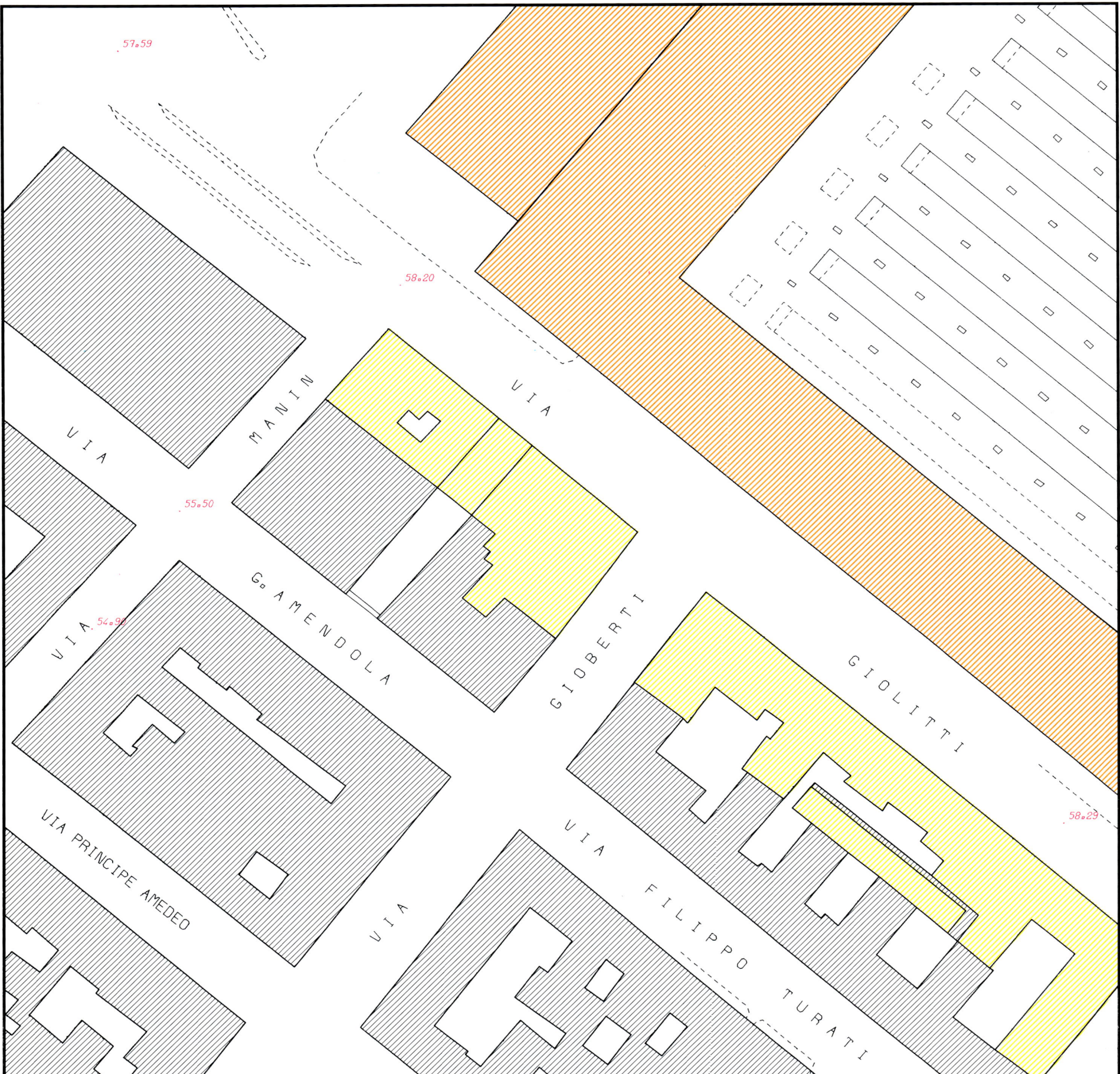

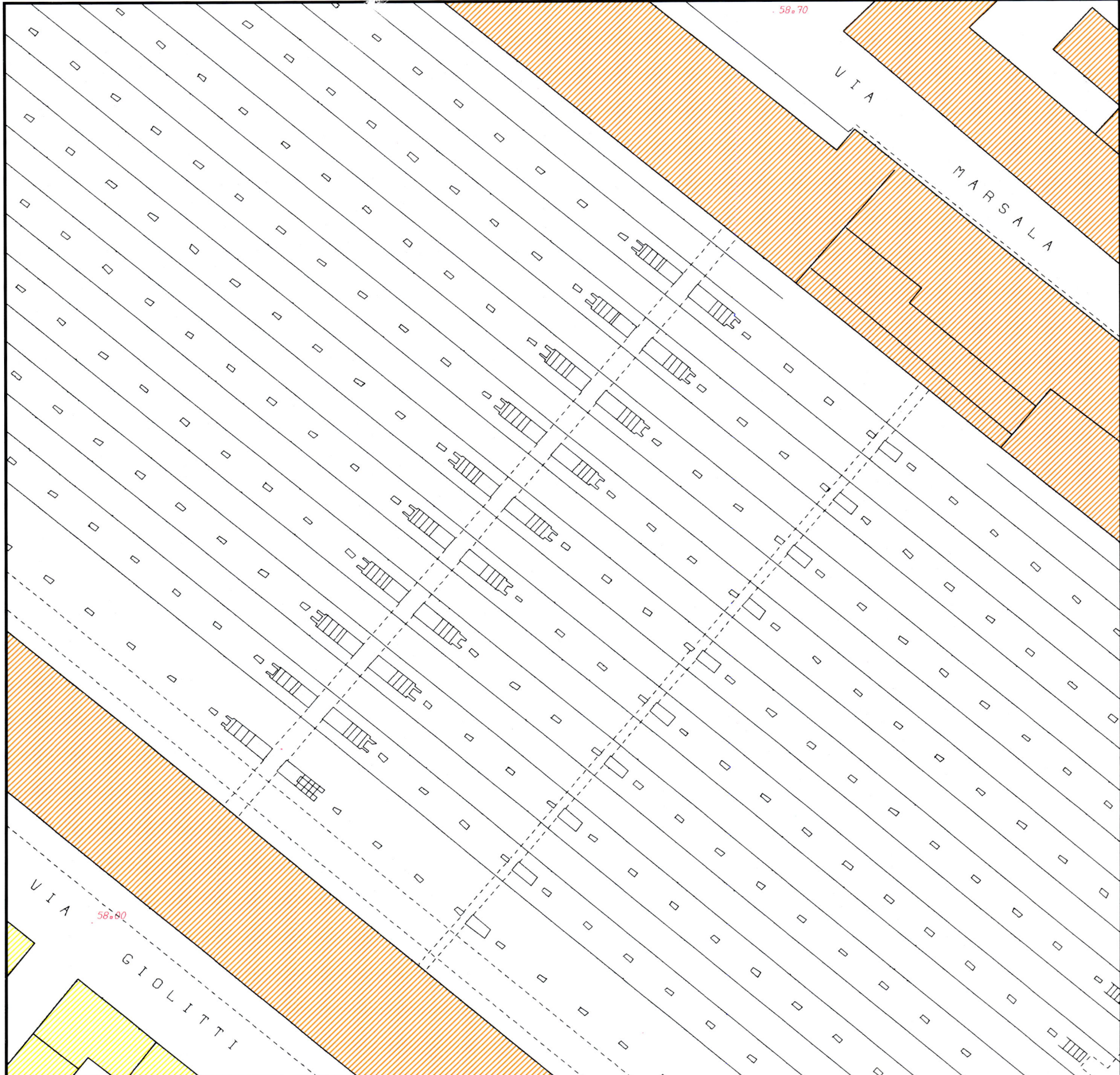

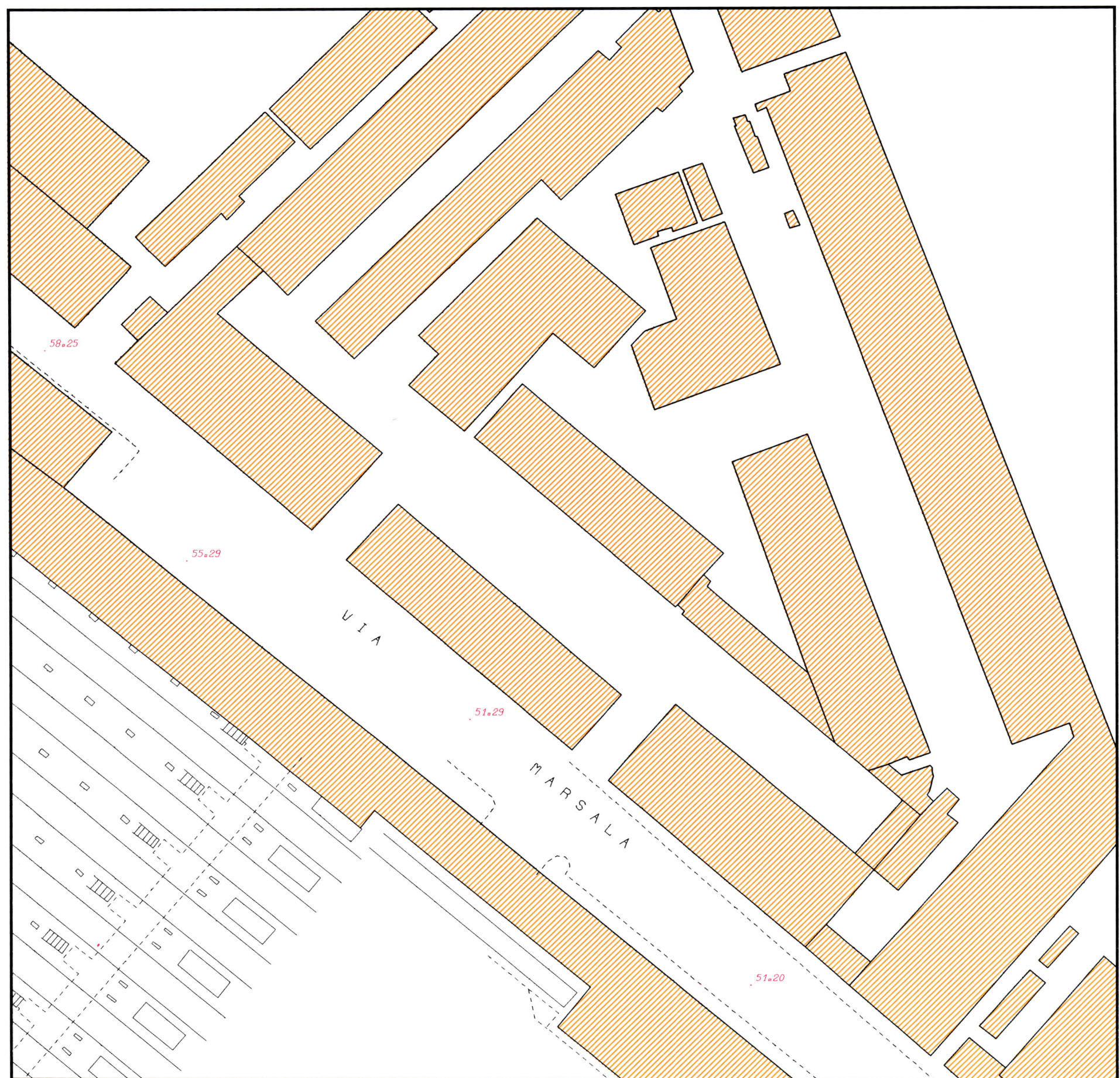

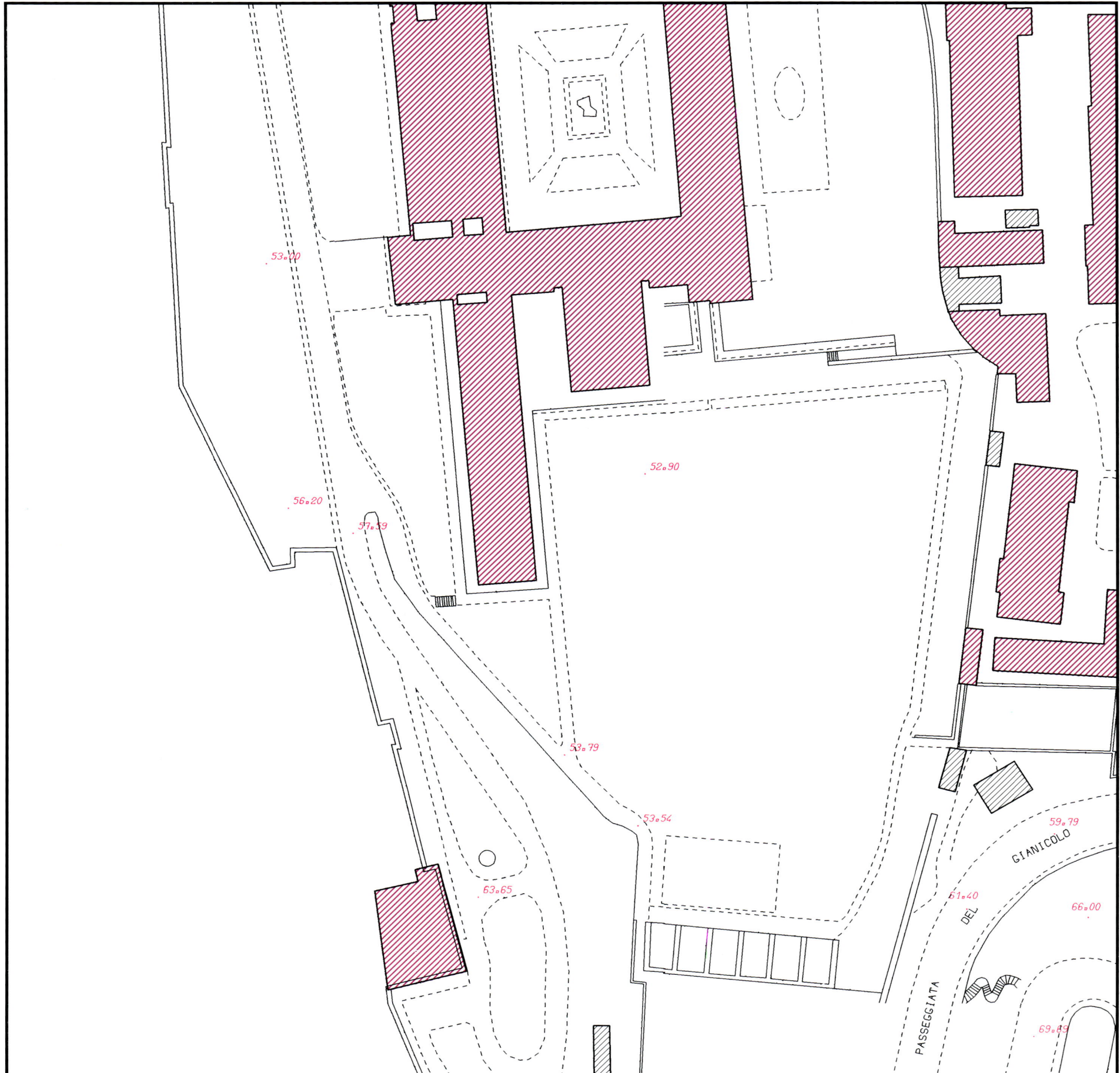

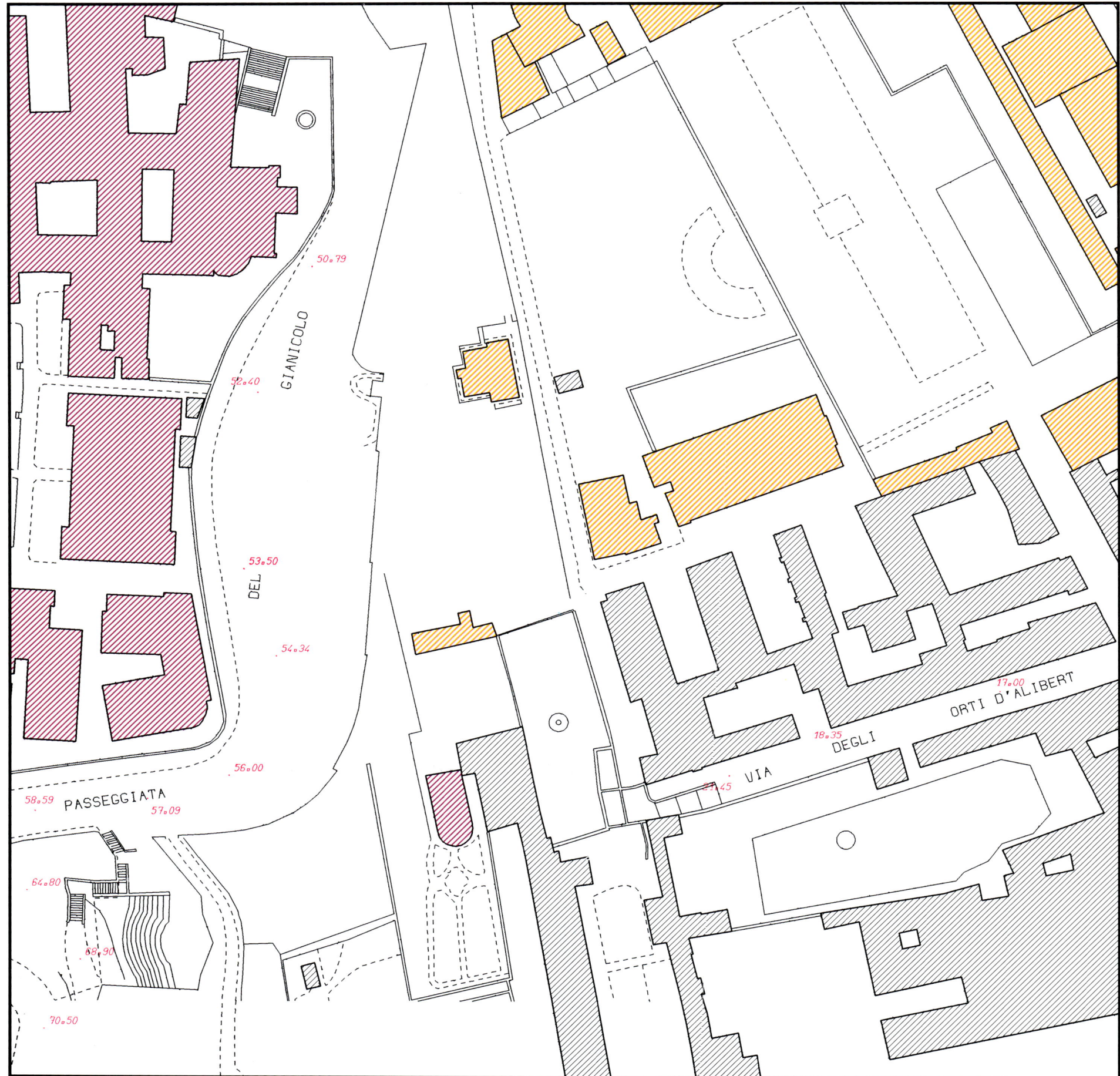

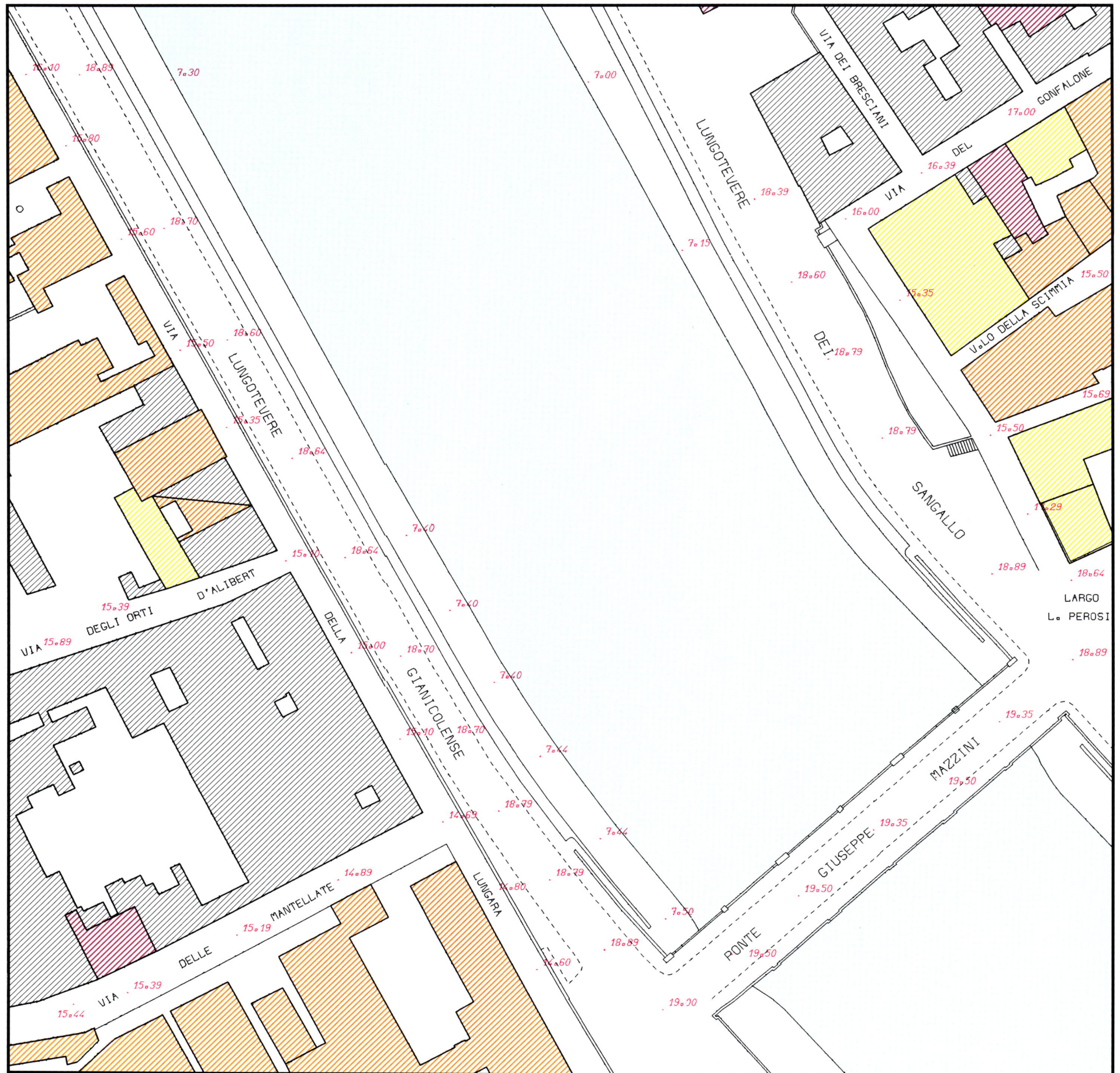

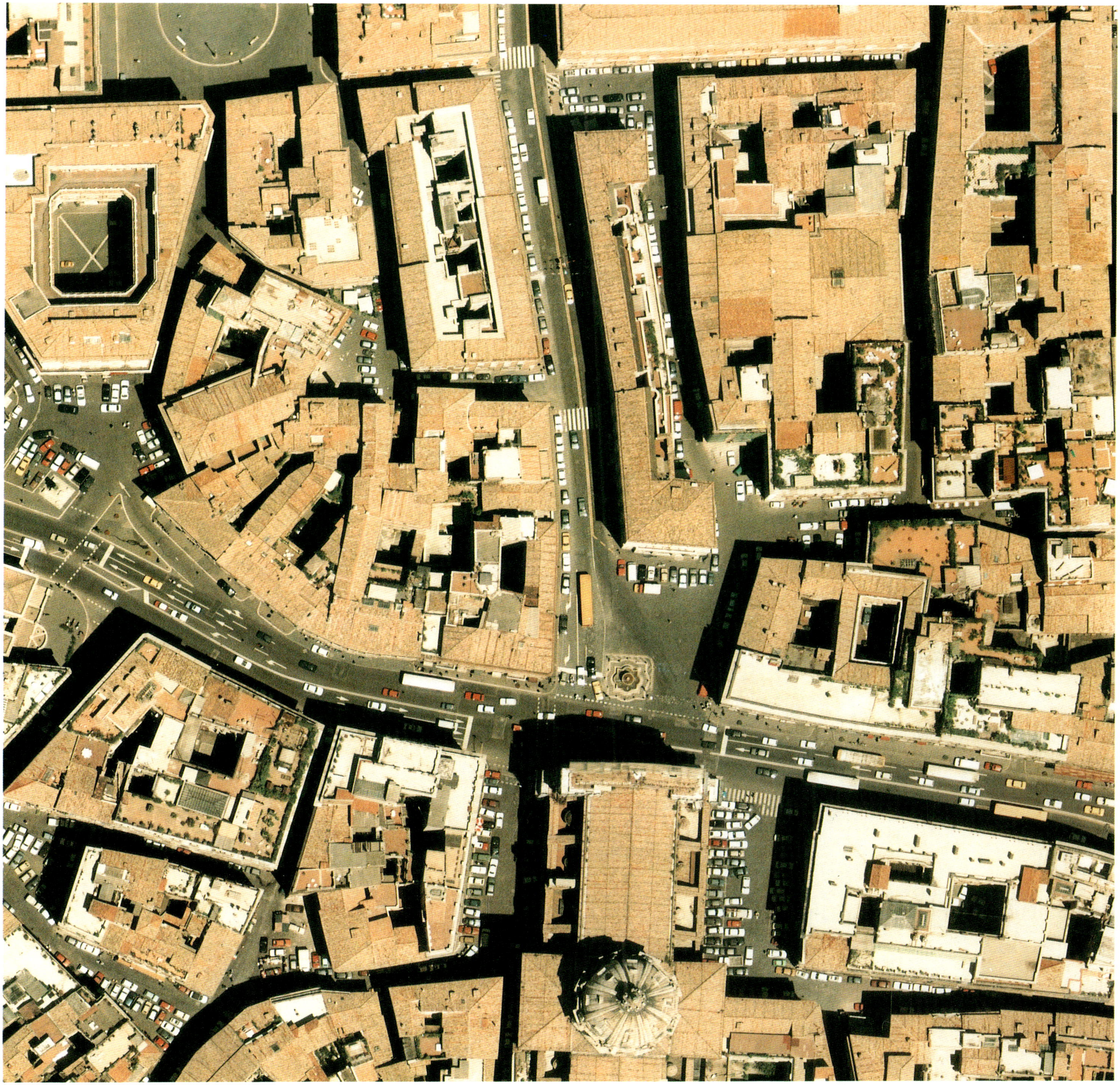

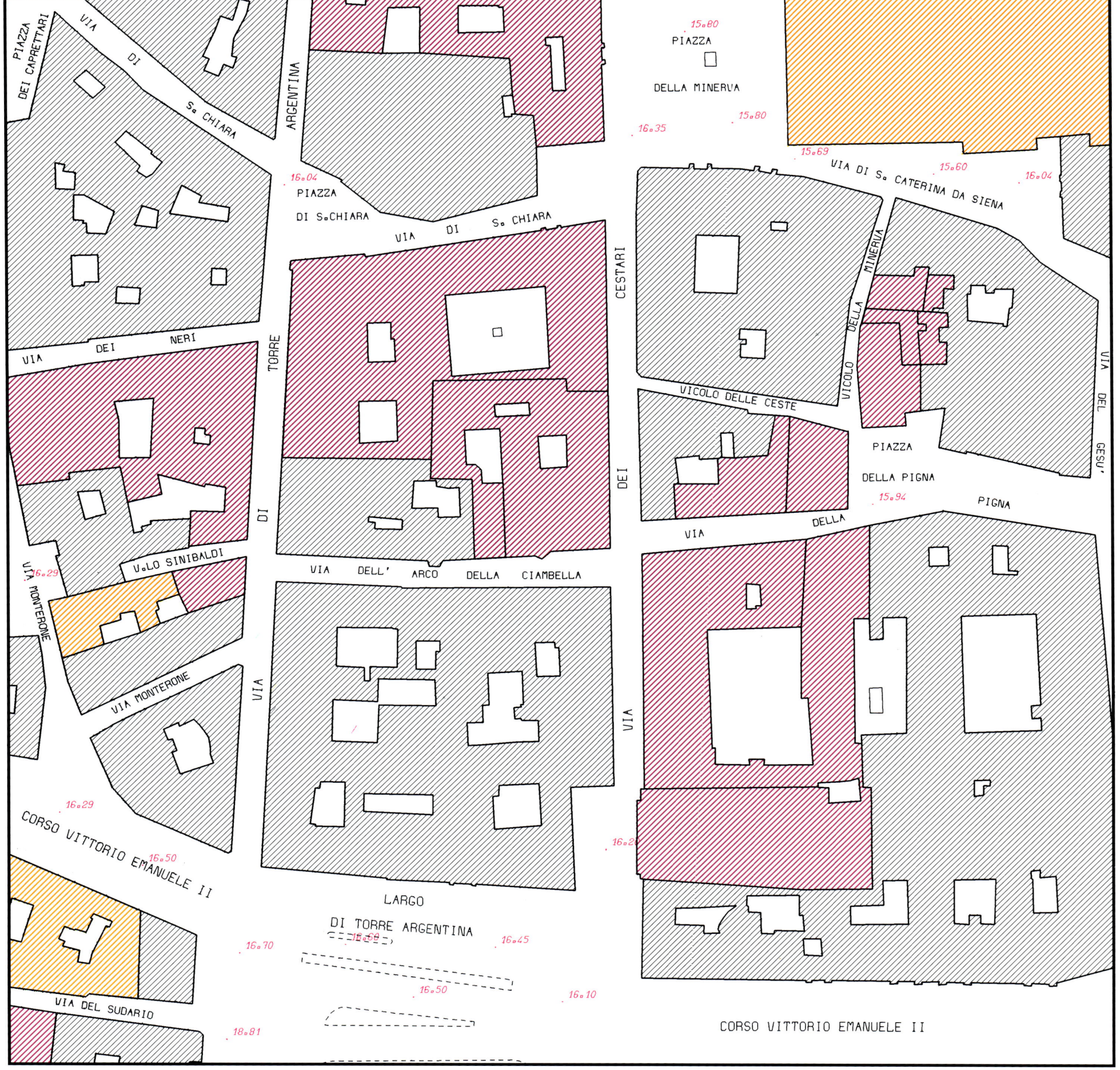

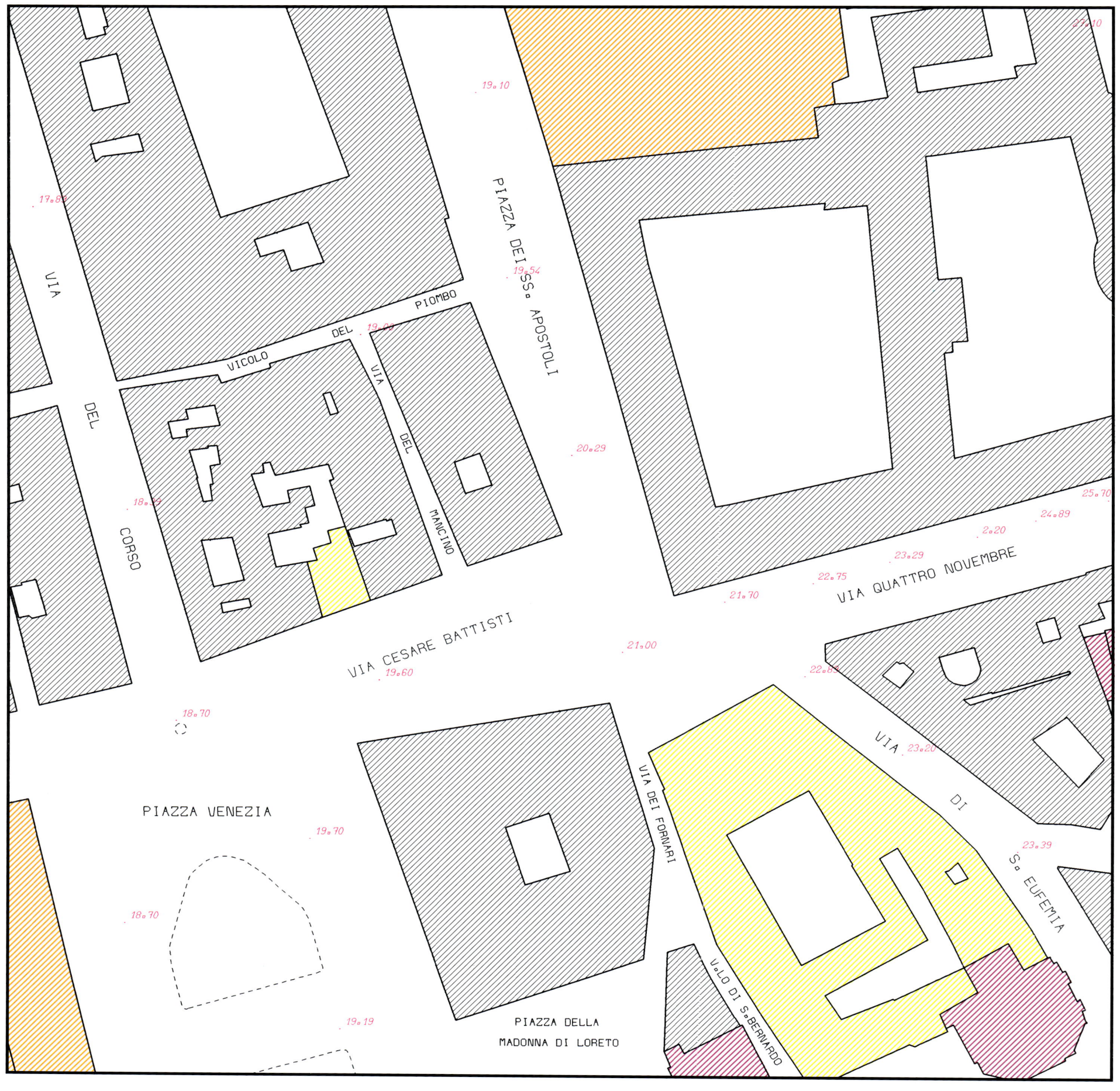

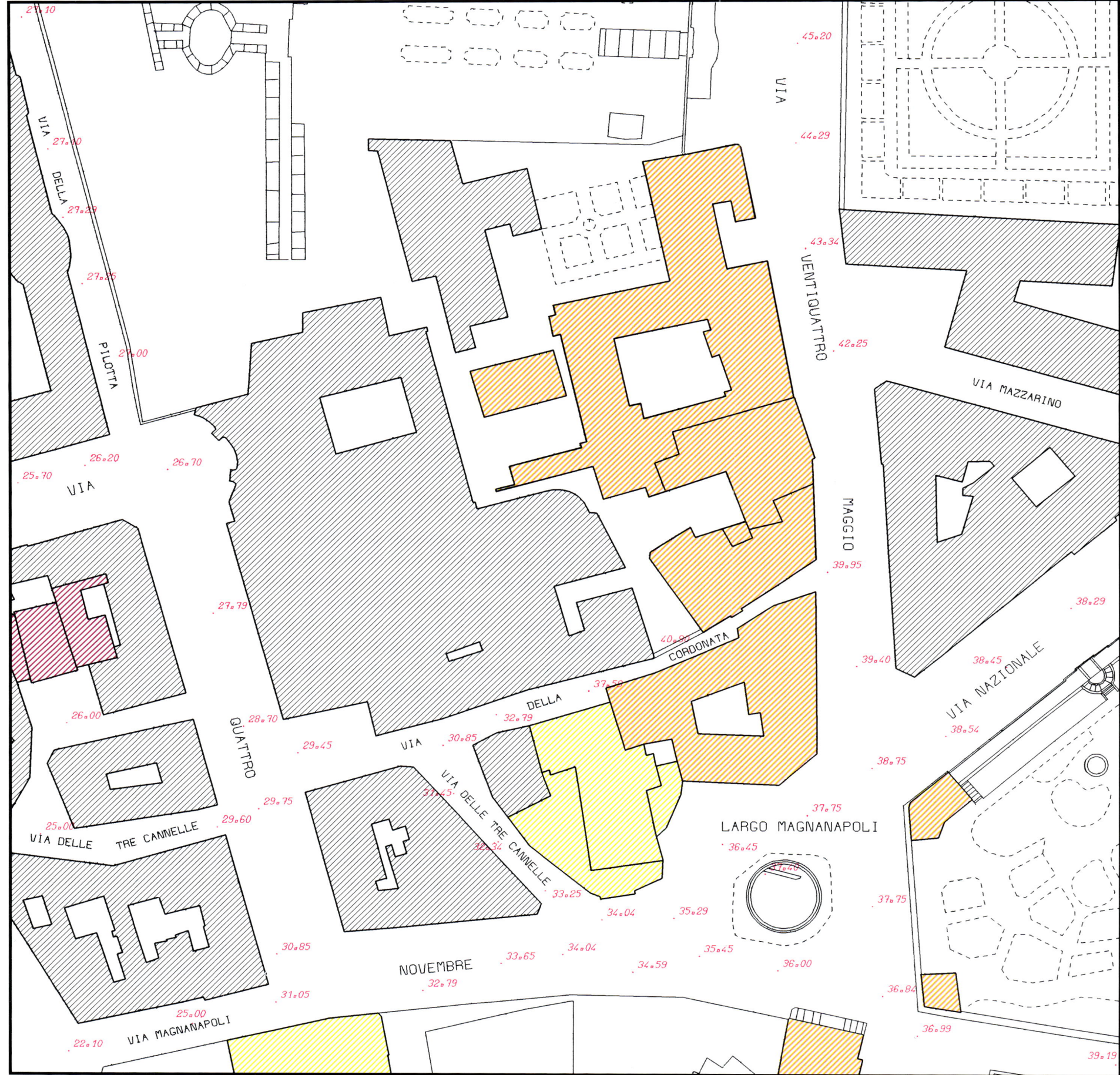

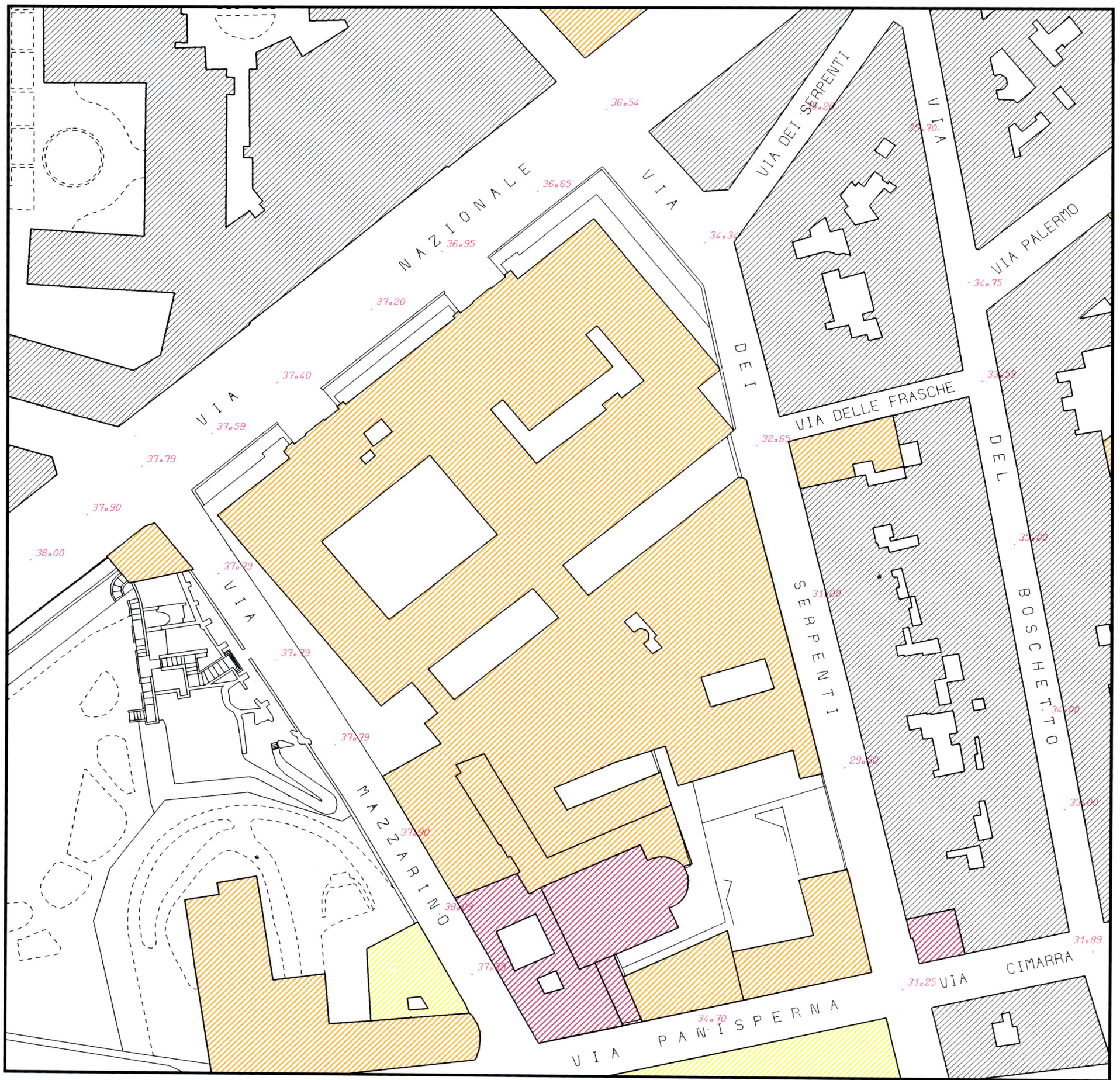

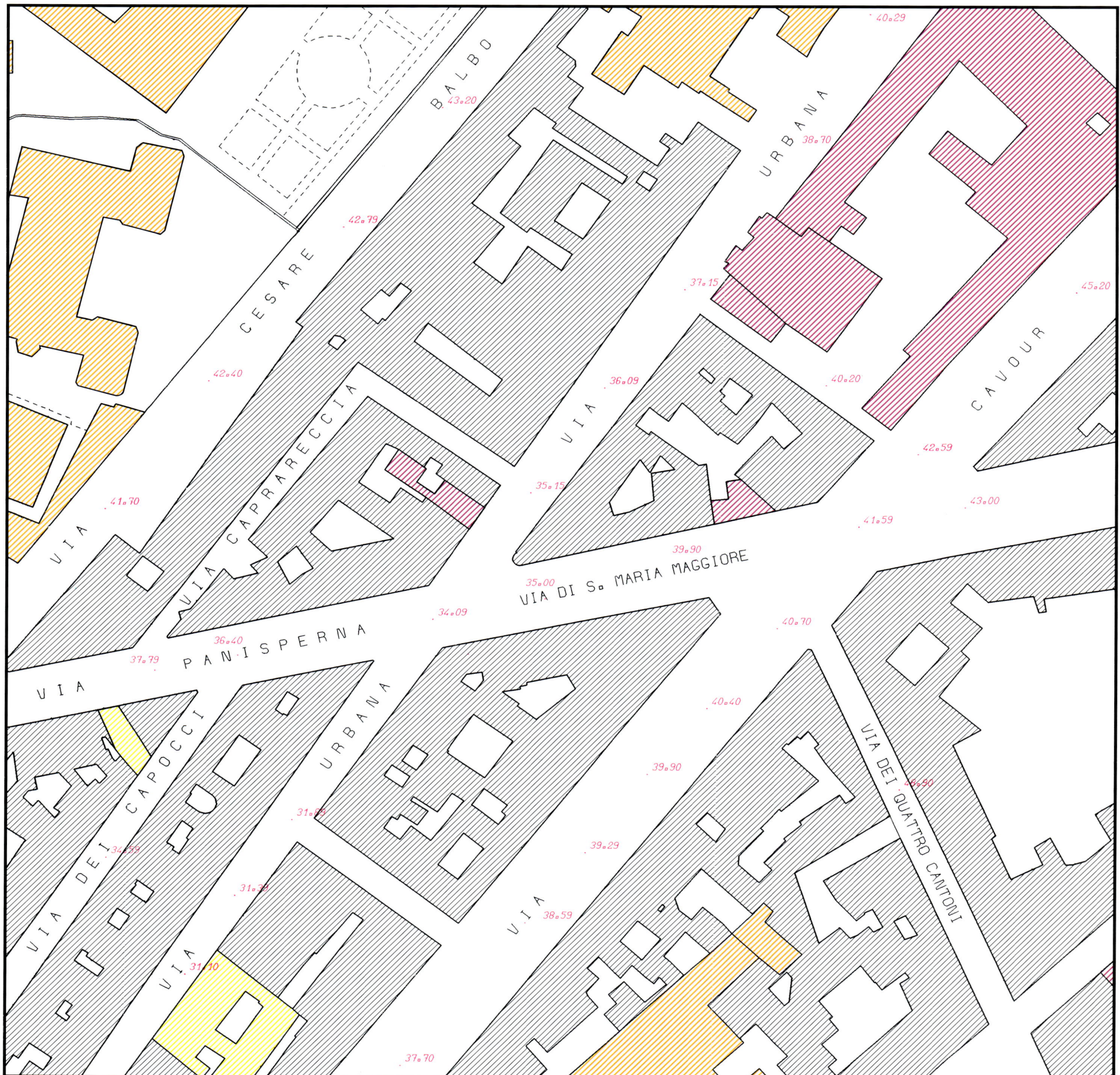

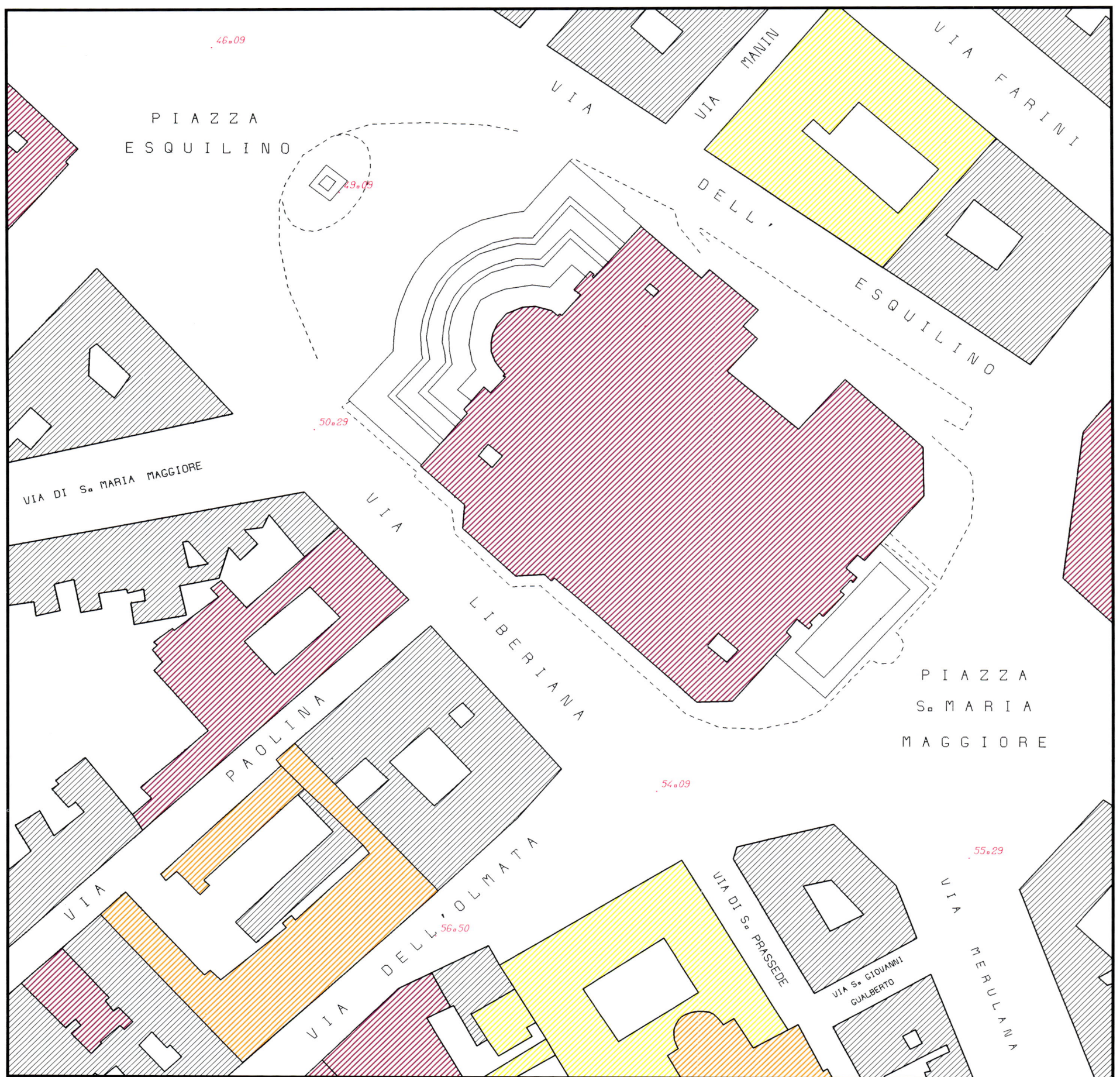

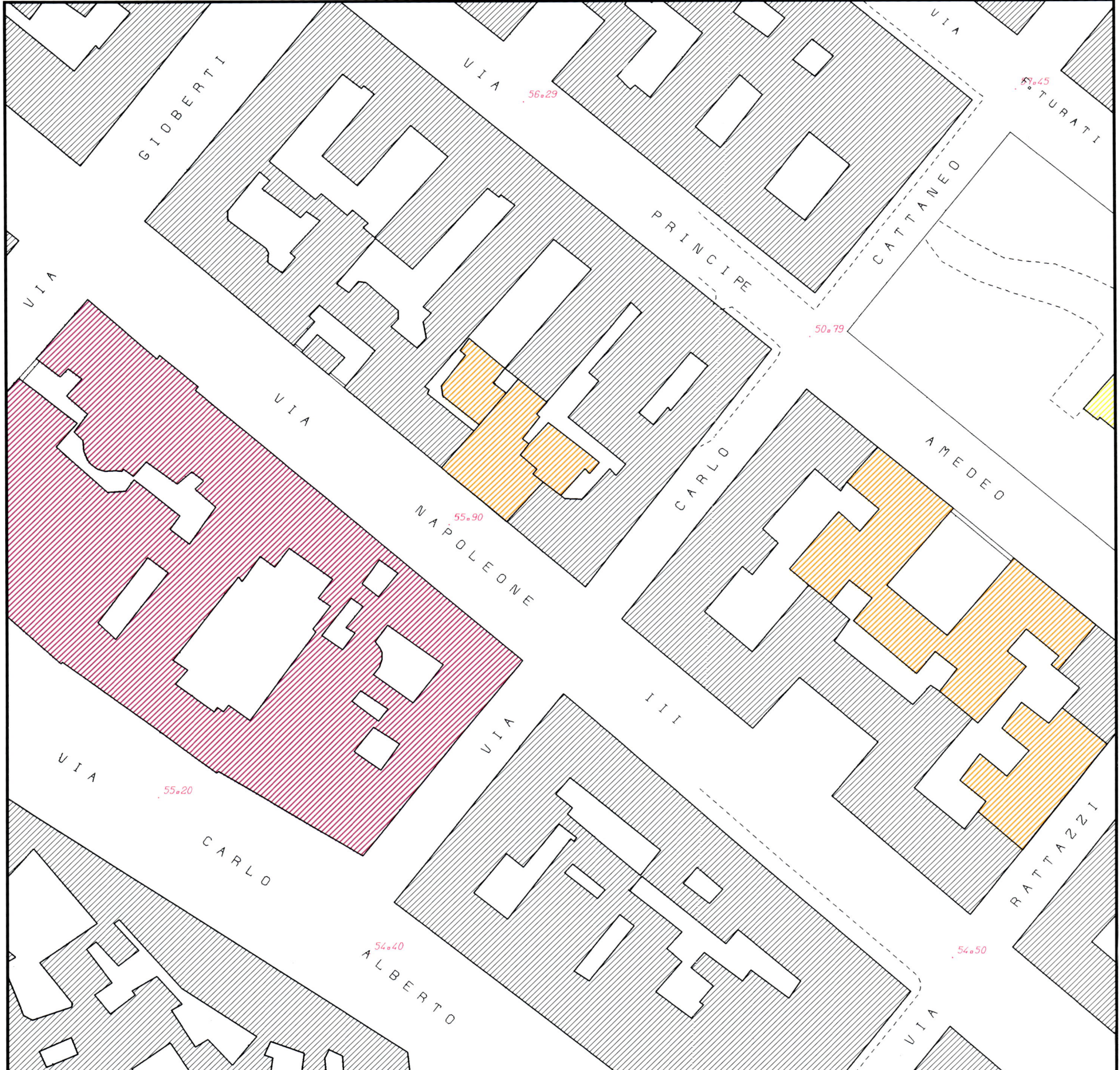

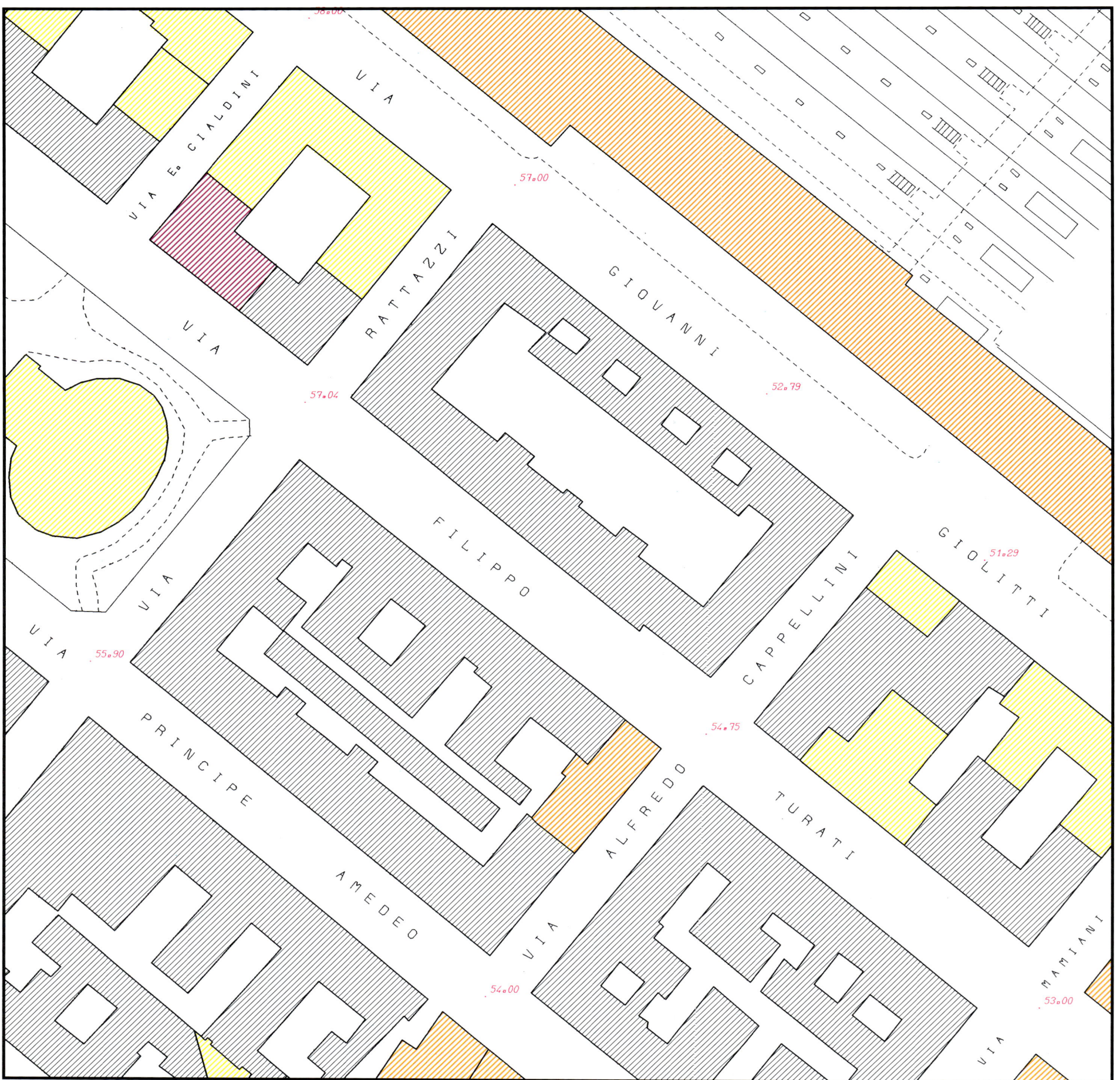

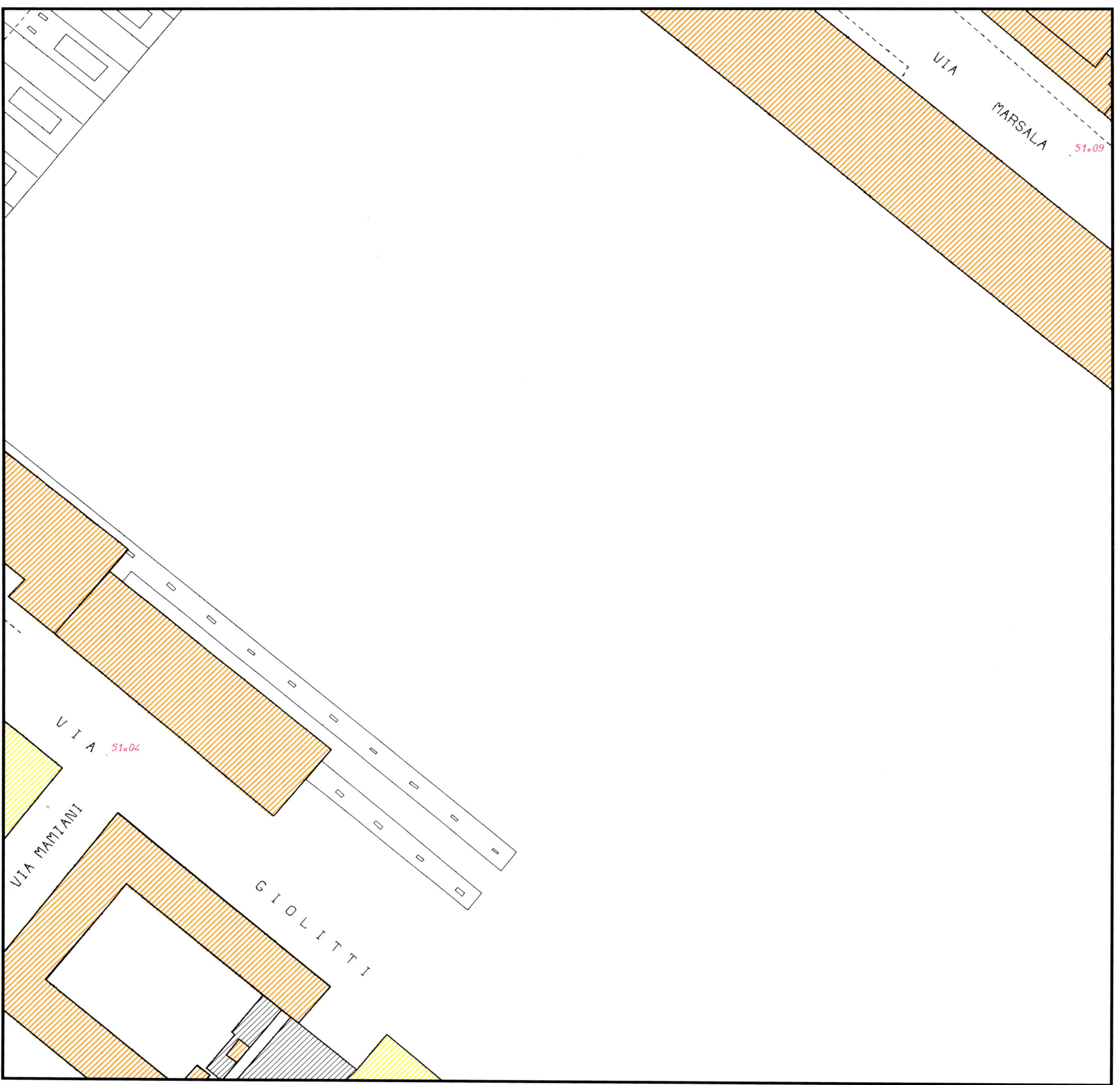

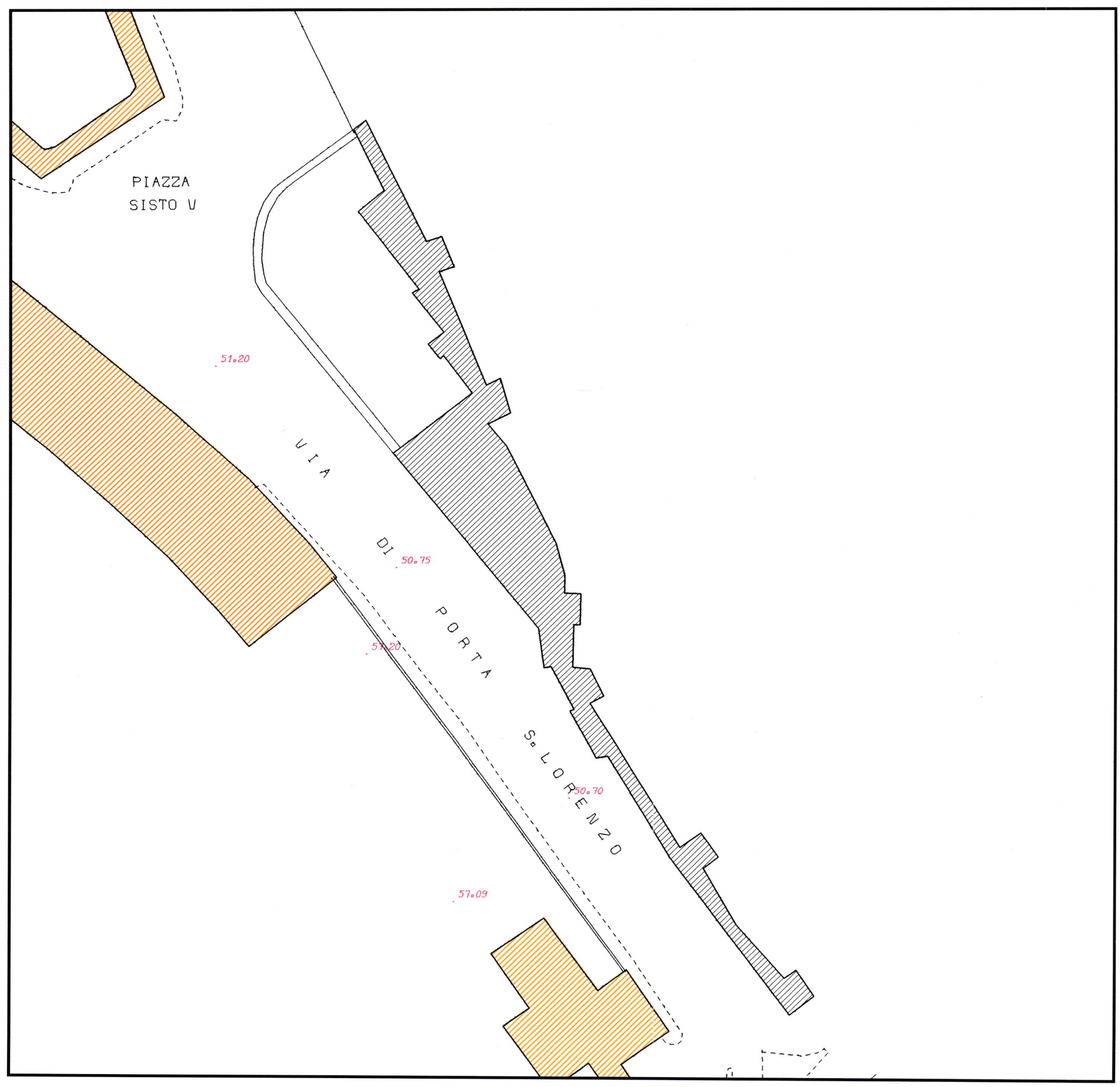

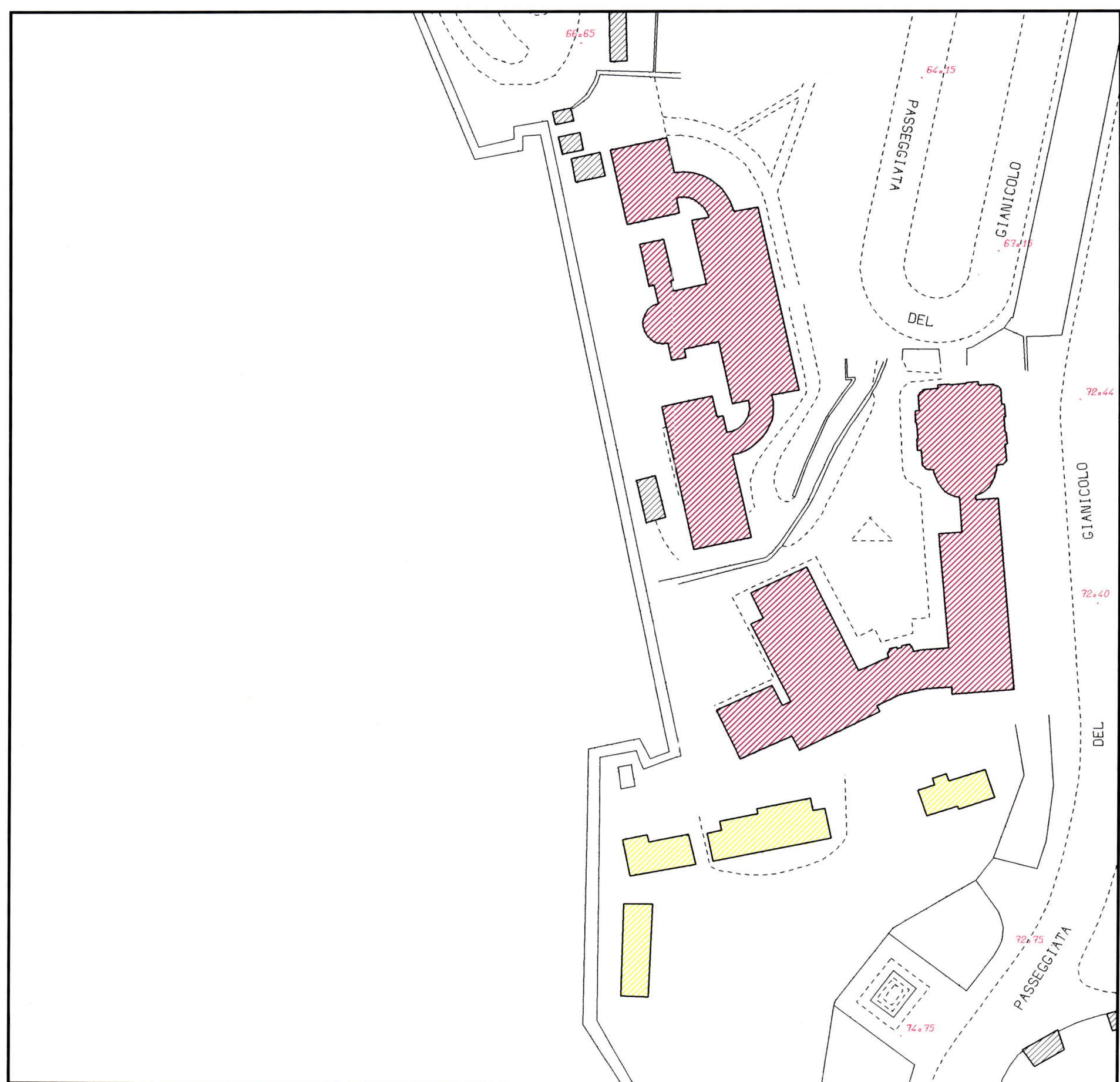

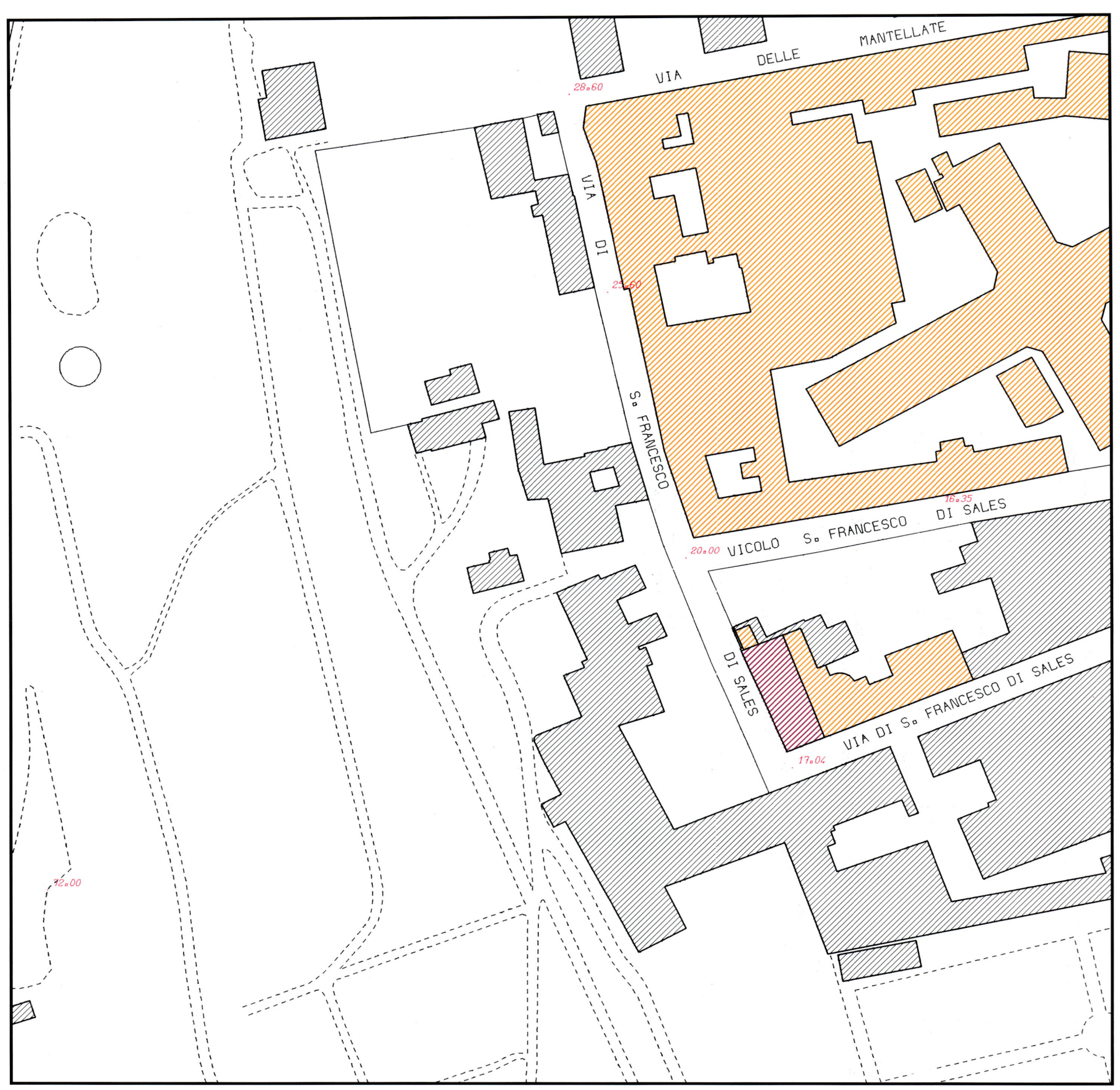

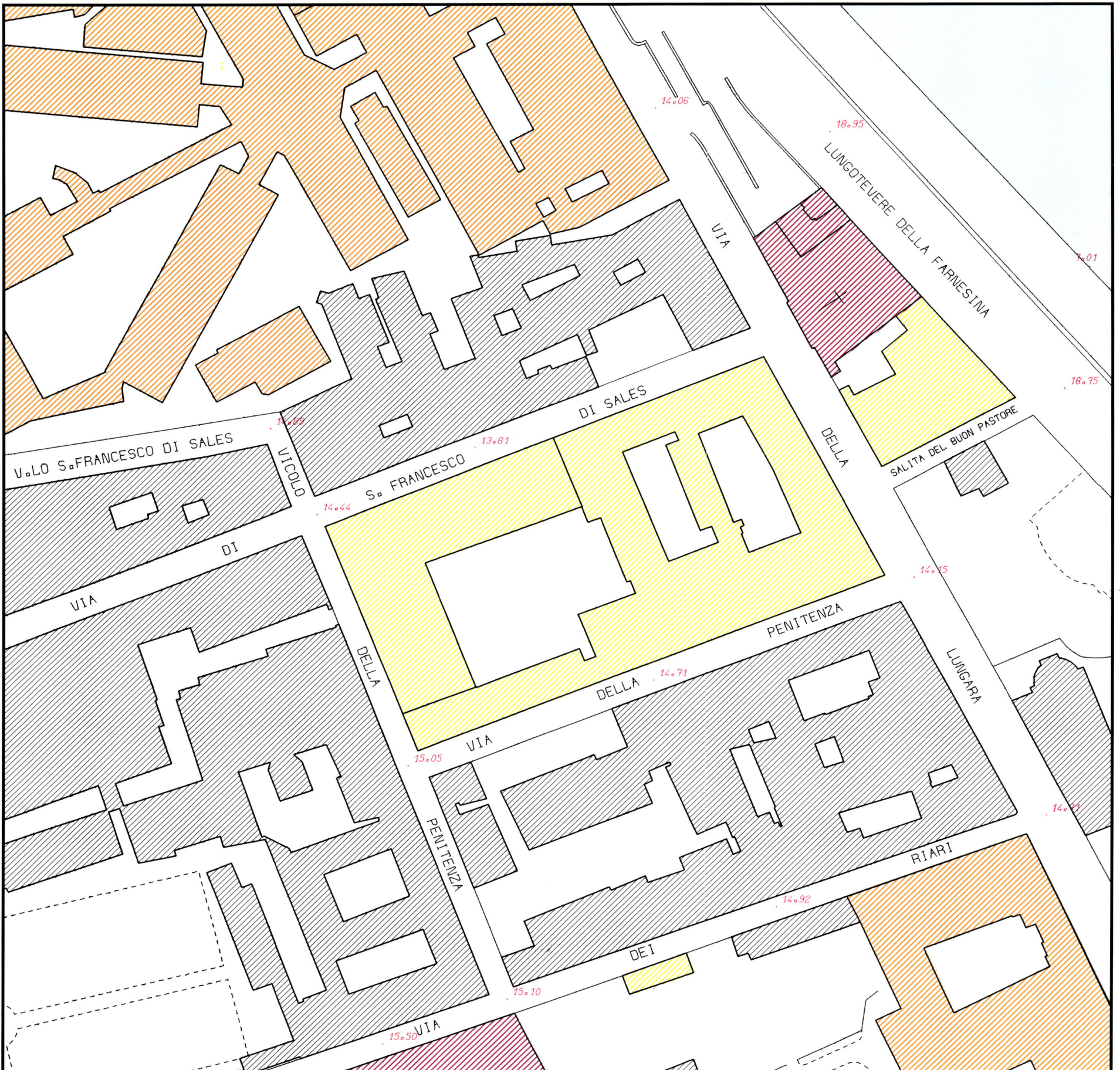

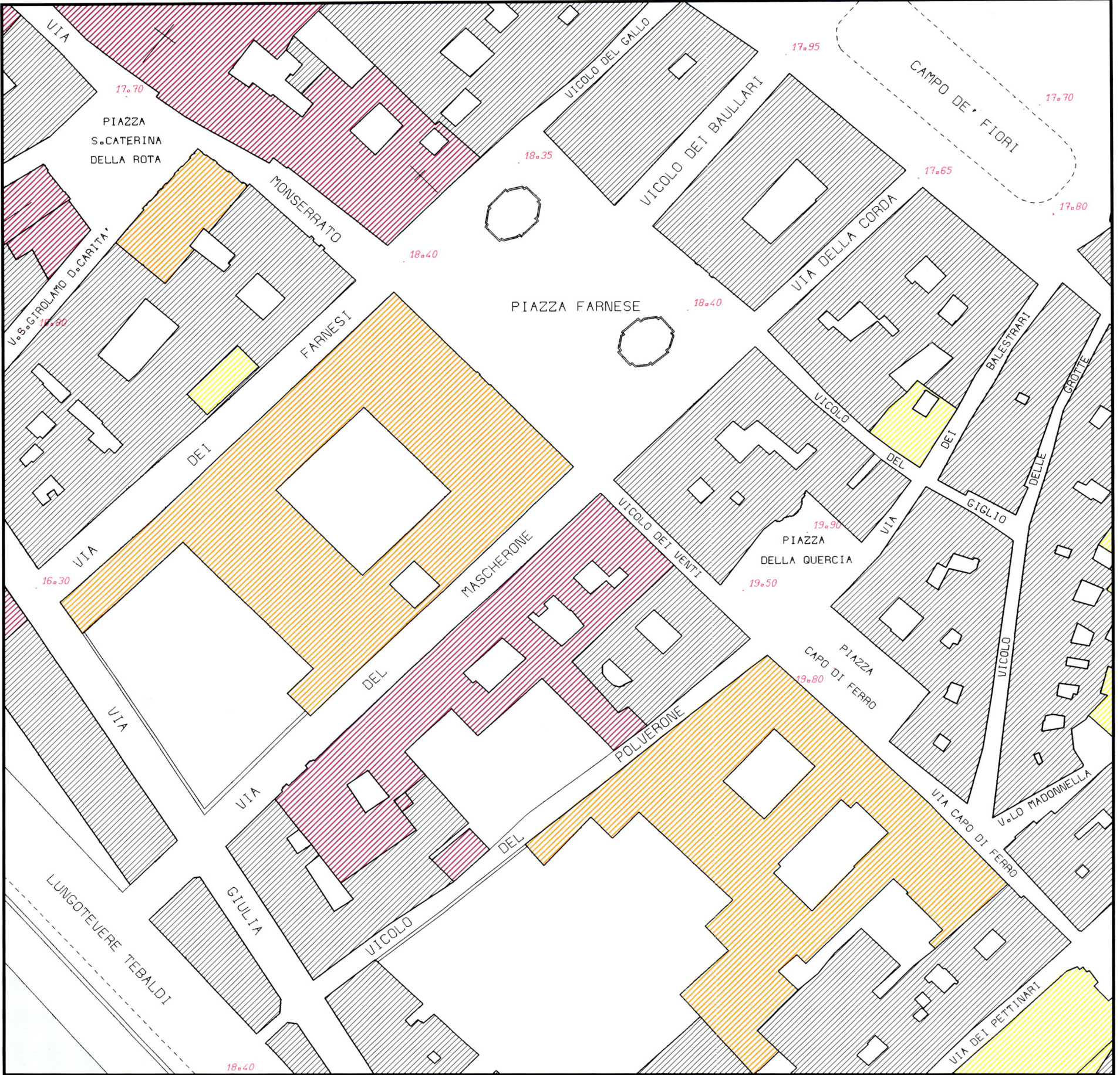

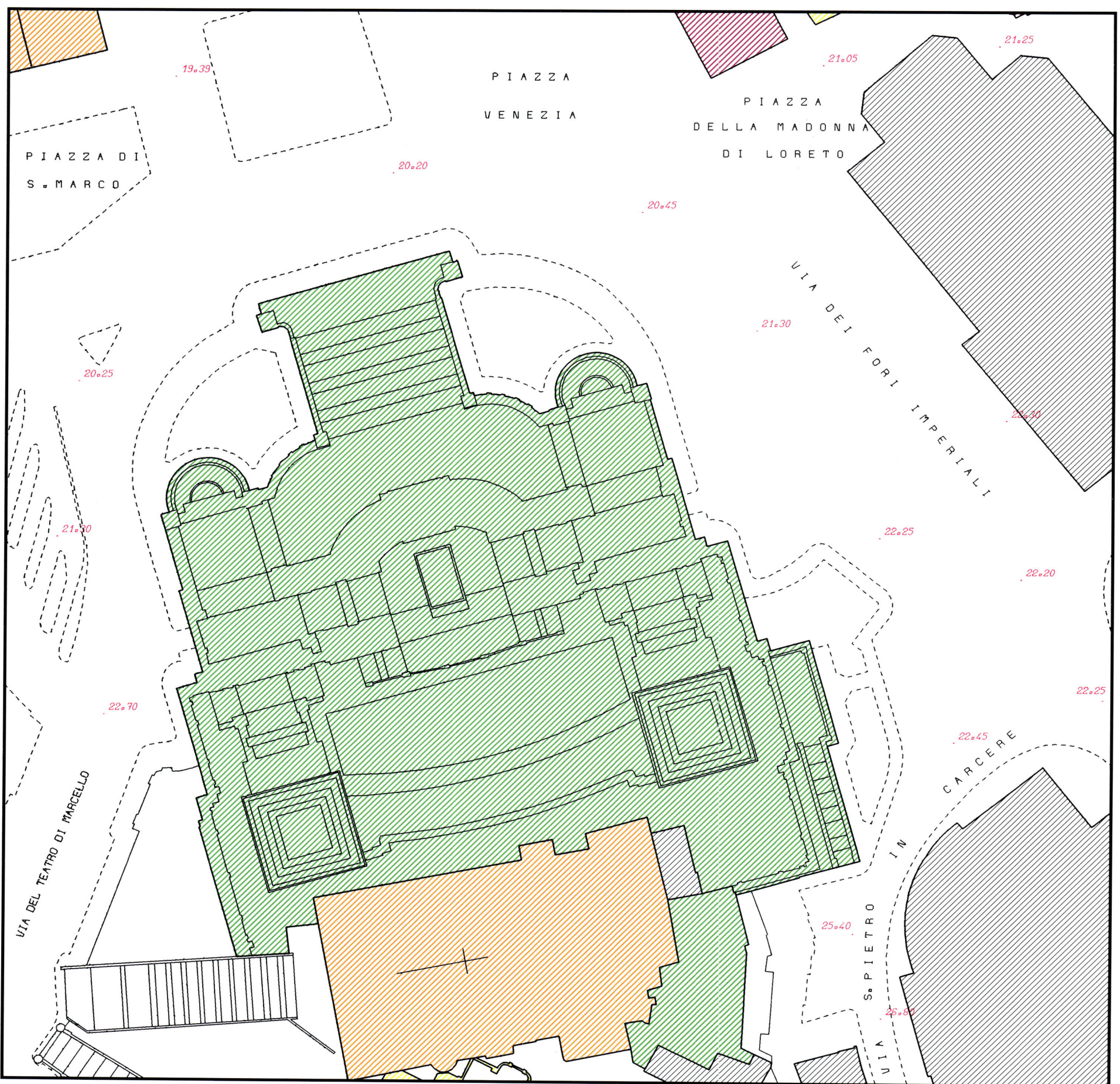

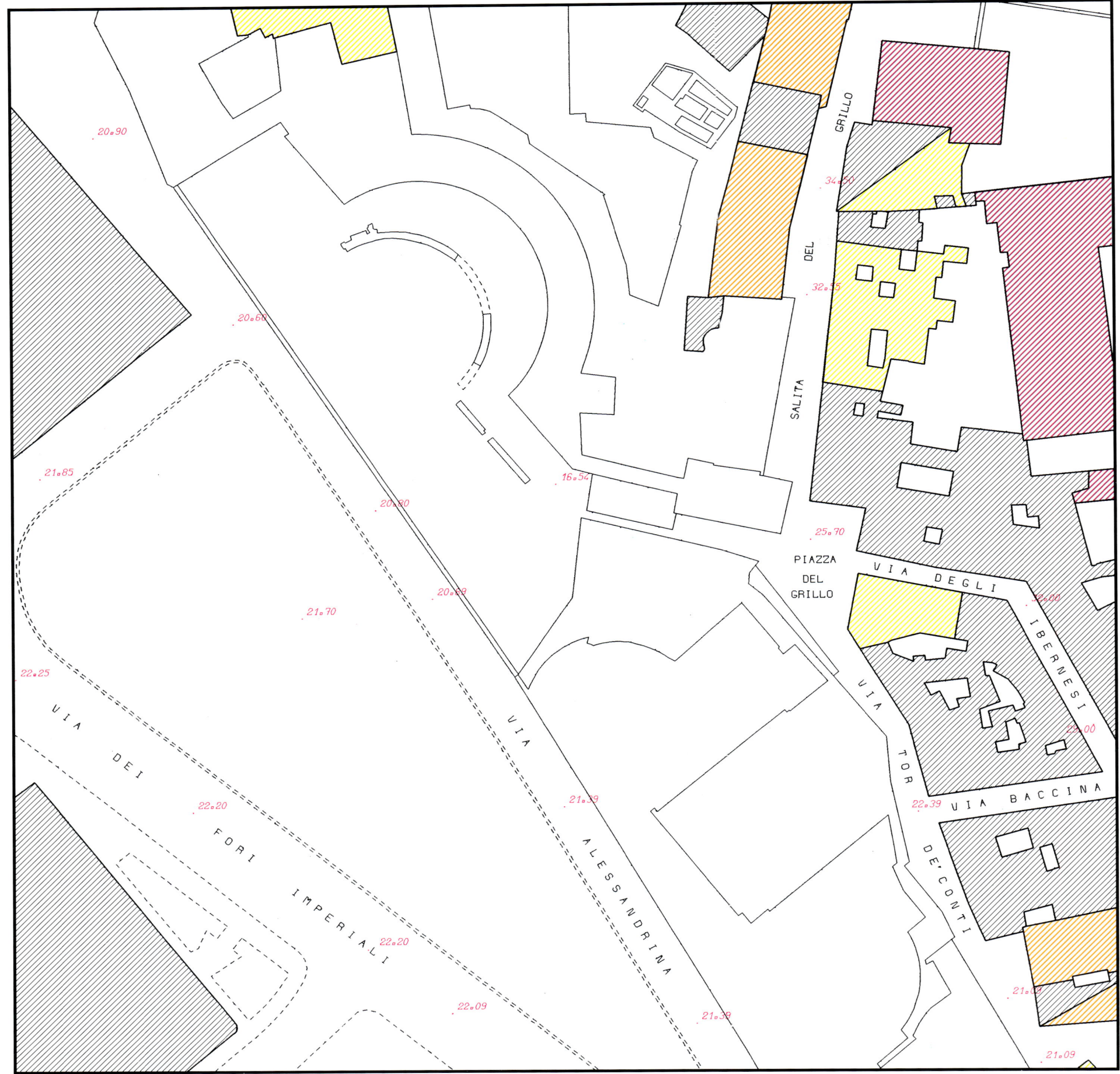

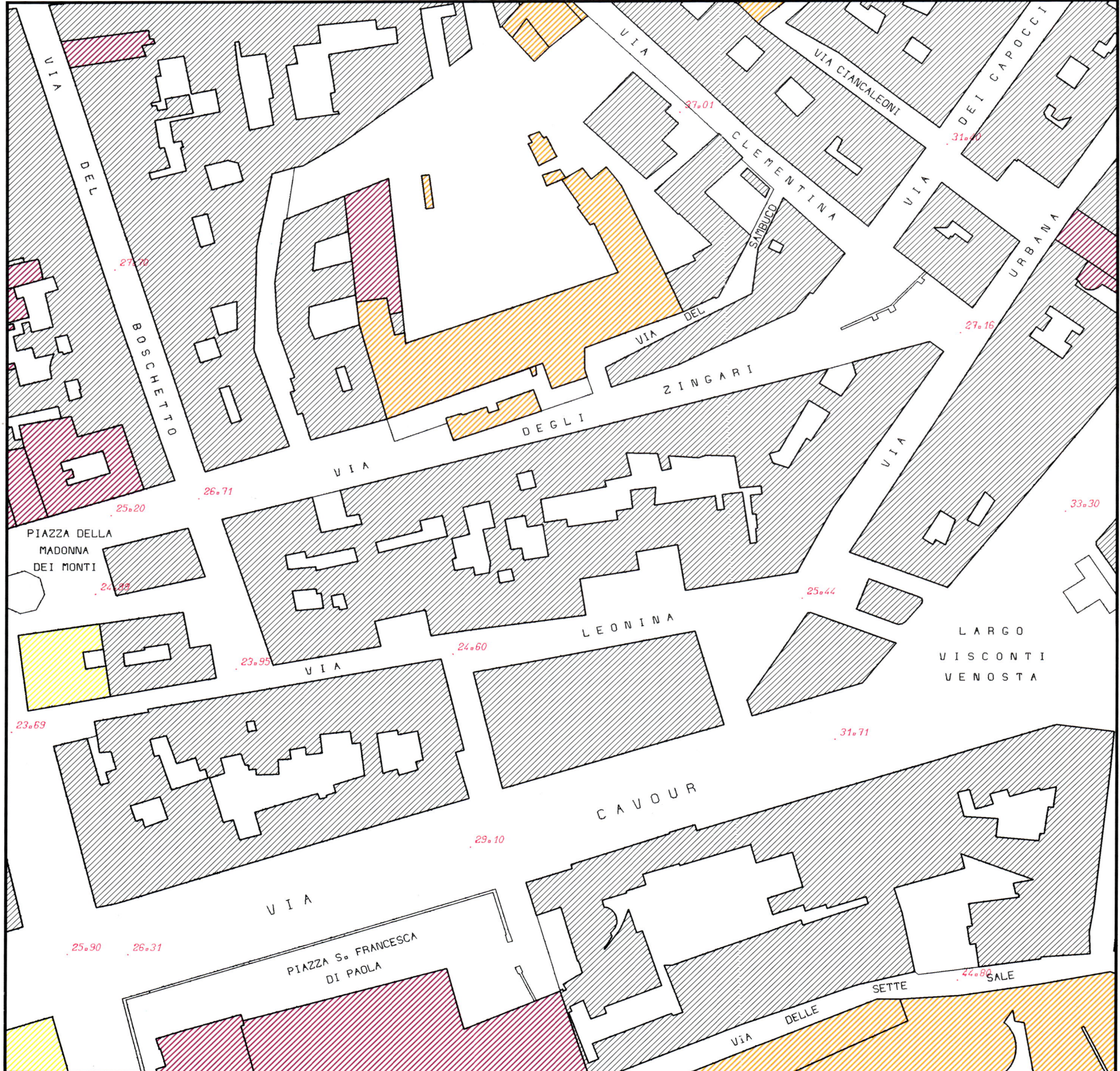

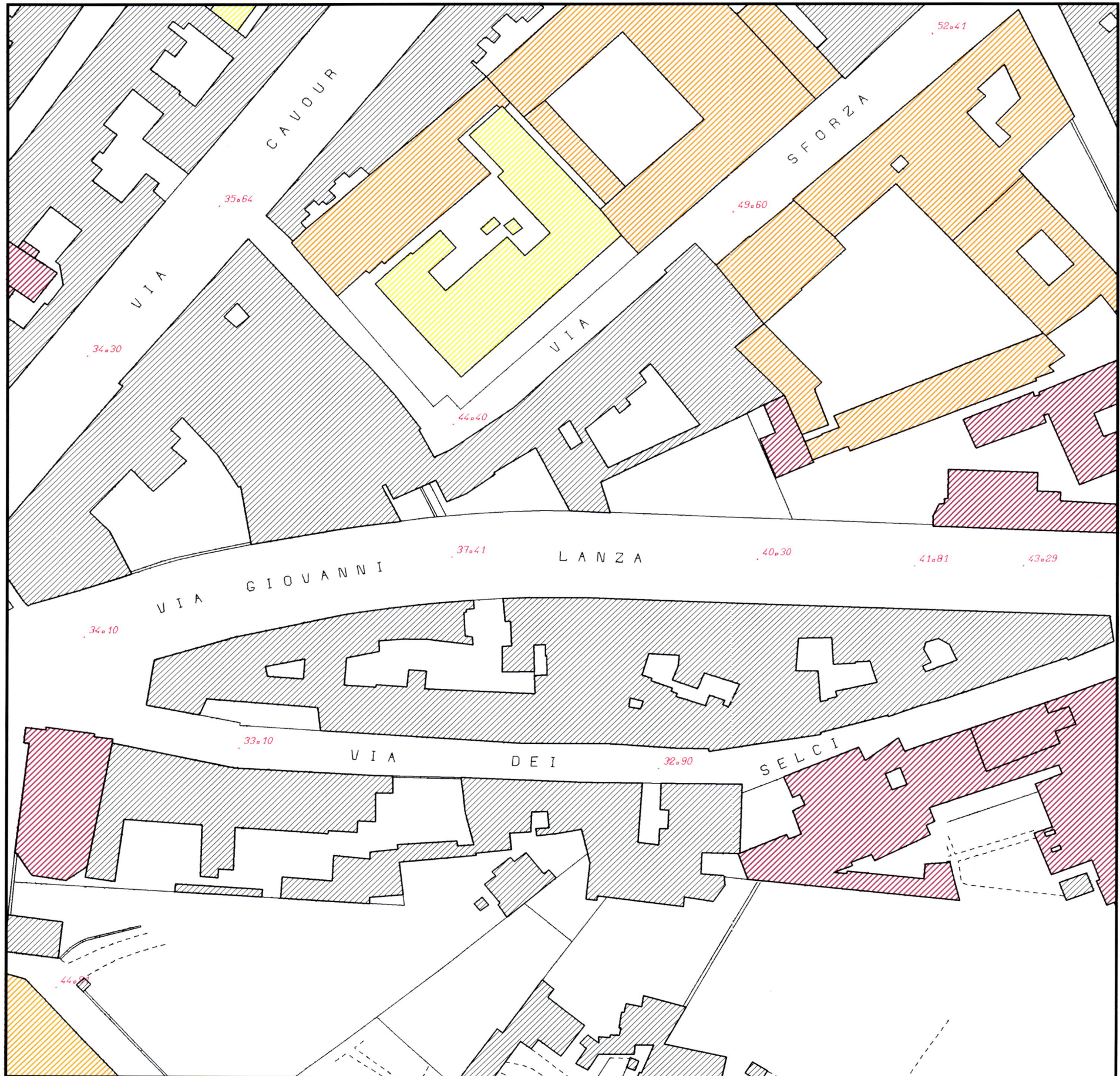

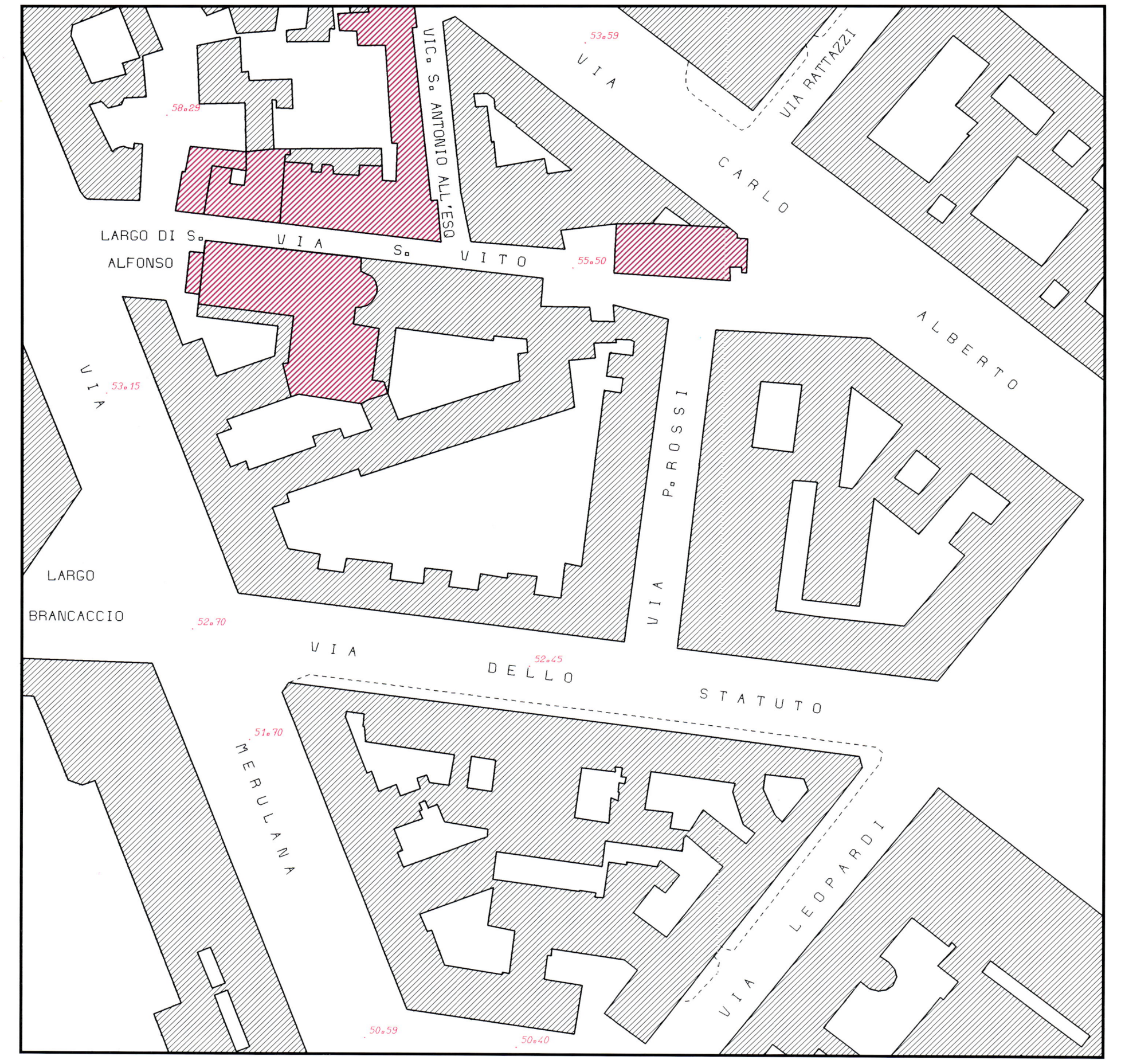

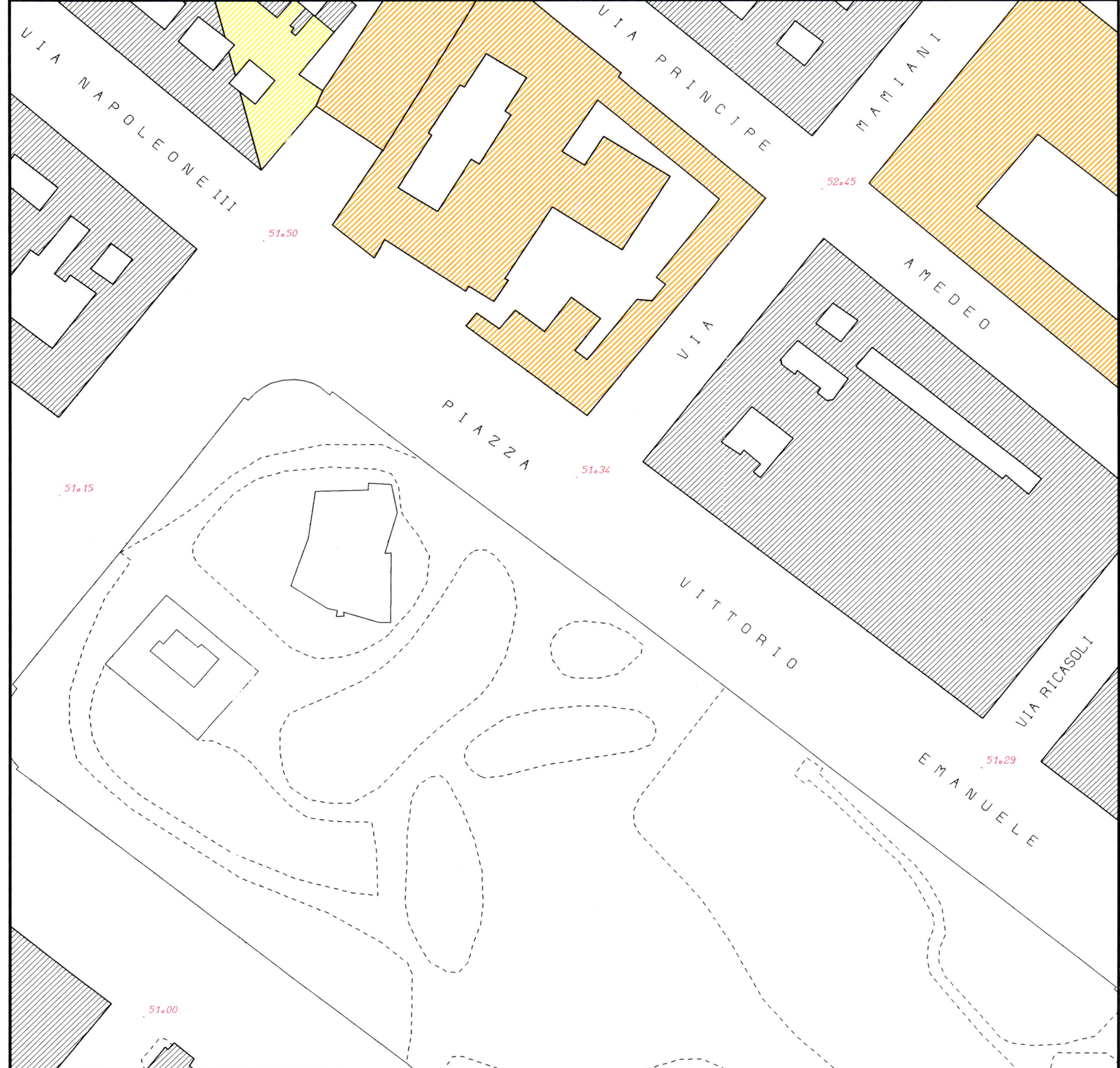

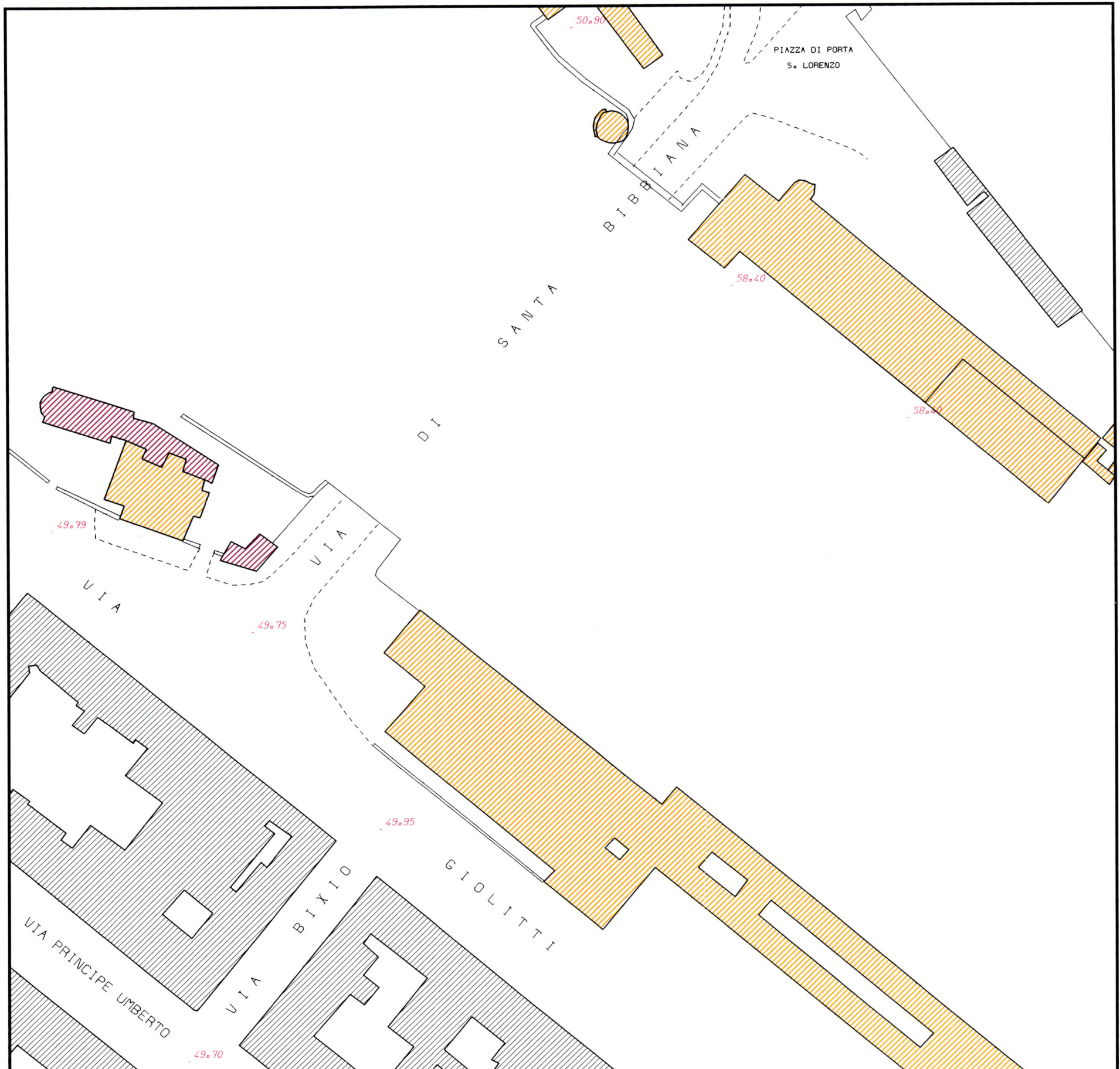

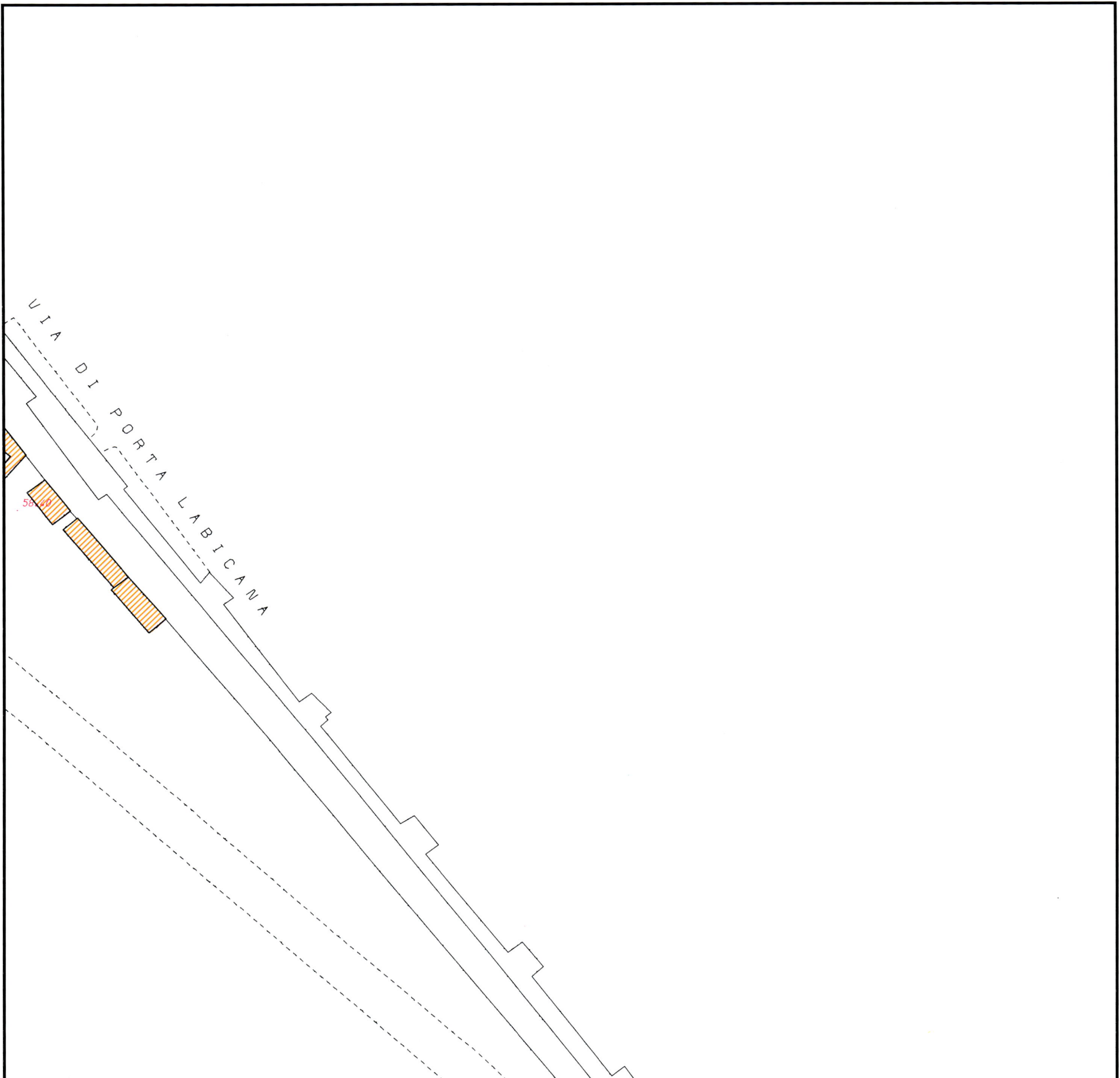

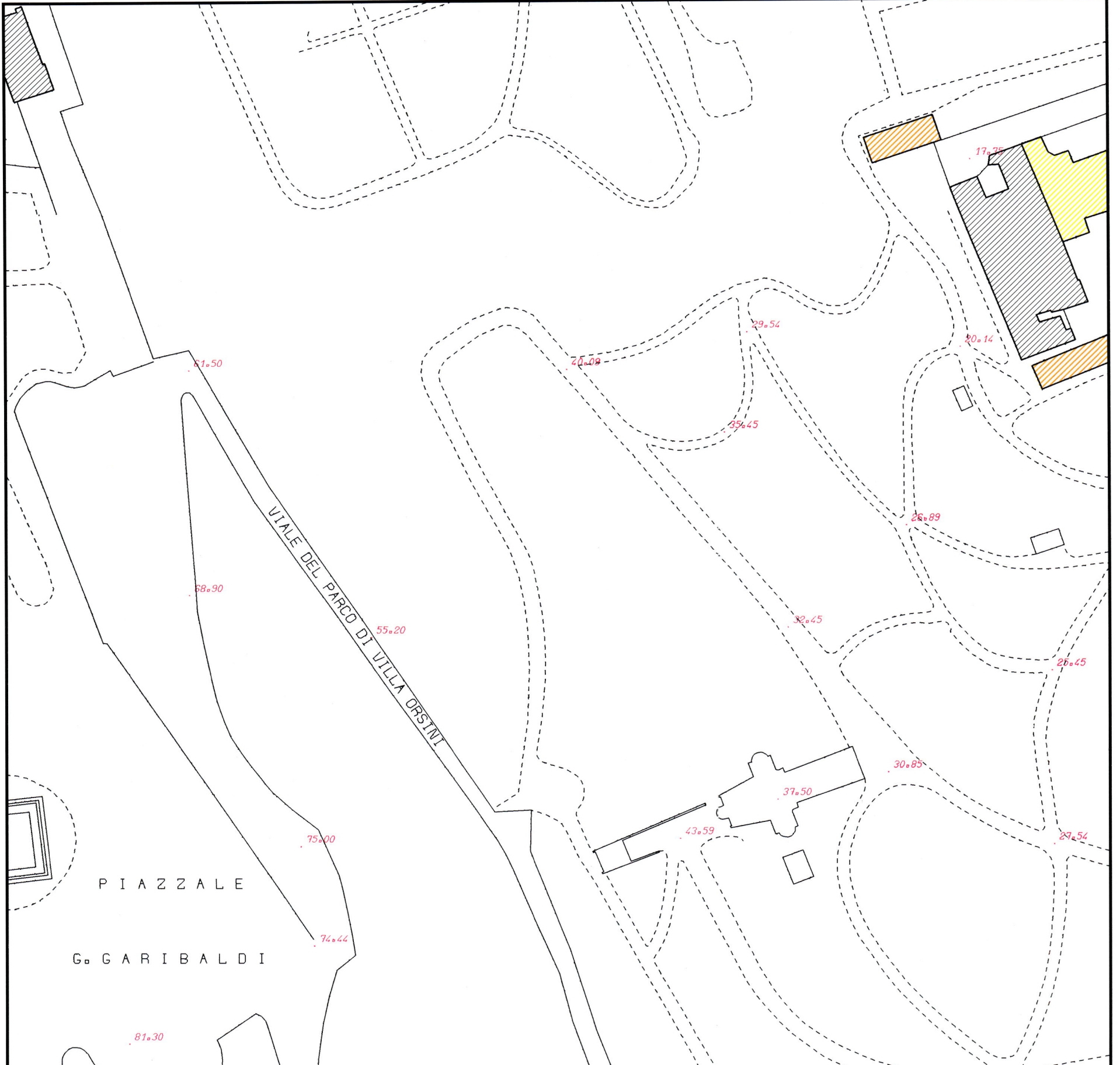

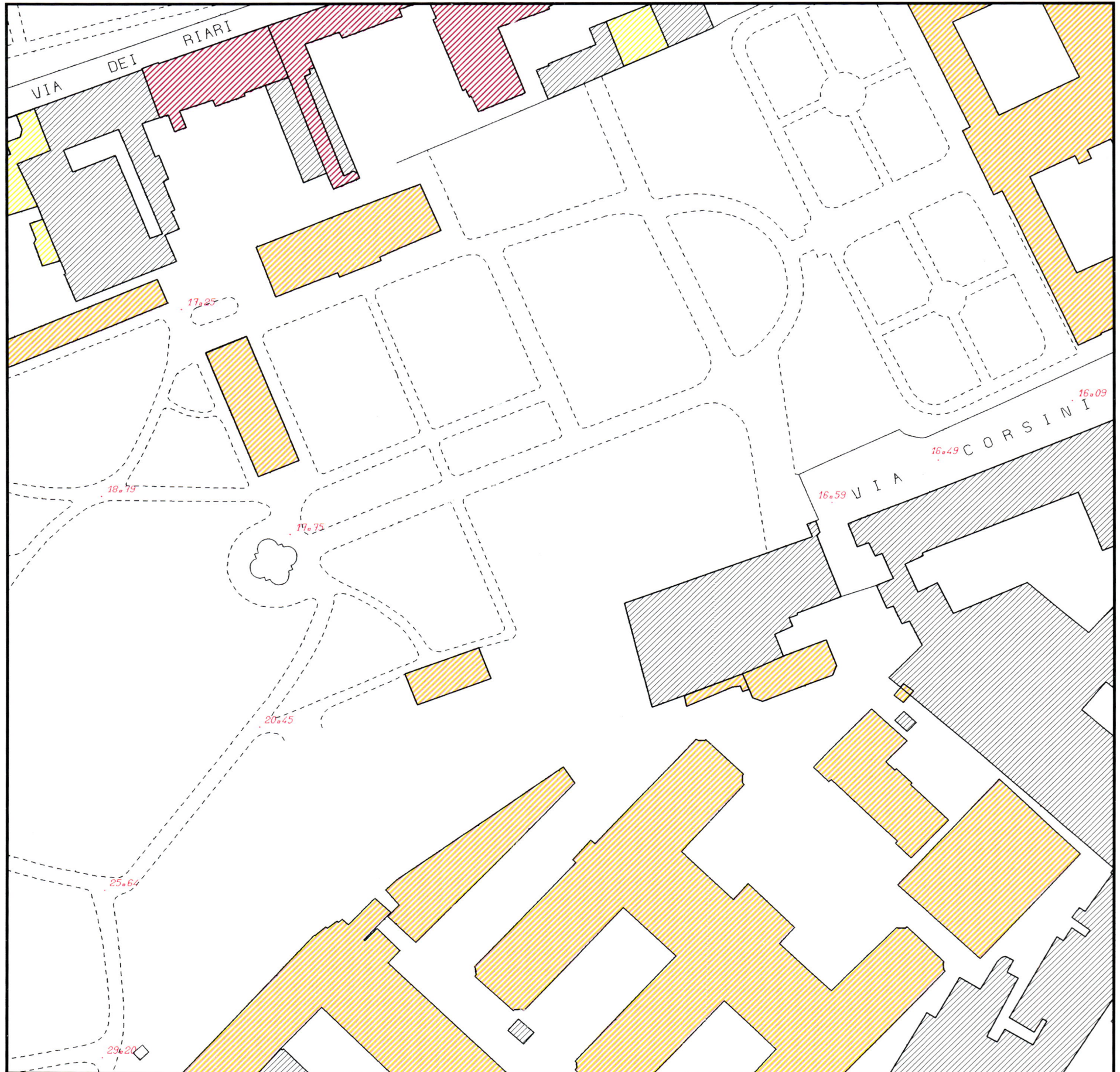

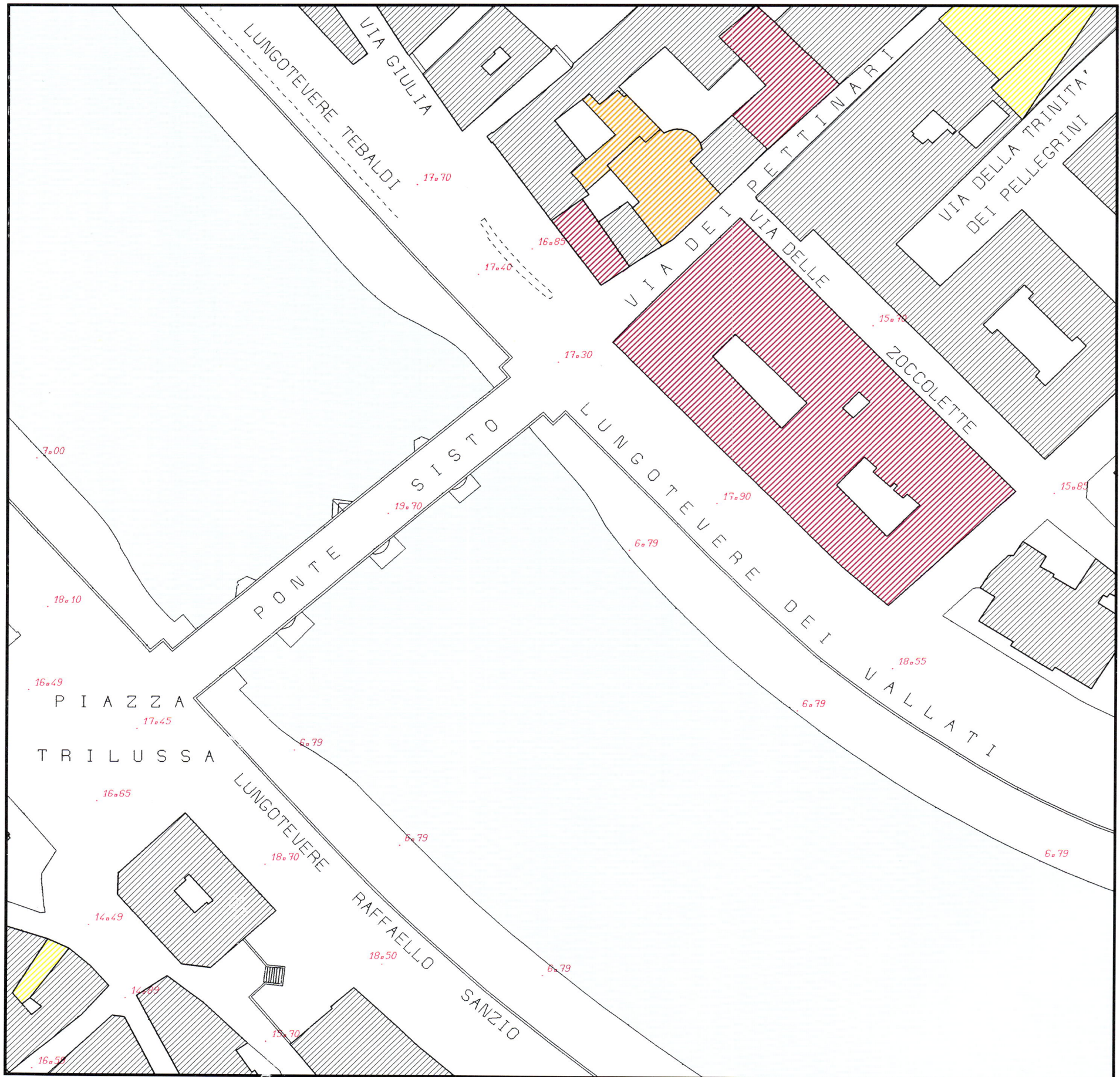

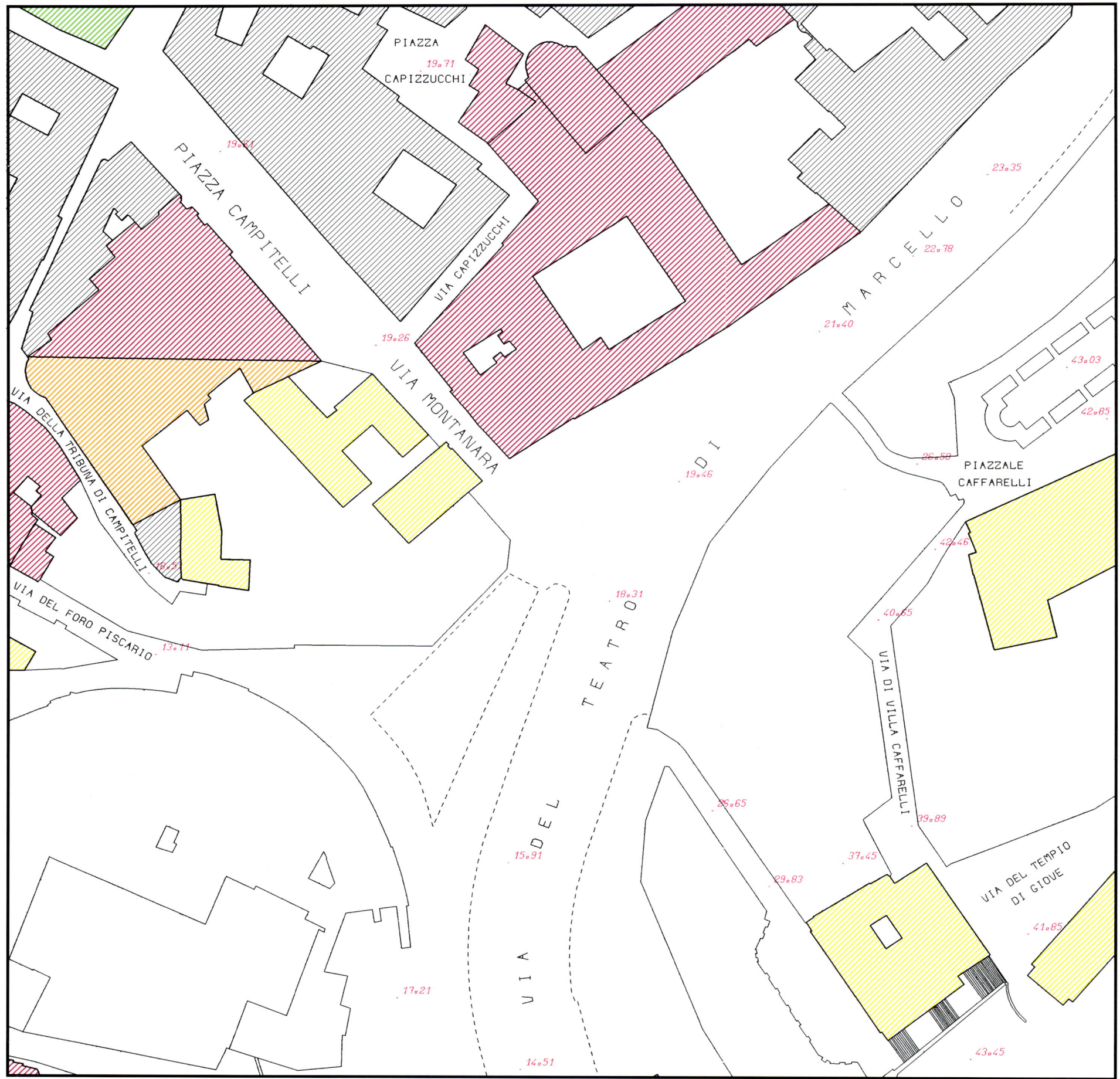

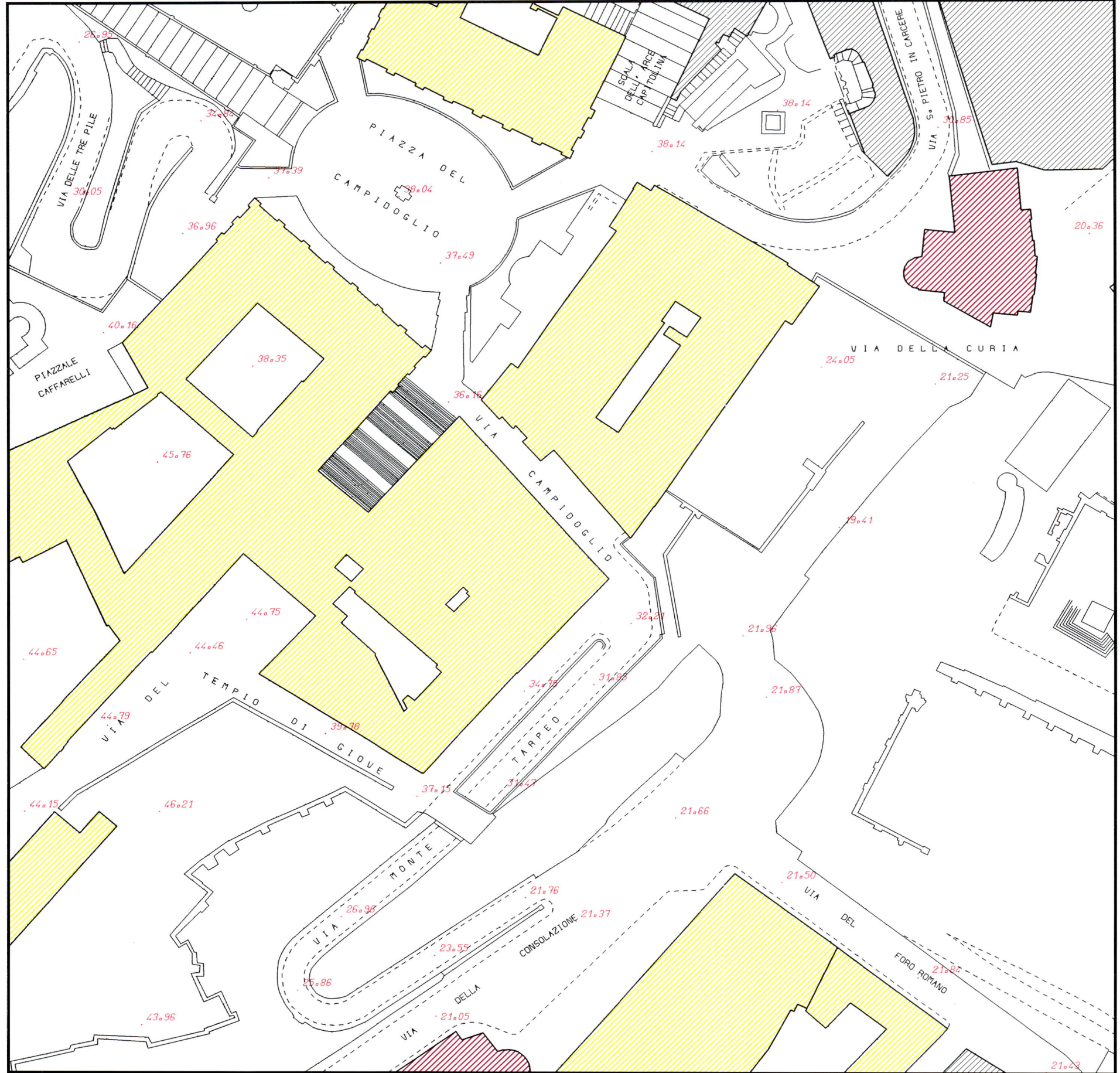

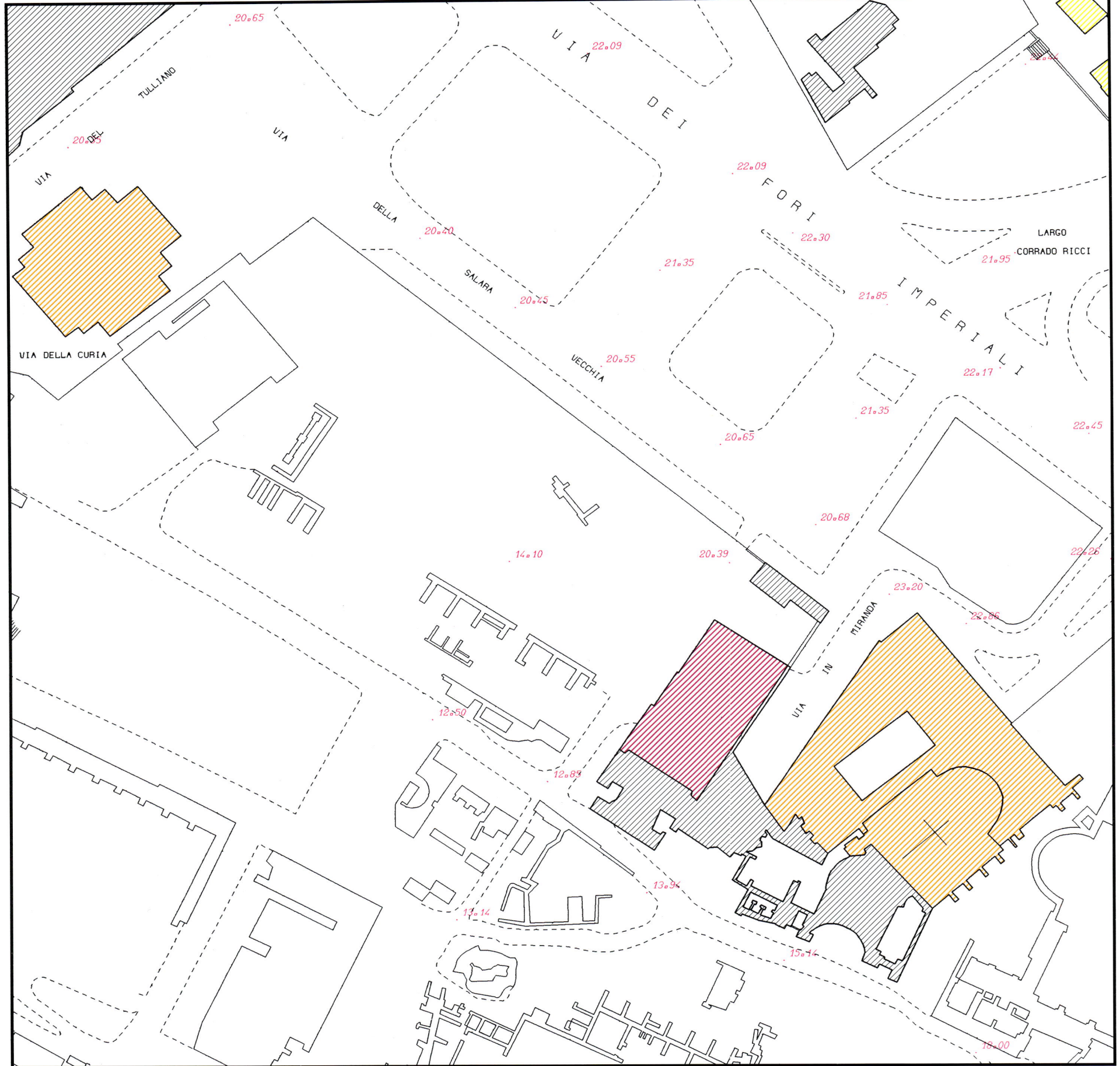

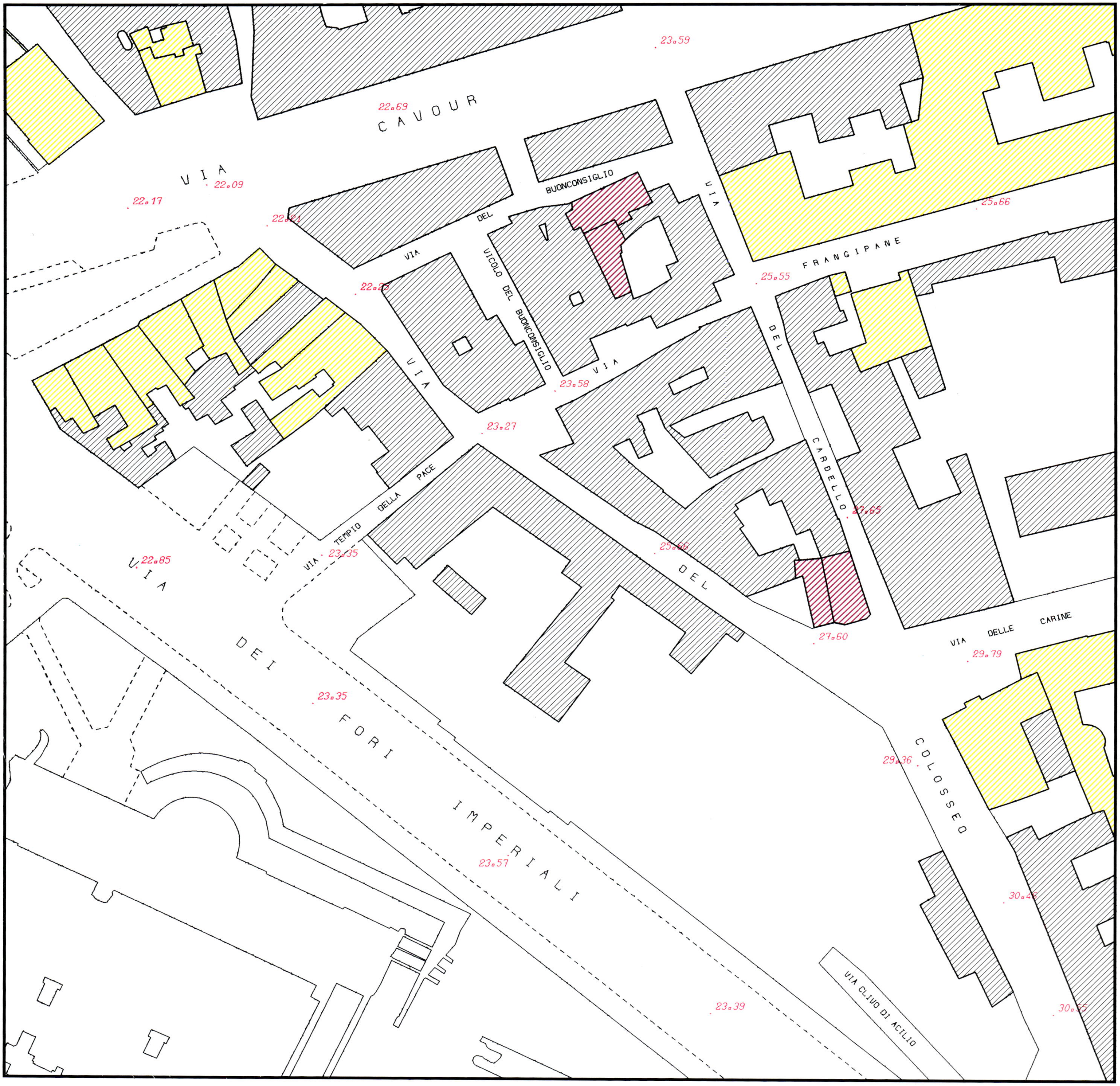
VIA CAVOUR
VIA DEL BUONCONSIGLIO
VICOLO DEL BUONCONSIGLIO
VIA FRANGIPANE
VIA DEL CARDELLO
VIA DELLE CARINE
VIA DEL COLOSSEO
VIA TEMPIO DELLA PACE
VIA DEI FORI IMPERIALI
VIA CLIVO DI ACILIO
23.59
22.69
22.09
22.17
25.66
25.55
23.58
23.27
27.65
25.66
23.35
22.85
27.60
29.79
23.35
29.36
23.57
30.46
23.39
30.55

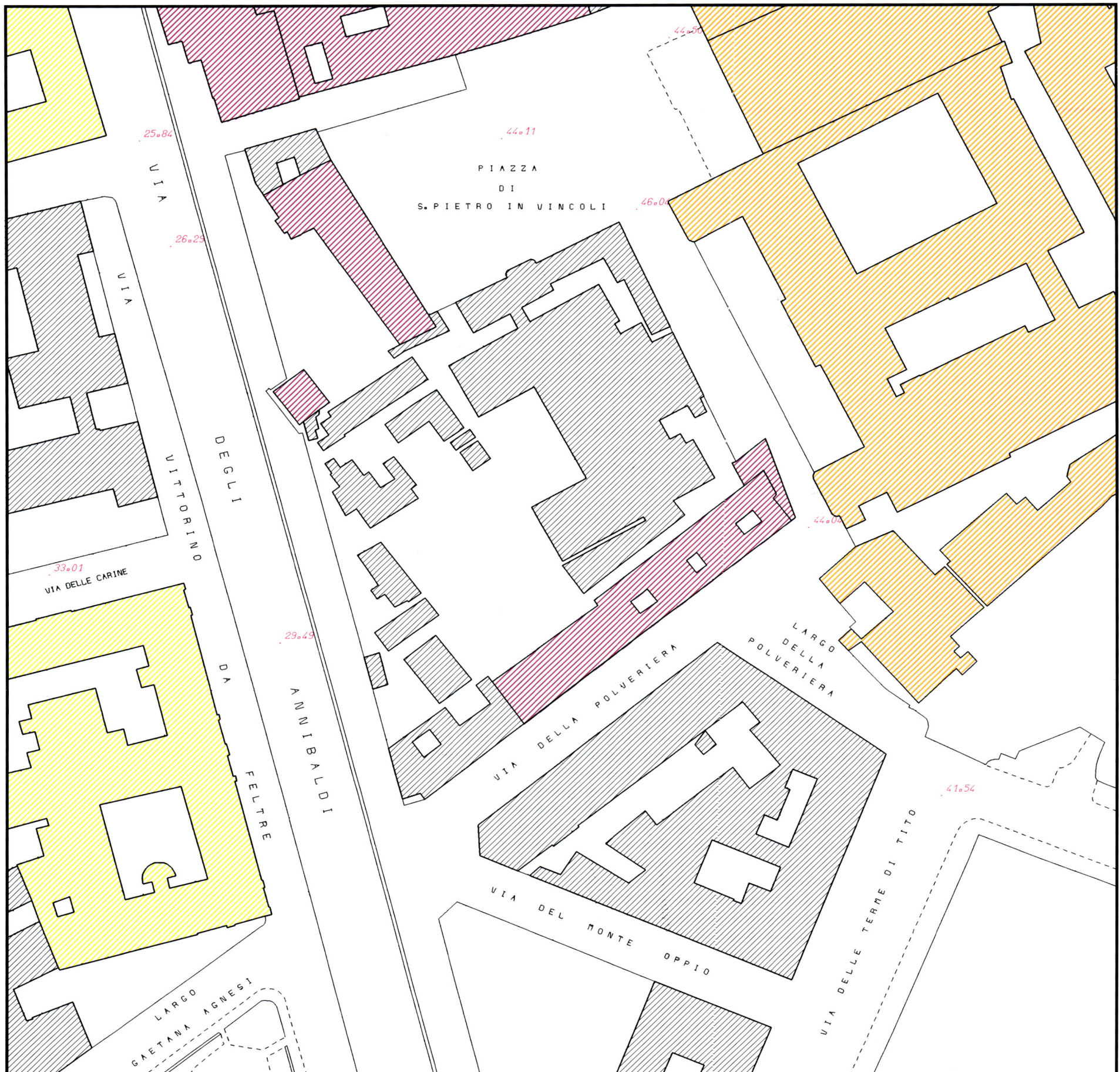

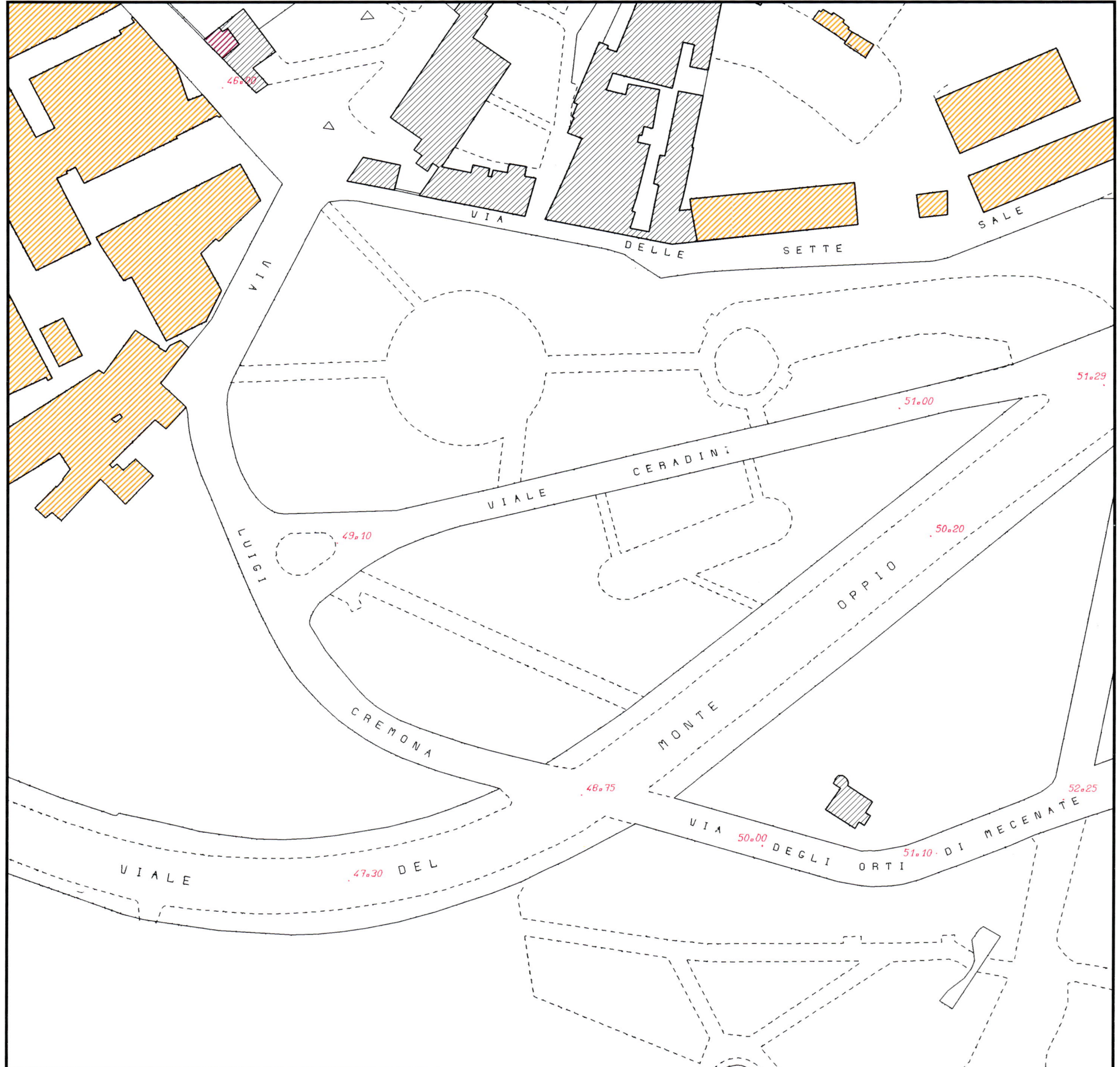

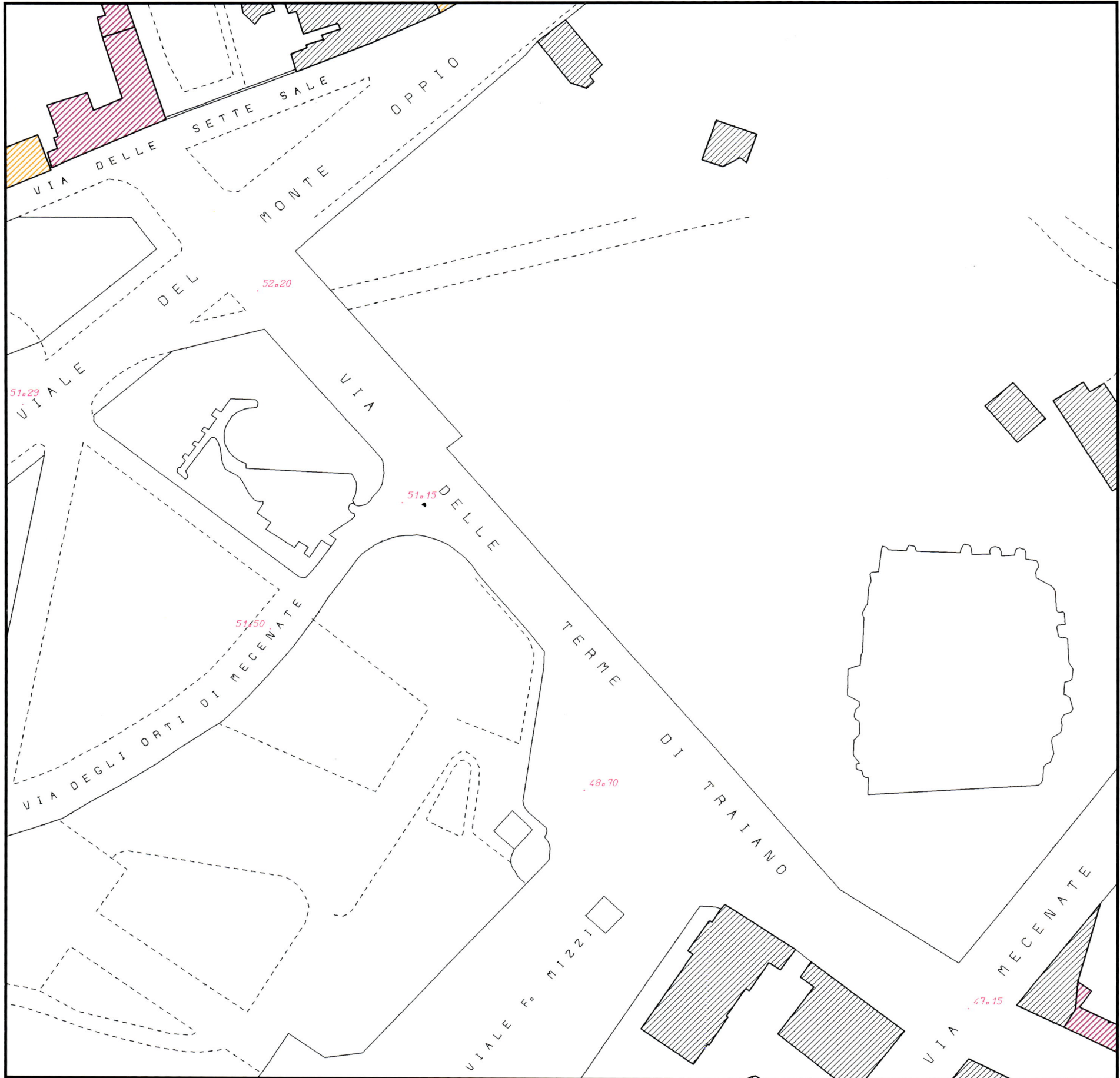

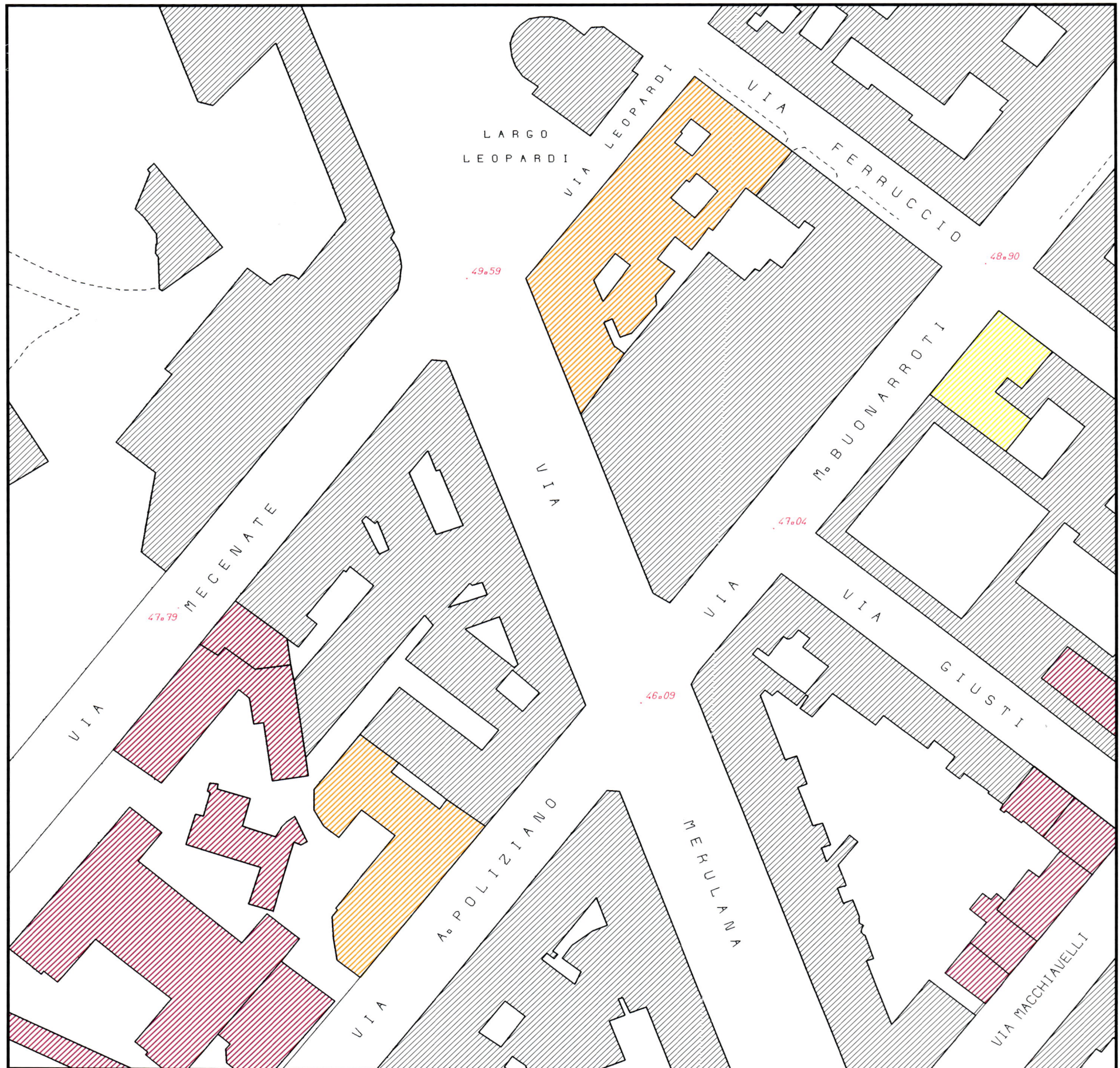

148

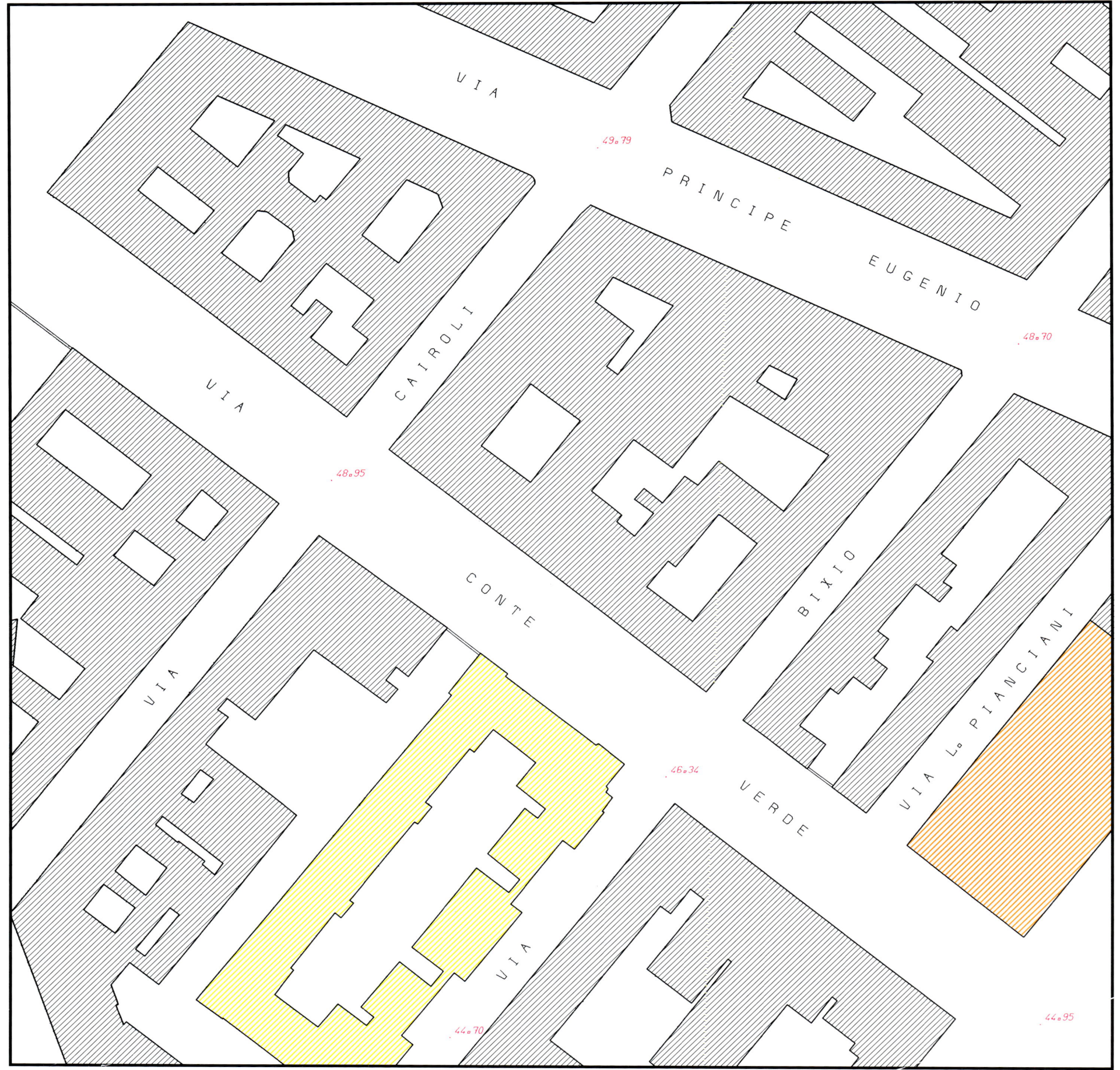

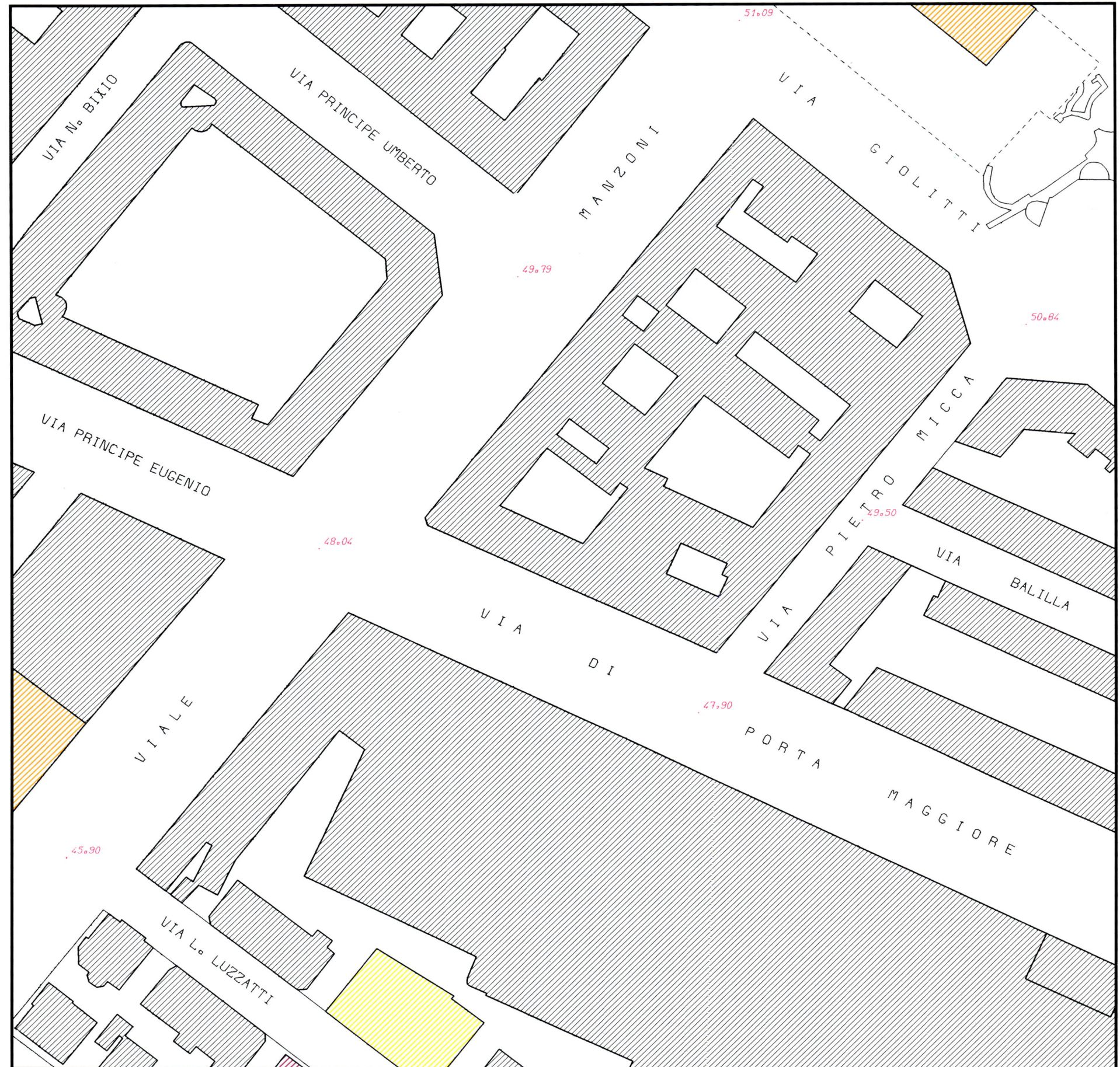

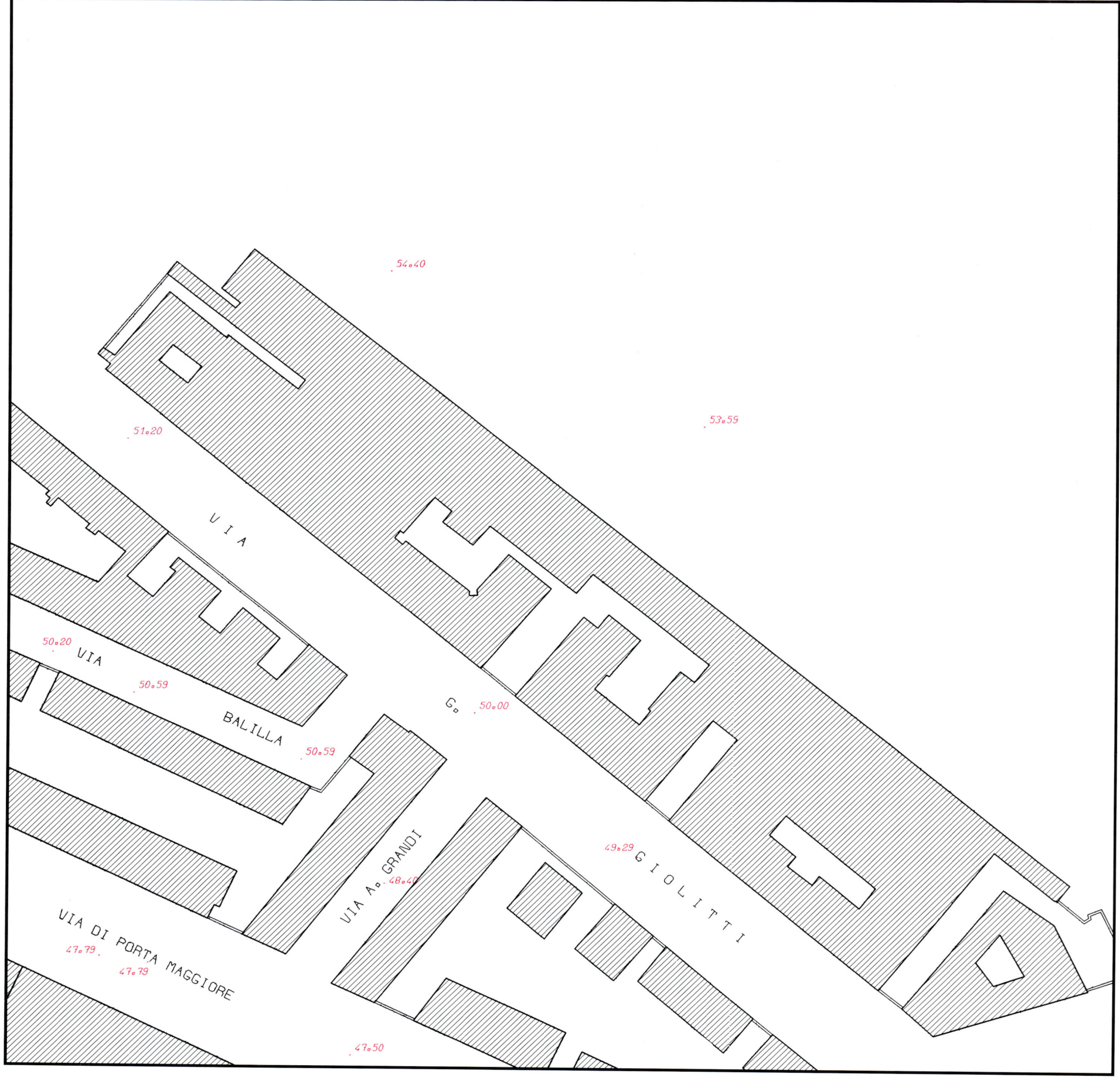

PIAZZALE

LABICANO

VIALE DELLE MURA AURELIE

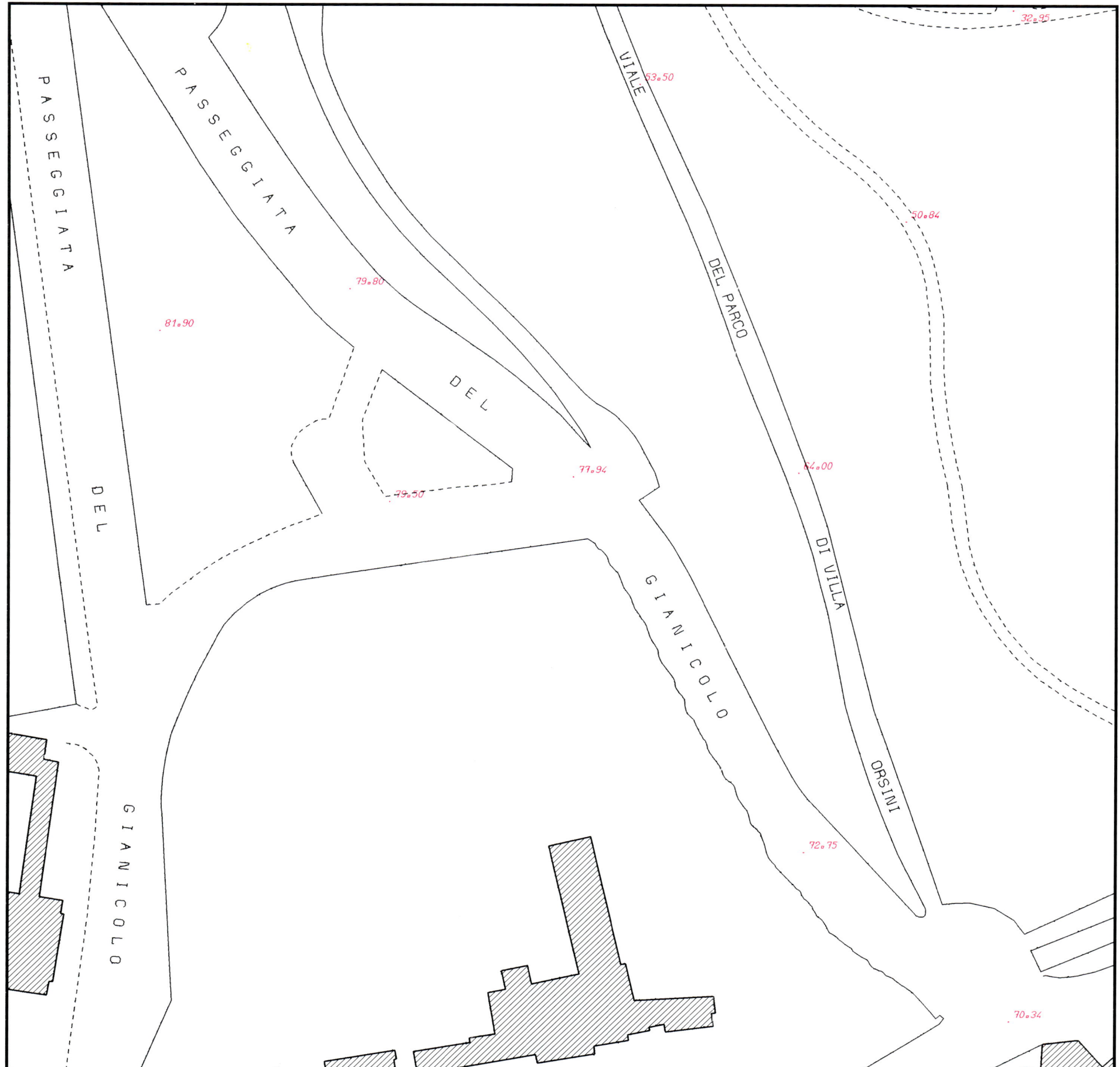

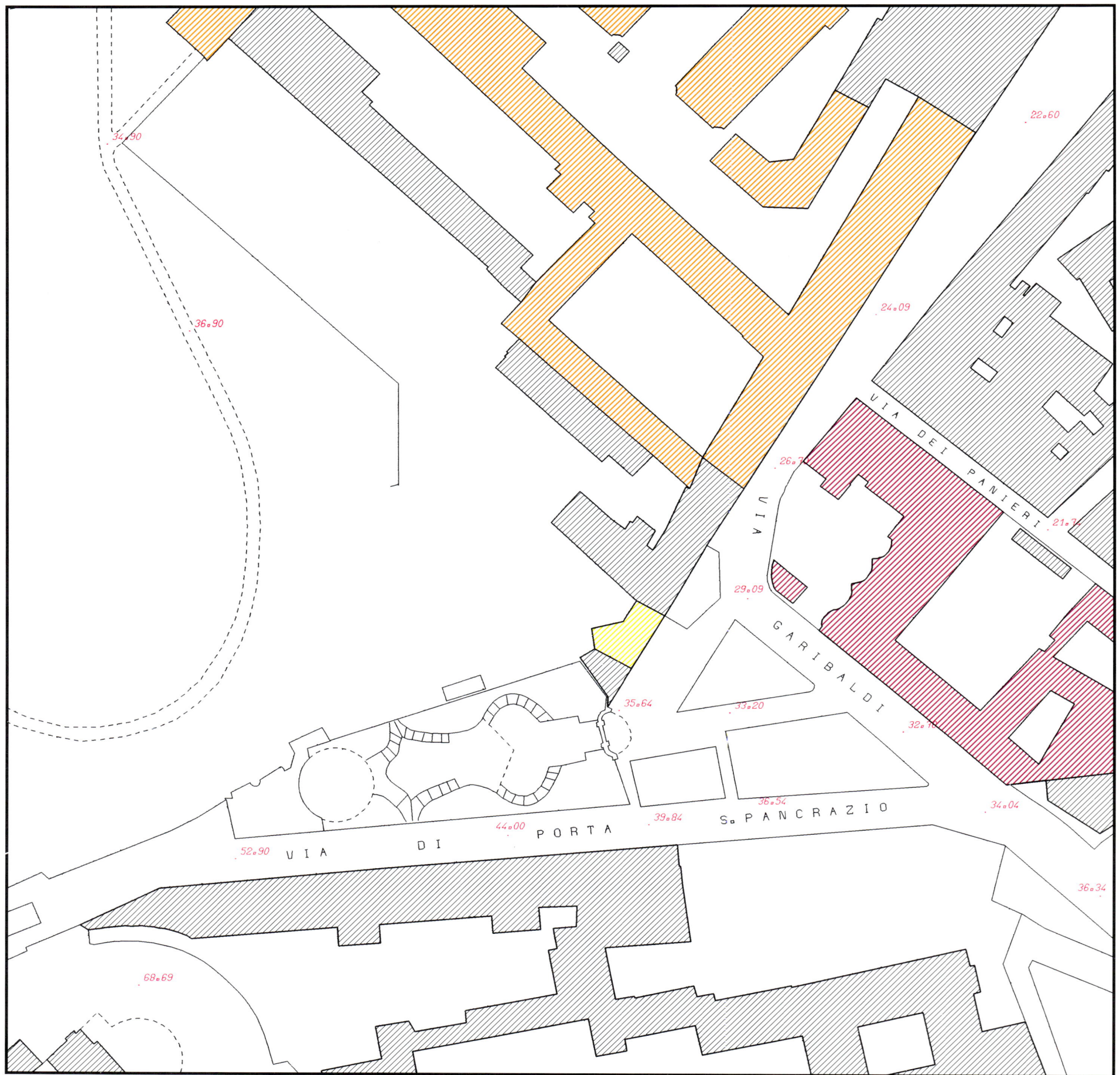

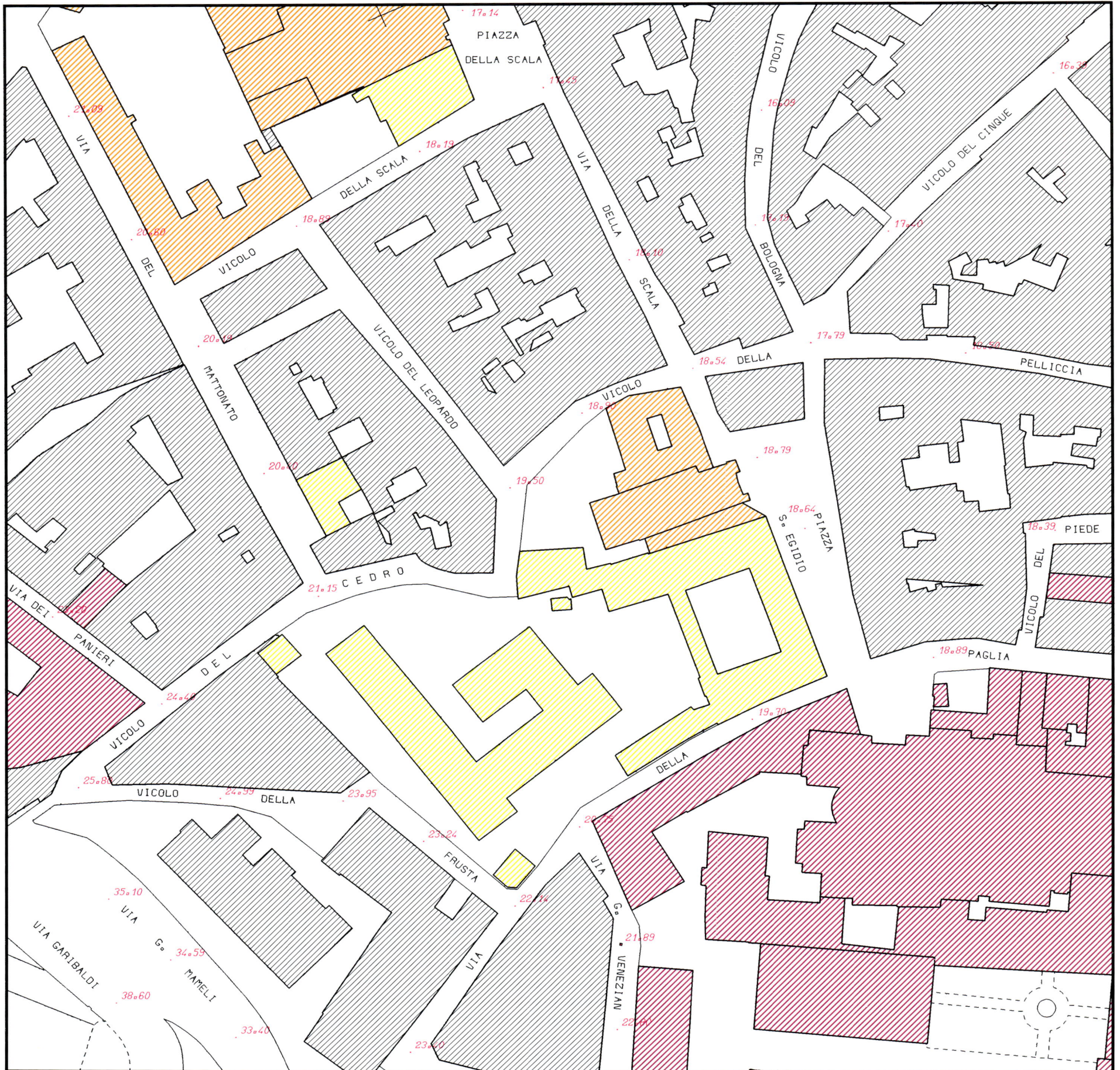

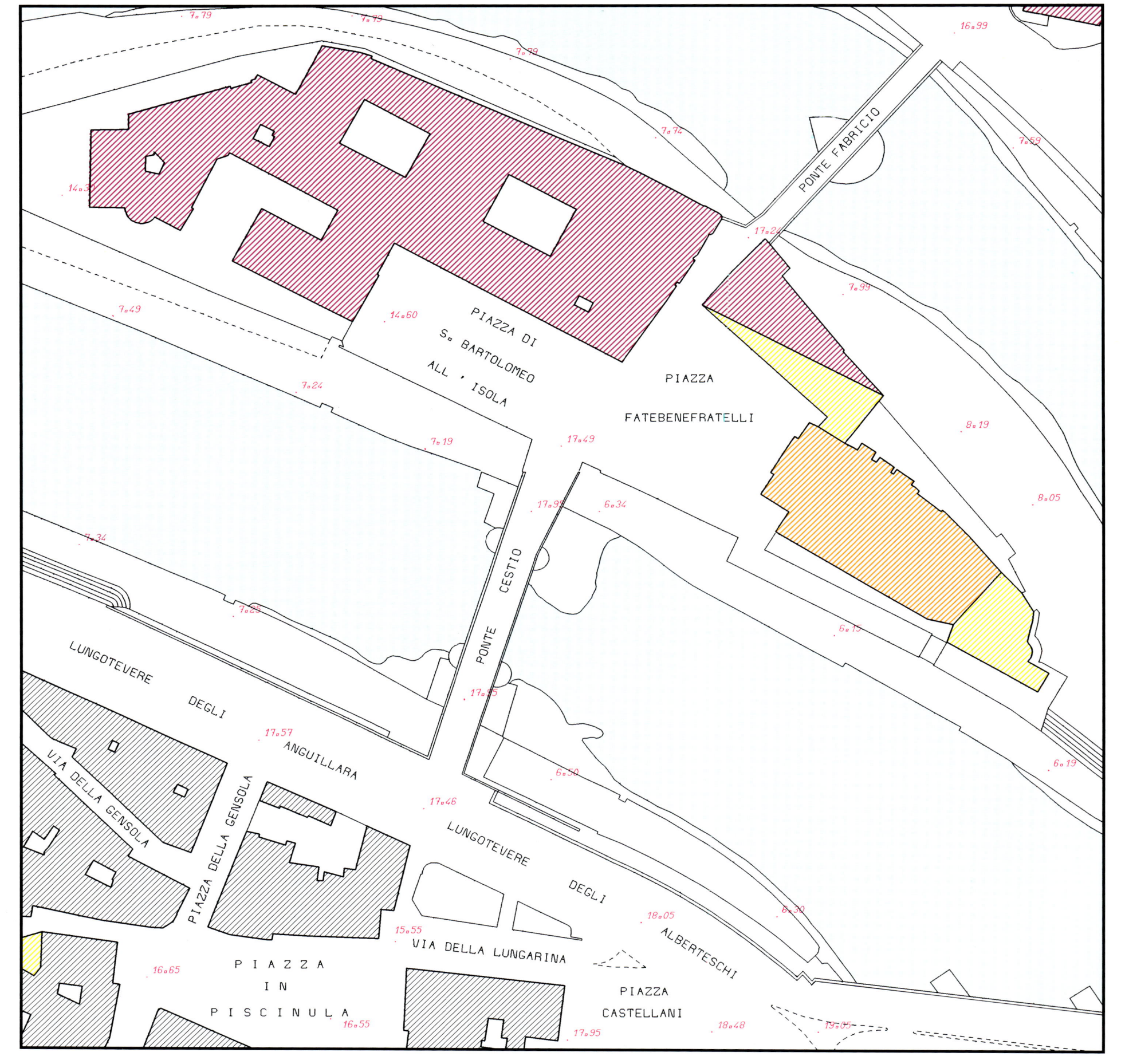

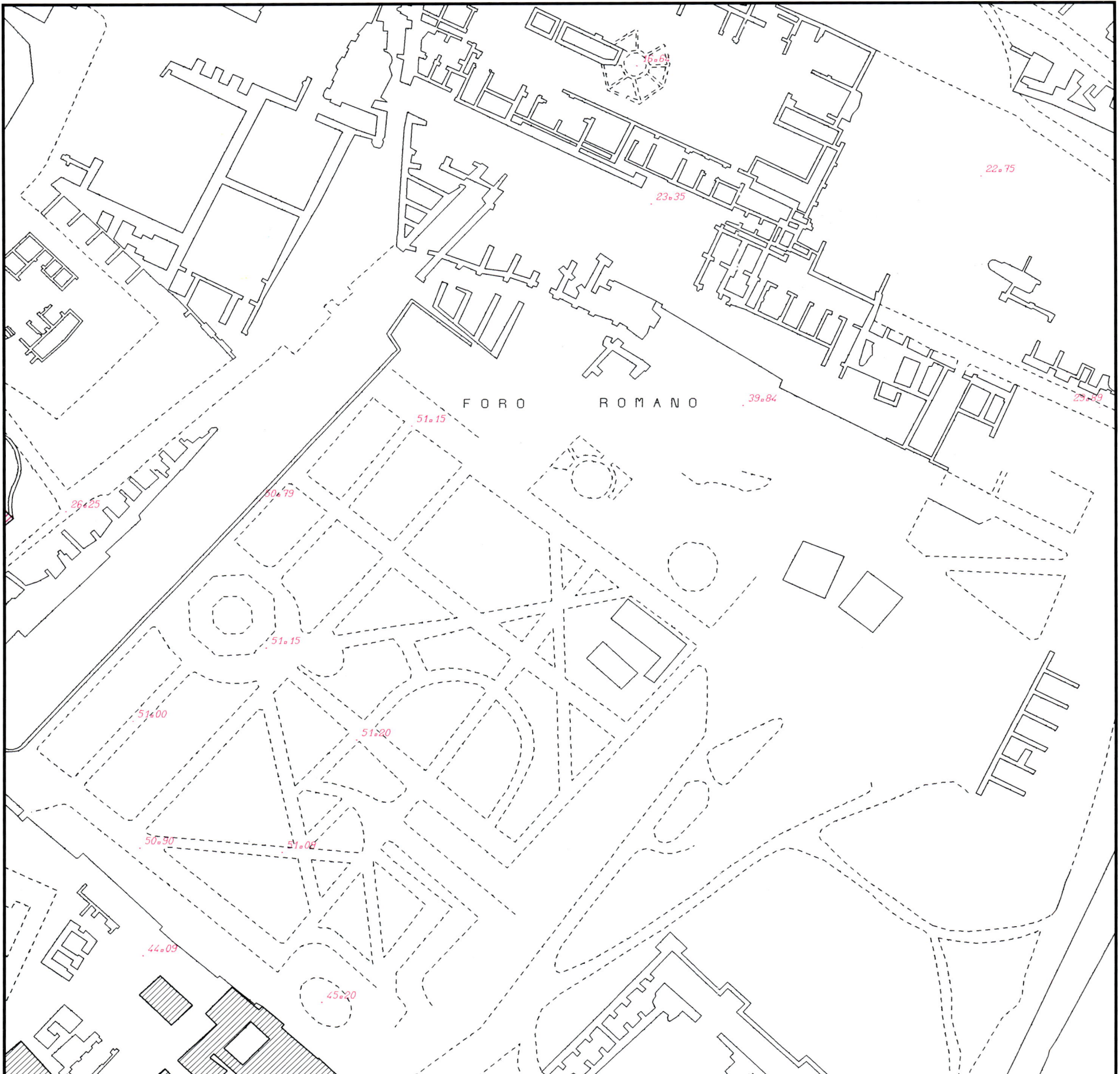

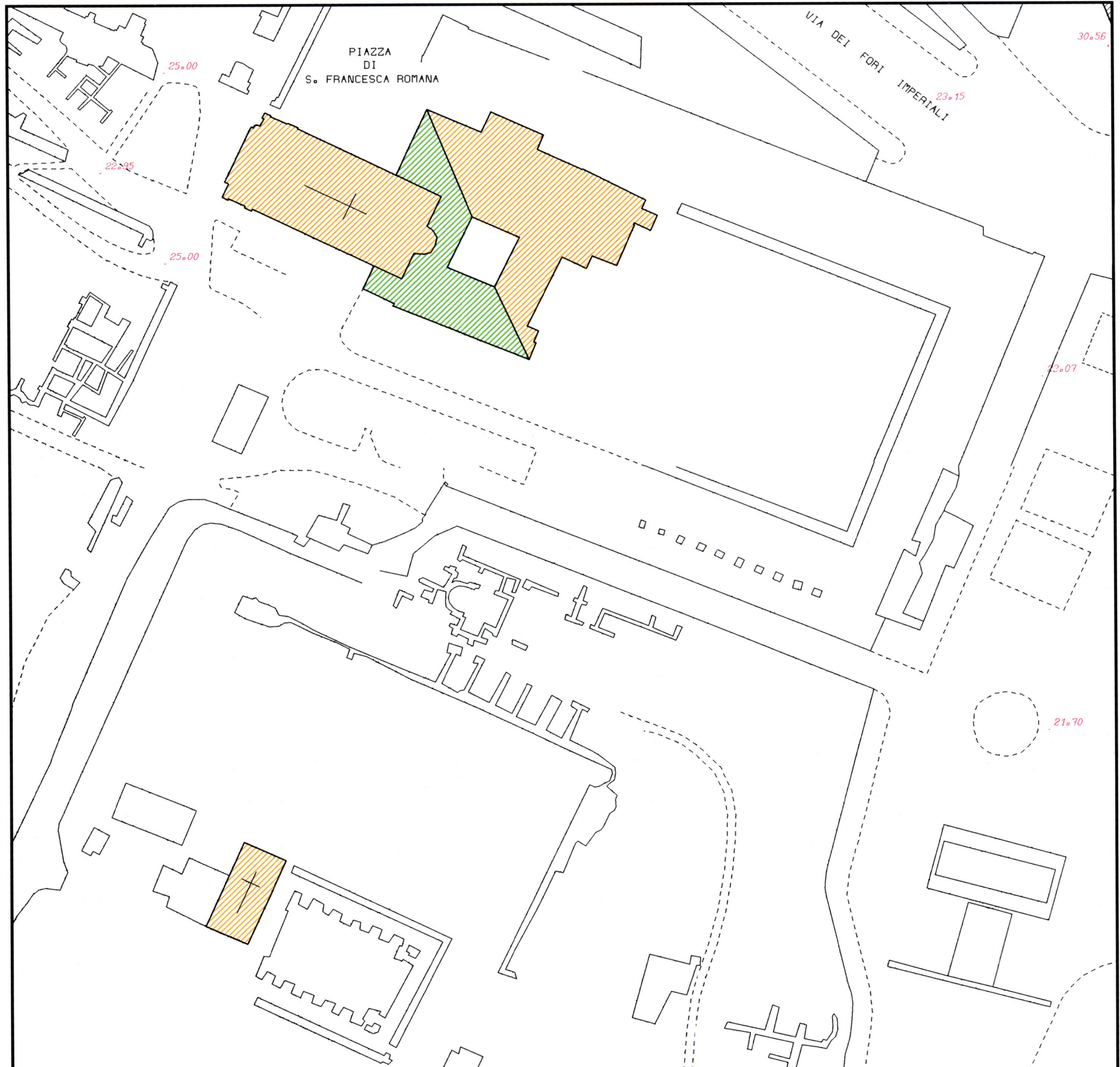

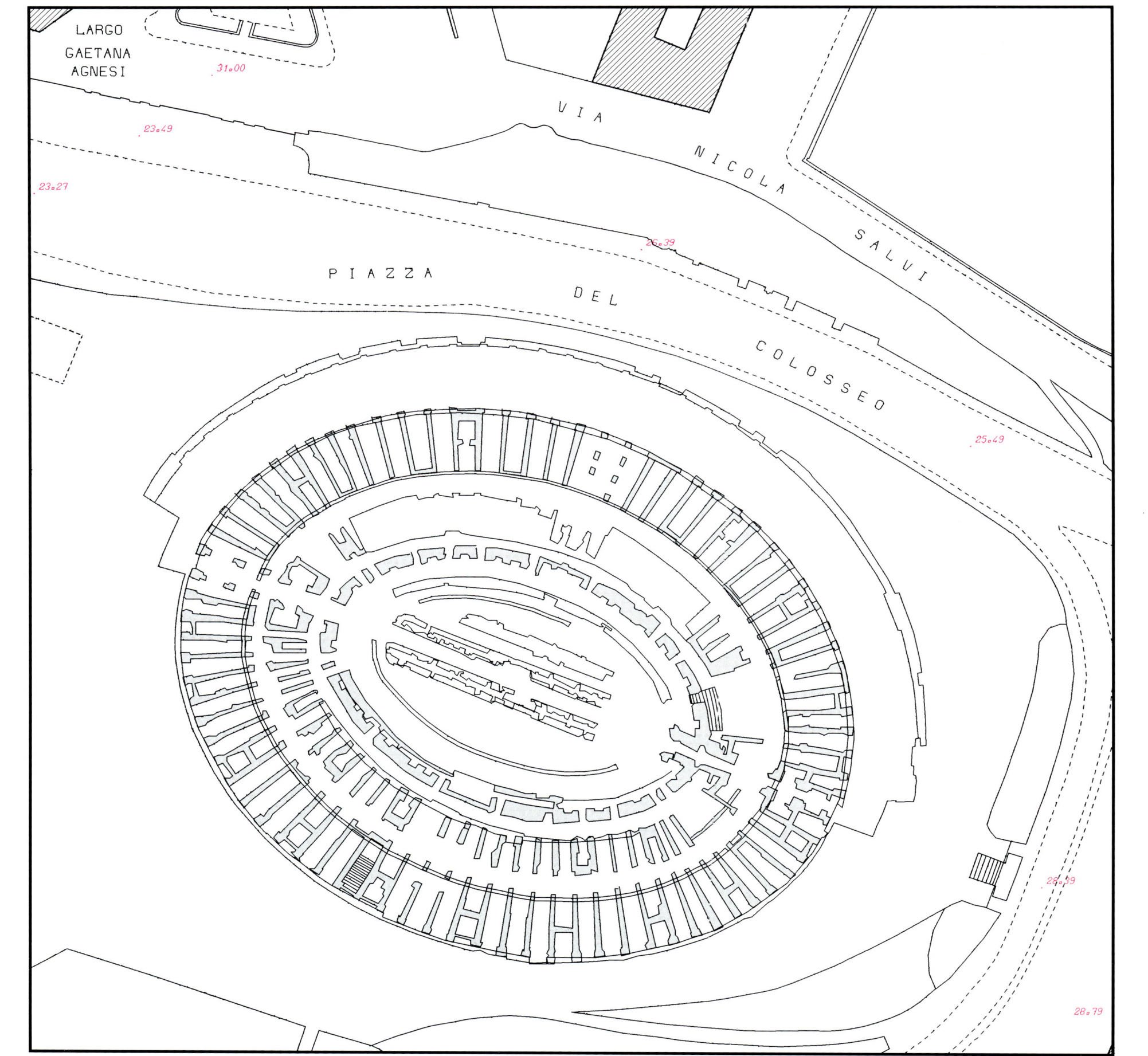

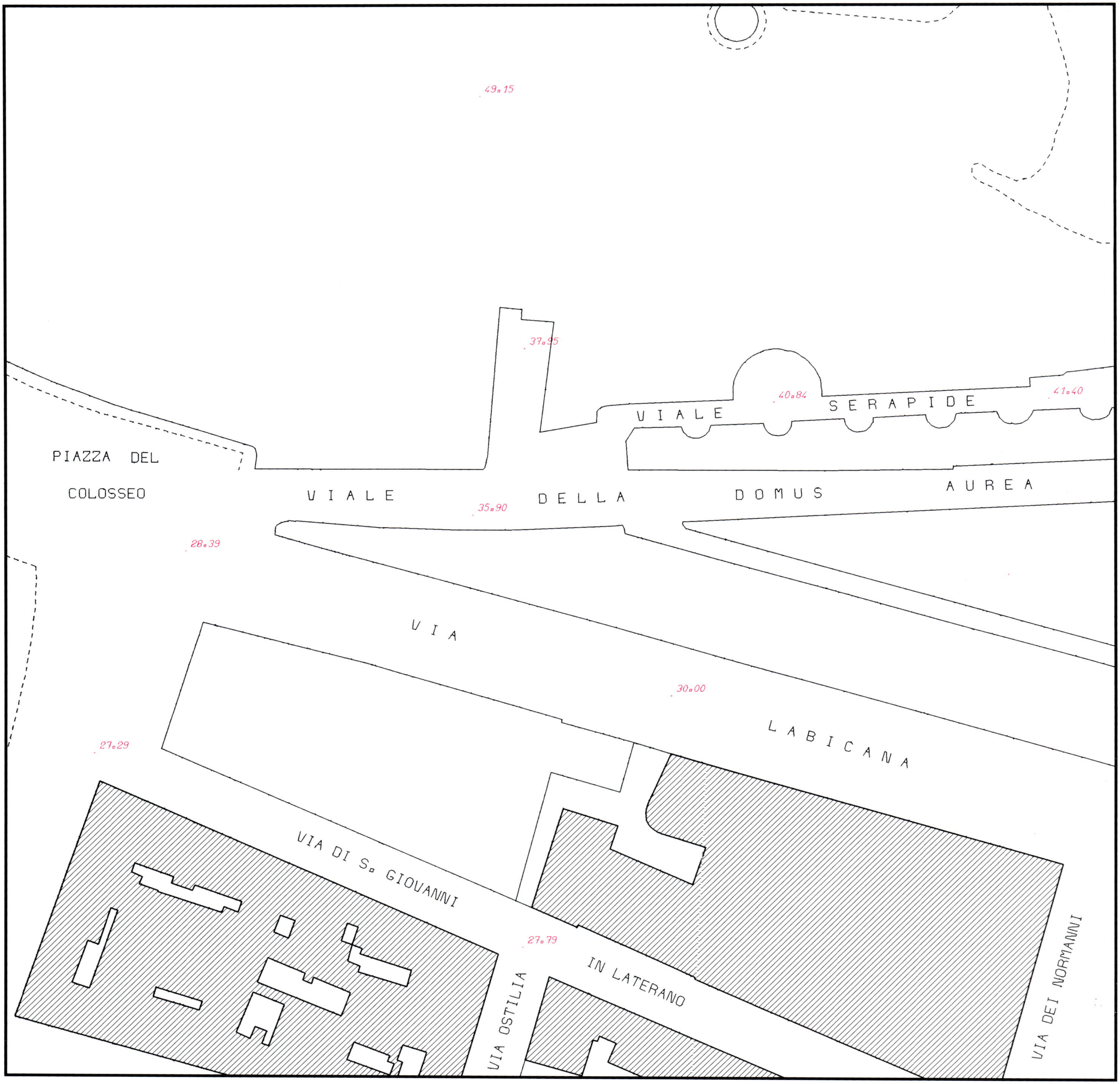

49.15

37.95

40.84 VIALE SERAPIDE 41.40

PIAZZA DEL COLOSSEO   VIALE   DELLA   35.90   DOMUS   AUREA

28.39

VIA

30.00

27.29

LABICANA

VIA DI S. GIOVANNI

27.79   IN LATERANO

VIA OSTILIA

VIA DEI NORMANNI

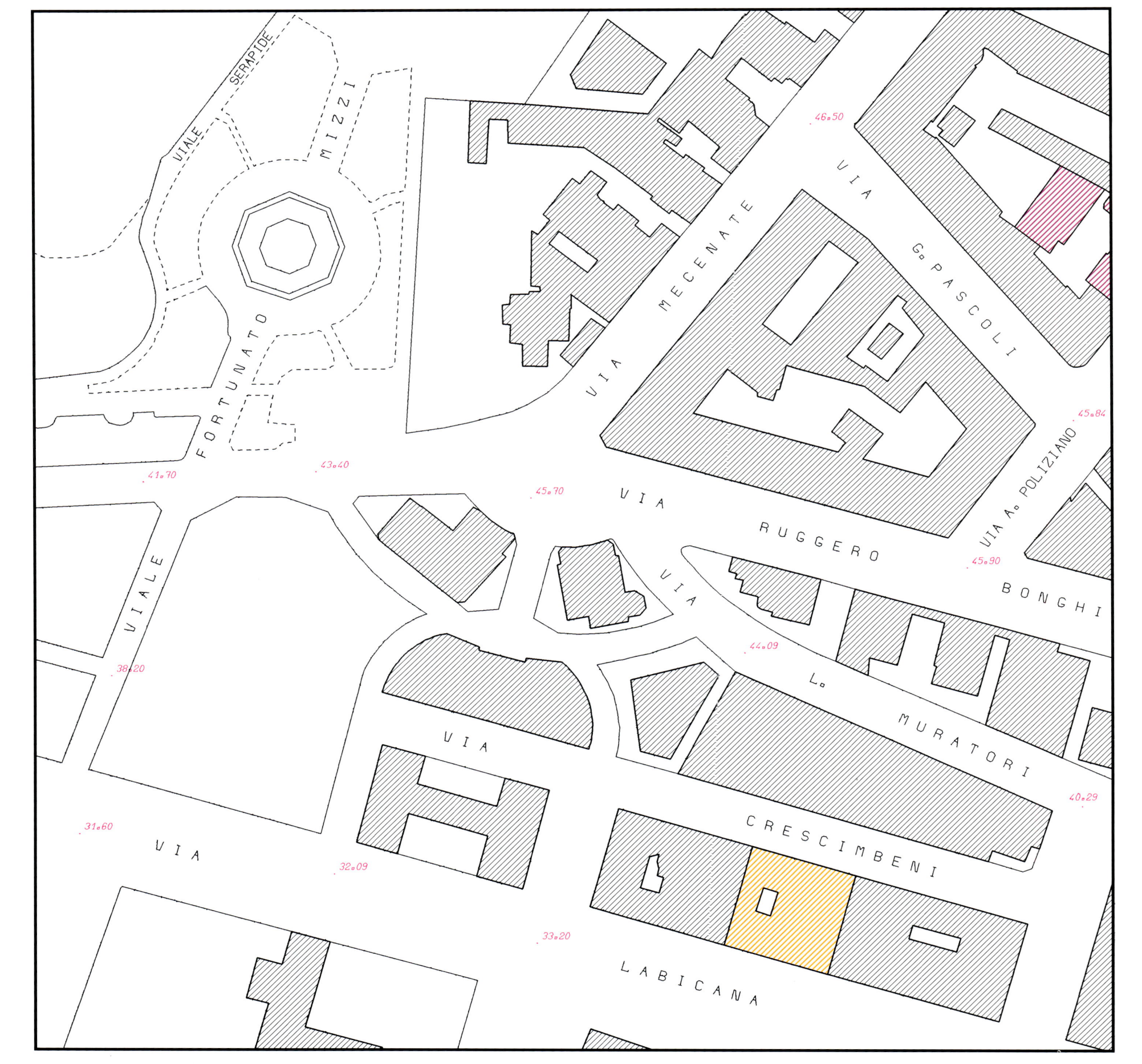

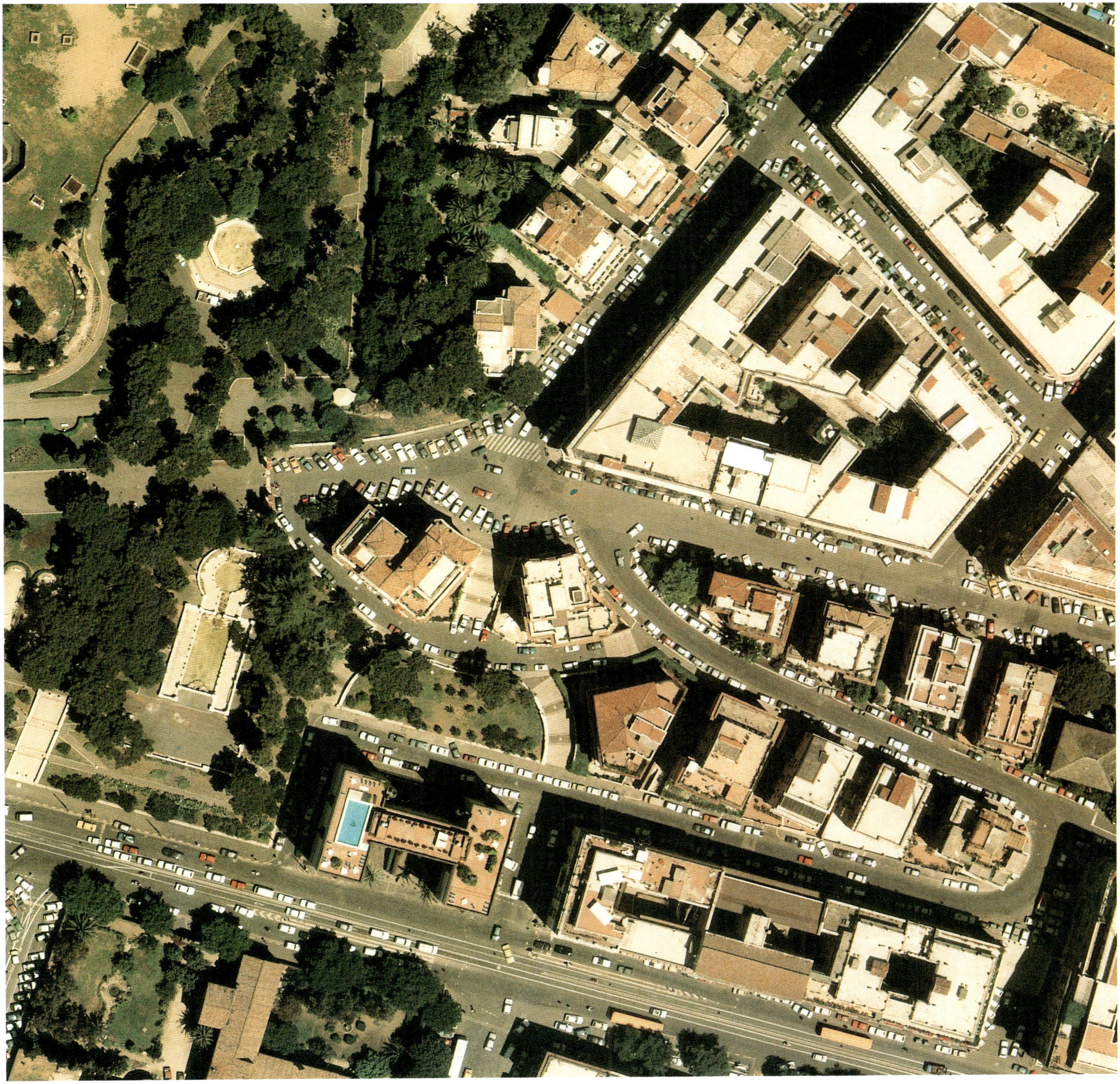

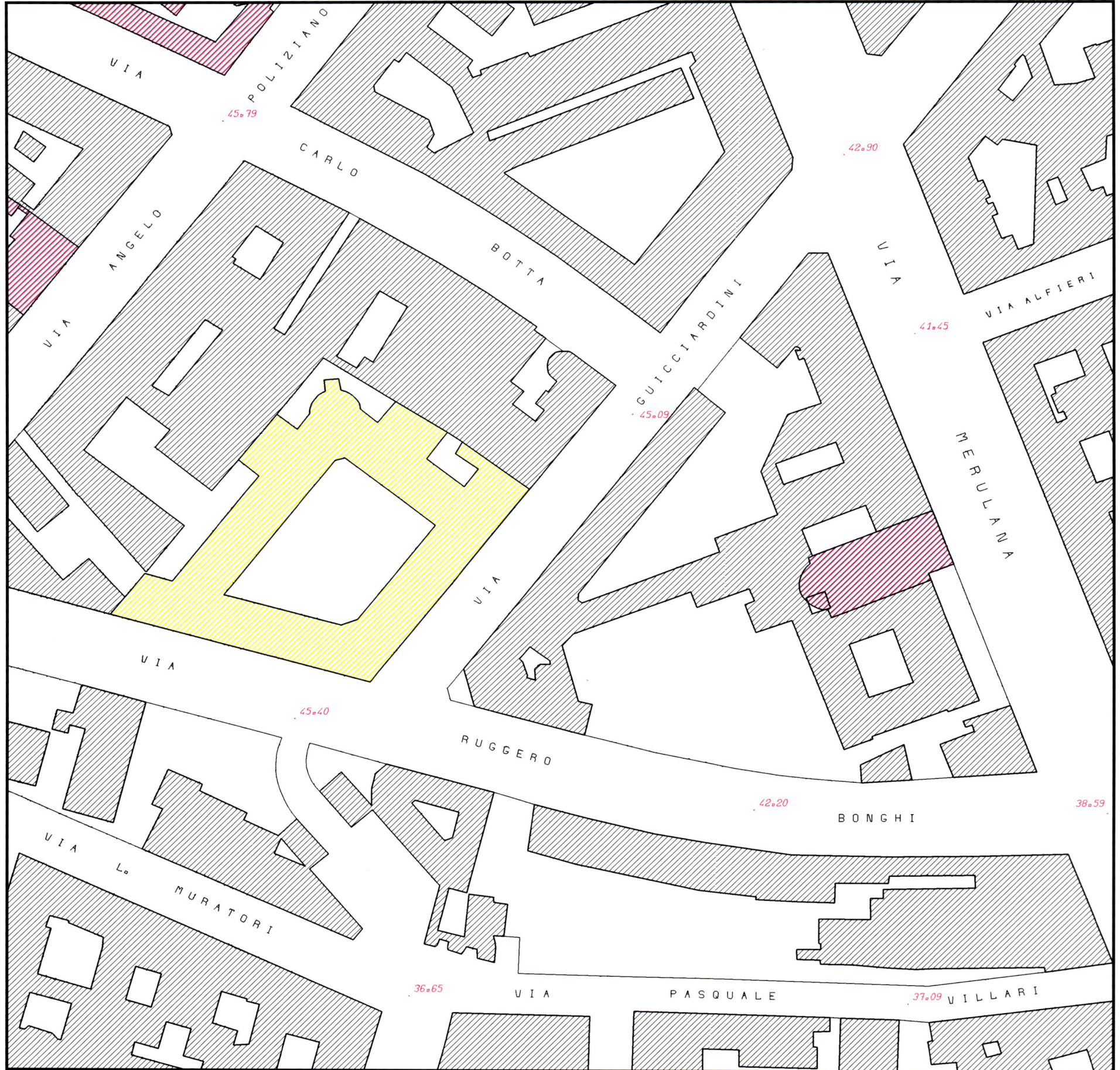

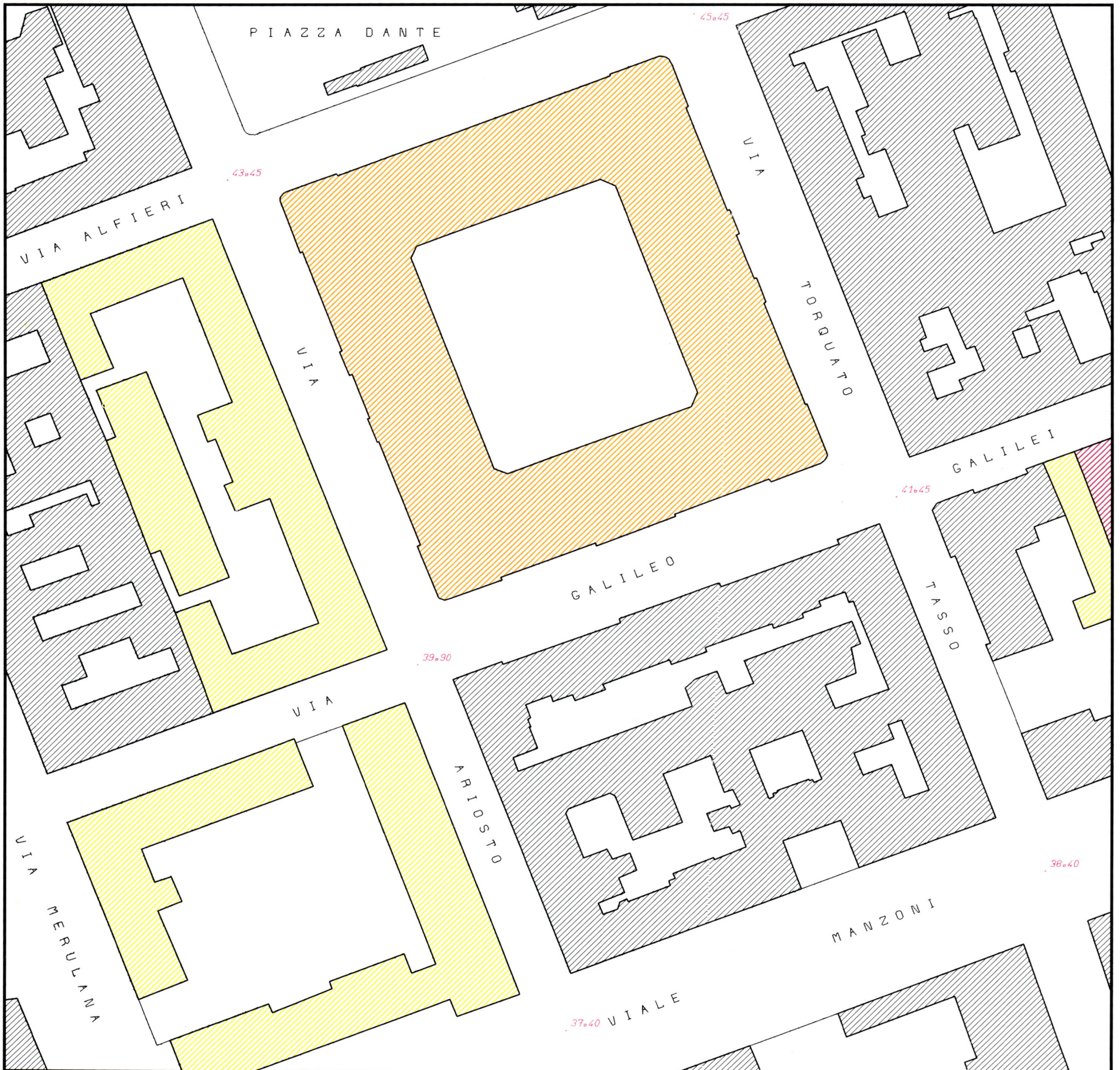

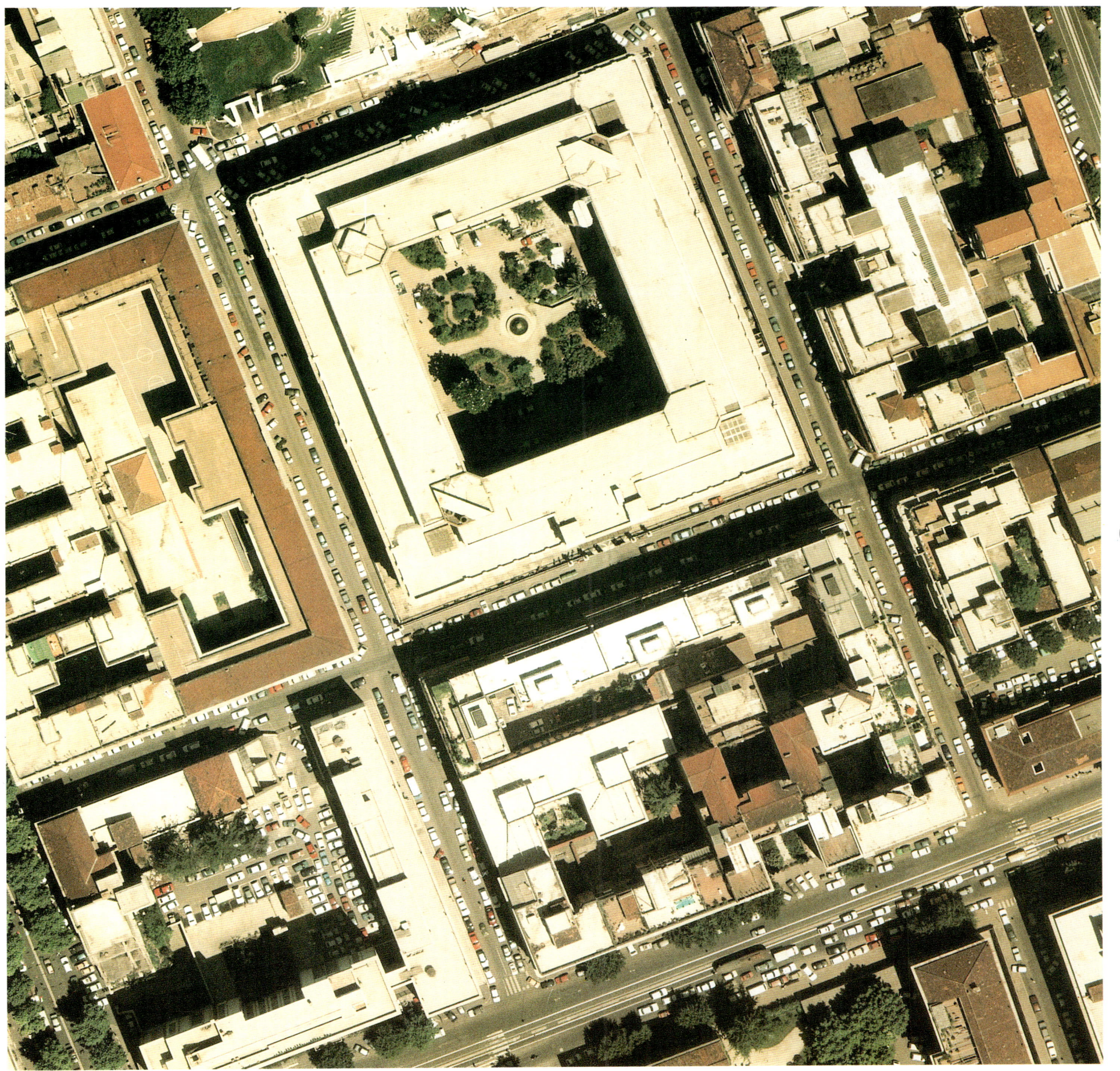

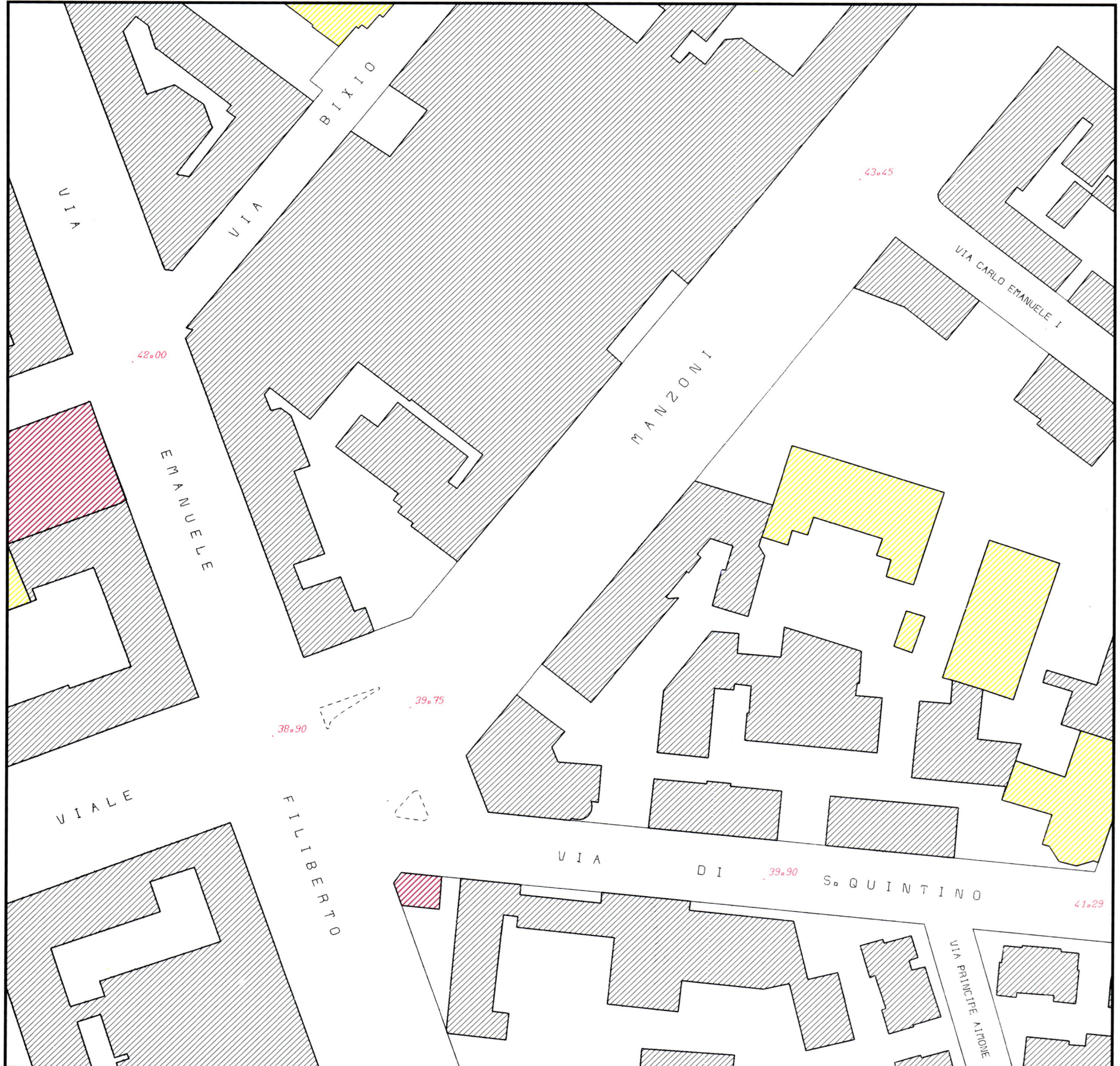

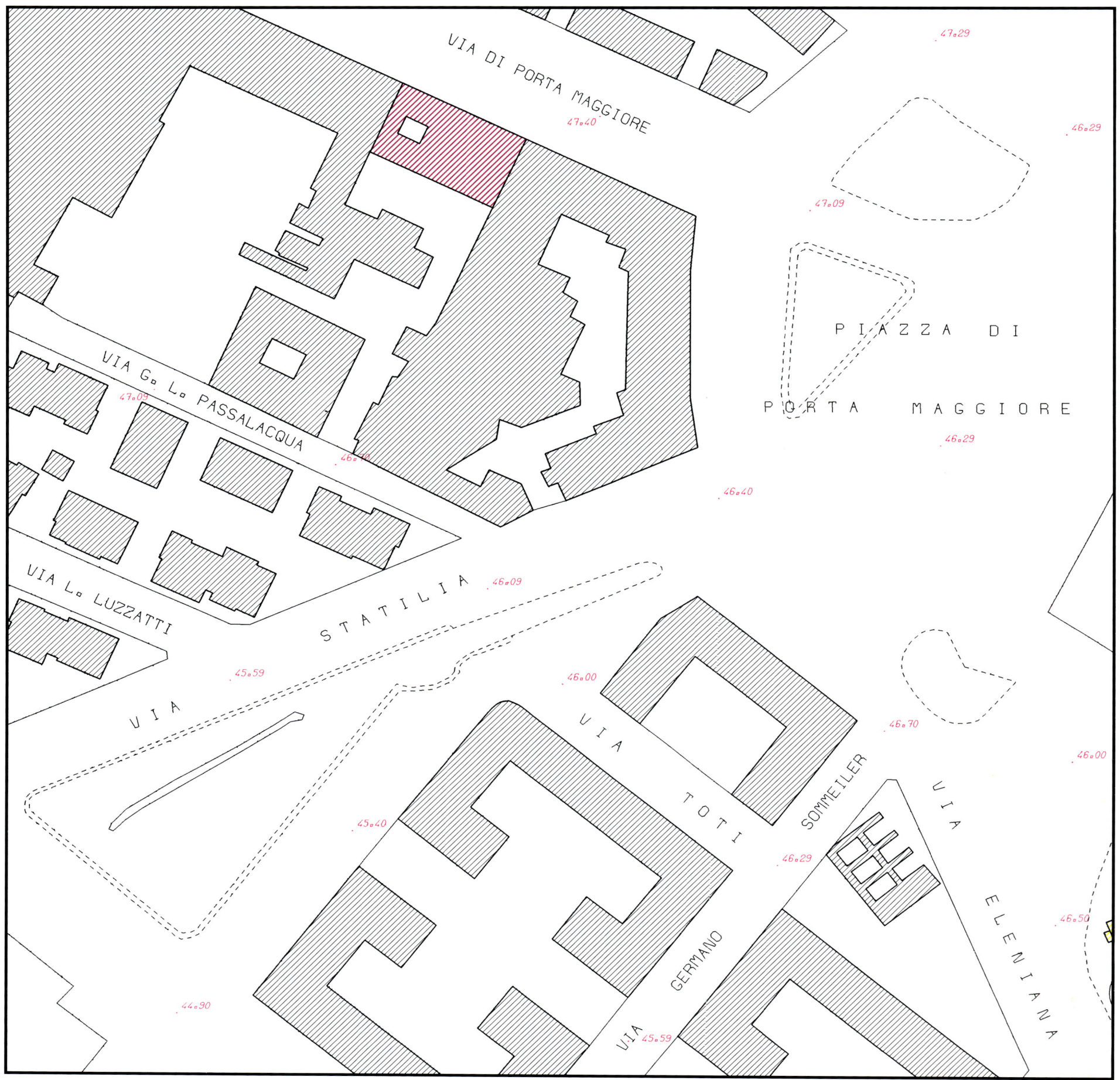

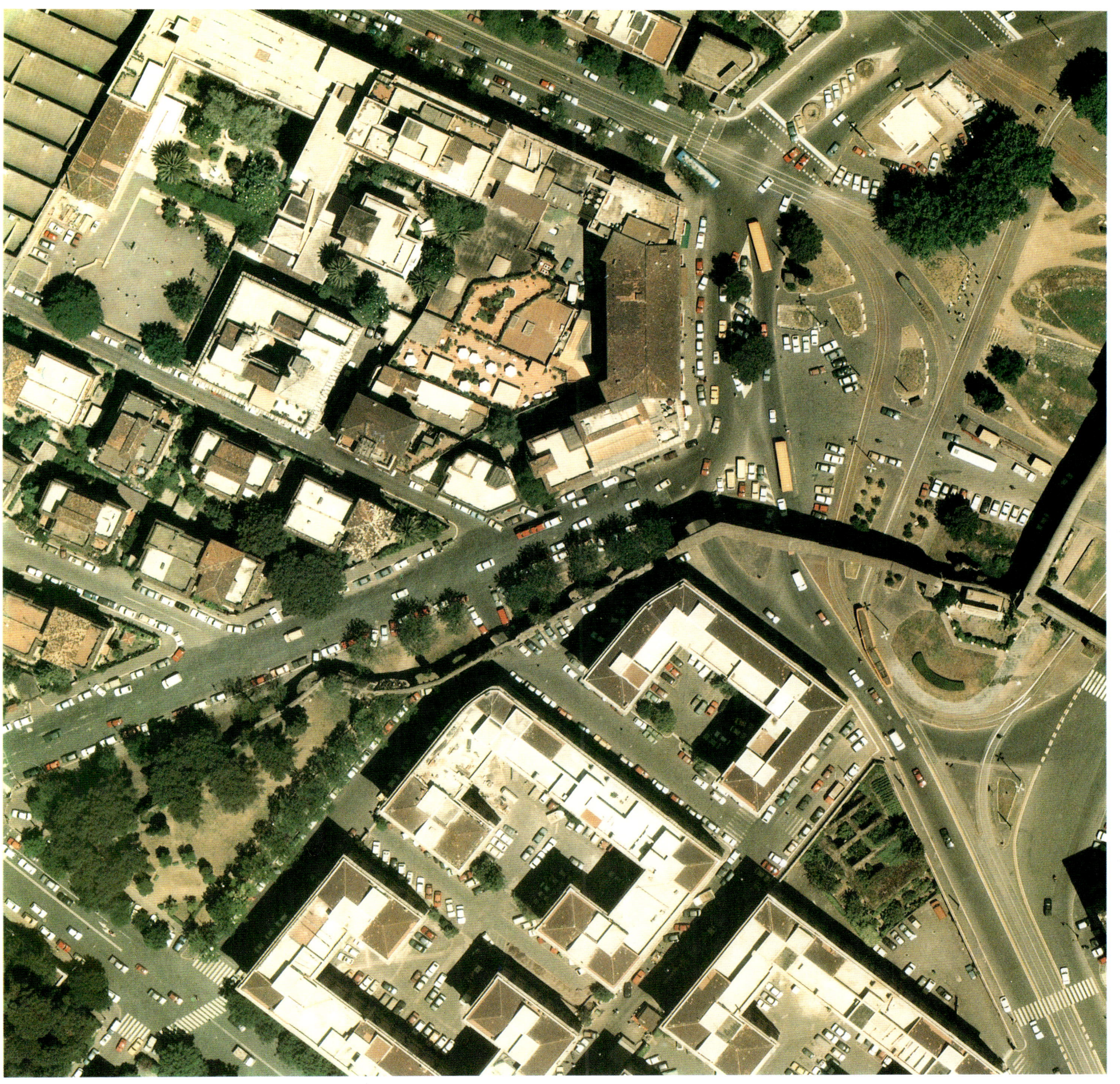

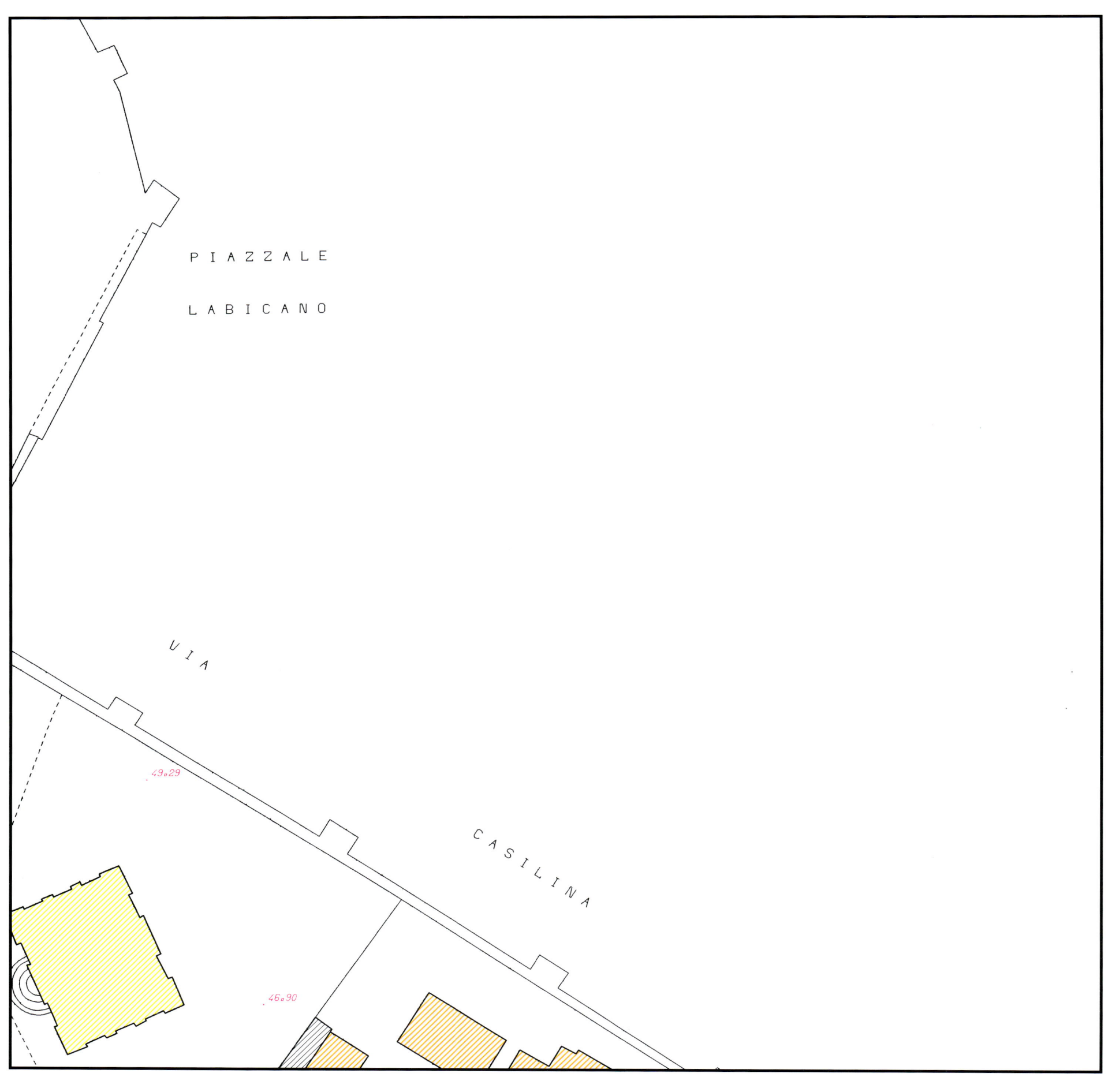

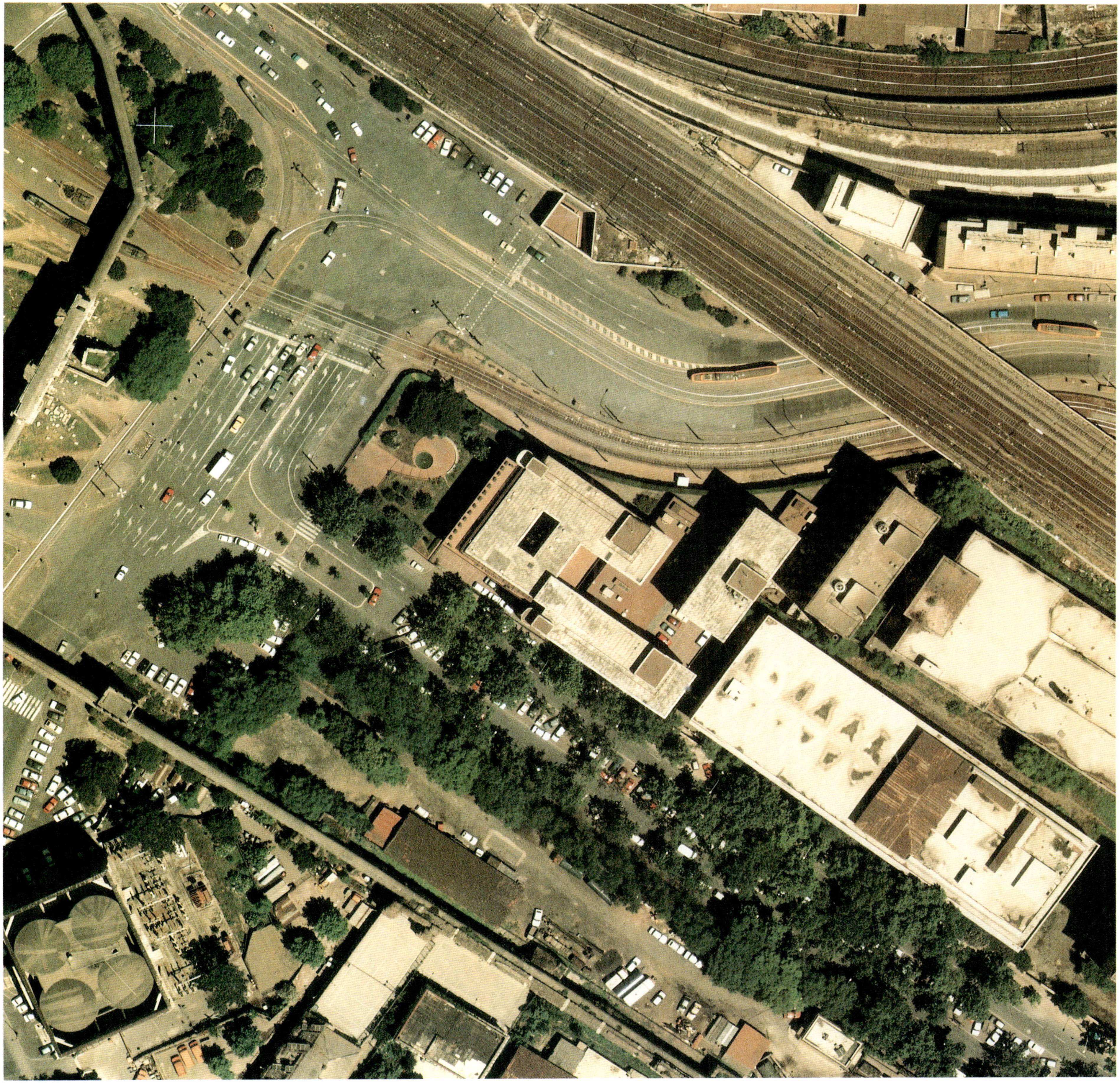

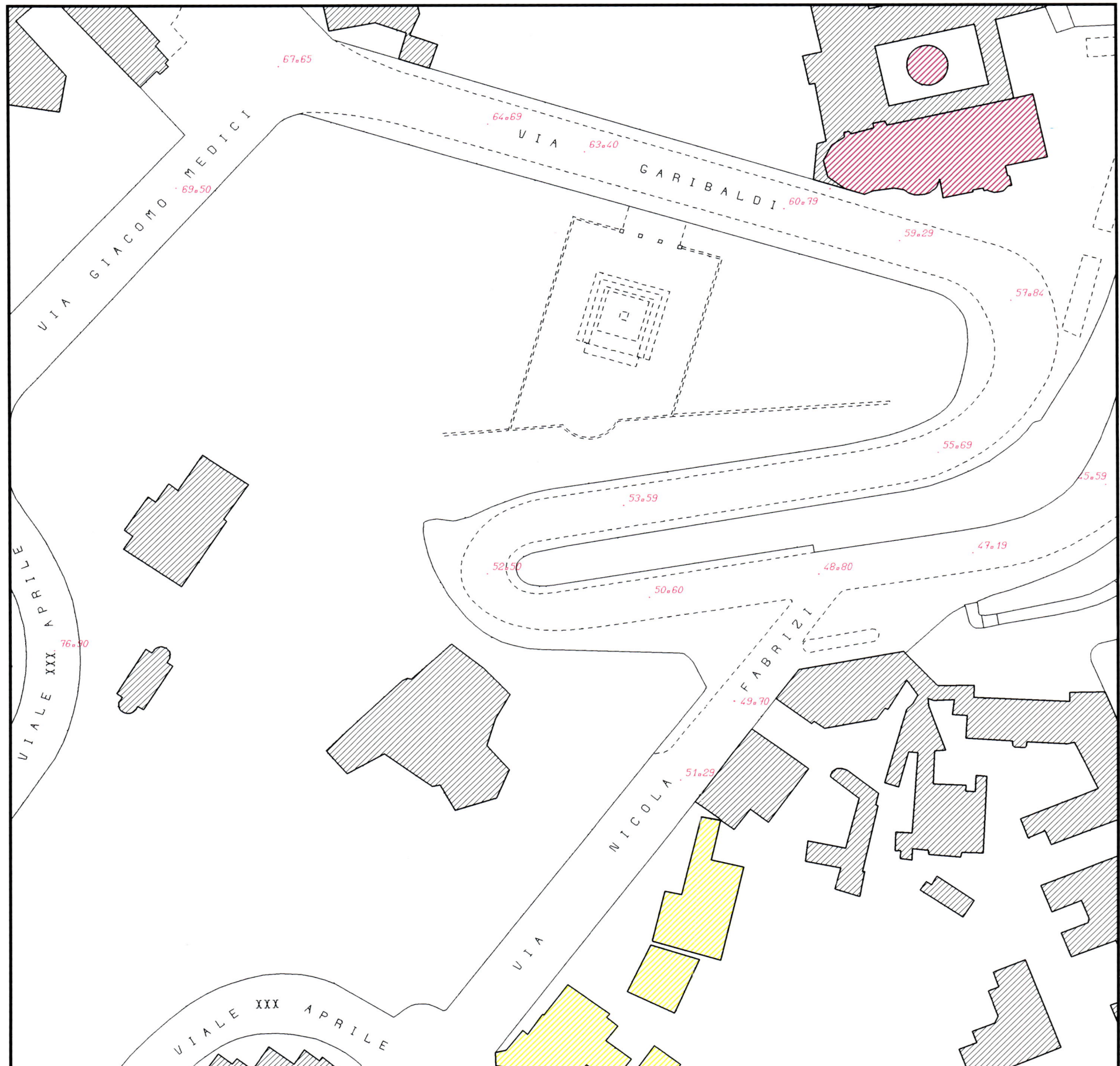

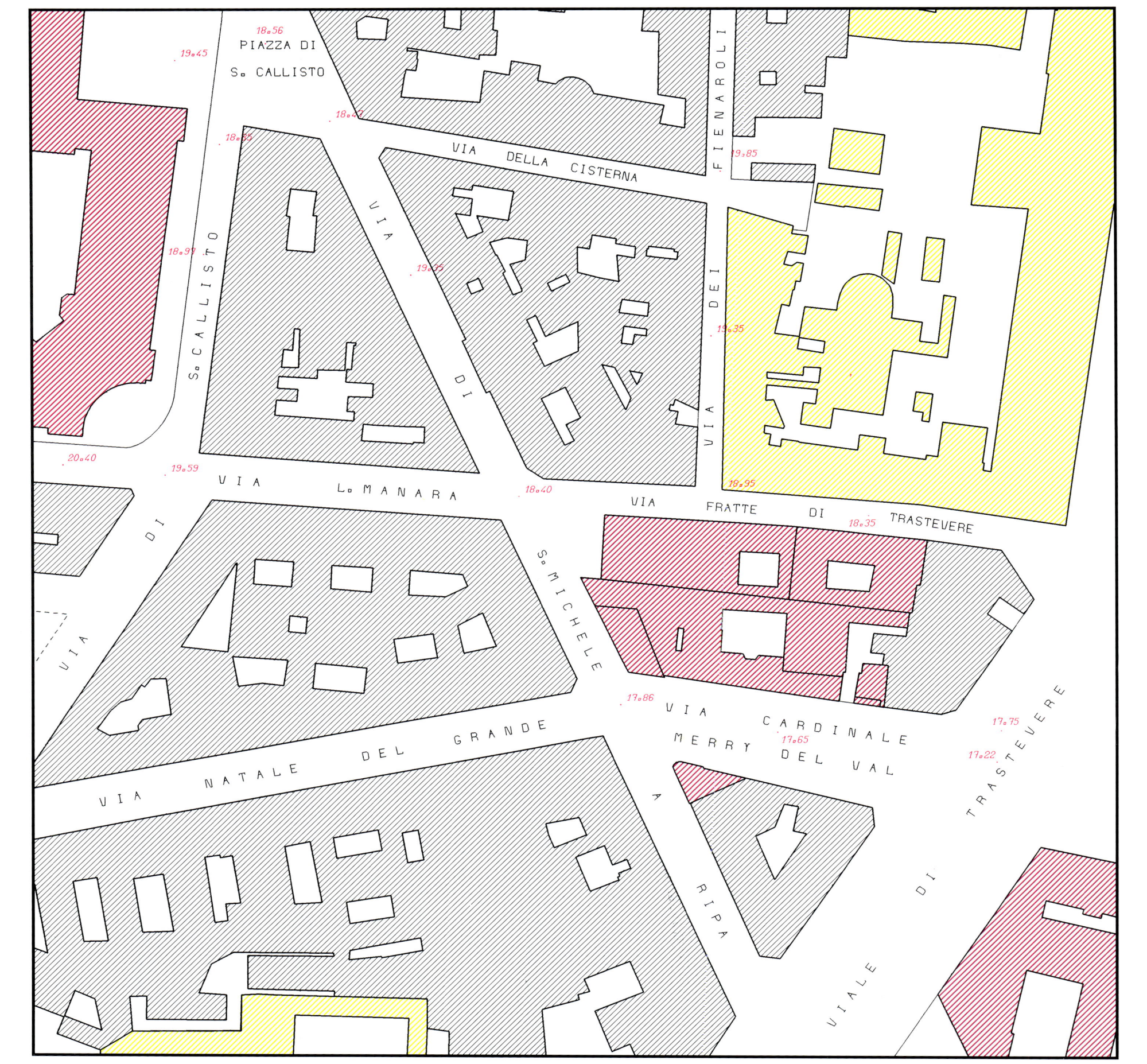

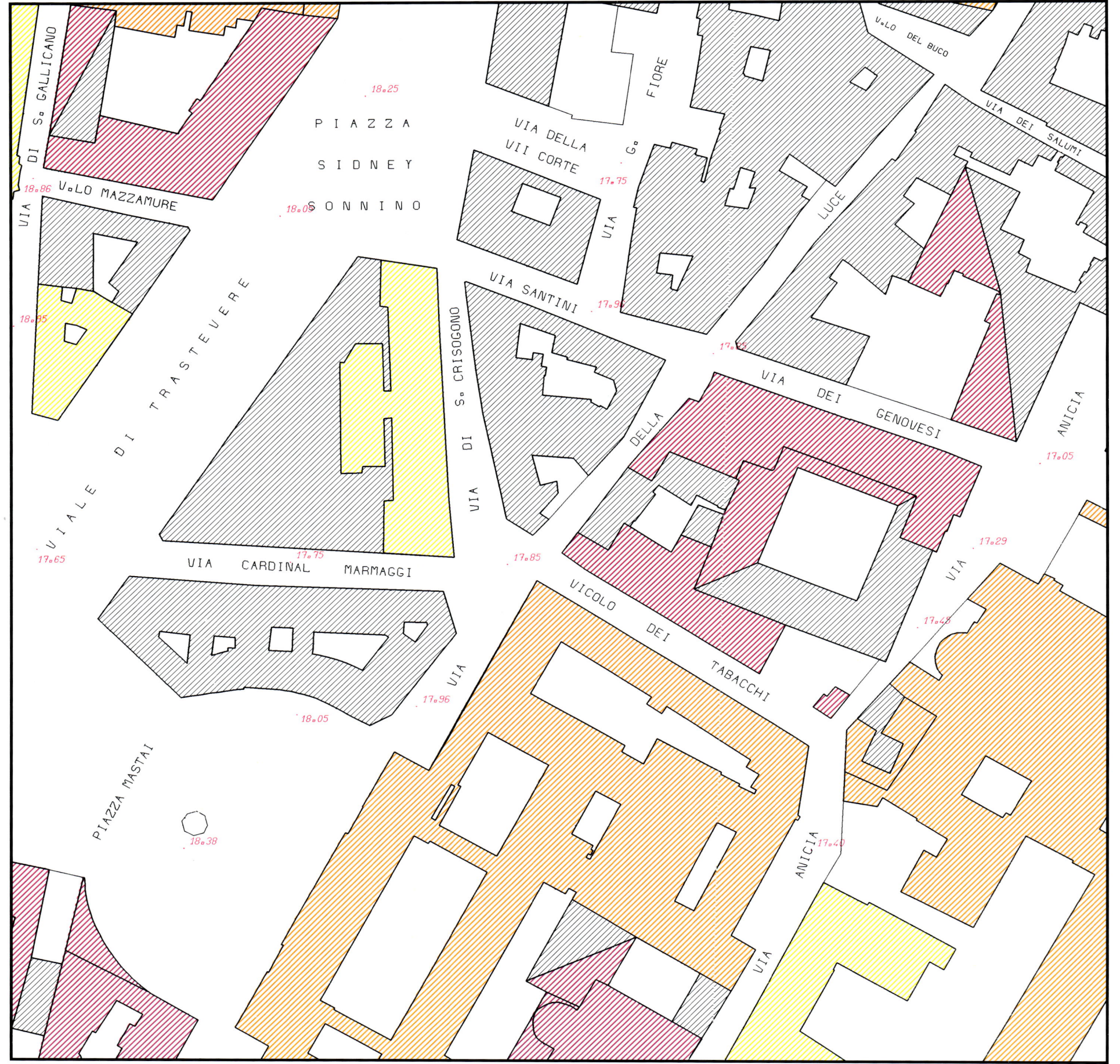

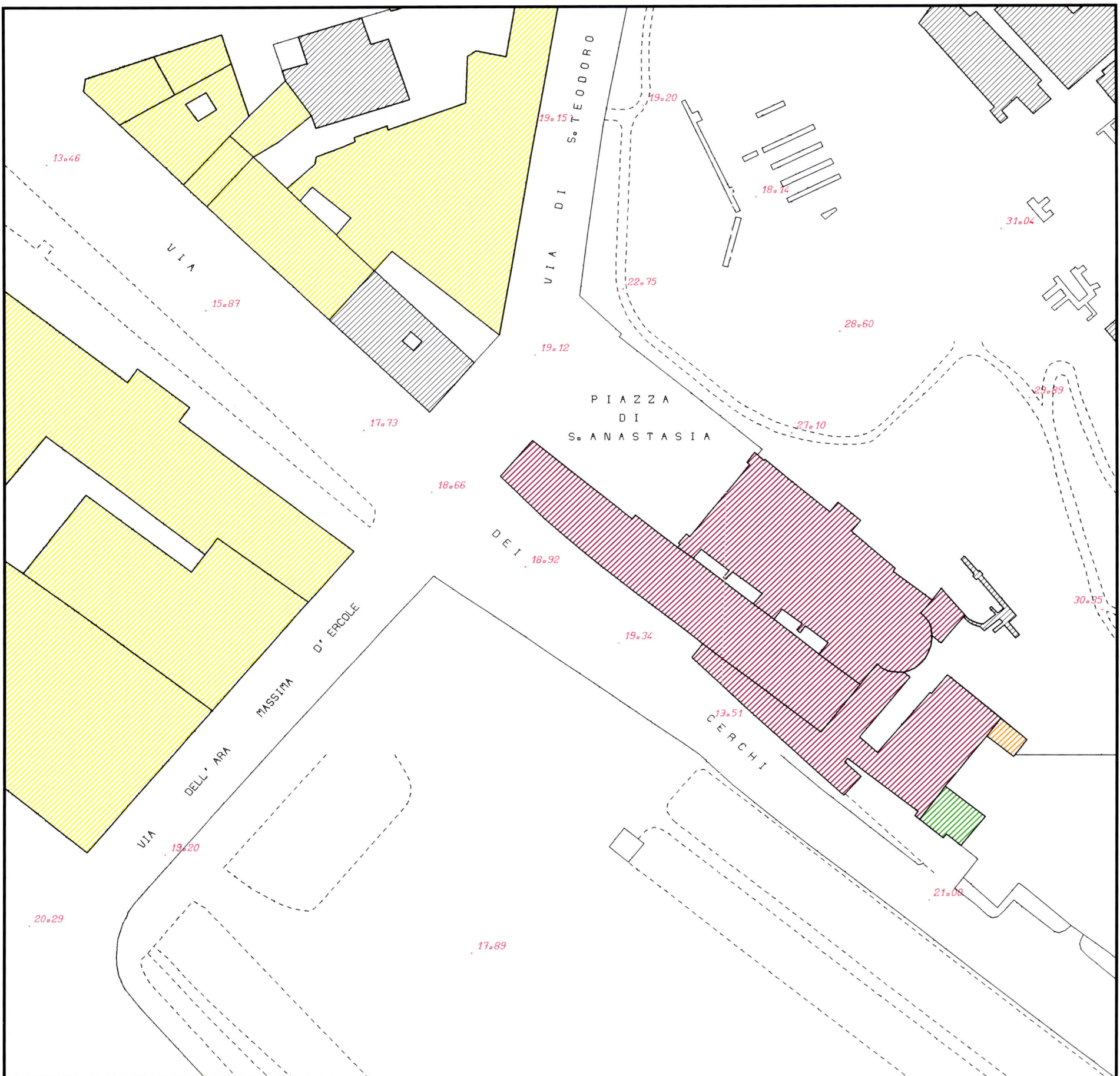

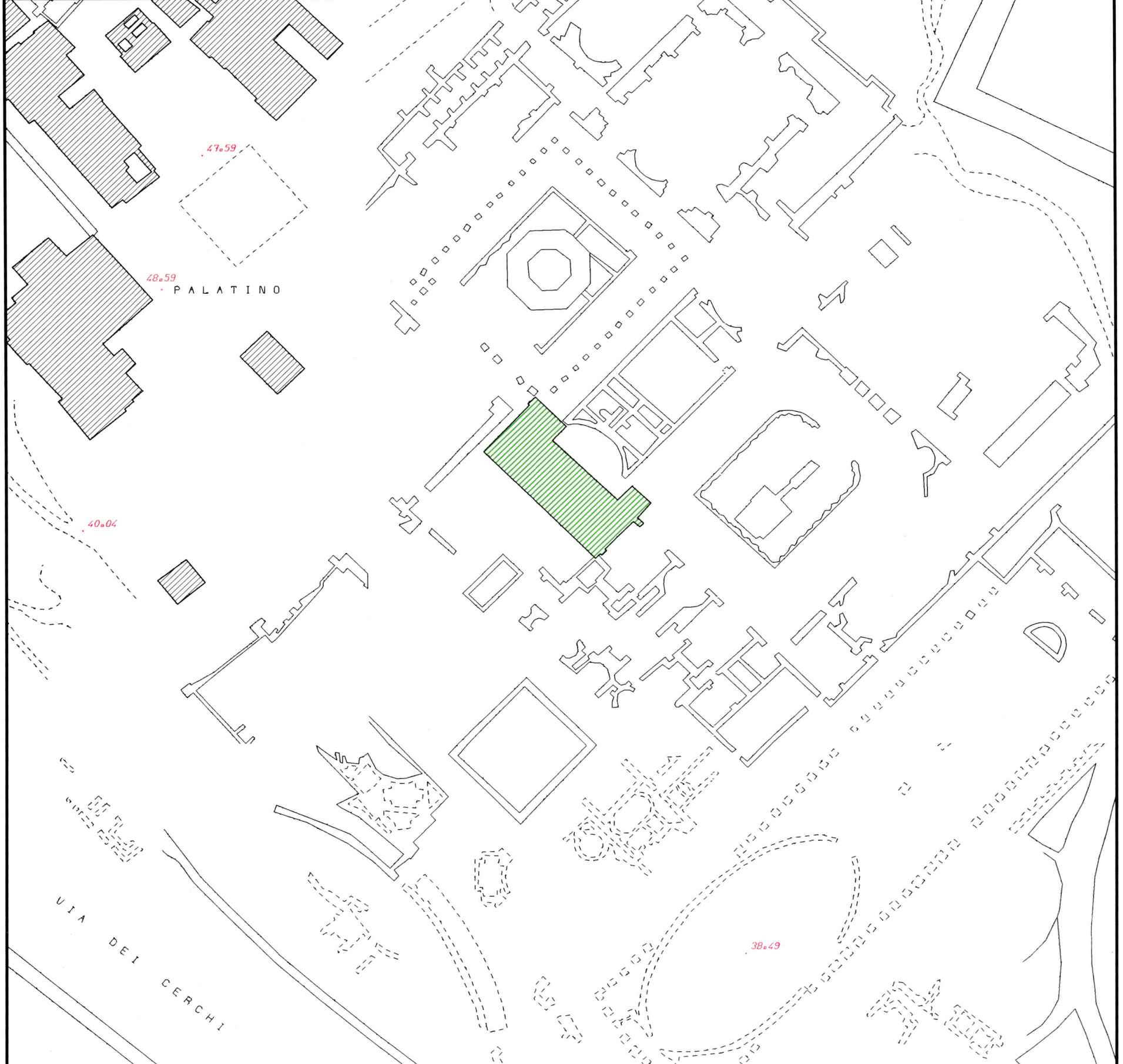

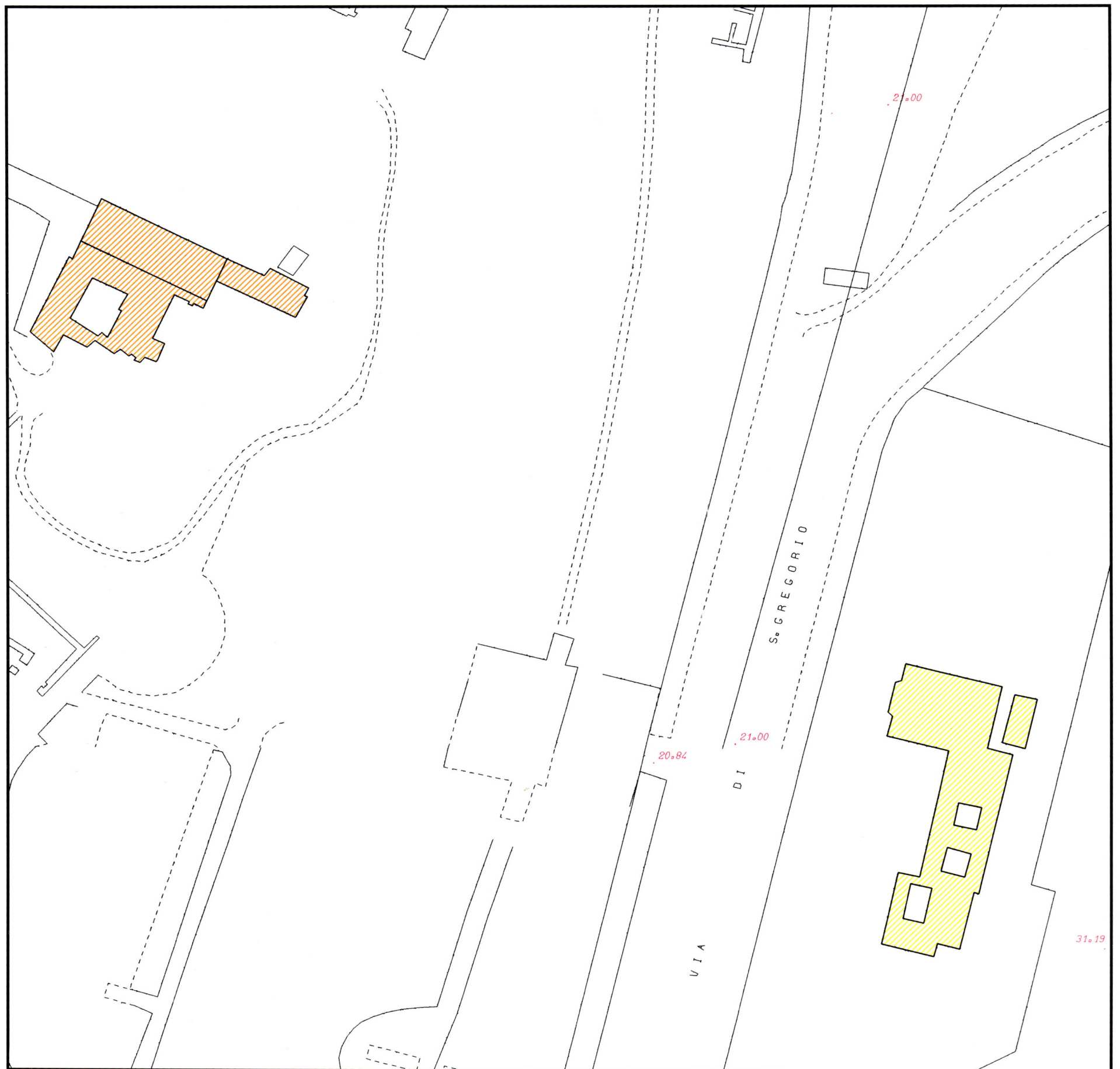

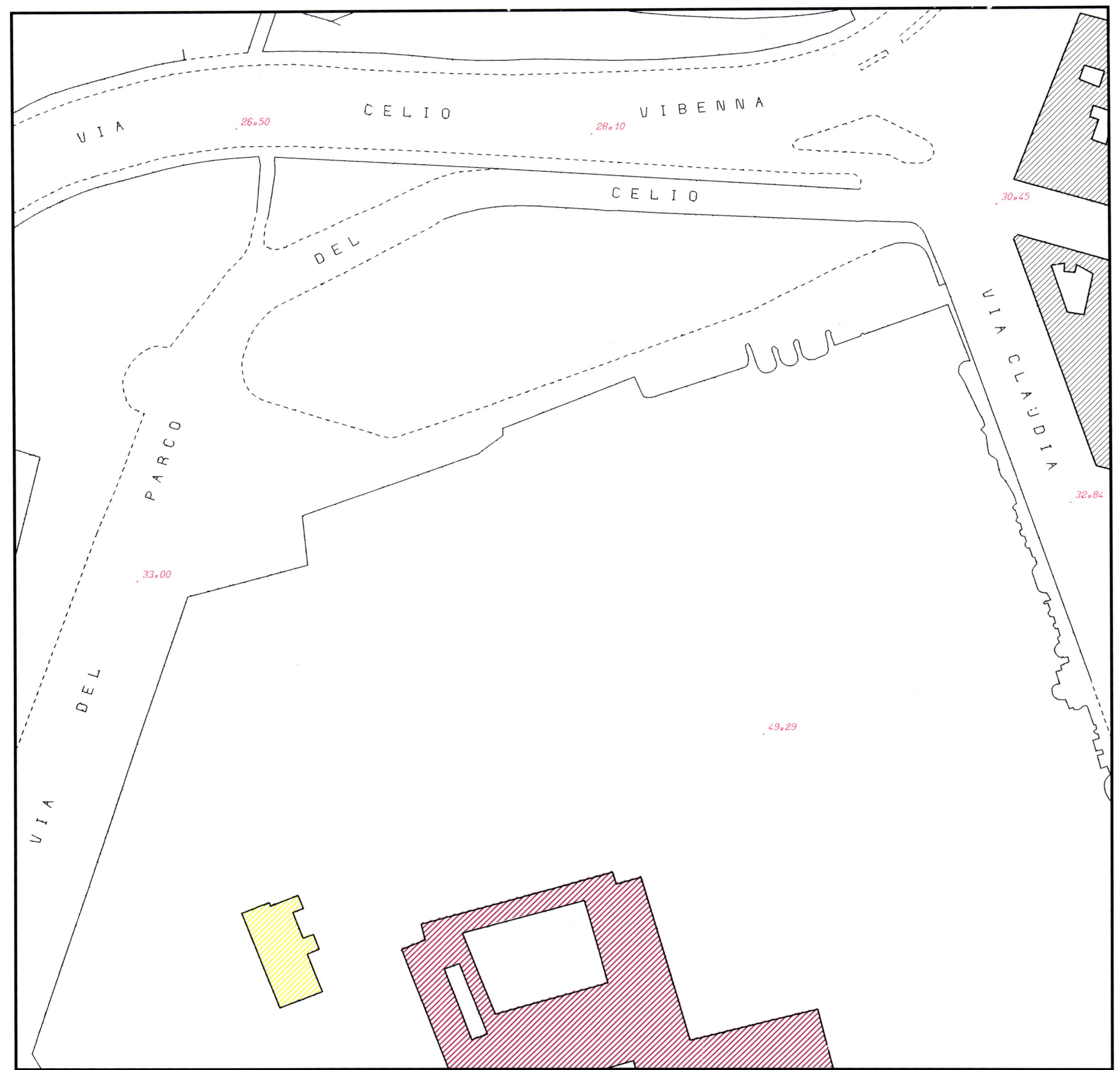

184

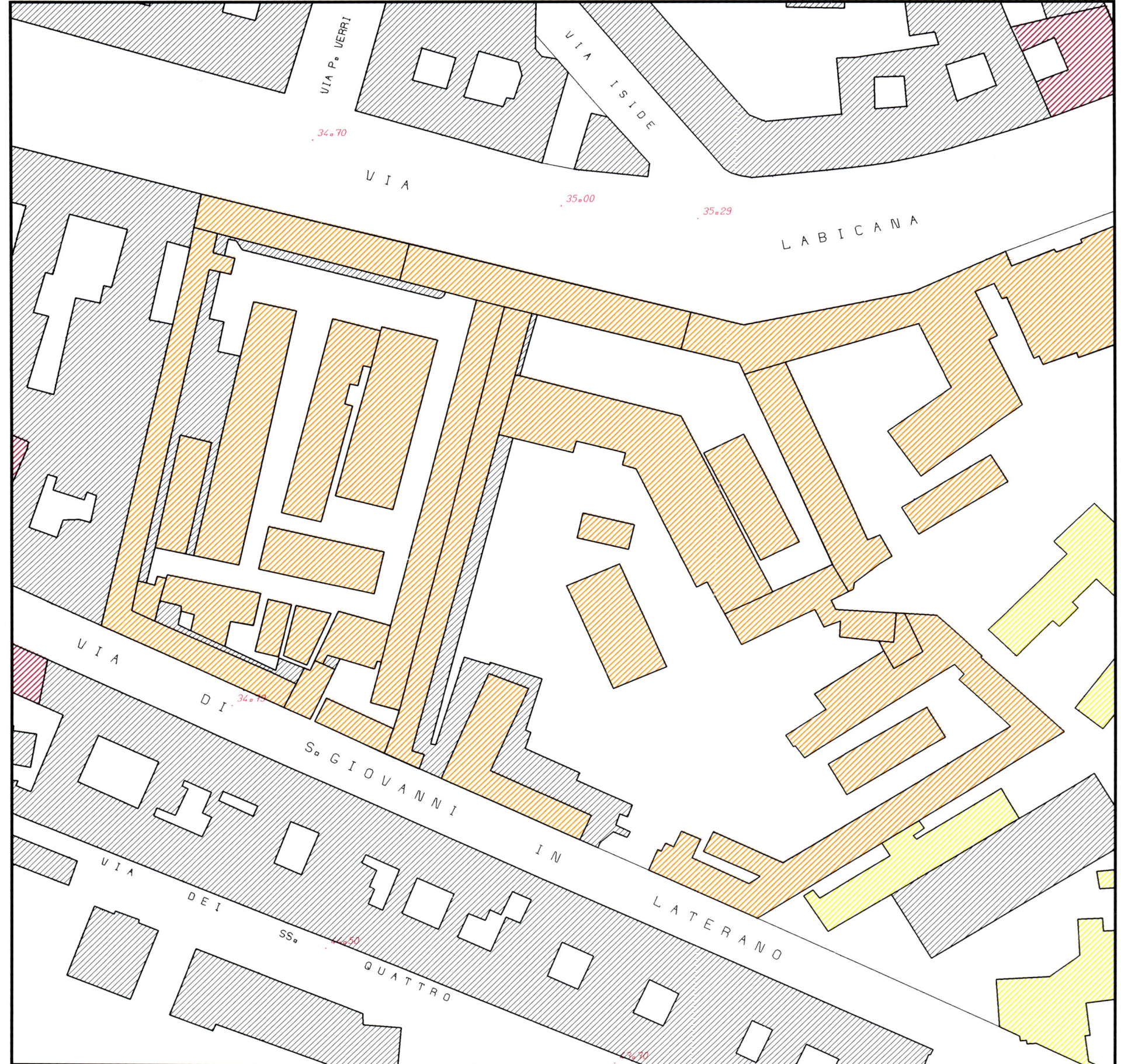

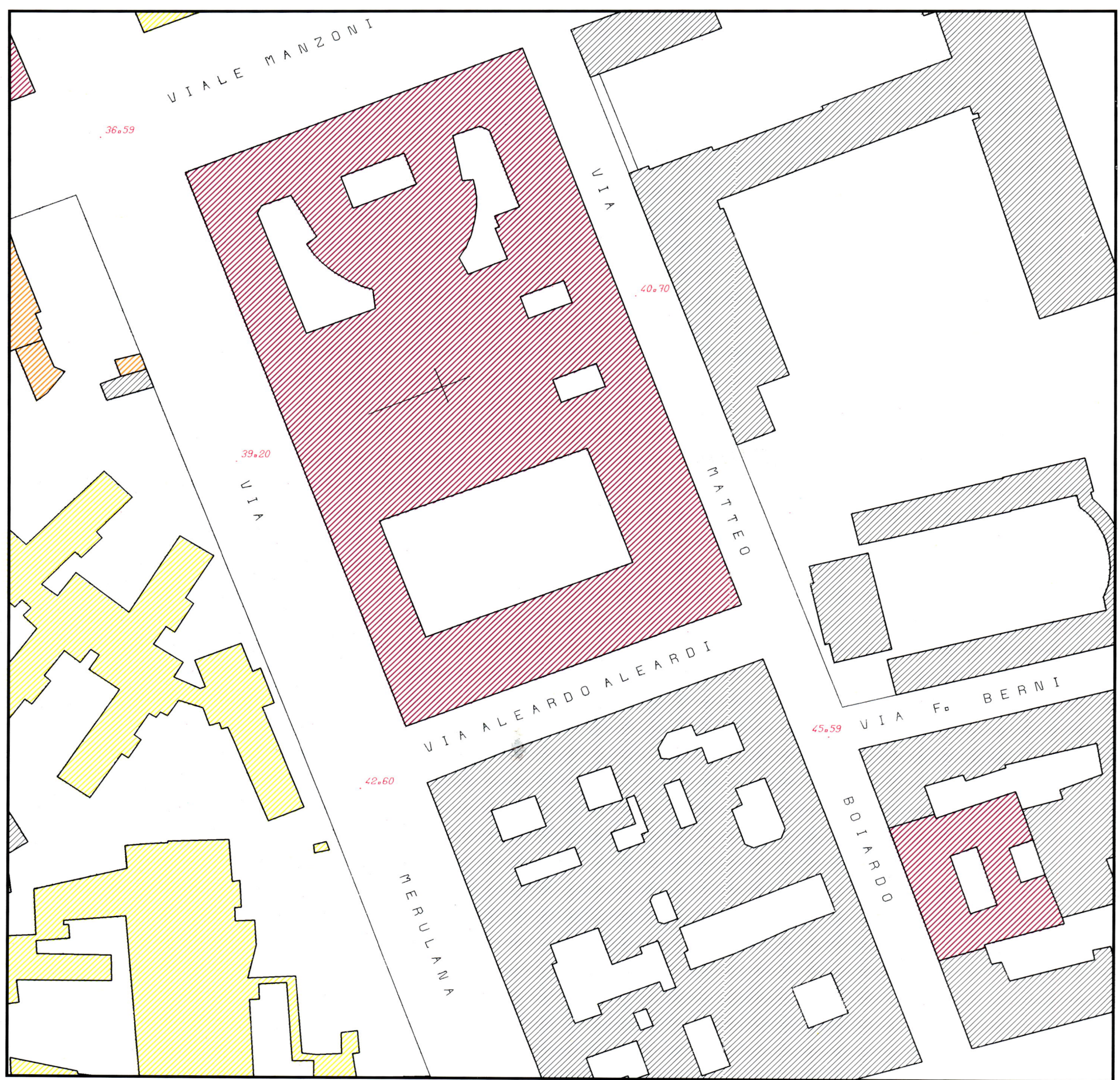

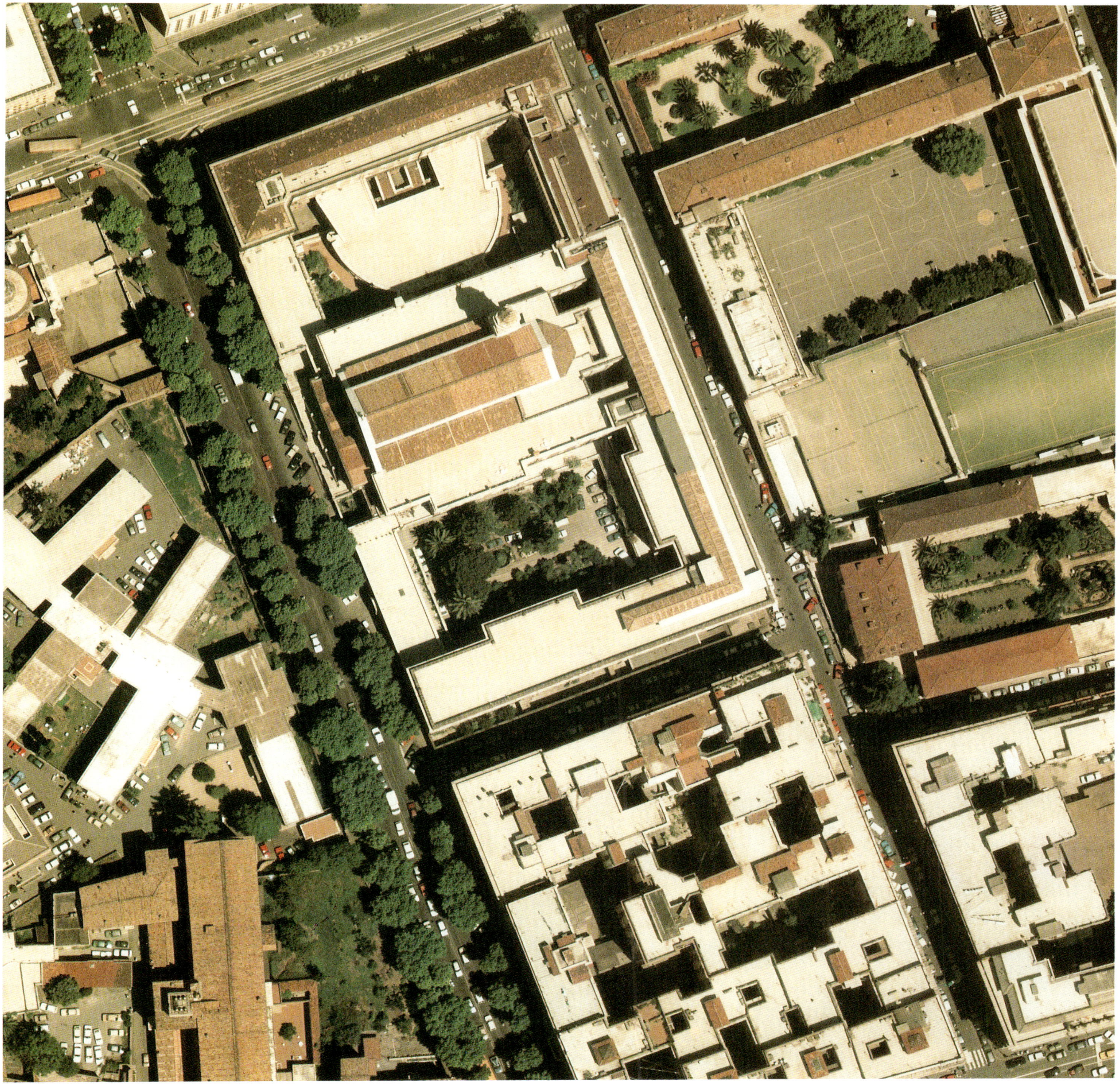

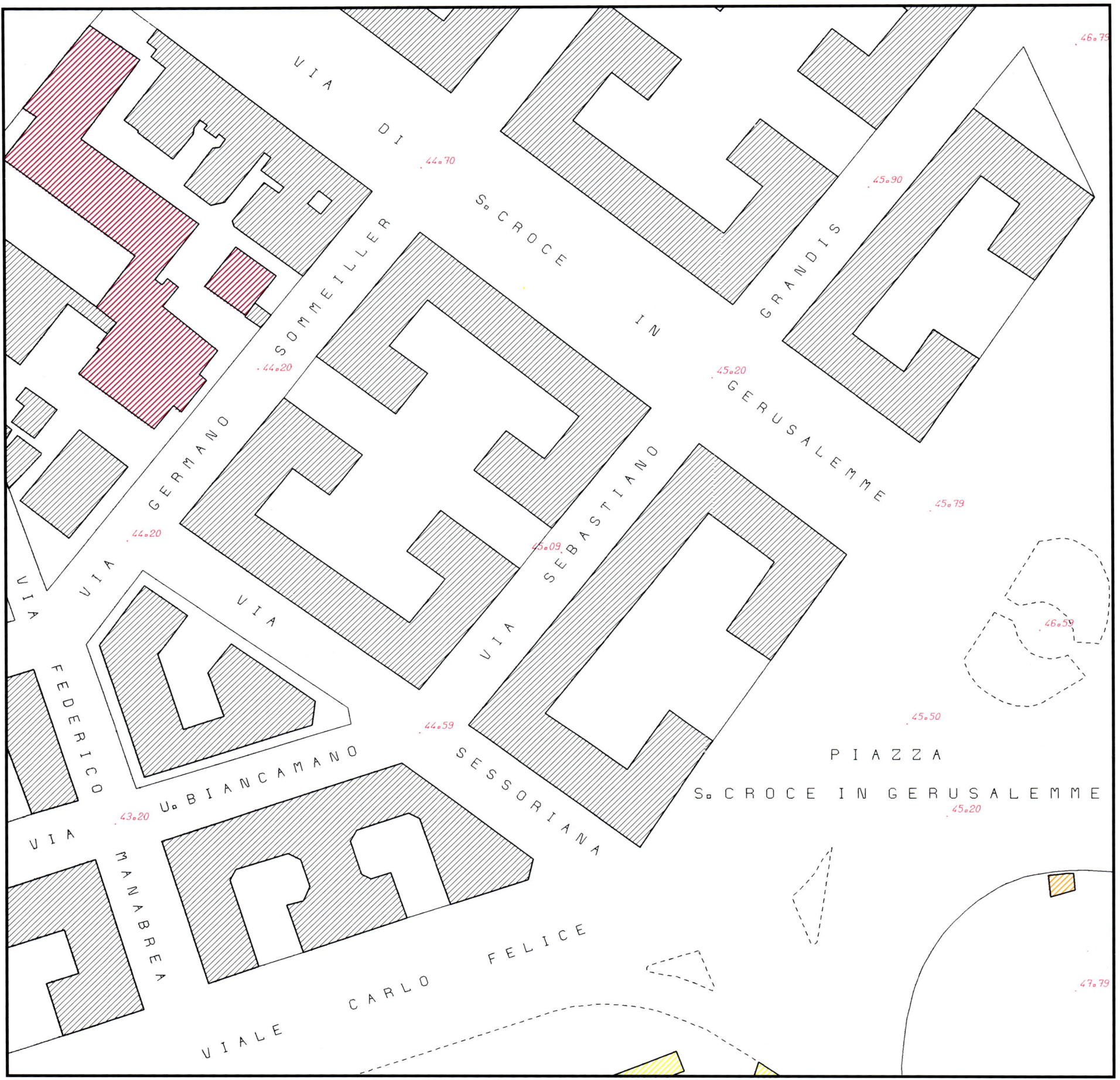

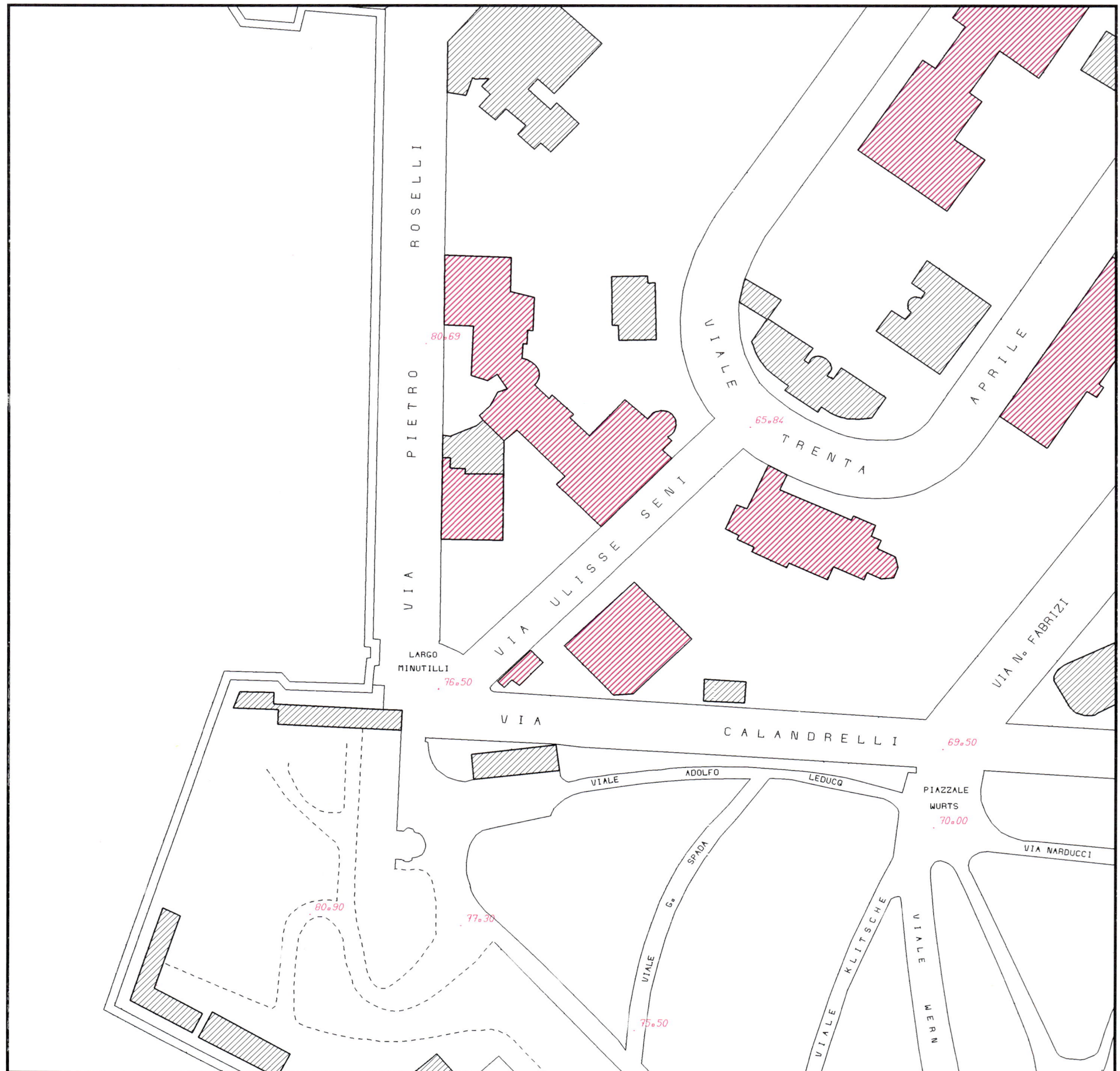

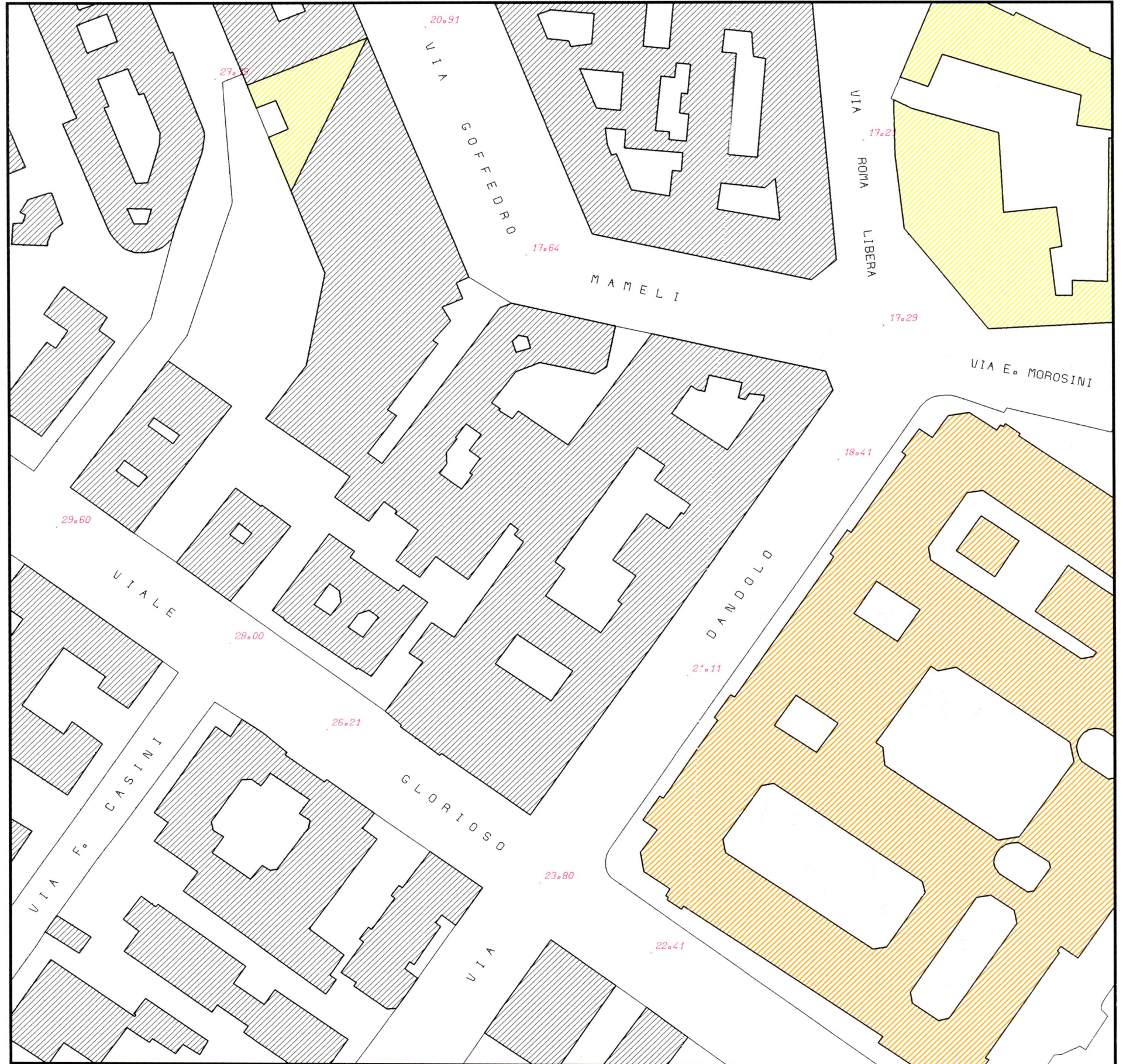

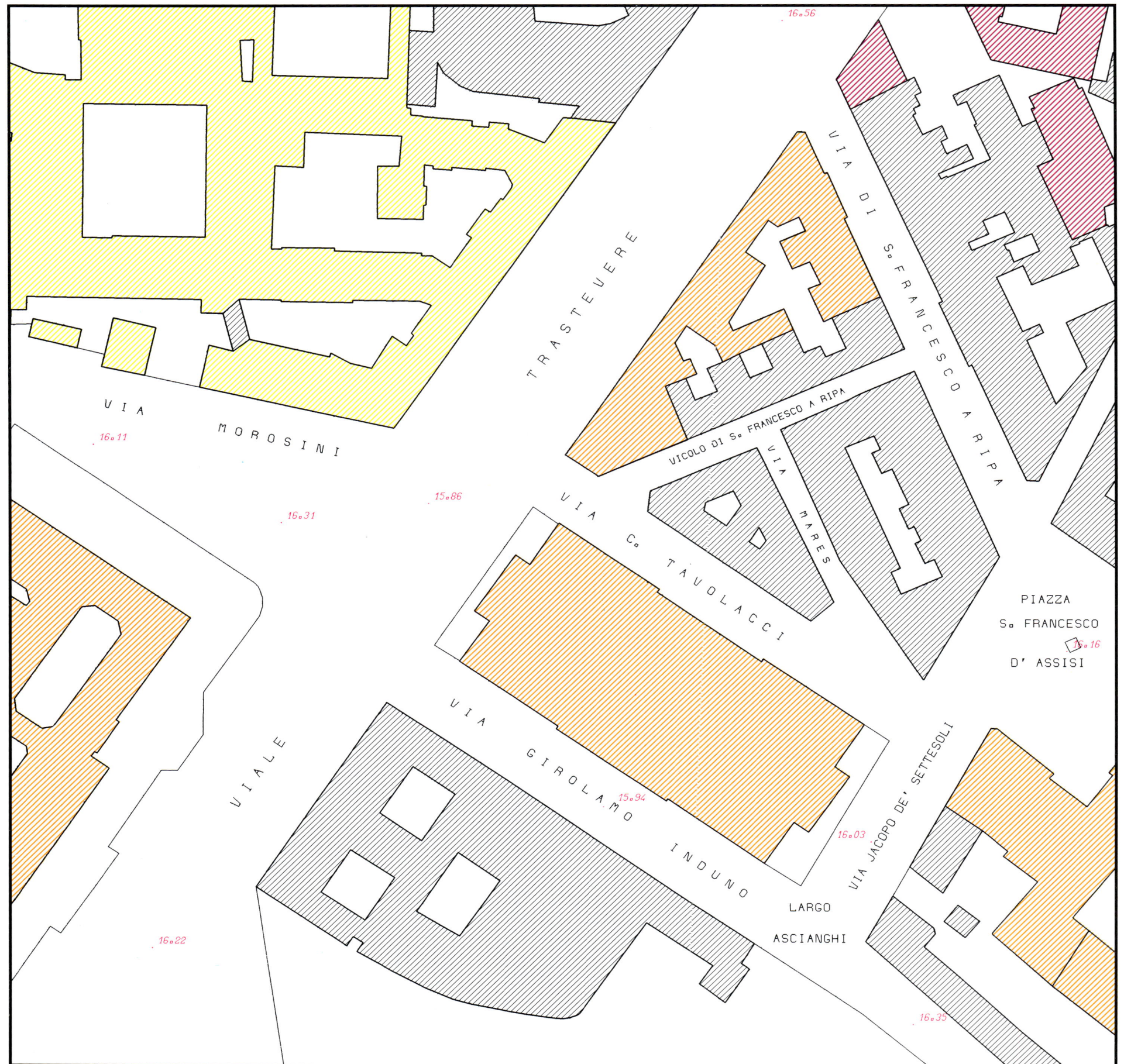

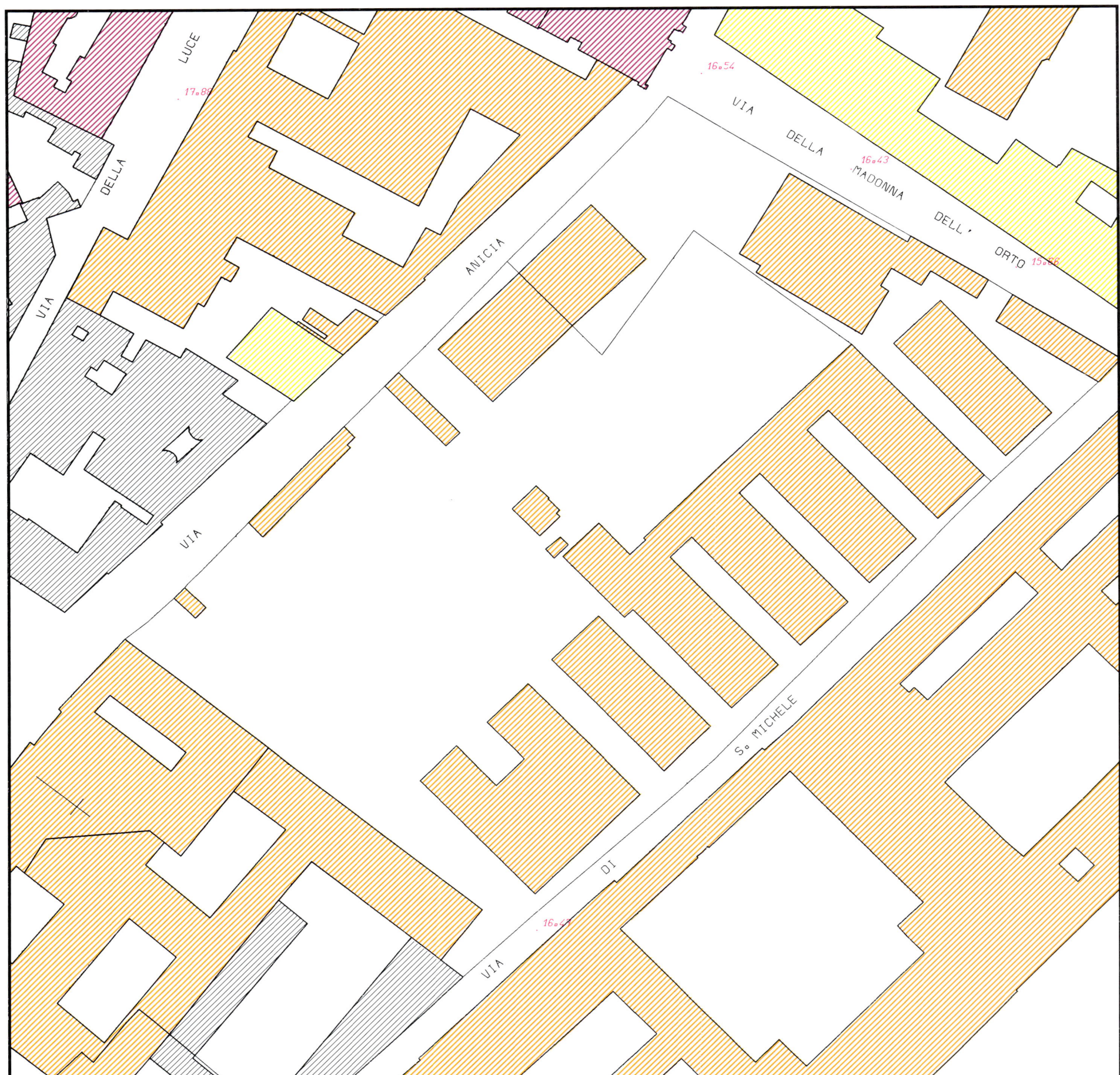

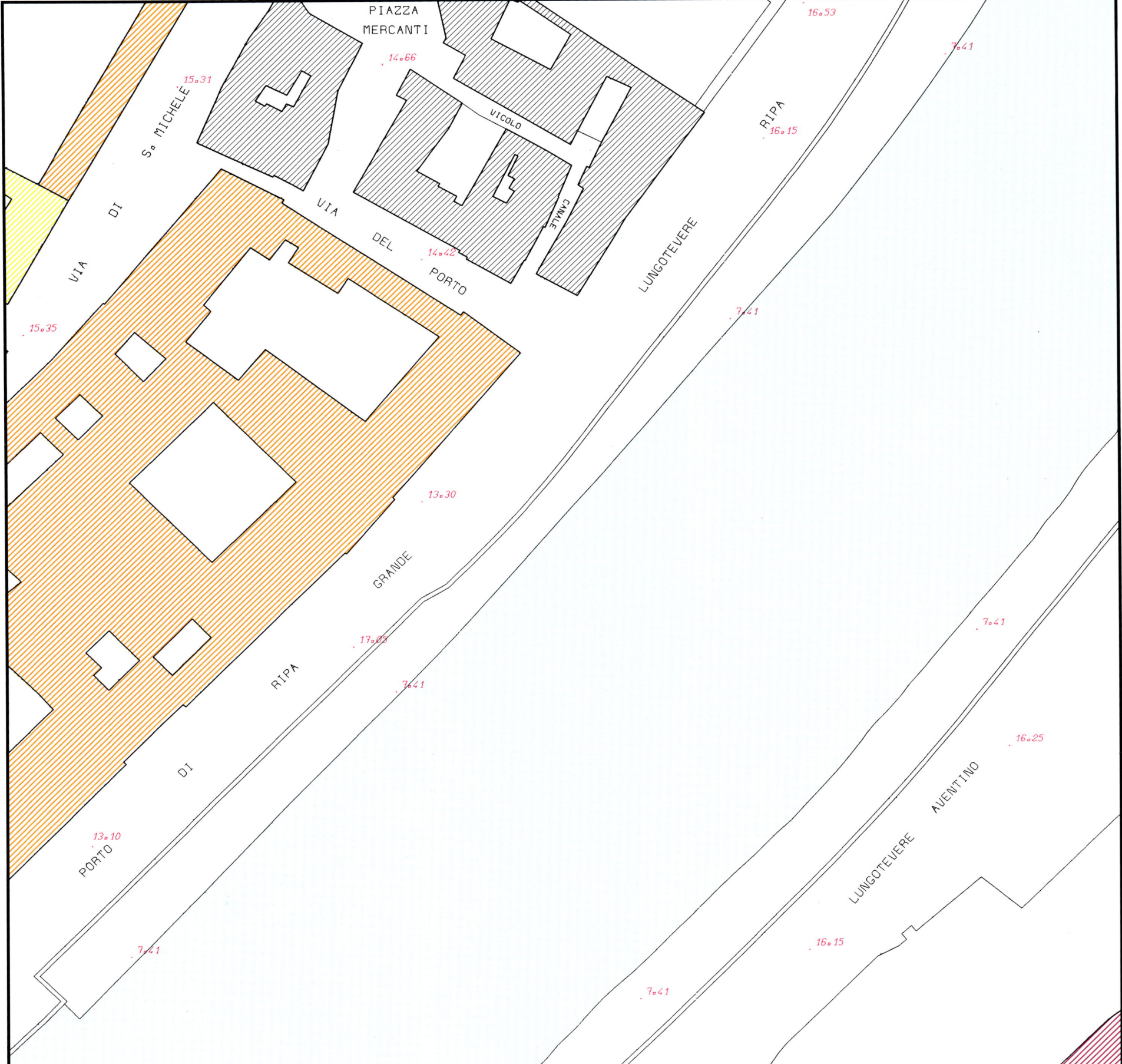

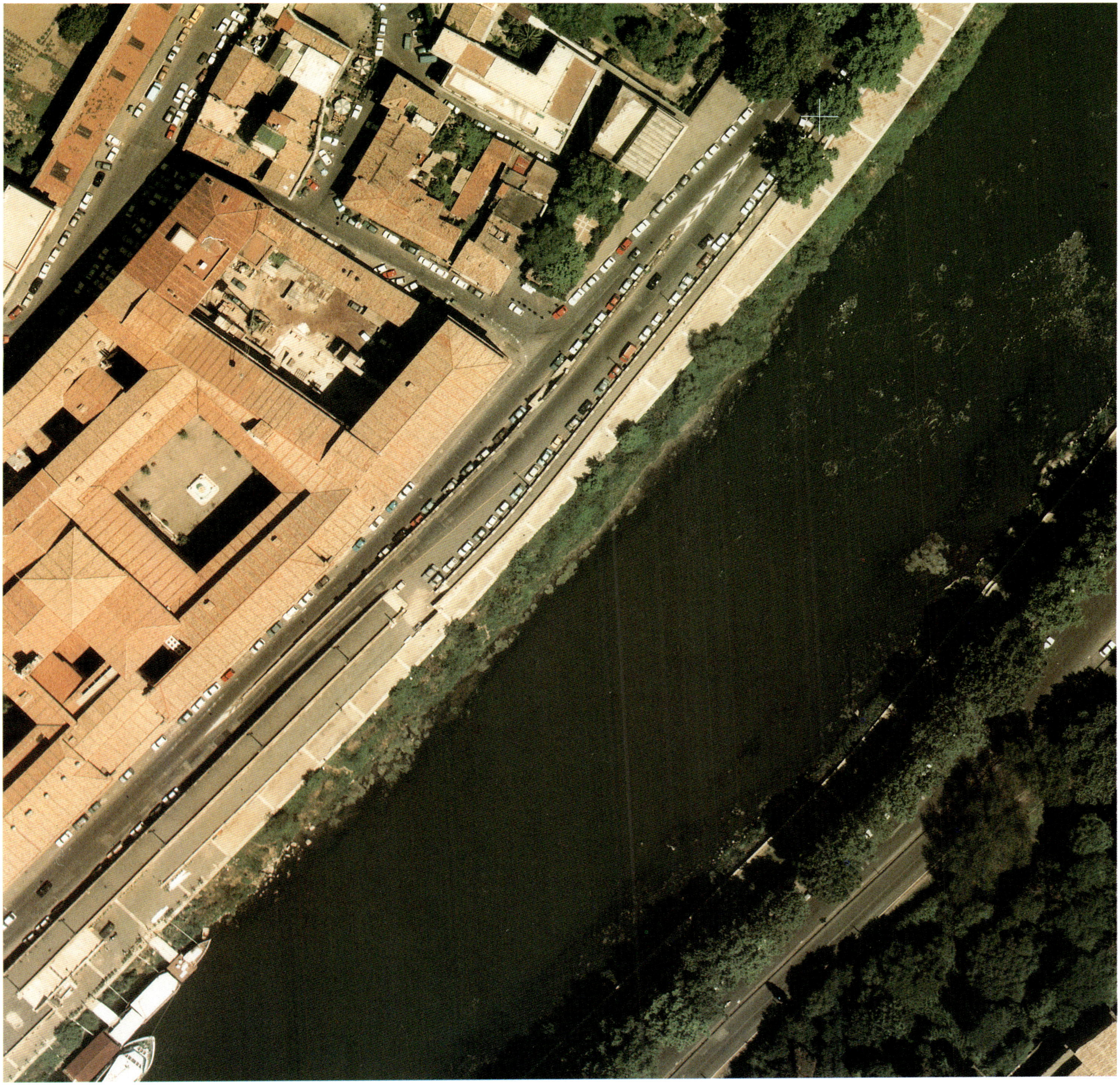

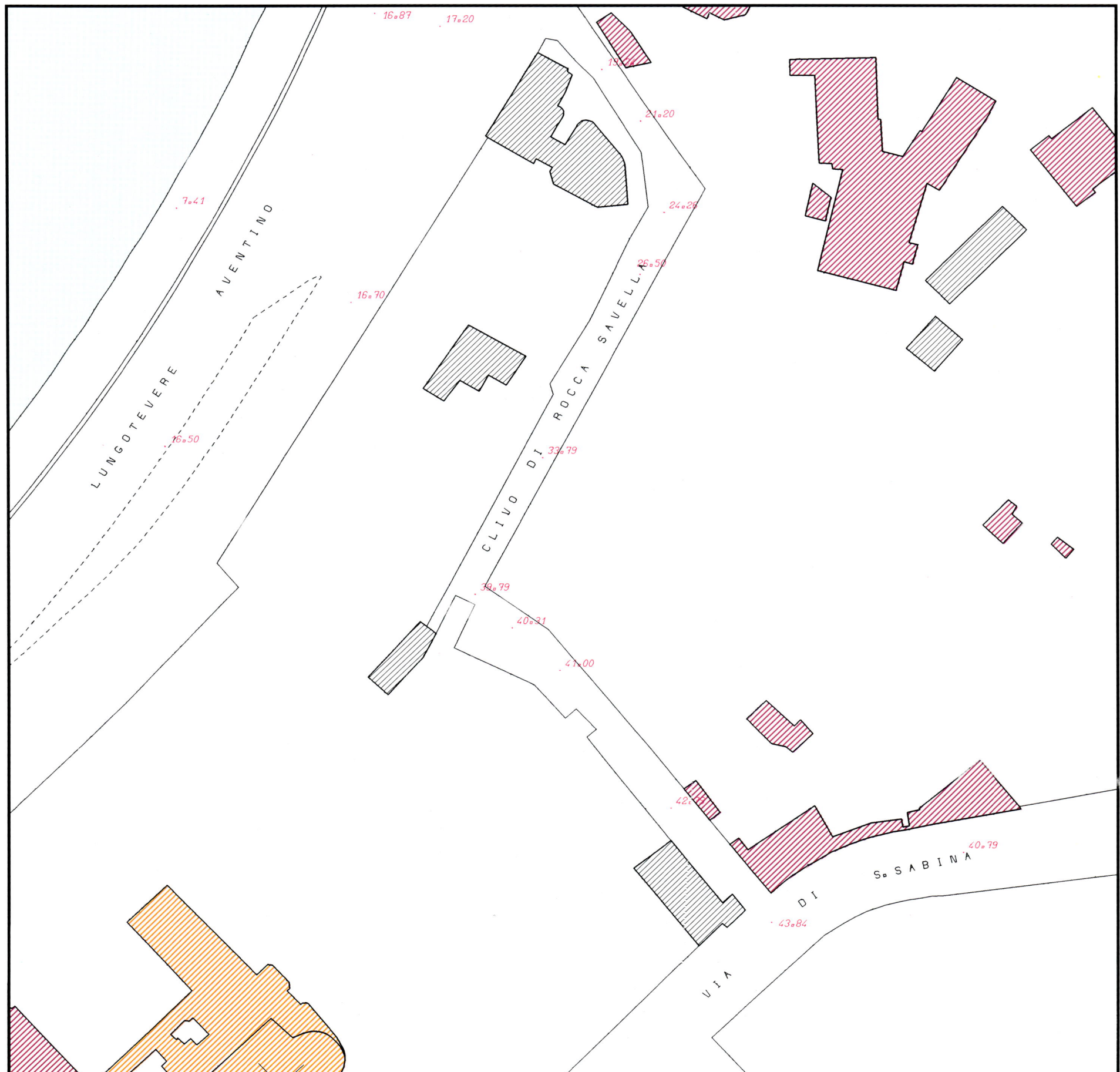

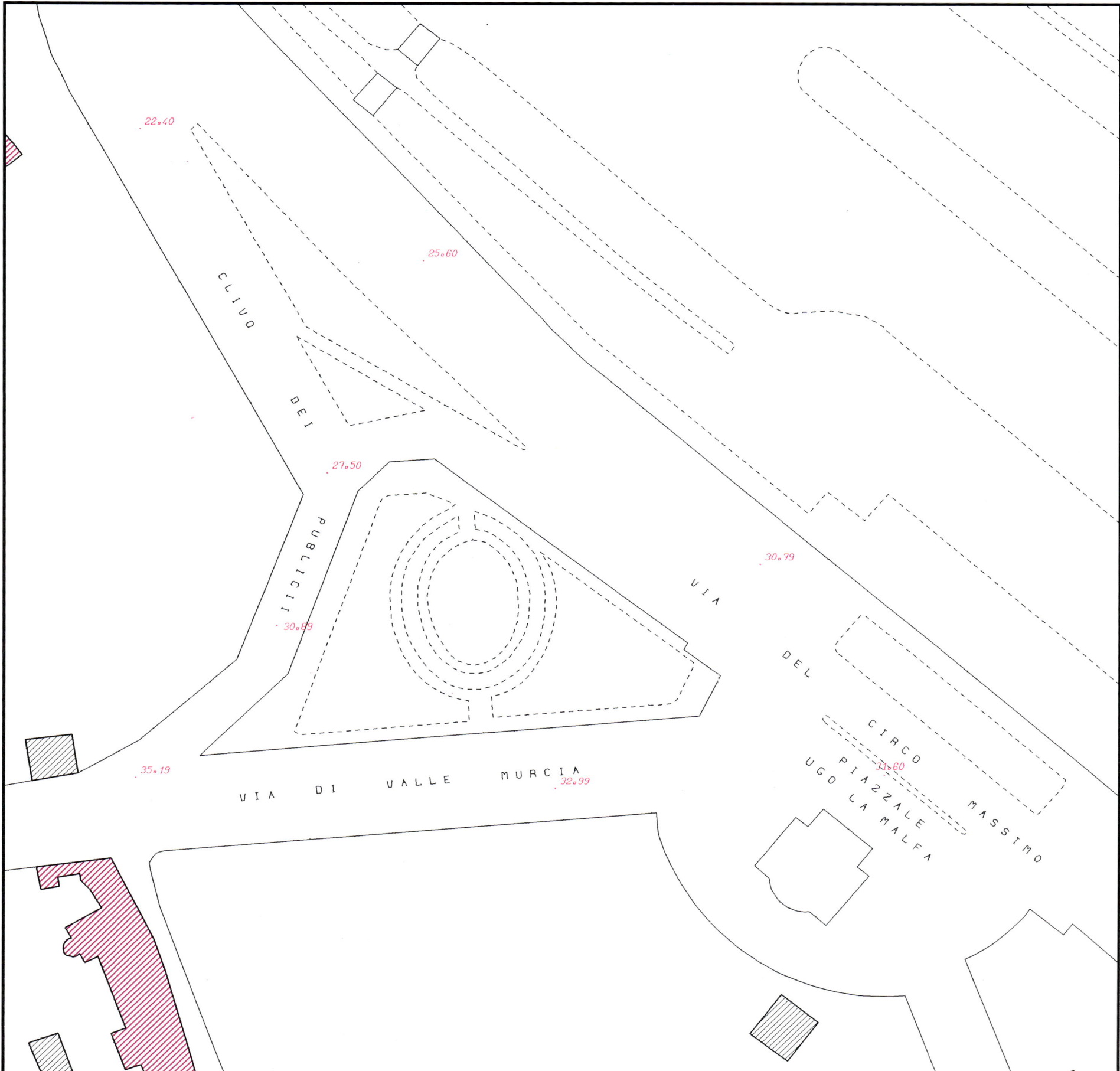

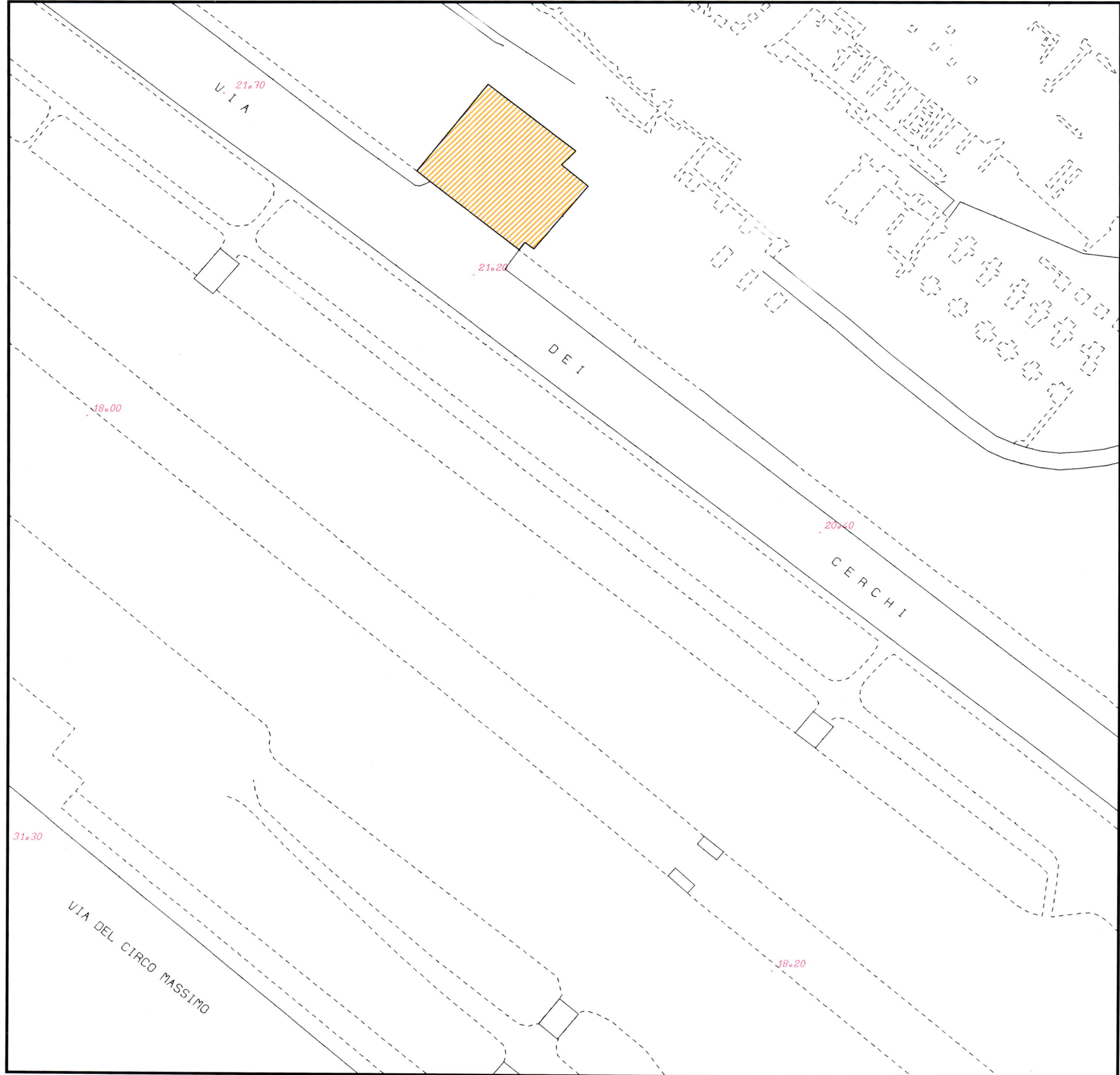

202

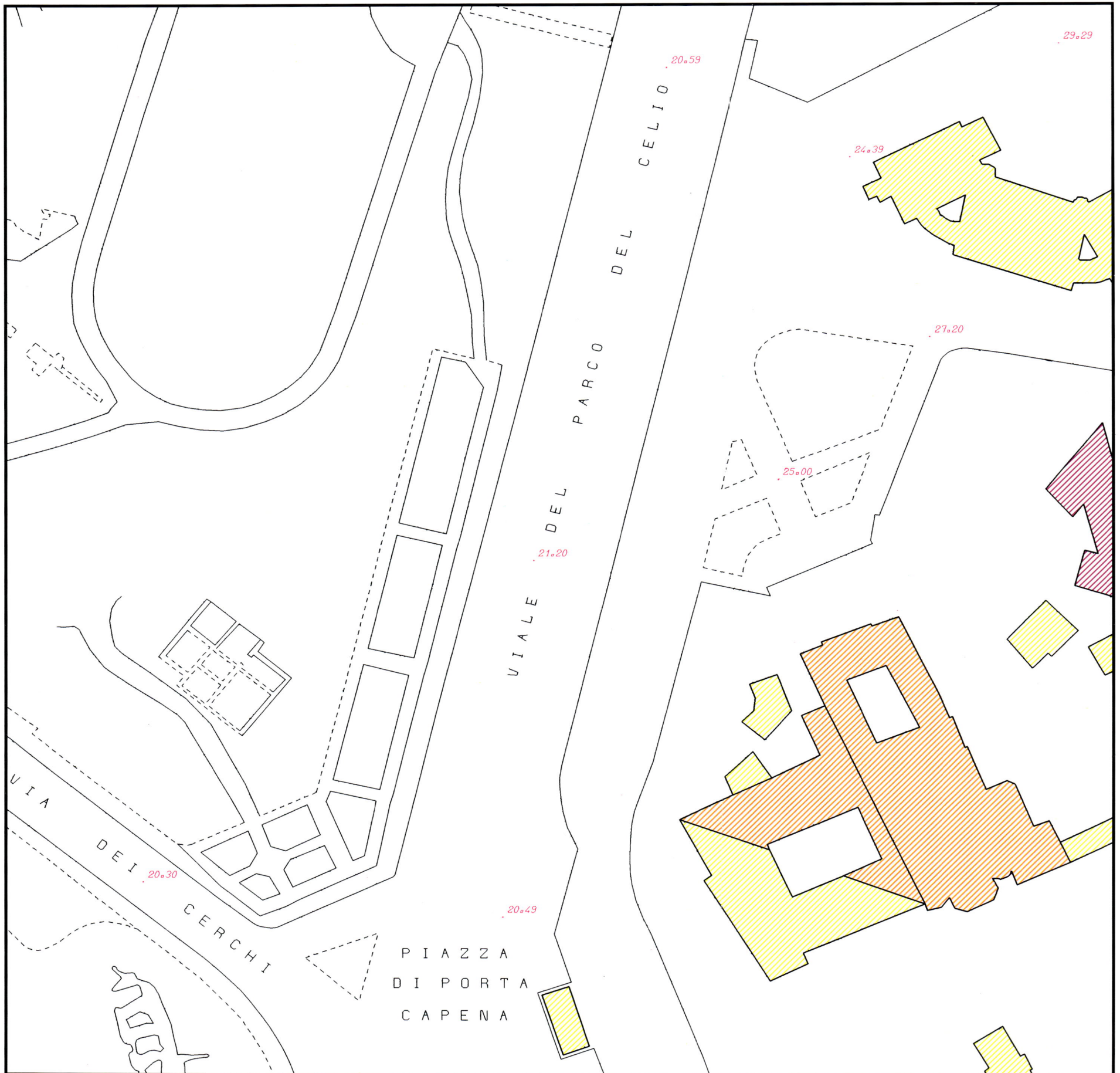

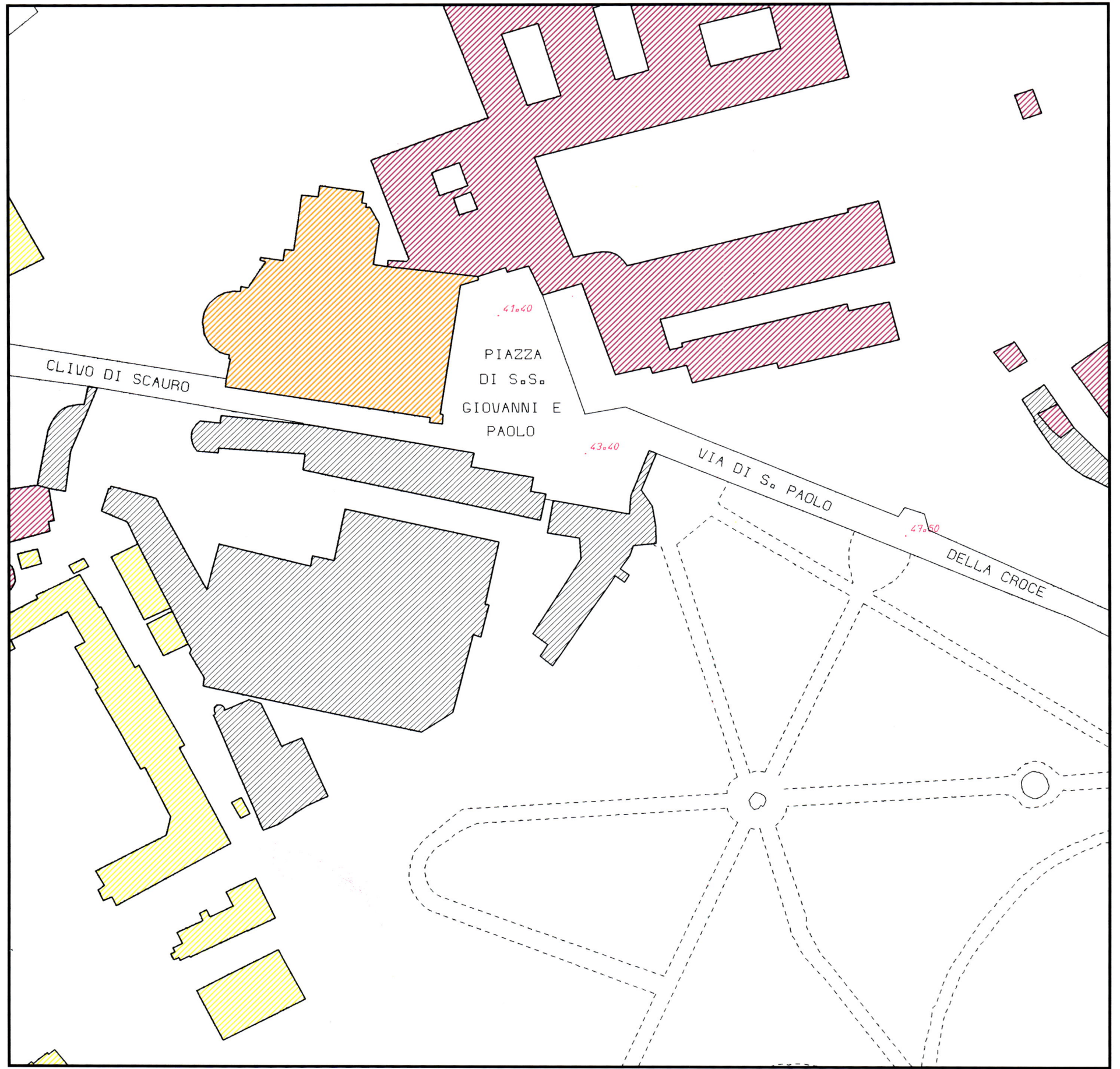

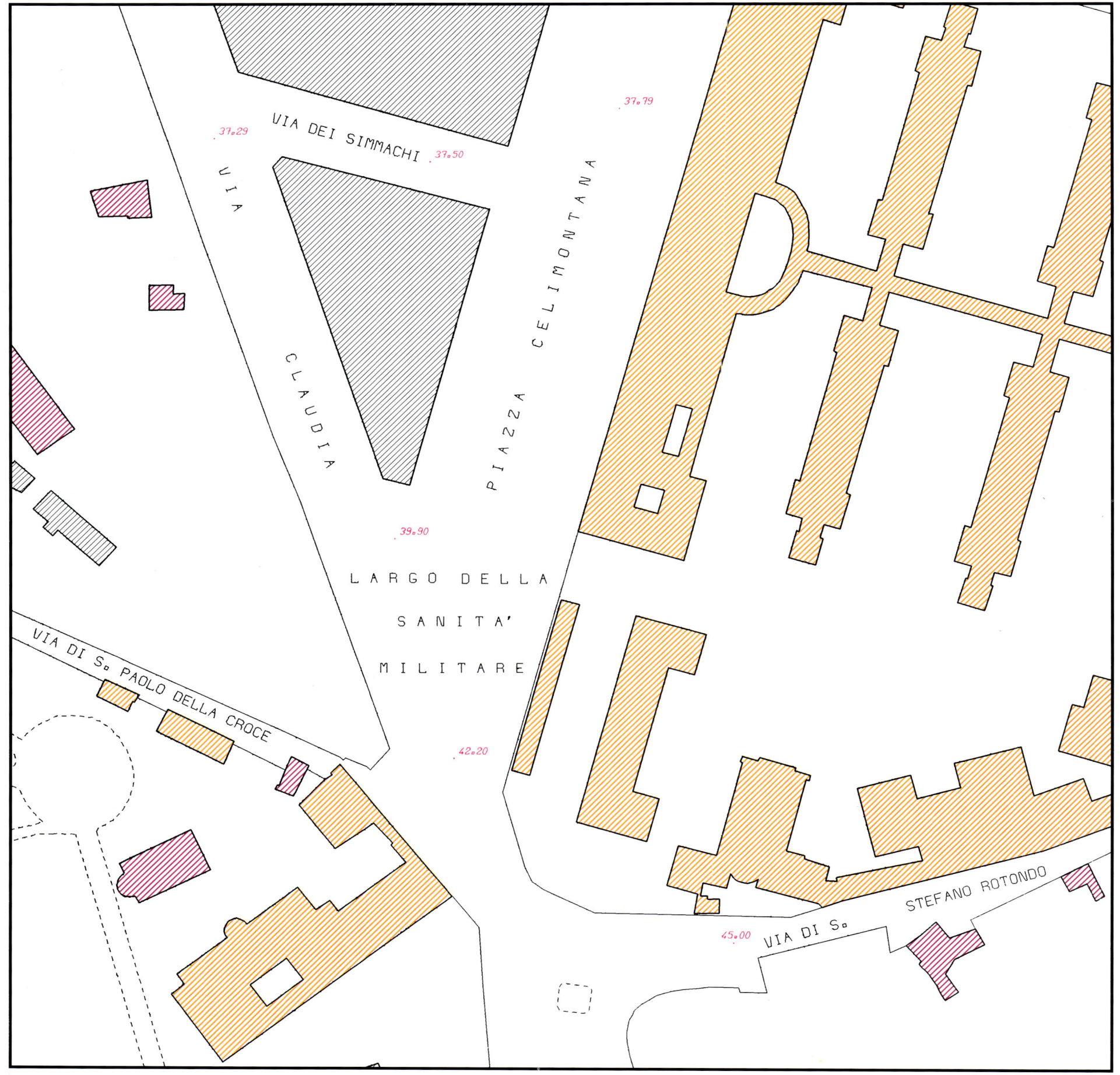

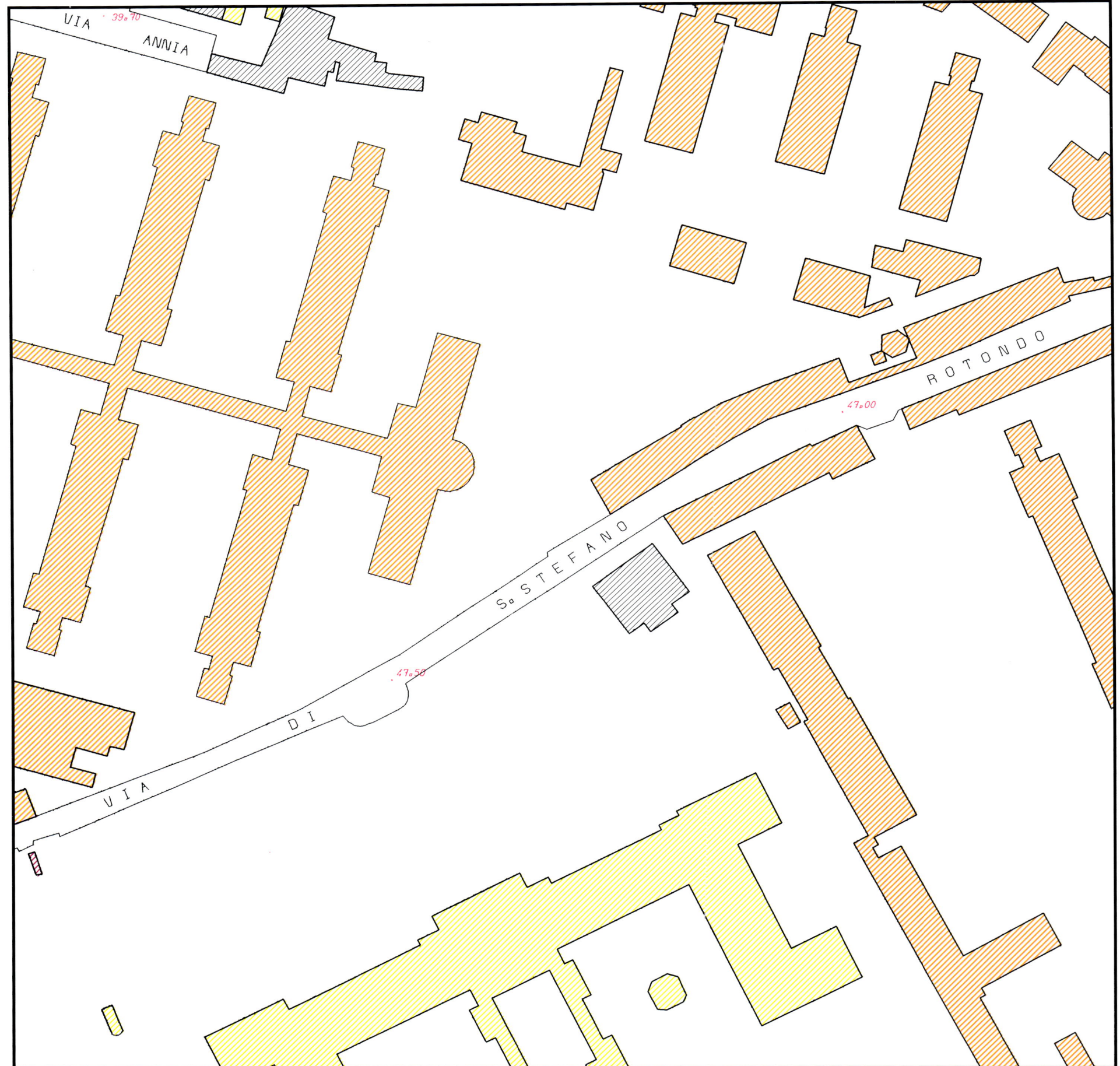

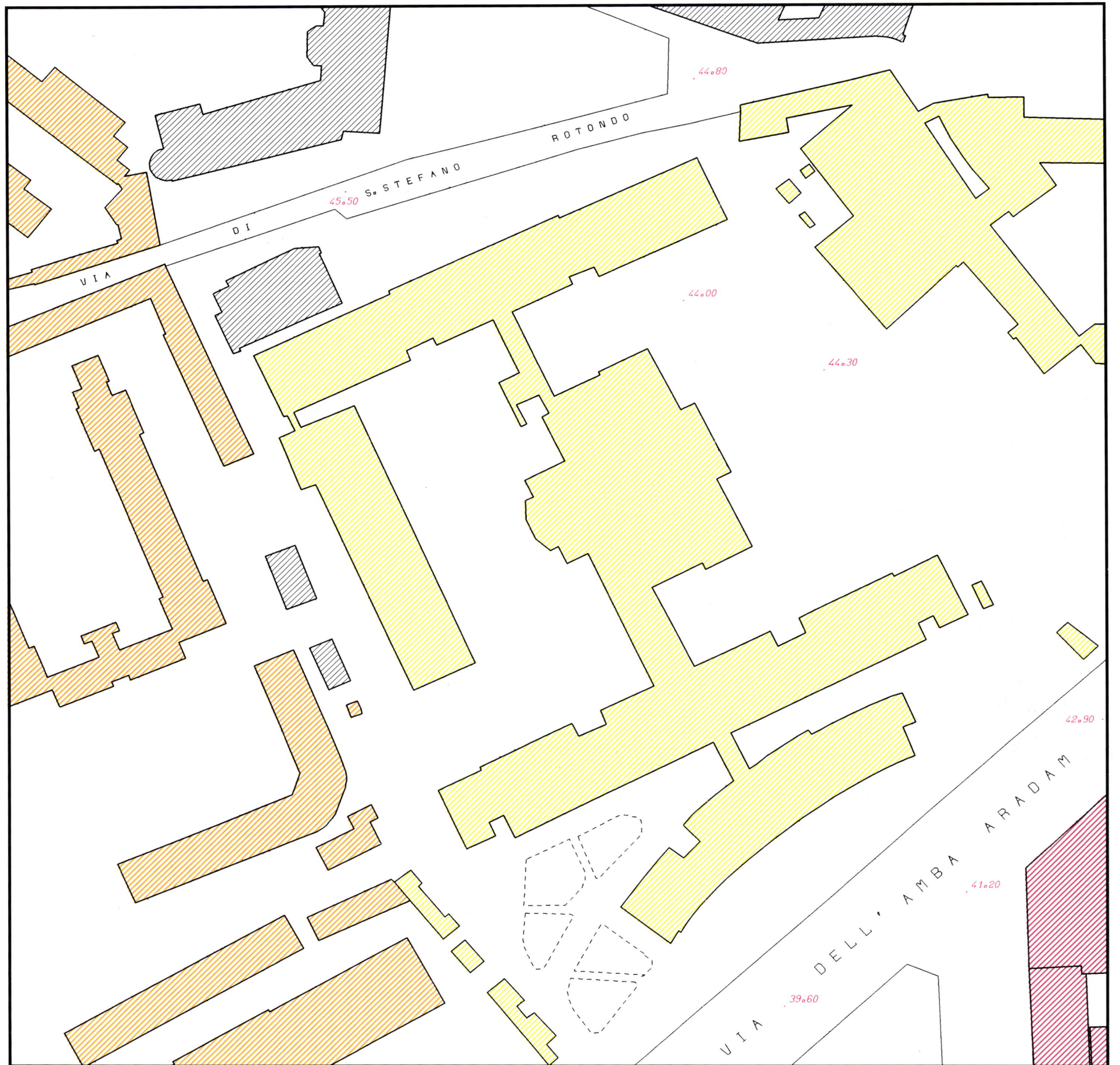

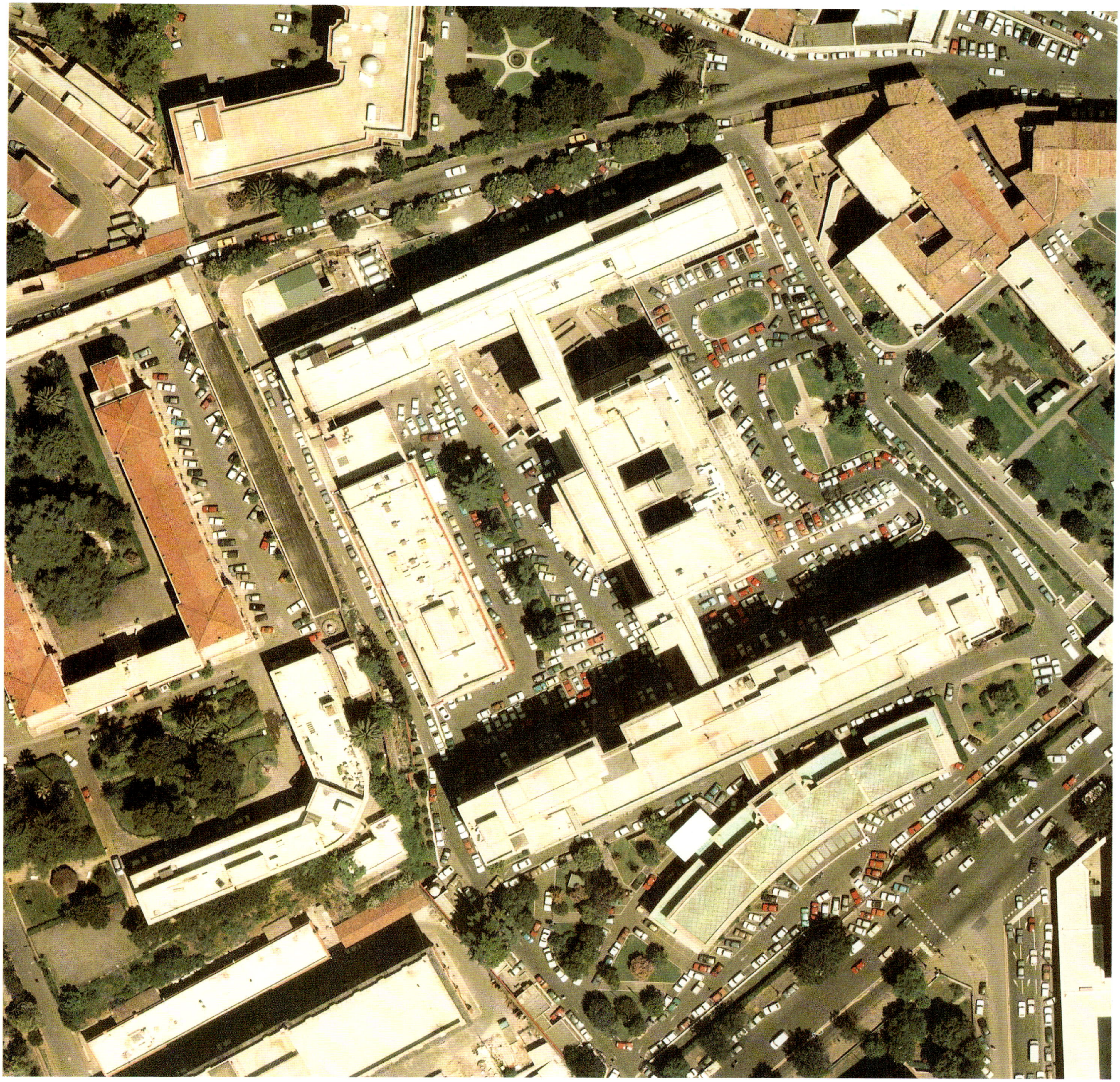

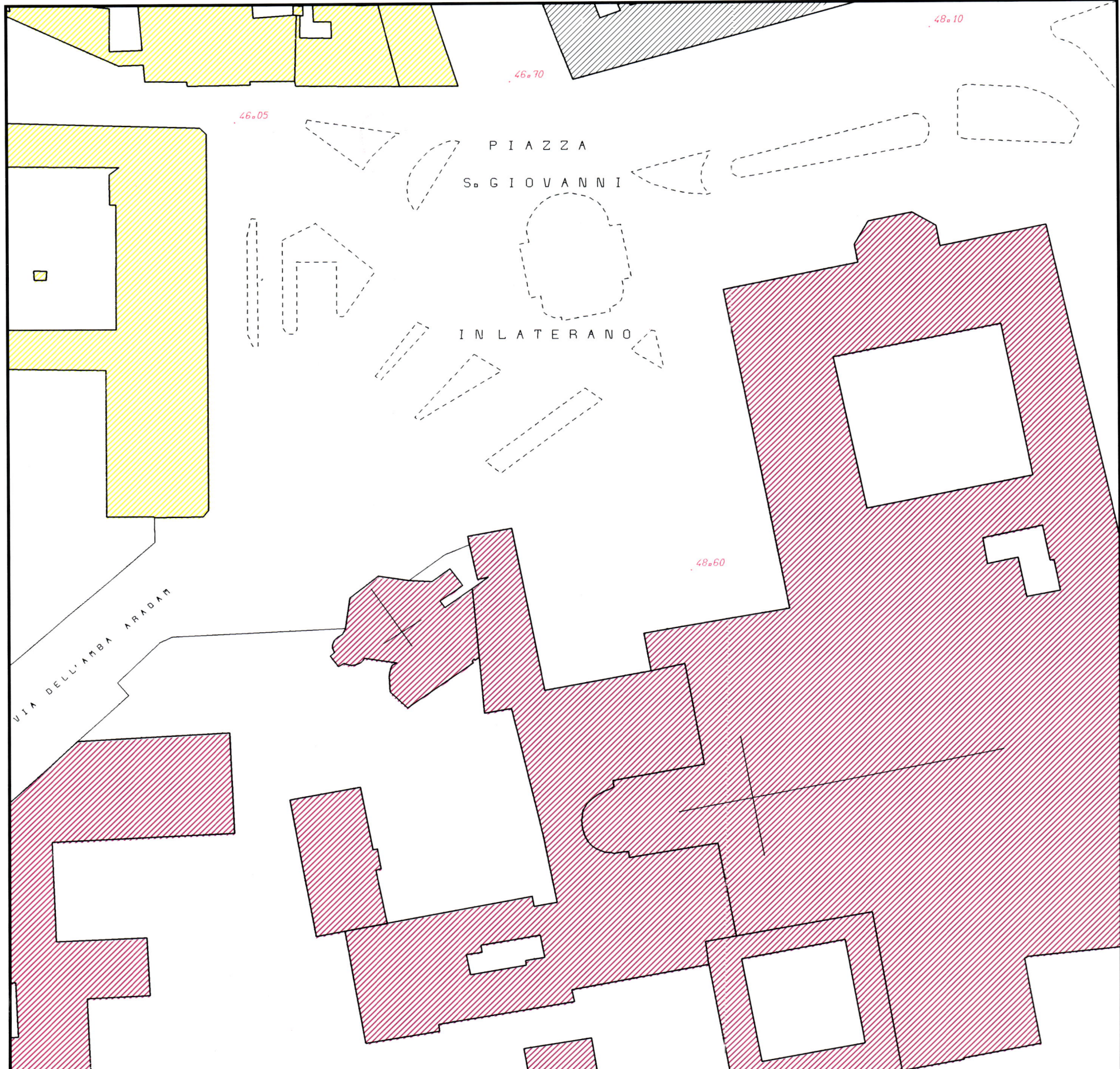

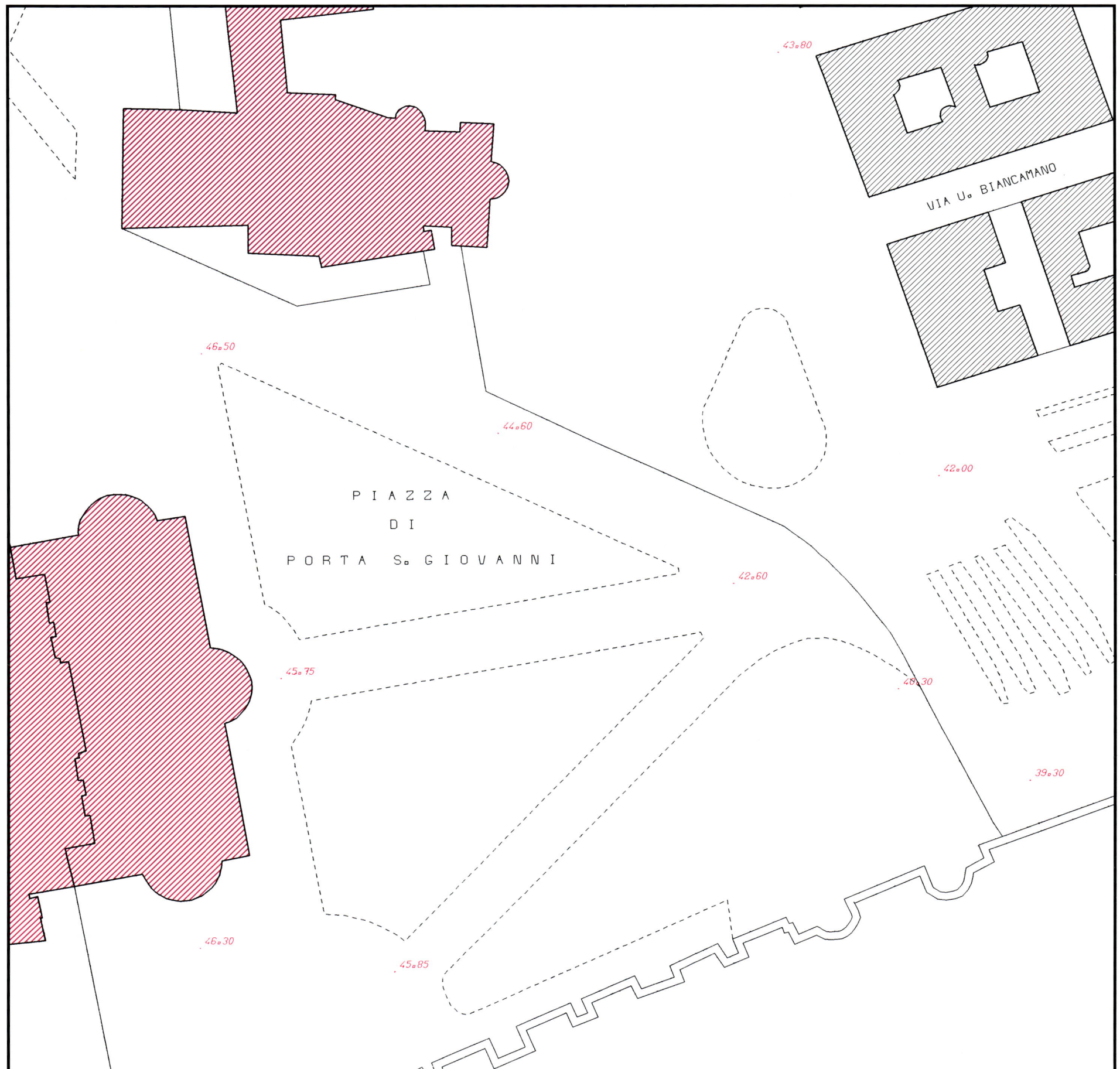

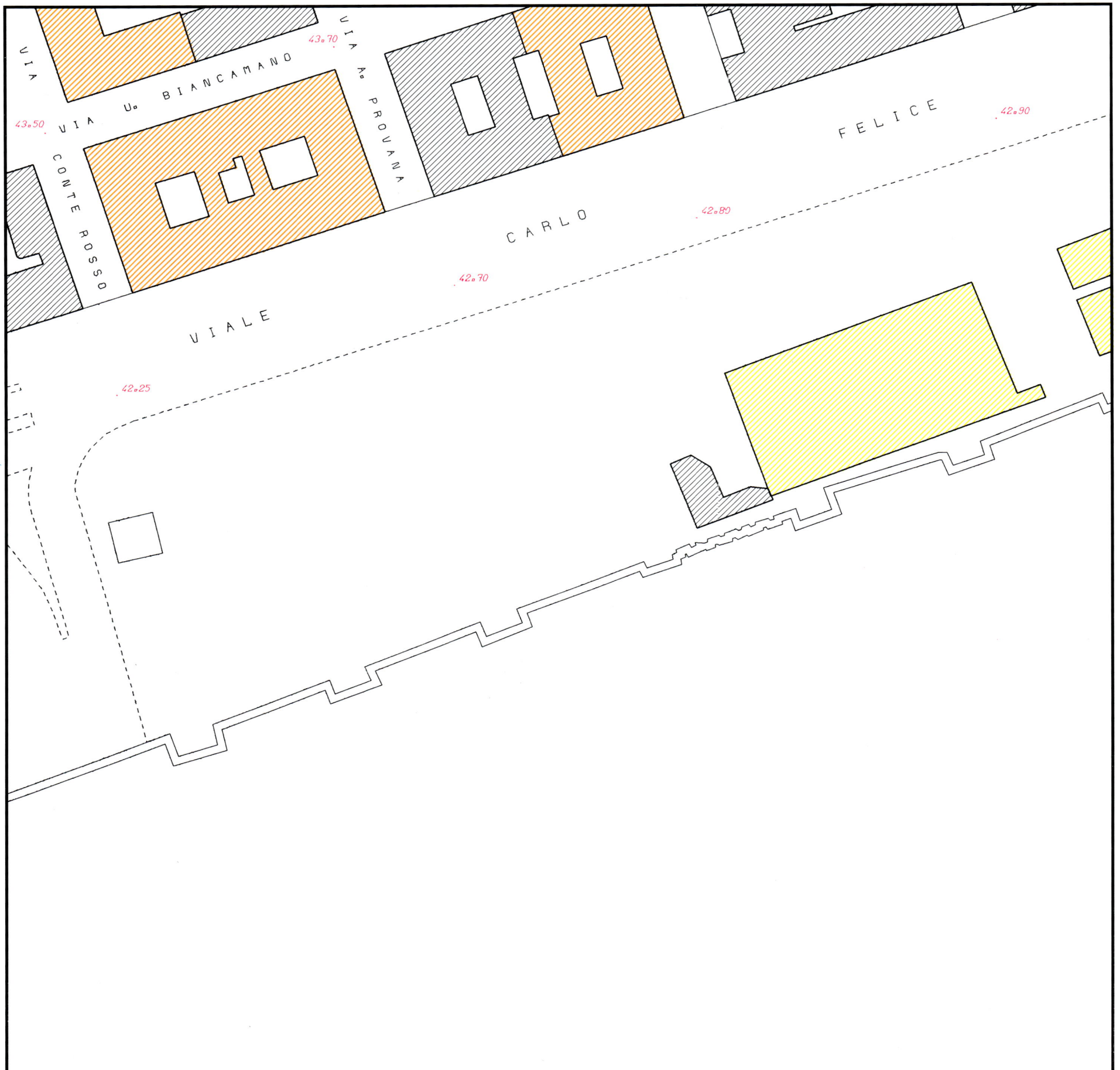

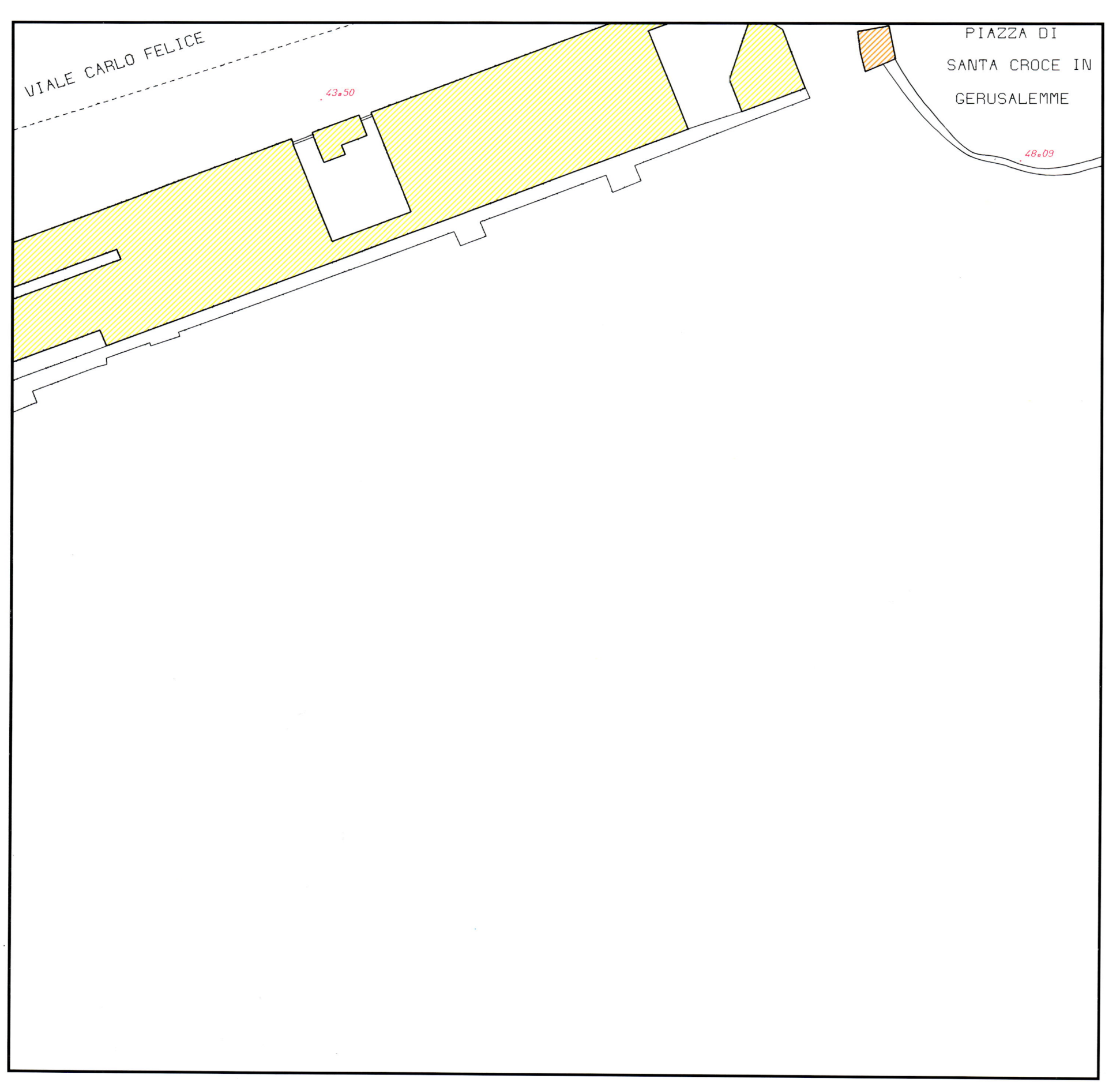

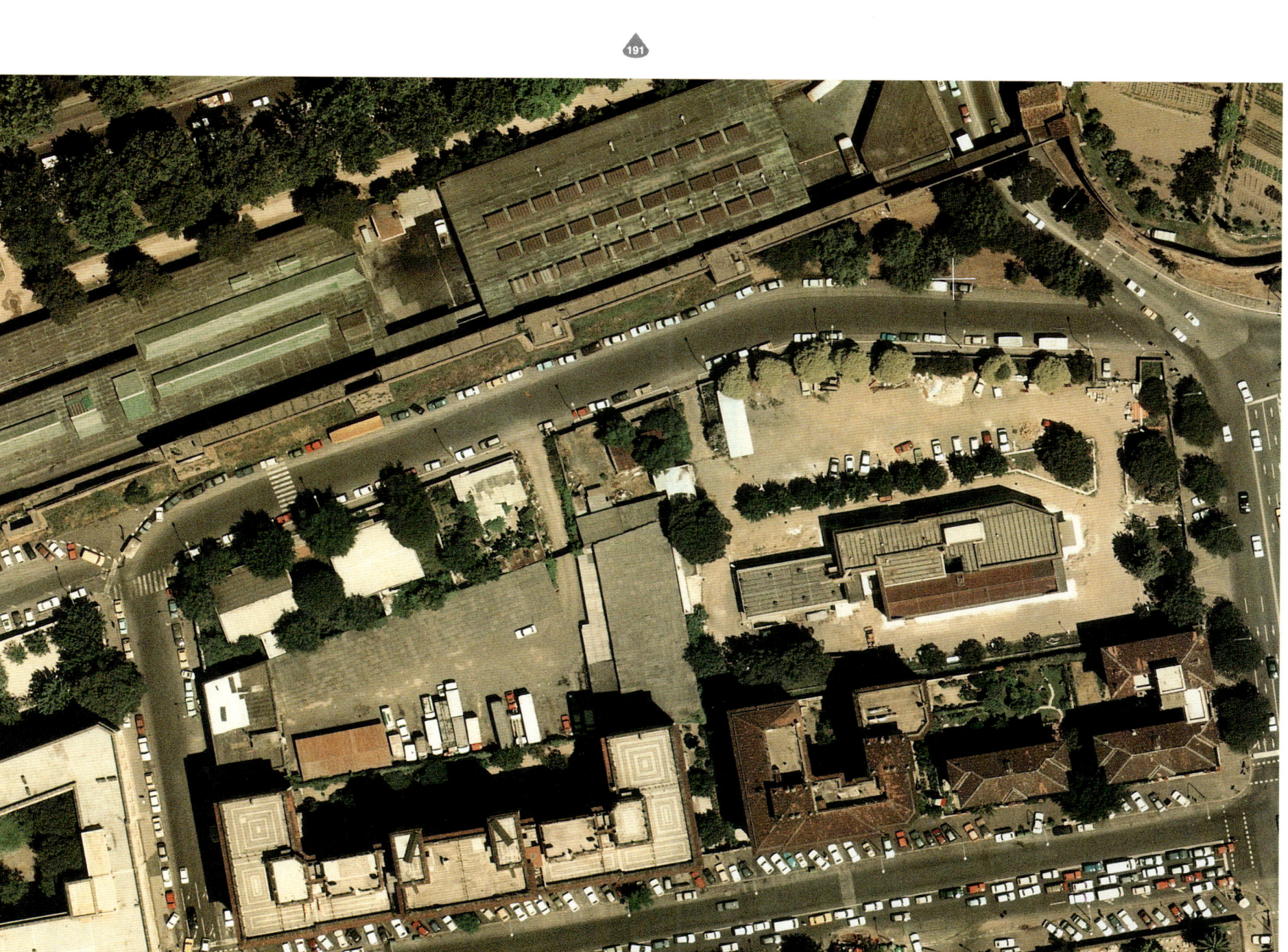

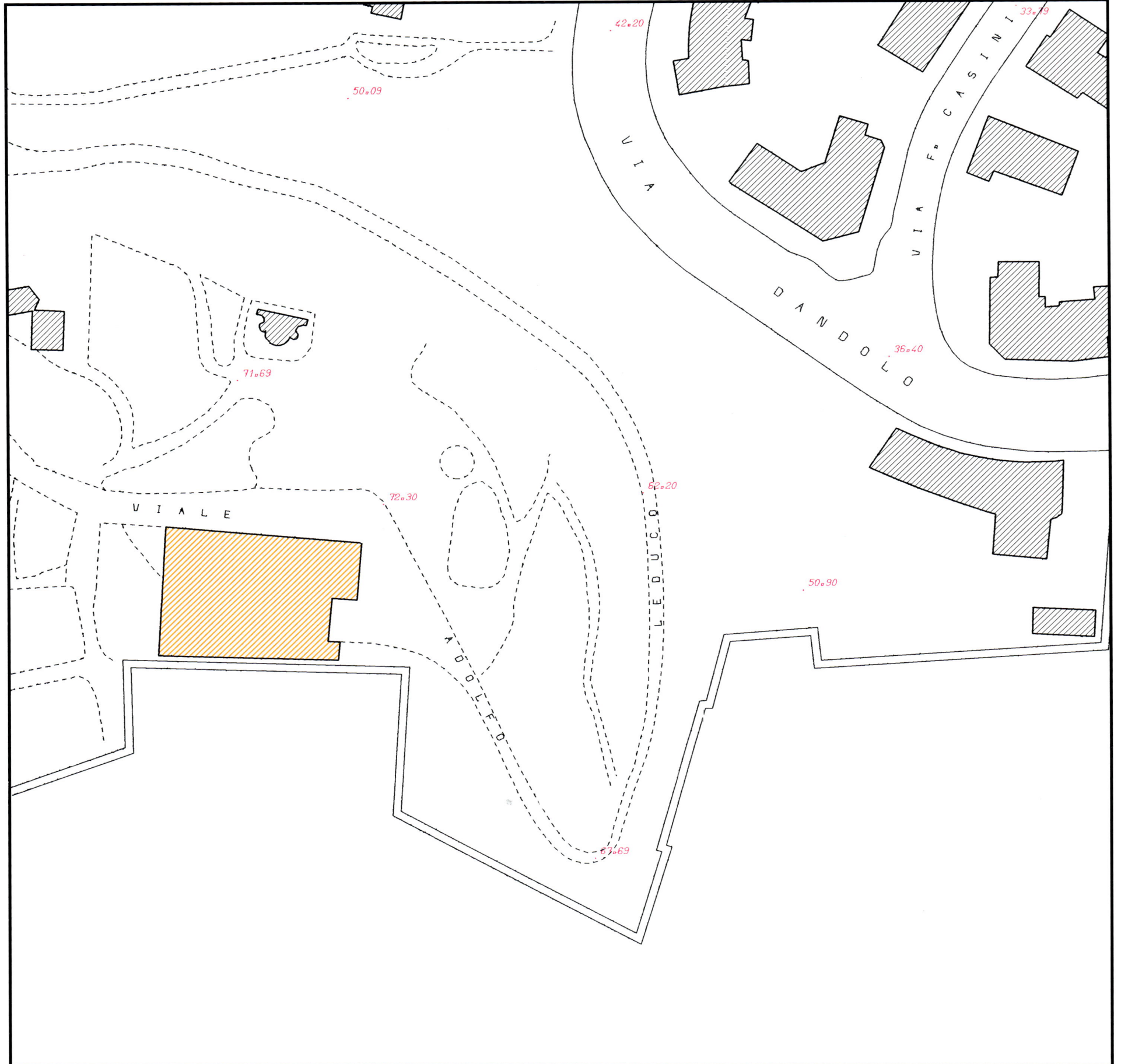

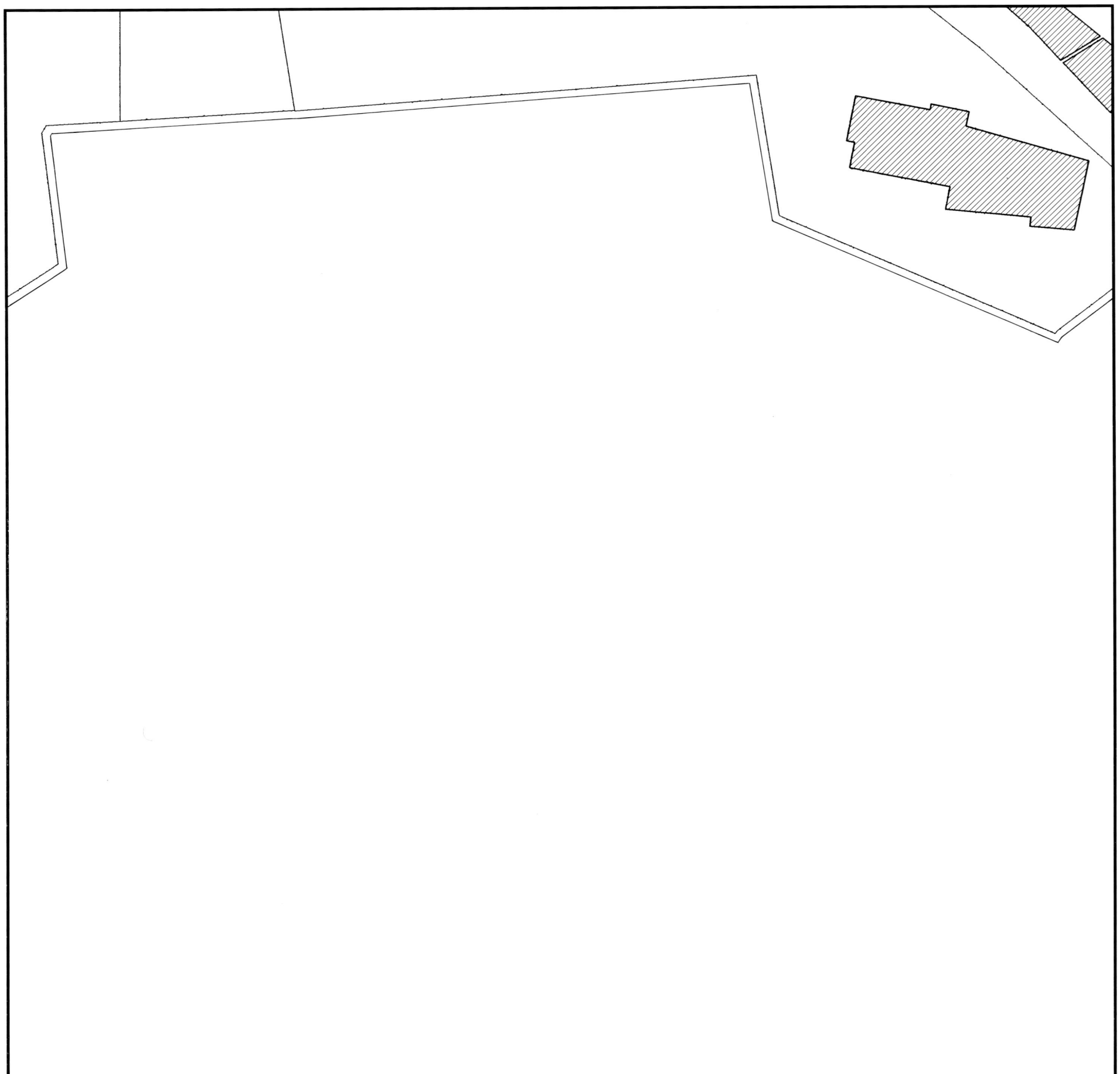

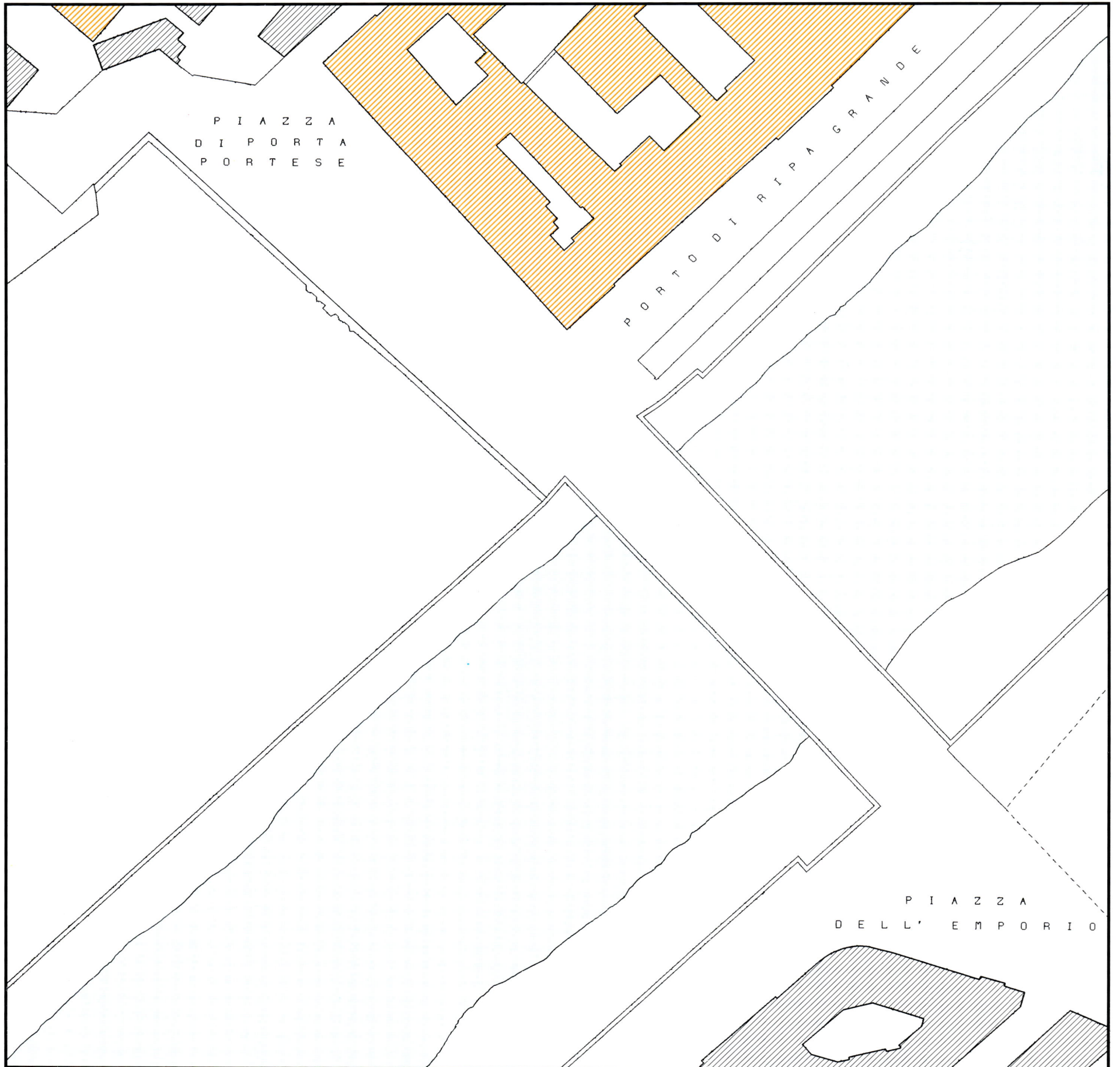

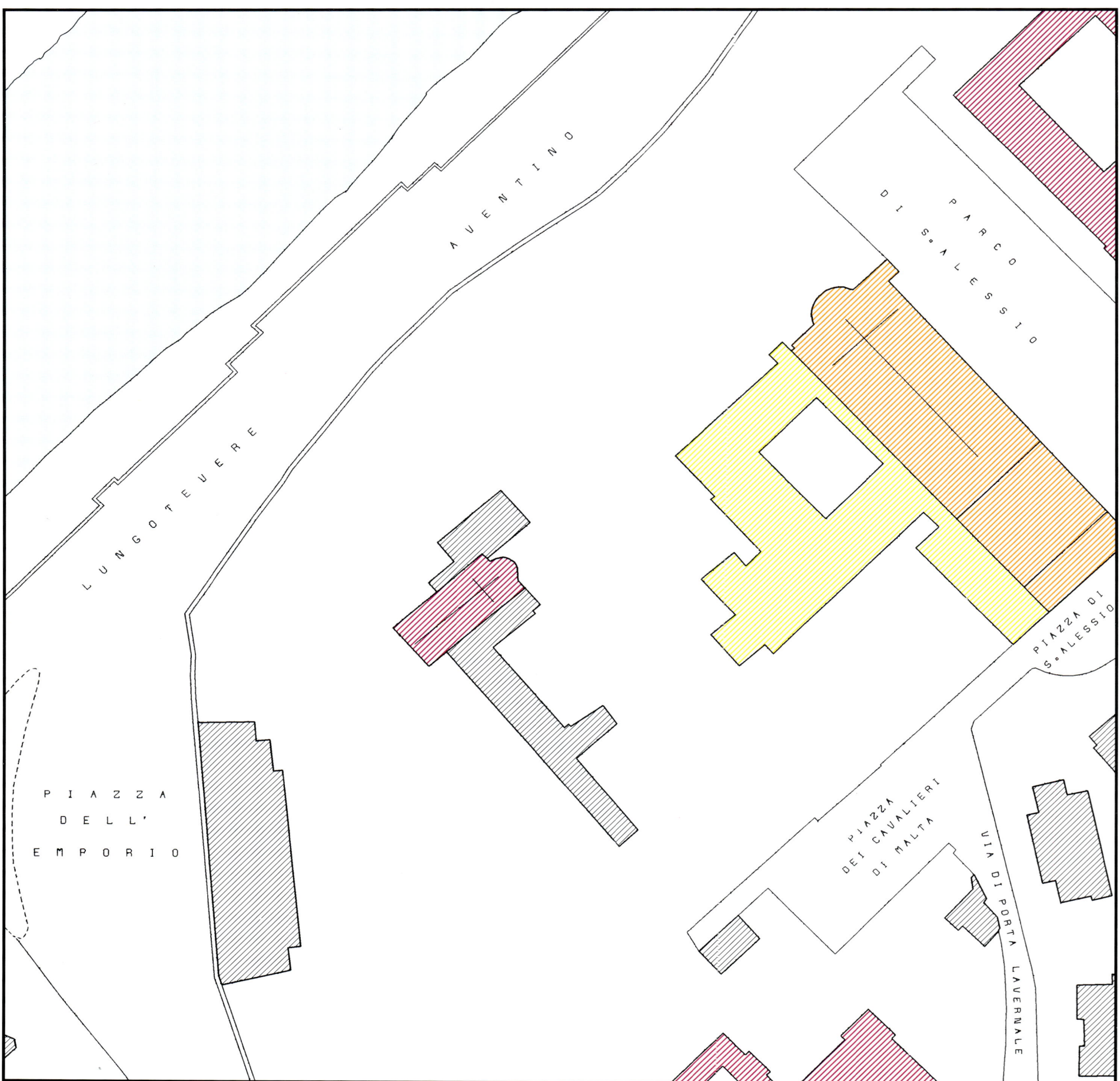

220

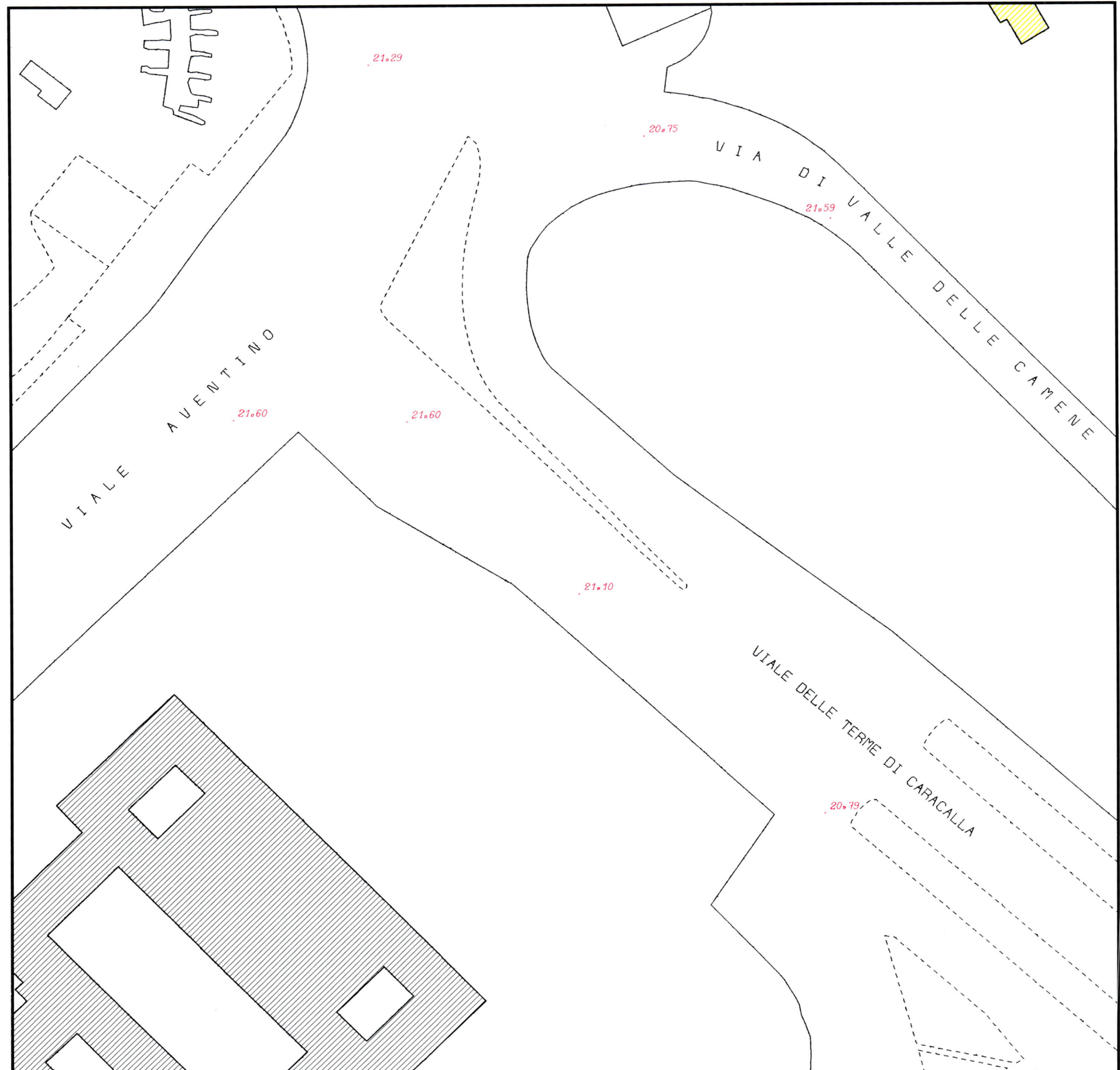

222

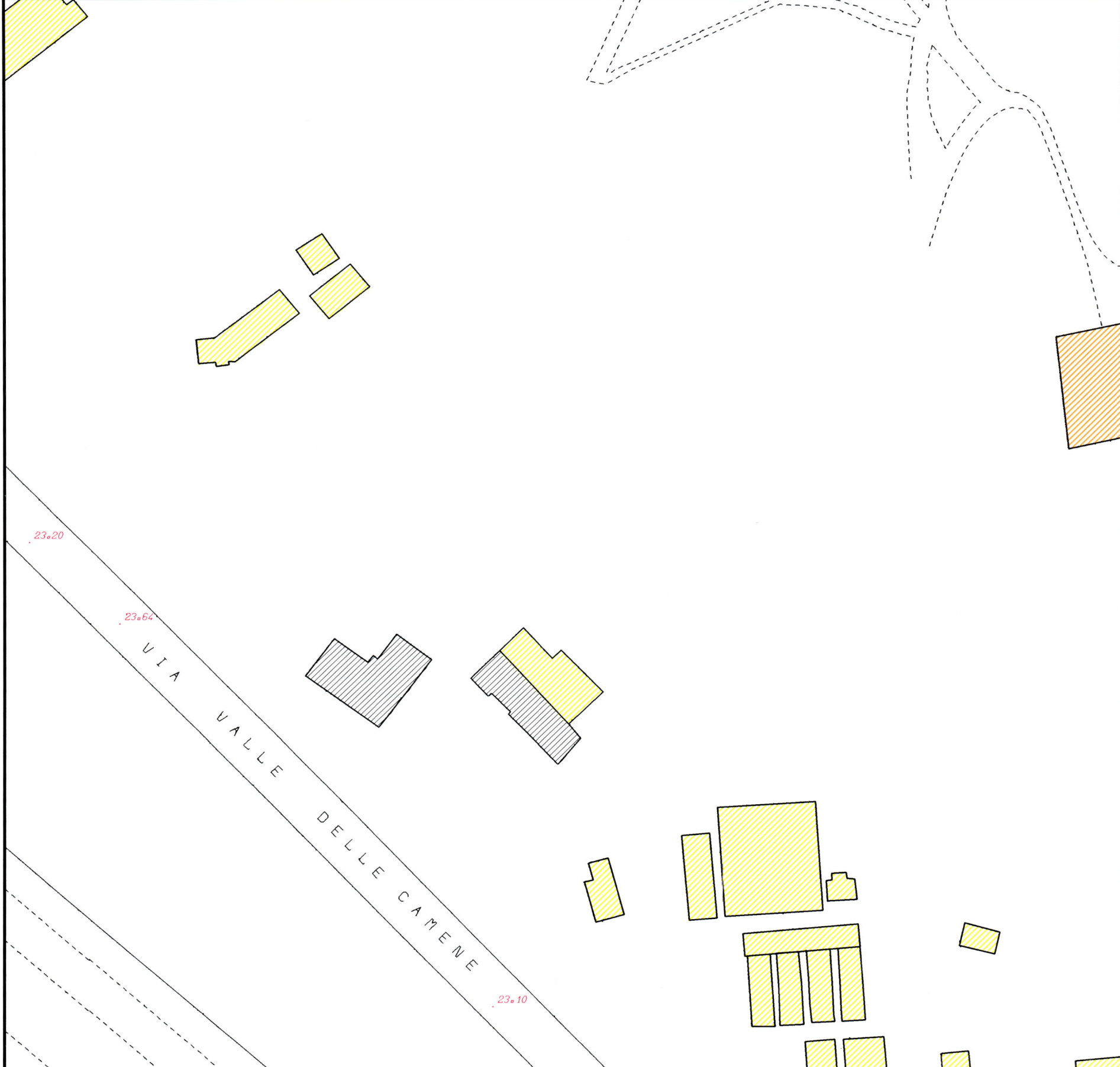

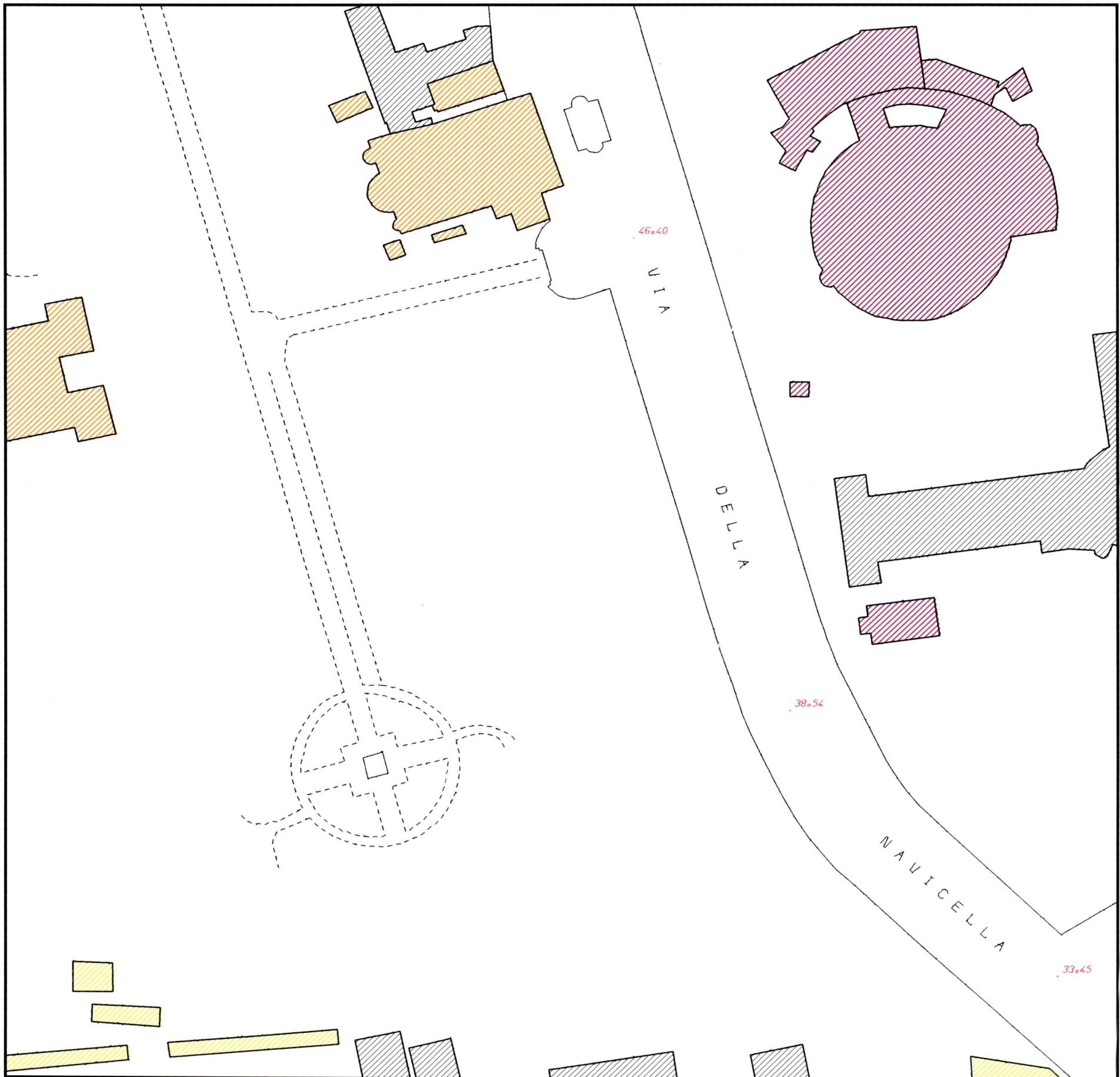

224

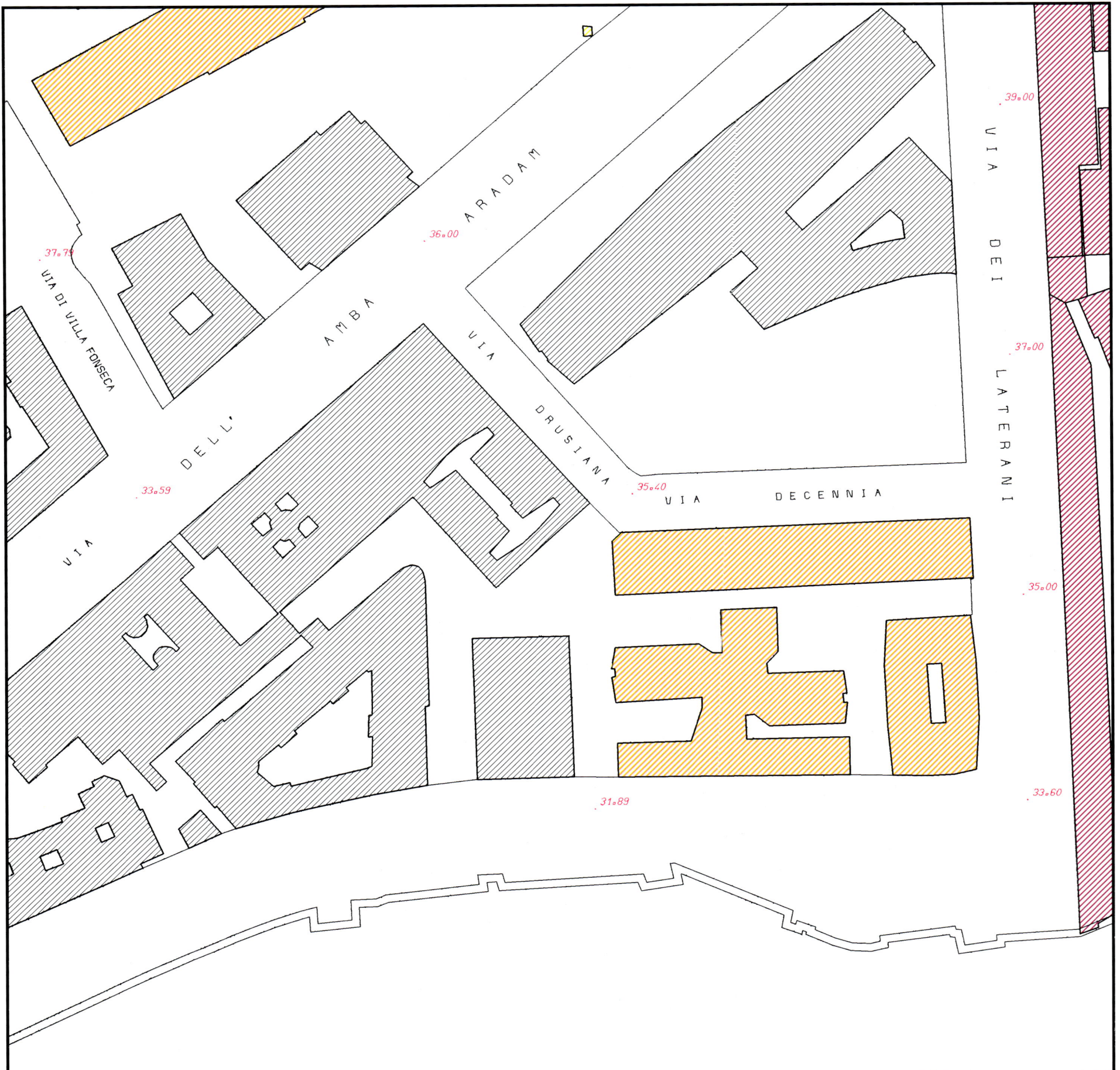

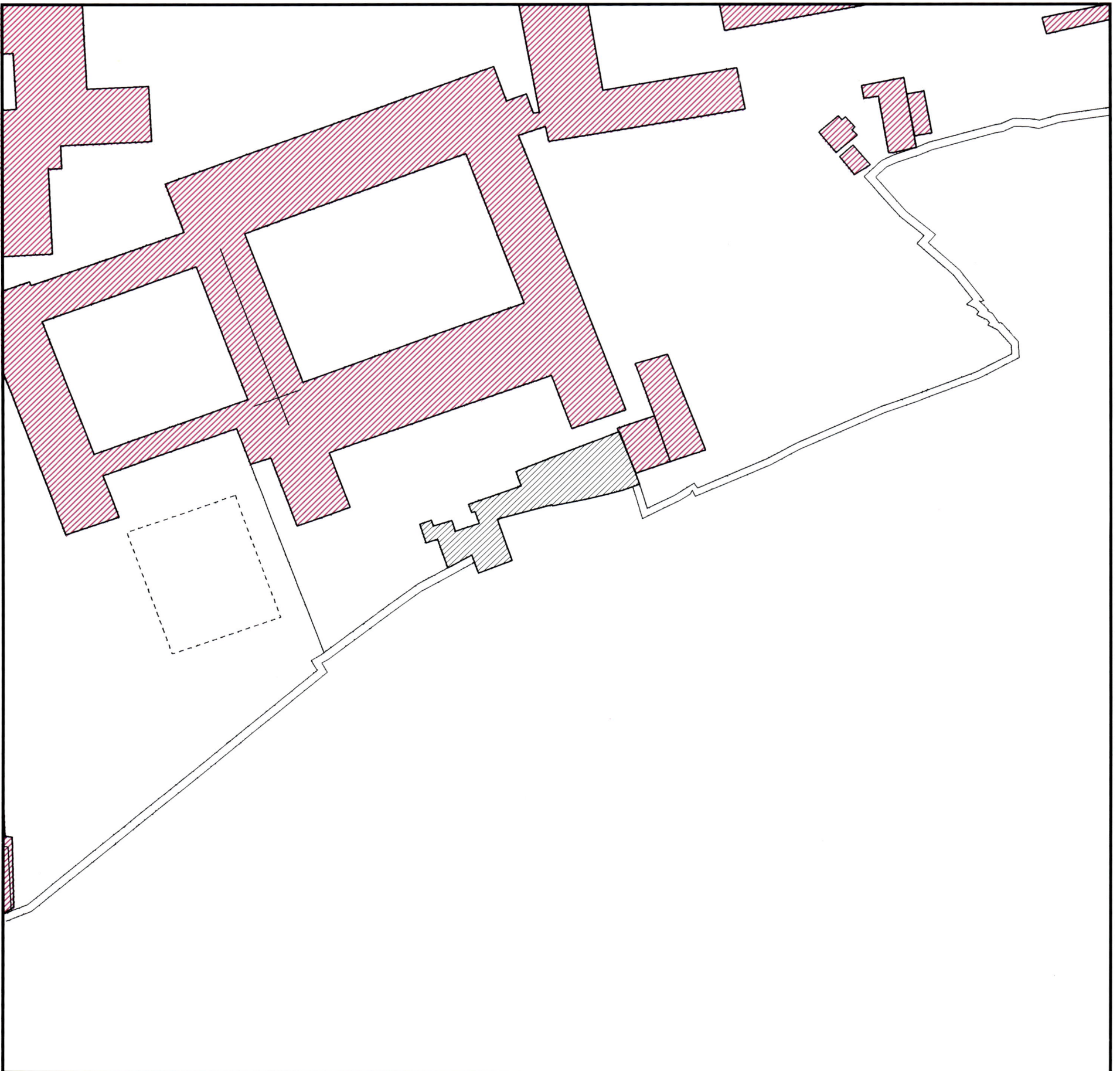

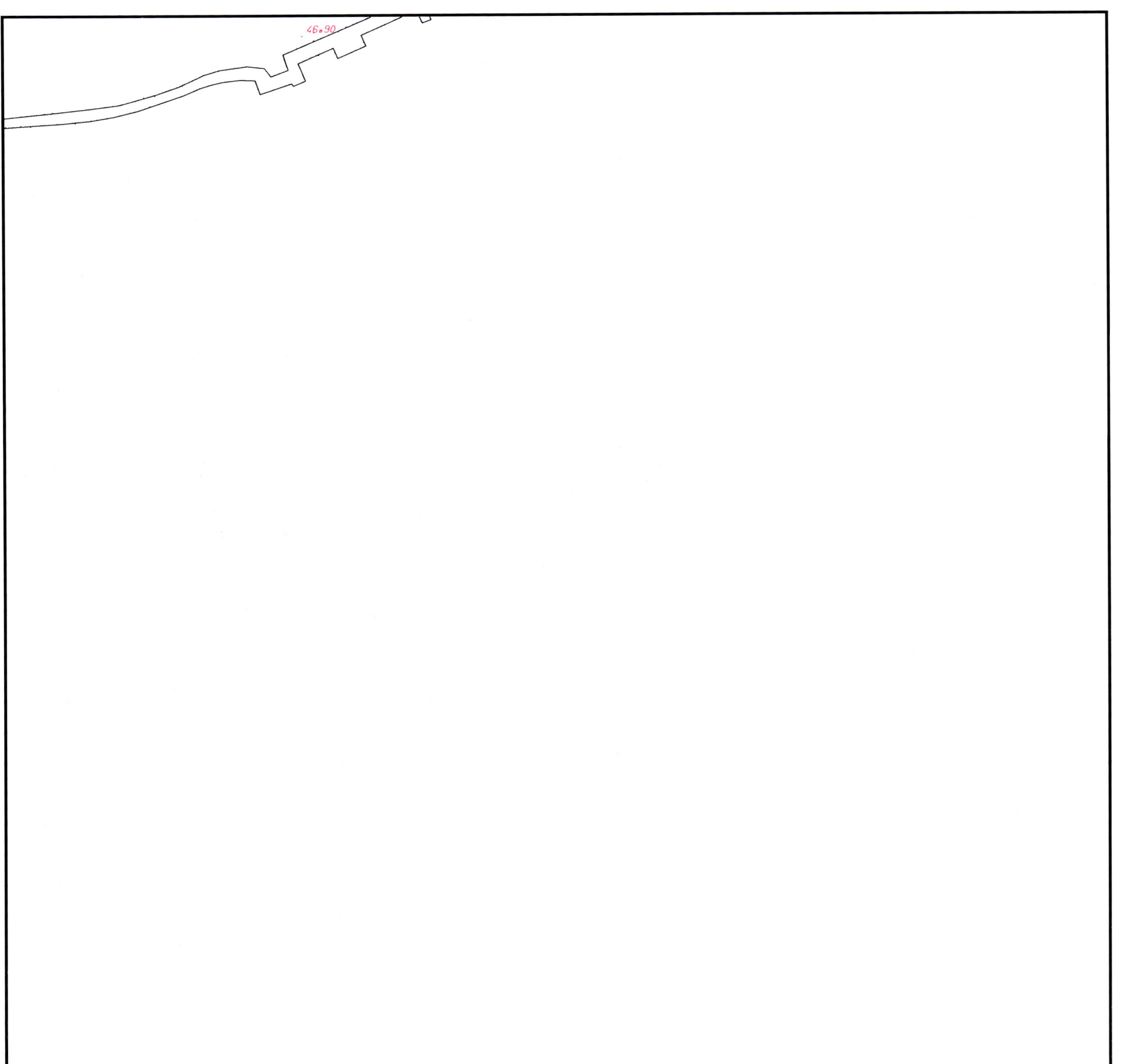

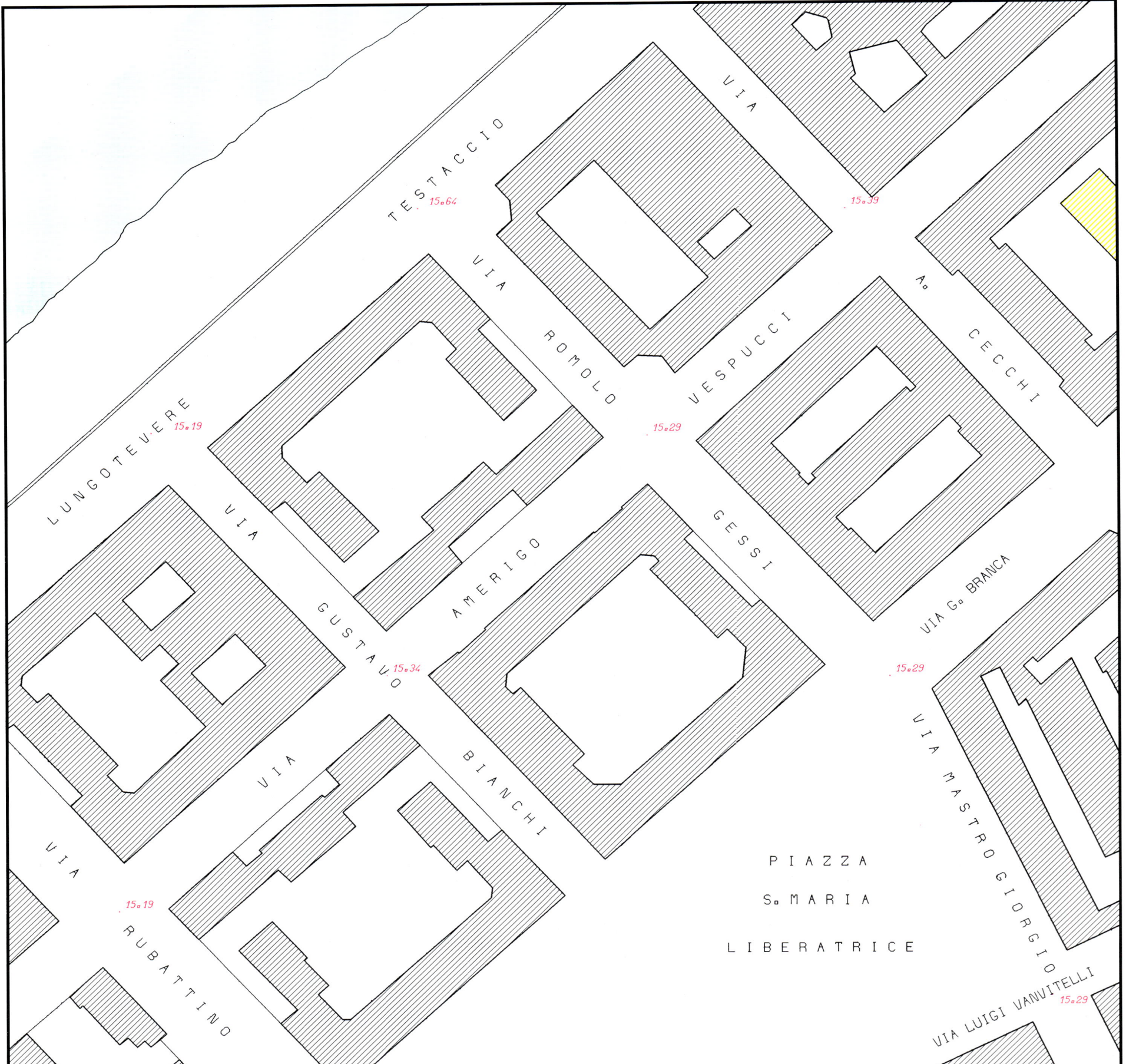

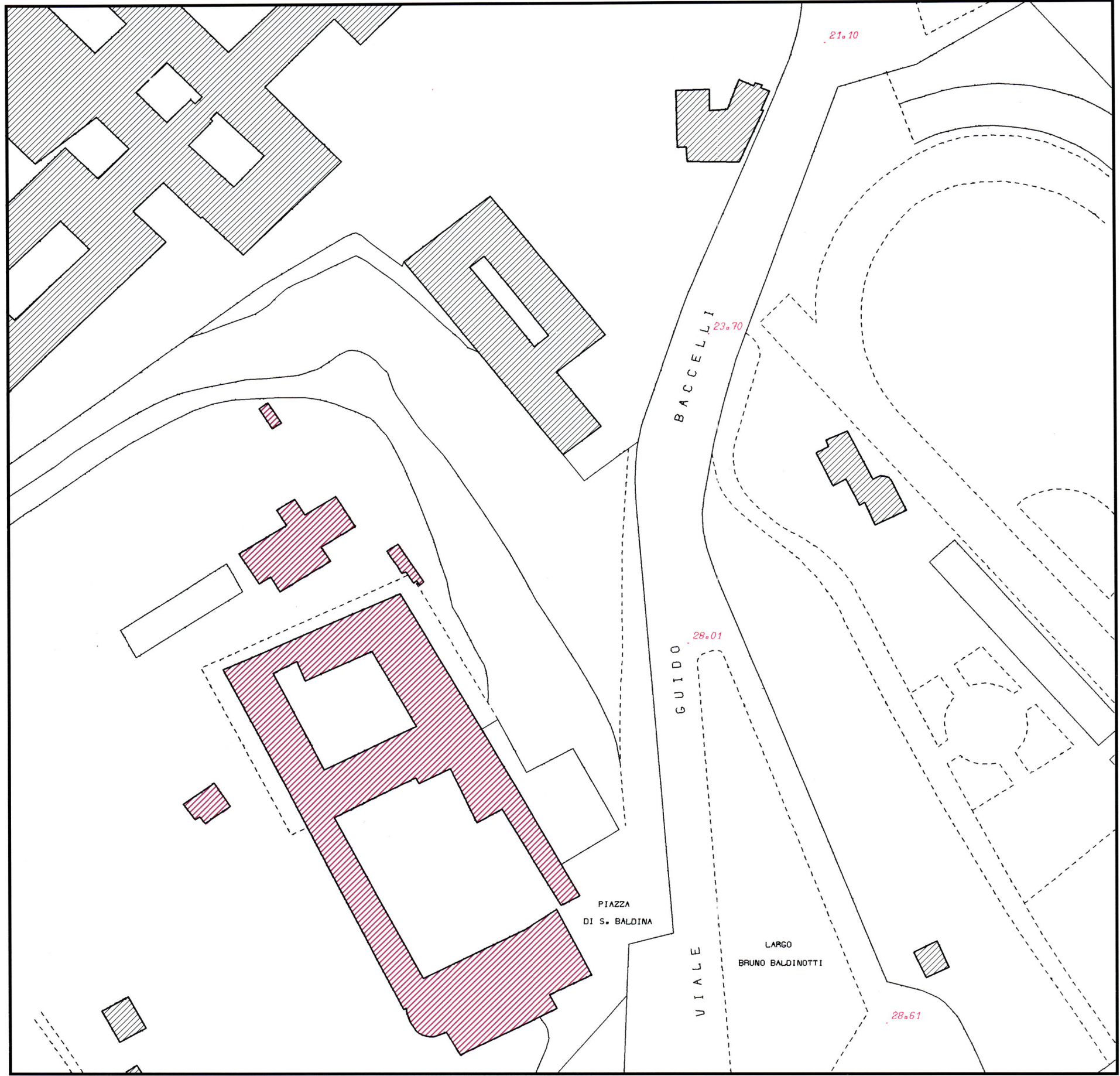

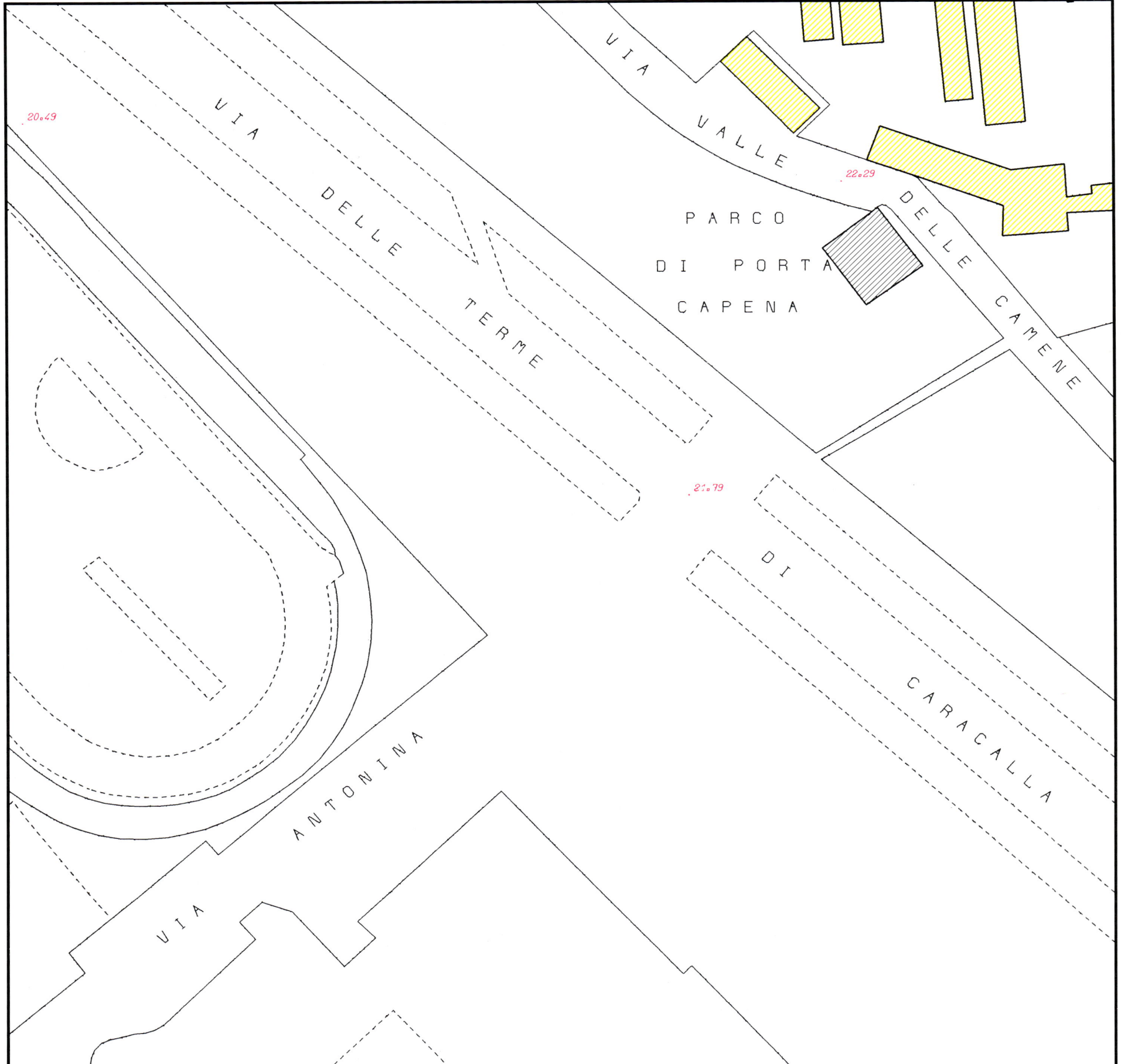

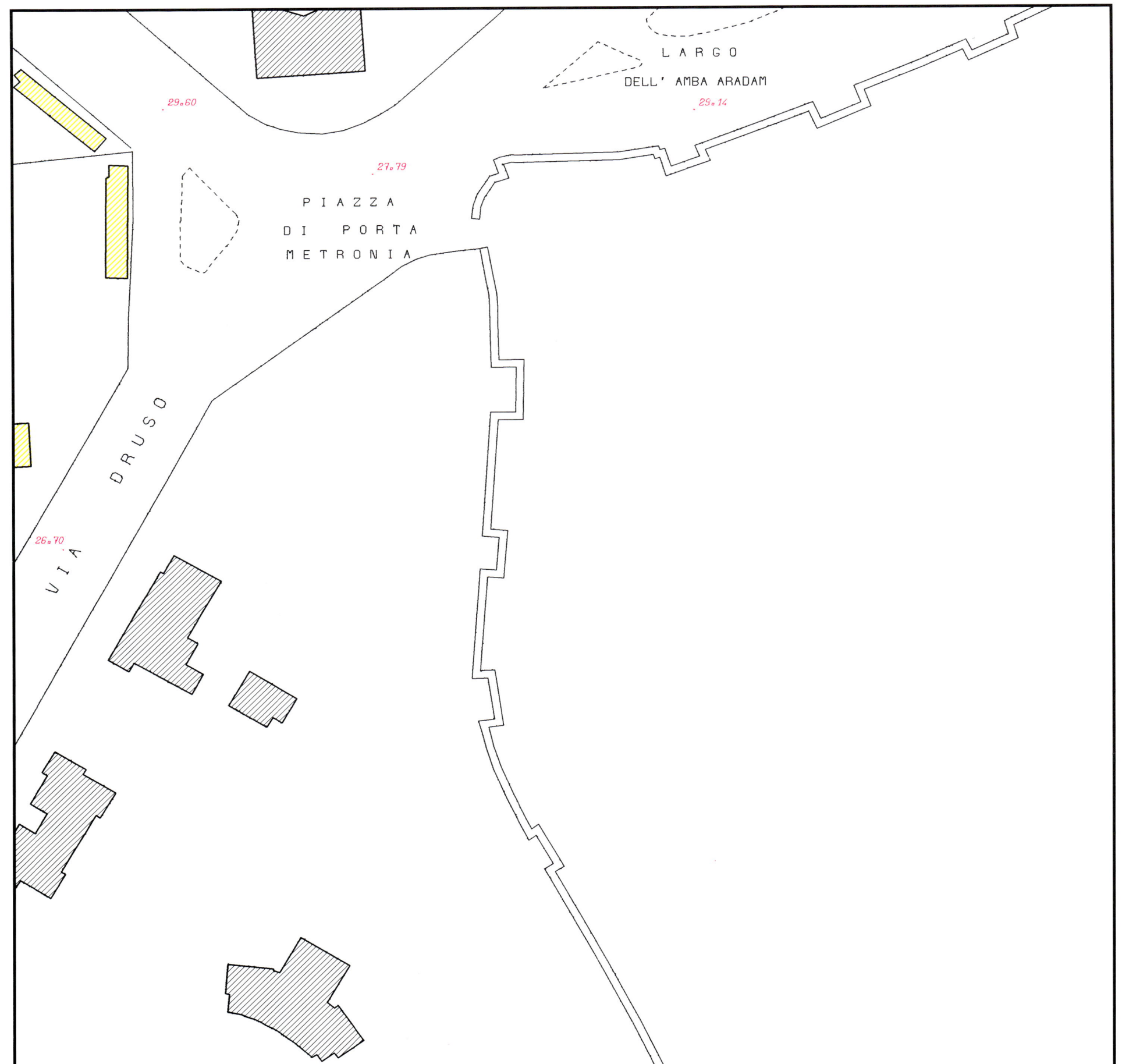

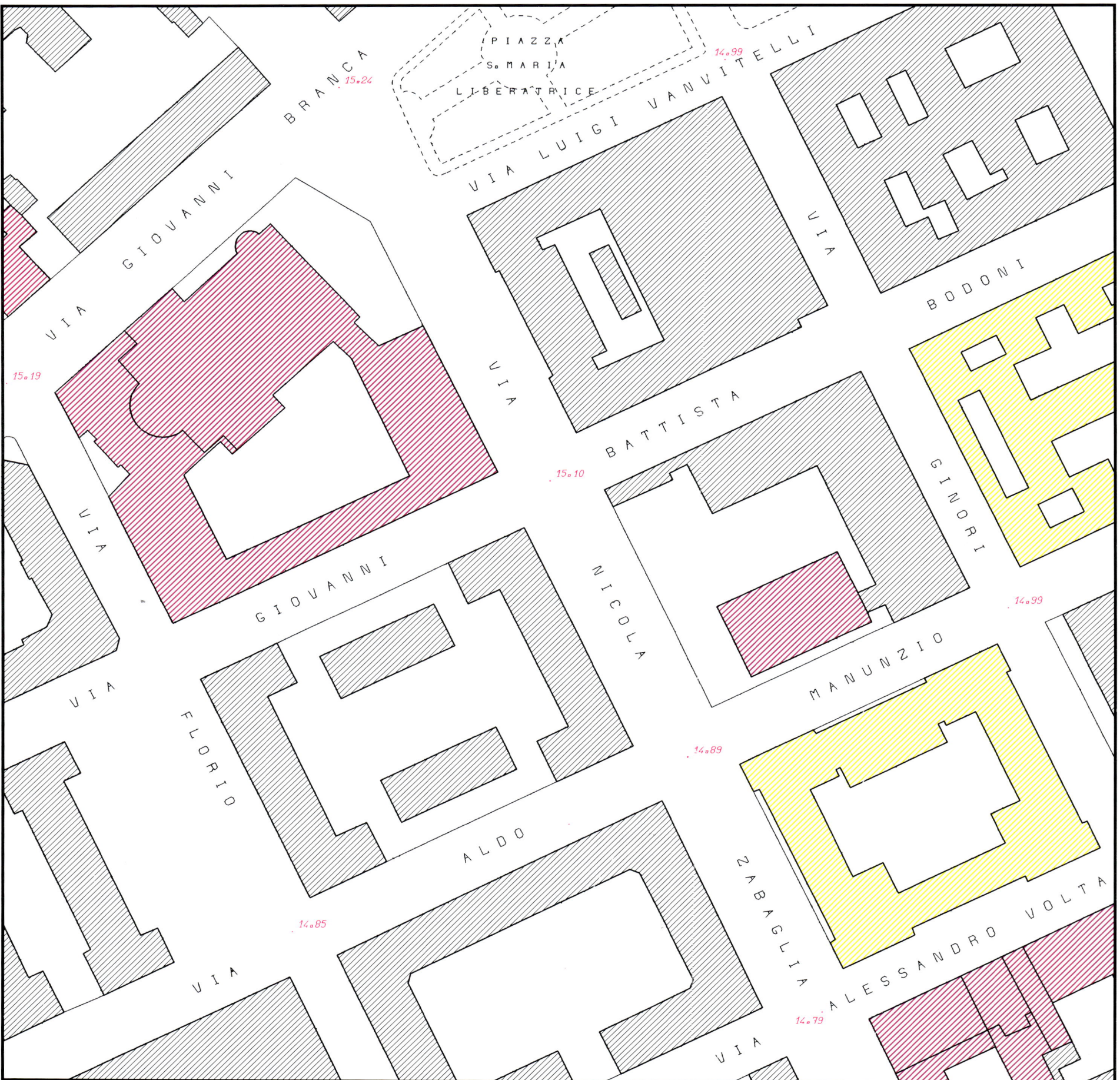

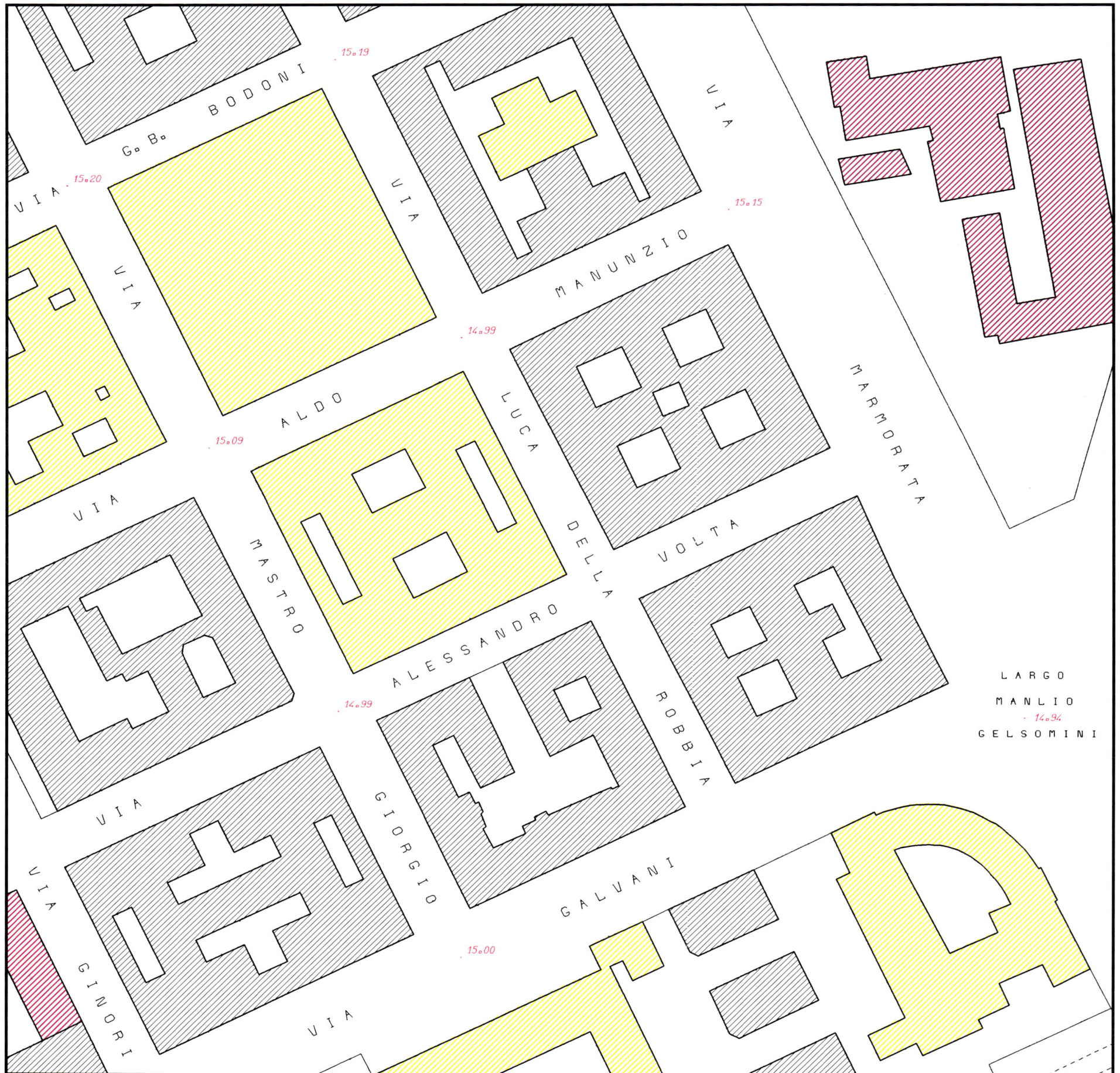

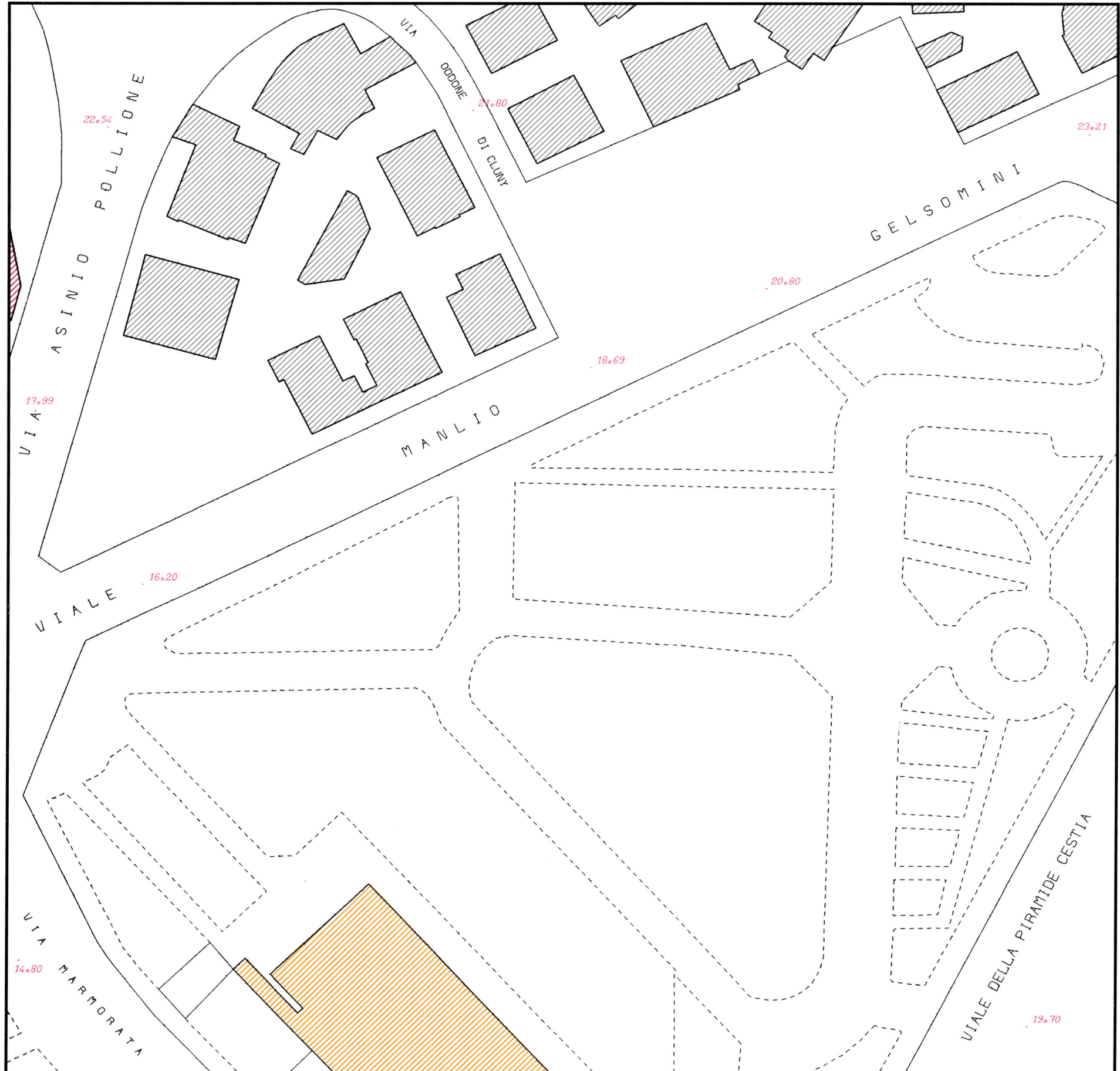

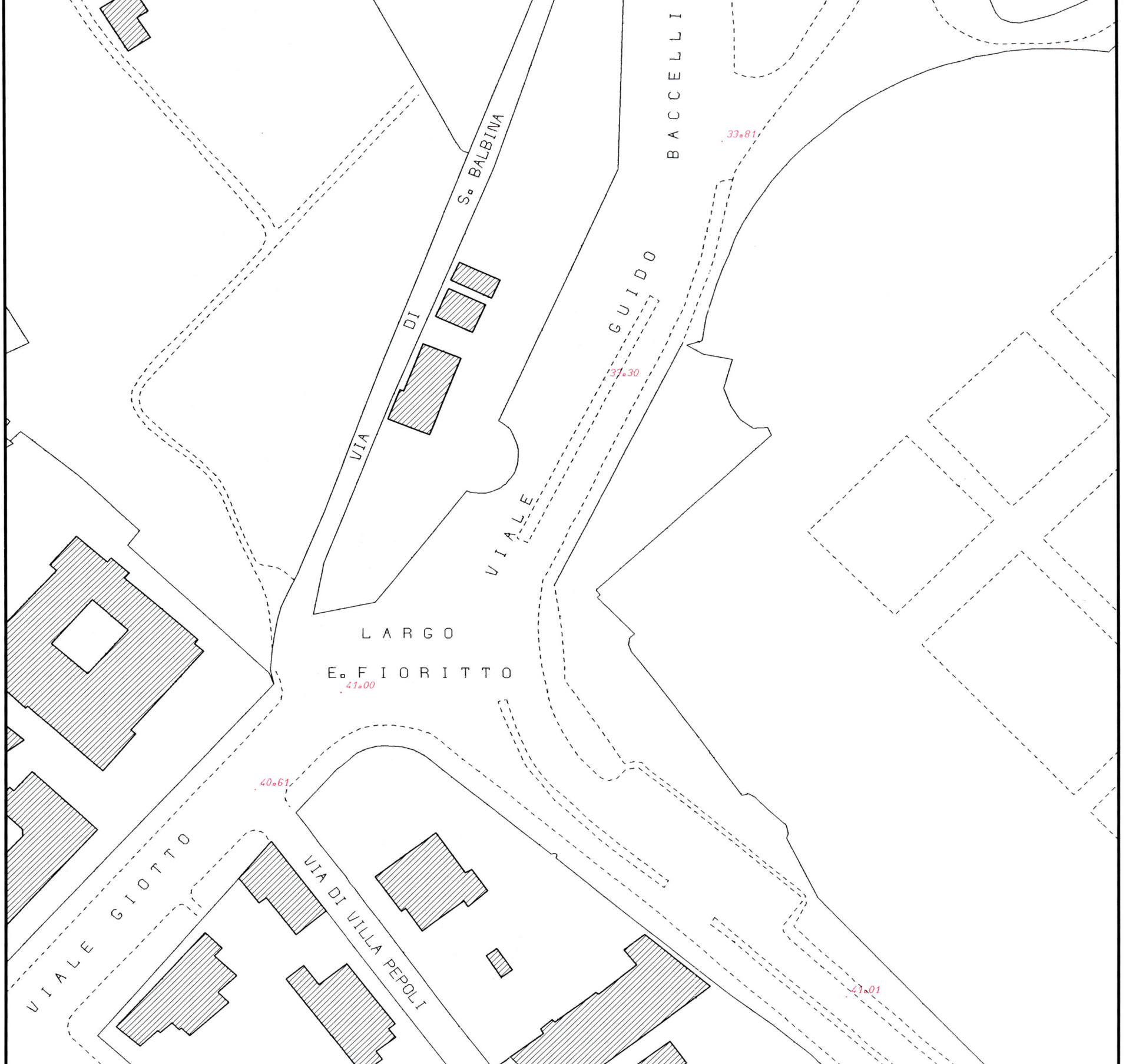

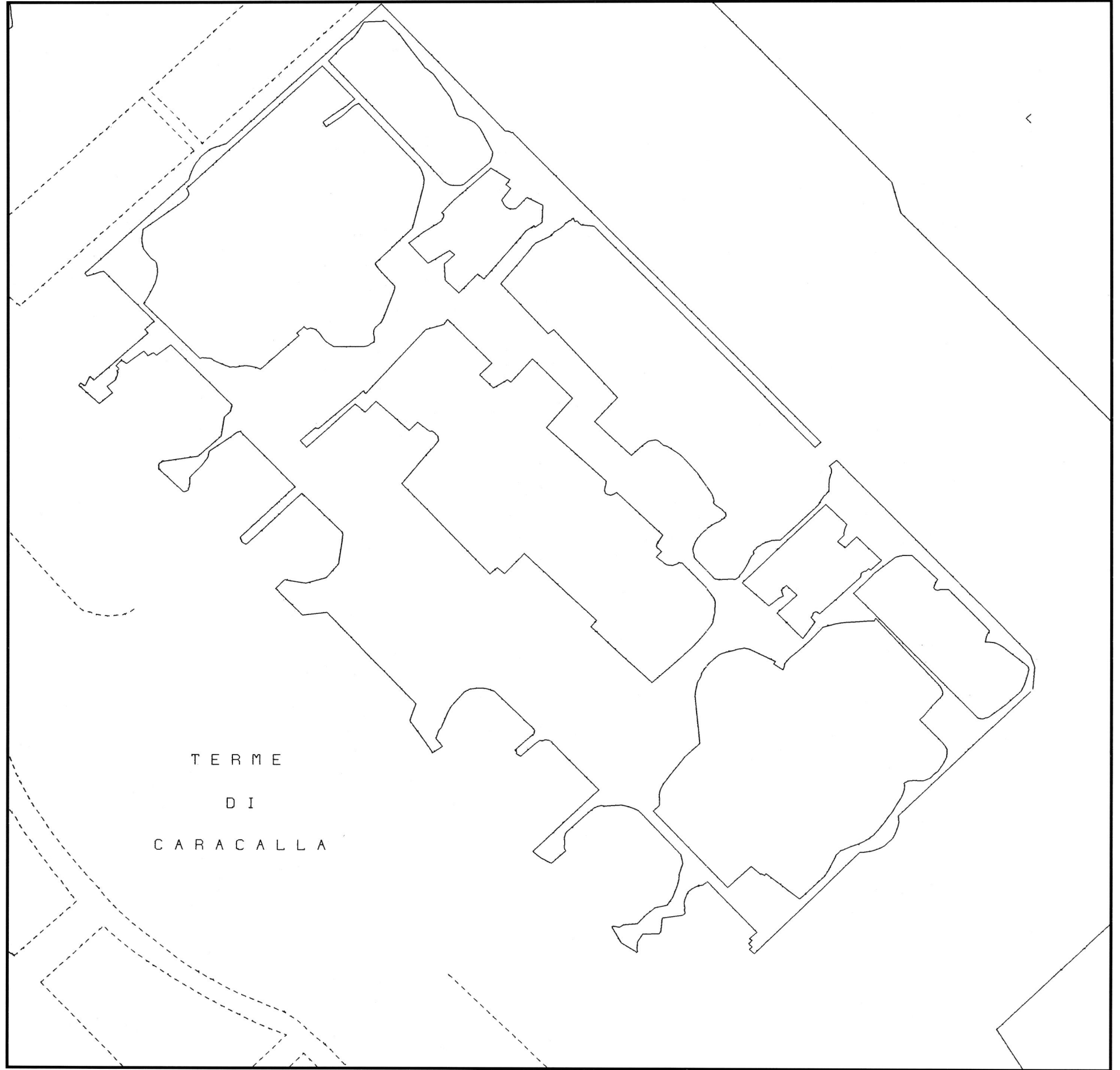

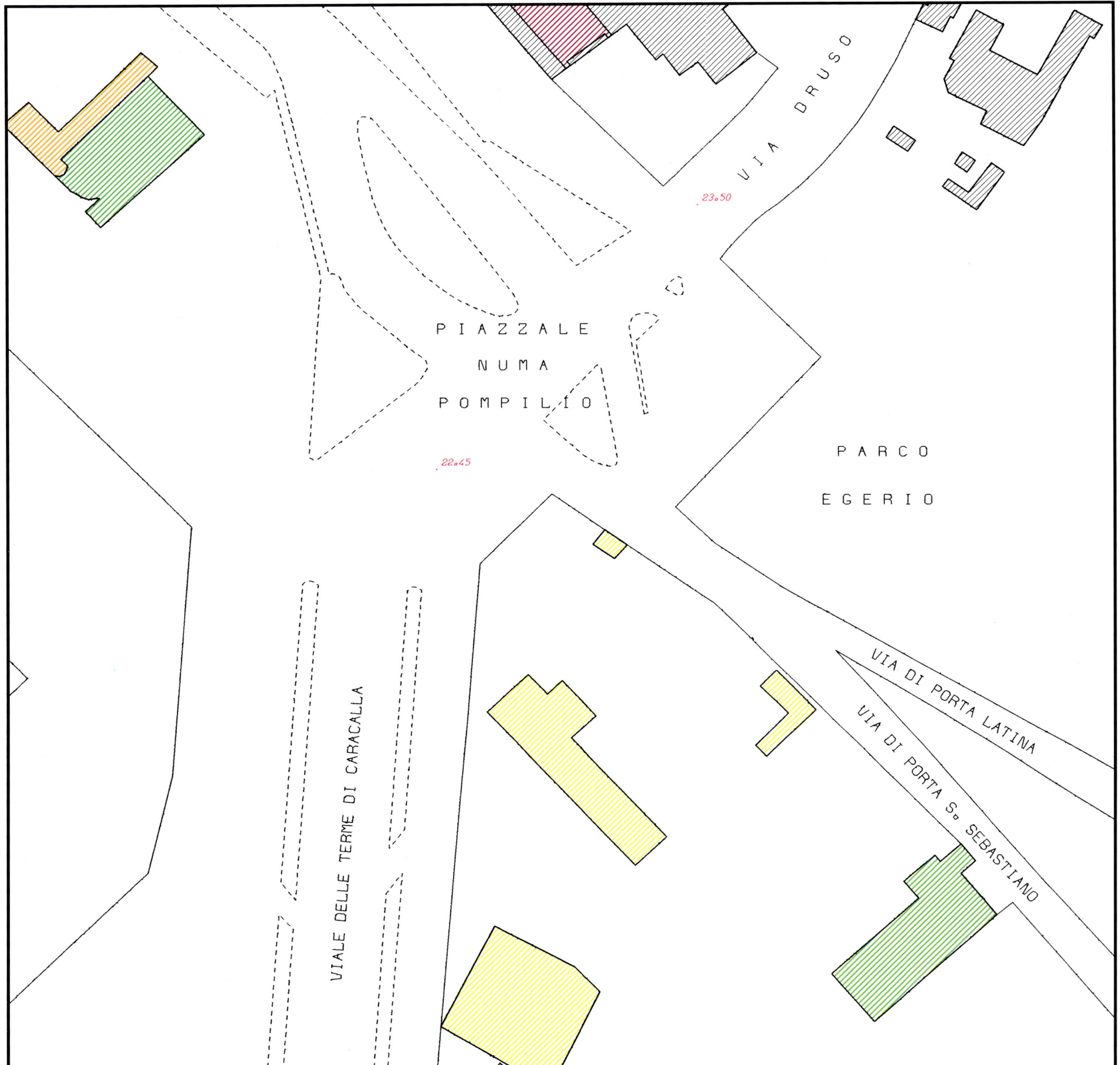

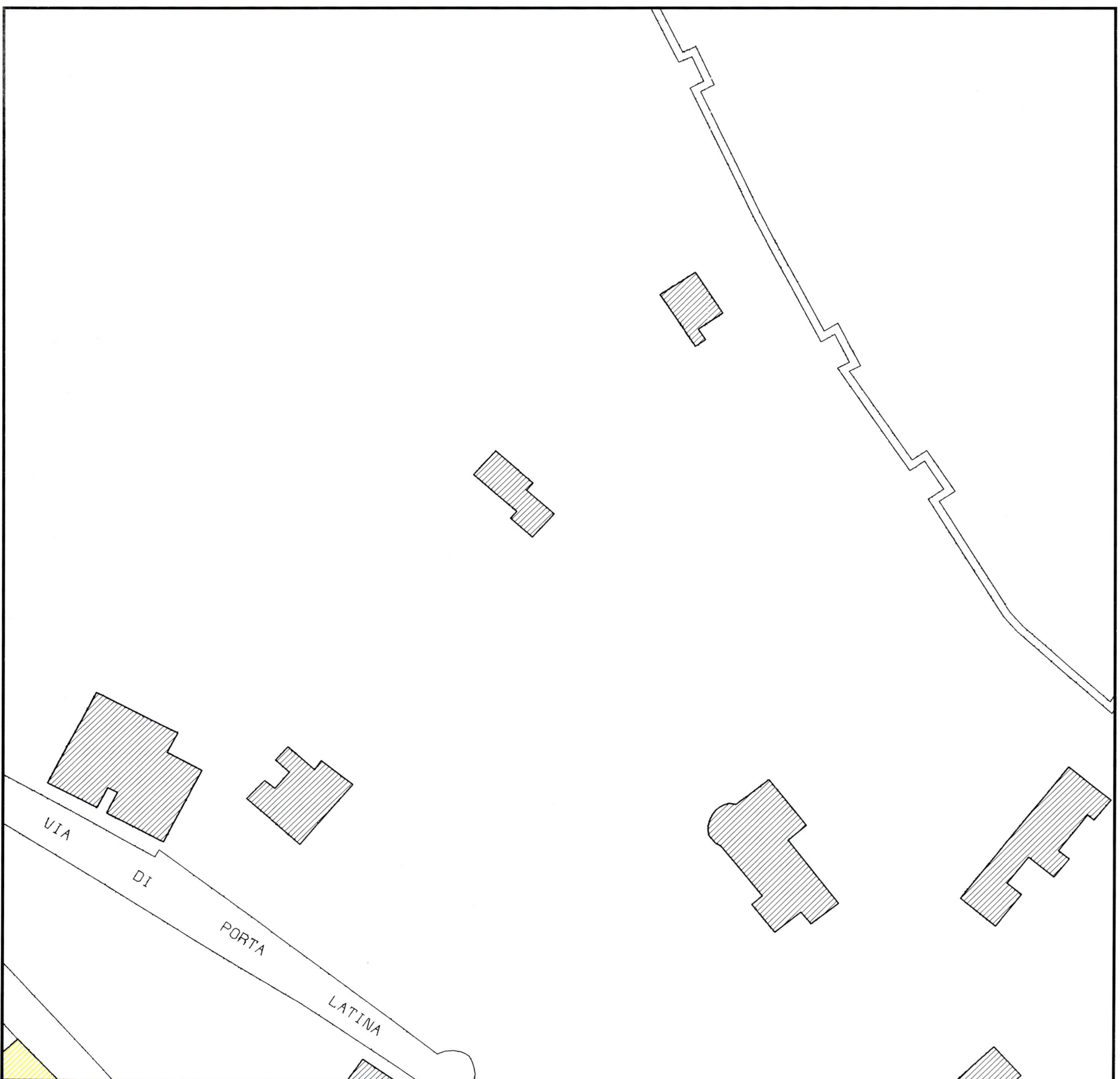

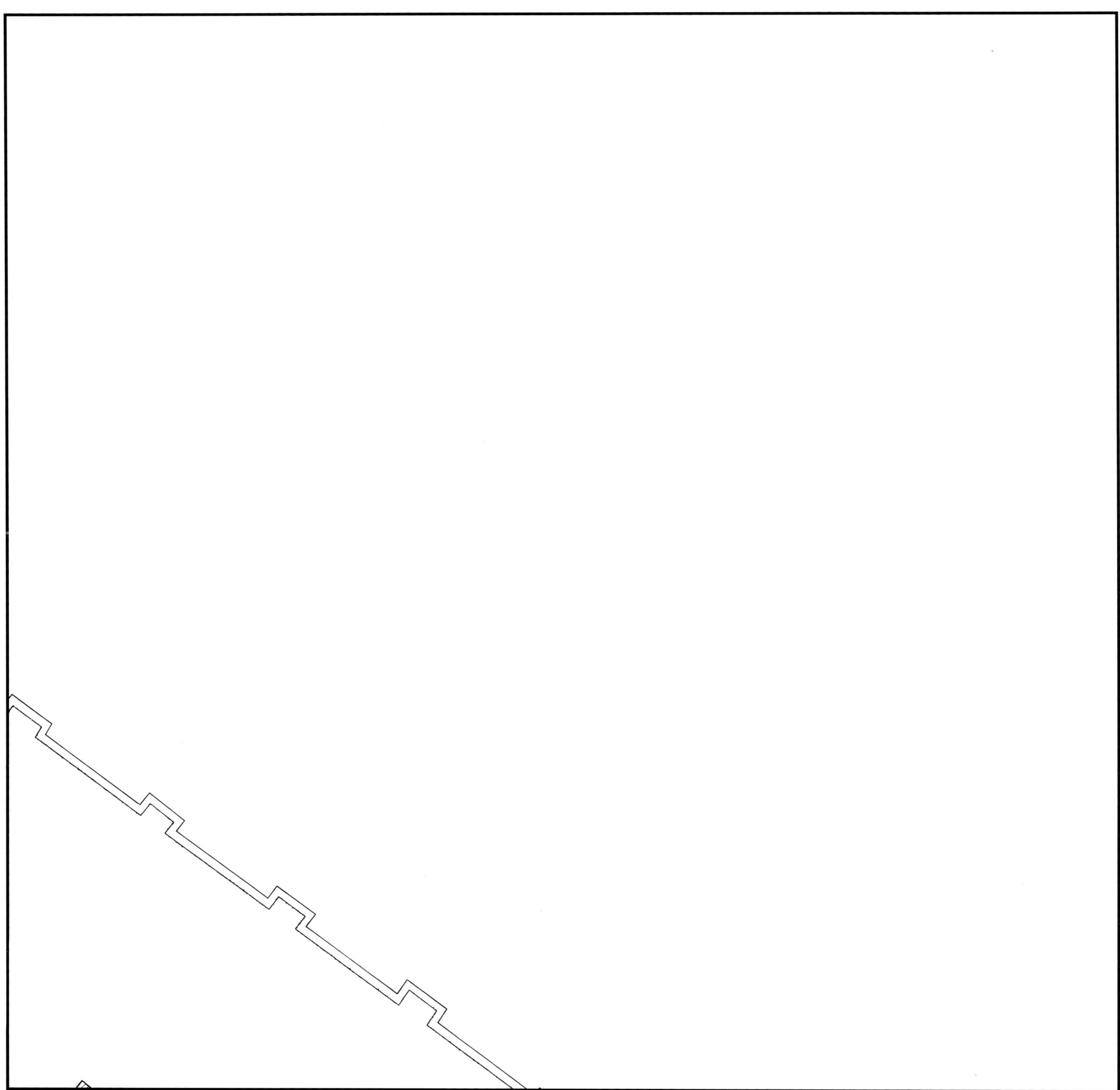

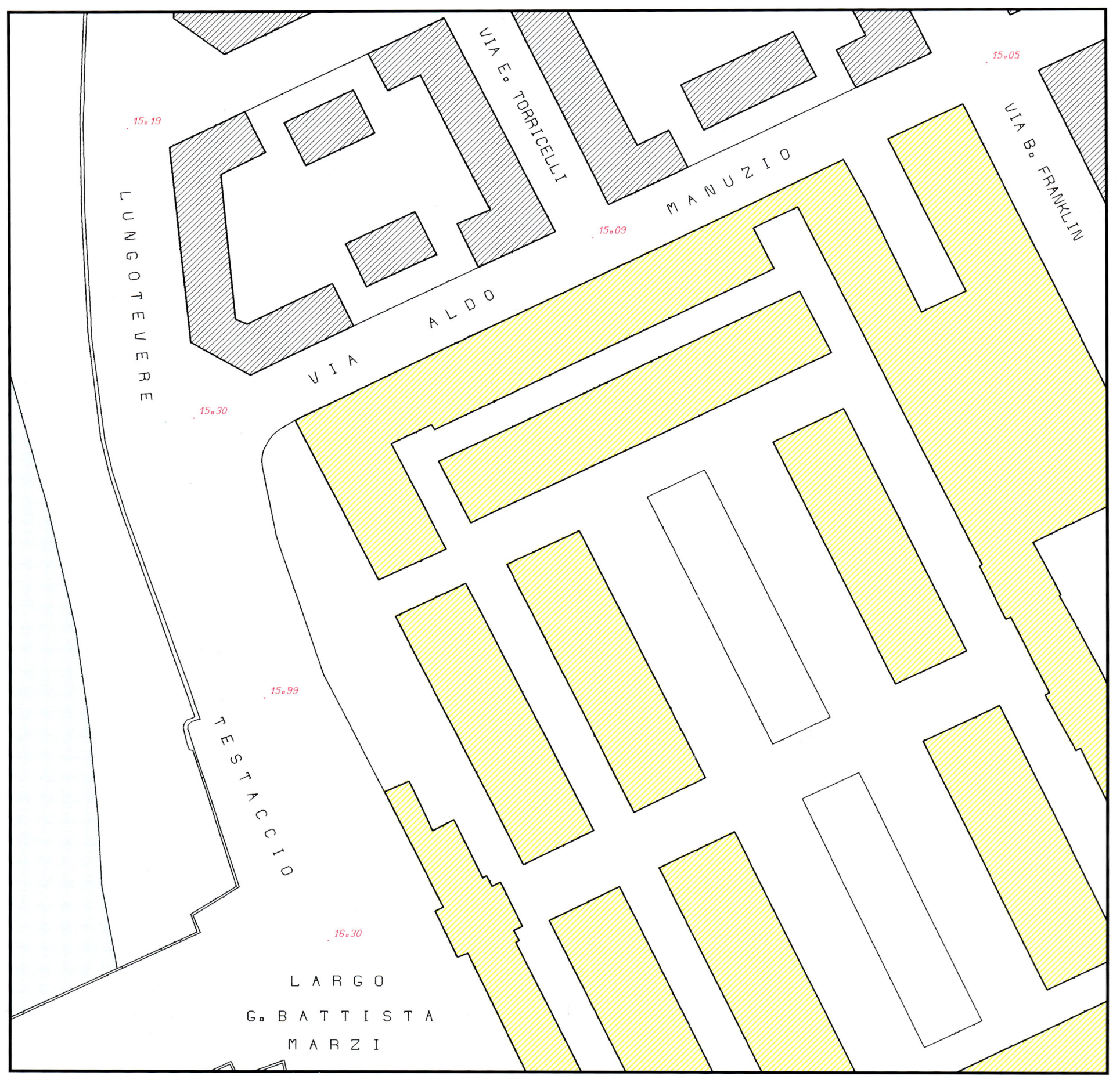

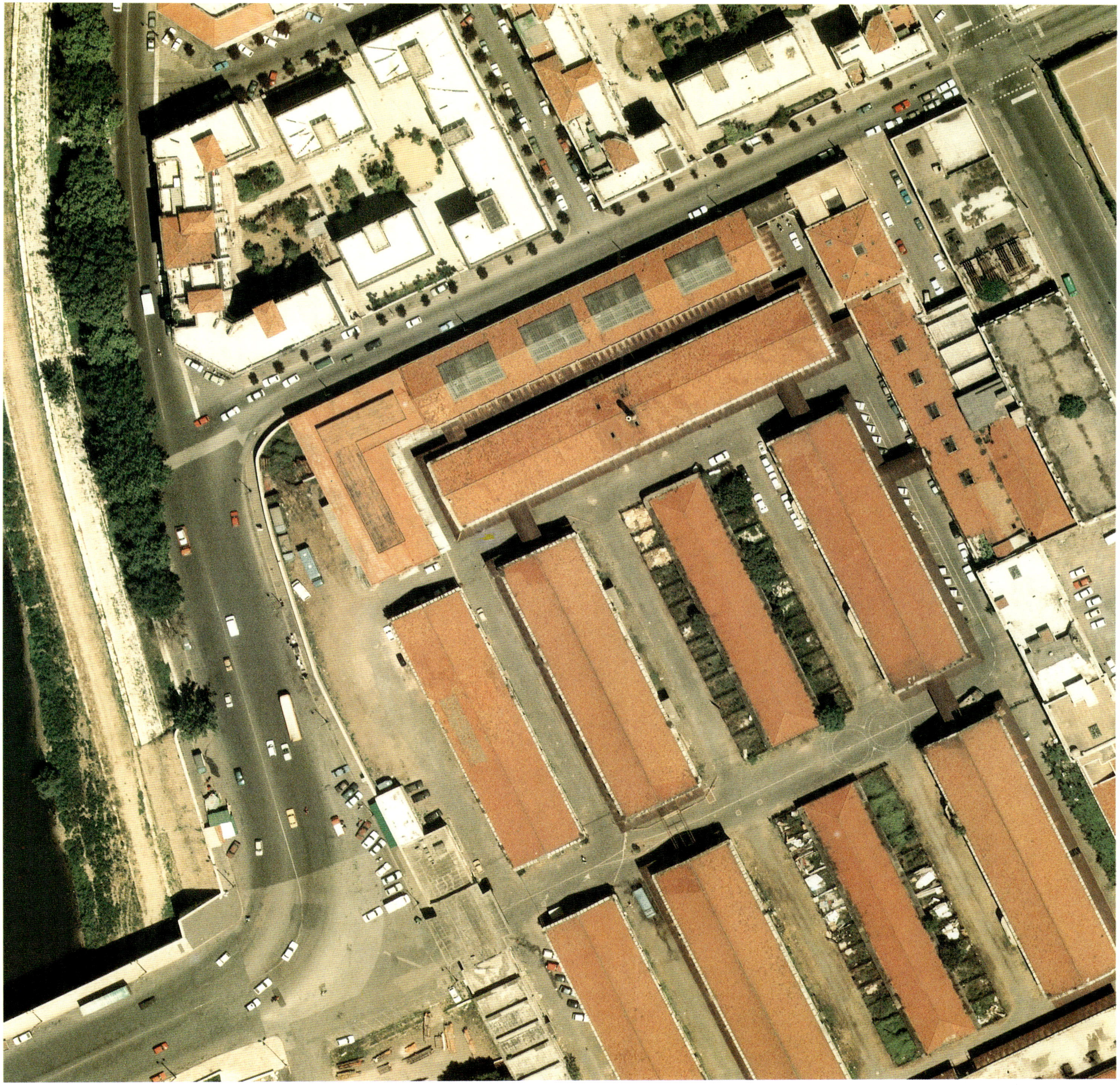

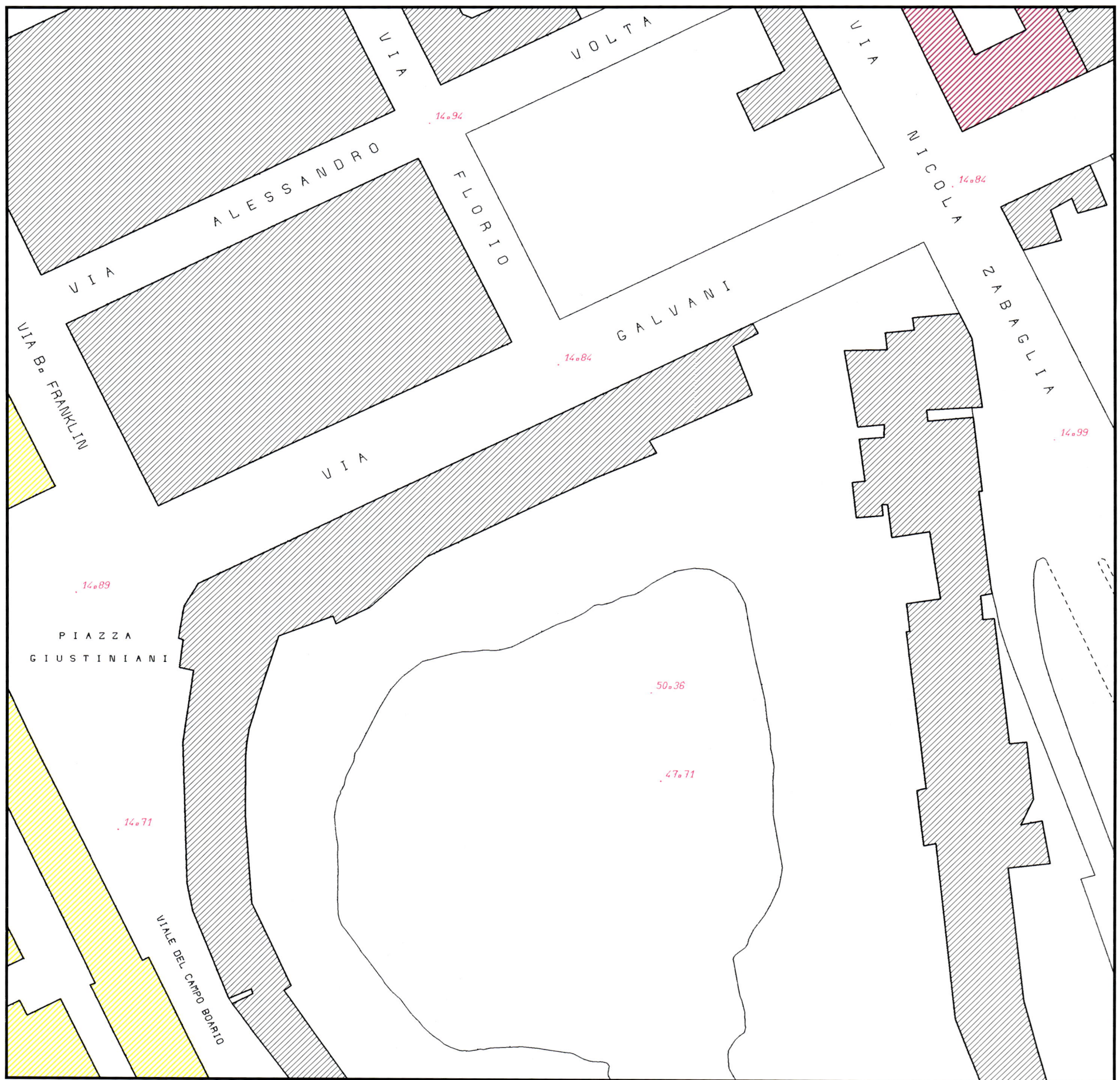

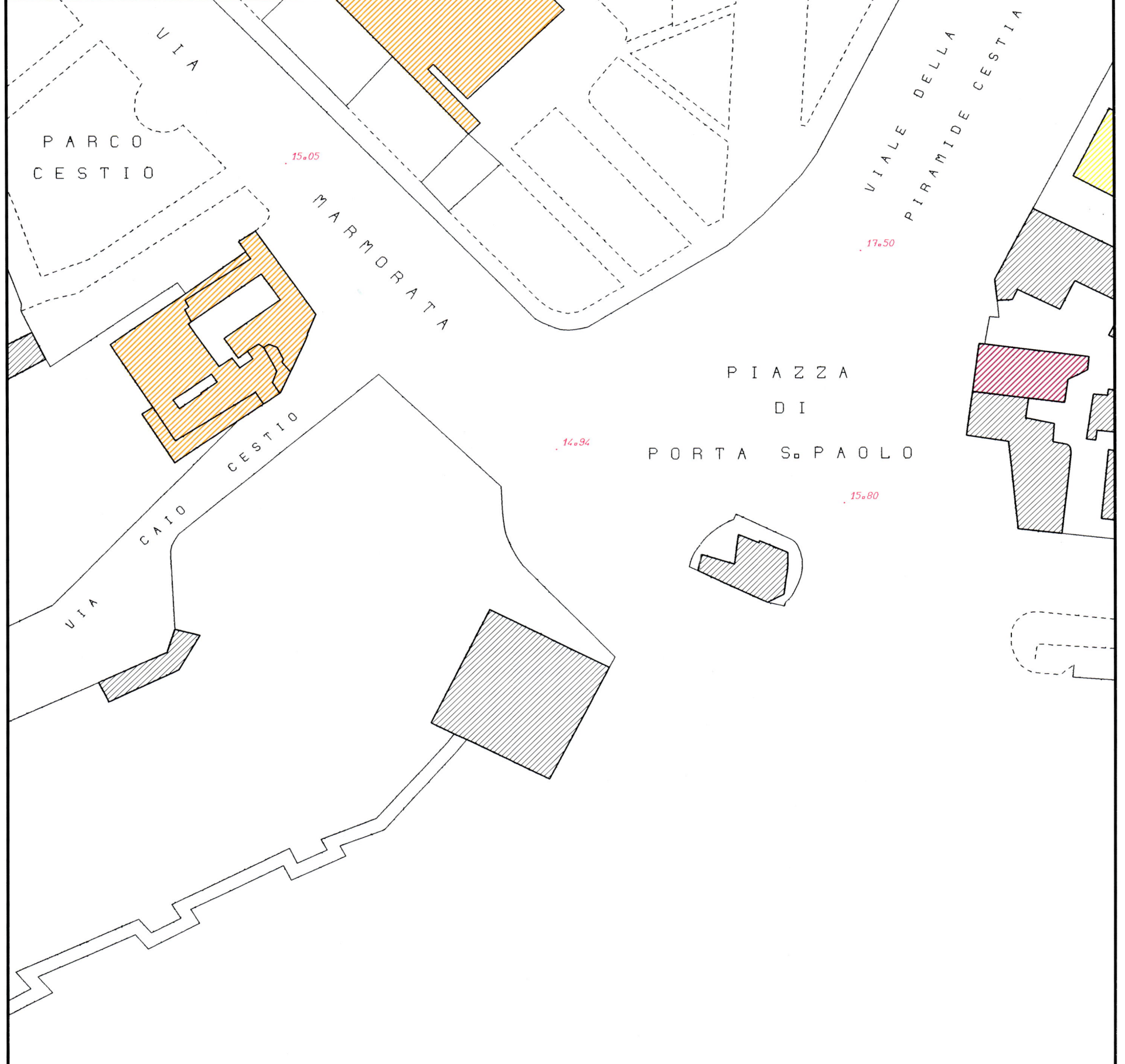

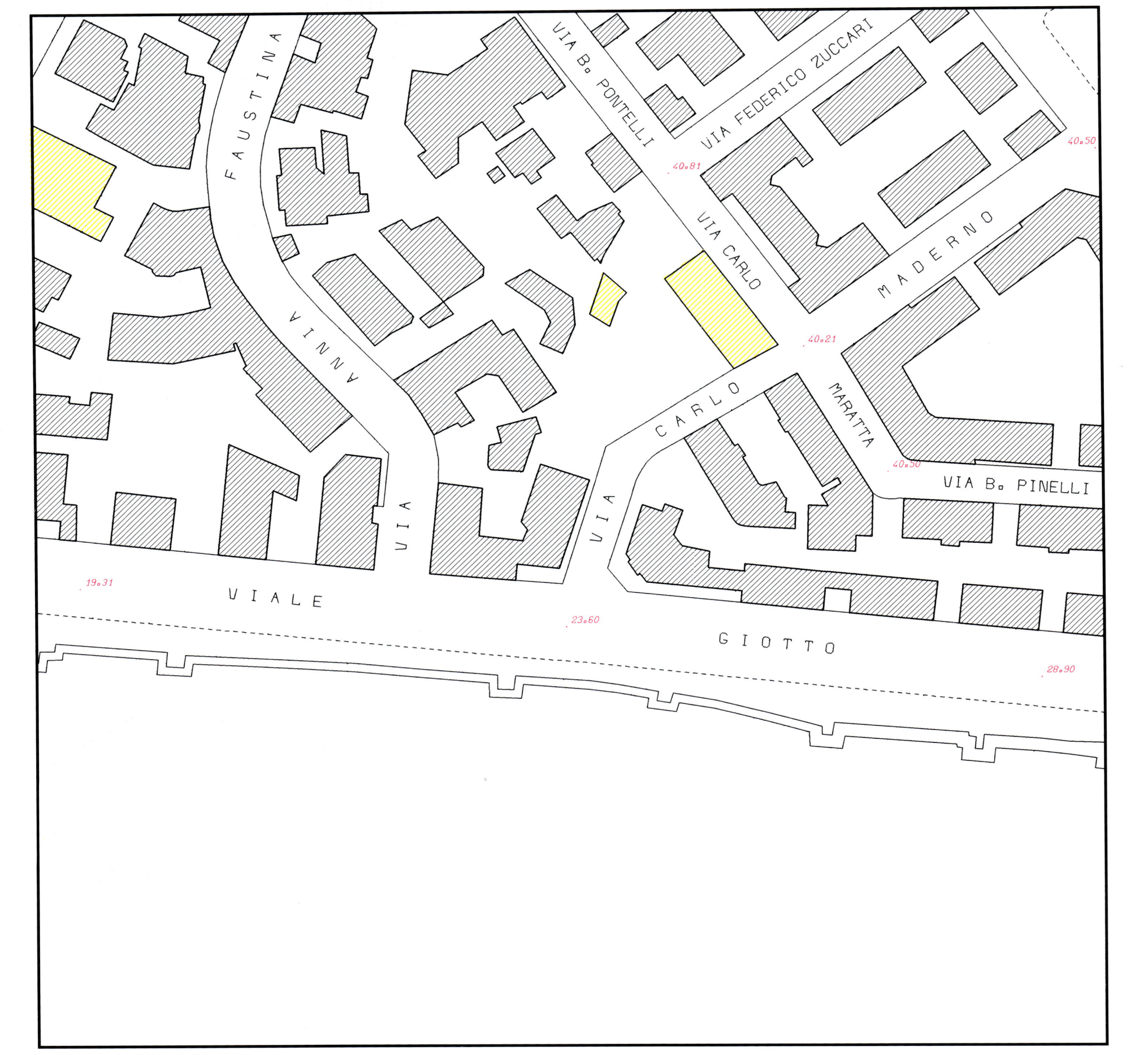

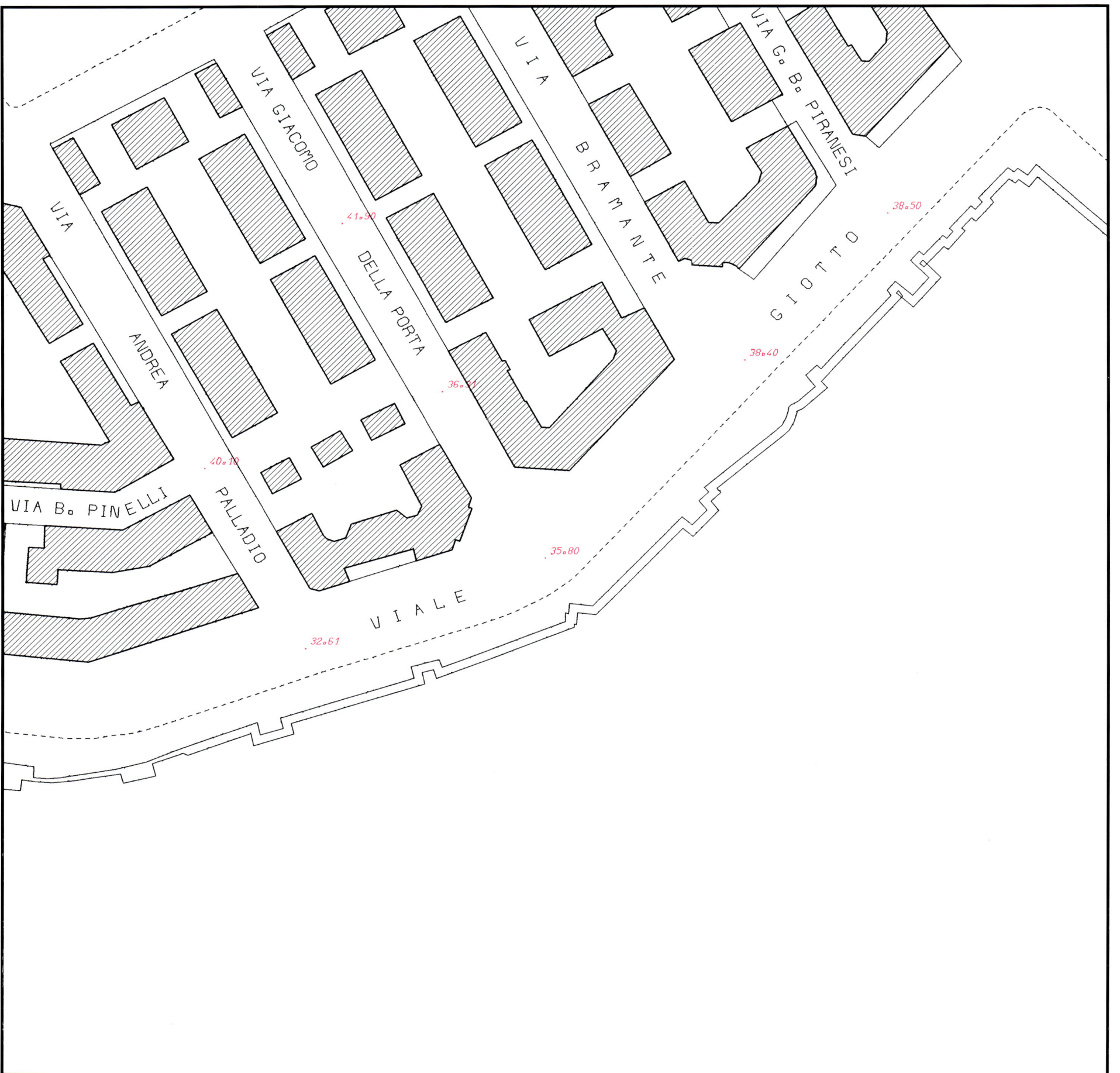

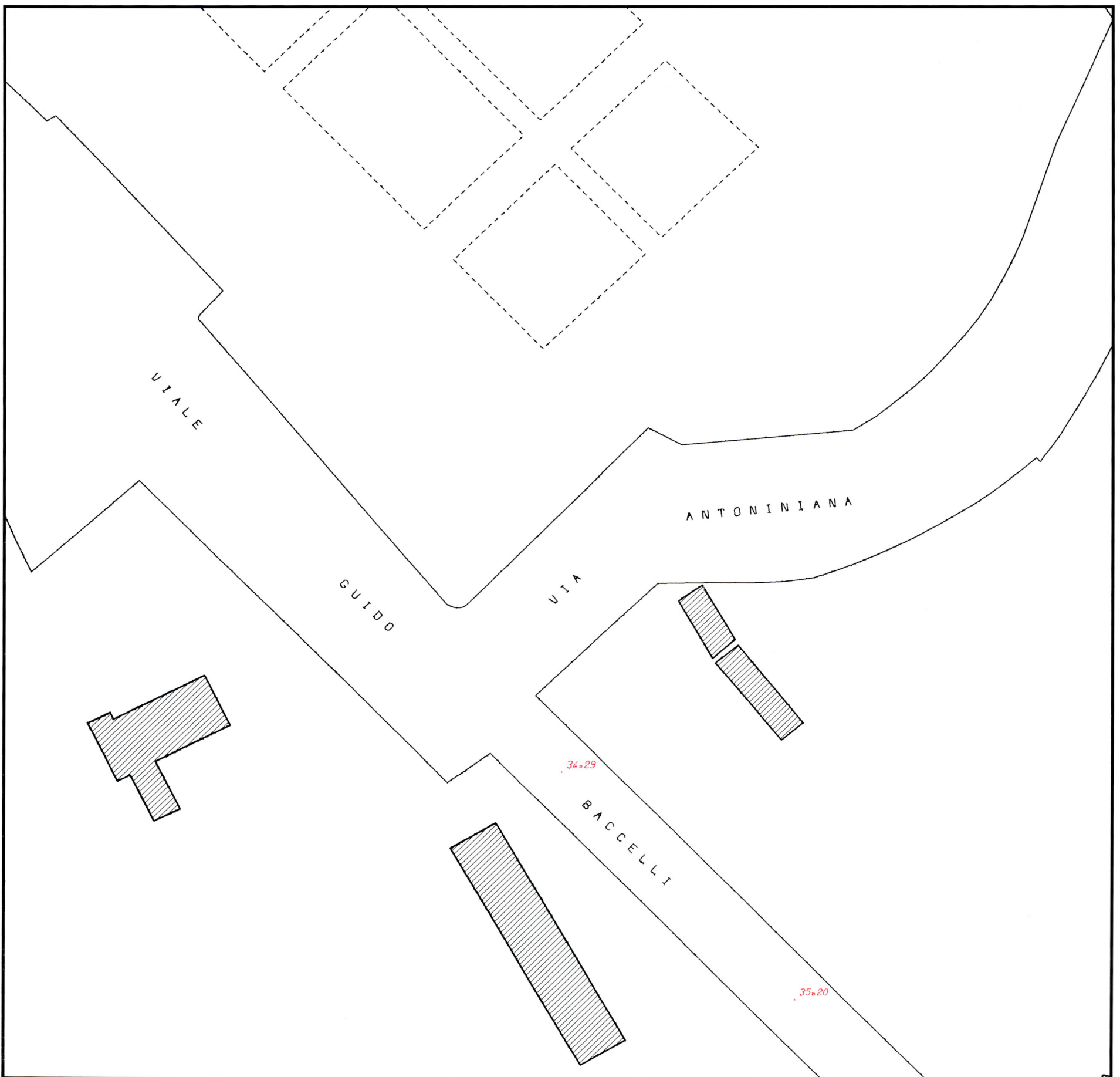

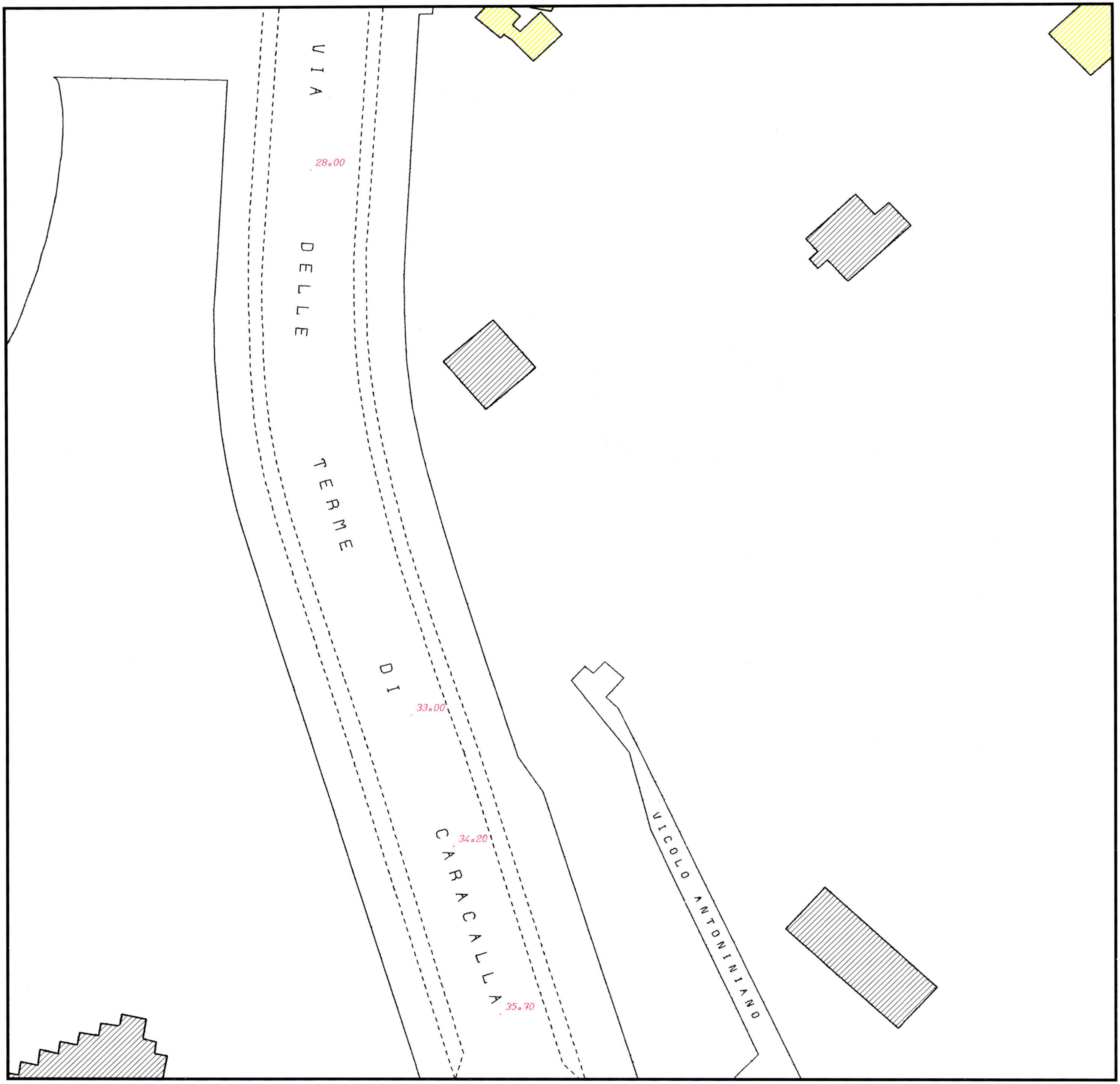

VIA DELLE TERME DI CARACALLA

28.00
33.00
34.20
35.70

VICOLO ANTONINIANO

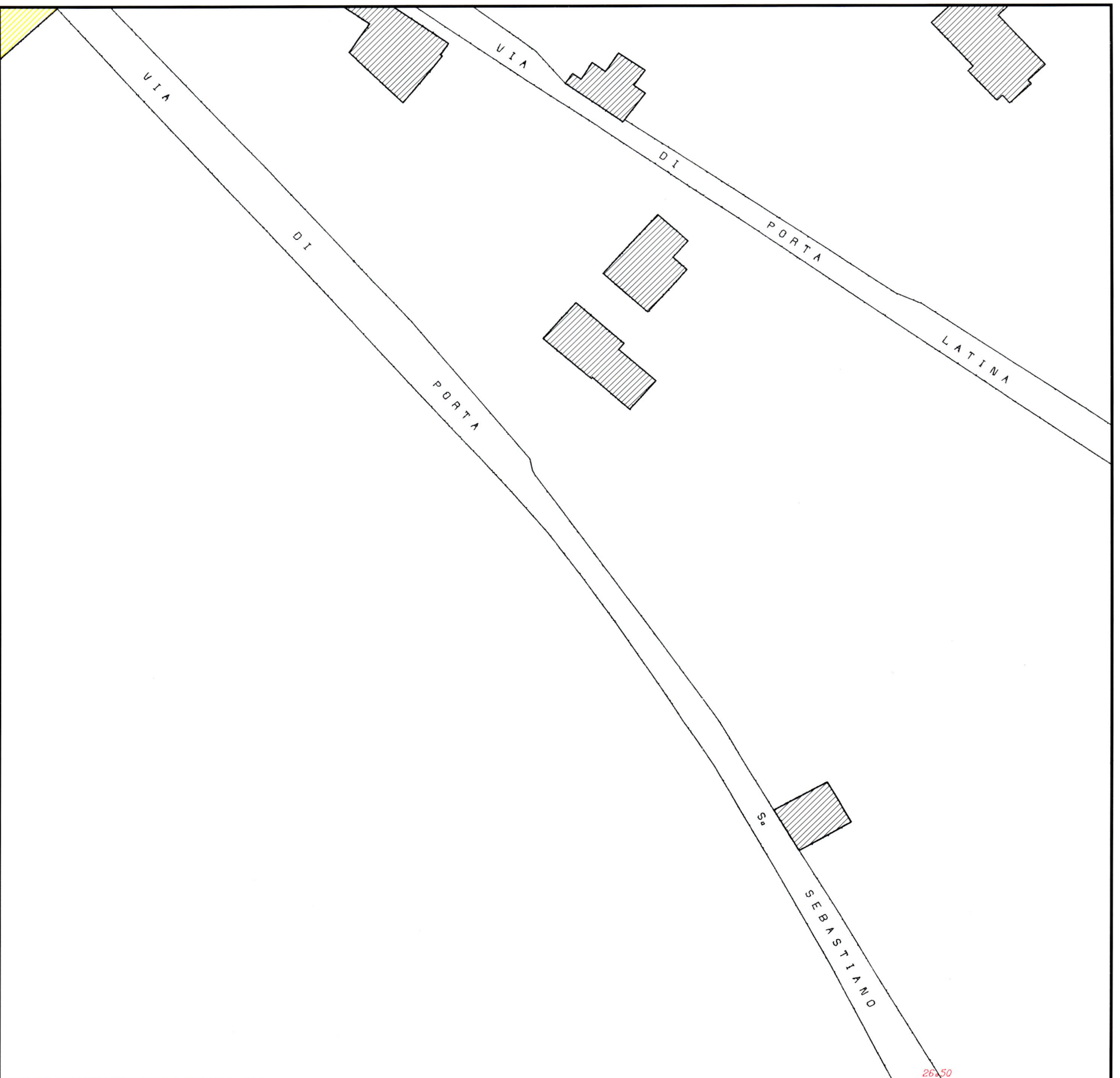

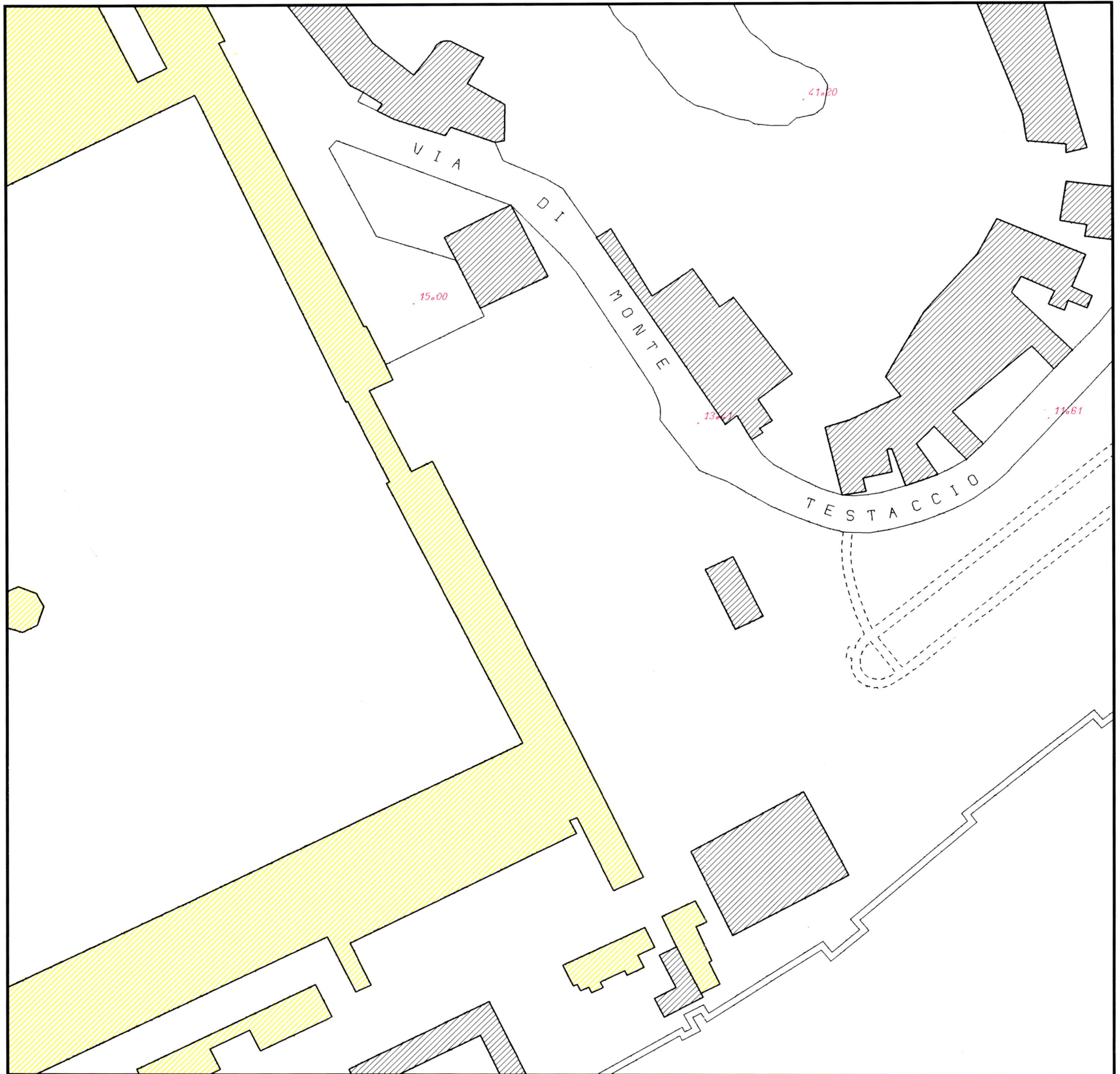

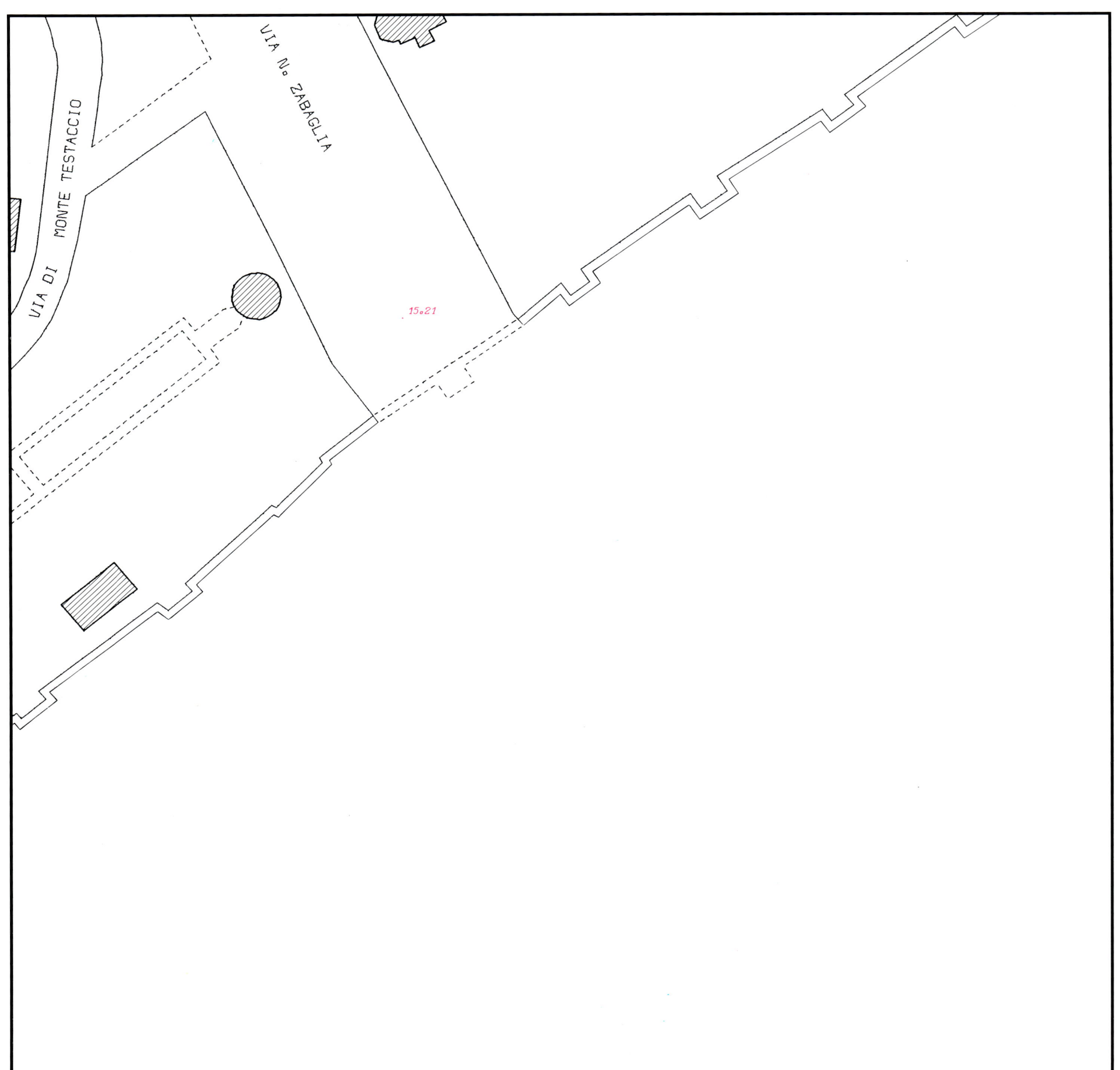

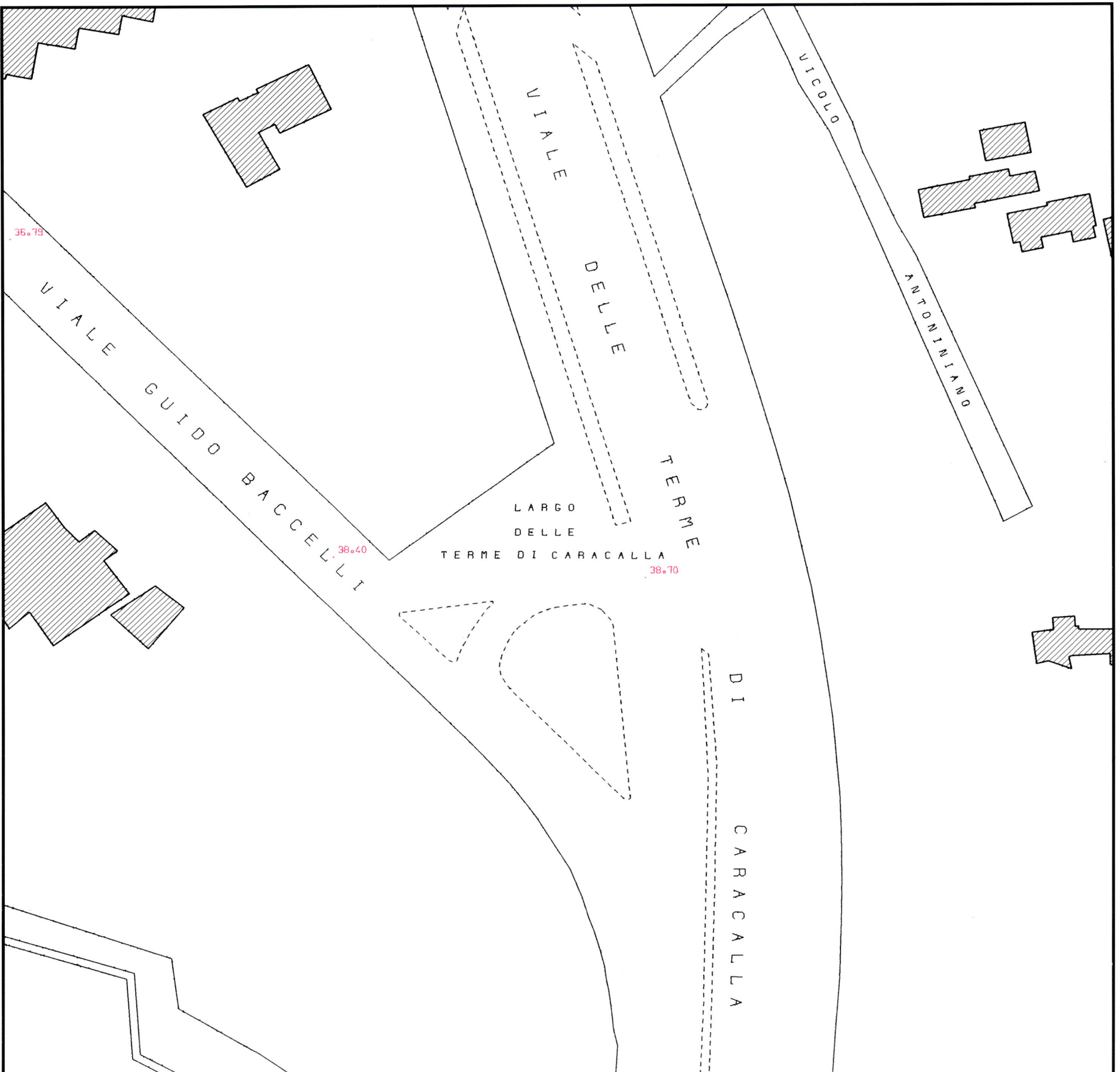

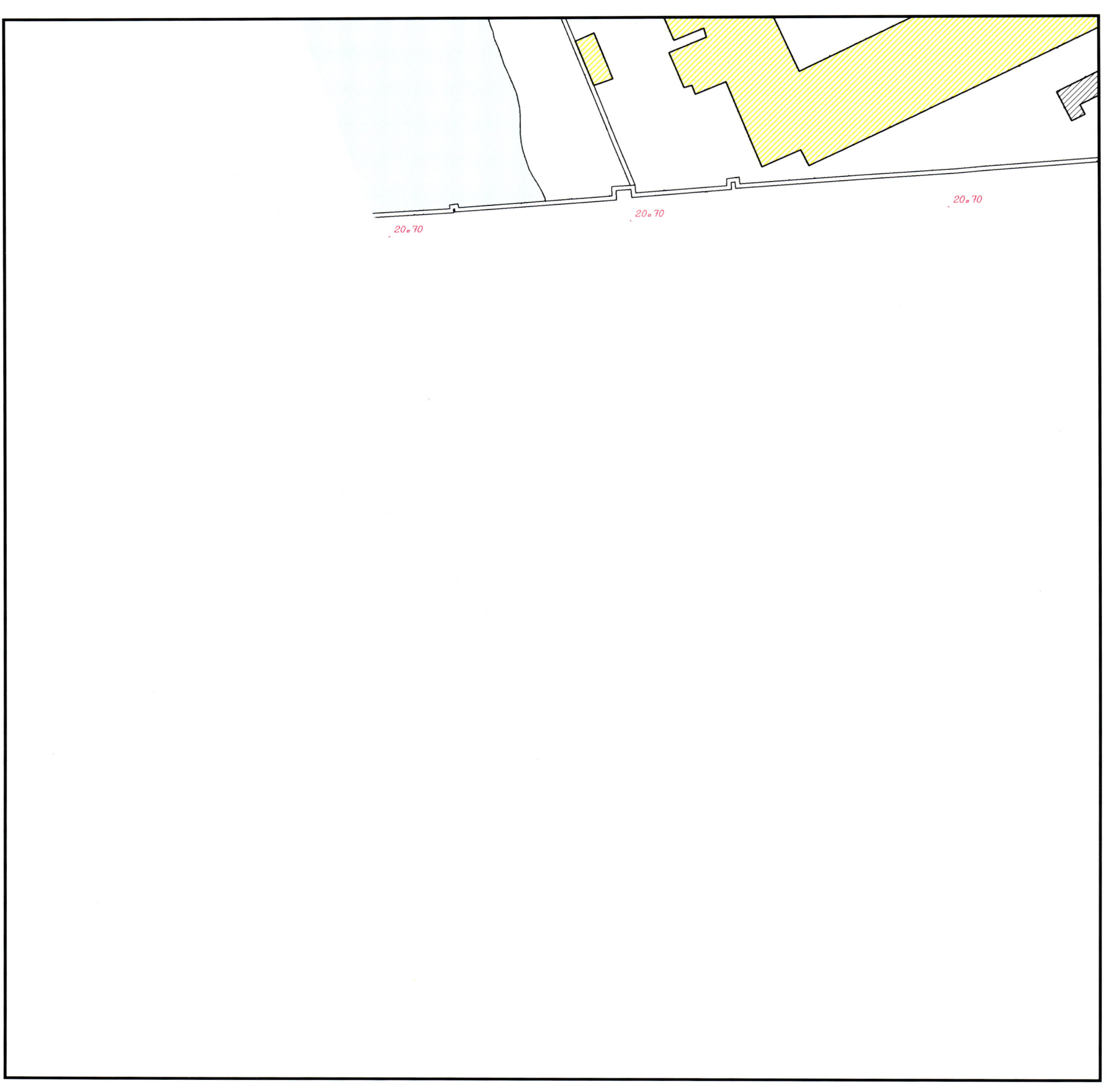

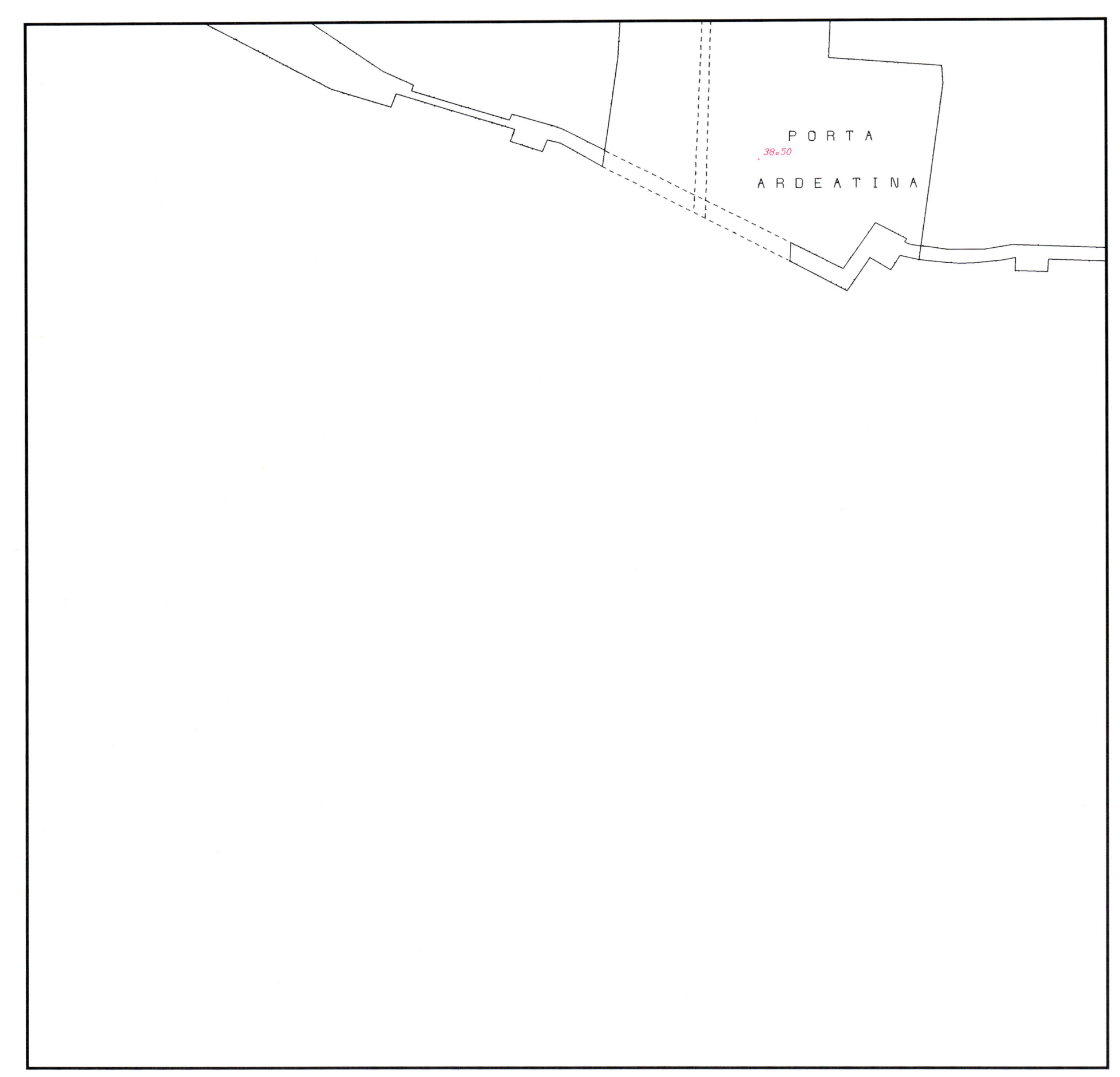

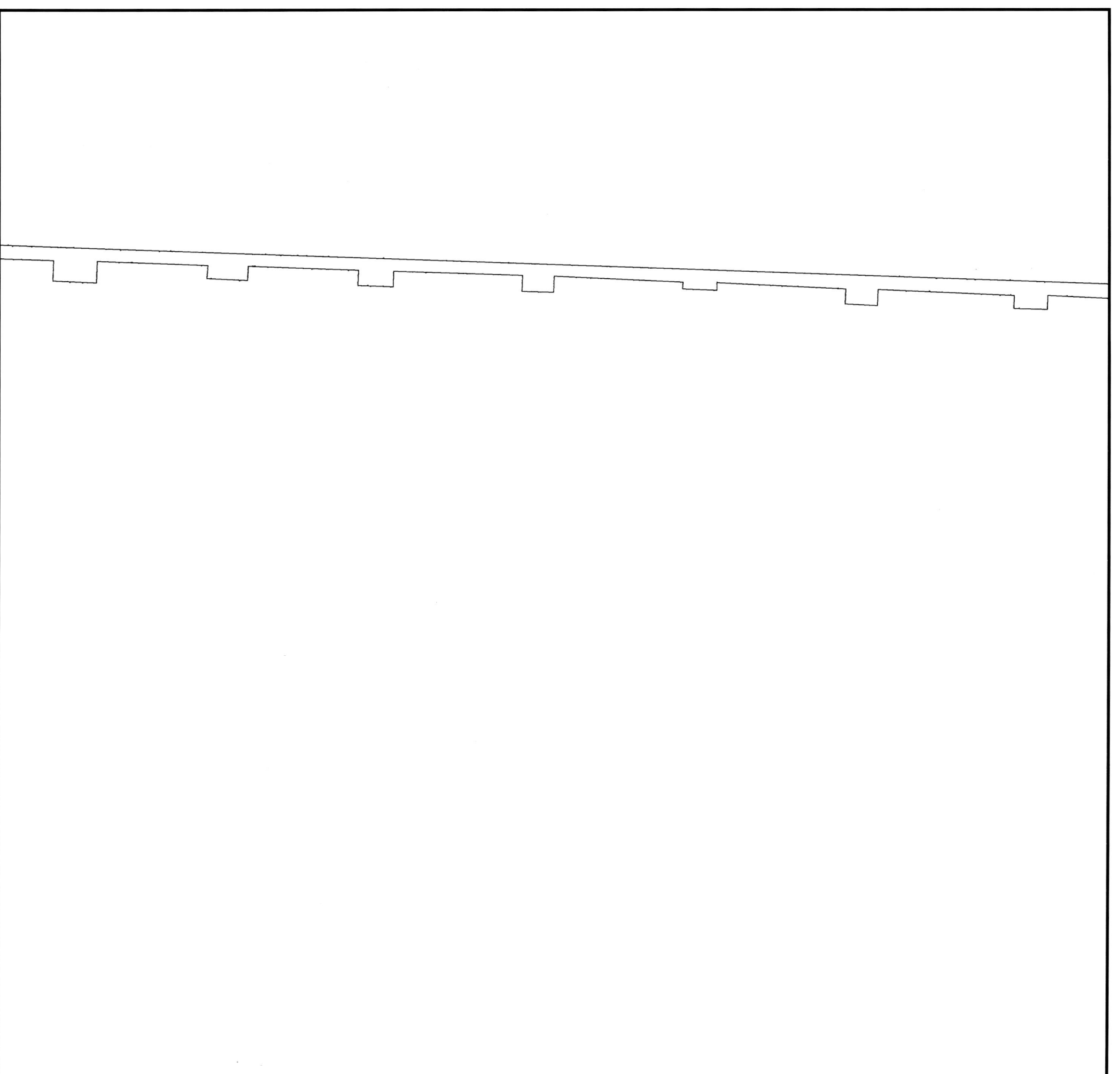

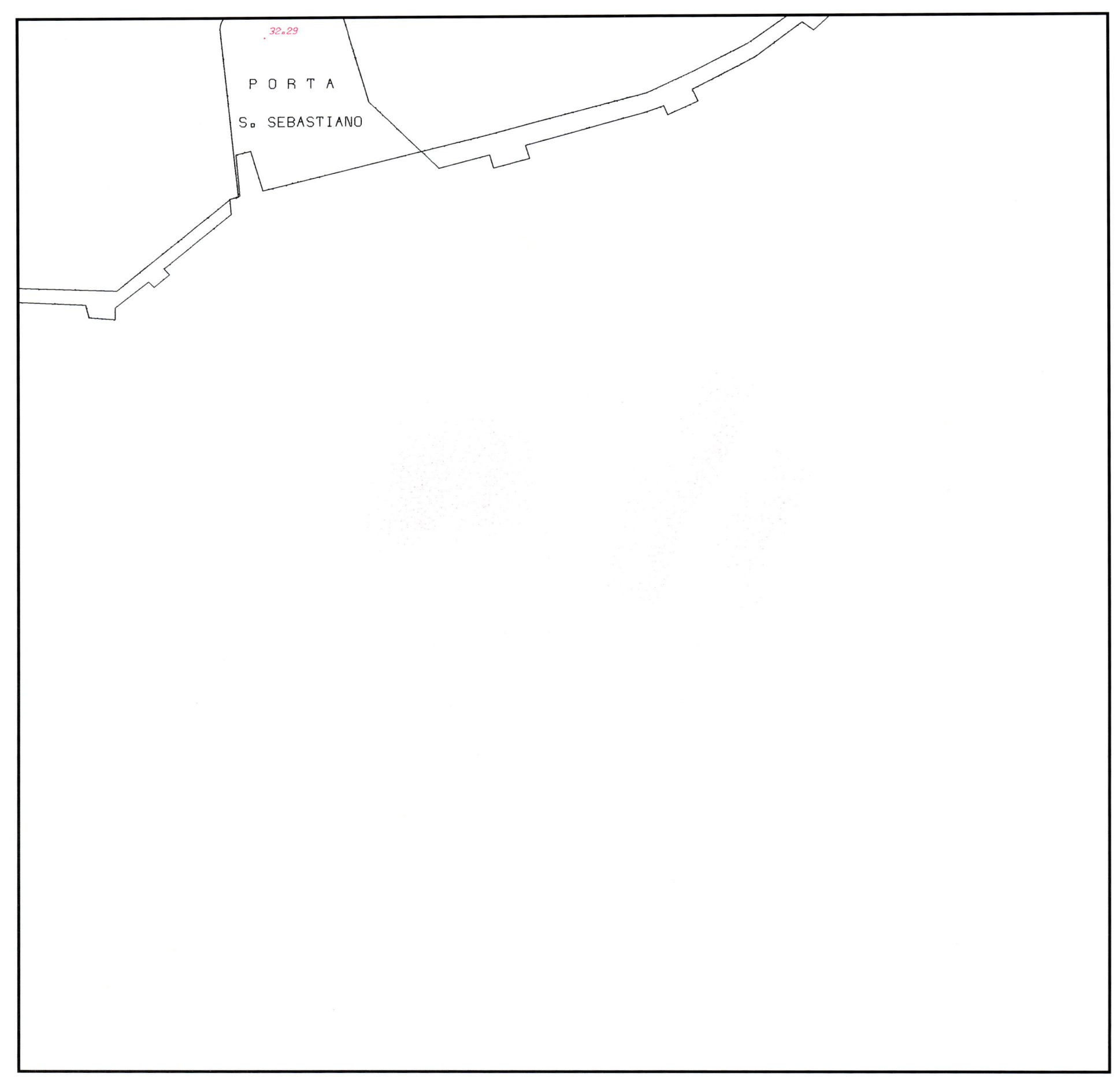

改善された都市のための新しい道具

特にアウグスツス時代以来、他のどの都市よりも西洋の中心と見なされてきたローマの発達は、質と量の両方において比類のない地図資料の豊富さを伴ってきた。このような資料の最良の出所は壮大なアマト・ピエトロ・フルータスの作品である。地形測量と地図製作に人生を捧げた後、フルータスは1962年にLe Piante di Rome（ローマの地図）という、分厚い3巻から成る本を出版した。セプティミアス・セヴェルスの時代から第2次世界大戦後までの何百という図面（上からの垂直投影）や「鳥瞰的観点」が、チベレ川がキャンパス・マルチウスや魚のような特徴のある形をしたチベリーナ島やコロシウムとその近くのロマン・フォルム、そしてトラストベレの小さな家々の間さえも曲がりくねって流れている姿を表している。

ローマは、あの頑固なボルテールが言うように、キリスト教の「メッカ」であり、それゆえ必然的に膨大な地図の放出を招いた。この都市が非常に偉大な建築物の宝庫となり、非常に多くの巡礼者（宗教巡礼者だけでなく、ヨーロッパ大陸巡遊旅行の非宗教的で文化的な巡礼者も含めて）の最終目的地であったという事実は、この町の地図が、何か新しい発展がある度に、それを利用する様々な人の必要に応じて絶えず改訂されてきたことを意味している。数えきれないほどの地図製作技術のほとんど総てがローマに応用されてきた。古代後期の「説話」絵巻、13世紀の象徴的な表現法（Rome a modo de lione）、上部からの投影による平面図、16世紀から18世紀の造形図の鳥の目のような視点、そして20世紀の航空写真などがそうである。最後の3つの図法では、正方形または長方形の背景に地図が刻まれたことから、主要点の位置に何らかの注意を払うことが必然的に要求された。このため、方位の配置は興味深いものとなり、しばしば宇宙地理的な哲学を表現している。図面の上部に誰もが知る北極として示されている北の位置は、比較的最近になって表れ始めたことがうかがえる。しかし、北の位置づけは世界の創造と同じ位古いものだと一般に信じられている。

平面図法で描かれた地図は土地台帳に特に適している。道や教会や家は、（メートル法に縮小されている以外は）「実際の」寸分違わぬ発展状況を示しており、あたかも設立時に地面レベルで描かれたように見える。この図法による地図では、垂直方向の建築の特徴や都市の高層化の成長度に関する情報は一切剥奪されている。この種の地図は、原始的ながらも正確な道具で作成されている。それらは建物間や地面間の水平距離をはかるのに役立つ。こうして集められた情報は、その後図面化される。上からのコントロールは誤差が累積されて図面が不正確になるのを避けるのにしばしば有効だが、これらは上からのコントロールを必要としない。

Forma Urbis Romae（AD203～211年、大きさ約13×18.10m）としてよく知られているセプチミアス・セヴェルスのローマ地図は、ローマを平面図法で表した巨大な大理石のモザイク板である。それは単なるガイドであっただけでなく、旅行案内でもあり、そして何よりもそれは土地台帳であった。それは為政者により作られた、全市民が参照できる公文書であった。防壁に囲まれたローマとそれを取り巻く地域を示すレオナルド・ブファリーニの1551年の木板もまた平面図法による。G.B.ノリの18世紀の地図も似たような平面図法ラインに沿って作られている。正確さと目的の違いをのぞけば（後の2つは土地台帳の目的で作られたのではない）、これらの平面図法による地図が造形図法による表現と異なる点は、それが測面の精密さにおいてはるかに上回っていることである。それらは表記されている物体の高さについては何の情報も与えないが、その欠点を精密な文献資料の豊富さで補っている。

物体を総観的かつ立体的に表すという論理以前の本能により起こったにもかかわらず、造形図法の地図は、平面図法では不可能であった詳細を提供することにより、都市についての情報に関して改善を施したと考えることができる。この図法は町の道路、家と煙突、屋根、木々などの高さに関する詳細も与えてくれる。このように総観的な情報はより深い知識を提供してはくれるものの、地図製作者にとっては処理が困難なものである。知識をより本能的に表現し、「鳥瞰的」遠近図法という比喩が示唆するように動物的ですらある反面、造形図法による地図は、ただ1つの観測点からでさえ物体を立体的に再成してしまえる軸測投像という近代的空間表現により近いものである。それゆえ、製図者は町や家を測量するだけでなく、高度や屋根や、地形が変化するところでは地点ごとの高さも測定しなくてはいけない。ところが彼らの作業はここで終わるわけではない。というのは、後部地面の高さを前部地面の高さで隠したりしないように注意を払って、高度段階を付けるという複雑な仕事に携わるからである。さらに、全体像を見失わず、かつ観測者に「向かった」高度を総て詳細に測定する必要を避けるため、図面化される姿をチェックする観測所として丘や鐘塔を定めるのも有効である。

事実、幸運にも町の成長を見下ろしてきた丘の存在は、ローマの地図の発達にとって非常に重大であったことがうかがえる。それは特に望遠鏡の発明と普及後何世紀もの時代において、方位の配置を規定することにもなった。言い換えれば、丘や丘の上にオープンの小屋を持つという利点は非常に重要であったため、地図や造形図の従来の作図における方角配置のチョイスを規定してしまったということである。16～17世紀の地図を見てとれるこの現象については、さらに詳細に立ち入って述べる価値がある。

しかし、「従来の作図における方角配置のチョイス」とはどういう意味なのであろうか。前述のセヴェルスのForma Urbis Romaeが明確な例である。ここでは南は上、北は下、東は左、西は右という配置で町が表されている。これは多少ともモンテマリオからの景色と一致しているが、平面図法を用いた表現法の精密さで描かれている。本書の写真による地図は、それから18世紀を経た後描かれたものであるが、北が上、南が下、東が右、西が左になっている。これはアベンチンからの景色と一致するかもしれないが、とにかく町の南部にある高地からの景色にあたる。ということは、後者は従来の製図法による古い地図を完全に逆転したものである。それならば、いつこのような逆転が起こり始め、なぜ近年になって北と南の位置が入れ替わったのであろうか。

この逆転は徐々に起こったものではなく突然のもので、啓蒙運動の頃に遡る。北を上にした最初のロ

ーマの平面図法による地図は、1736〜48年にG.B.ノリが自費で作成した地図である。この地図以前は、製図の伝統は一貫していなかったが、大部分は東が上になっていた。セプティミアス・セヴェルスの時代のように南が上になっていた平面図や造形図もあるが、それらは15〜16世紀に現われるだけで、アウグスツス時代に遡った建築に関するヴィトルヴィウスの論文の発見とその発表に明らかに影響を受けてのことであった。このローマの建築家の影響は非常に強かったため、ルネサンス時代の地図は南を上にしたものが主流であった。その例として、タッデオ・ディ・バルトロ（1414年）、15世紀初期の彫刻師（氏名不詳）、マソリーノ・ダ・パニカーレ（1453年）、1447年の彫刻師（氏名不詳）、G.ダ・ベソッツォ（16世紀初期）、ピエトロ・デル・マッサイオ（1469年、1471年、16世紀後半）等の地図がある。しかしヴィトルヴィウスを最も崇拝したのはレオン・バチスタ・アルベルチであろう。彼のDescriptio Urbis Romae（1423〜34年）の中で、彼はローマ式に南を上に置くことによって、ヴィトルヴィウスが方角の配置法を説明している個所（Ⅰ、6）を十分に理解していることを示した。このシステムは羅針盤が発明されるまで続くことになった。南を上にした地図を最後に作ったのはラファエルのサークルから出た古物研究家兼人文学者でもあるドシオであった。彼は近代に入ってからも、1561〜2年位まで古代の先人達について博識な言及をせずにはいられなかった。

けれどもヴィトルヴィウスの基本方位決定のテクニックとは何か、またいかなる理由で南が特権を得て地図上で上に置かれることになったのであろうか。事実、このような方法を用いたのはヴィトルヴィウス1人ではなかった。それは何世紀も前から実施され、ギリシャやローマの都市整備と土地分割の方法であっただけでなく、征服した土地を百分にも分けるためローマ軍隊に同行した土地測量技師が用いた有名な方法でもあった。この方法はき針（元来は真鍮のピンであったが今日では日時計の針）を地面に垂直に立てて正午の前後2時間に行なわれる。正午の約1時間前に地面に立てられたピンの影の先に印を付ける。それから1対のコンパスをピンの中心から影の端まで開き、それを半径とする円周を地面に描く。午後になりき針の影がしだいに離れて行き、再び前に描いた円周に触れた時、その交点に印を付ける。1対のコンパスをこの2点に置くと、「×」がなぞられる。ここから中心まで線を引くと、その線は南北を示し、影の2点を結ぶ線は東西を示す。当然のことながら、印を付けた2点が文字通り日の出から日の入りまでの太陽の動きを定義しているように、この作業の中心は太陽である。そして全作業が太陽に向かって行なわれるので、その結果を壁や紙の上に描くとなると、南を上にするのが最も自然であった。その反面、北は光が全く無い地平線のポイントであったため、南の反対として消極的な役を果たした。勿論これは習字法が上から下、左から右へとなっていた事実にもよる。イスラム世界のように習字法が「逆の」世界で状況を見ていたら、全く別の話になっていただろう。（しかし、それについて述べるとなると大きく不必要に話が逸れてしまう。）

南を上にする製図上の慣習は中世後期まで続いたが、11〜14世紀にかけてその間世界地図や造形図や平面図においては（ローマのも含めて）東を上にするというもう一つの方法があった。十字軍遠征の頃、地図は東が上になっていただけでなく、しばしば特別な挿入画でキリストの顔を東に描いたり、東という方向とキリストの顔とを関係づけることもあった。左右（北と南）には十字架に掛けられたキリストの手が、そして下（西）には脚が描かれた。同様に、世界の「臍」はエルサレムと一致するように作られた。また中にはアビニョン法王庁のオプチヌス・デ・カニストリスのように、地図の人格化を極端に解釈して、ヨーロッパと小アジアの地図を教化風に作る者もいた。「精神分裂ぎみ」とさえ言われたこの僧侶のある作品では、「イタリアの長靴」がキリストの脚、スペインが頭、ユーゴスラビアがもう一本の脚になった冠をかぶった騎士が、中東に居座るイスラムのような怪獣と戦う様子を描いている。神を人間の姿に具現化するというビジョンのこの錯乱したイメージは、その創造主と世界を同一視することから生まれた。それゆえ、世界の頭は必然的に人間の頭の位置に来ることに

オピチヌスのバチカンの写本から中世末期の世界地図に至るまで—地球がエルサレムを中心とする円で表されオリエントが上になった作者不詳の12世紀の地図や、再びエルサレムが中心でキリストの頭が上になった1255年頃のエブドルフ世界地図、そしてより非宗教的ではあるがそれでも厳密にオリエントを上にした15世紀後半のボルジア世界地図、等々—地図の方角配置（英語でオリエンテーション）は、（オリエントが最重要基本位置であるという）その言葉の語源を反映していた。アメリカ大陸の発見と羅針盤の商業的普及により、初めて「北」はアラブ人が与えた重要性を再獲得し、地図の上方に復帰することになった。

この広範に及ぶ変化は、ほとんどの特定地域地図や世界地図には影響を与えたが、16世紀中期以来ヨーロッパにおける印刷術の発明に伴って非常に流行した町や都市の地図製作ではそれほど当たり前のものではなかった。これらの印刷地図はたいていはその土地の出版者が収集するため、多少なりとも深く根ざした製図法の伝統の恩恵を多大に受けていて、必ずしも北に傾倒しているわけではなくむしろ東の方を好む傾向にあったということを認識するには、ピエール・モーティエーやブラウン＆ホーゲンベルグとその後継者により出版された、イタリア及び他のヨーロッパの都市の平面図や造形図の豊富なコレクションを見るだけで十分である。モーティエーのコレクションからランダムに例を挙げると、チェラスコ、ラキラ、ラ・バレッタ（マルタ）などがオリエントを上にして描かれている。明らかにこのコレクションは以前に彫られたブロンズ板を買った結果である。本来の作者名はそこで省かれるか、もしくは出版者が本来の作者の名前の上に自分の名前を入れた。不思議なことに、同じコレクションの中で、アスコリ・ピチェノは南を上に、グッビオは北を上に表されている。グッビオの方角配置は、町の北部にある丘が背後に来るため、南からでないとはっきり見えなかったという事実で説明がつく。ラキラにも同じことが言えるが、ラ・バレッタやチェラスコはそうはいかない。ラ・バレッタの場合、彫刻師が

最長の側が南北になる長方形のシートにうまく入るような景色を選んだ結果かもしれない。これらの製図を検討していくうちに、16世紀の方角配置は、そこから見える最高の景色や図面の形に合った景色などのように、「世俗的」で功利主義的な考慮にますます影響されていることが次第に分かってくる。ローマの地図も似たように功利主義的な背景を持っていたということは可能であろうか。

その答えはフルタスの巻にある地図を簡単に吟味してみれば与えられる。ユーフロシーノ・デラ・ボルパイアの特定地域地図（1547年）に基づいてその直後の1551年にレオナルド・ブファリーニにより作られた基本的な木板平面図から、前述の1748年に出版されたG.B.ノリ作の「啓蒙的」な平面図に至るまで、ルネサンス後のローマの地図は、ローマ様式で南が上のドシオ、西を上にしたベアトリゼット作（1557年）、ベリテリー・バリノ作（1567年）、ド・ペラック・ラフレリ作（1557年）等を除くと、総て東が上になっている。

東を上にした地図には、ピロ・リゴリオ（1552年）の有名な作品や、U.ピナード（1555年）、F.リチニオ（1557年）、F.パチオット（1557年）、S.ペルッツィ（1564〜5年）、G.F.カモチオ（1569年）、G.ブラウン、S.ノベラヌスとF.ホーゲンベルグ（1575年）、M.カルタロ（小1575年、大1576年）、A.ブランビラ（1590年）、A.テンペスタ（1597年）、T.デ・ブライ（1597年）、P.ベルテリ（1599年）、M.フロリミ（16世紀後半）、G.マージ（1600年）、A.ジョバンノーリ（1616年）、M.グルーター（1618年）、F.パオリ（1623年）、G.マージ（1625年）、G.バン・シャイック（1630年）、G.デ・ロッシ（1637年）、A.テンペスタ（再版1661〜2年）、G.ブレーユ（1663年）、V.バン・クルイル（1665年）、F.アグネリ（1666年）、G.B.ファルダ（小1667年、大1676年）、A.テンペスタ（1693年）、G.デ・ラ・フーイエ（1691〜1700年）、A.バービ（1697年）、N.デ・フェル（1700年）、F.ノド（1706年）、作者不詳（1727年）、ストリンドベック・ボデネー（1730年頃）等が含まれる。

これら総ての地図製作者が東を上にした理由は、ブファリーニの1551年の地図をさらに詳しく検討することで分かるのである。彼は羅針盤を持っていて、それを上手く利用したが、特定の基本方位に対するイデオロギー的嗜好は持っていなかった。実際、彼はジャニクルムの丘の都合良い土地の利点を生かし、天地学的な偏見のためにそれを放棄していられなかったわけである。その後ブファリーニは、ローマの中心の西まで羅針盤で2点離れた所にあるジャニクルムを観測点として選んだ。そのため、磁気羅針盤を用いて彼がシート上に描いた東北の線で完全に示されているように、図面の垂直方向は北東―南東となっている。通常東が上に来るという大まかな指示のある造形図では同じことが言えないが、ブファリーニの平面図の中で、この詳細は明らかである。

しかし、地図製作者達はいったいジャニクルムのどこで作業を行なったのであろうか。最も便利で適した地点は今でもビラ・ファルネシーナを見下ろす険しい岩山の上にある、ビラ・ランテのロジアである。モントリオのサン・ピエトロ教会のテラス、またはその鐘塔も素晴らしい観測点ではあるが、ロジアの方がもっと魅力的であったに違いない。法王レオ10世時代の掌璽院長で上品なヒューマニストでもあり、贅沢に耽っていたペシアのツリーニ枢機卿が自分と友人のために建てたこのビラは、ジュリオ・ロマノが設計し、ジョバンニ・ダ・ウーディネ作のスタッコがあった。1521年頃の昔から、ビラはUrbeの建設を測量してコントロールするための贅沢な観測点であったに違いない。

HINC TOTAL LICET AESTIMARE ROMAN
1531

この刻文は今日でもツリーニ枢機卿の保護者法王レオ10世とクレメント7世の行為やアエネアスとヌマ・ポンピリウスの話のイメージと共にロジアの中央のドアにある銘板に見ることができる。この壮大なビラは、恐らく1527年のローマ略奪後必要となった修復工事の年と思われる1531年以前に建てられた。そこを訪れる者は、メインサロンのフレスコ壁画上に刻まれた次のようなエレガントな落書きで思いだされるように、ビラは最初に陥落した建物であった。

a di 6 de magio 1527
fo la presa de Roma
（1527年5月6日ローマは略奪された）

ビラは、外部のスタッコ装飾は別として、少なくとも粗面仕上げに関しては、1521年までに完成していたのは確かである。ラテン語で書かれたぞんざいな落書きはマルティアーリスからの意訳である。

UNDE TOTAM LICET AESTIMARE ROMAN
ET LONGAM VALLEM NEBULAS TEGENTES

そして、これは今はもう見られない魅力的なジュリオ・ロマノの淫らなフレスコ壁画に囲まれて宴を楽しむべくビラにやって来た枢機卿の客人の誰かの雄弁なコメントを書いたものであることはほとんど間違いない。

ツリーニ枢機卿の時代以来、ロジアは地図製作者を北風ではないにしても雨から守ってくれるローマの観測所となった。ブファリーニの高度に正確な地図を始め、その後の建物の発展記録だけを加えた数々のバリエーションに至るまで、モントリオのサン・ピエトロと並んでロジアはルネサンス時代のローマの初期の地図に載っている。ジャニクルムの丘からは日の出が臨める。そのため、真に正確さを期すならば北東が上になると良心的なブファリーニが指摘するように、実際には羅針盤を少しずらさなくてはいけないのだが、東を上にした景色が必須となる。しかし、もし僅かにごまかすことで、すたれてしまったとはいえ一旦実行したら十分な魅力を発揮する方法で地図を作成する参考地点が得られるならば、どうして正確さにそれまでの努力を払わなければいけないのであろうか。キリストの姿を用いた象徴的な天地学の伝統に従ってきたが、それ以上に地図製作者に同伴してジャニクルムの丘をロバに乗って登るサンチョ・パンサのような人物の強い需要も満たしたに違いない。このような補助者は恐らく、簡単な目に見える測量旗で既に作られた観測結果を

探すプラエトルの表を手に持っているだけでなく、16世紀後半以降は、その発明者ガリレオのように事実上破門されることを免れた重いクリスタルと真鍮で作られた望遠鏡をも携帯していたことであろう。

ブファリーニの地図を優れた先例として、16世紀中期から18世紀中期にかけて、ローマの地図は溢れた。ウーディネ生まれ特有の勤勉さをもって、貧乏な大工、彫刻師、測量師、軍の設計士、そしてボルゴの壁の建設における事業家などが莫大な仕事を終えた後、まる2世紀の間地図製作者達は整った参考資料に恵まれた。当時利用できた手段を考慮すると、現在でも多くの人がその正確さに驚嘆する。彼らはブファリーニの製図を、自分達の鳥の目のような視点や、異なる詳細を持った他の平面図の基本とした。既に述べた例外は別として、それらの総ては東を上に置いた。

2世紀後、もう1人の北部出身の勤勉家が登場した。コモ出身のジョバン・バチスタ・ノリである。12年間をかけて自費による骨おりの実地調査を行なった後、ノリはもう一つの素晴らしいローマの平面図を描き彫った。これが北を上にした最初の地図で、天文学的なだけでなく磁気的でもある方角配置を伴った壮大な風配図も描かれている。ノリ以降、数多くの叙述的で土地台帳としてのローマの平面図は総て北を上に置いている。そして、事実、北極を世界地図の主役とする慣習が現われたのは18世紀中期からであった。

18世紀から20世紀初期にかけては、地図製作技術は偉大な発展を見せておらず、改良も光学的機器や印刷機を完全なものにする程度に止まっている。例えば、イタリア統一後のフィレンツェの軍事地理院で作成される洗練された正確な地理や地形のチャートは、今なお現地測量の結果をまとめたものである。しかしそれらは、それに隣接するシートが平行になっていることを保証する国全土の測地網の一部である。

この時点において、飛行機や写真などの技術的な発明と普及は多大な質の向上に通じる道を築いた。これにより、都市や地域はついに昔からの同じ観測点から開放され、完全に正主距離方位図法による地図上の正確さを許すことになった。地形図製作を目的に空中から写真撮影された最初の都市であったため、ローマは再び先駆を成すことになった。その結果、1900年に、イタリア陸軍技師第3連隊の写真部により1万分の1の地図が作られた。ほとんどの写真は空中に飛ばした風船から撮影された。というのは、飛行機からの測量は、第1次世界大戦後まで行なわれなかったからである。24才の無名の中尉ウンベルト・ニストリが、1万分の1の規模で最初の町の航空写真を製作するのに使われた写真のネガを使った。イタリア空軍は、騎士道精神をもって、その結果を当時（1919年）まだ生存していた有名な古代ローマの地形学者ロドルフォ・ランチアーニに捧げた。航空写真測量の発明者でその鋭敏な保護者であるウンベルト・ニストリは、1934年に高度3000メートルから再び航空写真を撮った。その結果は、1962年のローマの都市計画における補助資料として5000分の1の地図を製作するため、ETAが「ニストリ」システムを用いて航空写真測量を実施する基盤を形成することになった。この後者の測量調査は、1959年12月から1960年2月にかけて（冬至の頃）に撮影した写真のモザイクに基づいている。ニストリの最初の写真も、1919年2月のこの季節に撮影されている。

このタイミングのチョイスはどう説明できるだろうか。優れた白黒の航空写真撮影は地上が最も明らかに見える時、即ち空が澄んでいて（北風の時が最高）、植物ができるだけ裸に近い時に実行されるべきである。もう1つの条件は、前述の内容とは明確に相対するのだが、地面に写る屋根の影ができるだけ短いということである。しかしこの条件は、ほとんど北風が吹くチャンスがなく、草木が最高に生い繁っている夏至の頃にしか満たされない。

一般的に航空写真測量に適した最良の条件は、植物の成育が最小の冬に与えられる。それならば、なぜこの本のための測量は冬至ではなく夏至の頃に実施されたのか。答えは簡単である。明らかに白黒写真では、どの木の葉もほとんど同じに見える—カイガンショウはオークに似てくる—そして、煉瓦も瓦も全て似たような灰色の色合いになってしまう。非常に解像度の高い写真でないと、個々の物体の多様な色彩をそれぞれ表現することができない。それができてもなお、不確かな点は残る。ローマでは黄色っぽい屋根は、バチカンの近くのバレ・デレ・フォルナセから来たことを意味する。15世紀から1950年初めまで、これらの石切り場は、焼くと煉瓦や瓦が特徴ある金色になる粘土を産出してきた。赤っぽい屋根は、瓦がチベール谷の石切り場から来たことを物語っている。この石切り場は、便利の良いバチカンの石切り場が建設ブームや不動産投機プレッシャーの下、産業考古学の対象にしかなれないような古跡になって閉鎖されて以来、煉瓦や瓦を供給してきた。今日では、完全に黄色っぽい屋根はある意味で珍品である。それは屋根が埃をかぶっているという理由だけでなく、世界中の瓦葺き屋根がそうであるように、瓦の取り替えも含めて定期的に整備せざるを得ないからでもある。しかし、よく訓練された目は、黄色の「つぎはぎ」と赤の「つぎはぎ」を見分け、その年代も当てることができる。非常に大きな不動産プレッシャー下にある町では理解できることだが、このようにして年代を定める方法は、疑問を都合よく解釈して済ませてしまう文献資料よりも確かなことが多い。

屋根瓦について話を続けると、白黒写真では分からないもう1つの例は、パンテオンとピアッツァ・デル・ポポロにある2つの教会の亀甲型屋根の違いである。写真に表れるのはパターンの違いだけで、材質の違いは表れない。実際、ピアッツァ・デル・ポポロの屋根は、リグリアの枢機卿の頑固さからスレートで出来ており、僅かな色の違いで十分に、1450年の聖年にあがなわれ巡回の対象に含まれた異教徒寺院に法王ニコラス1世が贈った贅沢なパンテオンの鉛のシートと区別がつくはずである。

舗装に関しては、最近の消費者の動きがラチナの火山フリントよりもアルペン硬岩石の方を好む所では、鉄灰色が赤っぽい色に取って代わられている。ラチナの火山フリントは、溶岩が流れた地域に層になって分布しているため、大量生産の可能性がより少ない。それゆえ石切り場は、境界争いや、許可を持っていたり持っていない建設業者からの略奪の対

象になったり、溶岩流が曲がりくねっているため資源枯渇に陥ったりする。扇のように並んだ硬岩石の塊はより展性を持ち、均一な舗装材を生産し、その性質を解く手掛かりを与えてくれるが、形態的にはローマフリントに類似している。しかし、その赤っぽい色ですぐにそれと分かるため、非経済的なフリント舗装に対して、市議会が見返りや少なくとも改善を求めて遂行することを願う合法的な戦いに利用できる。しかし、なぜ競争力を持つ製品を選んでのみ改善が為されるべきなのであろうか。このような計画はどれもある製品を再び競争力のある物にする助けとなるか、少なくともその製品が単なる経済的な都合ではなく、批評眼のある嗜好にも基づいて決定が下されるような環境で、誇り高く生存できるような援助となるべきである。これは「援助産業」という概念が常織を全く侮辱しない領域である。何を置いても、そこには建築文化の遺産を守り、改良することに関わる中小企業を助け、冷酷の市場の論理が美的なクオリティーと厳密に繋がっている歴史的中心地区における生活水準を損ない簡単にそれを一掃してしまうような原料や技術を、彼らが生かしておけるよう助ける必要がある。

そこで結論として、植物生育に関して総て収集可能な情報を集め、前述の測量だけでなく木々の徹底的な測量も行なえるよう、6月から8月の間に航空カラー写真撮影が実施されなくてはいけない。そしてこの撮影は、たとえこの時期に木の葉がその下にある物体を覆ってしまうことがあっても、この期間に実施されなくてはいけない。カラー写真の利点で明確なのは、川の水の色も見分けることができるということである。例えばチベレ川のポンテ・シストとポンテ・サンタンジェロの間は緑色が広がっていることに注目してもらいたい。もし川が健全な状態であれば、川底の藻はこのようにはっきりと現われないであろう。ところで、「ビオンド」（美しい者）という昔流行った名前は、川の優良な状態を叙述る造語で、近年のトスカニーの水源まで広がった干ばつ状態のことを指すのではない。

カラー写真のタイミングもまた明確にそれなりの条件を持っている。たとえば影が最短になる夏至の頃に撮影するのが最良であるだけでなく、時間も太陽が頂点に来て影が絶対的に最短になるよう、できるだけ正午近くでなければいけない。それからウィトルウィウスの時代もそうであったように、記録は正午前後の1時間以内に行なわれなくてはいけない。本書に発表されている写真は、少なくともジャニクルムの丘の1枚については、それが撮影された時間をかなり正確に推測することができるため、そこから写真地図全体が記録された大体の時間も推し計ることができる。ジャニクルムの丘のガリバルディの記念碑がある広場の下で、旅行者が身を乗り出している擁壁の近くに、透明なもやの断片が浮いている。これは実際に正午を知らせる大砲が打たれた証しである。この時間にはローマ市民は皆オフィスに着いているか商売を始めているので、町の交通は最小限にとどまっている。市民の車は舗道に沿って1～2列に駐車しており、焼けるような太陽は既にタールマックや不動のメタルの車体を熱している。

さて、ここで家路を急ぐ交通ラッシュ前のほとんど静止した町に目を向けてみよう。都市の綴れ織りの中で最もはっきりと目につくのは屋根とテラスの状態である。写真地図はそれらについて、その高さも含め非常に精密な情報を与えてくれるし、その主体は断片的なコメントの連続が与え得る以上の深さで取り扱われる価値を持っている。写真地図の助けを利用したローマの屋根の研究は、そこの政府当局が、抽象的に価値があるというだけでなく、実現する可能性が高く勝利の見込があある戦いに挑む動機を与えている。この戦いは不認可建築に対する戦いで、それは特に写真地図のように上から見ると、この町の建築上の腐敗の兆しとしてはっきりと認めることができる。

明かり取りの窓がある屋根裏部屋や、屋根から差し込んでくる日光、サンルーム、そして小さなプールさえも、屋根の上に散在している。しかし不認可建築で1番目につくのは、所謂「テクニカル・ボリューム」を非常に珍重される住居に変えた1960年代の不認可建築の波の時代に歴史的中心地区のてっぺんに建てられた「ペントハウス」である。都市開発計画の中で、これらの住居は、洗濯場や洗濯物を干す場所として隠されていた。それは、あたかも洗濯機が未だ市場に登場しておらず、洗濯場は新実在主義の映画からそのまま出て来たポーターにより決められた日に主婦が会し、大帆のような二重のシーツやペネロペーのペプロスに似た寝間着を陽の当たる所に干しているようだ。

デラックスに仕上げられた「テクニカル・ボリューム」がひしめく何千もの街角が存在するパリオリの丘を散らかした後、ペントハウス文化は歴史的中心地区に広がり、祭日のある週末の間や、中にはたった一夜にして隙間を見つけ、古いもので新しいものをカモフラージュする能力を伝えた。詩人ベリにより永遠の生命を与えられたピネッリの時代以来、昔の中心部は家賃凍結という形の生活保護のおかげで何とか生き残っている貧しい都市階級層の居住地域になっている。それに加えて、中心部は、議会、首相・大統領官邸、銀行、ローマや外部からの新聞社等の、政治経済力のイスに関連した誘発経済により、裕福な人々の流れも必然的に魅きつけることになった。様々な、ますます緊急な理由で、これらの力のイスに関係する人々は何よりも先に1階の店舗を占有し、入手可能な住宅とその改善を図った。伝統的な住居用の階—「ピアノノビーレ」や18～19世紀に異なった段階でその上に建てられたその他の階—には固定家賃のテナントが住んでいたため、唯一可能な解決策は、金持ちの住居を屋根の上下に移すことであった。これらの新しいペントハウスはフランスのように法律上の慣例で規制されることは全くなく、パリの屋根裏部屋とは全く異なり、「ボンヌ」（女中）や文無しの画家が住むのではなく、新支配者階級が利用することになった。

さらに、ペントハウスは、石造建築が物理的に耐えられる高さの限界に既に達している「自然の」高さの上にどんどん建てられていった。18世紀半ばから19世紀末にかけて、ルネサンス地域（貴重な歴史的建造物が最も密集している地域）の住宅に平均2階の高さが追加して建てられた。これと同様の建て増しは、アウレリアヌス城壁内にある町中の建物に及んだ。以前は、家の高さは、2階建ての住宅も多かったが、3階が平均であった。高さ規制に関する

最初の適用除外は、ルネサンス貴族達に与えられ、外交やレセプションの目的で使用する宮廷が対象であった。18世紀には5階建てにもなる賃貸住宅が、それらに寛大なピアッツァの端に現われた。その1例はピアッツァ・カプラニーカで、そこではこのような建物は、営利目的で建設を進め、元来あった建物を区画全体に拡張した宗教コミュニティーによる不動産取引の結果であった。試作と様式という観点からすれば重要性はあったが、これらは孤立した現象であった。最も興味深い建築工事は1870年に実施され、全道路が上方に拡張される結果を招いた。ビア・デル・コルソ、ビア・デル・バブイーノ、ビア・ジュリアはほんの3例である。新たに統一されたイタリアの支配階級エリート達は、ローマがコルソ・ビットリオ、プラチ街、エスキリーノ地区のように複雑で全体的に調和のとれた都市の変遷を進めていた頃、既にこれらの通りに目を付けていた。高さ平均は6階に制限されたが、これは当時の建築技術が許す最高の水準であった。そして、これに見合う割合で新しい道が建設された。

当時、建物は「自然の」技術と方法で建てられた。計画に類型的な変更が加えられ、玄関、ホール、階段のアレンジから始まり、それらは全て建設される階数に従って設計された。(これはジャンフランコ・カニージアの類型学で規定されているガイドラインにある方法で、都市計画史学者は利用が可能。)しかし1960年代の不動産投機の結果であるペントハウスには、それ自体自然や生理学的な要素は全く無い。それらははびこる雑草やキノコのように飾り気のない建物のてっぺんに群生し、カビが古い壁を侵食するように建物を痩せ衰えさせている。すでにゴミゴミしていた玄関にエレベーターが押し込まれた。余分な荷重が、1950年代頃まで通常質の悪い石灰華と煉瓦を混ぜて建てられた既に弱い上層階や壁を押さえ付けた。成金がゴミを捨てたり、彼らに冷水や冷房を供給する意図で急速成長するサービスの配管のために、床や梁の木材、しっくい、モルタル、もろい石灰華等の材料で作られている建物の古い部分を損傷したり失ったりする可能性など全く構わずに、狭い壁を打ち抜いてまで新しい通路を作った。秘かに物音を立てずに行なわれた上方への拡張は、その下の階を居住不可能にしてしまった。そして、ヘビが自分の尻尾を嚙んだというのは、まさにこのことであった。下の階に住めなくなればなるほど、居住生活はますます上に移動しなければならず、強制的な規制が無い中で、というより大抵はそういう規制があった所では、それを守る意志が欠如した中で、建物はどんどん高くなっていった。

歴史的中心地区の建物で日光が失われたことも写真地図で明るみに出たことである。前にも説明したように、写真地図は影が最も短い、即ち日光が最大に当たる季節と時間に撮影した写真の結果をまとめたものである。ここで、歴史的にも経済的にも興味深い建物が密集した歴史的中心地区を詳しく見てみよう。ビア・コンドッティはピアッツァ・デイ・スパーナから始まり、コルソ・ウンベルトと直角に交わって、トル・ディ・ノナに向かってまっすぐ走っている。ローマの良い「カルド」として、コルソ・ウンベルトはウィトルウィウスやローマの土地測量士が定めた通り、有害で厄介な風を避けるように南北(正確には西に点1つ傾いている)に走っている。それと平行に走る多くの道のように(この地域全体の道は碁盤の目のように走っているので、ここでは全道路の半分)、真昼のビア・コンドッティは影が落ちた深い溝のようで、昼下がりの、それも日の入りも間近という時になってやっと僅かな日光が当たっている。コルソとそれに平行する道は、真昼は沢山の光を浴びるが、それも長くは続かない。午後4時には、太陽は東に面した建物の屋根の後ろに永久に「沈んで」しまい、コルソはそれと直角に交わる道と同様に暗くなってしまう。

以上をまとめれば、固定した家賃は1960年代の「新興成金」を、歴史的中心地区に住んでいた「昔からの貧乏人」の頭上に住まわせることになり、その結果として、統計上や生活水準に関する限りでは到底耐えられない高さにまで家を上げてしまった。19世紀の開発で定められた限度内にとどまることが、人口統計上のプレッシャーにさらされていない町では最良の解決策であっただろうことは、疑いようがない。勿論、これは不動産市場の人工的な要素による今日のケースのように事態を悪化させるものでなく、建築物を修復したり改築したりするといった健全な経済政策に基づいていなければならない。このことはサービス・セクターとしてのこの町の未来に終止符を打つことを余儀なく示唆しているであろうか。しかし、ローマの少なくとも歴史的中心地区において、今までにそれ以外の活動が行なわれたことがあるだろうか。ローマは少なくとも2000年にわたって、典型的なサービス業の町であった。そこに住む人々は常にサービス業に従事してきた。宿屋、ホテル、銀行員、そして職人や専門家でさえもサービスをまとめる仕事に携わっていた。そして今日では、政治・経済関係のオフィスのマネージャー、官僚、国政から地域レベルまでの行政指導者等、ありとあらゆる職種レベルの専門家がそこに存在する。

これまでサービス・セクターの専門家達による、歴史的中心地区の襲撃の否定的な影響を挙げてきたが、彼らは非常に混乱した状況の中で動かなくてはいけなかったということにも触れた。市民の中には、今世紀に建てられた低コストの公営住宅よりも低い家賃で、ルネサンス貴族や18世紀の枢機卿達の由緒ある屋敷に今でも住む権利を持っている者がいる。またナポレオン時代になって始まった歴史的中心地区のプロレタリア化によって、17世紀末までこの町が目にした最も偉大で守護的な法王以上に王侯らしい生活を送った高級売春婦は言うまでもなく、銀行家や宮廷の侍従達の活動領域であった地域は、完全に退廃してしまった。16世紀のメジチ家の貴公子から法王ウルバン8世、イノセント10世、そしてアレクザンダー7世の時代まで、ビア・ジュリア、ビア・ディ・バンチ・ヌオビ、ビア・デル・コルソといった通りは、素晴らしい調和のとれた通りであったが、既に高さと幅が1対1の比になることを要するルネサンスの中庸よりも高くなっていた。ビラ・ファルネシーナ、パラッツォ・マッシーモ、パラッツォ・リアリオ(後のパラッツォ・デラ・カンチェレリア)等は、世界でも代表的な最高級住宅の中に入り、そこでの生活はブルジョアの私生活よりも宗教ミサの方に近い儀礼に従って営まれた。

今日では、宮殿のような家は郊外の緑の多い、

一マ時代の田園地域に移っている。新式の交通手段とコンピューター通信のおかげで、彼らは僅かに残った邸宅が、ほとんどどこの近代都市でも起こっているように、かつて枢機卿や諸侯が所有していたビラの土地や庭をついに手に入れたサービス業の専門家達やサービス業そのものに呑み込まれるのを、なすがままにしている。

この状況を考慮すると、ますます非ユートピア的なビジョンが浮かんでくる。幅ではなく高さにおけるルネサンス中心地域—政治的で行政的なパラッツィ—の「痩身化」である。事実1930年代に極度に革新的な横幅の痩身化があった。しかし現在の考えは、町の建物をイタリア王国創立時代の形に戻すことである。これは生理学的に自然な建物の高さとして既に述べたことに従って達成されるであろう。同様に、本来の建物の類型的で構造上の形に戻すことに存する生理的で自然な方法も用いられるであろう。

しかし、過剰な恩赦により、建物の状態は治癒不能なまでにひねくれた構造に固まってしまったであろうか。有害な恩赦の政策と断片的に公有の不動産という、息が詰まるような論理からの唯一の出口は市場を通すことである。当然のことながら、市場はいったん価格が規制されて初めて接収が可能になる。しかし、いかにも聖人ぶった態度や、急速に経済が変化する時代にはもはや適さない立法の道具を一般に与えるのを避けるためには、この方向を採るべきである。

適切な歴史と資料の研究により、現在では本来の建物の有機的成長を考慮に入れた最上の道路のプロフィールを再建することが可能である。その結果、近視眼的なペントハウス・ブームが起こした汚染を「剥ぎ取った」建築表象を再建することができる。そして、このようにして何百年も前ではないにしても19世紀にこれらの建物が有していた威厳のレベルまで回復することができる。

現在不動産市場では、所有者が1区画または屋敷全体を一括購入する傾向が認識され、ますます広がってきており、そうすれば何も邪魔するものもなければ、小口の所有者と分け合う必要もなくなる。当事者達は、ついに認められた自分達の資本を管理でき、彼らの1番の関心は、非常に高い金額で入手したばかりの資産を破滅に至らせるよりもむしろそれを有機的なユニットに回復させることに向くだろう。これらの新オーナー達は建物全体の全体的な善のために、喜んでくだらない有害な追加をすることを放棄するだろう。このような動きは所有者に税金の優遇措置を与えることにより、都市計画政策の中で奨励されるであろう。

しかし、これを全部行なうのは、長い週末の休み中に発効した建築恩赦と不動産取引の国「イタリエッタ」では少し野心が大きすぎるかもしれない。けれどもイタリアは間もなくヨーロッパの規準に合わなければいけなくなる国であることを念頭に置くと、これは実現可能であると信じたい。この写真地図の大きな価値は、これが将来の復元工事とローマの町から余分な高層部分を取り除く試みの第1の情報源となるであろうということである。この写真地図は、単なる夏の日の真昼の美しいが退廃した町の記念写真とは全く違い、より良い町を築くために使われる基本的な道具なのである。

パオロ・マルコニ

斜体で書かれた説明は、イタリア語の文献に付いている図版を指す。

1. セプティミアス・セウェルス時代（AD203〜11年）のローマの地図。この地図は大理石に彫られており、平和寺院に隣接する巨大なホールの壁に掛かっている。このホールはウェスペシアヌス時代に起源を置くが、セウェルスの治世下で修復された。色付きの大理石板で埋められた土台に載っていた大きな大理石の壁は、今では聖コスマと聖ダミアノのバシリカ聖堂の隣の修道院の外壁になっている。この彫刻の縮尺は約240分の1。現在993片残っており、原物の大きさは13×18.10m。方角配置は大まかに南東が上。このプレートはG.カレットニ、A.M.コリーニ、L.コッツァ、G.ガッティ編集による地図のより完全な版の複製である。La pianta marmorea di Roma antica etc., 1960年ローマ。(A.P.フルタズ著Le Piante di Roma、1962年ローマ、より) (p.11)

2. ポルティクス・リビアエとテアトルム・トライアーニがあるセプティミアス・セウェルス時代のローマ地図からの断片（イラスト1参照）。(A.P.フルタズより) (p.12)

3. レオナルド・ブファリーニ作1551年のローマ地図。今は残っていないオリジナルの木版のA.トレビジ・ダ・レッチェによる1560年再刷版。方角配置は北東が上。セウェルス時代の彫刻以来初の平面図法によるローマの地図は、ウーディネ出身のレオナルド・ブファリーニが行なった実地調査の結果。当時としては非常に精密地図で、おそらくブファリーニや多くの彼の模倣者が遅くとも1521年以降チベレ川の曲折を観測できるようにした地点であるジャニクルムの丘の上野ビラ・ランテのロジアからチェックしたものであろう。(A.P.フルタズより) (p.13)

4. 1748年ジョバンニ・バチスタ・ノリ作のローマ地図（小）。ブファリーニ後2番目のローマの平面図彫刻は、ピラネシとC.ノリにより作られ、大型の地図に随伴する（イラスト20、21、22参照）。方角配置は、ポルタ・ポルテセ地域に挿入された風配図から推論できるように、磁気北極が上。ノリの地図はブファリーニの地図に負うところが大きく、ノリはそれを部分的に再刷している。これはブファリーニと同じく、望遠鏡無しの後視や大型の地図に詳しく示されている三脚上の小テーブルを含む初歩的な光学操作を用いて作成された。（イラスト21参照）(A.P.フルタズより) (pp.14〜15)

5. タッデオ・ディ・バルトロ作の16世紀のローマ地図。シエナのパラッツォ・コミュナーレの内部チャペルの入り口に描かれている。(A.P.フルタズより) (p.16)

6．16世紀初期のローマ地図。サルストの作品も含む古写本の中の縮小図。方角配置は南が上。(A.P.フルタズより) *(p.17)*

7．中世のローマ地図。ファツィオ・デリ・ウベルティ作のディッタモンドを表すため1447年に作成された縮小図。方角配置は南が上。(A.P.フルタズより) *(p.18)*

8．1469年にピエトロ・デル・マッサイオが彩飾を施した15世紀のローマ地図。方角配置は南が上。(A.P.フルタズより) *(p.20)*

9．L.B.アルベルティの測量に従ったローマ地図。この地図は、ローマで1432〜4年の間にローマで書かれ、1879年G.B.デ・ロッシが出版した*Descriptio Urbis Romae*の小冊子を用いてD.ニオリにより表わされた。方角配置は南が上。(A.P.フルタズより) *(p.20)*

10．12世紀の作者不詳の世界地図。エルサレム中心でオリエントが上になっている。(L.バグロウ著 *History of Cartography*、1964年ロンドンより) *(p.21)*

11．1255年頃のエブドルフ世界地図。中心はエルサレムで大宇宙の絵を挿入しており、キリストの頭が上になり、手足が他の基本方位に向かって伸びている。方角配置は東が上。(バグロウ著*History*より) *(p.21)*

12．オピチヌス・デ・カニストリス。14世紀アビニョンの法王庁にいたパビア出身の僧。地中海とヨーロッパの近代史についての見解を表した「教化」地図。方角配置はキリストの頭で与えられ、それがこの地図に形式を与えている。(*Palatino Latino*、*No.6435*、ノンブル69v、バチカン法王庁図書館) *(p.22)*

13．オピチムス・デ・カニストリス。地中海があからさまに悪魔のような様相を呈し、一方それがヨーロッパとマグレブの性別を変えている。(同上、ノンブル84r) *(p.23)*

14．1557年のローマ地図。ナポリの戦いを連想している。ニッコロ・ベアトリゼット製図及び彫刻。1557年A.ラフレリ出版。暫時的な補強をしているのが目立つ。地図をチェックするのに使用した観測所はトリニタ・デ・モンティ（ピンチオ）であったかもしれない。方角配置は西が上。(A.P.フルタズより) *(p.24)*

15．1561年のローマ地図。G.A.ドシオ製図、S.デル・レ彫刻。F.ファレティ出版。この作者の骨董品に対する関心の深さが、古代の史跡の強調や方角配置の選択を説明している。方角配置は南が上。(A.P.フルタズより) *(p.24)*

16．1552年のローマ地図。ピロ・リゴリオ製図、G.L.A.とだけイニシャルのある無名の彫刻師による彫刻。M.トラメジーノ出版。「ビラB.デ・ペシエ」という刻印と共にリゴリオが指摘しているように、当時ペシアのバルダサーレ・トゥリーニ枢機卿が所有していたビラ・ランテをかなり詳細に描写していることに注目。ビラは両切妻屋根と本館の南の庭にある小さな小屋がある。最終的な屋根は寄せ棟式だったので、この屋根葺きは仮のものであったに違いない。この製図は建設途中に描かれたものかもしれない。ビラは1531年まで完全に仕上ってさえいなかった。この情況の中でビラに置かれている重要性は、ロジアはローマで最高の景色が臨めるところであったことのもう1つの証明であるようだ。方角配置は東が上。(A.P.フルタズより) *(pp.24〜25)*

17．1557年のローマ地図。F.パチオッティ（パチオット）製図、N.ベアトリゼット彫刻。1557年A.ラフレリ出版。造形図ではあるが、ブファリーニの作品に基づいている。「ビラ・バルド・デ・ペシエ」と刻まれているように、ここでもビラ・ランテが目立つ。今度は屋根は寄せ棟で、多分リゴリオが描いた後さらに修正が行なわれたのではないかと思われる。方角配置は東が上。(A.P.フルタズより) *(p.26)*

18．1575年のローマ地図（小）。M.カルタロ製図。ここではビラ・ランテにはキャプションが付いていないが、パチオットが描いたのと同じ屋根―顕著にファサードを縁取る2本の特徴ある柱のある寄せ棟屋根―がある。入口の通景を縁取る2つのアーチ型の亭も描かれている。方角配置は東が上。(A.P.フルタズより) *(p.26)*

19．1551年のローマ地図。A.ブファリーニ設計及び彫刻（イラスト3参照）。この板目木版はビア・サラリア地域の平面図の上を走る南北線を強調している。この方角配置を選んだことで、ブファリーニがどれだけ、他の地図製作規準以上に、実地測定をコントロールしたジャニクルムのビラ・ランテにあるロジアの便利の良さを好んだかを明確に示しており、また彼は羅針盤に依存できたことで、疑いなくその選択に助けられている。多くの地図製作者はブファリーニの地図を手本にしたが、特に造形図においては、東を上にした。方角配置は北東が上。(A.P.フルタズより) *(p.27)*

20．1748年のローマ地図（大）。G.B.ノリ作。口絵。(A.P.フルタズより) *(p.28)*

21．1748年のローマ地図（大）。G.B.ノリ作。ラテラノのサン・ジョバンニとエルサレムのサンタ・クロス地域を示すシート。風配図はノリが磁気北極に方角を定めていることを現わしにしている。これを行なったのはローマの地図製作の歴史ではノリが最初。(A.P.フルタズより) *(p.28)*

22．1748年のローマ地図（大）。G.B.ノリ作。ピアッツァ・デル・カンピドリオ、聖ペテロのドーム、ポルタ・ラティーナがある建築的背景を描写したシート。簡単な後視のある三脚の上で、地図製作者コ

モが素晴らしい測量を行なうのに使用した「プラエトルの表」で遊ぶキューピットもいる。ノリはブファリーニの作品に負うところが多く、彼の大小の地図彫刻と共に再製することによりその「手本」に感謝の意を表現している。(A.P.フルタズより)(p.28)

23. *1900年のローマ地図。*1900年陸軍技師第3連隊作。スカッチア、スカルフォニ、フルタズの3者は、この地図は「空中に静止した風船からの測量の助け」により描かれ、イラスト24の空中写真がそれを確証付けているようだという意見である。方角配置は磁気北極が上。(A.P.フルタズより)(p.29)

24. *1919年のローマの景色。*1919年2月11日、ウンベルト・ニストリ中尉の飛行機から撮影。オリジナルの縮尺は約1万分の1。方角配置は磁気北極が上。(A.P.フルタズより)(p.30)

25. *1934年のローマの航空写真。*1934年にパリで開催された国際空中ショー及び航空写真測量法会議の間、高度3000メートルからウンベルト・ニストリが撮影。この詳細写真はプラティ、フラミニオ、ピンチオ、パリオリの各地域を示している。方角配置は磁気北極が上。(A.P.フルタズより)(p.31)

26. *1961年のローマの航空写真測量地図。*ローマの都市開発新計画のために *Ente Topografico Aerofotogrammetrico (ETA)* が撮影、印刷を行なった。中心部は5000分の1の縮尺で、約1万分の1の縮尺で再製。方角配置は磁気北極が上。(A.P.フルタズより)(pp.32〜33)

ローマのための新しい地図製作システムの目的と内容

序文

老子曰く、「家はそれを見る者に属し、それに住む者に属すに非ず。」町の建て込んだ地域全体についてもこの格言は当てはまる。勿論、それは土地の所有権のことを言っているのではなく、町の造型的な性質の文化面と美的面についてのことで、それは楽しく充実した精神的経験面において、相当の重要性を持っている。さらにこれは、ル・コルビュジュの言葉を借りれば、"raison d'être des choses"、即ち築かれた環境に構造と生命を与えるもっとも内奥の「意味」を把握することができる限りにおいてのみ、真実なのである。ゲーテが鋭く指摘したように、「我々は理解できないものは所有できない」のである。従って事物はわれわれがそれを理解しない限り、いつまでも異質なものであり続けるのである。

下に説明する機能に加えて、写真地図と線状地図が含まれているこのローマの地図帳が、この町が少しでもわれわれにとって異質のものでなくなり、通常とは違った角度から現われた構造をよりよく理解するための助けとして利用されて欲しいと思っている。本書はまた、「建築学のつづれ織り」や「都市形態学」や「建築の言語」等、どれほど論議を交えても未解決のままの問題に繋がる、多種多様な具体的な問題と関わっているローマの歴史的アイデンティティーという一般的な問題に焦点を当てようと試みる「専門家」にとっても役立つべきである。

この主題について、芸術史学者G.C.アーガンが市長としての経験に触れて述べた言葉を引用する価値がある。「ローマはユニークな町である・・・経済学者や社会学者の計算に従って設計されたことはなく、常に想像されてきた・・・1870年以降、ローマはもはや想像されるものではなくなった。そこには町を形成する欲望があった。不幸にも、その開発を計画した支配者達は皆不動産投機に賛成し、町は調和を保って成長しなかったばかりか、その発達はその搾取と厳密に結び付いてしまった・・・ローマはその歴史的なアイデンティティーを失った。」

逆説的なイメージ

ボルヘスはある作品の中で、どのようにして地図製作者のグループが対象とその描写を正確に一致させるという神話に盲目的になり、現実と寸分違わない実物大の実に完璧な地図を作ったかを物語っている。その結果は、全く実用目的にそぐわない、現物を忠実に表すといえども役に立たない巨大な地図となった。逆説はさておき、ボルヘスは言葉と物の関係という無限の問題に焦点を当て、もし科学が発達するとしたら、それは一部には、完全な複製となるようにモデルをオリジナルに非常に近く作りたいと願う者達の不誠実な努力のおかげである、という推測にわれわれを導いていることが分かる。

本書を出版するのに要した努力は、ボルヘスの逆説的物語に照らして見ることができる。この場合は、従来の地図と航空写真を統合することによるが、たとえどのような形式を採ろうとも、実物とそのイメージを完全に一致させようという、同じように非現実的な試みがここにはある。

詩的イメージに加えて、現在まで少なくとも20年間、都市ゾーン化の機能とテクニックに沿った純粋な経済分析もしくは分類の試みに関わった後、単に物理的な物としての町のイメージを提供することにより大きな強調が置かれたが、その主な目的はそれらのユニークな性格について具体的な情報を提供するためであるということも、言わなくてはいけない。

アルド・ロッシのL'architettura della città、ジョセッピ・サモノのL'urbanistica e l'avvenire della città、ジャンフランコ・カニッジアのLe strutture dello spazio antropicoのように現在では定評のある作品と並んで、この方面の他の作品は「3世代計画」までのベルナルド・セッチの研究など、最近の分析的都市研究を含んでいる。これらと共に、写真測量調査で作成した市街地図（マルシリオ）だけでなく、他の出版社が製作した個々のイタリアの町に関する数えきれないほどの研究（エイナウディによるStoria dell'arte italianaの第8巻、ラテルザのモノグラフや専門的評論）も、バチスチが始めて出版（エディルスタンパ）により再度送り出され、最終的にローマ市議会史跡地域特別事務局により編集されたManuali del recuperoなどにあるような建築技術や様式を研究していることも述べる必要がある。

ローマ地図は、都市の具体的でユニークな性質を表すモデルを確立しようとするプロジェクトの範疇に入る。このようなプロジェクトはコンピューター・サイエンスのおかげで可能になったことは疑いようがない。本書で発表されている地図は、記号インフォメーション（インフォメーション・エントリー）を関係づける（コンピューターでプロセスし、管理された）地図製作の基本的な部分である。さらにこのシステムは、特に効果的な立体景観とモデルを生み出す能力がある。

この主題については、この先さらに深く追及するが、その前にボルヘスのことに戻りたいと思う。「言葉と物」という題名の作品の中で、彼は動物を次のように分類している「中国の百科辞典」を紹介している。ア）皇帝に属するもの、イ）はく製もの、ウ）柔順なもの、エ）子豚、オ）人魚、カ）伝説上のもの、キ）野犬、ク）現在の種分けに含まれるもの、ケ）熱狂的なもの、コ）無数なもの、サ）非常にきめ細かなラクダの毛の筆で描かれたもの、シ）その他、ス）交尾をするもの、セ）遠くから見ると蝿のように見えるもの、という分類である。

地図製作の逆説のように、この馬鹿げた皮肉っぽい分類は、いくつかの科学的かつ哲学的な観念並びに隠された文学的な真実を含んでいる。実際、フーコーはこの文献に基づいて人間学の考古学を発見しようとした。この馬鹿げた分類法は、われわれコンピューター人間への具体的な教訓を含んでいる。ほとんど無限に近い分類シリーズを創ることは可能だが、その総てが役に立つ／実用的な真実を含んでいる訳ではない。多くは、ボルヘスのありそうもない「中国の百科辞典」の分類よりもわずかにまともなだけで（全く皮肉っぽくない）ことさえある。マクラクリンが言うように、無限に大量の「データ」を集めるのは良識に欠けることである。それらはモデルを製作するにはあまりにも数が多すぎてかつ完全に利用価値のないものなので、できるだけシンプルでうまく方向づけができた、コントロールできる数

の変数から成るべきである。

ローマの歴史的中心地区の場合、満足のゆく実体の概測を成し遂げようと度々試みた後、部分的ではあるが異なる形式の知識の必要を満たせるモデルを見つける試みが行なわれている。これらの中には、主題地図や立体モデルがある。もしわれわれがボルヘスの完全に正確な製図者の立場であったら、ここで多くの疑問を挙げなければいけないだろう。主題地図は役立つ情報を与えてくれるが、非人間的で、故意に部分的になっている。その一方、立体モデルは建物の具体的実体やその肌や材料を捉えることができない。

私は、個人的には、ノリの地図が非凡だと常に思っている。この17世紀の作品では、屋根付きのピアッツァとして見られる外部の都市スペースと内地図は隣接して現われている。ベニスを含め他の都市についてもまたこれと似た地図が作られている。部分的ではあるが、このような地図は個々の公共スペースを理解する道具を与えてくれる。というのは、当時の教会は屋外スペース同様、公共の場所や空間であった。これを裏付ける証拠は放蕩者の回想にも出ているし、さらに時代を遡って、教会が陰の密会や非道徳行為を可能にする、余分なネーブやチャペルを削除しようとした勧告にも見られる。

同等に素晴らしいのは、数多くの鳥の目のような視点の立体図などで、それらは正確さにはほど遠いが、町の物理的な感覚や色やユニークな特徴を提供してくれる。

ここに述べられている地図製作者や彫刻師のより直感的な作品と比べるとまだまだ多くの欠点があるが、コンピューターによる地図製作は、その分類と情報を常に認識しながら、将来発展し成長する能力を持つ道具となる利点と可能性を備えている。

ローマの中心部の地図：単純な概念モデル

コンピューター・サイエンスの世界へ新たに足を踏み入れた者が、とにかくどれだけの情報が管理され、処理され、そして合成されるかに気づき始めると、彼らはしばしば高度に複雑で明瞭な実体はた易くコントロールできると信じさせられてしまう。そしてそこから単一で、絶対的で、完全に客観的な要素として見られている「データ」を求めて一種の追跡が始まる。しかし、これらの要素は単一や客観的とはほど遠いということが、やがて彼らにも分かってくる。ある決まった目的のために集められれば、即座にその客観性は失われるし、大まかな規準に添って集められれば、信頼性に限界を定めることになってしまうからである。

コンピューターシステムのハードウェアとソフトウェアの両方が持つ大きな力からさらに生じる誤解は、異なった使用目的のために膨大な量のデータを管理するのは易いと思ってしまうことである。その結果、何千ものユーザーとなり得る人達のニーズに応えられるよう、複雑な資料を作ろうとする誘惑にかられる。その結末は、巨大な伝統的な公立資料館の埃っぽい廊下で感じる戸惑いのようなものである。そこには驚くほど豊富で興味深い資料があることは分かっているのだが、必然的にあまりにも単調に分類されていて、求める項目を捜し出すことが非常に困難である。

しかし、われわれのケースはもっと単純である、というよりむしろ、われわれの関心事は数少なく、きちんと定義されている、といったほうがいいだろう。それは、何千もの商品を置いている大きなデパートに行っても、1度に欲しいのはほんの数品だけ、というようなものである。もし要るものだけを書いた買物リストを持って来なかったら、要らない物を袋一杯買い込んでしまうことになりかねない。

本書の「地図帳」は、いくつかの簡単に識別できて一般に使われている要素に基づいている。そして、その根本的な情報システムについても同じことが言える。しかし、新しい地域の発達や新たなビル建設で絶えず発展を続けているローマ市の治権下にある膨大な地域（15万736ヘクタール）の発達について行くのは、白地図でさえ大変なことである。毎日この状況と取り組んでいるにもかかわらず、その事情説明に頭を痛める役人や技術者や専門家も、同じような困難に遭遇している。この古代都市は世界一広い歴史的中心地域（約1500ヘクタール）で、非常に密に都市のつづれ織りを成している。建物の中には何世紀もそこにあるものもあれば、2千年存在しているものもあるが、それらでさえ認可・不認可の高層化や取り壊し、道路備品、舗道、歩行者区域、公園や庭園という形式の緑化地域の改変が行なわれる度に、絶えず変化している。

航空写真の始まりは今から70余年の昔に遡る。しかし、人の手による優れた航空写真の作図は大都市地域にとっては時間がかかり過ぎる。その一方自動処理システムは、公共機関にとってはかなり経済的で、それを管理する専門的人材もほとんど要らない。このようにして、飛行計画や写真測量は、コンピューターで更新したり修正したりするための簡単で迅速な手段を提供してくれる。

ローマの歴史的中心地域の線状地図や写真地図に適用されたアプローチの根底にある原則は比較的率直である。最初の正確で伝統的な構図は数字に変換され、その後引き続いて飛行を行ない更新される。その段階は適当な時間の間隔を置いていくつかに分けられ、コンピューター処理で自動的に管理された更新が直ちに行なわれる。

写真地図と反対側のページの地図は、大部分のユーザーには全く興味のない情報で一杯になる訳ではない。それは建物の内部と外部の形（外部の輪郭、中庭など、航空写真では必ずしも分かり易いものではない）や、通りの名称、地点の高さ（丘や坂や階段が沢山ある）、そして公共の場所についての情報を単に示すものである。

その結果は、必要に従って断片的な従来の地図よりも確実に読み易い道具になる。縮尺は、正確な全景図（各シートは6ヘクタール、即ち6万2500平方メートルを網羅している）が作れるほど小さいが、最も小さい家や車や木さえ判別できるほどの大きさでもある。

ローマの歴史的中心地域の地図製作システムは、表されるべき基本的な要素の簡潔さに基づいている。論理の基本になるのは、都市の区画（道路や広場で境界を定められたユニットとして識別可能な建物や住宅区画）である。この基本ユニットは、さらにサブユニット（中庭、回廊、屋内スペース、屋根の要

素など）に分けられる。基本ユニットは、「リオーネ」（地区）や国勢調査地域などのように、抽象的だが一般に使われている行政地区より直接に関連しているが、場所の名称で定められている。これにより、わずかの要素から複雑なデータ資料を作り上げることが可能になる。

データ処理のおかげで、建物の表面積や容積やその他の特徴、人口統計、そして所有者のデータなどを直接引き出したり、簡単に結合、クロスチェック、確認することができる。もっと間接的には、単純な論理的操作ステップを踏めば、簡単な識別要素から複雑な資料を築くことが可能である。このように、われわれが持っているのは少数の複雑なモデルではなくて、個別にも全体的にも入手しやすく共通の地形マトリックスに相互に同化できるモジュールなのである。これはまた、研究であろうが、デザインであろうが、公共事業であろうが、個々のユーザーの多様なニーズに従って、表象やモデルを創ることも可能にした。

歴史的そして伝統的な地図は確かにより人間的で、厳密な描写の中では、その場所の特徴だけでなくその見方というか表現法を反映した豊富な絵画的イメージを与えてくれる。そのような地図には、ペン書きで個人的な注釈があったり、水彩画や線書きの絵が描かれていたりすることが多く、その結果、比類のない魅力を持った研究道具になる。近代の地図製作はこのような魅力を提供することはできないが、（自動製図と合わせた）写真イメージは、はるかに非凡な町のアイデアを与えてくれる。というのは、写真に写ったイメージは十分に物や人を見分けられる近さのものであるが、特別な非正統的な視点から撮影されているからである。

写真イメージや絵画的な景色や宮殿や場所—伝統的な観点からのイメージは、コンピューターが作ったイメージとはほとんど別の世界のものである。だからといって、後者を単に非人間的だと片付けてしまうのは、少し単純化し過ぎている。そこに表れる各要素はペン（と言ってもここではコンピューターのプログラムの中の視覚磁気ポインターのことだが）で置換する前に、頭の中で入念に設計されてい

る。その速度と出力によって、コンピューターは数時間、時には数分で、異なる明暗の立面図をいくつも作成することができる。この場合、コンピューターは計画用に使われる。それはわれわれや他の人達が建築デザインのインパクトや、広場や道または地域への変化のインパクトを理解する助けとなる。昔は、立面図は視覚的な表現やコミュニケーションの手段で、非常に印象的である一方、立面図そのもの自体が自身の目的である場合もあった。現在は、それらは視覚化、理解、そしてコミュニケーションのための急速な技術の一部である。

ローマは非常に表現が複雑な都市で、他の多くの都市のように常に前進している。現在では確立した写真技術とデータ処理という新しい道具を用いることにより、その地域全体が完全な客観性という幻想の餌食に陥ることなく表される。結果的に得られるイメージは従来通りの構造になっているかもしれないが、大きな縮尺の公共スペースや広場や旅行案内書が使われれば、それも好奇心をそそったり、一般の想像を興奮させたりできる。

技術、資料そして問題

具体的な応用プログラムの進化やハードウェアの発達に伴って、専門的な市場が現われた。ユーザー・インターフェイスは改良を重ね、ハードウェアとソフトウェアの両方ともより簡単に入手し利用できるようになった。処理コストが大幅に低下し、数年前までは高度に専門的なコンピューター・センターの非常に高額のハードウェアでしか可能でなかった技術や管理システムが下方に広がっていった。

今では、スピードやスクリーンの質の規制はいくつかあるものの、専門家ではない個人ユーザーが利用できる低コストのコンピューターで、かなり大規模の地図製作資料が管理できる。処理結果はそれから紙の上または写真の支持体に、個人ユーザーには高価すぎるけれども、専門的なサービスセンターでは十分経済的に生産できる技術や手段で移される。

これは総て、ローマの歴史的中心地域のために開発された地図製作システムが、コンピューター市場

がまだ大学生や研究者のようなユーザーのために低コストのハードウェアを提供していなかった頃にも、これらの要因を総て考慮して最初からデザインされていたため可能になったのである。このような理由で、開発すべき優先事項の１つは、簡単にしかも迅速に他のいかなる環境にも移せる形式のデータと資料を提供することである。

ここでわれわれはこのシステムのおそらく最も重要な特徴の所にやって来た。控え目な経済資源で作られたため多くの初期段階の欠陥（後に修正）を含んでいた資料の初期の質は別にすると、最重要要因は、この産物が多くの場合当事者が実施する直接の高額ではない測量の結果修正され更新できるほど非常に容易である。

立体モデルはもっと具体的な訓練を要求する。このモデルの主目的は、たいてい都市規模で進行中のデザインのバックアップやチェックポイントとしての役割を果たすことである。組織的な目的のために必然的に図式的であるが、これらのモデルは、通常は似たような伝統的な技術を以て長年働いてきた者だけが本当に獲得できる全体的なビジョンを備えた能力を要求する。しかしそこで再び、製図や敷地割りの経験がほとんどない者でさえ、かなり確かな結果を得ることができる。

資料と処理

文学的な逆説に加えて、都市計画者と行政官は、何世紀もの間町の建物に関する知識、使い道、管理、コントロールを支配してきた司法業務や規制法そして限られた資金の上で合意しなければいけない。中世都市の法律に体系化され、早くも15世紀にはいくつかの（重荷叙述的な）土地台帳に大まかに書かれてさえいた、建設工事と都市の建物のコントロールに関する慣習と義務は、常に都市コミュニティーの発達において最初の要素となってきた。そして、建物の幾何に関する大まかな情報や、公共と個人両方の所有権の詳細を、製図や地図に含める誘惑がある。ローマの歴史的中心地域の場合、建物に関する量的な情報（表面積、容積、地理的な所在地）に優先が

与えられた。そのような情報は、航空写真地図から得たり、必要に応じて上に置かれた土地台帳からの所有権に関する情報を伴った。これらの情報をさらに研究して、新たな主題地図（ローマの歴史的中心地域内の公共が所有する不動産の地図）が生まれた。

もっと最近になって、上述の情報システムの直接的な結果、公共サービス企業の資料（SIP、ENEL、ITALGAS）などのように、他の資料館の情報を入手したり引照することが可能になった。これらの資料は町の日常の公共生活の複雑で機能的な写真を提供したり、空間やルートやサービスの改善を試みる基盤を形成したりすることができる。

航空写真測量に基づいた地図は1980年に遡るが1990年5月の特別調査飛行により修正され更新された。約1500ヘクタールの面積の縮尺は1000分の1で、約530ヘクタールの面積のそれは500分の1である。このベースに、1400の地名が加えられた。

土地台帳は財務省（Direzione generale del catasto e dei servizi tecnici erariali）が出しているオリジナルから得られる。土地台帳から直接に得られない不動産に関する主題的情報がそれに加えられる。この情報は現在処理が進行中である。正式な試行は適切な登記事務局が計画を立てている。

建築物や歴史的遺産をより効率よく管理する目的で、研究機関（CNRやCommissione per la valutazione del rischio anbientale）や文化遺産監督地域、大学教授陣（Departimento di storia e analisi della città）、そして計画機関と多くのプログラムやオペレーション関係の同意に至った。これらの機関のうち、市の建築物を研究しコントロールするために特別に任命された後者の機関は、立体表現用の計算システムは広範囲の空間や地形モデルも提供できるので、このシステムから非常に大きな援助を受けている。

この町の形態と構造についてわれわれが持っている知識の一部の将来は、現在ではある程度の財源ででも可能になった資料収集管理の似たようなシステムの発達と普及に疑いなく結び付けられるだろう。それによって得られる機能的モデルや図示的モデルは、ダイナミックな認識補助としてそれ自身の自主性を持つだろう。それらは企画の代替ではないし、またそうなれるとも言えないが、増大する情報の流れを迅速に処理する本質的な能力のおかげで、質的には限りがあるものの量的には有用で効果的な計画の情報を生成することができる。

システム設計

類似したプロジェクトのアプローチにおける基本的な問題は、既存または将来のモデルとシステムを1つにまとめるシステム設計の研究と開発である。

極端に速く回転するハードウェアとソフトウェアの性質を考慮すると、容易に輸出し応用できるシステム設計をデザインするのは不可能である。それでもなお、ここで示そうとしてきたように、柔軟性を念頭においた資料や過程やモデルを組み立てることは可能である。地図製作と文字数字両方の記録資料は、数多くのスタンダードな形式（ASCII、DXF、IGESなど）で輸出することができる。その過程は、最も普及した仕様と標準化した派生言語にできるだけ従い、次第に標準でない言語の内部のマクロ命令または、それよりもひどいのは、プログラムの資質を最適化するがその使用を特別な1機種のハードウェアに限ってしまうシステムのコール—ハードウェアのメモリーのある分野へのアクセス—を次第に削除していながら、Cとフォートラン77で書かれた。

これらの特性は既にシステムに広く習得されていて、行政、研究機関、デザイン・企画会社、そして中小の設計事務所や技術スタジオなどにさえもおけるまたたく間の情報のコンピューター処理化を特に考慮すると、その使用がすでに広範囲に及んでいる産物の最終階段で理想的な状態だと考えられる。

処理または最処理すべきデータの普及のためのプロトコールを製作することから得られる利点は、皆にとっても利益をもたらす。このことは、最終的にそれを使用する人間の異なった範疇を考えた時に明確になったが、地図製作や都市計画や設計の応用プログラムを売ったり作ったりしている企業には最近まで明確ではなかった。事実、そこにはプログラムを限られた同種のハードウェアに拘束するという行為が、暗黙の了解において実践されていた。もし、過去において、これが最高の性能を持つハードウェアを最大限に利用する必要で正当化されたならば、標準的なオペレーション・システムや言語（UNIXシステムV、DOS、ウィンドウズ、Xウィンドウズ、C、フォートラン）の事実上の強制に伴う、新型の驚くほど高性能のシステムの出現や市場水準の崩壊は、ただ1つの方向を押しつけることを主張してきた者達をその主張を固持できない立場へと追いやった。

性能や価格が基本的に類似していることを考えれば、1つの特別なハードウェア・システムに固執するのはもはや経済的に成り立たないし、重要でもない。そして、客を長期のサービス契約に頼らせることを試みたり強制するのは大きな間違いである。これは、大部分のソフトウェア業者が持っていない組織における柔軟性を前提としている。さらに、それはできるだけ迅速に自分達のシステムの特性を変更するという永久の追跡に、人材を捧げてしまうことを意味する。ハードウェアとソフトウェアの両方を作っている親会社でさえ、マーケティングの限界はおろか、一定の生産量の限界をも越えられないグループが製造した特によく売れる可鍛性のハードウェア部品（特別なグラフィック・アダプター、特別に開発されたグラフィック・マイクロプロセッサー）だけでなく、既に市場でよく売れているソフトウェア製品を直ちに取り入れる傾向が今日ではますます強まっている。

このようにシステムを取り巻く環境をざっと見てきたが、性能や特性の一部に関しては、コンピューターの系統間における区別はだんだん消えていっているということも付け加えなくてはいけない。かつては（そして今でもそうだが）、パーソナルコンピューター（PC）やマイクロコンピューター、ミニコンピューター、メインフレームのコンピューター等の間で、しばしば与えられた過程の処理スピードや、様々な仕事を同時に管理したり（マルチタスキング）、この可能性をいくつかのユーザーに提供したりする（マルチユーザー・モード）両方の能力

において、違いがあった。この可能性の複合体により、コンピューターの系列とそれぞれのオペレーション・システムの境界が定義された。今日、これらの分類パラメーターは消えていっている。なぜなら、マルチタスキングは今では優れたパソコンで可能だし、マルチユーザー・モードも低コストのハードウェアにUNIXを使えば利用できるからである。これは、パソコンはお互い同士や自分よりも強力な処理ユニットを持ったユーザーと結べるので、ローカル・ネットワーク（LAN）は、さらに遠隔地のネットワークでさえも、事実上（依然としていくつかの制限はあるが）マルチユーザー・モードを持っていることを意味している。名目上は優れたものの範疇に入るハードウェアの特性に匹敵する「小さく」て、安く、非常に速いコンピューターが、現在市場で積極的に売り出されている。

困難無しにという訳ではなく、ローマの歴史的中心地域の都市計画と設計企画だけでなく、都市規模の地図製作の自動化プロジェクトにおいても、現在の市場の状態と合意する努力が成されている。なぜなら、このプロジェクトは一般の人々や専門的なユーザー達に非常に異なったシステムで呼び掛けなければいけないからである。行政が組織化された数字による情報の要求の増加を示すかたわら、計画者や研究者や学生は、資料館が自分達の限定された設備に適応してくれることを期待し、紙上に書かれた形式だけでなく数字の形式でもデータや過程が得られることを必要とする。

従って、歴史的中心地域事務局の地図製作及び計画システムの設計は、２つのもっともありふれたオペレーション・システム（DOSまたはUNIX）を使い、一定の環境（Xウィンドウズ、ウィンドウズ）において、（データの獲得と修正のための）グラフィック・プリンターやプロッターやデジタイザーなどの周辺機器と結ばれたパソコンで、グラフィック・データと文字数字式の記録資料を結合できるプログラムを持って、ローカル・ネットワークのLANの中で作業ができるように組まれている。さらに、近い将来には、当地の行政機構（ローマ市議会）や国（史跡管理局）の他の部門の資料やシステムと長距離で結ばれる可能性もある。

行政の適用努力は、モラルの面では満たされているが自分達が取り組まなければならない問題のダイナミックな性質とはかなり違った毎日のお役所式の面倒な手続きでしょっちゅう悩まされている意気揚揚のテクニシャンと行政組織の側の柔軟性を前提にしている。

一見では地図製作の産物には限界があるが、更新と修正の可能性を示すために妥協に達した。その一方で、歴史的中心地域事務局に間に合うように製作された選ばれた資料（公共が所有する不動産の資料）は、やがて革新的に更新され統合されることになっている。

一般的に複雑なオペレーションにはよくあることだが、間違いや省略があるかもしれない。非常に専門的なユーザーの中には、もっと専門的で詳細にわたった地図の必要を感じる者もいるかもしれない。そのような地図は入手可能だが、それを読むことに関心があったり、実際にそれを読める「読者」は何人いるだろうか。

大量の情報をより特殊化された別の場所で提供することに決めて、本書ではわれわれは誰にも分かりやすい完全に新しく貴重な道具を単に提供しただけである。最終的な結果は昔の製図のような絵画的な美しさを総て持っている訳ではないかもしれないが、航空写真の珍しい視点から、現実の客観的なビジョンとその実用的な従来通りの表現が効果的に比較できる。最後に、この道具は、ダイナミックに更新された製作システムの一部で、根本的な技術の紛れもなく複雑な性質にもかかわらず、それは容易に利用でき普及されるということで、一層役に立つものである。

エウゲニオ・バルダニ、
ブルーノ・クッシーノ、
ルイジ・プレスチネンツァ・プリーシ

斜体で書かれた説明は、イタリア語の文献に付いている図版を指す。

27. ピアッツァ・デラ・マドンナ・デ・モンティ。フォンタナ・ディ・ジアコモ・デラ・ポルタ。立体のコンピューター・イメージ。（F.ペコラーロ、F.ベルティ、M.パヌンティ設計）(p.36)

28. ピアッツァ・デラ・マドンナ・デ・モンティ。フォンタナ・ディ・ジアコモ・デラ・ポルタ。新しいレイアウトと道路用備品計画の詳細。（F.ペコラーロ、F.ベルティ、M.パヌンティ）(p.37)

29. ピアッツァ・デラ・マドンナ・デ・モンティ。フォンタナ・ディ・ジアコモ・デラ・ポルタ。新しいレイアウト。（F.ペコラーロ、F.ベルティ、M.パヌンティ）(p.37)

30. ピアッツァ・マンフレード・ファンティ。アクアリオ・ロマノの前の新しいレイアウトと道路用備品計画の立体のコンピューター・イメージ。（F.ペコラーロ、F.ベルティ、M.パヌンティ）(p.38)

31. ピアッツァ・マンフレード・ファンティ。アクアリオ・ロマノの前の新しいレイアウトと道路用備品計画の立体のコンピューター・イメージ。（F.ペコラーロ、F.ベルティ、M.パヌンティ）(p.39)

32. ピアッツァ・コロンナ。ワイヤーフレームの遠近図。新しいレイアウトと道路用備品計画の立体のコンピューター・イメージ。（A.シンボロッティ、M.マルティーニ。コンピューター処理はF.ブラメリーニによる）(p.40)

33. ピアッツァ・コロンナ。ワイヤーフレームの遠近図。新しいレイアウトと道路用備品計画の立体のコンピューター・イメージ。（A.シンボロッティ、M.マルティーニ。コンピューター処理はF.ブラメリーニによる）(p.41)

34. ピアッツァ・コロンナ。パラッツォ・ウェーデキントの正面の詳細のワイヤーフレーム等角投影図。（コンピューター処理は*F*.ブラメリーニによる）(*p.41*)

35. ピアッツァ・コロンナ。影付遠近図。（処理は*F*.ブラメリーニによる）(*p.42*)

36. ピアッツァ・コロンナ。パラッツィオ・チーギの正面の詳細。影付ワイヤーフレームのコンピューター・イメージ。(*F*.ブラメリーニによる)(*p.42*)

地図製作技術

ベニスに関する依然の作品（1989年、マルシリオ）とは違って「ローマ地図」の中では、航空写真は、その地域の地形的要素を表すだけでなく、この場合は公共体という特別な範疇に入る使用者達が建物やスペースをどのように使用しているかというような非地図的な要素から派生した珍しい主題的特徴を数多く含んだ地図を伴っている。

この主題的内容は、歴史的中心地域事業特別事務局が行なった数多くのその地域の分析のほんの１つを表しているにすぎない。そのような分析の目的は、今日のローマの歴史的中心地域の複雑な都市システムにおける変遷のパターンに対する知識を深め、より効果的にその統制が行えるようになることである。

この分析の計画や監督に用いられたシステムは、Sistema Informativo Territoriale (SIT)である。ローマのオートマップとアエロフォト・コンサルトがデータベース開発の目的で創案したこのシステムは、地図製作、建築、司法、社会経済、行政などの情報の複雑で詳細にわたる資料を統合し管理するためのマルチメディア技術を使用している。

このシステムの「心臓部」になるのはGEODIS（ジョグラフィック・ディストリビューテッド・インフォメーション・システム）というオートマップが総て開発したシステムで、これはIBMコンピューター・システムとRISCの技術という２つの「脳」を動かし、データのインプットとアウトプットのためにグラフィックや文字数字式の変数と結ぶものである。これらの機器のおかげで、何年にもわたるデータの合理化と相互連結が進行中である。ここで問題となるデータは、長年にわたって市議会事務局で集められてきたものであるが、様々なまとまりのない形式でしか存在しなかったため、骨の折れる解釈によってやっと関連づけられるものであった。

このような作業条件を頭において、SITの３つの主な構成要素—データバンク、ソフトウェア、ハードウェア—について説明してみたいと思う。しかしその前に、ここに採用されている全体的なアプローチについての一般的なコメントから始めたいと思う。

全体的な特性：データバンクと局所地域データバンク

「データバンク」とは一般に、データが個別にも集成的にも使えるよう設計された構造の中にまとめられた特定の主題に関するデータのセットだと考えられている。

研究方法がデータの集合全体を取り巻くことに制限されないようにするだけでなく、それはしばしば特別な項目の情報特有の相互関係に決定されたより詳しい情報の「自然容器」であるため、多少は複雑な構造が不可欠になる。この構造は、多くの場合実際の基本的情報よりも重要な「メタ情報」の容器であると言っても、大した誇張ではない。データ構造のデザインは、データバンク自体の特定の目的と厳密に関わっている。

ペーパー・データバンクでは、構造は必然的に固定してしまう。これは、計画的に多少なりとも革新的な変化は、資料の大々的な再構成の問題を抱えることを意味している。大量のデータの場合、そのような操作は時間と労力を伴うのがほとんど常なので、時間の無駄になってしまう。これは電子資料でも同じである。しかし、電子資料で密度の高い複雑な構造を作り管理するほうが、ペーパー資料よりも簡単である。さらに近年では、もっと柔軟性のある構造を確実にしたり、特定の分類目的への依存を少なくする構造を作るため、多大な努力が成されている。

当初、データベース構造を管理するソフトウェア（DBMS、データベース・マネージメント・システム）は、内部構造が目に見えるようにすることを意図した規準に従い、ユーザーに主動でそれを管理させた。これはヒエラルキー、つまりネットワークDBMSの実情で、これもまた１種の硬直性に苦しんだ。その結果、設計段階で熟考されなかった研究規準の応用は、常に問題のあるものとなった。

現在最良の結果は所謂「関連」コンセプトから得られる。そこでは、構造は既存データに何からの形式で既に含まれている情報に基づいてさえいれば、未修正データからでもダイナミックに作ることができる。これがローマ市議会地域で採用された解決策であった。

関連DBMSでは、基本的なコンセプトは表である。非常に単純な縦と横の列から成る表で、横の各列は情報の項目を表し、縦は記述領域を表している。関連DBMSは、領域の「観点」—論理的な等式と様々な種類の機能（数学的、ストリング、その他）に基づいた選択基準—の定義により、（データ自体における暗黙の構造だがそのようにコード化されていなかった）データ間の関係の発見を可能にした。観点はデータベースを設計する際に事前決定されるのではなく、特定のニーズに応じて定義が可能になり、データに適用される。特定の「観点」がデータに適用される度に、DBMSは要求されるリストを製作する。（観点の定義の時点ではなく適用の時点で）ダイナミックに生成されているので、このリストはその直前まで起こった総ての修正事項（取り消し、訂正、挿入など）をすべて考慮に入れる。

コンピューター化されたデータベースへのアクセスが固定されている限り、その適用はデータが密に集められている分野に必然的に限られて、そして概念的には非常に単純で見通しのきく標準的なアクセスのものであった。結果的に、それらは型にはまった使用しかできなかった。その典型的な例は市議会登録局から与えられる。ここは非常に密度の濃い基本データ（市民１人１人に関する総てのデータ）を持っているが、たいてい通常標準的で暫時的に定まった過程を必要とするのである。

関連システムの偉大な柔軟性は、非常に野心的な目的をも達成させることができる。このことはわれわれのプロジェクトの目的に直接影響を与えた。というのは、もしそれが大きな柔軟性とダイナミックなアクセスを有していなかったら、与えられた地域における現象の説明を試みるデータベースの価値—即ち局地的な関係を含む構造を使用する試み—は、非常に疑わしいものになるからである。

行政的にも地理的にも「局地」という言葉にカバーされる現象は非常に多様で、流動的で、変化しやすいので、決まりきった照会の固定した設計は完全に無駄である。問題となる地域の自然なロケーションにおけるデータの多様な類型について考える意志、もっと正確に言うならばその必要は、その極度にダ

イナミックな現象を支配できるソフトウェアを使用する必要を示唆している。ここにおけるその考えとは、その中で各データがある位置づけを持っているだけでなく、何よりも先に、極端な合成手段により集まりその領域で見られる横の現象を確認し発見できるようにする構造を通じて、管理され統合された、1種の容器モデルを作ることである。

上で説明した必要と厳密に対応させるために関連ソフトウェア・システムの概念を故意にここで紹介したが、コンピューター化された使用という観点からは、関連データ管理システムは不可欠ではあるものの、われわれの目的には十分とは言えない。データが表になっていることを考慮すると、関連DBMSは、ある種の情報に表が要求されるのと同様、1種のユーザー・インターフェイスを必要とするのが当たり前な（地理的にも幾何学的にも）完全に局所地域の情報を操作するのが困難である。ここで要求されるのは、グラフィックというよりもむしろ地図的なインターフェイスである。関連システムの表が紙の目録に似ているように、局所地域を表すことを要求するシステムは、地図製作の形式でそうしなければいけないのである。これはわれわれが地図の使用に慣れているからという理由よりも、むしろその反対に、地図が人がその必要を満たすために何千年にもわたって働き完成させてきた地域を表す方法だからである（つまり、地図が人に「慣れている」のであってその逆ではないということである）。

局所地域DBMSは、その全ての関連スペースの地域を表す必要を考慮し損なうことは許されないし、関連システムがそれ自身のデータを（自然な）表の形で提示するのと同様、それらを地図の形で外部世界（ユーザー・インターフェイス）に提示しなくてはいけない。また、このシステムはより多くの「従来通りの」情報を表の形で管理しなくてはならないばかりか、表と「局所地域」（空間的）関係のおかげで表の項目と相関関係のある参照点を持つ地図の両方で項目の参照の保存もしなければならない。このシステムは表と局所地域（空間的）両方の混合された基準を用いて、表と地図の両方の形でアウトプットが出されるようなデータの「観点」が簡単に作れなければいけない。

必要とされる総ての情報レベルのデータベースが一旦入れられると、この種のシステムは、容易にその地域の様々な現象の状態の確認調査を提供してくれる。そしてもし関連DBMSに基づいて表のデータを保存すれば、そこで生じた現実的な必要に従ってデータベースを次第に作り上げていくだけでなく他の情報レベルからの追加補足要素を加えることも同様に簡単に行なえる。

ローマ市議会局所地域データバンク

こうして、当時ローマの歴史的中心地域用のデータバンクを作る背景の根底にある論理ができあがった。これらのデータバンクは、情報システムが地域全体をカバーし完全に統合されるよう総て地理的参照事項を付けた地図、グラフィック、そして文字数字による資料から構成される。

データバンクを築く上で、次の地図資料が使用された。

＊全国測地学システムに含まれガウス・ボアガ座標を使用した、部分的に500分の1と1000分の1の縮尺の1980年の航空写真測量結果。
＊カッシーニ・ソルドナー平面座標に基づく1000分の1の地籍図。ベース地図から異なって切り取られ、シート全体に不規則に分けられているのではなく境界線で区画分けされている。
＊2000分の1の市の地名研究図。地理的な背景がなく、完全な道路計画とその周辺と国勢調査地域と道路区画の正式な番地が書かれている。

全体的に200足らずのシート地図から成る資料で、それは高性能デジタイザーを用いたアエロフォト・コンサルトと、データを統一された情報セット（建物、区画、地籍区画、国勢調査地域等）にコード化することによりデジタル化された。相互参照の目的で総ての地図データは、最も正確な地図―航空測量地図―を参考とした統合された形式で管理されている。建物、橋、記念碑などの端、40近い特徴ポイントが各シートに明記されており、それらのガウス・ボアガ座標が直接データベースから読める。これらの数値は、データベース作成の全段階で使われたオートマップソフトウェアの回転―並進処理を使って1つの座標システムに総て移せるよう、他の地図の対応点の上に重ねられる。

このデータベースは、デジタル化の際に与えられたコードで区別された統一カテゴリーでまとめられたデータのセットから成っている。独立的、具体的もしくは抽象的な「対象的」はこれらのカテゴリーに入っている。具体的な対象物というのは、現場で見たり測量したりでき、それゆえ写真地図に載っている自然または人工的な物体・現象を直接指す。一方、抽象的対象物とは、行政境界線のように現場では見えないが人の決定や計算プロセスの結果を含む基本的文献資料からのみ調査できる、人が発明した項目のことである。

上に説明した地図レベルの情報に加えて、現場の対象と関連したりもしくは関連させられるデータを含んだ文字数字レベル―または表レベル―の情報もある。しかし、この文字数字レベルの情報は実地で直接表されることはないが、しばしば進行中のプロセスを識別する基本的な現象を説明する。

前の段階で述べた論理に従って、地図製作用データベースにおけるデジタル地図の編成は、これもまた関連データベースでまとめられた1連の既存データや測量データ全体を局所地域中に分布させることになった。既に存在していたり、ローマ市議会で特別に調査を行なったデータには次のものがある。
＊所有権を示す地籍データ。
＊歴史的中心地域にある公有もしくは公共の統制下にある建築物のデータ。
＊国勢調査からのISTATデータ。
＊輸送手段やタイム・ゾーンに細分された移動性に関するデータ。
＊特有の一定地域に属するその他の色々な情報。

ハードウェア

このシステムのハードウェアは、コンピューターの性能をずっと上げるため限られた数の基本的な指示を使用する最近の構造アプローチであるRISC技

術を持った２つのIBMシステムに基づいている。大型フォーマットのカラー・グラフィック・スクリーン付きの6150とRISC6000の２システムは、大量記憶装置（620MB）と２台のPS／2ターミナル、文字数字式ターミナル、プロッターそしてキャルコンプのデジタイザー（どちらも大型フォーマット）から成る周辺装置両方の共通管理ができるようつながれている。

ソフトウェア

RISC IBMの操作システムは標準UNIXのIBM版であるAIXである。オートマップが全体的に開発したGEODISソフトウェアは、局所地域の管理にはこのシステムを使う。

GEODISは（文字数字データだけでなく）地図製作に基づいた局所地域のデータバンクの自動管理プログラムのパッケージである。このパッケージをもって、数式地図や、その複雑性や建築や構造がどうであれ、現地の（具体的または抽象的な）対象に関した文字数字式データの関連データベースや、文字数字式データベースと地図の関係のセットを管理することが可能になる。さらに、地理的データベースと文字数字式データベースの一貫性が適当な更新を作業により保証される。

GEODISを使用することで、その地域にとって重要性を持つどんな情報も、地図上で（そして現場においても）位置付けや視覚化することが可能である。それとは逆に、幾何学的な情報はコード化した情報の形で文字数字式データベースに移せる。その典型的な１例は、図式で定められたゾーンの中でそれらの包含関係を比較して得られた、建物の記録にあるゾーン化コードを移すことである。さらに、文字数字式データベース検索の結果は地図製作サポート上で視覚化され、局所地域データが「読める」ようなシステムを作る。

１つ以上の表や観点は、表の縦列と横列の対象と関連する一義のコードにより、各クラスの対象と関連づけられる。

またGEODISは、使いやすいシンプル・メニュー・システム、組織化されたフロー・コントロールを持つパワフルなマクロ言語、進んだ「プリミティブ」などが備わった、相互作用を持つグラフィック環境も供給する。これらのプリミティブは、外部プログラムのライブラリー管理や文字数字式データベースとの統合だけでなく、地図製作上の対象に関した複雑な操作（面積と容積の計算、全体的な幾何・位相幾何学的な操作や変換）を実行するために人工知能技術を使用している。

ユーザーは状況に応じて色々な方法でこの環境を利用することができる。ユーザーはキーボードから直接マクロ指令を送れるし、標準メニューシステムを使ったり、反復的な操作をスピードアップするためにそれをあつらえたりすることもできる。さらにマクロ言語と外部設備を利用して複雑な手続きを設計することもでき、それは効果的にその先の指示や複雑なプリミティブになる。

それらの管理上の機敏さと操作上の即時性を前提として、結果的に同じ技術がローマ市議会やローマ管区やラティウム地域の事務局に普及したために、これらの能力は、異なる地方行政体によったりもしくはそれらの行政当局間で一貫して作られている、同数の複雑な情報システム核を作ってきている。そのような事務局はそれぞれ異なる仕事を行なうかもしれないが、彼らは皆、共通した遺産のイメージを守る同じ論理に従って、その共同遺産に取り組んでいるのである。

ガブリエラ・マルテーセ、
ダニエーレ・ティナッチ

斜体で書かれた説明は、イタリア語の文献に付いている図版を指す。

37. ローマ。歴史的中心地域。国勢調査地域と道路区画の地図。地域の情報シートの重ね刷り。（1981年ISTAT国勢調査データ）(p.43)

38. ローマ。歴史的中心地域。国勢調査地域と道路区画の地図。住民が100人以下の地区は水色、200人以下の地区は紫で表している。（1981年ISTAT国勢調査データ）(p.44)

39. 100以上の業者がいる地区のハイライト。（1981年ISTAT国勢調査データ、小売り・卸売り業者データバンクから）(p.44)

40. 公有地地図からの抜粋。(p.45)

41. ローマ。歴史的中心地域。1000分の１屋根レベルの地図。(pp.46〜47)

写真地図の製作

　1000分の1のローマのカラー写真地図は、アウンリアン城壁に囲まれた地域をカバーしている。合計81枚の50×50cmのフォーマットのプレートが、ガウス・ボアガ座標に従ってデカルト直角格子を成している。Venezia forma urbisに既に使われているこのフォーマットの選択は、多くの要因を考慮した上で決定した。主な関心事は、オリジナルのフォトグラムに近いフォーマットを使うということであった。写真が撮られたその瞬間を反映した正確な直線並列の必要を前提とすると、個々のプレートについて均一の中心投象と解像度を保証するため正方形のフォーマットが選ばれた。中心投象の影響を最小にとどめ、解像度を最高にするため、各写真の中心部分だけが使われた。

　この航空写真測量オペレーションとそれに伴う処理の全責任を負うパルマのCompagnia Generale Ripreseaereeにより写真地図の撮影と現像は最小の詳細まで計画され、達成された。

　測量は1990年6月11日に、焦点距離305.38mmでフォーマット23×23cmのツァイスRMK.A30/23を備えた2エンジンのパルテナビアP681-ANCPから行なわれた。写真は約1800メートルの相対的高度から、縦のオーバーラップ平均80％で、高感度コダック・エアロカラー・ネガティブ・フィルム2445（エスター・ベース）を使って撮影され、このフィルムはその後エアロネグ連続自動現像機で処理された。ローマの歴史的中心地域の航空写真測量範囲は東西に向かった出撃機10台を必要とし、平均5700分の1の縮尺で合計308枚の写真を作成した。

　写真測量は午前10時58分から午前11時43分（夏時間）という非常に限られた時間の中で実行された。光の状態と太陽の位置は、最短の影で最高のカラー結果を保証し、カメラの視点に太陽光線が反射する状況（所謂ホットスポット）を避けるには、理想的であった。飛行計画のグラフが示すように、8回目の飛行は2階段に分けられた。ローマ上空の交通量が多かったため、撮影を完了する許可が下りなかった。撮影し損なった部分は約10分後に撮影された。

　1000分の1の縮尺に拡大・修正するための完全な方角配置を得るために、IGMI全国ネットワークに含まれているより高い高度における特別写真と直接測定により定められた後者に連結したポイントで行なわれた航空三角測量を用いて、適切なフレーミングが実施された。

　ツァイスRMK.A30/23、焦点距離305.38mm、コダック・ダブルX気象パンクロフィルム2405を使って、絶対高度3000メートルで行なわれたこの測量は、ストリップ5枚とフォトグラム132枚を撮影し、修正毎に8つのコントロールポイントを与えた。拡大と修正作業は、色の正確さのために細かく調節された高解像パワーレンズだけでなくカラーヘッドと投影コントロールユニットが備わったツァイスSEG VI機器で行なわれた。敏感な資料の処理は可能なかぎりの均一性と正確な解像度を確実にするため特別な注意を払わなければならなかった。

　写真地図の各セクションは、最終誤差が平地で±0.4グラフィック・ミリメートル、ローマ市の形態の典型ある丘陵地はそれを少し越える値になるまで、最低6の地面レベルの既知ポイントでチェックされた。各セクションはまた、色の均一性と詳細の表現についてもチェックされた。許容限界を越えた最終誤差値も、この地図帳作成用に優れた資料を提供するには十分な低さであった。50×50cmフォーマットの紙に印刷するためにコダック・エクタカラー紙が使われた。

　各カラー写真地図から4枚の25×25cmプレートが得られ、対応する同じ縮尺の線状地図と共に本書の本質を形成している。

リチニーオ・フェレッティ

斜体で書かれた説明は、イタリア語の文献に付いているイラストを指す。

42. 1990年6月11日午前10時58分から午前11時43分の間に撮影され、ローマの歴史的中心地域の写真地図の81枚のプレートを作成するのに使われたフィルムの10枚のストリップの図表。(p.48)

43. 各フィルムストリップに要した時間の表。8回目の撮影は2度に分けて行なわれなければならなかった。(p.49)

44. 3枚のストリップ中18枚の写真にカバーされた地域の図表。暗い灰色の帯は上張りを示している (p.49)

45. 3枚の写真から成るストリップ3の断片の図表。フォトグラム285と287は図式的な形式で提示されている一方、フォトグラム286はその実物大に再生されている。フォトグラム286の中心部分だけが写真地図の最終プリントに使われた（プレート63、64、81、82）。できるだけ多くの資料を得るため、明らかに非常に広い重複（80％）がある。写真地図に実際に使われている写真は、中心投象法の影響を最小にとどめ最高の解像度を得るため、各フォトグラムの中心部分からのものである。(pp.50〜51)

Color separations by La Fotomeccanica *Padua*
and T. Zaramella *Padua*
Printed by Offset Invicta *Padua*

Printed in July 1992
by Marsilio Editori, Venice

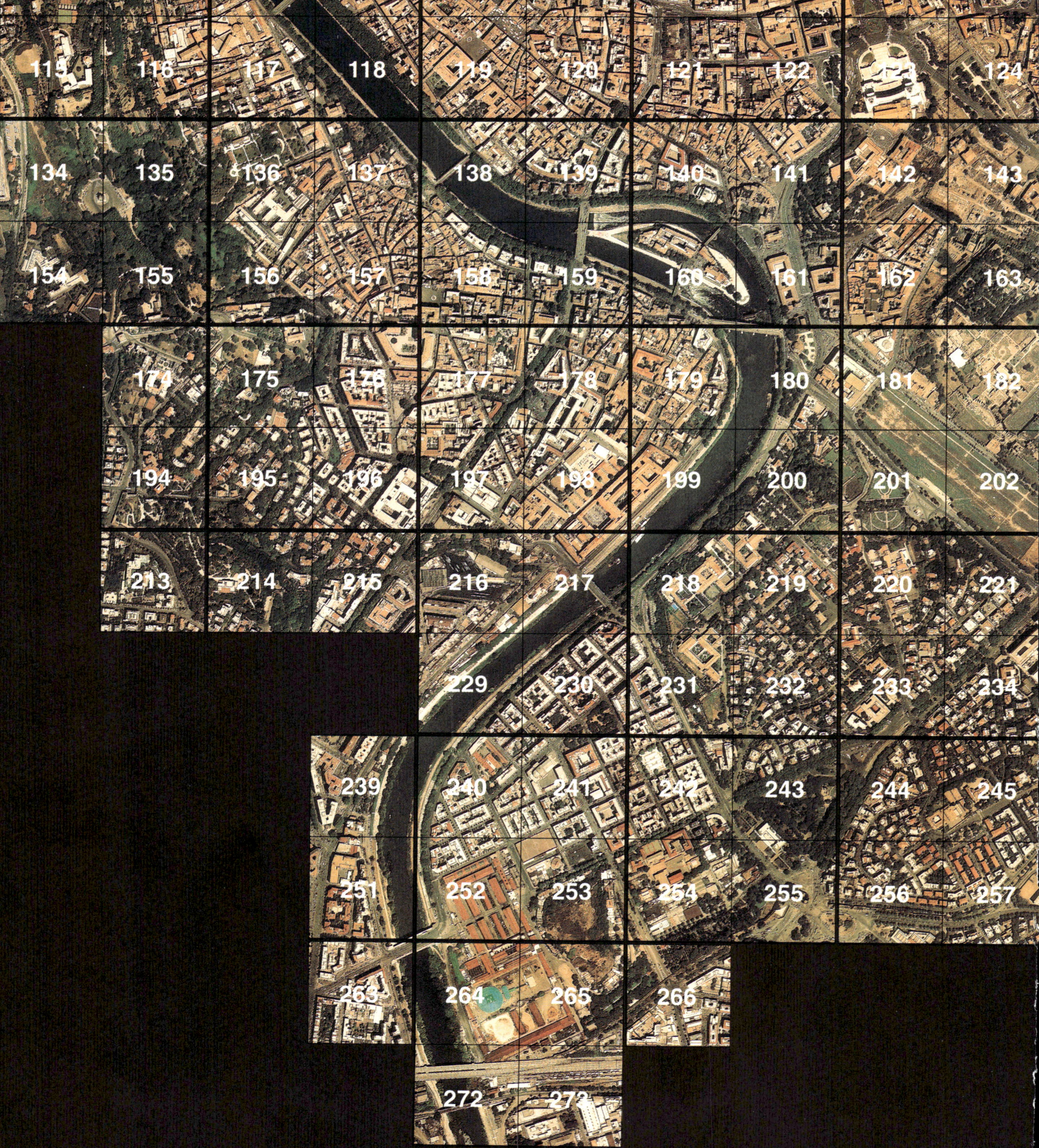